Hm 430 MAN   Staffs

Safeguarding Adults and the Law

2nd edition

Michael Mandelstam

D1353803

Jessica Kingsley *Publishers*
London and Philadelphia

Book No.   **05107014**

30121 0 05107014

This publication contains public sector information licensed under the Open Government Licence v1.0.

First published in 2008
This edition published in 2013
by Jessica Kingsley Publishers
116 Pentonville RoadLondon N1 9JB, UK
and
400 Market Street, Suite 400
Philadelphia, PA 19106, USA

www.jkp.com

Copyright © Michael Mandelstam 2008, 2013

Front cover image source: iStockphoto®. The cover image is for illustrative purposes only, and any person featuring is a model.

All rights reserved. No part of this publication may be reproduced in any material form (including photocopying or storing it in any medium by electronic means and whether or not transiently or incidentally to some other use of this publication) without the written permission of the copyright owner except in accordance with the provisions of the Copyright, Designs and Patents Act 1988 or under the terms of a licence issued by the Copyright Licensing Agency Ltd, Saffron House, 6–10 Kirby Street, London EC1N 8TS. Applications for the copyright owner's written permission to reproduce any part of this publication should be addressed to the publisher.

Warning: The doing of an unauthorised act in relation to a copyright work may result in both a civil claim for damages and criminal prosecution.

Library of Congress Cataloging in Publication Data
Mandelstam, Michael, 1956-
  Safeguarding adults and the law / Michael Mandelstam. -- 2nd ed.
    p. ; cm.
  Rev. ed. of: Safeguarding vulnerable adults and the law / Michael Mandelstam. 2009.
  Includes bibliographical references and index.
  ISBN 978-1-84905-300-6 (alk. paper)
  I. Mandelstam, Michael, 1956- Safeguarding vulnerable adults and the law. II. Title.
  [DNLM: 1. Vulnerable Populations--legislation & jurisprudence--Great Britain. 2. Aged--Great Britain.
3. Community Health Services--legislation & jurisprudence--Great Britain. 4. Disabled Persons--Great
Britain. 5. Mentally Ill Persons--Great Britain. 6. Social Work--legislation & jurisprudence--Great
Britain.
  W 32.5 FA1]

  362.941--dc23

                                    2012045059

British Library Cataloguing in Publication Data
A CIP catalogue record for this book is available from the British Library

ISBN 978 1 84905 300 6
eISBN 978 0 85700 626 4

Printed and bound in Great Britain

Acknowledgements

The author would like to thank Jessica Kingsley, Victoria Peters, Rachel Menzies and all the other staff involved at JKP for their support and expertise.

Thanks also to Tim Spencer-Lane for so helpfully looking over Chapter 9. All mistakes of course, in that chapter or any other, are the author's.

I am grateful also to the staff at the public library in Sudbury, Suffolk, whose continued helpfulness, assiduousness and courtesy remain constant.

Contents

Preface

Since the last edition of this book, published early in 2009, the profile of safeguarding adults has risen. Accordingly, this new edition continues to consider neglect and abuse across a broad spectrum of settings, circumstances and law. Yet, in early 2013, one issue warrants singling out, following the public inquiry into Mid Staffordshire NHS Foundation Trust: systemic poor care and neglect in health (and social) care, suffered by older people. It is a pressing matter for several reasons.

First, the evidence of the last 15 years points beyond reasonable doubt to a problem serious in its nature and extent.[1] The type of health care exposed at Stafford is no isolated instance or mere outlier.

Second, to delineate the problem in this book is not to criticise unduly the National Health Service and local authorities but to point out pitfalls to avoid, with a view to maintaining all that is good in these services. Of this good, there is a great deal. But the existence of the good does not preclude the bad.

Third, those many deniers and evaders of accountability, within the NHS, local authorities and central government, have much to answer for. An unacknowledged problem cannot be solved. The ills gain ground before they break out virulently, as has happened at Stafford and elsewhere in the NHS.

Forty-six years ago, a book on the treatment of psycho-geriatric patients in hospitals was published, entitled *Sans everything*. It is unsettling, not just because of what was going on in 1967 – including patients being stripped of their hearing aids, spectacles, dentures and dignity – but because there are far too many parallels today. The book acknowledged the harm, distress and anxiety that could be caused by its content; yet it needed to be published, if only to benefit us all in the future.[2]

Of course, things have since moved on. We seek now to enable people to remain at home longer and out of hospital, where appropriate; although, contrary to Department of Health utterance, older people – just like anybody else – do need to be in hospital for acute needs(!). But even shorter hospital stays do not preclude inhumane treatment or avoidable death, nor do they make up for the inexcusable marginalisation of geriatric medicine.

Besides which, nursing homes continue to be capable of the worst excesses – and for people in their own homes, community health services are often inadequately resourced, whilst social services help ever fewer people on grounds of 'ineligibility'. The risk is real of warehousing older people, not in hospitals or care homes, but in their own homes where poor care and neglect are out of all sight. The setting may have changed, but the song remains the same.

---

1   Mandelstam, M. *How we treat the sick: neglect and abuse in our health services.* London: Jessica Kingsley Publishers, 2011.

2   Robb, B. (presenter/editor). *Sans everything: last scene of all, that ends this strange eventful history is second childishness and mere oblivion; sans teeth, sans eyes, sans taste.* London: Nelson, 1967, pp.ix–xi (Foreword written by Dr R. Barton).

Fourth, we look to the State, the NHS and social services to safeguard vulnerable adults from external threat; for example, the dishonest neighbour or sadistic carer. But the State must look to itself as well; State-perpetrated poor care and neglect raise the stakes – legally, morally and of course politically. In tackling these ills, 'safeguarding adults' as an activity is currently on the side-lines, a bystander raising the occasional shout. This is the harsh conclusion reached if one compares the magnitude of the problem with the limited inroads made into it – by the NHS, local authorities, the Care Quality Commission, Health and Safety Executive, General Medical Council, Nursing and Midwifery Council, the police and the Crown Prosecution Service.

Lastly, safeguarding adults boards, responsible for steering local safeguarding activity, need to ask themselves searching questions about their direction and priorities in relation to systemic poor care and neglect. This is so particularly if those ills flow from key partners within the local board itself, that is, the NHS and social services who – through provision or commissioning of care – may be causing the very harm they are meant to be combating.

If these boards are to grasp the nettle, they will have to take on vested interests and be prepared to upset people. In the wake of the Stafford public inquiry, they could do worse than read an incisive article published in *Private Eye*: 'Return to the killing fields: a chronicle of death foretold'.[3] Amongst other things, it indicates the forces you are up against in challenging poor care, neglect, death, denial and lack of accountability in the NHS. If in doubt, turn also to Dr Heather Wood, undaunted inspector of the Healthcare Commission, who has written of the 'deep rooted pathology [which] is the stranglehold that managers, many apparently devoid of an ethical code and certainly without a regulatory body, have on the NHS'.[4] Or to Professor Brian Jarman's equally eye-opening article, 'When managers rule'.[5]

Formidable obstacles there may be, but to be worthy of their name and the statutory status which they will in future enjoy, safeguarding boards surely need to develop hard-hitting strategies to counteract systemic poor care and neglect. For instance, at present they conduct serious case reviews when individual, vulnerable adults are abused or killed by acquaintances, or perhaps when a person dies of neglect in the family home. And they oversee local safeguarding aimed at 'low hanging fruit'; for example, unfairly targeting 77-year-old local care home owners, themselves vulnerable, for apparently lesser infringements of rules.[6] Instead of tackling bigger game.

February 2013

---

3   M.D. 'Return to the killing fields: a chronicle of death foretold.' *Private Eye*, 22 February–7 March 2013.

4   Wood, H. 'Mid Staffs is evidence of all that is wrong with NHS management: the balance of power must shift back to the clinicians.' *British Medical Journal*, 6 February 2013.

5   Jarman, B. 'When managers rule.' *British Medical Journal*, 19 December 2012.

6   *Davis v West Sussex County Council* [2012] EWHC 2152 (QB).

I

Introduction

KEY POINTS

This book is about how law can safeguard and protect vulnerable adults from neglect and abuse. It deals with the law and practice in England only. To the rest of the United Kingdom – Wales, Northern Ireland, Scotland – the book is relevant to varying degrees.

The term 'vulnerable adult' continues to be used in this book. It remains, at the time of writing, the term used in Department of Health guidance about safeguarding.

This introductory chapter outlines who these vulnerable adults are, who may need safeguarding or protecting, and what the law is that both enables and places limits on safeguarding activity and interventions.

VULNERABLE ADULTS

It might seem intuitively obvious who vulnerable adults are. But one needs to consider the definitions provided by legislation, by central government guidance and by the courts. These are teased out in detail in Chapter 2.

At the most general level, current government guidance called *No secrets* states that vulnerable adults are people who may need community care services (arranged by local authorities) because of age, disability or illness and who are at significant risk of harm or exploitation because they cannot look after themselves or protect themselves from others.[1]

Typically, people who may be in need of community care services include those who are elderly, physically or learning disabled, sensorily impaired, mentally disordered or lacking mental capacity.

This definition will cease to apply if and when the draft Care and Support Bill 2012 becomes law and comes into force (probably in 2015).

WHAT DO VULNERABLE ADULTS NEED PROTECTING FROM?

The government's *No secrets* guidance states that vulnerable adults need to be protected from abuse. This is a loose term but is said to include abuse that is physical, sexual, psychological, financial or material, discriminatory, institutional and which can include neglect and acts of omission.

At one extreme is harm perpetrated by neglectful, reckless, sadistic, bullying or dishonest individuals, whether known to the victim or sometimes strangers who pick deliberately on vulnerable adults.

Equally, there is more 'respectable' and systemic neglect perpetrated or tolerated by institutions and organisations, including NHS hospitals, care homes and care providers generally. Respectable, because such neglect has become accepted by politicians, senior managers and many staff in health and social care, no matter the suffering of those who fall victim to it.

Respectable and accepted such neglect may have become, but of course not acceptable.

It should be noted at the outset that this book is about neglect and abuse, where it occurs. The many examples included are not uplifting. However, it must be remembered that there are equally many good things being done by carers, family, social services and the NHS. The purpose of the book is to point to typical neglect and abuse patterns and to indicate what can be done about them – not to claim that all is gloom and doom.

Note. The term 'vulnerable adult' continues to be used in this book. It remains the term used in Department of Health guidance about safeguarding.

However, as already noted, it is likely to be omitted from the future social care legislation affecting local authorities primarily, and to some extent other organisations such as the NHS and the police.

The term remains in other legislation such as the Safeguarding Vulnerable Groups Act 2006, which governs the barring of people from working with vulnerable adults. The law courts continue to use the term frequently to refer to – well, vulnerable adults.

---

1   Department of Health. *No secrets: guidance on developing and implementing multi-agency policies and procedures to protect vulnerable adults from abuse.* London: DH, 2000.

FINANCIAL ABUSE

Financial abuse might involve a whole range of people in positions of trust: close family members, friends, neighbours, carers, care home managers, health care workers, social services care managers, social workers, solicitors, clergy or bank staff.

Theft, forgery, fraud, false accounting, robbery, burglary might be committed by those (a) already in a long-standing position of trust, (b) who have recently but rapidly gained the victim's trust, or (c) who, as complete strangers, have deliberately targeted vulnerable, often older but also younger, adults because of that vulnerability.

Examples are numerous and varied. For instance, a nurse steals from a patient, a war hero, dying in hospital. Carers, trusted absolutely and treated like daughters, steal from 76-year-old blind women. Families may be driven to distraction and to the installation of hidden surveillance cameras in pink teddy bears in order to catch NHS health care assistants stealing money in the home of 75-year-old women suffering from leukaemia.

A man of low intelligence is taken by his carer to the building society every day for six months until he has transferred to the carer £60,000, his inheritance from his father. A friendly neighbour takes under her wing a vulnerable, elderly man next door, exercises 'undue influence' and deprives him in a short space of time of £300,000, constituting 90 per cent of his liquid assets. Carers in care homes quietly relieve residents with dementia of their wedding rings.

A church minister forges the wills of parishioners on their death bed in hospital, and social workers steal by abusing a power of attorney. An old friend gets a mentally incapacitated person to change her will – in favour of the old friend. Mother and daughter carers in a private capacity from the next village persuade a mentally incapacitated woman to sign over her £300,000 house to them, thereby depriving a children's hospital, to which she had left the house in her will.

A former senior civil servant, suffering from Alzheimer's disease and cancer, is tricked fraudulently out of his £500,000 life savings by a builder. Rogue traders get an older person to agree to roofing work that is not needed, sit on the roof all morning and then drive the person to the bank to be paid hundreds or even thousands of pounds. Or even extract the payment up front and then disappear without even pretending to carry out the work.

Less obviously, but still unlawfully, local authorities take a reckless and cavalier approach to legal rules and thus make unlawful charges for services. For instance, they might charge, wrongly, for reablement services, for mental health aftercare, for 'topping up' fees for care homes – or, without demur, for care home placements that should clearly be funded, free of charge, by the NHS.

And the NHS – at the effective bidding of central government – has, in the last 20 years or so, too often made arbitrary decisions about whether it will provide 'NHS continuing health care'. This has happened not on the basis of clear law, clinical need and principle, but on the basis of expedience, the desire to make savings to please the Department of Health. It reveals a profound antipathy for older people (the main victims of this 'policy').

No matter that older people then have to use up all their savings and sell their homes, even though legally they should not have had to do this. Or that, at the very least, they should have had transparent, fair and rational legal rules applied to them – rather than opaque and arbitrary judgements.

PHYSICAL (AND PSYCHOLOGICAL) ABUSE AND NEGLECT

An 89-year-old man might be left to die in an upstairs care home room, with suppurating pressure sores down to the bone, the care home owner hacking off rotting flesh with a pair of scissors, wearing gloves with which he had just scooped faeces off the sheets. Alternatively, five care home residents all die in the same week from a combination of pressure sores and malnutrition.

Carers might wilfully neglect people with severe learning disabilities by leaving them locked up in a car on a hot day for hours while the manager and his assistant go to a betting shop.

The care might move beyond neglect, typically associated with omission, to more active abuse. For instance, care workers might force medication down people's throats, so that they have to swallow to stop from choking, throw residents across the room or pinch them. They might kick, push, shove, beat, handle roughly, verbally abuse, neglect, deceive and steal. Managers of care homes may stand back and do nothing even when receiving reports about this.

A care home worker might taunt and distress residents with learning disabilities. Or sleep when she is meant to be on duty – during which time a resident catches his head between the headboard and rails of his bed, suffers brain damage and dies – before falsifying the night-time record.

Local authorities might commission services, systematically, knowingly or at least recklessly, in such a way as to result in ultimately neglectful care affecting people's dignity, safety, nutritional state, cleanliness and hygiene, as well as their fundamental emotional and psychological well-being.

People with learning disabilities – sometimes left to their own devices by local authorities in the name of independence, autonomy, choice and mental capacity – might subsequently be stolen from, harassed, bullied, exploited, assaulted, tortured and sometimes murdered. By their 'friends'.

Systemic shortcuts in basic care are rife within the NHS, particularly in hospitals – that is, in relation to compassion, nutrition, hydration, bowel and bladder function, cleanliness, hygiene, infection control, tissue viability and pressure sores, falls, assessment, diagnosis, treatment, monitoring, dignity, discharge from hospital – leading not just to appalling care and suffering, physical and psychological, but also to scores or even hundreds of avoidable deaths in a single hospital.

LAW AND SAFEGUARDING

Practices and occurrences such as the above, and how the law can be used to protect people from them, lie at the heart of the book.

Law is not necessarily a magic wand but is nevertheless an essential tool with which to work out and guide interventions by local authorities, the NHS, the police and other organisations.

Equally, the limitations and boundaries of the law must be delineated. Otherwise, it is all too easy for agencies of the State to intervene not only unlawfully but to the detriment of the person they are trying to protect.

Law can be used to prevent, ameliorate, remedy or punish. For instance, preventatively, assessment of vulnerable people and their informal carers by local authorities, under community care legislation, may provide support and advice that averts neglect or abuse.

If matters have already deteriorated, compulsory (ameliorative or remedial) intervention might be appropriate – for instance, under the Mental Capacity Act 2005 if a person lacks capacity to take relevant decisions to protect himself or herself from harm.

If, unfortunately, the situation nevertheless results in a criminal offence being committed, then the criminal law might provide a punitive measure in response, for example, to theft, assault or wilful neglect.

The breadth of law considered in the book is wide, in summary:

- social services and NHS functions

- regulation of health and social care providers

- the banning and barring of people from working with vulnerable adults

- mental capacity

- mental health

- human rights

- environmental health

- civil torts (negligence, trespass to the person, false imprisonment)

- undue influence

- the inherent jurisdiction of the courts to protect vulnerable people

- information disclosure and confidentiality

- the giving of evidence by vulnerable people in court

- assault, battery

- manslaughter, murder, assisted suicide

- theft, fraud, false accounting

- sexual offences

- wilful neglect or ill-treatment

- restraint.

To cover each area of law exhaustively would not be practical. Instead, the book picks out principles, legal cases and examples relevant to safeguarding adults.

THE STATE, ITS AGENCIES AND SAFEGUARDING

There is a further crucial factor to consider and understand. This is about the role of the State – that is, central government and local statutory bodies such as local councils, NHS hospitals and the police.

In particular, it has become clear over the last few years that two of the key statutory agencies charged with safeguarding – namely, local authorities and the NHS – are themselves sometimes ensnared in, contributing to or even wholly responsible for the very abuse and neglect from which they are meant to be protecting people.

If neglect and abuse at the hands of the State were incidental and isolated, occasional and inadvertent – or deliberately perpetrated but only by rogue or maverick elements (statistic outliers, as it were) – it would be unsurprising and not remarkable. However, when such involvement is systemic, it is of a different order.

This factor adds undoubted complexity to an understanding of safeguarding. It also brings with it significant problems, both practical and legal.

LEGAL REMEDIES

It is beyond the scope of this book to set out detailed procedures about legal actions and how to take them. However, the following is a very short summary.

It will be seen that there are various divisions. One such is that between criminal and civil cases and the standard of proof required: criminal proof is 'beyond reasonable doubt', civil 'on the balance of probability'. In percentage terms, the balance of probability literally would require 51 per cent; beyond reasonable doubt, if expressed in such terms, would amount maybe to 75 per cent or more.

In other words, a criminal case might fail for want of sufficient proof, but a civil case (e.g. for compensation in negligence) might succeed on the same facts.

JUDICIAL REVIEW: HIGH COURT (ADMINISTRATIVE, QUEEN'S BENCH DIVISION)

Judicial review is a type of civil legal case that can be brought in the High Court against public bodies only. The purpose of such cases is not to win financial compensation. It is to get the court to overrule the decision of a public body, usually on the grounds that there was something wrong in the decision-making process. The public body usually then has to retake the decision.

The courts apply common law principles to examine decisions for fault; chiefly: irrationality (the public body taking leave of its senses), not taking account of relevant factors (a very basic common-sense principle), illegality (*ultra vires*: doing what the legislation prohibits) or 'fettering of discretion' (rigid application of a policy without considering exceptions). Permission is required from the courts to bring a judicial review case.

Human rights cases will normally be brought in the form of a judicial review case, since human rights legislation applies only to public bodies (or to bodies carrying out functions of a public nature), with one or more articles of the European Convention on Human Rights being referred to, in addition to any common law traditional grounds of judicial review. The courts do sometimes award modest financial compensation on human rights grounds.

MENTAL CAPACITY: COURT OF PROTECTION

The Court of Protection's jurisdiction is concerned with the Mental Capacity Act 2005. Various people, including a person thought to lack capacity as well as a range of other interested parties, can bring a case. Some require permission to do so; others don't. The Court has a variety of functions, including making orders and declarations.

VULNERABLE ADULTS WITH CAPACITY: HIGH COURT (INHERENT JURISDICTION: E.G. FAMILY DIVISION)

Applications can be made to the High Court, asking it to exercise its 'inherent jurisdiction' in respect of adults with mental capacity but otherwise vulnerable and in need of protection.

DISPUTED WILLS OR TRANSFER OF PROPERTY: HIGH COURT (EQUITY: CHANCERY DIVISION)

The validity of wills or gifts can be challenged in the High Court on grounds of lack of capacity or undue influence.

NEGLIGENCE CASES AND OTHER CIVIL TORTS: HIGH COURT (QUEEN'S BENCH DIVISION)

In contrast to judicial review, civil negligence cases are about seeking financial compensation for harm that has been suffered – usually physical, sometimes psychological or financial – because of breach of a duty of care by somebody who owed that duty.

CIVIL ORDERS AND INJUNCTIONS: COUNTY COURT, MAGISTRATES' COURT

A victim of some sort of harassment, abuse, domestic violence or persecution can seek a civil order, often called an injunction, from the law courts – for instance, protection from harassment injunctions, non-molestation orders, occupation orders or forced marriage protection orders. Sometimes, another person can seek the order to protect a victim; for example, a local authority or the police might apply for an anti-social behaviour order or a forced marriage protection order.

CRIMINAL LAW PROSECUTION: MAGISTRATES' COURT, CROWN COURT

The Crown Prosecution Service is responsible for bringing most prosecutions, although local authorities (e.g. trading standards officers) can do so sometimes. The Care Quality Commission has powers to prosecute care providers, if necessary. Likewise, the Health and Safety Executive prosecutes under health and safety at work legislation.

Exceptionally, private criminal prosecutions can be taken, by virtue of s.6 of the Prosecution of Offences Act 1985, but these are rare. Private prosecution of some offences requires permission from the Director of Public Prosecutions (e.g. s.127 of the Mental Health Act 1983).

2

Overview of themes and chapters

Key points
Overall observations
    Extent of the law
    Application of the law
    Loopholes in the law
    Protecting vulnerable adults but treating workers fairly
    Information sharing and disclosure
    Degree to which the State should interfere with people's autonomy
    Autonomy, free markets and vulnerable adults
    Direct perpetration by the State of poor care and neglect
    Criminal offences and elderly or otherwise vulnerable people
Summary of the book
    Chapter 3: Safeguarding law and policy
    Chapter 4: Proportionate interventions, the State, human rights
      (and discrimination law)
    Chapter 5: Local social services authorities: pivotal role in safeguarding
    Chapters 6 and 7: The National Health Service
    Chapters 8–12: Regulation of care providers and care workers
    Chapter 13: Mental capacity
    Chapter 14: Inherent jurisdiction of the High Court
    Chapter 15: Interventions and removal of people from their own
      homes (including in circumstances of self-neglect)
    Chapter 16: Civil orders and housing matters
    Chapter 17: Sharing and disclosure of personal and other information
    Chapter 18: Criminal justice: prosecution, evidence, protecting
      victims, coroners
    Chapter 19: Criminal justice support for vulnerable victims and witnesses
    Chapter 20: Criminal justice support for vulnerable suspects
    Chapter 21: Physical harm and abuse: criminal offences
    Chapter 22: Sexual offences
    Chapter 23: Financial harm and abuse: criminal offences
    Chapter 24: Undue influence: gifts, wills (law of equity)
    Chapter 25: Harm and civil wrongs, including negligence
    Chapter 26: Restraint

KEY POINTS

This book is about the law and how it can be used to safeguard adults from abuse or neglect. So it needs to cover both what is happening in practice and what, legally, can be done about it.

As to the occurrence of neglect and abuse – financial, physical, emotional or psychological – it is a sorry and unpleasant tale.

The many cases summarised in the book exemplify unsavoury characteristics of human behaviour. In themselves, they are nothing new. And, in the context of vulnerable adults, it is perhaps even less surprising that these characteristics should be so much in evidence. And yet, even so, particularly because of that vulnerability, some of what is going on is shocking in the true sense of that word. These stories continue to startle and disturb, even after one has digested hundreds, perhaps thousands, of them. And it is, of course, important that they should.

Stories of greed, desperation, temptation, opportunism, deceit, dishonesty, forgery, fraud, undue influence and blatant abuse of position abound. Terrible and sometimes fatal neglect, sadism, cruelty, violent loss of temper, torture and murder, likewise.

All directed towards people who – through disability, age or some other vulnerability – are less able to protect themselves than other people. And week in, week out, as perpetrators are convicted, judges employ terms such as despicable, hard-hearted, callous, evil, cruel, ruthless, merciless, cynical to describe the people they are passing sentence on.

To repeat, unless one has a particularly optimistic view of human nature, none of this is a cause for wonder. Its prevalence is anybody's guess. There is a dearth of reliable information for a number of reasons. But it is clear that neglect and abuse of vulnerable adults is a more than trivial phenomenon.

This chapter picks out a few overall themes and threads running through the book, before summarising each chapter.

OVERALL OBSERVATIONS

A number of general observations need to be made about the law: its extent, its application and loopholes within it.

In addition, a number of aspects of the State's role stand out. These include the balance to be struck between the autonomy of the individual and interference by the State, as well as the unexpected role of State bodies themselves – such as the Department of Health, the NHS and local authorities – in contributing to or perpetrating neglect or abuse.

EXTENT OF THE LAW

There is a remarkable amount of law relevant to the safeguarding of adults. It might seem daunting. However, there is a silver lining. If one bit of law is not appropriate or applied successfully, another might be.

So, for example, if a person with mental capacity to handle money is grossly exploited by an acquaintance, intervention under the Mental Capacity Act 2005 might not be possible. But a prosecution under the Theft Act 1968 might be, if the circumstances of the 'gift' being made amount to dishonesty.

Likewise, a mentally disordered person might be judged to have capacity to engage in unwise sexual relationships. A local authority and the Court of Protection would therefore be unable to utilise the Mental Capacity Act to protect the person. But if the sexual activity is associated with inducement, threat or deception, then a prosecution under the Sexual Offences Act 2003 would still be possible, notwithstanding the presence of mental capacity.

And if a person is living in a state of self-neglect, at least seven pieces of legislation are relevant in considering whether to intervene or not. One has in mind s.47 of the National Assistance Act 1948 (due to be repealed), the Mental Capacity Act 2005, Public Health Act 1936, Environmental Protection Act 1990, Human Rights Act 1998, Mental Health Act 1983 and NHS and Community Care Act 1990. The applicability of none, one or more of these Acts will depend on all the circumstances.

APPLICATION OF THE LAW

In considering all this law, a useful distinction can be made: that is, loopholes in the law, where relevant law does not exist, as opposed to relevant law existing but not being used effectively in practice.

For example, the Mental Capacity Act 2005 is about how decisions should be made if people lack the capacity to decide for themselves. In its application, however, it continues to be too often misunderstood or, for some other reason, not applied properly. The consequence sometimes is to cause even greater harm to the vulnerable adult.

Alternatively, there might be inconsistent and selective application of the law, not through misunderstanding but for other reasons.

For example, there continue to be domestic manslaughter convictions involving isolated and 'inadequate' family carers (typically a son or daughter) who have not called for assistance when a parent is dying, say, of pressure sores. Yet no manslaughter prosecutions are brought when NHS Trust Boards, either knowingly or at least recklessly, reduce drastically standards of care – or even explicitly refuse to isolate infected patients – and many patients die (e.g. 38 at Stoke Mandeville, 90 at Maidstone and Tunbridge Wells and many hundreds at Stafford Hospital).

Or take the somewhat uneven approach to larger-scale, corporate financial misdeeds and those committed by individual rogues. For instance, HSBC were fined some £10 million and agreed to pay £30 million compensation to elderly people who had been swindled. That is a large sum of money and represents financial harm and exploitation on a large scale. Elderly people had been sold bonds to pay for care home fees, irrespective of their short life expectancy, which meant that the bonds were entirely inappropriate.[1] Nobody was sent to prison. Yet when a fraudster sold useless or faulty alarm systems to a number of elderly people, and gained dishonestly some £28,000, he was sentenced to 54 months in prison.[2]

LOOPHOLES IN THE LAW

On the other hand are the genuine loopholes which explain the absence of legal remedy and action, in contrast to misapplication of the law or unwillingness to use it.

One such glaring loophole is revealed by the fact that, in English law, the criminal offences of wilful neglect or ill-treatment apply only to people who are mentally disordered or who lack mental capacity. Otherwise, no matter how badly treated and no matter how vulnerable a person is, no such criminal offence exists.

Likewise, given the extent of systemic neglect in health care, brought about by decisions of senior managers, the absence of an offence of corporate neglect (compare the offence of corporate manslaughter) is also a lacuna.

Another perceived gap is the inability of a local authority to gain compulsory entry (with a court order) to the home of a vulnerable adult, with mental capacity, perceived to be at risk of abuse or neglect. At the time of writing, Scotland has long since filled this hole, Wales is proposing to do so to some extent, and England is consulting about whether to.[3]

PROTECTING VULNERABLE ADULTS BUT TREATING WORKERS FAIRLY

The extent of State intervention is a hot topic in relation to the regulation of health and social care providers and workers.

Care providers, for instance, are arguably regulated too lightly, given the evidence of inadequate, poor, degrading, inhumane and sometimes fatal care that vulnerable adults are regularly subjected to in care homes, in hospitals and in their own homes. This is not for want of potentially effective legislation, more about the way it is being used.

Furthermore, central government has in any case given a push in the direction of less regulation in social care by encouraging the use of 'direct payments', given by local authorities to people so that they can buy their own care. They are free to use the money to employ personal assistants who do not come within the Care Quality Commission's remit and so are underneath the regulatory radar.

In contrast is the danger of legislation, designed to regulate employees working with vulnerable adults, functioning in a disproportionate and unfair manner. This has become evident, for example, in the context of the extent of information that

---

1   Financial Services Authority. *FSA fines HSBC £10.5million for mis-selling products to elderly customers.* London: FSA, 2011. Accessed on 4 September 2012 at: www.fsa.gov.uk/library/communication/pr/2011/105.shtml.

2   *R v Kalian* [2012] EWCA Crim 652.

3   Adult Support and Protection (Scotland) Act 2007. Also: Welsh Government. *Social Services (Wales) Bill: consultation document.* Cardiff: WG, 2012, p.66. Also: Department of Health. *Consultation on new adult safeguarding power.* London: DH, paras 9–10.

can be included in enhanced criminal record certificates. These certificates are required and considered by an employer when taking on a person to work with vulnerable adults.

Likewise, the same sort of issue has surfaced in terms of the restricted grounds on which workers are now able to appeal against their being placed on the 'barred list' by the Disclosure and Barring Service (formerly the Independent Safeguarding Authority). If they are on the list, workers are prohibited from working with vulnerable adults; and central government has narrowed down the grounds on which they can appeal to a tribunal.

INFORMATION SHARING AND DISCLOSURE

They say that information is power and perhaps, in the modern world, with more information than ever available and conveyed so easily by means of computer and the internet, this is even more so.

Mention has already been made, immediately above, as to how sharing information – on criminal record certificates or referral to the Disclosure and Barring Service – can have a huge impact on people's lives. There are, in addition, other considerations.

SHARING INFORMATION BETWEEN AGENCIES

Legally, agencies such as local authorities and the police have to strive continually for a balance in deciding whether to share safeguarding information between themselves or with third parties. It is a matter of balancing the wider public interest (which might be served by sharing or disclosure) with interests of confidentiality. The Data Protection Act 1998 and the Human Rights Act 1998, as well as established common law rules, are relevant.

FREEDOM OF INFORMATION

However, there is another piece of legislation to do with information that is of great importance in the context of safeguarding.

The Freedom of Information Act 2000 governs requests made to public bodies about information that is non-personal (in relation to the requester). It might be information requested about somebody else (e.g. a dead relative or hospital staff who treated that relative). Or it might be non-personal (or at least anonymised) information – for instance, statistics on serious incidents, deaths from infection, pressure sore incidence.

There seem to be at least two key points to make.

First, the Act understandably contains a number of provisos, on the basis of which a public body can refuse to disclose the information sought. These provisos may relate to law enforcement, compromising an investigation, prejudice in the conduct of public affairs, health and safety, personal information or information originally given in confidence. In addition, requests that would be too expensive to process or vexatious requests also constitute grounds for not making the information available.

So, when the Information Commissioner and, beyond the Commissioner, the Information Tribunal hear disputes, they consider these provisos and whether non-disclosure is justified in the particular case. On their face, the provisos are reasonable and attempt to strike a balance between complete openness and legitimate limitations.

Second, however, this balancing exercise, as framed in the Act, presupposes that public bodies will, by and large, act in good faith. And the approach of the Information Commissioner and of the Information Tribunal seems generally – other than in blatantly obvious instances – to assume that this is indeed the way in which the public bodies act.

The problem is that such an assumption can, these days, not be made. In other words, it is arguable that too many public bodies would think nothing of cynically undermining the principles of the Act, as well as taking advantage of the Information Commissioner's or Tribunal's understandable inclination not to attribute bad faith to such a body.

One has only to think of the huge cover-up, which emerged in 2012, orchestrated by South Yorkshire Police in relation to the Hillsborough football disaster, or of so many NHS hospitals adept at concealing widespread poor care.

DEGREE TO WHICH THE STATE SHOULD INTERFERE WITH PEOPLE'S AUTONOMY

A persistent theme in safeguarding is the extent to which the State – for example, in the form of a local authority – be given legal powers to interfere in people's lives on grounds of their diminished mental capacity, mental disorder or other vulnerability.

If somebody with mental capacity wishes to live in a state of self-neglect and malnutrition leading to their death, should he or she be allowed to get on with it undisturbed?

Or suppose an elderly couple are being oppressed, bullied and perhaps assaulted by their middle-aged son. If they have the mental capacity to decide to do nothing about it, should the local authority have the legal power to step in against their wishes?

AUTONOMY AND DIGNITY

Autonomy and dignity would seem obvious enough principles on which safeguarding might rest. They would also appear to go hand in hand, the latter following from the former. Though not mentioned explicitly in it, the two concepts are often associated with the European Convention on Human Rights and, in particular, article 8 which refers, amongst other things, to people's right to respect for their private lives.

Autonomy can be defined as self-determination or self-government. Dignity is defined in the dictionary as a sense of pride in oneself, self-respect or the state or quality of being worthy of honour or respect.[4]

Nevertheless, autonomy and dignity might not always dovetail and, when it comes to safeguarding, might even jar.

The Mental Capacity Act 2005 states that a person, with capacity to do so, might make unwise decisions, which in themselves do not necessarily signal a lack of capacity. However, what if those decisions are made by a vulnerable adult, with mental capacity, leading to what onlookers would deem to be a degrading and undignified outcome? Or, indeed, to abuse, violence and murder – as has happened on some occasions?

Undue influence or coercion might be in play in such circumstances, in which case interference by the State might be more obviously justifiable. Thus, the courts have signalled their readiness to intervene in such cases – at least up to a point – using their own common law power called the 'inherent jurisdiction'. This would be to protect the vulnerable person's human rights under article 8 of the European Convention. But, there again, suppose there is no undue influence or coercion – or at least none obviously identifiable?

There is also an obvious disconnection between autonomy and dignity in another situation; that is, when the person concerned lacks the mental capacity to take a truly autonomous decision. Does the concept of dignity apply to a person who is unable to understand what is happening?

The answer, according to the law courts, is yes. They have stated that it is not just the 'sentient or self-conscious who have dignity interests protected by the law'. Dignity extends even to unconsciousness (let alone to a conscious but mentally incapacitated person); it is 'demeaning to the human spirit to say that, being unconscious, he can have no interest in his personal privacy and dignity, in how he lives or dies'.[5] This surely must be the right approach.

In turn, there then needs to be some objective notion of dignity as well as a subjective one.

This means that, in principle, notions of dignity might clash with pure autonomy. If so, this then poses the further question as to what the State should do about it, if anything. The free-market approach in health and social care increasingly puts great store by the notion of autonomy.

AUTONOMY, FREE MARKETS AND VULNERABLE ADULTS

Notions of autonomy and indeed of dignity and the right not to be unduly interfered with by the State are associated in law with human rights.

Yet these notions are being taken in another direction as well: namely, to support the idea of a society run on free-market lines. Which is by no means an

---

4   *Concise Oxford Dictionary of Current English* (8th edition). Oxford: Clarendon Press, 1990.

5   *Airedale NHS Trust v Bland* [1993] AC 789 (House of Lords).

inevitable corollary of human rights. This is sometimes called neo-liberalism and it is increasingly being applied to health and social care, as well as to society at large.

The underlying premiss envisages self-reliant consumers making their way through life and the markets, exercising choice, stimulating competition and so driving up the quality of services. It is an ideology that seeks to reduce greatly the role of the State.

However, in the case of vulnerable adults, there is a serious concern that, taken to an extreme, this ideology is not appropriate. If this is the case, then the implications for safeguarding activity are significant in at least two ways.

First, if the market-based model of health and social care is not suitable for older people with complex needs, there is a high risk of poor care and neglect proliferating at the hands of both State and private sector care providers. Which is exactly what has been happening.

Second, if vulnerable adults are being left with ever less support, then they will be even more at risk from financial, physical or sexual abuse.

FREE MARKETS AND PRIVATE PROVIDERS ARE NOT A PANACEA

It would, of course, be erroneous to suggest, for example, that the inhumane and neglectful treatment of elderly people is the result of the private sector and free-market approach to health and social care.

There have been plenty of examples of State-run NHS hospitals treating patients extremely badly. However, equally, the blind assertion and dogma that the private sector will do better than the public sector is borne out by no evidence at all. In fact, it is quite clear that, to the extent the private sector has become involved in health and social care, it too has sometimes become steeped in highly neglectful or abusive practices toward elderly and other vulnerable adults.

It is not at all clear how well the free-market model fits vulnerable adults, particularly elderly people who – ill, sick, mentally weakened and with complex needs – are not the happy shoppers, exercising choice and finding value in the marketplace, which the model envisages. Likewise, people with learning disabilities or mental health problems.

Central government, of course, retorts that local authorities and the NHS should give added support to those who are more vulnerable and need additional help to achieve this control, choice and independence.

Given, however, the general shortage of resources to cope with demand in health and social care – and the prevailing ideology of self-reliance – this is clearly wishful thinking. It is not happening.

LEAVING PEOPLE TO SAFEGUARD THEMSELVES

Government has stated that there is no place for a paternalistic welfare state.[6] It maintains that 'self-care' will enable people to have 'maximum choice and control' and that the State and its agencies will be 'more active and enabling, less controlling'.[7]

This sounds attractive, but in practice it carries the undoubted danger that vulnerable people in need might – in the hurly-burly and financially harassed world of social and health care – be left to sink or swim, with minimal intervention and assistance. For example, a statement made in May 2011 talked of protection for vulnerable adults – but also noted that:

> The Government wishes to empower individuals to take responsibility for their own lives. This includes enabling them to protect themselves from harm and abuse, with and without assistance from others.[8]

In combination with protection from statutory agencies, there is nothing objectionable in such a statement. The peril is that local authorities will seize on it, in this age of the consumer, and decide that basically people should safeguard themselves – whilst the welfare state shrinks.

More generally, the idea that the State should recede in favour of family, friends, neighbours and local community networks – the Big Society – is attractive in one breath. But in another, taken as an excuse for swingeing cuts to health and social care services, it is barely realistic. Not least because (a) vulnerable adults may simply not have family or friends at all or be able to provide support, and (b) it is quite clear that the family, friends and neighbours – sometimes invested with halos by central government – may be the very people exploiting or otherwise harming the vulnerable adult.

Put simply, one possible outcome of current government thinking is to leave, increasingly, vulnerable people with health and social care needs in some sort of Wild West, prey to a mounting tide of abuse and neglect. With those involved in safeguarding activity left to try to pick up the pieces.

CONSUMERS, COMMODITIES AND VULNERABLE ADULTS

There is one last, but major, ramification of this ideology of the free market and the consumer. The last decade or more has seen what we might call an increasing trend of viewing adults with health and social care needs as commodities – the very converse of 'consumers' – who need to be priced up and sold off to the lowest bidder. And both the State and the independent sector are active in this process.

---

6   Department of Health. *Putting people first: a shared vision and commitment to the transformation of adult social care.* London: Her Majesty's Government, 2007, p.2.

7   Skills for Care. *Common core principles to support self care.* London: Skills for Care, 2008, p.2 (Foreword written by two government ministers).

8   Department of Health. *Statement of government policy on adult safeguarding.* 16 May 2011, Gateway Reference 16072. London: DH, 2011, p.5.

Once you view people, especially vulnerable people with complex needs, as such commodities, the path to poor and neglectful care beckons.

Local authorities, for example, have long been trying to save money by contracting out care to the private sector. There is a temptation to pay as little as possible to care providers, thereby driving down not just cost but also quality.

Private sector care homes, in turn, have a duty to make a profit to satisfy shareholders. The result, of this combination of unrealistic commissioning and the need to make a profit, is shortcuts. That is, shortcuts with the amount of care allotted, its quality and, with the quality, the competence and pay of care staff.

And this is why, for example, in 2012, we find judges convicting senior carers of wilful neglect in care homes but also referring to the background of large companies, some of them owned by private equity concerns, taking shortcuts with people's care.

For instance, when a care home manager wilfully neglected an elderly person with dementia and was sent to prison, the judge roundly criticised BUPA for attempting to fill as many beds in the home while cutting costs.[9] Similar comments were made about the manner in which Southern Cross was running another care home, where a conviction for wilful neglect also resulted.[10]

The story of another company, Castlebeck Ltd, is illuminating. In the search for viable commodities and profit, it carried out market research in 2002–2003 and decided that State-funded people with learning disabilities constituted just such a business opportunity. To the extent that it opened a private hospital, called Winterbourne View, for the purpose and charged the NHS £3500 per week per patient.

This is, of course, a substantial sum of money, even for caring for people with complex needs. The commissioners, largely the NHS, seemed only too pleased to 'get rid' of these patients and carried out little review and monitoring of what was going on. And the regulator (the Care Quality Commission), apparently operating so as to give the private sector as much leeway as reasonably possible without officious interference, stood off – despite concerns being raised by a whistleblowing nurse.

Yet, for this money, patients were systematically bullied, kicked, slapped, taunted, sat on and variously humiliated. Following exposure by the BBC programme *Panorama*, 11 carers were eventually convicted of ill-treating persons lacking mental capacity.

In 2006, Castlebeck had been bought at a cost of £255 million by Lydian Capital Partnership, a Swiss private equity firm. In 2007, profits made by Castlebeck (which owns other care homes and hospitals) stood at £18.9 million; in 2009,

---

9   Bunyan, N. 'Bupa put profit first at filthy and understaffed care home, says judge.' *Daily Telegraph*, 17 March 2012.
10   Kennedy, R. 'Nurse at Southern Cross home did not call doctor and Joyce Wordingham died, court hears.' *Evening Chronicle*, 3 March 2012.

profits stood at £13.3 million.[11] Much of the profit is generated from the State, from taxpayers' money, since the NHS and local authorities provide the vast bulk of the funding.

In late 2012, following on from a Freedom of Information Act request to the Care Quality Commission, it was revealed that the Commission knew about at least 217 care providers in England employing workers not properly qualified. In particular, one company alone was employing 23 workers with criminal convictions including theft and assault. One worker had no fewer than seven convictions. And eight companies in the Midlands alone weren't carrying out criminal record checks.[12]

All this is unedifying. Coupled with the well-reported neglect and abuse endemic in care homes and amongst domiciliary care workers, it does not suggest that the private sector is the simple answer to giving us humanity and dignity. Certainly, the Department of Health's final report on the Winterbourne scandal did not limit its scathing criticism to the statutory sector, including the NHS and the Care Quality Commission. It noted of Castlebeck's role:

> While most organisations providing care put in place governance arrangements that support safety and quality, some do not pay sufficient attention to this area. Where the leadership of an organisation allows a culture to develop that does not foster safety and quality in care, the people providing that leadership have to be held to account for the service failings. In the words of the serious case review, 'Castlebeck Ltd's appreciation of events…was limited, not least because they took the financial rewards without any apparent accountability.' This is an unacceptable situation and must change.[13]

STATE CARE SECTOR GROOMED FOR PRICING PEOPLE UP

Which is not to say that the public sector has covered itself in glory.

It was, after all, the NHS at the heart of scandal and death at Mid Staffordshire NHS Foundation Trust. Even so, it could be argued that an increasing free-market approach, even within the NHS, was in some ways responsible.

This is because of the grooming of the NHS, over the last decade, to organise, plan and deliver services on a purely business model, with competition for the tendering out of services in mind.

This has involved 'payment by results', 'care pathways' for patients (into which people with more complex needs do not easily fit) and the imperative of hospitals balancing their books. And it was this grooming that led to the scandal in Stafford;

---

11   Slack, J. and Kisiel, R. 'Profits before patients: care home residents subjected to horrific abuse went to A&E 76 times in three years – but private owner did nothing.' *Daily Mail*, 7 August 2012. And: Flynn, M. *Winterbourne View Hospital: a serious case review*. Bristol: South Gloucestershire Safeguarding Adults Board, 2012.

12   'Home care workers "not properly vetted".' *BBC News*, 15 October 2012. Accessed on 15 October 2012 at: www.bbc.co.uk/news/health-19944217.

13   Department of Health. *Transforming care: A national response to Winterbourne View Hospital Department of Health Review: Final Report*. London: DH, 2012, paras 5.6–5.7.

the business model demanded that the hospital become a foundation trust. In order to do that, it cut care so drastically that it started to inflict suffering and death on patients. And, until the NHS Trust got caught out, the Department of Health gave full backing to the hospital and its financially driven cuts to services.[14]

Perhaps this pricing up of people's needs, this crude valuation of what they are worth in terms of time, expertise, humane care and, really, the milk of human kindness – whether in the private or public sectors – promises a disastrous moral outcome. And maybe figures such as Professor Michael Sandel have got it right when they warn about the moral impact of such market forces – and that there are some things that money can't buy.[15]

DIRECT PERPETRATION BY THE STATE OF POOR CARE AND NEGLECT

There is a striking dichotomy in the role of the State between protecting adults from neglect and abuse and – in flat contradiction, of course – its other role in perpetrating the very same systemically.

Integral to such systemic neglect and sometimes abuse are disingenuousness and concealment on a significant scale, which prevent a solution. This latter trait makes the question of public access to both personal and non-personal information all the more acute – and the rules about this, under the Freedom of Information Act and the Data Protection Act, all the more important.

This dichotomy surfaces particularly in the provision and commission of health care by the NHS and of social care by local authorities. Politically, morally and legally, the stakes are raised hugely if it is the State itself that is responsible not for unavoidable, rare occurrences of neglect but for its systemic perpetration.

For example, convincing evidence points to systemic neglect of older people within acute hospitals over many years. Yet very little is done about it. A culture of denial, concealment and disingenuousness is as common as the neglect itself. This culture emanates from politicians downwards, through the Department of Health and down to various levels of regional and local NHS management.

The problem is systemic in the sense both that it is widespread (which does not. of course, preclude plenty of good practice) and also that very little effective is being done about it.

On the financial side of things, too, the Department of Health and the NHS have for many years, behind the scenes, continued to try to avoid paying for what is termed NHS continuing health care and left it to elderly people and their families to pay for care, which, rightfully and legally, should have been free of charge. Likewise, local authorities have played fast and loose with rules about charging top-up fees for care homes, for intermediate care and for reablement. In any other

---

14   Francis, R. (Chair). *Independent inquiry into care provided by Mid Staffordshire NHS Foundation Trust January 2005–March 2009.* London: TSO, 2010.

15   Sandel, M. *What money can't buy: the moral limits of the markets.* London: Allen Lane, 2012.

setting, such a deliberate or reckless approach to the law and to vulnerable people's finances would be regarded as financial abuse.

Local practitioners in health, social care and the police might sometimes stand back and congratulate themselves on catching villainous, private individuals who prey on vulnerable adults, such as the carer who steals rings from the fingers of elderly people in a care home. And yet they remain silent and inactive concerning far worse when it comes to systemic physical or financial harm and abuse perpetrated by the State.

In sum, it is no exaggeration to say that it is now possible for an elderly person to be unlawfully charged tens of thousands of pounds by a local authority in a care home, for care that the NHS should have funded. They might then be admitted to hospital, where they are poorly assessed, are not cared for properly and subsequently die, depressed, lacking in dignity – finished off by pressure sores, dehydration and malnutrition.

But, for some reason, we do not consider any of this to come within the scope of safeguarding.

CRIMINAL OFFENCES AND ELDERLY OR OTHERWISE VULNERABLE PEOPLE

The later chapters of this book, covering criminal offences involving financial or physical harm, reveal apparently significant levels of criminal offences committed against older people or younger adults otherwise vulnerable.

One should be wary of drawing unwarranted or simplistic conclusions about why this happens. However, at least one pattern is that of very low-paid care workers, who are asked to care for people (in their own homes or in care homes) with very complex and demanding needs. These care workers may also have a minimum of training and skills, something that is all too easily associated with low pay.

A common result is twofold. Facing financial hardship at home, carers succumb to temptation and opportunism and start to borrow or simply take money – by means of theft, fraud or forgery – from the vulnerable victim (who may or may not be relatively wealthy). Alternatively, faced with very difficult behaviour, low-paid and low-skilled staff lose their temper and start physically to abuse their charges – either in isolated incidents or, inured to it, more regularly.

It is, of course, no excuse, legal or otherwise, to plead low pay and difficult work in justification of criminal offences. Nor are these factors the sole cause. Nonetheless, if care of older and other vulnerable people were more valued, morally and financially, then perhaps the pattern might change for the better.

SUMMARY OF THE BOOK

With the above themes and issues in mind, the following paragraphs provide a brief summary of the whole book.

CHAPTER 3: SAFEGUARDING LAW AND POLICY

This chapter covers a number of general points about safeguarding. These include the policy background, definitions and principles – including abuse, neglect, harm and vulnerable adults. It also looks forward to changes to social care law as outlined in the draft Care and Support Bill 2012.

CHAPTER 4: PROPORTIONATE INTERVENTIONS, THE STATE, HUMAN RIGHTS (AND DISCRIMINATION LAW)

Proportionate interventions constitute almost the holy grail of safeguarding: that is, trying to avoid too much or too little State intervention in a person's life. The cornerstone of proportionality is the Human Rights Act 1998.

Relevant human rights include article 5 (deprivation of liberty) and article 8 (right to respect for private life). Other rights, not so closely linked to proportionality but just as – perhaps more – important because they are absolute, are article 2 (right to life) and article 3 (right not to be subjected to inhuman or degrading treatment or punishment).

CHAPTER 5: LOCAL SOCIAL SERVICES AUTHORITIES: PIVOTAL ROLE IN SAFEGUARDING

This chapter outlines the statutory basis for the safeguarding activity of local social services authorities and the range of assistance and intervention they can provide under community care legislation. It also looks forward to the changes that will be made if and when the draft Care and Support Bill 2012 becomes law.

In addition, it considers the extent to which local authorities themselves sometimes perpetrate, cause, contribute to or are associated with neglect or abuse.

The chapter draws attention – with reference to legal cases – to the common pitfalls, legal and practical, to be avoided in safeguarding. Pointing out mistakes and things going wrong is not to take a negative approach; if obvious pitfalls are avoided, then by default local authorities are much more likely to get things right.

CHAPTERS 6 AND 7: THE NATIONAL HEALTH SERVICE

These chapters on the National Health Service are of particular importance: first, the NHS is meant to be treating and looking after people's health; second, it is run by the State; and yet, third, it continues to be responsible for perpetrating, systemically, poor, harmful, degrading and neglectful hospital care. And the chief victims of this are vulnerable elderly people. Fourth, in terms of safeguarding, it remains the great blind spot.

These chapters therefore spell out in some detail the evidence of neglect within NHS hospitals, together with contributory causes, in order to be clear just what it is to which safeguarding activity generally, and the law and guidance in particular, needs to be applied. They link, logically, the key factors, one following from another: (a) the extent of poor care and neglect, (b) the model of health care that is systematically marginalising older people with complex needs, (c) the denial and concealment that takes place, (d) the lack of accountability, and (e) the ruthless treatment and suppression of whistleblowers.

In the author's view, tackling neglect of vulnerable patients in the NHS is, currently, the biggest challenge facing those who are engaged in safeguarding.

The point of these chapters is not to condemn the NHS. Precisely the opposite. First, because there remains a great deal of good care, even for older people, although this is being fast eroded. Second, because it is such a venerated and fine institution that it needs saving from a new generation of managers and politicians who are steadily but surely destroying an ethos of public service, care, compassion and dedication – and thereby cranking up levels of poor care and neglect.

CHAPTERS 8–12: REGULATION OF CARE PROVIDERS AND CARE WORKERS

Regulation of health and social care providers, as well as of professionals and workers in the field, has, in principle, a key role to play in protecting and safeguarding adults.

Rogue individual workers might be involved in dishonesty, incompetence, cruelty, sadism and so on. Equally, it might be organisational, institutional failings behind poor care and neglect – in hospitals, in care homes or people's own homes.

The regulation is fivefold.

First (Chapter 8), health and social care providers are regulated currently by an organisation, notionally independent but under the political thumb of the Department of Health, known as the Care Quality Commission.

Second (Chapter 9), there is a system of criminal record certificates, which are required when people wish to work with vulnerable adults and before they can take up such employment.

Third (Chapter 10) is a barred list, held by the Disclosure and Barring Service (DBS). Inclusion on this list means that a person is legally unable to work with vulnerable adults (or with children, for whom there is a separate list).

Fourth (Chapter 11) is the system of regulation for health and social care professionals, operated by the General Medical Council, the Nursing and Midwifery Council and the Health and Care Professions Council.

Fifth (Chapter 12) is an irregular, informal and problematic, but hugely important, element of regulation: whistleblowing by staff.

CHAPTER 13: MENTAL CAPACITY

The Mental Capacity Act 2005 is set out in some detail because, by definition, adults lacking mental capacity to take decisions about their everyday welfare and finances are likely to be more vulnerable.

Furthermore, the Act is meant to be both protective and empowering for the individual who does or may lack capacity. In practice, however, a tension sometimes emerges in safeguarding when these two concepts jar.

A number of key issues are covered and illustrated with case law, including the test for mental capacity, unwise decisions, acting in a person's best interests, restraint, depriving people of their liberty, lasting powers of attorney, Court of Protection interventions to safeguard vulnerable adults lacking capacity, advance refusals of medical treatment, independent mental capacity advocacy. The offences of ill-treatment and wilful neglect are explained and illustrated in a later chapter.

In the last two years or so, a slew of legal cases has streamed through the courts; at their heart has lain the attempt of local authorities and their staff to marry up their safeguarding concerns with the rules of the Mental Capacity Act 2005.

CHAPTER 14: INHERENT JURISDICTION OF THE HIGH COURT

Many decisions previously taken by the Family Division of the High Court under common law – the inherent jurisdiction – are now made by the Court of Protection under the Mental Capacity Act 2005. However, some issues that might arise in safeguarding fall outside the 2005 Act and so still call for the exercise of the jurisdiction.

Primarily, the inherent jurisdiction comes into play either when a person effectively lacks capacity, but, for some reason, the matter in hand does not come under the rules of the Mental Capacity Act, or when a person has capacity to take a decision but circumstances mean that he or she is being prevented from exercising that capacity.

CHAPTER 15: INTERVENTIONS AND REMOVAL OF PEOPLE FROM THEIR OWN HOMES (INCLUDING IN CIRCUMSTANCES OF SELF-NEGLECT)

This chapter covers a clutch of legally based interventions that might assist in protecting and safeguarding vulnerable adults in certain circumstances, including that of self-neglect. These include removing people from their home under the National Assistance Act 1948, environmental health law and interventions under the Mental Health Act 1983.

CHAPTER 16: CIVIL ORDERS AND HOUSING MATTERS

This chapter considers the use of civil orders for safeguarding and protection purposes, including non-molestation, occupation and forced marriage protection (all under the Family Law Act 1996), protection from harassment and anti-social behaviour. It also summarises steps that housing providers can take to manage safeguarding issues.

The chapter also looks ahead to the set of orders, including criminal behaviour orders, that are expected to replace anti-social behaviour orders and injunctions.

Civil orders might play a crucial preventative role and be an alternative to criminal proceedings for various reasons, including the absence of a criminal offence, weakness of evidence or the unwillingness of the victim to participate in criminal proceedings.

CHAPTER 17: SHARING AND DISCLOSURE OF PERSONAL AND OTHER INFORMATION

This chapter covers the law about the sharing and disclosure of personal (and other) information – between agencies and to individuals.

Agencies may need to share information in order to protect people, yet those people also have rights to confidentiality. In addition, people who believe they have been wrongly vilified or accused may wish to have access to information held about them. And sometimes when harm (including death) has come to their relative, family members may do their own investigating to try to find out what happened or is still happening (e.g. in a hospital or care home) and to disinter the relevant information.

All this brings into play various laws, including the common law of confidentiality, Human Rights Act 1998, Data Protection Act 1998 and the Freedom of Information Act 2000.

This chapter summarises some key legal 'rules', illustrating them with a range of cases from the courts, the Information Commissioner and the Information Tribunal.

CHAPTER 18: CRIMINAL JUSTICE: PROSECUTION, EVIDENCE, PROTECTING VICTIMS, CORONERS

This chapter summarises prosecution codes and rules relevant to vulnerable victims, including standard of proof, evidence, public interest and prosecution policies relating to particular groups of people.

Also outlined in this chapter are victim support, sentencing and multi-agency public protection arrangements (MAPPA), which involve managing the risks posed by a convicted offender who has been released from detention.

The role of coroners is also summarised, with examples of verdicts relating to the deaths of vulnerable adults.

CHAPTER 19: CRIMINAL JUSTICE SUPPORT FOR VULNERABLE VICTIMS AND WITNESSES

This chapter summarises the main provisions for assisting vulnerable witnesses to give evidence, starting with police interviews right through to court cases.

Special measures relating to criminal trials are contained within the Youth Justice and Criminal Evidence Act 1999, including, for instance, the giving of video evidence or of other help to the witness.

Other assistance available, right through the criminal justice process, is detailed in the guidance from the Ministry of Justice, aimed at achieving 'best evidence'.

CHAPTER 20: CRIMINAL JUSTICE SUPPORT FOR VULNERABLE SUSPECTS

Sometimes, a vulnerable adult is a suspect in criminal proceedings rather than a witness. This chapter summarises some of the ways in which the criminal justice system responds to that vulnerability, including the provision of appropriate adults, special measures, diversion away from the criminal justice system and sentencing.

CHAPTER 21: PHYSICAL HARM AND ABUSE: CRIMINAL OFFENCES

Physical harm and abuse might constitute a criminal offence, including assault, battery, manslaughter, murder and assisted suicide.

In addition are the wide-ranging offences of wilful neglect or ill-treatment which are contained in both the Mental Health Act 1983 and the Mental Capacity Act 2005.

And, under the Domestic Violence, Crime and Victims Act 2004, there is an offence of causing the death of – or serious physical harm to – a vulnerable adult, either by causing this directly or failing to take reasonable steps to prevent it.

These offences are summarised in this chapter and illustrated with examples.

The role of the Health and Safety Executive is also considered and how it could, and should, be using health and safety at work legislation to prosecute in circumstances of neglect, or even abuse, when this is due to a poor system of work.

CHAPTER 22: SEXUAL OFFENCES

Under the Sexual Offences Act 2003 there are various basic offences (rape, sexual assault, etc.), as relevant to vulnerable adults as to anybody else.

However, in addition are offences specifically related to victims with a mental disorder. These offences have special rules attached. Of particular note is that, of these three sets of offences, two do not require that the victim lacked capacity to consent to the sexual activity. Lack of capacity is not required when there is inducement, threat or deception involved or the perpetrator is a care worker.

CHAPTER 23: FINANCIAL HARM AND ABUSE: CRIMINAL OFFENCES

This chapter covers financial abuse of vulnerable adults. It is perceived to be a serious and widespread problem.

Perpetrators typically include a range of individual people in positions of trust, including close family members, friends, neighbours, both informal and paid carers, nurses, social services staff, bank staff, solicitors and even church ministers. The chapter also covers offences committed by rogue traders and by 'cold callers'.

In criminal law, financial abuse might come in the form of theft, burglary, robbery, fraud, false accounting and forgery. The number of legal cases easily identified and involving financial abuse, both by carers and other professionals in positions of trust, suggests that the problem is more than trivial.

Under the radar, and rarely regarded as a safeguarding matter or as financial abuse (let alone a criminal matter), is systemic, unlawful charging for services by some local authorities, the NHS or large companies.

CHAPTER 24: UNDUE INFLUENCE: GIFTS, WILLS (LAW OF EQUITY)

In civil law, and apart from lack of capacity, there is sometimes an alternative ground on which a transaction may be set aside. This is on the basis of a legal, equitable concept known as undue influence. It can provide a legal remedy in relation to suspicious, improper transactions.

This chapter illustrates undue influence with legal cases and also summarises in what circumstances cases might be brought and by whom.

CHAPTER 25: HARM AND CIVIL WRONGS, INCLUDING NEGLIGENCE

This chapter covers civil torts. These are legal 'wrongs' that give rise to civil actions for damages. Two such torts are trespass to the person and false imprisonment. Negligence is another.

They are relevant to safeguarding for two reasons. First, they require a lower standard of proof than is required in criminal proceedings. So a failed criminal prosecution does not necessarily preclude a civil action. Second, such cases may achieve significant and important financial compensation for the victim who has suffered harm.

That said, there are circumstances in which the courts protect local authorities (and sometimes the NHS) from findings of negligence if the alleged harm is associated with difficult statutory, policy or financial decisions made by the authority.

CHAPTER 26: RESTRAINT

The physical restraint of adults remains a substantial issue. On the one hand, total prohibition of restraint might sometimes result in harm to both the service user and other people. Equally, improper restraint runs the risk of injury to the restrained or the restrainer, breach of human rights, the criminal offence of assault and battery, and the civil tort of trespass to the person.

This chapter refers to the rules under the Mental Capacity Act 2005, to Department of Health guidance on restraint and to a number of key legal cases illustrating the importance of a careful approach to restraint – and also to the sometimes fine line between legally acceptable and unacceptable practices.

Safeguarding law and policy

Key points
Adult protection and safeguarding adults: legal underpinning
    Proposals for inclusion in legislation
    Welfare functions under community care legislation underpins safeguarding
No secrets: Department of Health guidance and its implications
Definition of vulnerable adult under current legislation and guidance
    Vulnerable adults or adults at risk of harm – or neither?
Harm: abuse, neglect, acts of omission
Self-neglect
Institutional, systemic neglect and omissions
When to intervene
Inter-agency approach to adult protection
Information sharing
Prevalence of abuse or neglect of vulnerable adults
Draft Care and Support Bill 2012: key points in relation to safeguarding
    General well-being duty: including protection from neglect and abuse
    Information and advice: including about safety
    Efficient and effective market in care and support services
    General duty to cooperate: including for protection of people from
        abuse or neglect
    Duty to cooperate unless incompatible or it would have adverse effect
    Provision of services in the local area: prevention, delay or
        reduction of need
    How to meet people's care and support needs
    Duty to assess
    Duty to assess carers
    Refusal of assessment: lack of capacity
    National eligibility criteria
    Duty to meet the needs of carers
    Care plans and support plans
    Abuse or neglect: duty of local authority to make enquiries or cause
        enquiries to be made by others
    Safeguarding adults boards
    Safeguarding reviews: deaths or other concerns
    Abolition of old power to remove people from their homes
    Protection of people's property

KEY POINTS

This chapter sets out the current legal underpinning to safeguarding and looks at the draft Care and Support Bill, published in 2012 and possibly becoming law by 2015.

In particular, the chapter covers the current guidance – called *No secrets*, issued in 2000 by the Department of Health – on the nature of neglect and abuse, definition of a vulnerable adult, multi-agency working and the sharing of information.

ADULT PROTECTION AND SAFEGUARDING ADULTS: LEGAL UNDERPINNING

Adult protection, or safeguarding adults, has only relatively recently been identified as a concern and area of work in its own right. Its boundaries are unclear; it remains relatively ill-defined.

In England, it has hitherto been recognised only by the absence in social services legislation of any reference to it. Nonetheless, it is a fast-growing activity for local social services authorities, to which central government – through guidance rather than legislation – has given the lead in dealing with the issue.

This situation has contrasted with child protection provisions contained in the Children Act 1989, which explicitly confer significant protective functions on local authorities in relation to children.

Central government has so far failed to adopt proposals originally made by the Law Commission in 1995 that local authorities in England should be given explicit, statutory protective powers for adults. This lacuna in England has, for some years now, contrasted with the position in Scotland, where the Adult Support and Protection (Scotland) Act 2007 gives Scottish local authorities explicit duties and powers of intervention.

PROPOSALS FOR INCLUSION IN LEGISLATION

Nonetheless, in 2012, the government announced its decision to legislate for England, although the proposed changes do not go as far as Scottish legislation. (The Welsh Government has made its own proposals, which, on balance, will probably turn out to be closer to the English than the Scottish model.[1])

In 2011, the Law Commission made specific proposals about safeguarding, as part of recommendations for wider reform of adult social care law. Although not going as far as some of its proposals from 1995,[2] they nevertheless included a proposed duty on social services to 'investigate' in relation to safeguarding and also the setting up of local statutory safeguarding boards.[3]

In 2012, the government in England finally published a draft Care and Support Bill, based on these proposals, placing a duty on social services to protect adults

1   Welsh Government. Social Services (Wales) Bill: consultation document. Cardiff: WG, 2012, pp.65–67.
2   Law Commission. *Mental incapacity*. Law Com. no. 231. London: HMSO, 1995, paras 9.1–9.28.
3   Law Commission. *Adult social care*. Law Com. no. 326. London: TSO, 2011, Part 9.

from neglect and abuse, 'to make enquiries' when adults are at risk of neglect and abuse and also to set up local safeguarding boards.

WELFARE FUNCTIONS UNDER COMMUNITY CARE LEGISLATION UNDERPINS SAFEGUARDING

All this said, and rather confusingly, the absence up to now of explicit reference in social services legislation to safeguarding has *not* meant a lack of an implicit legal or policy basis for local authority safeguarding work. Safeguarding functions have largely been carried out under a local authority's powers and duties contained within community care legislation: to assess people in need and to provide advice, support and services.

In fact, even under the draft Care and Support Bill 2012, the advice, support and services to help a person at risk of neglect and abuse would still be provided under the general care and support provisions of the Bill, rather than under the dedicated safeguarding clauses. This is because the clause in the Bill covering the making of enquiries about abuse and neglect says nothing about actually providing any help.

Assuming the draft Care and Support Bill becomes law, it is likely to come into force in 2015. The remainder of this chapter therefore tackles the law and guidance as it currently stands but, where relevant, with reference to the expected future changes. It then summarises key points from the draft Bill at the end of the chapter.

NO SECRETS: DEPARTMENT OF HEALTH GUIDANCE AND ITS IMPLICATIONS

The Department of Health published policy guidance in 2000 under s.7 of the Local Authority Social Services Act 1970. It remains extant and applicable, probably until, and if, the draft Care and Support Bill becomes law and is brought into force.

Entitled *No secrets*, the guidance states that local authority social services departments should take the lead in inter-agency working to combat abuse of vulnerable adults. It sets out a framework only, on which local authorities could base more detailed local policies and procedures.

Although only guidance, as opposed to legislation, it has the status of being statutory. This is because s.7 of the 1970 Act requires a local authority to act under such guidance, and substantial deviation from it may result in the authority acting unlawfully.[4] Its statutory status therefore gives it legal clout.

However, the guidance is generally broad-brush in approach; so, despite its statutory basis, it does not impose, explicitly at least, an onerous and detailed burden on local authorities. For example, it suggests that local authorities may wish to set up adult protection committees but does not require this.

Furthermore, the statutory nature of this guidance applies in any case only to local social services authorities; it does not have such status in respect of other

---

4   *R v Islington London Borough Council, ex p Rixon* [1997] 1 ELR 477.

agencies referred to in the guidance as having a role in adult protection – for example, NHS bodies, the police and housing providers.

DEFINITION OF VULNERABLE ADULT UNDER CURRENT LEGISLATION AND GUIDANCE

No secrets states that it is concerned with the protection from abuse of vulnerable adults. The draft Care and Support Bill 2012 (see above) does not use the term 'vulnerable adult'. It simply talks about protecting adults who are experiencing, or who are at risk from, neglect and abuse.

So the current guidance, and its definition of vulnerable adult, may soon be a thing of the past. However, the term 'vulnerable adult' surfaces in other legislation. In addition, the courts frequently make use of the term in mental capacity and other related cases involving adult protection.

Currently, therefore, before the advent of new legislation, a vulnerable adult is defined – for the purposes of local social services authorities at least – as a person:

> …who is or may be in need of community care services by reason of mental or other disability, age or illness; and who is or may be unable to take care of him- or herself, or unable to protect him- or herself against significant harm or exploitation.[5]

People's eligibility for help depends on a two-stage test: first, whether they come under the groups of people defined in the community care legislation; and, second, whether they are judged, under eligibility criteria, to be eligible for help.

This current two-step test will change if and when the draft Care and Support Bill 2012, in its current form, becomes law.

Eligibility will then, it seems, no longer depend on an adult coming within a defined category, such as disability, age or mental disorder. Instead, the test will simply be whether any adult's need for care and support is sufficiently great to qualify under the national eligibility framework, applied by each local authority. At the time of writing, it is not clear what any such eligibility rules will look like.

VULNERABLE ADULTS OR ADULTS AT RISK OF HARM – OR NEITHER?

The Law Commission proposed that the term 'vulnerable adult', in current guidance, should be replaced in future legislation with the term 'adult at risk of harm' (who has health or social care needs). This was partly because of a largely incomprehensible notion that the term 'vulnerable adult' is patronising or disempowering, applies a permanent stigma to a person and somehow suggests the adult is at fault for his or her plight.[6]

---

5   Department of Health. *No secrets: guidance on developing and implementing multi-agency policies and procedures to protect vulnerable adults from abuse.* London: DH, 2000, p.8.

6   See: Department of Health. *Safeguarding adults: a consultation on the review of the 'No secrets' guidance.* London: DH, 2008, p.49. And: Law Commission. *Adult social care.* Law Com. no. 326. London: TSO, 2011, para 9.21.

The draft Care and Support Bill 2012 avoids both terms. It simply talks about protecting people from abuse or neglect.

Nonetheless, the term 'vulnerable adult' will survive in other legislation, including the Safeguarding Vulnerable Groups Act 2006 (under which rogue workers are barred from working with vulnerable adults), the Police Act 1997 (criminal record certificates), the Domestic Violence, Crime and Victims Act 2004 and the Housing Act 1996. And 'vulnerable witness' is a term used in the Youth Justice and Criminal Evidence Act 1999.

HARM: ABUSE, NEGLECT, ACTS OF OMISSION

Abuse is characterised by *No secrets* as physical, sexual, psychological, financial, material, neglect and acts of omission, discriminatory or institutional.

Some forms of abuse are criminal offences – for example, physical assault, sexual assault and rape, or fraud.[7]

The draft Care and Support Bill 2012 defines the word 'abuse' but not the word 'neglect'. Even the definition of abuse is sketchy. The Bill does not provide a denotation (core meaning), merely a connotation (example). It illustrates the term by stating that abuse includes certain types of financial or property abuse. But this gives a lopsided feel; it could even be taken to suggest that physical abuse is not covered.

Confusingly perhaps, health and social care providers, with a duty under regulations to protect users of services from abuse or neglect, are given a more helpful steer, albeit only illustrative. Abuse is defined in these regulations as:

(a) sexual abuse;

(b) physical or psychological ill-treatment;

(c) theft, misuse or misappropriation of money or property; or

(d) neglect and acts of omission which cause harm or place at risk of harm.[8]

SELF-NEGLECT

The import of the *No secrets* definition appears to be that self-neglect is not part of safeguarding or adult protection work. This is because the guidance identifies two key ingredients: a vulnerable adult and abuse. The definition of a vulnerable adult is capable of including self-neglect because it refers to the inability of a person to look after himself or herself. But the definition of abuse definitely rules out self-neglect: 'Abuse is a violation of an individual's human and civil rights by any other person or persons.'[9]

---

7   Department of Health. *No secrets.* London: DH, 2000, p.9.
8   Quoted from: SI 2010/781. The Health and Social Care Act 2008 (Regulated Activities) Regulations 2010, r.11.
9   Department of Health. *No secrets.* London: DH, 2000, para 2.5.

The government has confirmed that its intention, in its draft Care and Support Bill 2012, is not to include self-harm or self-neglect within the ambit of safeguarding. This is because it believes that safeguarding should be about neglect or abuse perpetrated by another person.

In fact, though, the draft Bill as published does not define neglect at all. So the duty to protect people from neglect, self-neglect or otherwise, remains on the face of the Bill. Therefore, whether or not local authorities include self-neglect within what they call safeguarding activity is, according to the government, ultimately up to them.[10]

In fact, under the draft Bill as it stands (subject to any eligibility framework or statutory guidance issued in the future), there is a duty to make enquiries in relation to neglect. It might be argued, therefore, that failure to do so in relation to self-neglect – which is a species of neglect after all – could be a breach of duty.

INSTITUTIONAL, SYSTEMIC NEGLECT AND OMISSIONS

The *No secrets* guidance refers to neglect, omissions and institutional abuse.

Even so, sometimes harm in a wider sense – typically institutional and with less discernible ill-motivation – seems to be less easily recognised and even to occupy a blind spot.

It may, these days, be easy enough to invoke adult protection procedures in respect of the care home assistant who is physically rough with residents and is suspected also of stealing their personal property. It becomes more problematic, however, in the case of an NHS trust which, struggling in good faith to meet performance and financial targets, loses sight altogether of standards of care and indeed its patients. The result may be loss of dignity and even large-scale loss of life.

Indeed, the general thrust of government policy on safeguarding has been to recognise the need to protect patients from being harmed by individual rogue practitioners or ill-motivated private individuals, but to ignore or play down the more significant issue of institutional and systemic neglect.

In the case, for example, of systemic neglect in care homes, the government has little to say, even though part of the problem lies in how the State (local authorities and the NHS) commissions care and how the private sector – in whose ability to deliver dignified care central government of any hue continues to place blind faith – provides it.

It seems, therefore, that adult protection concerns are more likely to be triggered, for example, by the actions of a dishonest care home assistant than by the practices of an NHS trust that has lost perspective on basic, humane care.

---

10   Department of Health. *Reforming the law for adult care and support: the Government's response to Law Commission report 326 on adult social care.* London: DH, 2012, para 9.16.

WHEN TO INTERVENE

Currently, the Department of Health's *No secrets* guidance states that the following factors should be considered in deciding whether to intervene: the vulnerability of the individual, the nature and extent of the abuse, the length of time it has been occurring, the impact on the individual and the risk of repeated or increasingly serious acts involving the vulnerable adult or other vulnerable adults.[11]

Combining this part of the guidance with reference in the guidance to 'significant harm', there is clearly judgement and discretion involved. One serious case review, following the murder of a vulnerable young woman by 'friends', noted that significant harm – and possible need for intervention – needs to be measured not just in single episodes but also a succession of lesser occurrences which may cumulatively point to more significant harm.[12]

Separate statutory guidance, on eligibility for social services help generally, makes it clear that legal obligations to intervene will be triggered not only by serious abuse or neglect (considered by the guidance to be a 'critical' issue) but also by bare, non-serious abuse or neglect (still a 'substantial' matter).[13] Either way, serious or non-serious, the neglect or abuse must still presumably constitute 'significant' harm for the purposes of the *No secrets* guidance if the two sets of guidance are to be reconciled. In which case, the threshold for local authority intervention in neglect and abuse cases is low.

Under the draft Care and Support Bill 2012 (see below), a local authority would, following assessment, have a duty to meet people's needs for care and support – including protecting them from neglect or abuse – if the person meets the eligibility criteria, whatever they may be. The draft Bill itself carries no detail.

A local authority would also have a duty to make enquiries, or to cause enquiries to be made, if it has reasonable cause to suspect that an adult is being abused or neglected or is at risk of being so, and is unable to protect himself or herself against it.

INTER-AGENCY APPROACH TO ADULT PROTECTION

Currently, the Department of Health's *No secrets* guidance stresses the importance of inter-agency working at local level, between various organisations including the NHS and social services, sheltered and supported housing providers, regulators of services, police and Crown Prosecution Service, voluntary and private sector agencies, local authority housing and education departments, probation service, DSS benefit agencies, carer support groups, user groups and user-led services,

---

11   Department of Health. *No secrets*. London: DH, 2000, para 2.19.
12   Warwickshire Safeguarding Adults Partnership. *Serious case review: the murder of Gemma Hayter*. Warwick: WSAP, 2010, para 4.4.
13   Department of Health. *Prioritising need in the context of Putting People First: A whole system approach to eligibility for social care: guidance on eligibility criteria for adult social care, England 2010*. London: DH, 2010, para 54.

advocacy and advisory services, community safety partnerships, legal advice and representation services.[14]

The guidance states that collaboration needs to take place at all levels, involving operational staff, supervisory line management, senior management staff, different parts of the local authority (i.e. corporately), chief officers/chief executives and local authority members. In particular, the director of adult social services has a particularly important role to play.[15]

It suggests the formation of adult protection committees but does not make this a requirement, stating instead that agencies 'may consider there are merits to establishing a multi-agency management committee (adult protection) which is a standing committee of lead officers'.[16] This is in contrast to the local safeguarding children's boards that were made obligatory by the Children Act 2004.

The lack of statutory obligation placed upon local authorities and other agencies has been criticised.

Detachment of NHS from safeguarding. For example, in the case of the NHS, the chairwoman of the serious case review into the murder in Cornwall of a man with learning disabilities made a number of points, which, in her view, may have underlain the apparent failure of the NHS in that case. She noted that there was no requirement that the NHS have a lead officer for adult protection, no guidance on expenditure of resources in making sure NHS staff are properly trained, an apparent lack of monitoring and scrutiny of safeguarding processes in NHS trusts, and that there were questions about whether safeguarding was integral to all contracting arrangements of primary care trusts and whether GPs were charging for submitting evidence to and for attending strategy meetings (and, if so, who should pay).[17]

The draft Care and Support Bill 2012 proposes that safeguarding adults boards be put on a statutory footing and also a statutory duty of cooperation between agencies (see below).

INFORMATION SHARING

The Department of Health guidance emphasises that, as part of inter-agency working, agreement on the sharing of information will be required, in order to balance, on the one hand, confidentiality and, on the other, the importance of sharing information (even in the absence of a person's consent).

It notes that information must be shared on a 'need to know' basis only and that confidentiality should not be confused with secrecy. Informed consent should be obtained but, if this is not possible and other vulnerable adults are at risk, it might be necessary to override this requirement. Assurances of absolute confidentiality should not be given where there are concerns about abuse.[18]

---

14   Department of Health. *No secrets.* London: DH, 2000, p.20.
15   Department of Health. *No secrets.* London: DH, 2000, pp.16–17.
16   Department of Health. *No secrets.* London: DH, 2000, para 3.4.
17   Flynn, M. 'How the NHS is failing vulnerable adults.' *Health Service Journal,* 8 April 2008.
18   Department of Health. *No secrets.* London: DH, 2000, p.24.

It also goes on to state that principles of confidentiality designed to safeguard and promote the interests of service users should not be confused with those 'designed to protect the management interests of an organisation'.[19]

(This last statement could usefully be taken to apply not only to the personal information of the person making the request – disclosure of which is regulated under the Data Protection Act 1998 – but also information about other people or non-personal information, requests about which come under the Freedom of Information Act 2000. Thus, information more generally – for instance, about standards of care, mortality rates or infection rates, neglect or abuse statistics, safeguarding activity and investigations – come under the 2000 Act.)

PREVALENCE OF ABUSE OR NEGLECT OF VULNERABLE ADULTS

Given the hazy definitions surrounding adult protection and safeguarding adults, information about the prevalence of harm, abuse and neglect is also sketchy. Likewise, it seems uncertain whether there is an increasing problem in society, whether people are now simply talking about and reporting it more, or whether for some reason we think we should do more about it now than in the past.

It is beyond the scope and purpose of this book to consider statistics in detail.

Nonetheless, a few points about prevalence are as follows. For instance, one major study surveyed some 2100 people in the United Kingdom living in private households, aged 66 years or over. On the basis of this sample, it concluded that, in one year, some 227,000 people (2.6% of the relevant population) had suffered neglect or abuse.

The categories of abuse used in the study were financial, psychological, physical and sexual. Neglect was also included. However, this study did not cover what it termed 'stranger abuse' or institutional abuse; care homes and hospitals were excluded, although sheltered accommodation was included.[20]

Whilst such exclusions may have been expedient in terms of that particular study, they mean that a significant part of the equation was missing. The potential level of harm, through abuse and neglect, in care homes and hospitals is considerable. Furthermore, it is clear that certain groups of people may be more vulnerable to harm even if it emanates not from people known to them but from 'strangers'. For instance, a burglar was jailed having raided 600 homes and targeted elderly people in their nineties, concentrating in particular on people who were blind, deaf or partially sighted.[21]

In 2004, Action on Elder Abuse stated that it could not say whether abuse was increasing or was of epidemic proportions but that it was certainly more widely recognised. It identified inadequate care as an issue of great concern. This was on

19   Department of Health. *No secrets.* London: DH, 2000, p.22.

20   O'Keefe, M., Hills, A., Doyle, M., McCreadie, C. *et al. UK Study of abuse and neglect of older people.* London: Comic Relief and Department of Health, 2007, pp.3–15.

21   Bird, S. 'Conman jailed for 600 raids in just 18 months.' *The Times,* 8 February 2003.

the basis of calls to its helpline. It, too, excluded stranger, but not institutional, abuse. It defined elder abuse as 'a single or repeated act or lack of appropriate action occurring within any relationship where there is an expectation of trust, which causes harm or distress to an older person'.[22]

It is the author's view that there is almost certainly a larger problem than anybody has been able to put their finger on. For instance, the convictions for financial or physical abuse of elderly people or people with learning disabilities – reported in local and sometimes the national press – are numerous. Yet it is more than likely that many occurrences of criminal abuse go undetected, and, of those that are detected, many will not make to it court for want of evidence or because of the unwillingness of the victim to press the complaint and participate. Similarly, persistent reports, over many years, of neglect in care homes continue and suggest a widespread malaise.

The evidence of the last 15 years shows beyond any doubt a systemic problem of neglect of older people within the health service.[23] Indeed, there is a respectable view that even a major breakdown in humane care, as happened at Stafford Hospital and which was associated with many hundreds of deaths, would not necessarily be detected again, such is the entrenchment and acceptance of poor care in some hospitals.

DRAFT CARE AND SUPPORT BILL 2012: KEY POINTS IN RELATION TO SAFEGUARDING

The following are the key provisions of the draft Care and Support Bill 2012 that are particularly relevant to safeguarding, some explicitly, some by implication. Assuming it becomes law, it is expected to come into force in 2015.

GENERAL WELL-BEING DUTY: INCLUDING PROTECTION FROM NEGLECT AND ABUSE

In clause 1, there is a general duty placed on local authorities relating to the well-being of adults who come within the ambit of the Bill – that is, those adults who may require care or support.

Well-being is defined to include 'protection from abuse and neglect'. The local authority, in carrying out its functions towards relevant adults, has to have regard to various matters including 'the need to protect people from neglect and abuse'.[24]

This means that, at a general level, protecting people from neglect and abuse, legally, will be part and parcel of adult social care. However, it should be noted that duties expressed as being 'general' are notoriously difficult to enforce by individuals in the courts.

---

22   Action on Elder Abuse. *Hidden voices: older people's experience of abuse.* London: AEA, 2004, pp.11, 16.

23   Mandelstam, M. *How we treat the sick: neglect and abuse in our health services.* London: Jessica Kingsley Publishers, 2011, Chapter 4.

24   Draft Care and Support Bill 2012, clause 1.

INFORMATION AND ADVICE: INCLUDING ABOUT SAFETY

Clause 2 states that local authorities must have an information and advice service covering various matters including (italics added) 'how to raise concerns about the *safety* of an adult who has needs for care and support'.[25]

EFFICIENT AND EFFECTIVE MARKET IN CARE AND SUPPORT SERVICES

Clause 3 is entitled 'Promoting diversity and quality in provision of services'. It states that a 'local authority must promote the efficient and effective operation in its area of a market in services for meeting care and support needs'.[26]

This might sound as if it has little to do with safeguarding. However, there is a concern that the way the market in social care currently operates results in cost cutting and tends to produce poor standards of care, which in turn can lead to neglect or abuse.

Clause 3 could, pessimistically, be interpreted as an open invitation to a further deterioration in standards of care; local authorities are wont to take words such as 'efficient' to mean 'cheapest', without paying too much attention to the quality of what is being provided.

Furthermore, sick, physically and mentally frail and vulnerable older people are not the active, free-wheeling consumers on which the idea of a 'market' is premissed.

GENERAL DUTY TO COOPERATE: INCLUDING FOR PROTECTION OF PEOPLE FROM ABUSE OR NEGLECT

Clause 4 creates a duty to cooperate: on the local authority with its relevant partners and on the relevant partners with the local authority.

The cooperation is to be exercised generally, as well as specifically. Listed purposes include 'protecting adults with needs for care and support who are experiencing, or are at risk of, abuse or neglect'. Relevant partners are district councils, NHS bodies, the police, the prison service and the probation service.[27]

This is a useful clause to have, since protecting people from neglect and abuse might cut across different agencies. Even so, general duties to cooperate in legislation of this type can be difficult, if not impossible, to pin down and enforce.

DUTY TO COOPERATE UNLESS INCOMPATIBLE OR IT WOULD HAVE ADVERSE EFFECT

Clause 5 therefore strengthens clause 4. It states that if a local authority requests cooperation of a relevant partner, that partner must comply unless it believes that to do so would be incompatible with its own duties or have an adverse effect on

---

25   Draft Care and Support Bill 2012, clause 2.
26   Draft Care and Support Bill 2012, clause 3.
27   Draft Care and Support Bill 2012, clause 4.

the exercise of its functions. The same rule applies if a relevant partner makes such a request of a local authority.[28]

The explanatory notes on clause 5 state that it is relevant to safeguarding enquiries:

> This duty supplements the duty in clause 4. It is intended to be used by local authorities or partners where their co-operation is requested in relation to an individual adult or carer who has needs by either the local authority or one of the 'relevant partners' in clause 4. The duty is not limited to particular situations but could be used, for example, in relation to adult safeguarding enquiries...[29]

Hitherto, there has been no explicit, statutory basis for local authorities to try to put pressure on the National Health Service or other agencies in relation to safeguarding. In combination with clause 34 (see below), through which a local authority can make enquiries or cause enquiries to be made by others, there is now such a basis.

PROVISION OF SERVICES IN THE LOCAL AREA: PREVENTION, DELAY OR REDUCTION OF NEED

Under clause 7, local authorities must provide or arrange services, facilities or resources – or take other steps – to help prevent, delay or reduce the needs for care and support of adults in its area.[30]

Since many adults suffering neglect and abuse will have care and support needs (either pre-existing or as a result of, or in connection with, the neglect or abuse), this clause is relevant. Not least, it points to local authorities intervening before a crisis point is reached, since it refers to prevention.

However, although it is a duty, it is another one of these general duties – to the local population rather than each individual – and therefore difficult to enforce.

HOW TO MEET PEOPLE'S CARE AND SUPPORT NEEDS

Clause 8 gives examples of how local authorities can meet people's care and support needs: (a) accommodation in a care home or in premises of some other type, (b) care and support at home or in the community, (c) counselling, advocacy and other types of social work, (d) goods and facilities, (e) information and advice.[31]

Information, advice and support are, at first blush, very obvious forms of services needed by people at risk of neglect or abuse – quite apart from the other services listed.

This means that a person suffering abuse or neglect, without any other pre-existing care and support needs, but now in need of information, advice, support or

---

28   Draft Care and Support Bill 2012, clause 5.
29   Draft Care and Support Bill 2012, Detailed Notes, Annex B, para 14.
30   Draft Care and Support Bill 2012, clause 7.
31   Draft Care and Support Bill 2012, clause 8.

any other service because of that abuse or neglect, would, in principle, qualify for help from the local authority (subject to the application of any eligibility criteria: see below).

DUTY TO ASSESS

Clause 9 imposes a duty to assess if it appears to a local authority that an adult may have needs for care and support. The authority must determine whether the person has needs and what they are.[32]

So a person who might be suffering from neglect or abuse, thereby being in possible need of information, advice, support or any other service, would be eligible for an assessment.

DUTY TO ASSESS CARERS

Clause 10 contains a duty to assess carers if it appears to the authority that a carer may have needs (current or future) for support. The authority must determine whether there are needs and what they are (current or future).[33]

Timely support for carers under stress can in practice prevent crises, involving domestic neglect or abuse, arising.

REFUSAL OF ASSESSMENT: LACK OF CAPACITY

Clause 11 clarifies that if a person, with capacity to do so, refuses an assessment, the local authority is not required to assess. However, this rule does not apply if the person lacks capacity to refuse and the assessment would be in his or her best interests. Nor does it apply if the 'the adult is experiencing, or is at risk of, abuse or neglect'.[34]

This means, for example, that if the local authority were to take the view that a person with capacity was being abused, neglected or at risk of being so, it should attempt nevertheless to assess. However, this clause as it stands does not afford the local authority any power of compulsion – for instance, to enter premises without consent and then to assess.

So it will not be able to enforce a face-to-face assessment unless there is doubt about the person's capacity (in which case the Mental Capacity Act comes into play) or unless it seeks an order from the High Court under the latter's inherent jurisdiction. Or unless the compulsory provisions of the Mental Health Act 1983 apply.

At the time of writing, however, the government is consulting as to whether a local authority – as part of its duty to make enquiries into abuse and neglect –

---

32   Draft Care and Support Bill 2012, clause 9.
33   Draft Care and Support Bill 2012, clause 10.
34   Draft Care and Support Bill 2012, clause 11.

should have a power of entry to a person's home if it believes that somebody else is preventing the authority talking to the person: see below.[35]

NATIONAL ELIGIBILITY CRITERIA

Clause 17 imposes a duty to meet a person's needs if those needs meet the eligibility criteria applied by the local authority.[36]

The Bill gives the government the power to pass regulations, setting out a national framework of eligibility.[37]

Neglect and abuse will presumably be defined as coming within the higher reaches of any such eligibility scheme, thus making people at risk of them legally entitled to help.

DUTY TO MEET THE NEEDS OF CARERS

Clause 19 imposes a duty to meet the needs of carers who fulfil the eligibility criteria applied by the local authority.[38]

This will represent a significant change in the law. Under the current legislation, the Carers and Disabled Children Act 2000, there is a duty to assess, but not to provide services for, carers. And, as already pointed out, timely help for carers can help prevent poor care turning into neglect or abuse because of the physical and mental stresses placed on the carer.

CARE PLANS AND SUPPORT PLANS

Clauses 23 and 24 cover care and support plans for adults in need and support plans for carers.[39]

ABUSE OR NEGLECT: DUTY OF LOCAL AUTHORITY TO MAKE ENQUIRIES OR CAUSE ENQUIRIES TO BE MADE BY OTHERS

Clause 34 is specific to abuse or neglect. It therefore warrants reproducing in full:

> Where a local authority has reasonable cause to suspect that an adult in its area (whether or not ordinarily resident there) –
>
> (a) has needs for care and support (whether or not the authority is meeting any of those needs),
>
> (b) is experiencing, or is at risk of, abuse or neglect, and
>
> (c) as a result of those needs is unable to protect himself or herself against the abuse or neglect or the risk of it,

---

35   Department of Health. *Consultation on new adult safeguarding power.* London: DH, 2012, paras 9–10.
36   Draft Care and Support Bill 2012, clause 17.
37   Draft Care and Support Bill 2012, clause 13.
38   Draft Care and Support Bill 2012, clause 19.
39   Draft Care and Support Bill 2012, clauses 23, 24.

it must make (or cause to be made) whatever enquiries it thinks necessary to enable it to decide whether any action should be taken in the adult's case (whether under this Part or otherwise) and, if so, what and by whom.

'Abuse' includes –

(d) having money or other property stolen,

(e) being defrauded,

(f) being put under pressure in relation to money or other property, and

(g) having money or other property misused.[40]

This clause, though potentially important, is additional to the general duty to assess people who might have care and support needs. Legally, it should be seen as over and above the basic duties, outlined immediately above, to assess and meet people's needs, including those arising from neglect or abuse.

The explanatory notes to the Bill seems to view this duty to make enquiries as very much connected to the role of other agencies and to the fact that the local authority can 'cause' those other agencies to make enquiries:

This clause places a duty on local authorities to make enquiries, or to ask others to make enquiries, where they reasonably suspect that an adult in its area with care and support needs is at risk of abuse or neglect. The purpose of the enquiry is to establish what, if any, action is required in relation to the case. This clause supplements the existing obligations on other organisations to look after the people in their care effectively, or, in the case of the police, to prevent and respond to criminal activity. It applies to adults currently in its geographical area, whether or not the person is ordinarily resident there, and regardless of whether the authority is meeting their care and support needs.[41]

The definition of abuse is curious. It does not in fact attempt a real definition, but merely gives examples of what might be included. The examples are lopsided, since they are concerned with property and finance only; no mention is made of physical abuse. However, that is not to say that physical abuse is not covered.

At the time of writing, the Department of Health is consulting as to whether the duty to make enquiries should be extended so as to give local authorities a power of entry, with a court-issued warrant. This would be when a local authority believes that a person with mental capacity is experiencing abuse or neglect but that someone else in the property is preventing the local authority from speaking with that person. The purpose would be to enable the local authority to speak to the person alone and to give them information and advice which they otherwise might be unable or unwilling to ask for.[42]

---

40   Quoted from: Draft Care and Support Bill 2012, clause 34.
41   Draft Care and Support Bill 2012, Detailed Notes, Annex B, para 63.
42   Department of Health. *Consultation on new adult safeguarding power.* London: DH, paras 9–10, 17.

SAFEGUARDING ADULTS BOARDS

Clause 35 is likewise specific to safeguarding, including the duty on the local authority to establish a safeguarding adults board:

(1) Each local authority must establish a Safeguarding Adults Board (an 'SAB') for its area.

(2) The objective of an SAB is to help and protect adults in its area in cases of the kind described in section 34(1).

(3) The way in which an SAB must seek to achieve its objective is by co-ordinating and ensuring the effectiveness of what each of its members does.

(4) An SAB may do anything which appears to it to be necessary or desirable for the purpose of achieving its objective.[43]

Key members of the safeguarding board are the local authority, the police and the NHS; other organisations can be appointed members as well.[44]

Hitherto, safeguarding adults boards have existed but have been non-statutory. One of the challenges facing such boards, statutory or otherwise, is how to deal effectively with systemic neglect or abuse emanating from one of the key agencies on the board. For instance, if there is such neglect in a local NHS hospital, and a representative of the NHS sits on the board, a conflict of interest may well arise.

SAFEGUARDING REVIEWS: DEATHS OR OTHER CONCERNS

Clause 36 covers safeguarding reviews following death or other concerns:

(1) An SAB must arrange for there to be a review of any case in which –

(a) an adult in the SAB's area with needs for care and support (whether or not the local authority was meeting any of those needs) was, or the SAB suspects that the adult was, experiencing abuse or neglect, and

(b) the adult dies or there is reasonable cause for concern about how the SAB, a member of it or some other person involved in the adult's case acted.

(2) Each member of the SAB must co-operate in and contribute to the carrying out of the review with a view to –

(a) identifying the lessons to be learnt from the adult's case, and

(b) applying those lessons to future cases.[45]

---

43   Quoted from: Draft Care and Support Bill 2012, clause 35.
44   Draft Care and Support Bill 2012, schedule 1.
45   Quoted from: Draft Care and Support Bill 2012, clause 36.

Many local authorities already conduct serious case reviews about the deaths of vulnerable adults. This clause adds, however, another ground for establishing such a review, irrespective of a death: namely, concern about how the board, a member of it or anybody else involved responded to the neglect or abuse.

ABOLITION OF OLD POWER TO REMOVE PEOPLE FROM THEIR HOMES

Clause 37 abolishes s.47 of the National Assistance Act 1948, an old power enabling local authorities to remove people in need of care from their own homes.[46] At the time of writing, the government is intending to consult about whether a similar type of power should be included in the new Act.

PROTECTION OF PEOPLE'S PROPERTY

Clause 38 places a duty on local authorities to protect the property of adults in need of care and support, which is being provided in other accommodation or in hospital. The duty is triggered if it appears to the authority that there is a danger of loss or damage to movable property belonging to the adult in the authority's area because the adult is unable to protect or deal with the property and no suitable arrangements have been or are being made. The local authority must then take reasonable steps to prevent or mitigate the loss or damage.

This power is similar to that currently in s.48 of the National Assistance Act 1948, which will be abolished if and when the new legislation comes into force.

---

46   Draft Care and Support Bill 2012, clause 37.

Proportionate interventions, the State, human rights (and discrimination law)

KEY POINTS

Local authorities and other agencies tread a fine and sometimes difficult line. The identification of abuse and safeguarding needs to be taken seriously, but at the same time proportion and balance are required. Intervene too little and it can all go wrong legally and practically; intervene over-zealously and likewise.

For local authorities and other agencies, a crucial check on proportionality, and a guard against disproportionality, is the law. There are cases that find their way to court where things have gone awry. This is not to say that there are not countless instances where local authorities get it right, but it seems that there are at least a more than trivial number of cases in which significant problems surface.

Legal rules, to be found in a range of legislation, including the Human Rights Act 1998, the Mental Capacity Act 2005 and community care legislation, provide help. Yet there is not always sufficient awareness of the depth and application of the principles involved, and ignorance, or, alternatively, a tick-box approach to these, does not suffice.

It is not that practitioners should become quasi-lawyers for the sake of it or indeed at all, but it is to recognise that when decisions are made and actions are taken about fundamental aspects of a vulnerable adult's life, safeguards are required. Otherwise, as has been pointed out, not least by the judiciary, the State can end up making things worse.

In addition to human rights and mental capacity law, a further legal dimension comes in the form of the Equality Act 2010 and its anti-discrimination provisions. Already covering matters such as disability, race and sex, from 1 October 2012 the Act extended its reach to cover discrimination on grounds of age. This is significant in the context of safeguarding because of prevailing discrimination against older people in health and social care.

HUMAN RIGHTS

Closely allied to the protection of vulnerable adults are human rights.

The Human Rights Act 1998 had the effect of bringing the European Convention on Human Rights directly into United Kingdom law.

The human rights under the European Convention, relevant to the protection of vulnerable adults, include, in summary:

- right to life (article 2)

- right not to be subjected to torture or to inhuman or degrading treatment or punishment (article 3)

- right not to be deprived of liberty other than in specified circumstances and only then in accordance with legal procedures (article 5)

- right to a fair hearing (article 6)

- right to respect for a person's home, private and family life. However, interference with this may be justified if it is in accordance with the law and is necessary in a democratic society. In addition it must be (a) in the interests of national security, public safety or the economic well-being of the country, (b) for the prevention of disorder or crime, (c) for the protection of health or morals, or (d) for the protection of the rights and freedom of others (article 8)

- right to freedom of expression (article 10)

- right to marry (article 12)

- right not to suffer discrimination (article 14).

PUBLIC BODIES

Only public bodies, or other bodies carrying out functions of a public nature, have human rights obligations. This is significant.

For example, in the past the courts stated that a resident of a *local authority care home* could legally argue a human rights case against the authority in its role of care home owner. However, the resident of an *independent care home* could not bring a human rights case directly against the care home, even if the resident had been placed there by the local authority (a public body). This was because the care home was deemed not to be carrying out functions of a public nature.[1]

Section 145 of the Health and Social Care Act 2008 then changed the effect of this legal ruling by stating that care homes are, after all, deemed to be carrying out functions of a public nature – and are thus subject to the Human Rights Act 1998 – but only in respect of residents placed by local authorities under ss.21 and 26 of the National Assistance Act 1948.

This legislative amendment does not cover those adults (a) placed in an independent care home by the NHS, (b) placed by local authorities and the NHS in an independent care home under s.117 of the Mental Health Act 1983, (c) who are self-funding residents who have their own contractual arrangements with the independent care home, or (d) who receive services in their own home from independent domiciliary care agencies (rather than from the local authority or NHS body).

Central government maintains in the case of the NHS that human rights would automatically apply, but this does not seem necessarily to be so, given the reasoning of the courts in the *YL* case. It is of concern that, applied to vulnerable adults, a policy of market-based consumerism, with ever more contracting out of services to the independent sector, may bring with it a dilution of the human rights of vulnerable adults – the very people most in need of such protection.

HUMAN RIGHTS AND ADULT PROTECTION

The link between human rights and adult protection seems clear enough.

For instance, the Parliamentary Joint Committee on Human Rights drew attention to a wide range of concerns about the poor treatment of older people in health care, much of it in the context of care and treatment directly provided or commissioned by the NHS.

The Committee associated aspects of this poor treatment with particular rights under the European Convention. There appears to be a close correlation between this list and what would be considered adult safeguarding matters involving harm, abuse and neglect. The list set out by the Committee included:

- malnutrition and dehydration (articles 2, 3, 8)
- abuse and rough treatment (articles 3, 8)
- lack of privacy in mixed sex wards (article 8)
- lapses in confidentiality (article 8)

---

1   *YL v Birmingham City Council* [2007] UKHL 27.

- neglect and poor hygiene (articles 3, 8)

- inappropriate medication and physical restraint (article 8)

- inadequate assessment of a person's needs (articles 2, 3, 8)

- over-hasty discharge from hospital (article 8)

- bullying and patronising attitudes (articles 3, 8)

- discrimination on basis of age, disability or race (article 14)

- communication difficulties particularly for people with dementia (articles 8, 14)

- fear of making complaints (article 8)

- eviction from care homes (article 8).[2]

There are many examples throughout this book involving actual, or potential, breach of people's human rights at the hands of public bodies, by action or omission.

RIGHT TO LIFE

Article 2 (the right to life) demands that the State take reasonable steps positively to safeguard people's right to life:

> Everyone's right to life shall be protected by law. No one shall be deprived of his life intentionally save in the execution of a sentence of a court following his conviction of a crime for which this penalty is provided by law.

This has been held by the courts to include setting up independent enquiries in certain circumstances where people have died in connection with potentially untoward acts or omissions of public bodies.

For instance, had the Healthcare Commission not independently investigated scores of avoidable deaths of elderly people in hospital from *Clostridium difficile* in Buckinghamshire and Kent,[3] an article 2 challenge could possibly have been made. Likewise, it was only the threat of a legal challenge by the organisation Cure the NHS, under article 2, that led the government in 2009 to appoint an independent inquiry into events at Stafford Hospital, where hundreds of patients had died.[4]

In a 2008 case, the European Court of Human Rights considered the adequacy of legal remedies, available and used, in a case involving the disappearance of a person with dementia from a nursing home.

---

2   Quoted from: Joint Committee on Human Rights (House of Lords and House of Commons). *A life like any other? Human rights of adults with learning disabilities. HL 40–1.* London: TSO, 2007, p.9.

3   Healthcare Commission. *Investigation into outbreaks of Clostridium difficile at Stoke Mandeville Hospital, Buckinghamshire Hospitals NHS Trust.* London: HC, 2006. And also: Healthcare Commission. *Investigation into outbreaks of Clostridium difficile at Maidstone and Tunbridge Wells NHS Trust.* London: HC, 2007.

4   Leigh Day & Co. 'Judicial reviews and the Mid Staffordshire inquiries.' *News,* 12 May 2010. Accessed on 23 November 2012 at: www.leighday.co.uk/Our-expertise/human-rights/Mid-Staffordshire-Inquiry/Judicial-reviews-and-the-Mid-Staffordshire-inquiri.

Disappearance of man's mother from nursing home: human organ gang possibly involved. The European Court stated that there was an obligation by the State to:

> ...make regulations compelling hospitals, whether public or private, to adopt appropriate measures for the protection of their patients' lives and to set up an effective independent judicial system so that the cause of death of patients in the care of the medical profession, whether in the public or private sector, can be determined and those responsible made accountable.

In a case involving the disappearance and death (presumed, since she was never found) of a woman with Alzheimer's from a nursing home, the European Court interpreted this requirement broadly and as applicable to the circumstances. Her son suspected abduction by a criminal gang trading in human organs. Although legal remedies, disciplinary, civil and criminal, were in principle available, in practice they had not been used to 'secure an effective possibility to establish the facts surrounding the disappearance'.[5]

INHUMAN OR DEGRADING TREATMENT

The courts normally regard article 3 as setting a high threshold; in other words, it is not easily breached. It is absolute, rather than qualified, and reads:

> No one shall be subjected to torture or to inhuman or degrading treatment or punishment.

The European Court of Human Rights has stated that inhuman or degrading treatment means that the ill-treatment in question must reach a minimum level of severity and involve actual bodily injury or intense physical or mental suffering. Degrading treatment could occur if it 'humiliates or debases an individual showing a lack of respect for, or diminishing, his or her human dignity or arouses feelings of fear, anguish or inferiority capable of breaking an individual's moral and physical resistance'.[6]

The European Court has found a breach of article 3 in relation to the distress and hardship caused to a heroin addict in prison who subsequently died there. Amongst the key reasons for this finding were the inability accurately to record her weight loss (through dehydration and vomiting), a gap in monitoring by doctors, failure to admit the person to hospital to ensure medication and fluid intake, and failure to obtain more expert assistance to control the vomiting.[7]

It was a breach also in the case of a severely physically disabled person subjected to degrading treatment in a police cell.

Degrading treatment of severely disabled woman in police cell. A severely physically disabled person had been sent to prison for contempt of court. She had failed to disclose her assets in a debt case. In the police cell she was unable to use the bed and had to sleep in her wheelchair where she became very cold. When she reached the prison hospital, she could not use the toilet herself, the female duty officer could not manage to move her alone, and male prison officers had to assist. The European Court concluded that to detain

---

5   *Dodov v Bulgaria* [2008] European Court of Human Rights, case no. 59548/00.

6   *Pretty v United Kingdom* [2002] 2 FCR 97 (European Court of Human Rights).

7   *McGlinchey v United Kingdom* [2003] Application 50390/99 (European Court of Human Rights).

a severely disabled person – in conditions where she is dangerously cold, risks developing pressure sores because her bed is too hard or unreachable, and is unable to go to the toilet or keep clean without the greatest difficulty – constituted degrading treatment contrary to article 3. Damages of £4500 were awarded.[8]

The unnecessary use of handcuffs on a prisoner receiving chemotherapy treatment in a civilian hospital has been held to be degrading, inhumane and a breach of article 3, where there was no adequately founded risk of escape or harm to the public.[9]

The following examples, identified in the context of the NHS, were not taken to court as human rights cases, but arguably involved breach of article 3 rights.

For instance, the right not to be subjected to inhuman or degrading treatment may arguably be engaged if a person with learning disabilities is restrained excessively in a wheelchair for 16 hours a day or has his arms tied to his wheelchair eight hours daily,[10] if hospital patients are told to relieve their bowels and bladder in bed and then left for hours in wet or soiled bedding,[11] if a dying man is nursed in the hospital dining room in front of other patients eating their meals,[12] and if hospital patients are tied to commodes for extended periods and given their meals on them.[13]

More recently, it has been reported that legal cases have been settled out of court with Stafford Hospital, on both article 3 grounds and in negligence.[14]

In 2012, another group legal action was being taken against the Worcestershire Acute Hospitals NHS Trust, which runs the Alexandra and Kidderminster and Worcester hospitals. The basis of the action was appalling and humiliating treatment, including patients left dehydrated, food left out of their reach, insufficient staff and those present not seeming to care.[15] The action was settled out of court, with an apology and compensation in 38 separate cases amounting to a total of £410,000.[16]

DISTINCTION BETWEEN MINIMUM CARE AND DEGRADING TREATMENT

What is acceptable in terms of dignity and degrading care has been called into some question by the decision of the Supreme Court in relation to a retired ballerina living in Kensington and Chelsea. She was not incontinent but required assistance

8   *Price v United Kingdom* [2001] Application 33394/96 (European Court of Human Rights).

9   *R(Graham) v Secretary of State for Justice* [2007] EWHC 2940 (Admin).

10   Healthcare Commission and Commission for Social Care Inspection. *Joint investigation into the provision of services for people with learning disabilities at Cornwall Partnership NHS Trust.* London: HC, CSCI, 2006, pp.42, 55.

11   Healthcare Commission. *Investigation into outbreaks of Clostridium difficile at Maidstone and Tunbridge Wells NHS Trust.* London: HC, 2007, p.4.

12   Mental Health Act Commission. *Risk, rights, recovery: twelfth biennial report, 2005–2007.* London: MHAC, 2008, p.19.

13   Commission for Health Improvement. *Investigation into the North Lakeland NHS Trust.* London: CHI, 2000, p.29.

14   Leigh Day & Co. 'All Stafford Hospital claims accepted.' *News,* 17 November 2010. Accessed on 12 January 2012 at: www.leighday.co.uk/News/2010/November-2010/All-Stafford-Hospital-claims-accepted.

15   Dayani, A. 'Families to sue over standards of care at Alexandra Hospital, Redditch.' *Birmingham Post,* 10 November 2011.

16   Donnelly, L. 'Hospital apologises to 38 families for appalling care that saw a patient starve to death.' *Sunday Telegraph,* 22 December 2012.

to get on to the commode at night because (a) her mobility was compromised following a stroke and falls, and (b) she had a smaller bladder than usual. The local authority provided her with night-time assistance to do this but then changed its mind on grounds of cost. It offered her incontinence pads instead. She argued that this was contrary to dignity and human rights.

Four of the five law lords in the Supreme Court sided with the local authority. None of them considered article 3; they also doubted whether article 8 was even engaged, let alone breached. If the local authority's actions did constitute an interference under article 8, then that interference was justified with reference to its being (a) in accordance with the law (the community care legislation), (b) for the economic well-being of other service users, and (c) proportionate in that her basic needs were still being met despite the substantial cost savings represented by incontinence pads.

The fifth judge, Lady Hale, did not see it this way at all. She was troubled by the view of the other four judges:

> A person in her situation needs this help during the day as well as during the night and irrespective of whether she needs to urinate or to defecate. Logically, the decision of the majority in this case would entitle a local authority to withdraw this help even though the client needed to defecate during the night and thus might be left lying in her faeces until the carers came in the morning. This is not [the] problem at the moment, but her evidence leaves one in no doubt that this is one of her fears. Indeed, the majority view would also entitle an authority to withdraw this help during the day. The only constraint would be how frequently (or rather how infrequently) it was deemed necessary to change the pads or sheets, consistently with the avoidance of infection and other hazards such as nappy rash. The consequences do not bear thinking about.[17]

The nature of this decision may call into some doubt how successful human rights cases about such matters might be in the future – for example, when hospital patients, who are not incontinent, are left in their own bodily waste for many hours or subjected to other indignities.

HUMILIATION, CRIMINAL JUSTICE AND ARTICLE 3

In the following case, the court held that the Crown Prosecution Service (CPS) had not followed its own Code when deciding not to prosecute a case in relation to a mentally disordered victim. The consequences of the failure to do so were a breach of article 3 because of the humiliation of being treated like a second-class citizen by the criminal justice system.

---

17   *R(McDonald) v Royal Borough of Kensington and Chelsea* [2011] UKSC 33.

Failure to prosecute assault against a man with mental health problems. A man suffered from a history of psychotic illness, which involved paranoid beliefs and auditory and visual hallucinations. On Boxing Day, part of his ear had been bitten off. On the basis of a doctor's report, to the effect that his mental condition might affect his perception and recollection of events, the CPS decided to discontinue the case. The court found that the CPS had not adhered to Part 5 of the Code for Crown Prosecutors; its decision was irrational. Either it had misread the medical report or it had stereotyped the man as having mental health problems that rendered him a non-credible witness.

In addition, the court held that this constituted a breach of article 3 of the Convention. This was because abandonment of the case on the eve of the trial added insult to his injury. It was a humiliation, causing him to feel like a second-class citizen. Far from protecting him against serious assaults, the criminal justice system had in fact increased his sense of vulnerability and of being beyond the protection of the law.[18]

UNLAWFUL DEPRIVATION OF A PERSON'S LIBERTY

Article 5 concerns deprivation of liberty.

Deprivation of liberty can be lawful but (a) it must be according to legally based procedures and thus not be arbitrary; (b) it can be justified only for people falling into certain categories (such as people of unsound mind or people suspected or convicted of a criminal offence); and (c) there must be speedy procedures available through which to challenge the detention:

1. Everyone has the right to liberty and security of person. No one shall be deprived of his liberty save in the following cases and in accordance with a procedure prescribed by law:

    (a) the lawful detention of a person after conviction by a competent court;

    (b) the lawful arrest or detention of a person for non-compliance with the lawful order of a court or in order to secure the fulfilment of any obligation prescribed by law;

    (c) the lawful arrest or detention of a person effected for the purpose of bringing him before the competent legal authority on reasonable suspicion of having committed an offence or when it is reasonably considered necessary to prevent his committing an offence or fleeing after having done so;

    (d) the detention of a minor by lawful order for the purpose of educational supervision or his lawful detention for the purpose of bringing him before the competent legal authority;

    (e) the lawful detention of persons for the prevention of the spreading of infectious diseases, of persons of un-sound mind, alcoholics or drug addicts or vagrants;

---

18   *R(B) v DPP* [2009] EWHC 106 (Admin).

(f) the lawful arrest or detention of a person to prevent his effecting an unauthorised entry into the country or of a person against whom action is being taken with a view to deportation or extradition.

2. Everyone who is arrested shall be informed promptly, in a language which he understands, of the reasons for his arrest and of any charge against him.

3. Everyone arrested or detained in accordance with the provisions of paragraph 1 (c) of this Article shall be brought promptly before a judge or other officer authorised by law to exercise judicial power and shall be entitled to trial within a reasonable time or to release pending trial. Release may be conditioned by guarantees to appear for trial.

4. Everyone who is deprived of his liberty by arrest or detention shall be entitled to take proceedings by which the lawfulness of his detention shall be decided speedily by a court and his release ordered if the detention is not lawful.

5. Everyone who has been the victim of arrest or detention in contravention of the provisions of this Article shall have an enforceable right to compensation.[19]

Thus, if a local authority deprives a person of his liberty, by placing him in a care home or hospital and preventing him returning to his own home, without following a lawful procedure, it will breach article 5.[20]

Local authorities (and, hitherto, NHS primary care trusts) sometimes deprive people of their liberty. Not infrequently, such deprivations are linked to safeguarding concerns. In compliance with article 5, the Mental Capacity Act 2005 must be followed, in particular the deprivation of liberty safeguards (DOLS) it contains, or an application to the Court of Protection must be made.

Many legal cases have reached the courts, in a number of which important judgments and observations have been made. These are covered in Chapter 13.

There have been some high-profile cases in which local authorities have gone spectacularly wrong and not served the best interests of the adult they were trying to protect. For instance, cases in Manchester and Hillingdon stand somewhere near the top of this pile.[21]

On one view, such cases should not be considered too negatively, since, in the vast majority of instances, local authorities probably get things about right. In addition, such cases have the positive effect of pointing out the major pitfalls that need to be avoided.

---

19 Quoted from: Human Rights Act 1998, article 5.
20 *JE v DE and Surrey County Council* [2006] EWHC 3459 (Fam). And: *HL v United Kingdom* [2004] 40 EHRR 761 (European Court of Human Rights).
21 *G v E* [2010] EWHC 621 (Fam). And: *G v E* [2010] EWCA Civ 822 (Court of Appeal). And: *London Borough of Hillingdon v Neary* [2011] EWHC 1377 (COP).

On another view, these cases offer a sobering lesson in how well-intentioned decisions and actions can backfire. There is also the question of whether they are in fact representative of much more widespread, undetected, poor decision making that does not come to the attention of the courts.

RIGHT TO RESPECT FOR A PERSON'S HOME, PRIVATE AND FAMILY LIFE

Article 8 demands respect for a person's home, private and family life:

> Everyone has the right to respect for his private and family life, his home and his correspondence.
>
> There shall be no interference by a public authority with the exercise of this right except such as is in accordance with the law and is necessary in a democratic society in the interests of national security, public safety or the economic well-being of the country, for the prevention of disorder or crime, for the protection of health or morals, or for the protection of the rights and freedoms of others.

It can be seen that the rights are not absolute. Article 8 allows interference by a public body if certain conditions are met. The interference must be (a) in accordance with the law, (b) necessary in a democratic society, and (c) for a specified, listed purpose.

The courts have held that respect for private life includes physical and psychological integrity.[22]

For example, it was a breach of article 8 when a local authority failed to act for two years to alleviate the dire state of a physically disabled woman, with a family of six; having suffered a stroke, she was left largely immobile and doubly incontinent in her living room.[23]

Similarly, there was a breach when a local authority carried out a flawed assessment about where a 95-year-old woman should live. The court pointed out that the consequences of such a lapse could be fatal and so engaged article 8.[24]

JUSTIFYING THE INTERFERENCE WITH ARTICLE 8 RIGHTS

Nonetheless, if adult protection measures involve interference in home, private and family life, article 8 may provide the justification for that interference.

For instance, a local authority might wish to protect a vulnerable adult lacking capacity by removing him or her from the family home. It will not necessarily be acting contrary to article 8 as a whole if it can show that certain conditions are met, even though it might clearly be interfering with the right to respect for private life.

---

22   *Botta v Italy* [1998] Application no. 153/1996/772/973 (European Court of Human Rights).
23   *R(Bernard) v Enfield London Borough Council* [2002] EWHC 2282 (Admin).
24   *R(Goldsmith) v Wandsworth London Borough Council* [2004] EWCA Civ 1170.

First, it needs to show that it is acting in accordance with the law, such as the NHS and Community Care Act 1990 or Mental Capacity Act 2005. Second, that the intervention is 'necessary in a democratic society'; that is, the authority is taking steps that are proportionate in respect of the problem and risk – in effect, that it is not taking a sledgehammer to crack a nut. Third, it would need to indicate the purpose justifying the intervention – for instance, to protect a person's health or to prevent a crime.

Thus, if a local authority makes an unjustified intervention in the life of a person lacking mental capacity, it might not only breach article 5 as described above but also article 8. The *Manchester* and *Hillingdon* cases involved breaches of both articles 5 and 8. Both cases involved the local authority removing a young adult with learning disabilities from a family, domestic setting; and in both the local authority failed to follow the principles of both the Mental Capacity and Human Rights Act.[25]

The right to respect for private life also encompasses confidentiality, but interference with confidentiality is permitted if there is sufficient justification on the same basis: in accordance with the law, necessary and for a particular purpose (e.g. protection of health or prevention of crime). It is about balancing the competing interests of confidentiality and disclosure.[26]

The extent of information included in criminal record certificates[27] and the rules about barring people from working with vulnerable adults[28] have also been challenged successfully on the grounds of proportionality, with article 8 at the fulcrum.

Article 8 is chiefly about reining in State interference, imposing 'negative' obligations on public bodies. But the courts have held also that article 8 sometimes confers 'positive' obligations to interfere, in order to protect a person's right to respect for their private life – for example, if a person was being abused or neglected at home.[29]

ARTICLE 10: RIGHT TO FREEDOM OF EXPRESSION

Article 10 states that everyone has the right to freedom of expression. This right includes the freedom to hold opinions and to receive and impart information and ideas without inference from the State.

However, like article 8, this right is not absolute. It is subject to a number of provisos. Because freedom of expression carries with it duties and responsibilities, it can be subject to formalities, conditions and restrictions. However, these in turn are only justified if they are necessary in a democratic society for a number of specified

---

25   *G v E* [2010] EWHC 621 (Fam). And: *G v E* [2010] EWCA Civ 822 (Court of Appeal). And: *London Borough of Hillingdon v Neary* [2011] EWHC 1377 (COP).

26   *R v Plymouth City Council, ex p Stevens* [2002] EWCA Civ 388.

27   *R(L) v Commissioner of Police for the Metropolis* [2009] UKSC 3.

28   *R(Royal College of Nursing) v Secretary of State for the Home Department and the Independent Safeguarding Authority* [2010] EWHC 2761 (Admin).

29   *A Local Authority v A and B* [2010] EWHC 978 (Fam).

purposes. These purposes include public safety, the prevention of disorder or crime, the protection of health or morals, the protection of the reputation or rights of others, preventing the disclosure of information received in confidence.

The following case, about safeguarding issues, saw article 10 pitched against article 8 (the privacy of the residents) as a care home sought to prevent a BBC television programme, about poor care practices, being broadcast.

Secret filming in care home: balancing public interest with private life of residents. The right to freedom of expression might not readily spring to mind as a safeguarding issue, but it was raised in a case in which the media wished to broadcast a programme about standards of care in a care home. The care home sought an injunction to prevent the programme from being broadcast.

The BBC argued that it be allowed to show the programme in line with the freedom of expression and the fact that it was in the public interest to do so. The care home claimed that its objection was based on article 8; namely, that such filming, even with the identity of individual residents obscured, was still an interference with the private life of the residents. The court found in favour of the BBC and refused to grant an injunction to the care home.[30]

ARTICLE 14: FREEDOM FROM DISCRIMINATION

Article 14 states that the Convention rights and freedoms should be enjoyed free from discrimination on any ground such as sex, race, colour, language, religion, political or other opinion, national or social origin, association with a national minority, property, birth or other status.

The list of grounds contained in the article fails to include explicitly age or disability. However, the grounds are illustrative only; therefore, age and disability are implicit.

Article 14 cannot be argued in isolation but must be linked with one of the other articles in the Convention, although breach of that other article is not necessary in order to establish a breach of article 14. For instance, the following case related to disability.

Hospital treatment of person with severe learning disability: not making assumptions about clinical potential. An 18-year-old had the capacity of a five- to six-year-old child – with severe learning disability, autism and epilepsy. He was admitted to hospital for acute renal failure; haemodialysis was required. A dispute arose between the hospital and mother as to whether or in what circumstances a kidney transplant would ever be suitable for him and whether there was a possibility of a different form of haemodialysis by use of AV fistula.

The court found that the medical and nursing team's approach had been coloured by past experience with the man and the difficulties of verbal communication. However, other evidence in the case showed that steps could be taken to enable him to cope with certain treatment and that the possibility of an AV fistula should not be ruled out. Neither should kidney transplantation be ruled out on non-medical grounds.

The court made the point that it was crucial that he was not given less satisfactory treatment than a person who understood the risks, pain and discomfort of major surgery.

---

30   *BKM v British Broadcasting Association* [2009] EWHC 3151 (Chancery).

'To act in any other way would be contrary to the rights of a mentally incapacitated patient both under our domestic law and under the European Convention.'[31]

Although the court did not refer explicitly to article 14 (linked with article 2, right to life), implicitly it probably had it in mind.

In 2012, a family announced its intention to bring a case against the NHS after a DNR (do not resuscitate) order was placed on a patient's file, not just without consent and consultation but also because he had learning disabilities. Part of the legal argument could include article 14, linked with article 2 (and perhaps articles 3 and 8), as well as maybe the Equality Act 2010.[32]

EQUALITY ACT 2010

Aside from the Human Rights Act 1998 is the Equality Act 2010. It aims to prevent discrimination against people bearing 'protected characteristics'. These include age, disability, gender reassignment, marriage/civil partnership, race, religion/belief, sex, sexual orientation. The Act covers both direct and indirect discrimination against people with these characteristics.

In relation to disability, for example, discrimination is unfavourable treatment arising in consequence of person's disability, which is not a proportionate way of achieving a legitimate aim.[33] And there is a duty to make reasonable adjustments for disabled people relating to provision of services, criteria, practices, a physical feature or an auxiliary aid.[34]

Activity covered by the Act includes the provision of services to the public, disposal and management of premises including reasonable adjustments, employment, schools, further and higher education.

In addition is what is sometimes called a public sector equality duty. It means that public bodies must have due regard to the need to (a) eliminate discrimination, harassment, victimisation and any other conduct that is prohibited by or under this Act; (b) advance equality of opportunity between persons who share a relevant protected characteristic and persons who do not share it; (c) foster good relations between persons who share a relevant protected characteristic and persons who do not share it.[35]

TICK-BOX APPROACH TO THE LEGISLATION IS NOT SUFFICIENT

In relation to the provision of services for disabled people, the courts have shown themselves prepared to push local authorities reasonably hard to demonstrate that they are complying with the Act (or its predecessor, the Disability Discrimination Act 1995). The courts seem to have reacted against what could be termed a mere

---

31   *An Hospital Trust v S* [2003] EWHC 365 (Admin).
32   Mitchell, B. 'Down's Syndrome man takes legal action over "do not resuscitate" order.' *The Independent*, 13 September 2012.
33   Equality Act 2010, s.15.
34   Equality Act 2010, s.20.
35   Equality Act 2010, s.149.

tick-box approach. If a local authority has not thought, consulted or explained hard enough about the implications of its public sector equality duty, then it will go astray legally.

For example, two local social services authorities lost major legal cases when they tried to raise the threshold of eligibility for assistance for disabled people from the substantial level to the critical level only. In other words, people with low, moderate and substantial needs would receive no help; only those in the most critical of circumstances would do so. In each case, the High Court held that the local authority had paid insufficient attention, in its consultation process, to the implications of the changes for disabled people. Each local authority was told to go away; if it wanted to raise the threshold, it would have to consult all over again and this time do it properly.[36] The outcome was similar when another authority tried to remove its live-in wardens from sheltered accommodation.[37]

OLDER PEOPLE: AGE DISCRIMINATION

Of further and specific relevance to this book is the duty not to discriminate in the provision of goods and services against people on grounds of their age, which came into force in October 2012.[38]

It is widely recognised that older people are discriminated against in health and social care. In the context of this book, it is mainly older people who bear the brunt of systemic neglect within the health and social care system, in hospitals, care homes and in their own homes. It remains to be seen whether, and how far, the Act can be used to combat this.

---

36   R(Chavda) v Harrow London Borough Council [2007] EWHC 3064 (Admin). Also: R(W) v Birmingham City Council [2011] EWHC 1147 (Admin).

37   R(Bojevo) v London Borough of Barnet [2009] EWHC 3261 (Admin).

38   Government Equality Office. Equality Act 2010: banning age discrimination in services: an overview for service providers and customers. London: GEO, 2012.

Local social services authorities: pivotal role in safeguarding

Key points
    Community care assessment
    Balanced and proportionate interventions
    Perpetration of harm by local authorities
Community care assessment and provision of assistance
    Role of local authority in assessing or investigating
    Local authority's role to support, not to protect from violence, vulnerable adults
    Assessment and support rather than control and regulation
    Distinguishing service provision issues from safeguarding
    Eligibility for assistance from local authorities
    People who do or may need community care services
    Eligibility decision about level of need for assistance and services
    Application of the two-stage test to establish eligibility
    Misunderstanding of current legislation and who is eligible for help
    People who misuse alcohol and drugs
    Eligibility for assistance with safeguarding matters: draft Care and Support Bill
    Community care services: how people can be assisted
    Assessment and services for informal carers
Local authority investigations and responses: striking a balance
    Supporting evidence
    Proportionate responses and weighing up competing considerations
    Local authority procedures: importance of flexible approach
    Using the Mental Capacity Act
    Taking legally prescribed restrictions at face value
Systemic perpetration of harm by local authorities
    Local authorities: lack of insight into their own acts and omissions
    Local authorities linked to financial abuse
Failing to commission services adequately and to monitor and review contractual arrangements
Application of strict threshold of eligibility for assistance
Harm arising from failure to meet people's needs
Impact of personalisation and self-directed support
    Misuse of direct payments and safeguarding
    Independence and protection

KEY POINTS

When central government issued the *No secrets* guidance, giving local social services authorities the lead responsibility in local adult protection and safeguarding work, it did not accompany this responsibility with any new legislative powers for those authorities. Thus, currently, adult protection work by local authorities rests ultimately on existing community care legislation which does not mention adult protection or safeguarding.

As already highlighted, the draft Care and Support Bill 2012 will change this, if and when it becomes law. Unlike previous social care legislation, this refers explicitly both to protection from abuse and neglect and to safeguarding. However, despite the reference to the making of enquiries in cases of abuse or neglect, the substance of a local authority's help for people will remain grounded in the basic duty to assess and to meet people's needs.

Therefore, much of the following chapter will arguably remain relevant, in principle at least, even if and when the draft Care and Support Bill becomes law.

COMMUNITY CARE ASSESSMENT

The *No secrets* guidance states that a vulnerable adult is a person who may be in need of community care services. This is a direct reference to the same condition in s.47 of the NHS and Community Care Act 1990, which is the legal trigger for community care assessment of a person's needs.

What this means is that when local authorities are carrying out what they tend to call a 'safeguarding investigation', they are actually – in law – carrying out a community care assessment. So, in this sense, the community care legislation is directly relevant to adult protection, in terms of the duties to assess and to provide advice, information, support and services.

(The same remains true to an extent under the draft Care and Support Bill. Although there is a duty in the Bill to make enquiries in cases of neglect and abuse, assessment and the provision of services for people suffering neglect and abuse remain part of the local authority's assessment and service provision duties.)

However, this legal underpinning is not always appreciated. When it is not, there is a danger that local authorities misconstrue their role and function in safeguarding. This is not a matter of theoretical interest; the misunderstanding can sometimes lead local authorities down quite the wrong path.

For example, local authorities might in practice sometimes not help people when they should. Alternatively, if they do get involved but lose sight of their primary role – of assessing, working with, supporting, advising and providing services for vulnerable adults – local authorities can too easily find themselves taking an almost authoritarian, coercive and regulatory approach, which is not sanctioned by legislation and does nobody any good.

Furthermore, it is clearly the case that when local authorities concentrate successfully on these core functions, working with and supporting individuals and families, crises requiring the involvement of the courts might be less frequent. The difficulty for local authorities seems to be such high pressure, in terms of work and caseloads, that staff regularly complain that they simply don't have the time to work with people in this way.

BALANCED AND PROPORTIONATE INTERVENTIONS

A lack of appreciation of legal remit is sometimes responsible for a loss of balance and for an absence of justifiable, proportionate and lawful interventions. This chapter therefore makes reference to a number of legal cases in which local authorities have gone astray. It should be emphasised that this is not unduly to criticise local authorities, but merely to point out pitfalls that should be avoided.

Local authorities have an extremely difficult job on their hands, and, of course, for every one case that goes to court, there are countless that don't – and one would wish to assume that most of the time local authorities get it right. That said, there are sufficient numbers of cases getting to court as to be suggestive of a possibly wider malaise in the quality and lawfulness of decision making in safeguarding and mental capacity cases.

PERPETRATION OF HARM BY LOCAL AUTHORITIES

A further difficulty faces local authorities. It is not just a matter of sometimes misjudging attempts to safeguard vulnerable adults. Sometimes, they themselves directly perpetrate harm – not in the sense of the odd mistake here or there but more systemically.

This represents an underbelly which, unsurprisingly, local authorities do not tend to acknowledge, let alone regard as anything to do with safeguarding.

First, there is evidence of vulnerable people suffering financial harm when local authorities act in clear and persistent breach of legal rules about charging for services.

Second, the failure on the part of a local authority to monitor and review care providers, to whom they contract out care services, can lead to serious harm and sometimes even to the death of service users. It may, of course, be the care provider that ultimately fails the service user. However, if the local authority was aware – or should have been aware – of the poor quality of the provider, the blame lies at the authority's door, too. Equally, if the local authority was commissioning the bare minimum of service and help for vulnerable people, such that they would foreseeably suffer poor care and neglect, then the trail of fault can lead back to that local authority.

Third, local authorities are progressively applying more restrictive eligibility criteria, thus assisting fewer vulnerable people and potentially leaving them to significant risk of harm. And, even when people remain eligible, the amount of help allowed for by the local authority may sometimes be grossly inadequate – such that carers do not have time to do all that is necessary or, indeed, even to talk to the person.

Fourth, the failure sometimes to recognise a clear statutory duty to meet a vulnerable person's needs, either at all or in the appropriate manner, can also lead to severe detriment and, if not necessarily to abuse, to highly inappropriate alternative care and to harm.

Fifth, current government social (and health) care policy is awash with the mantra of giving people more control, choice and independence. There appears to be a danger that such a policy will be indiscriminate in practice and be applied too crudely, irrespective of the vulnerability of the adults concerned.

COMMUNITY CARE ASSESSMENT AND PROVISION OF ASSISTANCE

Local authorities have a duty to assess people who appear to be in need of community care services. This is under s.47 of the NHS and Community Care Act 1990. As already pointed out, what local authorities currently refer to as 'safeguarding investigations' are, at heart, community care assessments.

This means that safeguarding is not currently spelt out in social services legislation and that it is welfare – rather than regulatory – functions that underpin local authority safeguarding activity.

In relation to this, the points made below are likely to remain relevant even if and when the draft Care and Support Bill 2012 becomes law. Although the draft Bill does include a duty to make enquiries in relation to abuse and neglect, the heart of a local authority's duty – including towards those at risk of neglect and abuse – remains assessment and the provision of care and support.

ROLE OF LOCAL AUTHORITY IN ASSESSING OR INVESTIGATING

The courts have, in a few cases, spelt out what investigatory steps a local authority might take. The two examples below give an idea: the first in relation to a possible deprivation of liberty, the second to possible assisted suicide.

ASSESSMENT AND INVESTIGATION: POSSIBLE DEPRIVATION OF LIBERTY

For example, in one case there was a question of deprivation of liberty. It involved a local authority's reaction to a situation in a family home, in which the parents locked their daughter in her bedroom at night for her own safety. The court helpfully outlined the local authority's responsibilities as follows, in the light of concern about whether there was a deprivation of liberty.

The responsibilities included a duty to investigate (assess), to monitor, to provide support and to take the matter to court in some circumstances:

(i) These will include the duty to investigate, so as to determine whether there is, in fact, a deprivation of liberty. In this context the local authority will need to consider all the factors relevant to the objective and subjective elements [of deprivation of liberty]...

(ii) If, having carried out its investigation, the local authority is satisfied that the objective element is not present, so there is no deprivation of liberty, the local authority will have discharged its immediate obligations. However, its positive obligations may in an appropriate case require the local authority to continue to monitor the situation in the event that circumstances should change.

(iii) If, however, the local authority concludes that the measures imposed do or may constitute a deprivation of liberty, then it will be under a positive obligation, both under Article 5 alone and taken together with Article 14, to take reasonable and proportionate measures to bring that state of affairs to an end. What is reasonable and proportionate in the circumstances will, of course, depend upon the context, but it might for example... require the local authority to exercise its statutory powers and duties so as to provide support services for the carers that will enable inappropriate restrictions to be ended, or at least minimised.

(iv) If, however, there are no reasonable measures that the local authority can take to bring the deprivation of liberty to an end, or if the measures it proposes are objected to by the individual or his family, then it may be necessary for the local authority to seek the assistance of the court in determining whether there is, in fact, a deprivation of liberty and, if there is, obtaining authorisation for its continuance.

What emerges from this is that, whatever the extent of a local authority's positive obligations under Article 5, its duties, and more important its powers, are limited. In essence, its duties are threefold: a duty in appropriate circumstances to investigate; a duty in appropriate circumstances to provide supporting services; and a duty in appropriate circumstances to refer the matter to the court.[1]

ASSESSMENT AND INVESTIGATION: POSSIBLE ASSISTED SUICIDE

Assisted suicide is clearly relevant to safeguarding in terms of a criminal offence and the involvement of the police and the Crown Prosecution Service. The courts have set out what, in their view, a local authority should do when faced with a possible case of assisted suicide.

Assisted suicide and adult protection procedures. A woman was suffering from cerebellar ataxia. The condition was incurable and irreversible; it attacked that part of the brain controlling the body's motor functions. She had become increasingly disabled. She wished to be assisted to commit suicide. Her family was initially opposed to this; now,

---

1   *A Local Authority v A and B* [2010] EWHC 978 (Fam).

reluctantly, her family had decided to support her wishes. Her husband informed the local authority, which had been providing extensive support for his wife, that he was arranging to take her to Switzerland where assisted suicide is not a criminal offence.

The local authority applied to the courts for exercise of the inherent jurisdiction; an injunction was initially granted restraining the husband from removing his wife to Switzerland. The court then subsequently considered the situation. It concluded that the adult protection duties of the local authorities were as follows:

- to investigate the position of the vulnerable adult to consider her true position and intention
- to consider whether she was legally competent to make and carry out her decision and intention
- to consider whether (or what) influence may have been operating on her position and intention and to ensure that she had all the relevant information and knew all available options
- to consider whether to invoke the inherent jurisdiction of the courts to decide about the issue of her competence
- if she was not competent, to provide assistance in her best interests
- if she was competent, to allow her in any lawful way to give effect to her decision, although this should not preclude advice or assistance being given about what are perceived to be her best interests
- to inform the police if there were reasonable grounds for suspecting that a criminal offence would be involved
- in very exceptional circumstances only, to seek an injunction from the courts using s.222 of the Local Government Act 1972.[2]

By the time of the hearing, it had become clear that the woman had legal competence to take the decision. The court concluded that the local authority's duties extended no further than the above list and that the authority had no obligation to seek a continuation of an injunction under s.222; criminal justice agencies had all the powers. For its part, unless it was under an obligation, the local authority anyway did not wish to do so.

Nor would the court, of its own motion, continue the injunction where no one else with the necessary standing was seeking such an order, where the criminal justice agencies had the requisite knowledge and power, and where the effect of the injunction would be to 'deny a right to a seriously disabled but competent person that cannot be exercised herself by reason only of her physical disability'.[3]

LOCAL AUTHORITY'S ROLE TO SUPPORT, NOT TO PROTECT FROM VIOLENCE, VULNERABLE ADULTS

Legally, it is not the local authority's primary role to protect vulnerable adults from violence from third parties; that is the responsibility of the police.

2   *Re Z* [2004] EWHC 2817 (Fam).
3   *Re Z* [2004] EWHC 2817 (Fam).

This matter was considered in a case about a young man with Asperger's syndrome, known to social services, who had been found dead in a car park; an acquaintance was convicted of manslaughter. A judicial review case was taken against the coroner, the police and the local authority.

It was argued, amongst other things, that the local authority had a duty under article 2 of the European Convention on Human Rights 'to have in place appropriate systems to protect the lives of those with Asperger's syndrome from the risk from third parties'. The case failed. The judge set out at some length what he considered to be the extent of the local authority's duty in relation to article 2 of the European Convention (right to life). He was clear that 'The Council's obligation… was primarily one of support. The primary duty to protect him from a possibly fatal assault fell upon the Police Force.'[4]

Another case failed against a local authority when it was sued in negligence by two people with learning disabilities. They alleged that the local authority had taken inadequate steps to protect them from acquaintances who had physically tortured them one weekend. The Court of Appeal stated that not only had the local authority staff in fact taken adequate steps, but that, even had they not done so, the authority would not have been liable. This was, essentially, because, other than in special circumstances, it would not be in the public interest to hold local authorities liable for harm perpetrated by third parties.[5]

ASSESSMENT AND SUPPORT RATHER THAN CONTROL AND REGULATION

The courts have warned local authorities against overplaying their hand.

They have reminded them of their primary legal role under various pieces of community care welfare legislation, pointing out that these do not confer on local authorities 'any power to regulate, control, compel, restrain, confine or coerce. They are concerned with the provision of services and support.'

These comments were made in a case involving parents who locked their daughter in her bedroom each night for her safety; she had severe learning disabilities.[6] The comments bear some scrutiny. They constitute strong language.

The court underlined the importance of local authorities keeping their welfare role in mind and not seeking to assert control that is neither legally sanctioned nor productive:

> It is suggested that in a case such as this a local authority is not merely 'involved' with people in the situation of A and C and their families but that it may also have 'complete and effective control…through its assessments and care plans', given that the care plans deal with important aspects of their lives, their care, movement and, in C's case, social contacts. It needs to be

---

4   *R(AP) v HM Coroner for the County of Worcestershire, Worcestershire County Council, Chief Constable of West Mercia Police* [2011] EWHC 1453 (Admin).

5   *X & Y v Hounslow London Borough Council* [2009] EWCA Civ 286.

6   *In the Matter of A, In the Matter of C* [2010] EWHC 978 (Fam), High Court and Court of Protection, paras 51–54.

> said in the plainest possible terms that this suggestion, however formulated –
> and worryingly some local authorities seem almost to assume and take it for
> granted – is simply wrong in law. A local authority does not exercise 'control',
> it lacks the legal power to exercise control, over people in the situation of A
> or C or their carers.[7]

It continued by explaining that local authorities sometimes proceed on the basis of
a fundamental misunderstanding. Their role was to assess for and offer assistance,
advice and services:

> Moreover, the assertion or assumption, however formulated, betrays a
> fundamental misunderstanding of the nature of the relationship between a
> local authority and those, like A and C and their carers, who it is tasked
> to support – a fundamental misunderstanding of the relationship between
> the State and the citizen. People in the situation of A and C, together with
> their carers, look to the State – to a local authority – for the support, the
> assistance and the provision of the services to which the law, giving effect
> to the underlying principles of the Welfare State, entitles them. They do not
> seek to be 'controlled' by the State or by the local authority. And it is not
> for the State in the guise of a local authority to seek to exercise such control.
> The State, the local authority, is the servant of those in need of its support
> and assistance, not their master. As Ms Ball put it on behalf of the Official
> Solicitor in relation to someone in C's position, and in my judgment the
> same applies to someone like A, while the local authority performs important
> monitoring and safeguarding roles, its major function in relation to C and
> others like her is to assess needs and provide services. I agree.[8]

Routine talk of enforcement and threats was misplaced:

> This attitude is perhaps best exemplified by the proposition that 'in the event
> that the parents were to disagree with the *decisions* of the local authority
> (which will always be based upon the opinion of relevant professionals) it
> would seek to *enforce its decisions* through appropriate proceedings if necessary'
> (emphasis added). This approach, which to repeat is not the approach of
> the local authority in this case, though reflecting what I have come across
> elsewhere, reflects an attitude of mind which is not merely unsound in law
> but hardly best calculated to encourage proper effect being given to a local
> authority's procedural obligations under Article 8 of the Convention…[9]

And working with people and families was in any case likely to be more productive
than more coercive approaches:

---

7   *A Local Authority v A and B* [2010] EWHC 978 (Fam).
8   *A Local Authority v A and B* [2010] EWHC 978 (Fam).
9   *A Local Authority v A and B* [2010] EWHC 978 (Fam).

Moreover, it is likely to be nothing but counter-productive when it comes to a local authority 'working together', as it must, with family carers. 'Working together' involves something more – much more – than merely requiring carers to agree with a local authority's 'decision' even if, let alone just because, it may be backed by professional opinion. As Ms Ball comments, with what might be thought studied moderation, the use of the word 'enforce' may belie an overstated understanding of the degree of control which the local authority has in situations such as this.[10]

This court believed that too many local authorities suffered from serious misconceptions about their role and the law.[11]

DISTINGUISHING SERVICE PROVISION ISSUES FROM SAFEGUARDING

It is not only the courts that have detected the danger of stepping over the mark. The local ombudsman, too, has noted the importance of appropriate and proportionate responses. The local authority in the following case invoked the full weight of safeguarding procedures, including referral to the police, against the devoted parents of a young man with severe disabilities. The ombudsman found that this beggared belief since, in essence, it was a service provision rather than a safeguarding matter.

Manual handling of young disabled man by his parents: service provision matter rather than safeguarding. Local authority occupational therapists offered a portable hoist to the parents of a 21-year-old man; they were manually lifting him each morning out of the sofa bed in which he slept. They were also carrying him sometimes up the stairs. He could not walk, talk, stand or care for himself. The therapists insisted, on safety grounds, that the hoist be used with a hospital bed. The parents refused on grounds of lack of space.

Dispute with parents over hoist and bed. The therapists refused to provide the hoist without the hospital bed. The parents suggested that, instead, the local authority should make a direct payment to them for the hoist, so that they could purchase it themselves and take more responsibility for the situation.

Safeguarding referral made to the police. Concerned about the risk to the son (he appeared to lack the capacity to consent to it), the therapists made a safeguarding referral that was passed on to the police. The parents were informed this had happened only belatedly. The ombudsman referred to the local authority's lack of flexibility in what services it was prepared to offer, the absence of a social worker, the lack of a person-centred approach and the fact that the police had deemed the referral inappropriate. It was a service provision issue, rather than a full-blown safeguarding issue.

Maladministration: overreaction of local authority. The ombudsman found maladministration in respect of the adult protection referral, finding that it 'beggared belief'. He referred to the devotion of the family to their son's care, the local authority's procedural shortcomings (including poor record keeping), the family not being informed and their understandable distress and outrage when they found out.[12]

---

10   *A Local Authority v A and B* [2010] EWHC 978 (Fam).

11   *In the Matter of A, In the Matter of C* [2010] EWHC 978 (Fam), High Court and Court of Protection, paras 51–54.

12   Local Government Ombudsman. *Report on an investigation into complaint no. 07/B/07665 against Luton Borough Council, 2008.* London: LGO, 2008.

ELIGIBILITY FOR ASSISTANCE FROM LOCAL AUTHORITIES

The current position about 'eligibility' for support, under existing legislation, is set out immediately below. It is a two-stage test.

(The draft Care and Support Bill 2012 envisages in future the application of an eligibility test, as exists currently, to decide whether to help somebody. But it does not envisage the equivalent of the first stage of the test, which is currently applied and in effect determines whether a person will get an assessment at all.)

This is about whether the adult is a member of particular group of people, defined, for example, as disabled, old or mentally disordered.

Jettisoning reference to particular groups was a specific recommendation of the Law Commission, on the grounds that it would make it easier to understand when the duty of assessment was triggered.[13] However, it follows also that the ambit of the new legislation will be, in principle, wider than that of the existing legislation.

This might mean that certain vulnerable adults who previously have been passed over by social services – on the basis that they did not come within a certain 'user group' defined in legislation – will in future not be excluded. For instance, several serious case reviews involving the death of vulnerable adults have commented how the adult was not considered to come within social services remit, even to the extent of not receiving an assessment.[14]

PEOPLE WHO DO OR MAY NEED COMMUNITY CARE SERVICES

Currently, under s.47 of the NHS and Community Care Act 1990, local authorities have a duty of assessment, followed by a duty to decide whether the person's needs call for community care services. To be eligible for social services assistance, and indeed assessment, a person must first come within the groups of people covered by the community care legislation.

The relevant community care legislation is made up of the:

- National Assistance Act 1948

- Chronically Sick and Disabled Persons Act 1970

- Health Services and Public Health Act 1968 (section 45)

- NHS Act 2006 (schedule 20)

- Mental Health Act 1983 (section 117).

The groups of people covered by this legislation include, in the main, those with needs arising from age, illness, mental disorder, disability (physical, mental, sensory, learning), use of alcohol or drugs.

---

13   Law Commission. *Adult social care.* Law Com. no. 326. London: TSO, 2011, paras 12.31–12.33.
14   For example: Warwickshire Safeguarding Adults Partnership. *Serious case review: the murder of Gemma Hayter, 9th August 2010.* Warwick: WSAP, 2011. Also: Flynn, M. *The murder of Adult A (Michael Gilbert): a serious case review.* Luton: Luton Safeguarding Adults Board, 2011.

It is important to note, however, that if a person does not fall into what one could call the 'community care service user groups', then he or she will, by definition, not be even potentially eligible for help and assistance under the community care legislation – in relation to safeguarding or anything else. In fact, not even eligible for a full assessment.

This is not to say that if a referral is received the local authority should not react helpfully, first ascertaining the likely status of a person (which, of course, might anyway necessitate an assessment) and then referring the person to other appropriate sources of help.

ELIGIBILITY DECISION ABOUT LEVEL OF NEED
FOR ASSISTANCE AND SERVICES

So, once it is established that a person does fall within one of those groups (the first stage), and may be in need of community care services, then a statutory assessment is required by s.47 of the 1990 Act.

Following such an assessment, which might be relatively simple or more complex, a decision must be made about eligibility for services. This is the second stage and is completed by applying guidance on eligibility criteria.

The guidance is issued by the Department of Health. Although not legislation, it carries legal weight because it is made under s.7 of the Local Authority Social Services Act 1970. Such guidance must be generally followed by local authorities, unless there are cogent, perhaps exceptional, reasons for not doing so.

The guidance sets out four categories of risk to people's independence, or of need, which the local authority must assess for: critical, substantial, moderate or low. When people are assessed, the risks to their independence and their needs are allocated to one or more of the categories.

But it is down to each council to decide each year, by weighing up its limited resources in the light of local needs, which categories of need it will meet. For instance, the policy of many councils is to meet critical and substantial, but not moderate or low, needs.

The critical category in the guidance refers, amongst other things, to serious abuse or neglect that has occurred or will occur; the substantial category refers to abuse or neglect only, without it necessarily being serious.

APPLICATION OF THE TWO-STAGE TEST TO ESTABLISH ELIGIBILITY

The upshot of all this is that if a safeguarding issue has been identified in terms of abuse or neglect, then the person concerned is eligible for assistance (a) as long as they are in one of the defined groups of community care service users, and (b) even if they do not require any other community care services.

There are reports of local authority call centres turning away safeguarding referrals simply on the grounds that the person concerned is not receiving any other community care services (e.g. personal care, help with shopping). This is not legally justifiable.

Furthermore, a misunderstanding or misapplication of this two-stage legal test can be associated with catastrophic consequences. For instance, a serious case review in 2011, into the murder of a vulnerable young woman, considered both stages of the test.

First, social services had incorrectly stated that she did not come within its remit because she did not have a learning disability. On this ground, it had failed to assess her, even though a number of referrals and requests were made by the police. Yet she had a recognised mental disorder (although not a diagnosed mental illness) and this meant that she did come, in principle, within one of the community care groups, which include adults with 'mental disorder of any description'.[15]

Second, the incidents – on the basis of which the police had made their referrals and which indicated that all was not right – might have been regarded as falling short of 'significant harm', the term used in the *No secrets* guidance as part of the definition of a vulnerable adult. Nevertheless, the serious case review pointed out that a series of such lower-level incidents could cumulatively build up to a level of significant harm.[16]

In any case, under the eligibility guidance, 'serious' abuse is not required to trigger eligibility. This is because if the critical category in the guidance refers to serious abuse or neglect, then, logically, the abuse or neglect referred to in the substantial category is non-serious – and the person would still be eligible not only for assessment but also for assistance.

MISUNDERSTANDING OF CURRENT LEGISLATION AND WHO IS ELIGIBLE FOR HELP

An example of misunderstanding has been as follows. At one time, the House of Commons Health Committee recommended that the definition of 'elder abuse' be extended 'to include those individuals who do not require community care services, for example older people living in their own homes without the support of health and social care services, and those who can take care of themselves'.[17]

But, in fact, the guidance and the community care legislation already covered such people. This was because, first, older people generally (i.e. even without an obvious physical, mental or sensory disability) come within the legal ambit of community care under s.45 of the Health Services and Public Health Act 1968.

---

15   National Assistance Act 1948, s.29.

16   Warwickshire Safeguarding Adults Partnership. *Serious case review: the murder of Gemma Hayter, 9th August 2010.* Warwick: WSAP, 2011, paras 3.7.17, 4.4.

17   House of Commons Health Committee. *Elder abuse.* HC 111–1. London: TSO, 2004, p.9.

Second, support, information and advice are all community care services – even if the person is not actually receiving any other practical, 'hands-on' assistance.

Third, the guidance on eligibility states that abuse and neglect, serious or otherwise, constitute critical or substantial community care needs for the purpose of local authority intervention.[18] As already noted, there is no requirement that the person be receiving other community care services.

PEOPLE WHO MISUSE ALCOHOL AND DRUGS

The *No secrets* guidance talks of community care needs arising from age, illness or disability. It omits mention of people who are misusing alcohol and drugs, a group who nonetheless come under the community care legislation.

It might be thought the guidance has not deliberately omitted this group, until one realises that the Department of Health has believed that this group is indeed outside the ambit of safeguarding. This was highlighted when, in 2008, it consulted about safeguarding. It queried calls for a wider definition of vulnerable adult by stating that 'a wide definition may lead to homeless people, drug addicts, alcoholics and others being regarded as vulnerable adults'.[19]

However, those who use drugs and alcohol certainly do come, legally, within the ambit of safeguarding. This is easily demonstrated.

First, they come within community care legislation and so are a group of people who are potentially eligible for assistance.[20] This is clearly the government's view, as set out in directions issued under s.21 of the National Assistance Act 1948, referring to provision of accommodation 'specifically for persons who are alcoholic or drug dependent' – and likewise non-residential services, referred to in approvals made under schedule 20 of the NHS Act 2006.[21]

Second, any individual person, defined as within community care by this legislation, suffering abuse or neglect (serious or otherwise), is eligible for help under the Department of Health's own eligibility guidance.[22]

ELIGIBILITY FOR ASSISTANCE WITH SAFEGUARDING MATTERS: DRAFT CARE AND SUPPORT BILL

As already noted above, the draft Care and Support Bill 2012 does not define categories of service user by disability or any characteristic (such as age, or drug and/or alcohol abuse). Therefore, eligibility for help will in future simply depend on whether an adult comes within the eligible levels of need for care and support

---

18   Department of Health. *Prioritising need in the context of Putting People First: A whole system approach to eligibility for social care: guidance on eligibility criteria for adult social care, England 2010.* London: DH, 2010, p.21.

19   Department of Health. *Safeguarding adults: a consultation on the review of the 'No secrets' guidance.* London: DH, 2008, p.50.

20   They come under s.21 of the National Assistance Act 1948 and schedule 20 of the NHS Act 2006.

21   LAC(93)10. *Approvals and directions for arrangements from 1 April 1993 made under Schedule 8 to the National Health Service Act 1977 and Sections 21 and 29 of the National Assistance Act 1948.* London: Department of Health, 1993.

22   Department of Health. *Prioritising need in the context of Putting People First: A whole system approach to eligibility for social care: guidance on eligibility criteria for adult social care, England 2010.* London: DH, 2010, p.21.

as set out in a national framework, underpinned by regulations. This has already been discussed above.

COMMUNITY CARE SERVICES: HOW PEOPLE CAN BE ASSISTED

Community care legislation contains a wide variety of services that local authorities can potentially arrange for people – and which may be relevant in the context of safeguarding adults. For instance, they might place a person in a care home under s.21 of the National Assistance Act 1948 if the person is in need of care and attention and, for example, is old, ill, disabled, alcoholic, drug-dependent or has a mental disorder.

Alternatively, authorities have duties and powers to provide a wide range of non-residential services. These include practical assistance in a person's own home, day services and centres, travel, recreational activities, meals, assistive equipment, adaptations to the home – as well as advice, support and visiting services.

Such services, provided adequately and timeously, may play a crucial role in preventing or ameliorating situations that, in some circumstances, might otherwise tip into neglect or abuse.

These non-residential services are available for disabled people (including mental disorder) under the National Assistance Act 1948 (s.29) and the Chronically Sick and Disabled Persons Act 1970 (s.2).

Similar services are also available for older people generally, who are not disabled, under the Health Service and Public Health Act 1968 (s.45).

A range of other non-residential services are available under schedule 20 of the NHS Act 2006, including for illness generally, mental disorder in particular, as well as home help and laundry services for households where somebody is ill, lying in, an expectant mother, aged or disabled.

Under the draft Care and Support Bill 2012, services that a local authority can provide to meet needs are defined more simply and broadly than under the existing legislation, but, clearly, the services listed – accommodation, care, support, counselling and advocacy – would all be relevant to protecting people from neglect or abuse.

ASSESSMENT AND SERVICES FOR INFORMAL CARERS

The legislation referred to below will disappear if and when the draft Care and Support Bill 2012 becomes law.

However, the same general points made below about the importance of assisting informal carers (e.g. family or friends), in order to prevent the incidence of and escalation of domestic neglect or abuse, will still apply in the future. In fact, the new legislation will be more useful in this respect because, apart from containing a duty to assess, it also contains a duty (absent in the current legislation) to provide services for carers.

Local authorities are currently subject also to duties and powers in relation to people's informal carers. In summary, this legislation places a duty on local authorities to assess informal carers in their own right if (a) they are caring for a person who may be in need of community care services, (b) they are providing substantial care on a regular basis, and (c) they request an assessment.

The assessment must be about the person's ability to care and also take account of the carer's involvement in work, education, training and leisure activities. The legislation goes on to give the local authority a power, although not a duty, to arrange services for an informal carer. If the local authority asks the NHS to assist in respect of providing for carers, the NHS has a duty to give due consideration to the request.

The main legislation currently comprises the Carers (Recognition and Services) Act 1995, Carers and Disabled Children Act 2000 and Carers (Equal Opportunities) Act 2004. The current policy pursued by both local authorities and the NHS, of more care in people's own homes rather than institutional care, inevitably places a greater burden on families and informal carers. A build-up of physical and mental stress can sometimes lead to situations that threaten to descend into abuse or neglect by informal carers – or at any rate to harm suffered by the vulnerable, cared for, person.

Therefore, carers' legislation, as well as the community care legislation, can be used to assess and to prevent, defuse, or avoid a repeat of stress leading to harm, neglect or abuse. In the protection and safeguarding of vulnerable adults, it is arguably essential legislation. There has been a hint and sometimes more, in several safeguarding legal cases, of local authorities failing to provide adequate support for carers of vulnerable adults lacking capacity – contributing to the eventual crisis which precipitates drastic interventions and legal proceedings.[23]

COURT OF PROTECTION CASE REVEALING INADEQUATE SUPPORT FOR INFORMAL CARER

A recent Court of Protection case serves to highlight the plight of the informal carer.

A local authority was seeking to prevent the return home of a woman from hospital to her husband. It had convened a safeguarding meeting, such were the concerns, and now proposed to deprive her of her liberty in a nursing home – against her wishes (though she lacked capacity on this matter) and those of her husband.

---

23 *Newham London Borough Council v BS* [2003] EWHC 1909 (Fam). And: *B Borough Council v Mrs S* [2006] EWHC 2584 (Fam).

She had suffered two strokes and now lacked capacity to make the decision. One of the issues was that her husband had been struggling to care for her because of a lack of respite for him. But this lack was due to the outcome of the rigid policy of the local authority, which stipulated a maximum per week of three hours' respite to carers, irrespective of need.

The judge found the local authority's position perverse. He pointed out, bluntly:

> I can find no evidence which suggests that three hours' respite for carers per week is adequate, only evidence that the local authority has exercised its statutory discretion and, in the context of available resources, cannot afford to provide more. I make that interim finding because it is relevant to why Mr H has been worn down and frustrated, and disengaged from services, which did not help to promote his wife's best interests.
>
> The local authority's submission that Mrs H has care needs which Mr H cannot meet because of the 'lack of any…respite provision in his plan to care' is a gross distortion of the truth, given their decision to provide three hours' respite per week and his request for more respite care.
>
> The level of assistance provided to Mr H has placed him under great strain. Much of the conduct which the local authority complains of can be attributed to this lack of respite care.
>
> It is, I accept, for the local authority to determine whether he should be provided with more respite, having regard to matters such as their budget and the need to be fair to other service users. However, the solution to this problem, as they have in effect reminded me, lies in their hands, not mine.[24]

The local authority's argument for its strict three hours per week respite rule was, of course, based on the fact that it had limited resources. The judge had something to say about this, too, given (a) the costs to the local authority of deciding to go to court, and (b) the implications, otherwise, of depriving the wife of her liberty if she were placed, against both her own and her husband's wishes, in a care home:

> Although the cost of the difference in relation to the number of care hours amounts only to around £150 per week, which is considerably less than the public cost of this litigation, the local authority has expressed the view that any increase would amount to allowing itself to be 'blackmailed' and that it is 'a point of principle'. I cannot agree with the 'blackmail' point. When discussing their needs with people who have mental health problems and their carers, establishing agreement and a therapeutic rapport through a reasonable compromise of different perspectives is an important aspect of responding to the patient's needs. One also has to consider the issue of what action is necessary in the context of avoiding an avoidable deprivation of a citizen's liberty.[25]

---

24   *A London Local Authority v JH* [2011] EWHC 2420 (COP), p.46.
25   *A London Local Authority v JH* [2011] EWHC 2420 (COP), p.46.

STRESSES ON CARERS

The stresses on carers should not be underestimated.

In an article in *The Times* newspaper, a daughter revealed her feelings about the relentless care she was providing for her 98-year-old mother – though there was no suggestion of any actual abuse or neglect. It was a catalogue of bitterness, anger and despair; a 'living hell', exhaustion, depression, isolation, resentment felt toward 'this dreadful old crone'. Yet her conscience could not allow her to place in the strange environment of a care home her mother, who had failing hearing and eyesight, together with physical and mental frailties.[26]

The author of the book *The selfish pig's guide to caring* notes that anyone who has cared for somebody else, long-term, can understand the temptation to lash out verbally if not physically. He relates a conversation with a nurse from a care home – a good carer, who was cheerful, open, voluble and compassionate. She jokingly states how the residents drove her mad and that the only reason she hadn't pushed them down the stairs was that she would be found out. He wanted to ask her how serious she was being, but didn't dare – because he knew exactly what she meant, in relation to caring for his own wife.[27]

A judge recognised the strains of caring when he imposed a two-year community sentence, rather than a prison sentence, on a 78-year-old woman who had entered the court on a Zimmer frame. She had 'flipped' with the stress of caring for her 79-year-old husband who had Alzheimer's disease. She stabbed him 17 times, in their bungalow, with a carving knife. When police arrived, she would not let go of the knife and they used a taser gun to subdue her. He survived the attack. She pleaded guilty to wounding with intent to cause grievous bodily harm. The judge said:

> This is a highly unusual and extremely sad case. They had been happily married for 40 years and were devoted to each other. In 2003 [he] began to experience signs of memory loss. He eventually contracted dementia and it got progressively worse. She was his sole carer... Caring for anyone with dementia should not be underestimated. She found herself under a great strain and contracted a depressive illness. Plainly at the time of this incident the balance of her mind was disturbed against a background of great domestic upheaval. There are very exceptional cases when justice should be tempered with mercy. This is one of them. In almost every case of wounding with intent any defendant who either pleads or is found guilty can expect to receive a sentence measuring in years. For reasons I hope are obvious I am satisfied it would be contrary to the interests of justice to follow the guidelines in this case.[28]

---

26   'I resent her for still being alive.' *The Times (Times 2)*, 14 November 2007.

27   Marriott, H. *The selfish pig's guide to caring*. Clifton-upon-Teme: Polperro Heritage Press, 2003, p.189.

28   Bentley, P. 'Wife, 78, tasered twice after she stabbed her Alzheimer's suffering husband 17 times when she cracked under the pressure of caring for him.' *Daily Mail*, 21 May 2012.

LOCAL AUTHORITY INVESTIGATIONS AND RESPONSES: STRIKING A BALANCE

Safeguarding vulnerable adults has become a major activity in adult social care, second only to the policy of personalisation (see below).

It is about protecting vulnerable adults from sometimes very serious harm; equally grave and sometimes drastic are the interventions that local authorities must make. For this reason, a balance needs to be maintained between under- and over-intervention. An essential tool in trying to maintain this balance is the law. It is precisely legislation – for example, the Mental Capacity Act 2005 and the Human Rights Act 1998 – that contains principles and rules for this very purpose.

There is a common sentiment within social services to the effect that 'you are damned if you do and damned if you don't'. There is obviously truth in this, but equally the phrase is sometimes used as an excuse. There seems little doubt that an increasing number of legal cases, particularly involving mental capacity, have revealed local authority decisions and actions that have paid scant regard even to the most basic of legal safeguards, rules and principles.

In other words, local authorities and their staff have too often come legally adrift, not on the finer and more difficult, but rather on some of the most basic, points of the law. When this fact is coupled with draconian intervention, it adds up sometimes to significant abuse of power.

Such occurrences should be clearly distinguished from those cases in which local authorities do adhere to the law, do try to take a balanced approach – but then something still goes wrong. In such cases, there is not the same degree of legal approbation. Indeed, there may be none; sometimes things go wrong and it is nobody's fault.

SUPPORTING EVIDENCE

Part of a proportionate response to a safeguarding concern depends on a reasonable approach to allegations and evidence. Assumptions and premature conclusions need to be avoided, without going to the other extreme of inaction in the face of obvious abuse or neglect. It can be a hard task.

TAKING ALLEGATIONS TOO READILY AT FACE VALUE

Proceeding without reasonable evidence resulted, in the following local ombudsman case, in the local authority turning on the messenger. This was maladministration. It concerned a relative who had raised adult protection issues about his sister-in-law, who had learning disabilities and lived in a care home. He was in turn made the subject of unsubstantiated allegations by a care home owner, which the local authority too readily took at face value, without first investigating.

Unsubstantiated allegations: local authority going along with unsubstantiated allegations about a relative who had complained about the care of his sister-in-law. The sister and brother-in-law of a woman with learning disabilities complained that she had suffered abuse at two care homes. In the course of a long and protracted dispute, the owner of one of the care homes made unsubstantiated allegations about the behaviour of the brother-in-law, involving drunkenness, sexual misconduct and racist behaviour. A report by the council's registration and inspection unit repeated the allegations; the report came into the hands of members of another part of the family, which promptly ostracised the brother-in-law. The council wrote to the brother-in-law, repeating the allegations as if they were fact; he regarded the letter as defamatory.

The allegations were finally investigated and found to be without substance; subsequent legal action for defamation was settled by payment of a considerable sum of money and agreement by the council to purge its records and to pay legal costs. In the end, the ombudsman found that abuse had not in fact been suffered by the sister, but he was appalled at the 'almost complete lack of planning' behind one placement and the lack of reasonable social care work that went into it. It was more by luck than judgement that no harm befell her.[29]

SCRAPING THE BARREL FOR DUBIOUS EVIDENCE

The courts have sometimes been less than impressed with the evidence of abuse put forward by local authorities.

In one case, it appeared that social services had been scraping the bottom of the barrel by dredging up old and largely unsubstantiated allegations concerning abuse by a father against his daughter with learning disabilities. The court largely discounted this evidence, finding most of it not made out. However, the order sought by the local authority (to accommodate the daughter elsewhere) was given – albeit on general welfare, rather than on abuse, grounds. The local authority would have been better off arguing the basic welfare case only, without trying to gild the lily with dubious evidence about abuse.

Old and unsubstantiated allegations about the father's abuse towards his daughter. The father's case was that many of the local authority's allegations were old and unfounded and many related to the stressful time when his wife died from cancer. At the time, the local authority had not acted on any of these concerns. Furthermore, some of his complaints about the local authority's conduct had been upheld.

An incident going back to 1991, related by a support worker, when he allegedly threatened to beat his daughter with a belt, the judge discounted for lack of evidence on the file. A 1992 incident, reported by a nurse, that he had hit his daughter four times with his fist about the head and face, the judge also discounted on the evidence. The older allegations of drinking to excess, the judge also discounted, insofar as they came from his two other children, since they were so hostile to their father. A more recent allegation was also found to be unreliable; the judge took account of the fact that the witness, as a Muslim, did not drink alcohol; and a senior local authority community worker pointed out that the father's explanation was that he relieved pain in his neck and shoulder by rubbing them with Bay Rum, a preparation which can be used for medicinal purposes.[30]

---

29   Local Government Ombudsman. *Investigation into Bromley London Borough Council 2003* (01/B/17272). London: LGO, 2003.

30   *Newham London Borough Council v BS* [2003] EWHC 1909 (Fam).

SLANTING THE EVIDENCE IN BREACH OF DUTIES OF DISCLOSURE AND OF FAIRNESS

In another case, in which a local authority sought a court order preventing a woman interfering with her husband's removal to hospital in his best interests, it sought to bolster its case with unsubstantiated allegations that she abused him. It also withheld information from the court about the positive aspects of the wife's caring. The court criticised the local authority for acting 'in breach of its duties of full disclosure and fairness'. It had failed to particularise the allegations, to support them with evidence and to give a more balanced account.

Explanation was lacking about how the alleged incidents were raised with the wife or why they were not raised with her – and about why, if they had occurred, her husband had continued to be cared for at home. In addition, reference was not made to the good aspects of her care of and relationship with her husband. Particularly in the light of this unbalanced approach by the local authority, the court cautioned that 'without notice' orders – that is, not giving the other side a chance to dispute or respond at the time the order is made – should be exceptional. The court gave the order but on general welfare grounds, rather than on the allegations of abuse.[31]

TAKING CARE WITH FACTUAL ACCURACY

The concern about without notice orders arose more pointedly in another case, in which the local authority went badly wrong with the evidence. This involved the local authority seeking an order to transfer a 78-year-old man with dementia out of the care of his daughter and granddaughter and into a care home. He lacked capacity to decide for himself.

The first court hearing had granted the without notice order to this effect. At a second court hearing, the family challenged the making of that order. It transpired that virtually all the allegations with which the local authority had justified its initial, urgent application were incorrect. There was, simply, one factual and significant inaccuracy after another – so stark that the case warrants summarising in some detail.

Without notice application lacking evidence: preventing a man returning to the care of his daughter and granddaughter. A local authority sought a without notice order to transfer a man away from the care of his relatives (daughter and grand-daughter) into a care home.

It did so on the basis that (a) the relatives had obstructed a full 'mini mental state examination'; (b) his previous care home placement had been terminated by the care home because of the verbally abusive and threatening behaviour of the two relatives; (c) he had been assessed during a hospital stay as requiring 24-hour care in a nursing home; (d) the two relatives had removed him from hospital; (e) the relatives lived in a one-bedroom flat in which it would clearly be unsuitable for him to stay; (f) he had complex care needs; (g) his problematic diabetes required careful control but the relatives gave him unsuitable food; and (h) he would be at serious risk of harm in the care of the relatives.

---

31   *B Borough Council v Mrs S* [2006] EWHC 2584 (Fam).

Allegations by the local authority were badly flawed. The judge found that virtually all of these grounds had not been made out. The evidence did not support the claim about the mini mental state examination. The evidence about the behaviour in the care home might have been established, but it was highly regrettable that the local authority did not obtain first-hand evidence about the family's behaviour.

Lack of assessment. The assessment, concerning the need for 24-hour nursing home care, was found by the judge to have fallen short of a 'genuine and reasonable attempt to carry out a full assessment of the capacity of the family to meet the relative's needs in the community'. The authority had not in fact carried out such an assessment. When a thorough assessment was finally carried out, it concluded that he could be cared for in the community by his relatives.

Family had not removed man from hospital. It also transpired that the relatives had not removed him from hospital. He had instead been discharged by the hospital itself, and this had followed the non-attendance by a social worker at a case conference. The social worker had instead opted for court action.

Flat had two bedrooms not one. The flat turned out not to have one bedroom; in fact, it had two. The man clearly did have complex needs, but those did not necessarily rule out care in the community.

Diabetes more stable in the care of his family. And, on the question of diet, the local authority had claimed that he was regularly fed inappropriately by the relatives. In fact, no evidence was produced to the court about this. The relatives had received training and, by the time of the court case, when he was in the care of his relatives, his diabetes was now more stable than it had been in the care home.

Without notice application not justified. The judge concluded that, given the standoff with the family at the relevant time, a period in the care home might have been justified had the application been made by means of an 'on notice' order. However, a without notice process was not justified. The judge also noted that although a without notice order gives 'liberty to apply' to the other party, for relatives this may mean little. It should be spelt out to the other party that they can challenge the order.

Local authority's belated change of view about the man's bests interests. Finally, the judge pointed out that the last allegation, that he would be at serious risk of harm in the care of his relatives, was nonsense – given that, by the time of the second court hearing, all were agreed (even the local authority) that his best interests would be served by living with his relatives.

The judge pinpointed the core issue as being lack of communication on the part of the local authority and the failure by the relatives to make themselves physically and emotionally available to receive any communication.[32]

NUMBER OF ALLEGATIONS NOT NECESSARILY INDICATIVE OF THEIR STRENGTH

Appraising the strength of evidence may be difficult and number might not equate to strength.

For instance, in one case, allegations of assault were made against the father of a 30-year-old woman with learning disabilities. At an initial court hearing, involving a without notice application, an order was granted authorising the removal of the

32 *LLBC v TG* [2007] EWHC 2640 (Fam).

daughter from her parents. After this happened, a subsequent hearing was held to examine the allegations in more detail.

The allegations were 11 in number. However, of these, ten had the legal status of hearsay; that is, they were based on what the woman herself had told various professionals. The eleventh allegation was in the form of eyewitness (more precisely 'ear witness') evidence from two carers. In addition to the specific allegations, the local authority also sought to rely on observations of bruising as evidence of further abuse in addition to the 11 core allegations.

The court was extremely wary. First, it was clear from the evidence that the woman was physically vigorous and liable to bruise herself, which she did with some regularity. Second, whilst the court was prepared to admit hearsay as relevant evidence, the court was unconvinced by it. This was largely based on the unreliability of the woman's statements to these professionals. Third, the witnesses were not sufficiently reliable, and, on the balance of probability, the judge felt unable to conclude that – on the particular occasion in question – the father had slapped his daughter, causing a cut on her lip. Amongst the judge's reasons were the following:

> The very aspects of SA's intellectual functioning which render her incapable of being a witness must seriously compromise the ability of the court to rely upon hearsay accounts...
>
> SA's presentation during the ABE [Achieving Best Evidence] interview, and in particular her responses to questions about 'truth and lies', would seem to support the conclusion that she would not be capable of understanding the task of giving evidence...
>
> The local authority records are peppered with other allegations made by SA against professionals which are accepted by the local authority as not being reliable reports...
>
> SA is at times physically vigorous wherever she is, whether at home or in professional care. She sustains bruises and other injuries as a result. The local authority accept they cannot attribute any particular bruise to any particular incident. Since the proceedings began...the very good foster carers have had to withdraw from caring for SA because they considered that she was putting herself at risk of harm (and was being harmed) by physical behaviour in their home.
>
> In the circumstances it seems to me impossible to single the parents out in this regard and make negative findings about SA's safety in their home, which has been her home for some 30 years, when she is at much the same risk wherever she is because of her challenging behaviour.[33]

In short, the court 'did not find that any of the allegations of physical assault made by the local authority against the parents have been proved'. The judge did, however, go on to find that the parents had not cooperated with the local authority

---

33   *London Borough of Enfield v SA* [2010] 196 (COP).

and had also been making plans for her to get married, even though she lacked mental capacity to do so.

PROPORTIONATE RESPONSES AND WEIGHING UP COMPETING CONSIDERATIONS

Local authorities must judge what constitutes a proportionate response in relation to the risk of harm involved. Sometimes matters are more complicated when competing risks are in issue. So authorities have to try to act decisively but keep in focus the overall welfare of the service user.

DANGER OF KNEE-JERK REACTIONS AND THE NEED TO WEIGH UP COMPETING RISKS

In one case, the Care Standards Tribunal considered the reaction of the former Commission for Social Care Inspection (CSCI) and of three local authorities to adult protection concerns at a care home. It found the CSCI's reaction to have been disproportionate and that the local authorities who had placed residents in the home were excessively influenced by the CSCI.

Local authorities, under the thumb of the regulator, not acting in the best interests of service users. In order to be seen to be doing the right thing in principle by responding drastically to concerns that had arisen, the local authorities concerned appeared to achieve the opposite. The result was that the rights and welfare of the residents of the care home were not given sufficient attention, and they ended up being removed from the home without due procedure and against their best interests.

The case illustrated the fine line between protection and overreaction and also the sometimes unsatisfactory interaction between local authorities and regulators. The tribunal clearly took the view that the local authorities concerned, frightened of the regulator, had behaved in an unthinking and indiscriminate manner. This was particularly unfortunate since the CSCI had been proceeding on factual inaccuracies and on an apparently obsessive, excessive and unjustified determination to close the home.

The risks, actual or imagined, to the residents in the care home had not been balanced – by either the CSCI or the local authorities – against the detriment of sudden and compulsory removal of those residents to other care homes. The best interests of the residents suffered as a result.[34]

In the local ombudsman investigation immediately below, safeguarding concerns were responded to swiftly but in such a way that arguably placed the woman at greater risk and might have contributed to her death three days later. The local authority did respond very rapidly to the abuse allegations – an alleged slap by the mother and alleged unauthorised taking of money from a bank account – but lost sight of the very real and high physical vulnerability of the woman.

The case is worth summarising at some length, since it is illustrative of the difficult decisions sometimes facing local authority staff.

---

34   *Onyerindu v Commission for Social Care Inspection* [2007] EWCST 1041 (EA), [2008] 1269 (EA).

Judging a proportionate response to alleged financial and physical abuse. A severely physically disabled woman of 26 years lived with her parents. She suffered from spinal muscular atrophy, had severe curvature of the spine and was unable to use her legs. She was of very low body weight. Her mother (and father) had always been her main carer. She had specialist equipment and adaptations including a special ripple mattress, a customised electric wheelchair, a special alarm system, a wheelchair-accessible bathroom, a bath cushion and an adapted toilet seat. She was liable to chest infections, and care had to be taken with her posture both during the day in the wheelchair and during the night; sometimes her mother adjusted her position (but did not turn her over) in bed several times a night.

Alleged taking of money and slap. The woman attended a day centre run by a voluntary body on behalf of social services. This particular day, she was upset and explained to the manager of the centre that her mother had taken money from her bank account without her permission; and that when she had found out she had an argument with her mother who had slapped her legs.

Emergency placement organised. The centre manager contacted a social worker who knew the woman. The woman was adamant that she did not want to return home. The mother arrived to collect her daughter but was told that the latter did not want to return home, but not about the allegations. The mother went away and subsequently refused to return to the centre. The social worker talked to his manager and decided to arrange an emergency residential placement. A care home was identified that provided for people with severe physical disabilities.

Transport arrangements. The centre arranged transport to the home, though there was not an escort in the van; the social worker drove behind most of the way. On the way, they collected various belongings from the woman's home; the mother said she was not asked about any equipment her daughter might need or about her care needs. The journey lasted much longer than expected (some two hours) because of traffic jams on the M25.

First night in care home, sickness and death three days later. The woman spent her first night in the care home. She did not have a ripple mattress; a baby alarm was fixed up for her because she could not operate the emergency buzzer system. The notes stated that she needed turning several times a night. In the morning, she felt uncomfortable, sick, frail and unwell and wanted to go home. Her parents arrived to collect her. She died of bronchial pneumonia three days later.

Making enquiries before the placement. The local ombudsman pointed out that the mother had given unstinting care and love to her daughter all her life; that the daughter had been upset and that the local authority staff had been right to take her distress seriously. However, it was maladministration not to make proper enquiries before the placement and before deciding that the woman should travel without an escort. In particular, the woman's general practitioner and occupational therapist should have been consulted. This might have resulted in the placement going ahead, an alternative placement or her going back home. In any event, the ombudsman was not satisfied that she might still not have contracted the chest infection; thus, he could not blame the council for her death.

Considering a complicated case at a 'deep level'. The ombudsman also agreed with the view expressed by the local authority manager who had led the investigation into the events that the staff involved had failed to recognise at a 'deep level' that the woman's case was 'problematic'. They should have realised that only her parents had ever looked after her, and that, despite her being articulate and intellectually able, they should have talked to the GP and occupational therapist. They had also taken the woman's statements as 'absolute' without attempting to verify what had been said. The care home should have been checked for appropriate equipment, and also for its ability to assess the woman's needs, given that the local authority staff involved on the day knew little about her needs. Staff should have sensed that the case was 'more complicated than most'. Furthermore, he felt that the woman should have been accompanied in the vehicle during the trip to the care home.[35]

LOCAL AUTHORITY PROCEDURES: IMPORTANCE OF FLEXIBLE APPROACH

Most local authorities now have detailed, written, safeguarding policies and procedures, to which staff are meant to work. They are useful but a degree of flexibility is required.

For instance, in the case summarised immediately above, the local authority did not talk to the mother about the alleged abuse; in fact, talked to her barely at all – not even about the complex physical needs that her daughter had, particularly at night. Local authorities often have a policy that prohibits staff from talking to alleged perpetrators. The reason is typically to avoid jeopardising or contaminating any police investigation – or, alternatively, putting the victim at greater risk.

But taken to an unthinking extreme, such a policy will become counter-productive. Thus, there is nothing to stop local authorities talking to the perpetrator about other matters; in the above example, this would have been about the daughter's care needs.

In another case, the local authority had pulled back from talking to the husband of a woman with learning disabilities about contraception (there was a question over his wife's capacity to decide about whether to take it or not). The more he was cut out of the picture, the more obstructive he became. The reason the local authority gave for not talking to him was that there were also abuse concerns, including allegations that he was physically rough with her, threatened her and caused bruising on her arms.

The judge did not cast blame on the local authority and accepted that the husband was difficult to deal with. Still, the authority's approach was flawed because the matter that needed talking about was not the alleged abuse but the contraception:

> It is the fact that he was resistant to well-intentioned input, which made dealing with him difficult and created tension as regards the Local Authority's need to keep an eye on Mrs A's welfare. When Mrs A's reports of domestic violence started in October 2008, the Local Authority's 'safeguarding protocols' did not encompass anyone talking to Mr A about those reports, he being the alleged perpetrator. The rationale of this protocol (to avoid putting the complainant at increased risk) is perhaps one thing if domestic violence is the only issue. But here, the question of contraception was also in issue…

---

35   Local Government Ombudsman. *Investigation into Kent County Council 1999* (98/A/1612). London: LGO, 1999.

The result was that the husband felt increasingly sidelined and this in turn fuelled his lack of cooperation:

> In the result, and for whatever reasons, no-one has ever 'sat down with' Mr A to help him to feel part of the decision process. He told me that social service involvement made him feel there were 'three parties to the marriage'. His views about unwanted interference have thus grown and fed on themselves, creating split loyalties for Mrs A. Matters have been compounded by his rigid views about the status of marriage, and his sense of a personal responsibility for his wife, whose life-difficulties he has not been helped fully to understand. These various factors have created a vicious circle in the relationship of Mr A with the Local Authority, in which Mrs A has been caught up, until the couple 'pulled up the draw-bridge' earlier this year and useful communication with them became more or less impossible.[36]

Equally, there will in some cases be very good reasons for not talking to the alleged perpetrator, not just for fear of undermining police gathering of evidence but out of concern for the safety of the victim. For instance, in the case of a young woman murdered by her parents because of her westernised behaviour, it was suggested that the school and police had made things worse by talking to the parents at the wrong time.[37]

Flexibility might need to be applied to other rules or guidelines as well. In one case, the local ombudsman recognised the importance of adult protection policies, but reminded the local authority not to forget the needs and welfare of individual service users – which might call for exceptions to be made to an otherwise sensible policy.

Blanket policy on visits to home of staff. A local authority implemented a new policy, debarring social services staff from taking clients to their homes. The ombudsman recognised the persuasive arguments in favour of such a policy. However, it meant that a woman with learning difficulties could no longer spend seven hours a week with a family aide, employed by social services. Her parents complained that this arrangement had always worked well and was an essential part of meeting their daughter's needs; moreover, the change had now made her unhappy. The ombudsman concluded that the council fettered its discretion by applying the policy so rigidly that it gave no consideration to the individual circumstances of the case. Furthermore, before making the change, the local authority had failed to reassess the woman's needs and to consult with her parents. All this was maladministration.[38]

---

36   *A Local Authority v Mrs A* [2010] EWHC 1549 (Fam).

37   Jenkins, R. 'Catastrophic mistakes by school and police "led to honour killing of girl, 17".' *The Times*, 4 August 2012.

38   Local Government Ombudsman. *Investigation into Carmarthenshire County Council 1999* (99/0117/CM/210). London: LGO, 1999.

IMPORTANCE OF FAIR PROCEDURE – AND DANGER OF DISPROPORTIONATE FOCUS ON SMALLER, AND EASIER, TARGETS

The following case illustrates, in the main, the importance of local authorities acting fairly in their investigations, in relation to the evidence. It also shows how a local authority, in safeguarding, might tend to bring its full weight to bear on easy targets. A characteristic sometimes associated with bullying.

In this case, the target was the 77-year-old owner of a care home, whom it subjected to acute unfairness and what must be seen as coming close to a kangaroo court approach. It is worth pointing out that there are absolutely no circumstances in which a local authority would think about, let alone try, subjecting an NHS chief executive to such treatment – even if the hospital concerned was doing far worse than this care home. It is a case study of some note in unfairness.

Local authority allegations of poor care at care home: unfair, unsubstantiated allegations, care home owner given no chance properly to respond. In December 2010, the local authority concluded at a case conference that 15 allegations of abuse by various staff at a care home were substantiated (and ten were inconclusive), that the home should take 45 actions and that three members of staff should be referred to the Independent Safeguarding Authority (ISA) and Nursing and Midwifery Council (NMC).

This was despite the fact that the police had previously investigated and found nothing of concern. The Care Quality Commission (CQC) had investigated and found all essential standards being met. And the ISA and NMC subsequently took no action. In addition, the allegations were only given to the care home owner a day before the case conference – and crucial evidence was not allowed at the case conference.

Local authority refuses to give specifics of allegations. Back in May and June, the details of the allegations were sparse but seemed to revolve around nursing practices such as dressing wounds and syringing ears (which the local authority argued should have been the responsibilty of the community nursing service – since the care home was registered to provide residential but not nursing care). The care home owner was asked to suspend two members of staff, including the manager of the care home, the owner's daughter-in-law. Yet the local authority justified not giving details of the allegations, with reference to its procedures. When the care home owner asked for more information, the local authority characterised this request as non-cooperation.

In July, the local authority held a case conference, without even informing the care home about it, in contravention of the authority's own procedures.

Police and CQC take no action. Even while the police were still investigating in August, the local authority stated that many of its concerns were substantiated. By September, details of the allegations had still not been given. At the end of October, the police decided to take no action, and CQC had lifted its suspension on placements at the home and then found it to be meeting all essential standards.

Allegations given to care home at extreme short notice. One day before the case conference, a detailed 22-page set of allegations was finally given to the care home owner. Such short notice was in breach of the local authority's own procedures. Her solicitors asked for an adjournment. This was refused (although later the local authority would contrive to blame the care home owner for going ahead with the meeting). On the day of the case conference, the care home manager – who was familiar with the day-to-day running of the care home – was denied admission, as an alleged perpetrator. The 77-year-old care home owner – who was not familiar with the detail of daily work in the care home – went in alone.

Deplorable treatment of 77-year-old care home owner at day-long case conference. The conference went on for eight hours. There were ten other people present, from the 'safeguarding authorities', including eight from the local authority. Apart from the ten-to-one imbalance, informal comments made by the care home owner in the lunch break were abused. The conference drew adverse conclusions about the care home owner's suitability to own a care home, but these were based in part on detailed matters about patients and carers which it knew, or should have known, were outside the knowledge of the care home owner – given the short time (one day) to look into such detail.

The judge pointed out that the treatment of the care home owner was deplorable. And that it was rather odd for the local authority to refer to a family business as 'incestuous'.

Court finds local authority acted unfairly and unjustly. The allegations made by the local authority were serious, numerous and complex. The impact on the business was large, perhaps a loss of £150,000. Residents and families suffered disruption; three staff members were referred to their professional bodies (although they were subsequently exonerated).

The judge found, in summary, that the local authority had acted unfairly and unjustly. He declared that the conclusions of the case conference were unlawful and should be quashed, and ordered that the local authority withdraw its referral of the three members of the staff to the ISA and NMC.[39]

USING THE MENTAL CAPACITY ACT

In addition to the types of case illustrated immediately above, there have been a number under the Mental Capacity Act in which interventions by local authorities have been knocked back by the courts. What has emerged as a particular concern is that some of the most basic principles and rules were ignored or misunderstood by local authorities, even though their interventions were drastic and so warranted careful thought and scrutiny.

The courts take this seriously. In the *Hillingdon* case, outlined below, the court emphasised just how fundamental is the right to liberty, referring back to 1297 and Magna Carta:

> The ordinary powers of a local authority are limited to investigating, providing support services, and where appropriate referring the matter to the court. If a local authority seeks to regulate, control, compel, restrain, confine or coerce it must, except in an emergency, point to specific statutory authority for what it is doing or else obtain the appropriate sanction of the court… The origin of this basic legal principle is to be found in an era long before the invention of local authorities as we know them. Chapter 29 of Magna Carta 1297 provides that: '*No freeman shall be taken or imprisoned, or disseised of his freehold, or liberties, or free customs, or outlawed, or exiled, or any otherwise*

---

39   *Davis v West Sussex Council* [2012] EWHC 2152 (QB).

destroyed; nor will we not pass upon him, nor condemn him, but by lawful judgment of his peers, or by the law of the land.'[40]

MANCHESTER CITY COUNCIL CASE (G V E): ACTING ON UNSUBSTANTIATED SAFEGUARDING CONCERNS

Manchester City Council reacted to what were essentially unsubstantiated safeguarding concerns and removed a young man with severe learning disabilities from his adult placement carer, who had previously been his foster carer for many years. Three of the major concerns were as follows.

First, he had reportedly said that he was put in a wardrobe sometimes; yet a visit to the house disclosed no wardrobe in his room.

Second, it was alleged that when his carer picked him up from school, she wagged her finger at him, behaved aggressively and said that when he misbehaved, he should be put to the wall. The judge commented: 'Whilst I think it likely that F was cross with E and that she probably admonished him, I do not find that she was aggressive, or that this incident is indicative of a pattern of ill-treatment.'

Third, she had asked social workers for help with self-defence training, to help manage him when he became difficult and aggressive.

Fourth, the local authority argued a serious lack of cooperation on the carer's part; yet the judge came to a different conclusion and saw the carer's efforts in a different light:

> Overall, I do not find F has a history of generally poor cooperation with professionals. It is regrettable that there have been difficulties with the school, but in my judgment this is not a factor to which I should attach much weight in the balance against a return to F's care. On the contrary, the evidence shows that F is a carer who fights hard on E's behalf. It may be that sometimes she takes things too far (for example, by taking E to a professionals' meeting at which things were said that might have caused him anxiety). But it is in E's best interests to have a carer who genuinely cares for him and fights his corner. That is something to be placed in the balance in favour of a return home, in the interim and in particular in the long term.

None of this had stopped the local authority from removing the young man first into a care home and then into what was called supported living arrangements (although suspiciously appearing to be a care home under a different name). He was given medication to control his behaviour and subject to such restrictions and control that he was, in law, deprived of his liberty.

Yet the local authority neither used the deprivation of liberty safeguards (DOLS) within the Mental Capacity Act 2005, nor did they go to the court. Thus, not only was the 2005 Act breached but so too the Human Rights Act 1998. Under article 5 of the European Convention, he had been deprived of his liberty,

---

40   *London Borough of Hillingdon v Neary* [2011] EWHC 1377 (COP), paras 22–23.

but not according to procedures prescribed by law. Thus, too, had there been an unjustifiable interference with family life under article 8:

> For these reasons I find that the removal from F's care, the failure to give any or any adequate consideration to his family life with F at the time of the removal or for many months thereafter, the failure adequately to involve F in the decision-making process about E's future, and the impediments to contact between E and F for several months after his removal constituted a serious breach of his Article 8 rights.[41]

Unfortunately, the case illustrates another aspect of the approach to adult social care in some local authorities; this is a generally cavalier approach to law and legislation generally, not just in relation to human rights and mental capacity. This became evident because the local authority had sought to justify its decision in another way. It argued that it had a written policy, based on law, to the effect that the young man could not remain with his carer because restraint was not allowed in adult placements. Thus mental capacity and human rights aside, so the council seemed to argue, the man could not have remained.

What was extraordinary about this was that (a) both a social worker and a team manager referred the court to the written policy, (b) there turned out to be no such policy, and (c) the relevant legal adult placement regulations and associated government guidance at the time were to the opposite effect; they precisely permitted restraint in adult placements.[42]

NEARY V LONDON BOROUGH OF HILLINGDON: DRASTIC INTERVENTION NOT UNDERPINNED BY LAW OR FAIRNESS

The *Manchester* case, immediately above, has not been the only one to have hit the headlines.

In 2011, the London Borough of Hillingdon was castigated by a judge for having removed a young man with severe learning disabilities and autism from his father, contrary to the most basic principles of both the Mental Capacity Act 2005 and the Human Rights Act 1998.

In short, his father had agreed at Christmas time to a few days' respite for his son, because his son's routine had become disrupted (partly because of changed television programmes over the festive period). However, staff at the local authority residential unit rapidly formed the view that his behaviour was such that he should not be allowed home. The father was not informed for many months that this view had been taken. Furthermore, the judge later pointed out that the son's behaviour was not surprising given the sudden nature of the move to the unit.

Days turned into weeks, and weeks into months, until he finally made it back home in December, nearly a year later, following another court ruling. During this

---

41   *G v E* [2010] EWHC 621 (Fam).
42   *G v E* [2010] EWHC 621 (Fam), paras 161–162.

year, after he was left unsupervised in April, he walked out of the unit and knocked the spectacles off a passer-by.

Following that incident, the local authority sought formally to deprive him of his liberty and stopped his various activities outside of the unit. However, the judge ruled that not only had he in fact been deprived of his liberty before April, but that even after this time the local authority had continued to act unlawfully because it did not adhere to the basic rules of the Mental Capacity Act.

The court found that the local authority had not carried out proper best interests assessments because most of them did not properly consider, if at all, the least restrictive option – namely returning back home with appropriate support. Furthermore, the local authority failed to scrutinise these best interests assessments properly, and, given how flawed they were, it should have done so and not felt itself bound by them. Likewise, it should have conducted a review and also appointed an independent mental capacity advocate, under s.39D of the Mental Capacity Act.

Article 8 of the European Convention on Human Rights also demanded that close attention be given to enabling the son to live with his father, rather than substituting for this the care of the State.

The local authority had also muddled its separate legal responsibilities, consisting of three key elements. It acted as 'supervisory body' for the purpose of authorising deprivations of liberty; as service provider, since it was the local authority that ran the residential unit; and as providing overall social work support, through an allocated social worker. The authority had failed to ensure that these three functions were kept separate.

The judge found breach of the Mental Capacity Act 2005, as well as of articles 5 and 8 of the European Convention on Human Rights. He pointed out that the father and son nearly lost each other altogether. At one point, local authority staff were considering a distant, compulsory, placement for the son under the Mental Health Act 1983; and the judge believed that if the father had not been so exceptional in his approach, constructiveness and determination, this might have happened:

> It is very troubling to reflect that this approach might actually have succeeded, with a lesser parent than Mr Neary giving up in the face of such official determination. Had that happened, Steven would have faced a life in public care that he did not want and does not need.[43]

Unfortunately, Hillingdon seemed to be determined to dig a deeper hole than ever – a fear of damage to its reputation getting the upper hand – when it released an ill-judged media briefing, which attracted judicial ire:

> On 20 May 2011, the eve of the hearing, Hillingdon circulated a three-page media briefing note to most of the national media. The document was designed to counteract adverse publicity that Hillingdon has received, and

---

43   *London Borough of Hillingdon v Neary* [2011] EWHC 1377 (COP), para 28.

against which it had not attempted to defend itself. Nonetheless, it is a sorry document, full of contentious and inaccurate information, and creating a particularly unfair and negative picture of Steven and his behaviour. I learned about the document by chance on the last day of the hearing, expressed dismay, and asked for an explanation. I am told that it was authorised by the Director of Social Care, the Head of Corporate Communications and the Borough Solicitor. It is now accepted '*in hindsight*' that an error of judgment was made in issuing the briefing note. That is indeed so, though again hindsight has nothing do with it. In addition, Hillingdon has unreservedly apologised to the court. That courtesy is appreciated, although an apology for the document is in truth not owed to the court but to Steven and his father.[44]

BARRING PEOPLE FROM SEEING EACH OTHER: IMPORTANCE OF APPLYING RULES ABOUT CAPACITY, BEST INTERESTS AND LESS RESTRICTIVE OPTIONS

Local authorities have sometimes been quick to bar people from seeing each other, without applying the law either promptly or correctly.

For instance, a local authority was held to have breached human rights when it and a care home decided to prevent a man visiting a woman in the care home – ostensibly in her best interests. But the local authority had neither the law nor the evidence on its side.

In particular, it misapplied the Mental Capacity Act, failing to ascertain whether or not the person in question had mental capacity – and, even supposing she did, nonetheless failing to conduct a best interests test properly.

Banning a man from visiting his partner and childhood friend. An elderly man and elderly woman, after long separate marriages, had both lost their spouses. They now rekindled a childhood acquaintance. He moved in with her and a personal, intimate relationship developed. She then had to move into a care home. Concerns were then expressed about the way in which he spoke to her, to other residents at the home and to her daughters. A meeting was held and local authority staff looked into the matter.

Wrongly barring the man on the say-so of the woman's daughters. The social workers acknowledged that it had to be ascertained whether the woman had capacity to make a decision about the visits, but that in the meantime a decision was taken that the man and his family should be forbidden from visiting. The basis for this was that the woman's daughters, as next of kin, were entitled to take the decision. This was despite the fact that, more than once, the woman had said she wanted visits from both her daughters and the man. There was no evidence that the social workers had conducted a best interests decision. The local authority argued, however, that the care home had anyway taken a decision to prohibit him from visiting, so the local authority couldn't have done anything about it. The man was very unhappy and ended up not seeing the woman for nearly two years.

Unacceptable delay in mental capacity assessment. The local authority sought to obtain a medical assessment of the woman's capacity, but it took ten months for this to happen. This was unacceptable delay.

---

44   *London Borough of Hillingdon v Neary* [2011] EWHC 1377 (COP), para 155.

Consideration of less restrictive option. In any case, even if the local authority had taken the view from the outset that she lacked capacity, it should have considered her best interests, not just gone along with the daughters. And this would have involved not just considering whether the ban was justifiable but also whether some less drastic arrangement was possible – for example, supervised visits.

Extent of alleged harm. The alleged harm in question had only ever been words, not physical harm, but there was not even a record of this. The only recorded note was that, on one visit, when he left she had been distressed – but no record of why. It was this note that prompted the daughters to attend a meeting and ask for the ban. When her capacity was finally ascertained and the Court of Protection became involved, it was decided that she should see him (albeit observed): when he visited, she smiled and they got on very well.

Breach of article 8. In the event, the judge held that the man's human rights had been breached – namely, right to respect for private life under article 8 of the European Convention.[45]

PREVENTING A DAUGHTER FROM VISITING HER DYING MOTHER: ARBITRARY INJUSTICE

The sort of case summarised immediately above is not isolated.

For instance, the local government ombudsman found maladministration when a local authority prevented a daughter, for a period of about six weeks, from visiting her mother in a care home, between 19 December and 2 February. By the time she was allowed to visit, her mother had suffered a stroke, did not recognise her daughter and then died the next day.

The grounds for barring the daughter were specious. Social services were told by the care home that the woman's son, the daughter's brother, had written a letter saying that the daughter should not be allowed to visit the mother because she might take their mother from the home. The care home told the daughter that there were safeguarding issues and she could not currently visit. However, the brother withdrew his allegation within a couple of days. But by then it was too late.

When the daughter rang the care manager, who had placed her mother in the care home, the manager said she would ring back – but never did. The daughter then emailed, reiterating she had no intention of distressing her mother. Christmas passed, and, a month on from being barred from visiting, the daughter had heard nothing. It took the local authority that period to get round to doing a capacity assessment.

In the meantime, the authority had stated that, pending the assessment, any further decision making was frozen. The ombudsman criticised this, noting that without such an assessment there could be no basis for barring the daughter. Furthermore, the local authority had admitted that the assessment required was not specialist. The delay was therefore inexcusable. The ombudsman was scathing and straight to the point, referring to the difficulty of expressing or quantifying the

---

45   *City of Sunderland v MM* [2011] 1 FLR 712.

nature and scale of the injustice of denying the daughter the opportunity to talk to her mother before they were separated forever by death:

> Ms B was told unexpectedly – and without there being any evidence – that she was regarded as a threat to her own mother, denied access to her, made to hand over a Christmas gift outside the home and made to wait for over a month for the Council's processes before finally being told that she could see her mother. By then her mother was unable to recognise or communicate with her daughter.
>
> Two days before Christmas, officers…knew that Ms B's brother had withdrawn his allegation that she was a risk to their mother. From then there were no grounds for preventing mother and daughter from seeing each other.
>
> Knowing that Mrs B was dying, officers…arranged a specialist assessment of whether she had the capacity to decide whether she wanted to see her daughter. During the month that it took for this assessment to be done, Mrs and Ms B were prevented from seeing each other – although there was no legal power to stop Ms B from visiting her mother. The Investigating Officer was wrong to say that the effect of requesting the assessment was to 'freeze any further decision-making'…
>
> The maladministration deprived Ms B of the opportunity to speak with her mother before they were separated forever by death. The nature and scale of this injustice is difficult to express or quantify.[46]

OVER-ZEALOUS JUDGEMENTS ABOUT RISK, MENTAL CAPACITY AND BEST INTERESTS

Local authorities are understandably risk averse. Managers are afraid of getting the blame, and, in turn, frontline staff are sometimes afraid of being made scapegoats by higher management. But, perversely, excessive risk aversion gives rise to another risk: the censure of the courts.

In the following case, the judge found the local authority applying, over-zealously, the rules about capacity and best interests. In effect, the local authority was prepared to go to extraordinary lengths, including deprivation of liberty.

The authority sought to prevent an 82-year-old woman from going on a cruise with her long-standing partner of 20 years. It argued that she lacked capacity to make the decision, despite having been on many previous cruises. Her memory was impaired to some extent; she had been diagnosed with a severe degree of microvascular disease and bilateral hippocampal atrophy indicative of a mixed dementia. More recently, she had moved into a care home, but continued to spend weekends with her partner away from the care home.

The local authority relied on a social worker's evidence, and that of a psychiatrist, that she was unable to weigh up the relevant information about the cruise and

46   Local Government Ombudsman. *Investigation into complaint no 10 012 561 about Leeds City Council.* London: LGO, 2011.

its consequences. The judge summed these up as whether she would be safe and properly cared for during the holiday and whether the effect of the holiday would cause her distress because of the change of environment it would represent.

The test of capacity applied had been too rigorous in the circumstances:

> One must not forget that this is not a life-changing decision, or a choice between two evils or a decision over which an elderly person without Mrs Ross's impairment would be likely to agonise. It is a choice of whether to go on holiday or not, in familiar circumstances, with one's companion of the past two decades. In these circumstances I find myself unpersuaded that Mrs Ross, whatever her limitations, can be shown on the balance of probabilities to have lacked capacity to make this particular decision.

Perhaps a mountain had been made from a molehill. However, the judge considered also the position, in case he was wrong about her capacity, as to what her best interests would be. He understood the local authority's risk aversion but found that it had led them to taking an unduly negative and unbalanced approach to the cruise:

> That is understandable. They have the direct experience of dealing with Mrs Ross's daily care needs, of prompting her to take her medication (she is diabetic) and to attend to her other needs, and ensuring her safety and well-being. My strong impression is that her social worker and the staff at the home want to do the right thing for her but are focused on her safety and are acutely aware of things that might go wrong. Perhaps the prime example of this was the concern that Mrs Ross might 'wander' (as she undoubtedly has in the past when living alone) on the ship and go over the side. It was suggested, not without some force in my view, that this smacked of saying that her best interests were best served by taking every precaution to avoid any possible danger without carrying out the balancing exercise of considering the benefit to Mrs Ross of what, sadly, may be her last opportunity to enjoy such a holiday with Mr Davies. This led, in my view, to trying to find reasons why Mrs Ross should not go on this holiday rather than finding reasons why she should.

The judge went on to point out that 'concerns about her safety on board appear to have been given disproportionate emphasis'. Her partner would be with her, sharing her cabin, watching over her and attending to her needs. The risk of her 'wandering' was limited, given the confines of the ship. Her partner had formulated strategies at night-time to ensure she did not leave the cabin without his knowledge. She was familiar with cruises, had been on this ship before and would be with her partner; this allayed concerns that change of environment from care home to cruise ship would be distressing.

This case was not simply about a friendly discussion and modest protective measures. In order to prevent the woman from going on the cruise, the local authority had granted an authorisation, legally depriving her of her liberty; that is, the local authority was prepared to apply significant compulsion and restrictions in order to stop her going.[47]

In the end, the woman went on the cruise with her partner. It was reported that they enjoyed it, and that the woman was more mentally active than she would have been back in the care home.[48]

TAKING LEGALLY PRESCRIBED RESTRICTIONS AT FACE VALUE

When basic human rights, including restriction or deprivation of liberty, are at stake, the courts will be alert to excessive application of any such restrictions.

For instance, a man with learning disabilities was subject to a sexual offences prevention order. A number of prohibitions were contained within it. The order was as follows:

It is ordered that the defendant is prohibited from –

(a) approaching children under the age of 16;

(b) going to swimming pools unless accompanied by a responsible member of staff from a statutory agency...;

(c) going within 100 metres of a school or playground;

(d) being in the company of anyone under the age of 16 unless accompanied by a responsible member of staff from a statutory agency (eg, NHS or Social Services) or a contracted independent care provider...;

(e) residing at any address except that at which he has been directed to reside by Derbyshire County Council Social Services...

None of the above prohibitions will operate to prohibit contact with children or young persons under the age of 16 years that is inadvertent and unavoidable, in the course of the defendant's lawful daily activities.

The local authority implemented the order such as to prohibit him from leaving his residence unless accompanied; unless accompanied; without such accompaniment, he was effectively incarcerated. The case came to court because he was now being denied permission to travel, unaccompanied, to Blackpool to visit his sick grandmother. Given the potentially draconian effect of the local authority's approach to the man's liberty, the court held that the order should be taken at face value and no more. It wasn't even necessary to invoke the Human Rights Act because liberty had long been enshrined in common law:

---

47   *Cardiff City Council v Peggy Ross* [2011], Case no. 12063905, Court of Protection (Cardiff Regional Court).

48   Beckford, M. 'Elderly couple forced to go to court over council holiday ban.' *Daily Telegraph*, 20 January 2012.

It seems to me that when the liberty of the subject is at issue, a court order which imposes restrictions must be taken at face value. Unless the order contains the explicit restrictions to which the person is said to be subject, it is my very firm judgment impossible for them to be imposed. There is no need to invoke the support of the European Convention on Human Rights on the matter. This approach to the liberty of the subject has been long enshrined in the common law. Restrictions on liberty have to be clearly justified by law. In this case the operation of the order does not extend to these requirements which the County Council would seek, and so far has been able, to apply.[49]

SYSTEMIC PERPETRATION OF HARM BY LOCAL AUTHORITIES

The above examples illustrate the attempts by local authorities, in good faith, to safeguard and protect vulnerable adults – and how they lose their way by relying on insufficient or unreliable evidence, or by disproportionate intervention. However, there are other, different respects in which local authorities sometimes struggle.

Central government has given local social services authorities the lead in protecting and safeguarding vulnerable adults. As outlined already in this chapter, a substantial body of community care legislation underpins the ability of authorities to act.

Nonetheless, owing to the pressures placed on local authorities, they sometimes find themselves in situations when, far from protecting vulnerable people from harm of various sorts, they are themselves implicated, systemically, to greater or lesser degree in that harm.

Harm can come to vulnerable adults at the hands of local authorities in, for example, terms of:

- the imposition of unlawful charges for care

- failure of local authorities to monitor the care provided for highly vulnerable people

- application of strict criteria of eligibility so as to exclude vulnerable adults from assistance

- failure to carry out their duty to meet a person's assessed needs

- indiscriminate application of the mantra of 'independence, choice and control' in the context of 'self-directed support' and 'personalisation' – thus leaving some vulnerable adults at sometimes serious risk.

The paragraphs immediately below illustrate these five points. These are prefaced by a few cases illustrating also how difficult it can be for local authorities to show insight and investigate themselves.

---

49   *R(Smith) v Derbyshire County Council* [2008] EWHC 3355 (Admin).

LOCAL AUTHORITIES: LACK OF INSIGHT INTO THEIR OWN ACTS AND OMISSIONS

Local authorities might be, by nature, introspective, but this does not mean they are necessarily insightful and capable of recognising and investigating their own misdemeanours.

For instance, in the following case, adult protection procedures were apparently not followed, precisely because the safeguarding issue arose in warden-controlled sheltered housing, *owned and run by the local authority*.

Harassment by local authority warden: not investigated properly because it was a local authority service. Serious complaints, supported by cogent evidence, were made by two residents about persistent bullying and harassment by the warden. The council's response was inadequate. The complainants ultimately had to resort to the local government ombudsman. She found that the council had failed to follow its own adult protection procedures and did not launch a full investigation into the allegations against the warden. This was maladministration.

One of the local authority officers, providing information to the ombudsman, explained that he had pressed for a comprehensive investigation at the first adult protection strategy meeting about the case, but had been refused permission. He stated that in any other case there would have been a full adult protection investigation, but an exception had been made in this case because it was a scheme owned and run by the council itself.[50]

In another case, there was simply a failure to investigate and respond to the deliberately inflicted injuries suffered by a service user at a local authority respite care facility – and also a failure to adjust her care plan and consider alternative services.

Injuries suffered at a respite care facility. The woman involved was 30 years old. She had severe brain damage. She had been injured on two occasions at a respite facility run by the local authority. For the first injury, the local authority did not even consider whether to conduct an investigation. For the second, it did investigate but failed to identify the perpetrator; however, it was clear that the injuries were inflicted deliberately. Nevertheless, poor record keeping and communication and failure to implement a revised care plan were uncovered. All this was maladministration. The parents withdrew their daughter from the centre. The local authority should promptly have considered alternative care for her, even if this meant spending scarce resources, since it had a duty to meet her needs. Failure to do this was also maladministration.[51]

Also, if allegations are made, and local authorities do not follow basic procedures, the ombudsman will find maladministration.

Need to follow local safeguarding procedures about allegations that woman with learning disabilities was assaulted by her parents. A woman with learning disabilities was increasingly arguing with her parents, with whom she lived. The local authority had failed to draw up a care plan that might have identified a constructive way

---

50   Local Government Ombudsman. *Investigation into South Tyneside Metropolitan Borough Council 2008* (O6/C/18619 and 07/C/01489). London: LGO, 2008.

51   Local Government Ombudsman. *Investigation into complaint 02/B/16654 against Bedfordshire County Council, 2003.* London: LGO, 2003.

forward. She now alleged that her parents had hit her, locked her in her room and prevented her from seeing her friends. There was a clear written policy and also a procedure for such allegations. They stipulated immediate action to determine the risk and assess everybody's needs. The policy and procedure were not followed. The woman left her home precipitately and unplanned, ending up in an unsuitable adult placement with a person who lacked the skills to meet her needs. This was maladministration.[52]

In the following instance, local authority procedures were likewise not followed; neither the vulnerable adult's father nor the police were informed about serious assaults.

Failure to report assaults on woman with severe learning disabilities. A local authority placed a woman in a care home. Weighing only six stone, she was blind, of partial hearing, had virtually no speech and severe learning difficulties. In an 18-month period, she suffered a catalogue of injuries, including a fractured skull, broken fingers, cuts and bruises, and was assaulted by two members of staff.

The local ombudsman found that the care provided was inadequate. The father was only belatedly informed about the fractured skull. Neither the father nor the police were informed about the assaults. And the local authority had amended the investigator's report without telling her. The local ombudsman found maladministration.[53]

And the Public Services Ombudsman for Wales investigated in great detail the failure of safeguarding procedures in a local authority. The ombudsman found serious maladministration and concluded, amongst other things, that there was 'extensive evidence' that both individual social care workers and their employer (the local authority) were in breach of codes of practice published by the General Social Care Council, the registration body (at the time) for social workers.

Failure by local authority staff with appropriate knowledge and training to follow safeguarding procedures. There was an incident in a council-run day centre involving a vulnerable service user with learning disabilities and yanking, pulling and slapping by a member of staff. Other staff were worried about adverse consequences to them if they reported the incident. One eventually did so but only after a delay; the report was not well received and procedures were not followed in investigating it. One result of this was that the police were not informed promptly – this could have made a difference to a successful police investigation and justice being served.

After the incident, the same member of staff continued to abuse and mock service users, display outbursts of temper and deny food to service users. Some other staff simply didn't recognise this as abuse that should have triggered safeguarding procedures. A year later, there was another hitting incident by another member of staff. Again, there was a delay in reporting the second incident because the same staff member (who had reported the first one) was aware of the reaction to that first reporting.

In addition, the ombudsman found delays in investigation of the alleged incidents, failure to maintain records, failure to distinguish fact from hearsay or opinion, endemic poor

---

52   Local Government Ombudsman. *Investigation into complaint 98/C/0002 against Cumbria County Council, 2000.* London: LGO, 2000.

53   Local Government Ombudsman. *Investigation into complaint 99/A/4226 against Southwark London Borough Council, 2001.* London: LGO, 2001.

practice and poor management. Furthermore, staff charged with investigating the incidents themselves lacked appropriate knowledge, experience and expertise.

The ombudsman found serious maladministration by the local authority, with service users being left at risk of harm and the staff member who reported the abuse also suffering injustice (in the form stress, fear and anxiety).[54]

On the Wirral, a manager who raised whistleblowing concerns for a long period was finally vindicated when the council eventually and reluctantly commissioned an independent investigation which was made public (with significant details, including names of people and of organisations, omitted) – but only because he had been so persistent. Yet by 2008, when he approached the *Wirral Globe*, he claimed that he had been bullied out of his job and given a £40,000 payoff.

Financial and other abuse in supported living, and serious overcharging of vulnerable adults by the local authority. The scandal revolved around Supporting People services for people with learning disabilities. Concerns had included: (a) men with baseball bats turning up at a home run by an independent, unregistered 'service provider' and demanding money, involving an individual who had previously been investigated by the police for drug money laundering; (b) an allegation that a member of a 'service provider' staff had a conviction for assault with a deadly weapon; (c) an allegation of rape made by one of the vulnerable adults; (d) bank accounts being set up in the names of vulnerable adults and their benefits then removed from those accounts without permission.[55]

In addition, its chaotic approach to charging users of services meant that the local authority had eventually to repay 16 residents a total of £243,000 – which had been taken from them in improper charging practices. This was in fact the same amount of money the council paid for the independent review and report.[56] It transpired subsequently in 2012 that this repayment was an underestimate; a further £440,000 had to be repaid, making a total of some £700,000.[57]

There were also suggestions that social services had tried to avoid assessing certain service users, so as to avoid recognising their right to have services from the local authority, and thereby that the local authority was leaving it to the Supporting People providers to fill in the gaps, over and above what they should have been providing.[58]

When the whistleblower was finally vindicated, he had this to say about the cost to himself:

> Although I have always maintained that I did the right thing, I have recently, for the first time in 11 years, questioned this while my 13-year-old son was in hospital with a life-threatening brain tumour. I concluded that with the benefit of hindsight I might not have done the right thing if I had known

---

54   Public Services Ombudsman for Wales. *Report on an investigation into complaint no. 1999/200600720 against Carmarthenshire County Council*, 2009.

55   'Demand for sackings follows review that has shamed Wirral Council.' *Wirral Globe*, 12 January 2012.

56   'Whistleblower Martin Morton offered his job back by town hall chief.' *Wirral Globe*, 15 April 2011.

57   Murphy, L. 'Wirral Council to pay back an extra £440,000 to disabled people it overcharged.' *Liverpool Echo*, 22 August 2012.

58   Klonowski, A. *Independent Review of Wirral Metropolitan Borough Council's response to claims made by Mr Martin Morton (and others)*. Birkenhead: Wirral Council, 2012.

the impact that whistle-blowing has had on my health, my career and my family life. And that to me is the most damning statement that anyone could possibly make about this case.[59]

This manager had made his allegations all those years before and had referred justifiably to this systemic overcharging of vulnerable adults as 'financial abuse'.[60] The local authority did not see it that way; instead, it had chosen to silence and suppress the whistleblower.

LOCAL AUTHORITIES LINKED TO FINANCIAL ABUSE

As the case concerning Wirral Council, immediately above, illustrates, local authorities might sometimes be steeped in poor charging practices that amount to financial abuse of vulnerable adults.

The following paragraphs consider examples of local authority financial charging, including the topping up of care home fees, mental health aftercare services, NHS continuing health care and reablement services.

Clearly, if a local authority makes a genuine mistake in the odd case, it would not be sensible or fair to label it as an abuse. But when a local authority knows it is bending the rules, or should know but doesn't because it is taking a reckless or deliberately myopic approach to the law, then it becomes a different matter altogether.

Yet, in the field of adult safeguarding, unlawful charging by local authorities continues to occupy a blind spot.

CARE HOME CHARGES: UNLAWFULLY MAKING PEOPLE AND FAMILIES PAY EXTRA CARE HOME FEES

Evidence suggests that some, possibly many, local authorities have, over the past decade and longer, systematically – to greater or lesser extent – breached rules about care home charges. And continue to do so.

Under s.21 of the National Assistance Act 1948, local authorities place people in care homes. If a person wishes to go to a more expensive care home than the local authority is offering, he or she can do so – but only if a third party (typically a family member) agrees to 'top up' the difference between the amount the local authority is prepared to pay and the actual care home fees.

In other words, topping up is envisaged, and is lawful, under the rules, if a person chooses to go to more expensive accommodation – that is, over the usual cost that the local authority is prepared to pay to meet certain levels of need.

For there to be choice in this respect, there obviously must be a cheaper care home, charging a fee within the local authority's 'usual cost level', which could

---

59   'Martin Morton tells Globe readers why he endured 11 years of hell in his fight for justice.' *Wirral Globe*, 18 January 2012.

60   Murphy, L. 'Wirral Council to pay back an extra £440,000 to disabled people it overcharged.' *Liverpool Echo*, 22 August 2012.

meet the needs of the person (including, for instance, the need to be near close relatives). Otherwise, logically, there would be no choice involved.

So, sometimes a person may end up being placed by the local authority in a care home that is more expensive than the authority's usual cost level. And this might be because there is no other cheaper care home place, available and suitable, for meeting the person's assessed needs. In which case, it would be unlawful for a local authority to demand a top-up.

It is equally unlawful, under the rules, for the local authority to turn a blind eye by allowing the care home to extract a top-up in these circumstances. This is because the local authority must remain contractually responsible for the whole of the fee. All this is made quite clear under the regulations, directions and guidance.[61]

In the late 1990s, 14 per cent of residents funded by local authorities received third-party top-ups; by 2004, this had risen to 33 per cent. In addition, 40 per cent of local authorities believe that more top-ups are being paid than they know about because they were being negotiated directly between the home and the relatives. This is a practice that is consistent neither with the legal rules nor with the Department of Health's guidance. In short, this pattern seems to indicate 'widespread illegal conduct'.[62]

In 2007, the Commission for Social Care Inspection (CSCI) found that older people lacked adequate information about top-ups and that the prevalence of top-ups appeared closely related to the local care market. Where care home places were limited, up to 75 per cent of people placed by local authorities had to pay a top-up.

When care home places are so limited, it is much less likely that people would have been exercising a choice to be in a more expensive home. Therefore, this figure would almost certainly represent extensive and unlawful behaviour by the local authorities concerned. Indeed, CSCI confirmed in addition that councils felt forced to keep fee rates (usual cost levels) as low as possible.[63]

In some instances, this situation seems to mean that, in whichever home a person chooses to have his or her assessed needs met, it will be more expensive than the council is prepared to pay. Once again, in these circumstances, it is unlawful for the local authority to demand, or allow the care home to demand, a top-up.

At the very least, it was clear to CSCI that vulnerable older people and their families were bereft of information about top-up fees; indeed, such guidance was 'almost non-existent'. This opened the path to arbitrary decisions being made.[64]

61   SI 2001/3441. *National Assistance (Residential Accommodation) (Additional Payments and Assessment of Resources) (Amendment) (England) Regulations 2001.* Also: LAC(92)27. Department of Health. *National Assistance Act 1948 (Choice of Accommodation) Directions 1992.* London: DH. Also: LAC(2004)20. Department of Health. *Guidance on National Assistance Act 1948 (Choice of Accommodation) Directions 1992.* London: DH.

62   Continuing Care Conference. *Paying for care: third party top-ups and cross-subsidies.* London: CCC, 2007, pp.4, 17.

63   Commission for Social Care Inspection. *A fair contract with older people?* London: CSCI, p.5.

64   Commission for Social Care Inspection. *A fair contract with older people?* London: CSCI, p.78.

In 2012, the local government ombudsman found maladministration against a local authority for its cavalier attitude to top-up payments for a woman with dementia:

Careless attitude to suitability of care homes and to topping-up by a resident's family. A woman's daughter had looked at some care homes but rejected them as unsuitable, so the council exacted a top-up when the mother went into a more expensive home.

However, crucially, the council did not consider whether the daughter's objections to the cheaper homes were reasonable, nor was there evidence of the senior practitioner involved judging that any of those homes were suitable.

It was not reasonable for the council to expect the daughter to pay the top-up fees for a more expensive home since no suitable alternative placement had been identified (as the law demands before a top-up fee can be considered).

The local authority went wrong in another respect. When the care home approached it for the unpaid top-up fees, the authority did not take contractual responsibility as demanded by the regulations and guidance. Instead, it suggested the home take legal advice and pointed the home towards the daughter. The ombudsman found this abdication of its responsibility by the council 'wholly unacceptable'.[65]

Anecdotally, most local authorities are now more wary about directly applying unlawful top-up charges to families. However, it seems that, increasingly, those same local authorities are turning a blind eye to care homes exacting a top-up from families, contrary to the legal rules. As already noted above, a local authority should not be tolerating this. Further, the practices are becoming more disingenuous still, but equally dubious. This is when the care home, with the knowledge of the local authority, asks families not for a compulsory top-up but for a regular 'voluntary' donation – but indicates that without this donation the home will not be able to accept their relative.

In sum, the rules about care home fees and topping up are clear. They are meant to be applied by public bodies charged with caring for and protecting vulnerable people. Local authorities should know, adhere to and enforce the rules.

Yet, in reality, it seems likely that a significant number of vulnerable people, through their families, are (a) being deprived of crucial information about the rules and options, and (b) being asked improperly and unlawfully – sometimes effectively forced – to pay care home fees that are the responsibility of the local authority.

This results in financial harm; it is wholly unclear why, at least in some circumstances, this is not treated as financial abuse.

CHARGES FOR MENTAL HEALTH AFTERCARE

Aftercare services are provided under s.117 of the Mental Health Act 1983. These services are provided for people who have previously been detained under certain sections of the Mental Health Act 1983. There was, in the past, some genuine lack

---

65   Local Government Ombudsman. *Report on an investigation into complaint no. 10 018 968 against Walsall Metropolitan Borough Council.* London: LGO, 2012.

of clarity about the rules under s.117, certainly up to 1999, so that, even when local authorities levied unlawful charges, it would be harsh to characterise this past conduct as financial impropriety or abuse.

However, even since the law was clarified, cases have continued to come to light, which suggest a reckless approach to the rules and to people's money – always remembering the degree of vulnerability of the people concerned. Some local authorities have continued to persist with legally dubious attempts to find a way of charging people for services that should be free under s.117.

For instance, local authorities may maintain that, because s.117 services being provided have been successful in stabilising the person in the community – such that there is little risk of readmission to hospital – those services no longer need to be provided under s.117. Instead, they argue, the very same services can be provided under other community care legislation which allows charging – even though the very reason for the stability is those s.117 services. The courts have disapproved of this approach.[66] So too have the local government ombudsmen.[67] But this does not necessarily deter some local authorities from quietly ignoring both.

Alternatively, a local authority might claim, retrospectively, to have properly discharged a person from s.117 – but that it just didn't tell anyone at the time. However, this would mean that it had failed to consult with the person and carer as demanded by central government guidance[68] and the Mental Health Act code of practice.[69] When local authorities have done this, retrospectively, their actions are suggestive of attempts to get hold of large sums of money improperly (e.g. from a person's estate following death) and of an unconcern with the legal rules. The local ombudsman will find maladministration.[70]

Nor are the sums at stake paltry. In one case, the ombudsman recommended the council repay £60,000. In another case, £264,000 was found owing to one person.[71]

In a further case, the local authority attempted to place a woman in a cheaper care home that would not meet her assessed needs and the requirements of her care plan. If she wished to go into the more expensive home, she was told, she would have to top up. The local ombudsman found maladministration; the authority was obliged to cover the cost of a care home that would meet her needs.[72]

Another local authority, astonishingly, even persuaded the patient to sign away her statutory right to free placement under s.117 in a care home, telling her that

---

66   *R v Manchester City Council, ex p Stennett* [2002] UKHL 34.
67   *Clwyd County Council 1997* (97/0177, 97/0755). And: *Bath and North East Somerset Council 2007* (06/B/16774).
68   HSC 2000/3; LAC(2000)3. Department of Health. *After-care under the Mental Health Act 1983*. London: DH.
69   Department of Health. *Code of practice: Mental Health Act 1983*. London: DH, para 27.19.
70   *Wiltshire County Council 1999* (98/B/0341). And: *Leicestershire County Council 2001* (00/B/08307).
71   Commission for Local Administration in England. *Local Government Ombudsman: annual report 2003/4*. London: CLAE, 2004, p.4.
72   *North Yorkshire County Council 2007* (05/C/13158).

unless she did so she might have to wait 12 months in hospital before the council could place her. The ombudsman found maladministration.[73]

Yet, somehow, such malpractices are never referred to as financial abuse; they go by the name of honest mistakes. That is, if they are ever found out and acknowledged at all.

NHS CONTINUING HEALTH CARE

For some 20 years and perhaps longer, many people with what are termed 'NHS continuing health care needs' have been charged by local authorities for care that should have been funded free of charge by the NHS. The health service ombudsman has been investigating this pattern since at least 1994. Further detail is set out in Chapter 6.

However, although it is the NHS and Department of Health that have borne the main brunt of the criticism for this state of affairs, it is often overlooked that it is sometimes local authorities that have been charging unlawfully the people affected. Unlawfully because, as the law courts have pointed out, it is not just a case of what the NHS should have been paying for; it is about what local authorities are not legally permitted to do – namely, place (and charge) people in nursing homes who have primary health needs that are of the continuing care variety.[74]

Indeed, in one legal case about NHS continuing health care, the judge lamented the absence of the local authority as a party to the proceedings, since, in his view, the local authority was one of the key players.[75] Arguably, the local authority's absence from that case was symptomatic of the passivity and detachment of local authorities generally on this whole issue.

Nobody would accuse local authorities of having set out deliberately and unlawfully to cause financial harm to people in this way. Indeed, they would argue that they were merely acting in a humane and socially responsible manner by picking up the pieces improperly discarded by the NHS. But, until the end of 2007, when the Association of Directors of Adult Social Services (ADASS) issued guidance urging local authorities to be more assertive on the issue,[76] local authorities were, by and large, both individually and collectively silent for well over a decade. It seems that many still are.

The consequence of all this is that, by their inaction and readiness to take substantial sums from highly vulnerable people, local authorities have actively participated in conduct causing significant financial harm and injustice to many – perhaps tens of thousands of people over a period of some 15 years – including

---

73   *York City Council 2006* (04/B/01280).

74   *R v North and East Devon Health Authority, ex p Coughlan* [1999] 2 CCLR 285.

75   *R(Grogan) v Bexley NHS Care Trust* [2006] EWHC 44 (High Court).

76   Association of Directors of Adult Social Services; Local Government Association. *Commentary and advice for local authorities on the national framework for NHS continuing healthcare and NHS-funded nursing care.* London: ADASS/LGA, 2007.

the loss of their savings and homes in order to pay for care that should have been free of charge.

In this respect, it is notable that in one investigation the local ombudsman (as opposed to the health service ombudsman) found maladministration when a local authority social worker stood back and allowed a vulnerable service user to be unlawfully charged for a nursing home placement – a placement that should have been funded by the NHS.[77]

UNLAWFUL CHARGING FOR INTERMEDIATE CARE AND REABLEMENT

Another example of a reckless approach being taken by local authorities to the money of vulnerable (largely older) people has emerged in the last few years. It has concerned the provision of what have come to be known as reablement services.

In 2003, the government passed legislation that defined something called 'intermediate care' and stipulated that, for up to a period of six weeks, local authorities were legally prohibited from making a charge for it. The legislation was clear and the policy sensible; the government believed that it was cost-effective to make the service free because longer-term care costs could be avoided if people were assisted to regain or maintain independence through basic rehabilitation.

Furthermore, the rules were clear. A definition was given of intermediate care: it was and is 'a qualifying service [defined as a community care service] which consists of a structured programme of care provided for a limited period of time to assist a person to maintain or regain the ability to live in his home'.[78]

And then something strange happened. Local authorities increasingly renamed intermediate services and brought them under the heading 'reablement'. They then started to charge. But since what was being provided in most cases still fitted the definition of intermediate care, this was, obviously, legally impermissible. But this did not stop many local authorities doing it. The practice continued in a significant number of local authorities, until the Department of Health was shamed into acting – apparently in response to a story in *Community Care* magazine in the summer of 2010.[79] The guidance issued by the Department confirmed (a) that reablement was, in the main, likely to equate legally with intermediate care, and (b) that it could not be charged for, for up to six weeks.[80]

By analogy, what local authorities had done was take a tin of baked beans off the supermarket shelf, switch the label on it to sweetcorn and try to pass off the contents as the latter. But what remained inside, legally and actually, were baked beans.

Is this financial abuse? Yes. Local authorities are large organisations, with legal departments and well-paid senior managers. Even if they did not knowingly

---

77   *Hertfordshire County Council 2003* (00/B/16833).

78   SI 2003/1196. *The Community Care (Delayed Discharges etc.) Act (Qualifying Services) (England) Regulations 2003.*

79   Pitt, V. 'One in five councils illegally charge for reablement services.' *Community Care,* 20 September 2010.

80   LAC (DH) (2010) 6. Department of Health. *Local Authority Circular on the Personal Care at Home Act 2010 and charging for reablement.* London: DH, 2010.

breach the law, this was clearly a reckless approach; even the slightest glance at the legislation would have shown that the policy of charging for reablement was unlawful. Still in 2013, some local authorities continue to charge for reablement, notwithstanding the legal regulations that have been in place for virtually a decade and the government guidance issued in 2010.

No local authority known to the author has treated this as a safeguarding issue; it undoubtedly should have been treated as such. It is a strange logic for a local authority safeguarding team to seek to stop a carer from stealing £30 a week from a vulnerable adult, whilst the same local authority's finance team walks off with a greater weekly amount in glaringly unlawful charges.

LEGAL REMEDIES FOR UNLAWFUL CHARGING FOR SERVICES

There are legal remedies for unlawful charging by a public body.

Complaints can be made to local authorities and, if necessary, to the (independent) local government ombudsmen. The local ombudsmen can include compensation in their recommendations, following a finding of maladministration causing injustice. Alternatively, a judicial review legal case may also be possible, although the court would not normally award financial compensation directly.

If local authority senior managers could be shown knowingly to have (a) flouted the law and (b) therefore deprived the family of money dishonestly, then, in principle at least, this could amount not just to maladministration but also possibly to fraud. The fact that they might have acted with the best possible of intentions – for example, to make the local authority's scarce resources go further – would arguably be irrelevant. In practice, however, it is certainly difficult to see such a case being brought, let alone succeed.

Alternatively, it might also be possible in principle, but with a highly doubtful chance of success in practice, to bring a civil tort case involving what is called misfeasance in public office. This includes a public officer acting, knowingly, unlawfully.

Misfeasance in public office. The case law reveals two different forms of liability for misfeasance in public office. First, there is the case of targeted malice by a public officer – that is, conduct specifically intended to injure a person or persons. This type of case involves bad faith in the sense of the exercise of public power for an improper or ulterior motive. The second form is where a public officer acts, knowing that he or she has no power to do the act complained of and that the act will probably injure the plaintiff. It involves bad faith inasmuch as the public officer does not have an honest belief that his or her act is lawful.[81]

FAILING TO COMMISSION SERVICES ADEQUATELY AND TO MONITOR AND REVIEW CONTRACTUAL ARRANGEMENTS

Financial charging aside, local social services authorities these days commission most community care services from the independent sector, rather than providing

---

81   *Three Rivers District Council v Bank of England* [2003] 2 AC 1.

them directly. They do so by means of contracts, held with a range of care providers, including care homes, domiciliary care providers and day centres. Although the services are contracted out, local authorities retain at least a twofold responsibility.

First, they have a duty, under the NHS and Community Care Act 1990, ultimately to make sure that people's assessed needs are met adequately. Second, they are spending public money on contracts, the efficacy of which they should be ensuring.

One frequently hears local authority managers referring, off the record, to a 'race to the bottom' in terms of contracting out services: in other words, who will do it most cheaply? And this race is not only about the cheapest but also about what local authorities are asking contractors to do. In other words, local authorities contribute to poor quality of care by paring back on what they commission and what they are prepared to pay for it. Somewhere, in this unseemly race, poor care and neglect start to show themselves.

Whether through services commissioned and contracted out by local authorities or privately purchased from domiciliary care agencies or care homes (when the person is not eligible for help from the local authority), it appears that significant numbers of older people are increasingly being inadequately cared for.

The many reports of neglect or abuse in independent care homes, year in, year out, frequently concern residents who are placed and funded by local authorities (and the NHS). This calls into question the contracting, monitoring and reviewing role of the local authorities, for whom such residents – particularly the elderly – are too often out of sight and out of mind.

As to care in people's own homes, *Which?* published findings in 2012, referring to 'disgraceful' levels of care, including older people being confined to soiled beds, missed medication, food being placed and left out of reach and people being left unable to reach the bathroom.[82]

In 2012, it was reported that 73 per cent of care visits commissioned by local authorities lasted 30 minutes or less, and 10 per cent lasted 15 minutes only. Given that, in many local authorities, only people with high needs ('critical' or 'substantial') are eligible for anything at all, this is concerning.[83] Even 30 minutes, let alone 15, to get a person with physical frailty or disability, incontinence and dementia, up, washed, dressed and given breakfast, is going to be a tall order.

In 2011, the Equality and Human Rights Commission surveyed home care for older people. Their conclusions referred to hurry, inflexibility, lack of respect, being ignored, being put to bed too early, lateness, not turning up, unreliability – and the impact on medication, eating, not being able to get to the toilet.[84]

---

82   'Home care for elderly "disgraceful", report finds.' *The Guardian*, 16 March 2012.
83   Ramesh, R. 'Shortened care visits putting elderly and vulnerable at risk.' *The Guardian*, 5 July 2012.
84   Sykes, W. and Groom, C. *Older people's experiences of home care in England.* London: Equality and Human Rights Commission, 2011, pp.vi–vii.

LOCAL AUTHORITIES SHARE RESPONSIBILITY FOR THE DEATHS OF VULNERABLE ADULTS

Responsibility becomes all the more acute when one considers that local authorities deal with highly vulnerable people. And it is this latter consideration of vulnerability that has led the local government ombudsman to make findings of maladministration against local authorities when they fail to discharge the twofold responsibility, statutory and contractual.

For such failure, the ombudsman has pinned local authorities with a significant degree of blame for harm, including death, to service users. Clearly, such a level of detriment becomes – or should become – a safeguarding and adult protection matter. Typically, omissions and neglect are involved.

If a local authority has known full well about a care provider's failings but failed to act or acted inadequately, the ombudsman will fix the local authority with maladministration. The following case involved the death of a highly vulnerable service user.

Woman's death following council's apparent indifference to the fate of elderly people. The complainant's elderly parents were both in their nineties when they began to receive services provided by care agencies on behalf of the council. Even before his father died, he had been complaining to the council that agency staff frequently missed calls or arrived late – in which case, many elderly people like his mother tried to get up to make their own meals, putting their health in danger. On one occasion, his mother fell in the bedroom at 12.30pm. She was unable to get up, but expected a lunch-time visit, so lay on the floor waiting for the carer. After an hour, she realised nobody was coming. She then used her alarm. A few days later, there was no breakfast-time call; she managed to get herself up, but she went without breakfast or medication.

Carer arriving with no torch: woman startled and falls and dies. Finally, a home help made a tea-time call in January. She did not have a torch, which she was meant to carry, to illuminate the door entry keypad. So she banged on the living-room window. The woman was startled. As she tried to hurry into the kitchen to switch on the light, she fell on to the corner of a table. The home help let herself in, got the woman off the floor, made her a cup of tea and sandwich, wrote up the daily log without mentioning the fall, and left. Two hours later, the woman's son arrived to find his mother slumped in her chair unable to move. A doctor was called. She had suffered eight broken ribs as a result of the fall. The doctor made an incorrect diagnosis; appropriate treatment was delayed. She died two weeks later after the onset of pneumonia. The carer was dismissed for failing to report the incident.

Failure of council to respond to reports of missed or late calls: routine contract compliance checks not enough. The ombudsman was scathing. She stated that:

> …councils must respond to reports of missed or late calls by agency staff and follow up complaints by or on behalf of vulnerable service users as a matter of urgency. It cannot be left to routine contract compliance checks to find out whether planned services are really being delivered. It can never be acceptable for elderly people whose care is the responsibility of the Council to wait long periods of time for the next meal or for their medication to be given.

Maladministration: failure to act on previous complaints and make alternative arrangements. The council's failure to take up complaints of missed calls promptly was maladministration; likewise, its failure to consider whether to make alternative arrangements. When an agency is failing, the council 'must simultaneously look and act in two directions at the same time – to the contractor to improve performance and to the client to assess and respond to the risk posed to them by the contractor's failures'.

Furthermore, the way in which the complaint was then handled – including a failure to coordinate papers for the review panel stage – contributed to the complainant's impression that the council was merely going through the motions and that it 'did not care what was happening to its elderly and vulnerable clients'.[85]

In another case, the agency carers failed to turn up, resulting in the complainant's aunt lying all day on the floor and subsequently dying.

Council fails to do anything about an inadequate care agency: elderly woman lies on the floor all day and dies. The woman, 79 years old, used a wheelchair, having had both legs amputated. She had generalised arthritis, diabetes controlled by diet and a hearing impairment. She was highly dependent and required daily contact.

Stroke, heart attack, hypothermia. On one particular day in March 2003, the care agency contracted to provide care failed to visit in the morning. The carer, who had decided not to work that day, had not informed the agency. The early-evening visit did not take place either. Later that evening, she was found on the floor and admitted to hospital. During the period she lay on the floor, she had suffered a stroke, a heart attack and hypothermia. She died eight days later. The time the aunt spent on the floor before she was helped was some 13 hours after the time set for the morning visit. She was without food or water. The cause of the accident was probably because of the failure of the carers to visit her. 'She was badly let down by the Council and its provider.'

Known inadequacies of care agency. However, the inadequacies of the care agency on that particular day were not uncharacteristic. They were already well known to the council and included inappropriate and untrained staff, a failure to log in and out or report to the office, failure of the back-up telephone system, and failure to ensure all carers had access to a care plan explaining entry and emergency arrangements. In addition, a significant number of complaints had been made in the past about missed or late visits. These problems had existed for nine months, from the start of a block contract the council had with the care agency, yet the council's interventions had failed to protect service users.

Given the background of complaints during 2002 about the care agency involved, the council 'failed to understand that it was dealing with a provider that was acting dangerously towards some service users. It failed to understand the random nature of the problem. The Council failed to monitor the reports of missed visits.'

Previous survey revealing serious shortcomings in agency. By January 2003, an audit of the care agency had revealed that, of a survey of 20 service users, 75 per cent did not have care plans, 60 per cent lacked a written assessment by the provider, and 60 per cent had received no risk assessment. Of 20 staff files reviewed, there was no evidence that the company employed as many people as it claimed to, and staff were averaging considerably more than 48 hours per week of work. There was no evidence of induction training; no training schedule was in place. Complaints made by service users were not recorded on their files. For 25 of 43 visits surveyed, carers provided less than 25 per cent of the time they had been commissioned to spend.

---

85   Local Government Ombudsman. *Investigation into Sheffield City Council 2007* (05/C/06420). London: LGO, 2007.

Inadequate investigation of incident. In addition, the council's investigation of the incident involving the death of the woman was inadequate. It lacked a sense of urgency, and the responsible officer was content to leave matters largely with the company and to correspond with it over a number of months. The information the council did obtain showed that, in the week before the incident, the aunt had experienced the same failings experienced by other service users, including a lack of continuity in care because of the involvement of different carers, truncated visits, possible missed visits and use of inappropriate staff. The inappropriate staff comprised one who had been banned from working with service users and another who, in January (so the agency had informed the council), had been sacked for misconduct. Overall, the council failed to consider what measures to take to safeguard service users. All this was maladministration.[86]

In similar vein, national press coverage was given to the following example of serious shortcuts being taken, with potentially serious consequences.

Allegations that carers had falsified a log of daily visits made to the home of an 83-year-old woman. For nine days after the woman had been admitted to hospital, the carers let themselves into her home and signed the log saying they had seen and checked her, and that she was fine in bed – for example: 'Again staying in bed. Cat fed and watered.' It was only on the ninth day that a carer checked the bedroom to find that the woman was not there and recorded this. Devon County Council, which commissioned services from the care agency involved, and the Commission for Social Care Inspection were informed.[87]

CONTRACTING FAILURES: REMEDIES FOR FAILING TO PROTECT SERVICE USERS FROM HARM

Remedies other than the local government ombudsman might be possible. The Care Quality Commission might take action, although often arrives too late on the scene (see Chapter 8).

In addition, the Health and Safety Executive (see Chapter 21) has in the past prosecuted a local authority for poor contracting arrangements which led to a substandard contractor being used and to manual handling injuries to the contractor's employees. The contractor was, of course, itself prosecuted also for poor health and safety practices.[88] There would seem no reason why such a prosecution could not also cover harm to vulnerable service users (as opposed to paid staff) and lie against both the local authority and the contractor.

It might also be possible, in some circumstances at least, similarly to argue a civil negligence case be brought to seek financial compensation, against both contractor and local authority (see Chapter 25). This would, of course, depend on the degree of blame (legally, the extent of any breach of duty of care) and being able to show that this had directly caused the harm alleged.

Furthermore, if the harm suffered by a person – either in an isolated case or on an ongoing basis – amounted to a breach of human rights, then a case might lie

86   *Blackpool Borough Council 2006* (03/C/17141).
87   Morris, S. and Brindle, D. 'Carers accused of faking log of home visits to woman, 83.' *The Guardian*, 12 March 2008.
88   *Health and Safety Executive v London Borough of Barnet* [1997] unreported, Crown Court.

against the local authority. This might be possible if the local authority knew, or clearly should have known, that a person's human rights were being, or would be likely to be, breached. (The human rights case could also lie against the independent contractor, but only in limited circumstances: see Chapter 4.)

APPLICATION OF STRICT THRESHOLD OF ELIGIBILITY FOR ASSISTANCE

Owing to a mismatch between demands made upon them and available resources, local social services authorities struggle to reconcile their limited resources with their ability to meet people's needs. In the light of this, they commonly apply an eligibility threshold in order to establish what level of needs they are obliged to meet and which not. If this threshold becomes too restrictive, vulnerable adults are not assisted and may be put at risk of harm.

Typically, local authorities, under government guidance,[89] adopt policies to meet needs if they are deemed 'critical' or 'substantial', but not if they are 'moderate' or 'low' only. However, there is considerable variation between local authorities.

The higher a local authority sets its threshold, arguably the more consequences there are for safeguarding. For instance, the government guidance includes 'serious abuse or neglect' in the critical category, and just 'abuse or neglect' in the substantial category. If the guidance is taken at face value, the imposition of a threshold set at the critical level would result in a local authority not responding to abuse or neglect, unless it were serious. (The National Assembly for Wales avoided this particular problem by defining all abuse as a critical matter in its equivalent guidance.[90])

This point about the setting and application of the eligibility threshold is not hypothetical.

For instance, the serious case review into the torture and murder of a man with learning disabilities in Cornwall noted that a question had to be asked about why the ever-tightening eligibility criteria of services were rendering vulnerable men and women so unprotected.[91] It transpired that, although the service user had requested a discontinuation of local authority support sometime previous to his death, he would probably have lost his service anyway. This was because, had he been reviewed by social services at the time, he might not have been eligible under the local authority's fair access to care eligibility threshold. At the time, this had been set at the substantial level.[92]

---

89   Department of Health. *Prioritising need in the context of Putting People First: A whole system approach to eligibility for social care: guidance on eligibility criteria for adult social care, England 2010*. London, DH, 2010.

90   NAFWC 9/02; WHC(2002)32. National Assembly for Wales. *Health and social care for adults: creating a unified and fair system for assessing and managing care*. Cardiff: NAFW, 2002.

91   Flynn, M. *The murder of Steven Hoskin: a serious case review*. Truro: Cornwall Adult Protection Committee, 2007.

92   Cornwall Adult Protection Committee. *The murder of Steven Hoskin: serious case review*. Truro: Cornwall County Council, 2007, p.9.

Likewise, in 2011, another serious case review of the murder of a young woman found an increasing reluctance to assess, as well as the strictness of eligibility rules, to be associated with her death.[93]

More generally, the Commission for Social Care Inspection (CSCI), before it was wound up, outlined the adverse consequences of this approach for increasing numbers of older people, in terms of physical accidents, self-respect, mental health, emotional well-being and dignity.[94]

It is not too difficult to see that situations of harm and neglect could arise. For instance, a second report from CSCI noted how low-level needs – deemed ineligible for assistance – might escalate, how accidents might occur as people struggled to cope alone and how experiences might be dismal and very poor.

It concluded that the eligibility decisions of local authorities might fail 'utterly to meet people's needs for dignity and self-respect'. With some understatement, it records how a local authority visited a woman at home, assessed her as managing her own personal care and closed the case – having first recorded that she was unkempt, her knickers were around her knees, there was evidence of faeces on the floor and she was not taking her medication.[95]

Somewhere here, a line is being crossed, leading to vulnerable people, directly or indirectly, being placed at risk of harm by a glaring omission to assist – notwithstanding that local authorities are acting in good faith and subject to competing demands with limited resources.

HARM ARISING FROM FAILURE TO MEET PEOPLE'S NEEDS

If a person is judged to have eligible needs – that is, coming over the eligibility threshold – then, legally, the local authority will have a duty to meet that person's needs. This does not always happen – with consequences for safeguarding.

For instance, the local government ombudsmen have investigated a number of cases in which local authorities have refused to carry out their legal duty to meet a person's assessed needs on the grounds of lack of resources. These cases typically involved vulnerable younger adults with learning disabilities or autism and high needs. In one, the local authority's failure to pay for a suitable placement with the National Autistic Society led to the person being detained under the Mental Health Act 1983 compulsorily and inappropriately in a locked psychiatric ward.[96]

In another, the social worker found a suitable placement for a man with learning disabilities and autism. The social worker's recommendations were overruled by a manager on grounds of cost; instead, the person was placed in an alternative

93   Warwickshire Safeguarding Adults Partnership. *Serious case review: the murder of Gemma Hayter, 9th August 2010.* Warwick: WSAP, 2011.

94   Commission for Social Care Inspection. *The state of social care in England 2006–07.* London: CSCI, 2008.

95   Henwood, M. and Hudson, B. *Lost to the system? The impact of Fair Access to Care.* London: Commission for Social Care Inspection, 2008, pp.8–12.

96   Local Government Ombudsman. *Investigation into Bolton Metropolitan Borough Council 2004* (02/C/17068). London: LGO, 2004.

care home at half the cost, even though this conflicted with the findings of the assessment. The placement broke down, his condition deteriorated seriously and he was then detained under the Mental Health Act for some eight months in a psychiatric ward, where he was sedated with medication. Unnecessarily; that is, if the original assessment of need had been followed as, legally, it should have been. The ombudsman was highly critical.[97]

A third case warrants recounting in slightly more detail, leading as it did to neglect and abuse of a woman with learning disabilities. Once again, the ombudsman found the local authority had acted with maladministration in what came over as a fairly shocking case.

Woman wrongly kept in hospital for ten years. At the age of 18 years, a woman with severe learning difficulties was received into guardianship by the local authority; she resided at a care home. Following concerns about her behaviour, she was admitted, in March 1990, to hospital under s.3 of the Mental Health Act 1983; this compulsory detention replaced the guardianship order. Six months later, in September 1990, the consultant psychiatrist wrote to the local authority, stating that a further stay in hospital was not warranted; the s.3 detention ceased.

Local authority not wanting to pay for a placement. However, the local authority failed to put in place a plan for discharge because it was concerned about the cost of any such placement, and also argued with the NHS about who should be responsible for the funding.

The woman finally left hospital in 2001, having spent over ten years as an informal, compliant but incapacitated patient. As a consequence, aftercare duties under s.117 of the 1983 Act were never triggered and the local authority was never tested on its potential duties under s.117. The ombudsman concluded that, if it had been, the authority would have 'fallen far short' of its responsibilities.

Abuse of woman by other patients neither investigated nor prevented. The evidence suggested that the woman did not need to be a long-stay patient. A consequence of this unnecessary stay in hospital was that the local authority had neither investigated nor prevented the abuse the woman suffered at the hands of other patients during her inappropriate hospital stay. For example, as early as 1991, a local authority mental health management officer wrote to the director of social services about the woman's deteriorating welfare, bites on her legs inflicted by another patient and her shoddy clothing.

The ombudsman found that the local authority had failed in its duties, notwithstanding legal uncertainties during some of the period about NHS 'continuing care' responsibilities, and recommended £20,000 compensation.[98]

A fourth case focused, on the surface at least, on the failure to assess, review, supervise and manage the foster placement of a woman with learning disabilities. Underneath, however, lay a local authority learning disabilities team with one in three posts unfilled and a massive overspend. The consequences for the woman were dire and gave rise, belatedly, to an adult protection investigation.

97   Local Government Ombudsman. *Investigation into Southend-on-Sea Borough Council 2005* (04/A/10159). London: LGO, 2005.

98   Local Government Ombudsman. *Investigation into Wakefield Metropolitan District Council 2003* (01/C/15652). London: LGO, 2003.

Importance of reviewing and reassessing placements of vulnerable adults. For six years, a local authority had failed to assess and review a woman with learning disabilities in a foster placement (first as a child, then as an adult). The foster carers had not been registered as they should have been. The foster family obstructed her in contacting the previous foster family. She was not allowed to use sign language (her preferred means of communication), deprived of hearing-aid batteries, treated like a child, forced to share a bedroom, prevented from having a relationship with somebody at work and instead encouraged to have an inappropriate relationship with an older family acquaintance. The first assessment after all this time came when an adult protection investigation was launched.[99]

Possible remedies for such aberrations include complaints to the local ombudsmen (who might award financial compensation and recommend actions by the local authority) or judicial review legal cases to show the local authority is in breach of its duty.

If significant harm has been suffered directly, a civil negligence case may be contemplated, although might be difficult to win; obstacles to overcome would include showing the extent or even existence of the local authority's duty of care, a breach in that duty and the causation of the specific harm. It would also mean overcoming the courts' general reluctance to allow negligence cases to succeed against local authorities when resources, statutory functions or policy are in issue. See Chapter 25.

IMPACT OF PERSONALISATION AND SELF-DIRECTED SUPPORT

Department of Health community care policy talks currently and explicitly about greater choice, control and independence for people. To this end, its policy is that people should increasingly be assessing their own needs and should have the freedom to choose (a) how those needs will be met and (b) how to spend a sum of money that is allocated to them by local authorities. The amount of money is to be determined by the apparent level and type of need (self-assessed or otherwise) that a person has.[100]

Roughly, this summarises a policy that has come to be known variously as self-directed support, individual or personalised budgets, or simply personalisation.

A central, though not the only, plank of personalisation lies in the form of direct payments. These involve a local authority giving money to a person who then uses it to buy the services (or assistive equipment) that he or she has been assessed as needing. The person receiving the direct payment must have the capacity to consent to it, actually consent to it and have the ability to manage the payment, even if he or she needs help to do so.

The recipient of a direct payment is the person in need, although he or she can name somebody else as nominee to handle the money, as long as the recipient can still retain overall control of how the care is delivered.[101]

---

99 *Birmingham City Council 2008* (05/C/18474).
100 For example: LAC(DH)(2008)1. Department of Health. *Transforming social care*. London: DH, 2008.
101 Department of Health. *Guidance on direct payments*. London: DH, 2009, para 73.

Alternatively, if that person cannot consent to the payment, then somebody else – such as a person with a lasting power of attorney, a deputy or a family member – can receive it instead and apply the money on the person's behalf and in that person's best interests. Such a recipient must, however, be deemed 'suitable' by the local authority, which must also be satisfied that it is appropriate to make the payment.[102]

MISUSE OF DIRECT PAYMENTS AND SAFEGUARDING

There is no overwhelming evidence that direct payments are leading to widespread financial or other abuse, but there are nonetheless concerns and at least some evidence to suggest that direct payments can afford the opportunity for such abuse to take place.

PERSON LACKING CAPACITY: PAYMENT MADE TO SOMEBODY ELSE

If a person lacks capacity and payment is made to somebody else, the risk might increase of precisely 'unsuitable' people receiving the money and misusing it.

Donees of a lasting power of attorney or deputies appointed by the Court of Protection will automatically be deemed, as representatives of the person lacking capacity, to be suitable, although the local authority must still decide whether it is appropriate to make the payment. And, even in these cases, it must be borne in mind that a proportion of people with a lasting power of attorney are more than capable of abusing it. See Chapter 13.

DIRECT PAYMENTS AND CRIMINAL RECORD CHECKS

In any case, other 'suitable' people can receive the payment when the person in need lacks mental capacity; these may or may not be family members or friends already involved in providing care for the person lacking capacity. A criminal record check is necessary where the proposed suitable person is not a family member or friend providing care.[103]

However, this rule aside, adult direct payment recipients do not have a duty to ensure that a criminal record check is carried out. The guidance on direct payments states that councils should inform direct payment recipients of the benefit of such checks – but that those recipients will retain the choice about them.[104]

Direct payment recipients cannot request directly enhanced criminal record certificates themselves because only bodies registered with the Disclosure and Barring Service (DBS) can do so. Nonetheless, a request could be made by the recipient to an 'umbrella' body; that is, an organisation (such as a local authority or

---

102 Health and Social Care Act 2008, s.57. And: SI 2009/1887. The Community Care, Services for Carers and Children's Services (Direct Payments) (England) Regulations 2009.

103 SI 2009/1887. The Community Care, Services for Carers and Children's Services (Direct Payments) (England) Regulations 2009.

104 Department of Health. *Guidance on direct payments.* London: DH, 2009, para 129.

local voluntary body) registered with the DBS to request a check on other people's behalf.

DIRECT PAYMENTS AND FRAUD

In 2011, the Audit Commission produced a report on fraud perpetrated against local authorities; one section pinpointed direct payments as a factor in increasing levels of fraud.[105] And the City of London Police have alluded to the dangers if direct payments are not well managed, including the risk of systematic exploitation by organised criminals.[106] A few examples are as follows.

In Essex, a social worker was caring for her disabled husband and at the same time working for the local authority. She defrauded Essex County Council of £25,000. Via a direct payment, she claimed for a phantom carer for her husband, whom she interviewed but did not employ – but 'stole' her identity. She was given a 15-month prison sentence and struck off the register of social workers.[107]

In the following case, a man obtained direct payments apparently fraudulently, was then murdered by his son, who in turn continued to use the direct payments, effectively fraudulently, as well.

Fraudulent use of direct payments by father and son – and murder. A serious case review found that a direct payment continued to be paid for many months to a 70-year-old man – even after he had been murdered and buried in the back garden by his son. The father had serious health problems, including ulcerative colitis, heart problems, a problem with his salivary glands, the after-effects of pneumonia and rheumatism. He received nutritional supplements, had a stoma and required continence aids. Between August 2008 and February 2009, the man had no contact with social services or the NHS; despite this, the direct payments continued to be paid, stopping only when a police investigation began.

In addition, it transpired that the father had, in any case, probably been obtaining the direct payments fraudulently – that is, claiming for carers but relying instead on his son for support and not disclosing his financial affairs fully. After the father had been murdered, the son continued to use the direct payments, effectively fraudulently. The money was not recovered.[108]

A man was convicted of fraud involving over £12,000. The money was in the form of direct payments meant for his 73-year-old mother. Instead, he kept the money, altering bank payments to make it seem that he had used the money to pay for his mother's care.[109]

A particularly salient example of financial crime, involving a direct payment but leading on to worse, was as follows.

---

105   Audit Commission. *Protecting the public purse 2001: fighting fraud against local government.* London: AC, 2011, paras 41–50.

106   City of London Police; National Fraud Intelligence Bureau. *Assessment: financial crime against vulnerable adults.* London: Social Care Institute for Excellence, 2011, p.41.

107   McGregor, K. 'Jailed social worker struck off after admitting £25,000 fraud.' *Community Care,* 29 September 2009.

108   Flynn, M. *Executive Summary: the murder of Mr C: a serious case review.* Buckingham: Buckinghamshire Safeguarding Vulnerable Adults Board, 2011, pp.2, 4, 13–15.

109   'First direct payment cheat jailed.' *This is Croydon Today,* 8 April 2011. Accessed on 6 August 2012 at: www.thisiscroydontoday.co.uk/direct-payment-cheat-jailed/story-11368406-detail/story.html.

£36,000 of false claims set against a direct payment: and remortgaging, through forgery, of service user's house by carer without the disabled person's knowledge. A carer was employed through a direct payment by a mother of four children who had syringomyelia, a muscle-wasting disorder that had slowly robbed her of her mobility. She needed round-the-clock care. The carer put in false time sheets for care her husband allegedly, but not in reality, had provided – amounting to £36,000. In addition, the carer forged the woman's signature and remortgaged her house, without the woman's knowledge. The woman was now facing a £28,000 debt to be paid to the Alliance and Leicester Bank. It was hoped the bank would waive the debt. The carer was sent to prison for 18 months, after being convicted of false accounting, obtaining a money transfer by deception, and acquiring, using and possessing criminal property.[110]

INDEPENDENCE AND PROTECTION

There is a tension between the notion of people as active consumers of social care services and of protecting adults from neglect and abuse.

For instance, the serious case review conducted into the murder of a man with learning disabilities in Cornwall tackled this tension head-on. In this case, nearly a year before he was killed, the man had requested that his service from the local authority be discontinued. This duly happened. The review quoted from the White Paper about people with disabilities, *Valuing people*, which talked about independence but also stated that 'independence in this context does not mean doing everything unaided'.[111]

The review pointed out that his decision to terminate services was not discussed with him, even though such a choice might be compounding his vulnerability and might be made on the basis of inappropriate information or coercion from third parties. It noted the danger of policies about choice being translated into an attitude of admitting no restraints, adoption of an attitude of indifference and the promotion of unfettered independence.

In any case, in the particular circumstances, with social services receding into the background, the opposite outcome had in fact been achieved, as the police report had made clear. It found that the man had lost all control of his own life within his own home, had no say, choice or control over who stayed or visited him, no voice or influence over what happened to him, and had lost the little ability he had to make his own choices and decisions.

The review went on to be quite blunt about the lessons emerging from the man's murder. It challenged the dogma about 'choice' for adults who are apparently 'able' and stated that there were 'profound implications for the support of vulnerable adults in our communities'.[112]

---

110 Cowan, M. 'Acocks Green fraud victim wants bank to wipe "secret mortgage" debt.' *Birmingham Post*, 10 August 2009. Also: Washington, S. '"Cash for care" abuse warning.' *Radio 5 Live*, 18 October 2009. Accessed on 28 August 2012 at: http://news.bbc.co.uk/1/hi/health/8308782.stm.

111 Department of Health. *Valuing people: a new strategy for learning disability for the 21st century*. London: TSO, 2001, p.23.

112 Flynn, M. *The murder of Steven Hoskin: a serious case review*. Truro: Cornwall Adult Protection Committee, 2007, p.25.

Similarly, a more recent serious case review, which looked at the murder of a young woman with mental health problems, noted that a combination of (probable) mental capacity to take day-to-day decisions and personalisation should not just mean letting people go down the road to disaster. This conclusion followed after it had become clear that social services had persistently refused even to assess the woman:

> The new social care model of personalisation, based on self-directed support, provides opportunities for people to decide what support they need and how they want to be supported. However, it needs to be recognised that some people…are unaware of the risks presented by their lifestyle and repeatedly make decisions that place themselves at risk of harm. It is essential that the procedures for accessing community care assessments and services via self-directed care are based on robust risk assessments and do not further dilute the duty of care. This is not to suggest that services should become risk averse and ignore choice and self-direction, but that a balanced approach is taken based on positive risk taking that is underpinned by appropriate safeguards.[113]

Perhaps in similar vein, the Mental Health Act Commission quoted, from the *Wandsworth Guardian*, a coroner investigating the death of a schizophrenic woman who had been detained under s.2 of the Mental Health Act 1983 and then discharged into the care of a relative who also had mental health problems. She died of hypothermia in a freezing room. The coroner noted that 'time was when a person like this would have been cared for in a safe warm environment. But there has been a change, where people are not kept in institutions but are cared for in the community.'[114]

The trick seems to be not to minimise risk at all costs but somehow still to protect people. Yet it is understandable that local authorities might struggle to do this.

For example, one case centred on a local authority's care plan for a highly vulnerable woman with mental health problems and learning disabilities. The question was whether the local authority's care plan should allow continuation of a sexual relationship (to which she had the mental capacity to consent) with her long-standing partner. This would be a clear benefit to her, but it would also carry a number of risks in relation to her mental health and to other matters about which she lacked the capacity to decide. The court stated:

> The fact is that all life involves risk, and the young, the elderly and the vulnerable are exposed to additional risks and to risks they are less well

---

113 Warwickshire Safeguarding Adults Partnership. *Serious case review: the murder of Gemma Hayter, 9th August 2010.* Warwick: WSAP, 2011, para 4.2.5.
114 Mental Health Act Commission. *Risk, rights, recovery: twelfth biennial report, 2005–2007.* London: MHAC, 2008, p.25.

equipped to cope with. But just as wise parents resist the temptation to keep their children metaphorically wrapped up in cotton wool, so too we must avoid the temptation always to put physical health and safety of the elderly and the vulnerable before everything else. Often it will be appropriate to do so, but not always. Physical health and safety can sometimes be bought at too high a price in happiness and emotional welfare. The emphasis must be on sensible risk appraisal, not striving to avoid all risk, whatever the price, but instead seeking a proper balance and being willing to tolerate manageable or acceptable risks as the price appropriately to be paid in order to achieve some other good – in particular to achieve the vital good of the elderly or vulnerable person's happiness. What good is it making someone safer if it merely makes them miserable?[115]

The judge's reference to management of risk in this case was not superfluous. Concrete risks had indeed been identified – relevant to adult protection and on the basis of past events – that might arise from her having contact with her partner. These included the compromising of her compliance with medication and support, resulting deterioration in her mental health (and possible hospitalisation), homelessness and domestic violence resulting in bruising, marks and, on one occasion, being stabbed in the leg (her partner had been sentenced to four months' imprisonment for this wounding).

Notwithstanding the ruling of the judge, he was clear that, given there might be some physical risk as a trade-off for emotional well-being, it was not for the local authority to walk away. On the contrary, the court still expected the local authority to provide a supportive care package.[116]

115 *Local Authority X v MM* [2007] EWHC 2003 (Fam).
116 *Local Authority X v MM* [2007] EWHC 2003 (Fam).

The National Health Service: law, policy and guidance on safeguarding

KEY POINTS

Perhaps the major challenge in safeguarding policy and practice is how to deal with institutional and systemic poor care and neglect within the National Health Service (NHS). To date, those practitioners and managers in local authorities, the NHS and the police who regard themselves as involved in and supporting safeguarding have singularly failed to respond effectively.

With this in mind, this chapter sets out legislation, policy and guidance underpinning the NHS and relevant to safeguarding.

It also considers the issue of NHS continuing health care, and how the lack of clear rules, together with the disregarding of those rules that do exist, lead to a form of financial abuse of, largely, elderly people.

Chapter 7 then explains in detail the evidence of systemic poor care and neglect within the NHS, why it persists and its implications: practical, moral, professional, political and legal.

Note. It must be emphasised that the point of this chapter and Chapter 7 is not to condemn the NHS. First, because there remains a great deal of good care, even for older people, although this is being fast eroded. Second, because the NHS is such a venerated and fine institution and needs saving from a new generation of managers and from politicians who are steadily but surely destroying an ethos of public service, care, compassion and dedication – and thereby cranking up levels of poor care and neglect for the most vulnerable of patients.

SAFEGUARDING AND THE LAW

There is much talk of humane and dignified care – yet much of it remains tokenistic. As the next chapter shows, nobody wants to admit the extent of poor care and neglect within the NHS. This is why those who hold themselves out as involved in safeguarding – local authority staff, some NHS staff, the police and the Crown Prosecution Service – need to do their bit to try to tackle the problem.

However, local authority, police and NHS frontline staff often say that raising safeguarding issues in the NHS is discouraged. Police officers have related to the author how they don't have the resources or time to take on a large hospital, with all its defensive practices, in cases of possible neglect. It is much easier to go for smaller fry, such as a care home which is less organised and less able to throw up a defensive screen.

And social workers tell of how, if they were to raise safeguarding issues in hospitals, there would be so many that they would have no time to get on with their own work, and they would jeopardise their working relationships with their NHS colleagues.

Too often, the NHS is left to itself to investigate 'serious untoward incidents', about which nothing more is ever heard. It is clear that practitioners involved in safeguarding need to start putting pressure, in whatever form, on NHS hospitals. Perhaps at a strategic level, through safeguarding boards. There is no question, in the author's view, that too many local authority staff and perhaps the police also have become inured to, and almost complicit with, appalling care in our hospitals. Or that they simply look the other way.

More specifically, the law needs to be used far more effectively. Once a few hospitals, or even individuals, for instance, were convicted of manslaughter through recklessness, minds would be more concentrated.

Likewise, once a few senior managers were convicted of wilful neglect, on the basis of a 'couldn't care less' attitude, things might also start to change. Why? Because the prospect of a criminal conviction might just outweigh a manager's desire to get ahead and to hit a target. And because a conviction is a worse prospect than telling the truth and being victimised by managers further up the tree.

Yet the culture in the NHS of concealment, disingenuousness, threats and bullying of whistleblowing staff is largely driven by senior managers throughout the hierarchy right up to the chief executive of the NHS. This is set out in detail in Chapter 7.

We should therefore not characterise all senior managers as well-meaning individuals (many, of course, are) who are doing their best, honestly and transparently. The fact is that, in the worst cases, they conceal, threaten and lie to safeguard their own positions of power, status and salary. And the consequence is too often inhumane care, neglect, suffering and sometimes avoidable deaths on a large scale in our hospitals.

Until they are held accountable, nothing will change.

NHS LEGISLATION, GUIDANCE AND SAFEGUARDING

Legally, the NHS has a number of general duties under the NHS Act 2006 to provide medical, nursing, ambulance and aftercare services. These duties are vague and broad in nature but, ultimately, underpin the whole range of health services provided by the NHS. They do not refer to safeguarding patients from neglect and abuse.

This is perhaps unsurprising, because a State-run health service, operated for the health and care of the population, ought to be the last place you would expect to find systemic neglect.

More recently, NHS providers have become subject to regulations which set out the main obligations of health and social care providers. Included is the duty to safeguard service users from neglect and abuse.[1] These regulations are enforceable, in principle, by the Care Quality Commission (CQC): see Chapter 8.

DRAFT CARE AND SUPPORT BILL 2012

In the future, if and when the draft Care and Support Bill 2012 becomes law and is brought into force, three particular duties will affect the NHS.

First, it must be represented on statutory safeguarding adults boards. Second, it will have a general duty to cooperate with local authorities. Third, more specifically, this cooperation will include complying with requests from local authorities to make enquiries about neglect and abuse of patients – subject to those requests being consistent with NHS duties and not having an adverse effect on its functions.[2]

This new duty of the future is welcome. It is better than nothing. But it is by no means certain, however, that the provisions of the draft Bill will in fact make much difference.

---

1   SI 2010/781. The Health and Social Care Act 2008 (Regulated Activities) Regulations 2010.
2   Care and Support Bill 2012, clauses 4, 5, 34–35.

First, NHS bodies already are represented on local safeguarding adults boards, albeit non-statutory. Second, requests from local authorities will depend on a local authority (a) knowing what is going on and (b) having the will to make those requests.

This is not conjecture. Social services and the NHS are meant to work together; social services may be nervous about rocking the boat or be simply too timid. By way of example, the Healthcare Commission, having found serious failures in NHS services for people with learning disabilities in Cornwall, criticised social services. This was for having failed adequately to coordinate inter-agency adult protection arrangements, including referrals. The local authority was 'too willing to accept the opinion of staff at the [NHS] trust without challenge'.[3]

Third, the extent of concealment that takes place in the NHS about poor care would be consistent – in reality if perhaps not law – with not complying with the request from a local authority to make enquiries. This would be on the perverse grounds that damage to an NHS trust's reputation would have an adverse effect on the performance of its functions.

And, fourth, although the draft Bill says that local authorities can cause enquiries to be made by the NHS, and the NHS should generally cooperate, the NHS could always carry out half-hearted enquiries of some sort and do little about the problem.

GUIDANCE ISSUED TO THE NHS ABOUT SAFEGUARDING

Beyond both the current and prospective legislation, if NHS bodies look to government guidance on safeguarding, they do not find much assistance.

The *No secrets* guidance was issued to local authorities under s.7 of the Local Authority Social Services Act 1970, which makes it so-called statutory guidance carrying considerable legal weight – for local authorities. However, s.7 of that Act does not apply to the NHS; the guidance states only that it is 'commended' to the NHS.[4] It is wholly unsurprising that health service managers have taken little notice of it. Nonetheless, they should note that the health service ombudsman has, finding fault when an NHS trust reacted to complaints without a proper awareness of adult protection.

Rough handling on hospital ward: safeguarding matter. An elderly woman was admitted to hospital for repair of a fractured hip. She told her daughter that on Christmas Day a member of the night staff treated her roughly when attending to her because of vomiting and diarrhoea. Now she was frightened. The daughter made an oral complaint. The ward manager investigated and interviewed the staff member, but did not tell the daughter the result of the investigation. The daughter then made a formal complaint; the trust apologised for not telling mother and daughter the outcome of the investigation.

---

3   Healthcare Commission; Commission for Social Care Inspection. *Joint investigation into the provision of services for people with learning disabilities at Cornwall Partnership NHS Trust*. London: HC/CSCI, 2006, p.6.

4   Department of Health. *No secrets: guidance on developing and implementing multi-agency policies and procedures to protect vulnerable adults from abuse*. London: DH, 2000, para 1.3.

The health service ombudsman found that the trust's complaints procedures and documentation were deficient and that the trust had failed to realise that the mother and daughter viewed the incident as an assault. As such, the trust had not responded sufficiently robustly and should review its complaints policy in the light of the Department of Health's guidance *No secrets*.[5]

For what it is worth, NHS bodies are amongst those which, according to the guidance, should be participating in local inter-agency adult protection work, headed up by local authorities. This means that NHS bodies should have some sort of procedure in order to coordinate and act upon reports of incidents relevant to adult protection. The guidance states that in each local agency, including the NHS, roles and responsibilities need to be clear at a number of levels: supervisory line management, senior management staff, corporate/cross authority, chief officers/ chief executives.[6]

CLINICAL GOVERNANCE AND ADULT SAFEGUARDING

In 2010, the Department of Health issued further guidance, aimed specifically at the NHS, entitled *Clinical governance and adult safeguarding: an integrated process*. It states that when NHS trusts report serious incidents as 'clinical governance' matters, they should be picking out a subset of incidents to be reported as safeguarding. This would then mean informing the local social services authority (i.e. the local council), which has overall responsibility for coordinating local safeguarding activity.

Even this guidance does not have the status of 'statutory' guidance. But, more than this, the Department of Health's approach to systemic neglect is revealed to be, at best, ambiguous and, at worst, inadequate. For instance, it contains three detailed examples; two of these are about individual abuse, one from a member of staff, another from a patient's neighbour.

The third touches on pressure sores, which can be one of the indicators of systemic neglect in hospitals. This example speaks volumes because the details reveal that the pressure sores are linked to hospital policies, bed numbers and staffing and, in effect, to resource issues. The guidance then implies that this is therefore not neglect and not to be treated as a safeguarding matter.

Department of Health guidance: shortage of beds and poor care not to be viewed as neglect or as a safeguarding issue. The example explains how the subsequent investigation showed that the initial risk assessment for the patient, of developing pressure sores, highlighted a 'high' level of risk. The patient, however, was moved from ward to ward three times within the first week. A pressure-relieving mattress was identified as part of the care plan but was not applied until the fourth day after admission. The patient had a broken area by then. The mattress had been ordered, but, due to the numerous moves and shift changes, inadequate information had been passed on and reviewed. The equipment was therefore delayed in getting to the patient.

---

5   *Warrington Hospital NHS Trust 2001* (E.1846/99–00 in HSO 2001).

6   Department of Health. *No secrets*. London: DH, 2000, para 3.9.

A conclusion is reached in the example that, effectively because of the shortage of beds and associated chaos, there was no intentional harm or neglect. The inference appears to be, according to the guidance, that there would then be no formal safeguarding alert because the example states also that such an alert would be triggered only by neglect. The guidance is clearly hesitant; it flirts with the suggestion that the neglect of patients is a venial sin, as long as it occurs in the higher cause of finance, performance and patient throughput.[7]

It is well known that overcrowded hospitals (that is, running bed-occupancy levels too high) and moving patients rapidly from ward to ward for non-clinical reasons are not good for patients. Yet, too often, senior management in hospitals reduce bed and staff numbers to meet financial targets, whilst claiming blandly and optimistically that patient care will not suffer. This example in the guidance gives NHS trusts a green light to continue. Because the whole reason for issuing the guidance is that incident reporting alone within NHS trusts is often insufficient to trigger urgent remedies. Too often, incident reports – particularly in relation to systemic matters about poor care – are effectively buried within the clinical governance system of the hospital.

The implications of the guidance mean that the following patient death from pressure sores, brought about because of a lack of beds in a new hospital, would not be regarded as a safeguarding matter.

War veteran dying of pressure sores brought about by neglect. In 2006, a new hospital was opened – the Queen's Hospital, now run by Barking, Havering and Redbridge University Hospitals NHS Trust. It cost £261 million to build and was described by the developers as cleverly combining clinical values with aesthetic qualities.

At the time of opening it was also said to have 'an appearance and an atmosphere… more akin to a hotel than a hospital'. It was to be 'welcoming to patients and visitors alike'.[8] Indeed, it was an award-winning building. Another feature emphasised, in hindsight as a bit of an afterthought, was 'quick access to treatment'. In 2006, the Trust announced the loss of 190 beds and 650 staff because of a financial crisis; the chief executive, as chief executives are wont to do, stated that the reductions were clinically sustainable.[9]

In 2009, a coroner passed a verdict of death by natural causes contributed to by neglect at the Queen's Hospital. The deceased was an 86-year-old man, Mr Walter Gibson, veteran of the Normandy campaign in the Second World War. He had Parkinson's disease. In early 2008, he died a painful death at the hospital from infected pressure sores. These had been caused by his being left on two separate occasions (successive admissions, days apart, to the hospital) on a hospital trolley for 19 hours, after admission with a chest infection. The hospital had insufficient beds.

The result of his being on the trolley the second time was to exacerbate the sores that had developed on the first occasion. One of the sores was classed as stage 4, sufficiently deep to expose tendon and bone. The wounds were dressed, but a further 12 hours elapsed before he was admitted to a ward where a pressure-relief mattress was finally

---

7   Department of Health. *Clinical governance and adult safeguarding: an integrated process.* London: DH, 2010, p.11.

8   Catalyst Lendlease. *Queen's Hospital, Romford, Essex, United Kingdom.* 2010. Accessed on 2 September 2010 at: www.catalystlendlease.com/projects/queens-hospital.pdf.

9   '£24 million debt NHS trust cuts 650 jobs: up to 650 jobs are to be cut and 190 beds closed by an NHS trust that is trying to tackle debts.' *BBC News,* 28 April 2006. Accessed on 20 July 2010 at: http://news.bbc.co.uk/1/hi/england/london/4954818.stm.

made available. Too late. Mr Gibson died some days afterwards of septicaemia resulting from open sores.[10]

The coroner, referring to 'gross failings' and 'neglect', stated:

> It is quite clear from the evidence I've heard that the length of time Mr Gibson waited at A&E [accident and emergency] both the first and second time – the second time added insult to injury to a man already completely dependent – made a significant contribution to his death… He was at very, very high risk of pressure sores and he should have been provided with appropriate protection against worsening of the pressure sores.[11]

The logic of the Department of Health's guidance is that this sort of occurrence would not trigger a safeguarding alert. In practice, in fact, some hospitals are increasingly taking the incidence of pressure sores more seriously and triggering safeguarding alerts. For instance, some might involve the police routinely for stage 3 or stage 4 pressure sores, whether or not acquired in the hospital.[12]

Yet the practice of other hospitals reflects the limp character of the Department of Health's guidance. Taking their cue from it, some hospitals treat the occurrence of serious (stage 3 or stage 4) pressures sores as a safeguarding matter – but only if they have been acquired in a care home, not if they are acquired in hospital(!).[13]

DEPARTMENT OF HEALTH'S DETERMINATION NOT TO TAKE SYSTEMIC NEGLECT SERIOUSLY

The approach of the guidance has, therefore, arguably evolved little beyond the approach of *The NHS Plan* in 2000, which seemed to acknowledge the need to protect patients from individual rogue clinicians and health professionals, but not from systemic failings.[14] This way of looking at things echoes guidance issued in 2001 about the need to protect patients from a small number of 'problem doctors'; institutional mistreatment of patients was not highlighted.[15]

In short, the 2010 guidance does not grasp the nettle. It is illustrative of the fundamental failure of the Department of Health, as a whole, to take safeguarding seriously.

The Department of Health issued further guidance in early 2011. Three companion documents were issued for NHS practitioners, managers and commissioners. The guidance does emphasise the importance of safeguarding and

---

10   Schlesinger, F. 'Coroner's fury as great-grandfather, 86, dies after being dumped on A&E trolley for 19 hours TWICE.' *Daily Mail*, 22 May 2009.

11   Schlesinger, F. 'Coroner's fury as great-grandfather, 86, dies after being dumped on A&E trolley for 19 hours TWICE.' *Daily Mail*, 22 May 2009.

12   Phair, L. *An audit of disciplinary outcomes and incident reporting and the relationship with the vetting and barring scheme in the NHS.* London: Social Care Workforce Research Unit, King's College London, 2011, p.10.

13   Personal communication from an acute hospital safeguarding lead practitioner, December 2011.

14   Secretary of State for Health. *The NHS Plan: a plan for investment, a plan for reform.* Cm 4818-I. London: TSO, 2000, p.90.

15   Department of Health. *A commitment to quality, a quest for excellence: a statement on behalf of the Government, the medical profession and the NHS, 27 June 2001.* London: DH, 2001, p.1.

does make some reference to institutional abuse, without, unfortunately, spelling out for trusts what that would actually look like in detail (many trusts and their staff no longer recognise neglect). The guidance is vague, full of jargon and a classic token gesture. In any case, the guidance has the status of 'best practice guidance'; although better than nothing, the legal status and weight of such guidance is lesser rather than greater.[16]

OTHER LEGAL REMEDIES FOR POOR CARE AND NEGLECT

This book is about the law in relation to safeguarding. Whilst one would not wish to see a National Health Service operating in an over-legalised environment, the treatment of elderly people in our hospitals has now reached a pass where all tools should be used to do something about it. To an extent, when it comes to systemic poor care and neglect, there would seem to be a legal 'no go' area. That is, if any other organisation were to behave in this way, the law would be more readily applied.

In summary, the following laws could apply; they are teased out, separately, elsewhere in this book.

REGULATION OF HEALTH CARE PROVIDERS

The NHS is a health care provider and as such is subject to regulations and to registration and inspection by the Care Quality Commission.

The Commission and its predecessors, the Healthcare Commission and the Commission for Healthcare Improvement, have singularly failed to prevent the escalation and worsening of care for older people.

But, in principle, the regulatory legislation is there. Regulations set out a number of basic standards of service;[17] these are considered in Chapter 8. If NHS bodies adhered to them, even roughly, and CQC enforced them to a reasonable degree, then systemic neglect and abuse in the health service would not exist.

There are reasons for the failure of the Care Quality Commission and its predecessors. The constant reorganisation of these commissions illustrates what an expert report prepared for the Mid Staffordshire public inquiry pointed out: they have been created by, directed by and are beholden to the Department of Health. Their role has been more in the way of outsourced performance management than truly independent regulation.[18]

Sir Ian Kennedy, former chairman of the Healthcare Commission, gave evidence to the public inquiry. He explained that when that Commission replaced

16   Department of Health. *Safeguarding adults: the role of health service practitioners.* London: DH, 2011. Department of Health. *Safeguarding adults: the role of health service managers and their boards.* London: DH, 2011. Department of Health. *Safeguarding adults: the role of NHS managers.* London: DH, 2011.

17   SI 2010/781. The Health and Social Care Act 2008 (Regulated Activities) Regulations 2010.

18   Walshe, K. *The development of health care regulation in England: a background paper for the Mid Staffordshire public inquiry,* 2010, p.18. Accessed on 20 December 2010 at: www.midstaffspublicinquiry.com/hearings/s/120/week-two-15-18-nov-2010.

its predecessor, the Commission for Health Improvement, he had been told by government that the latter had been too independent.

In addition, the Healthcare Commission then had criteria for grading hospitals imposed upon it by the Department of Health. The Minister of Health at the time expressed concern about the number of trusts that had been given low grades; he requested that the Commission revisited the categories so that a more politically acceptable message would emerge. Sir Ian Kennedy noted that:

> When the Department of Health was told about what had happened at Stafford its reaction was that this was an awful story rather than it being an opportunity to shape up the NHS. My experience of the Department of Health is that they have a tendency to shoot the messenger. The politicians were most interested in how any story would be received and this was also true of Mid Staffordshire.[19]

In 2012, the House of Commons Public Accounts Committee was scathing about the Care Quality Commission. It is worth quoting from its conclusions:

> The Commission has more responsibilities but less money than its predecessors. Despite this it has consistently failed to spend its budget because of delays in filling staff vacancies. It is overseen by the Department of Health (the Department), which underestimated the scale of the task it had set in requiring the Commission to merge three bodies at the same time as taking on an expanded role. The Commission did not act quickly on vital issues such as information from whistleblowers. Neither did it deal with problems effectively, and the Department is only now taking action. We have serious concerns about the Commission's governance, leadership and culture. A Board member, Commission staff, and representatives of the health and adult social care sectors have all been critical of how the Commission is run.
>
> Neither the Commission nor the Department have defined what success would look like in regulating health and adult social care. This makes it hard for us to know whether the Commission has the resources it needs to operate effectively. In addition, while the Commission reports what it does, it does not measure the quality or impact of its work. Where information is available, it is not presented in a way that allows the public to make meaningful comparisons between care providers. As a result, the public are unclear what the Commission's role is and lack confidence that it is an effective regulator.[20]

What is disturbing is that it could be argued that the failing organisation depicted by the Commission is exactly the logical result of what the Department of Health set up and wanted. The Department has never wanted a Commission that would

---

19 'Deaths figure "removed from Stafford Hospital report".' *BBC News*, 4 May 2011. Accessed on 24 July 2011 at: www.bbc.co.uk/news/uk-england-stoke-staffordshire-13288896.

20 House of Commons Public Accounts Committee. *The Care Quality Commission: regulating the quality and safety of health and adult social care*. London: TSO, 2012, p.3.

expose too many failings either in the NHS – because of the political embarrassment – or amongst private sector care providers, in whom the government places so much store and is increasingly in tow to.

The role of the Care Quality Commission is set out more fully in Chapter 8.

HEALTH AND SAFETY EXECUTIVE

When the safety of NHS patients is put at risk by poor practice, and in particular poor systems of work (as opposed to individual clinical judgements), the Health and Safety Executive (HSE) could consider prosecution under, for example, s.3 of the Health and Safety at Work Act 1974.

There are indeed prosecutions in the case of individual mishaps, such as patients falling from windows, being scalded on radiators or dying when caught in bed rails. One might not categorise one-off incidents as coming necessarily within adult protection, but might do so if they recur with regularity and vulnerable people are particularly at risk.

It is perhaps noteworthy, however, that prosecutions appear not to have followed when health and safety breaches have been wholesale – for example, systemic abandonment of good standards of care and infection control and maintenance of equipment. This is even though such systemic defects are about failures in a system of work, which is the province of the HSE.

The role of HSE is analysed in Chapter 21.

MANSLAUGHTER

Where death has resulted from grossly negligent or reckless practice, manslaughter charges may be possible – either against individuals or against an organisation (e.g. an NHS trust) corporately.

Charges have been considered, and brought, in a few circumstances in the NHS involving grossly negligent individuals. But not in obvious cases of systemic neglect which call out for prosecution – such as at Stoke Mandeville Hospital, Maidstone and Tunbridge Wells NHS Trust or Stafford Hospital. This is considered in Chapter 7.

Militating against such prosecutions are at least two things. First, there is political sensitivity. If an NHS chief executive makes disastrous cuts to the standards of care, under acute and threatening pressure from the strategic health authority or Department of Health centrally, fingers will start to point back to senior civil servants and even ministers. Politically, central government will pull every string to stop such a turn of events.

Second, for the police and Crown Prosecution Service, taking on an NHS trust – which evidence tends to suggest will typically be large, defensive, obstructive and disingenuous – represents a daunting prospect, in terms both of ultimate success and committal of resources to investigate and to put together the evidence. The author has been informed by various police contacts that this is why a manslaughter case is much more likely in respect of neglect in a care home than in an NHS hospital.

Some of the care, neglect and death reported in the last 15 years has called out for a manslaughter case to be brought. Even a corporate manslaughter case, in which nobody is sent to prison but a fine exacted and reputation harmed, could have an extremely beneficial effect.

The law of manslaughter is covered in Chapter 21.

WILFUL NEGLECT OR ILL-TREATMENT

The separate offences of wilful neglect and ill-treatment can be charged if the person being ill-treated or wilfully neglected lacks mental capacity in relation to the care being given them, or has a mental disorder. The offences come under both the Mental Capacity Act 2005 and the Mental Health Act 1983. The offences are associated with strengths and weaknesses, which are juxtaposed in Chapter 21.

A glance at the cases prosecuted under these offences tends to suggest the same pattern as for manslaughter: NHS hospitals would seem to be barely represented, compared to care homes. For the reasons given in the next chapter, this is not because wilful neglect is absent from our hospitals.

NEGLIGENCE AND HUMAN RIGHTS CASES

When injury or death has resulted, civil negligence cases may also be possible if the poor practice can be shown to have been at least a substantial cause.

In addition, some of the highly neglectful care described above suggests clear human rights issues – for instance, under article 3 of the European Convention on Human Rights (right not to be subjected to inhuman and degrading treatment) and article 8 (right to respect for private life, including physical and psychological integrity; see 2.4), and indeed even article 2 (right to life). It has been reported, for example, that the Mid Staffordshire NHS Foundation Trust has settled numbers of compensation cases out of court, on human rights and negligence grounds.[21]

Human rights and negligence are explained Chapters 4 and 25 respectively.

JUDICIAL REVIEW

Judicial review is a type of legal case, through which the decision making of public bodies can be challenged.

In the context of neglect in the health services, one use of judicial review could be to challenge the decisions of public bodies – such as the police, Crown Prosecution Service, Care Quality Commission and Health and Safety Executive – about decisions not to investigate or prosecute certain types of occurrence, including

---

21   Leigh Day & Co. 'All Stafford hospital claims accepted.' *News*, 17 November 2010. Accessed on 20 December 2010 at: www.leighday.co.uk/News/2010/November-2010/All-Stafford-Hospital-claims-accepted.

large-scale deaths in hospitals (such as at Stoke Mandeville Hospital, Maidstone and Tunbridge Wells NHS Trust and Stafford Hospital).

Such cases clearly can be threatened and brought. For instance, a judicial review threat was used to force the government in 2009 to set up an independent inquiry into the Mid Staffordshire NHS Foundation Trust.[22] Likewise, it was used to challenge the Crown Prosecution Service over its decision not to prosecute anybody following the death by drowning of a person with learning disabilities in a care home.[23]

There is an argument that specialist lawyers should be looking more closely at this whole issue.

FINANCIAL HARM AND ABUSE: NHS CONTINUING HEALTH CARE

A footnote to the above comes in the form of NHS continuing health care. In a nutshell, the reason why this issue should be regarded as involving financial abuse is nothing to do with the political and moral question as to who should fund long-term health care – the individual or the State. But it is everything to do with a failure of transparency, fairness and adherence to the law.

The financial abuse arises twofold. First, at the level of central government, which has consistently refused to clarify the law, left matters opaque and, behind the scenes, encouraged local NHS bodies to extricate themselves from paying for long-term health care needs.

Second, the opacity means that, at local level, NHS bodies have been able to indulge in arbitrary and unfair decision making. Worse, insofar as there are ascertainable procedural rules in government directions and guidance, the NHS at local level often breaks them, usually with impunity, thereby making clearly unlawful decisions not to pay for people's care.

HEALTH SERVICES MUST BE PROVIDED FREE OF CHARGE UNLESS OTHERWISE SPECIFIED

Unless otherwise specified, in legal provisions for prescription charges, health services under the NHS Act 2006 must be provided free of charge.[24]

Yet for more than 15 years, many NHS providers – encouraged fully but quietly by the government – have gone out of their way to try to avoid providing and paying for 'NHS continuing health care'. This does not mean that the NHS has charged for the care, but that it has simply refused to provide it. This has resulted in many, largely older, people having to use up their savings and sell their houses in order to pay for care that should have been free.

---

22   Leigh Day & Co. 'Judicial reviews and the Mid Staffordshire inquiries.' *News*, 12 May 2010. Accessed on 23 November 2012 at: www.leighday.co.uk/Our-expertise/human-rights/Mid-Staffordshire-Inquiry/Judicial-reviews-and-the-Mid-Staffordshire-inquiri.

23   *Rowley v Director of Public Prosecutions* [2003] EWHC 693 (Admin).

24   National Health Service Act 2006, s.1.

TURNING AWAY OLDER PEOPLE FROM NHS CARE WITH NO TRANSPARENT DEBATE AND POLICY

As already noted, since at least the late 1980s, many long-stay NHS beds have been closed and older people with chronic health needs have gone elsewhere, largely to nursing homes. The theory was that they would still be the responsibility of the NHS and that their nursing home placements would be fully paid by the health service, and therefore be free of charge – just as hospital stays would be.

It has not worked out like this. Even for people with clearly complex and multiple health needs, the NHS began to say that they had 'social care' rather than 'health care' needs, in which case, if they had the money, they would have to pay nursing home bills themselves.

This has meant that whilst the NHS does still fully fund some patients, many others have wrongly been denied NHS 'continuing health care' status. They have instead had to pay for nursing home care from their savings and the equity of their homes; alternatively, local councils have had to pick up the tab of those lacking financial resources of their own.

This was, and is, not an official policy; it has been achieved on the quiet with no transparent, political debate, in or out of Parliament. It is this that has made it so objectionable; financial necessity and transparent, if controversial, policymaking are one thing, disingenuousness and political cowardice quite another. But what was happening did not go totally unnoticed. By 1994, the Health Service Ombudsman had issued a special report, aghast at the abandonment by Leeds Health Authority of patients with complex medical needs.[25]

In 1999, the Court of Appeal intervened in the case of Pamela Coughlan, again catching the NHS red-handed in denying responsibility for a person with clear health care needs.[26]

HEALTH SERVICE OMBUDSMAN'S CONDEMNATION OF SYSTEM; REPAYMENT OF LARGE SUMS OF MONEY

Hospitals, though, with the bit between their teeth, were undeterred in their determination to turn away the elderly. The ombudsman's continuing and many investigations culminated in a highly critical overview report issued in 2003.[27] It resulted in the Department of Health, reluctantly, having to repay £180–200 million to people or their families unlawfully charged for nursing home care.[28]

With safeguarding in mind, one should not, by the way, pass over this figure lightly; this was a huge amount of money exacted, essentially unlawfully, from vulnerable, elderly and dying people. Furthermore, it did not come about as a result of an honest mistake; it was the consequence of a chaotic and opaque system overseen and perpetuated quietly and deliberately by the Department of Health. As

---

25   Health Service Commissioner. *Failure to provide long term NHS care for brain damaged patient.* London: HMSO, 1994.

26   *R v North and East Devon Health Authority, ex p Coughlan* [1999] 2 CCLR 285 (Court of Appeal).

27   Health Service Ombudsman. *NHS funding for long term care.* London: TSO, 2003.

28   Womack, S. 'Elderly care blunders cost NHS £180m.' *Daily Telegraph,* 13 February 2008.

the ombudsman put it in her 2003 report, the system was not fair and transparent, the guidance was continually misinterpreted and misapplied, and injustice and hardship had resulted.[29]

Given that the government had encouraged the NHS to deny people the free care to which they were entitled, this should have been labelled financial abuse. Of course, it wasn't. It was left to a relative on a BBC *Panorama* programme to put her finger on it as 'State-sanctioned theft'.[30]

New guidance was issued in 2007 and then reissued in 2009.[31] Even so, this guidance is arguably inconsistent with major legal case law[32] – and there are undoubtedly many people in nursing homes, and in their own homes, who should have NHS continuing health care status but are denied it.

There has therefore been an inexorable and continuing shift of responsibility for people's health care needs away from the NHS. The unwritten policy and practice are nothing to do with whether a person has health care needs or not, and everything to do with the Department of Health's and local NHS trusts' determination to reduce their responsibility for older people with chronic health care needs.

In other words, the recategorising of health care as social care has no basis in diagnosis or condition, but is almost entirely political. This, in turn, means that NHS bodies will fight tooth and nail to avoid paying for people's care, hoping that they will die or their families give up. Irrespective of the law.

CONTINUING UNLAWFUL CHARGING BY THE NHS OF VULNERABLE PEOPLE

Nine years later, and the Department of Health has failed properly to remedy these faults, although some token effort has been made. Elderly people continue to be charged very large sums of money (by local authorities or care homes) as a result of decision making which, on examination, is often grossly flawed.

In the following case, it took seven years for the NHS to accept that it was responsible, by which time the patient was dead.

Seven-year fight to establish lawful funding for former auxiliary nurse who had suffered a stroke and was immobile, incontinent and unable to communicate. A family was repaid £117,000 after a former auxiliary nurse had been wrongly charged care home fees. The 88-year-old woman, who had suffered a stroke – and was immobile, incontinent and unable to communicate – died a few days after the NHS conceded that it should have funded her. The family had fought for seven years to establish what seemed obvious: that she was an NHS responsibility.[33]

---

29   Health Service Ombudsman. *NHS funding for long term care.* London: TSO, 2003, para 38.

30   BBC *Panorama*. 'A growing scandal.' First broadcast 26 July 2006.

31   Department of Health. *National Framework for NHS continuing health care and NHS funded nursing care.* London: DH, 2009.

32   Clements, L. 'NHS Funding for continuing care in England the revised (2009) Guidance.' *Journal of Social Care and Neurodisability 1*, 1, 2010, pp.39–47.

33   Williams, L. 'Halewood family awarded £117,000 for wrongly paid care home costs NHS should have funded.' *Liverpool Daily Post*, 10 November 2011.

In the following case, it was also a question of fighting tooth and nail.

£70,000 repaid for four years' care. Cornwall and the Isles of Scilly Primary Care Trust had to repay nearly £70,000 to a family who had been wrongly having to pay care home fees for four years for their female relative. She had dementia and had suffered a stroke and entered a nursing home in 2006, before dying in 2010. The NHS had conceded, nine months before her death, that she was eligible for NHS funding. But, after the family had requested a review, the Trust further ruled that she should have been funded from the beginning of 2008. With legal assistance, the family appealed to the strategic health authority, which ruled that she had been eligible for the entire four-year period and that her estate should be reimbursed all the care fees paid, amounting to almost £70,000.

The Primary Care Trust's statement speaks volumes about the sheer disingenuousness surrounding the whole issue of continuing care. To suggest that cash-strapped trusts welcome challenges such as this is, of course, nonsense:

> We are always happy to look into any cases where relatives feel the NHS should fund care as each case is different. When someone is deemed to have a primary health need, care is funded by the NHS after an assessment by a nurse. All of these cases are reviewed regularly to ensure that the care provided is appropriate, safe and of high quality. Where relatives do want funding decisions reviewed, we follow national guidance on the appeal process for NHS funding of care.[34]

It should be remembered that these cases involve large sums of money, which the NHS forces people to pay, without qualm, until challenged.

For instance, a woman with dementia was wrongly charged £90,000 for care home fees which should have been paid by East Lancashire Primary Care Trust over a five-year period. She was confused, agitated and required constant care. Her family fought the case and won, understandably believing that the only reason she was in the nursing home was because she required 24-hour nursing care. However, they needed help from lawyers to do it.[35]

Another protracted battle of four years' duration resulted in £100,000 being paid back to the family of a woman with dementia, but only after they had been obliged to sell her home. The family had to make a number of appeals and enlist the assistance of lawyers. Despite all this, NHS Sussex had the sheer nerve to state that the process was straightforward and accessible, that families should not go to lawyers (who would be taking a cut of the repayment), and that the NHS is only too happy to pay it back:

> There is a straightforward and easily accessible process for assessing the health needs of individuals. NHS Sussex does not believe legal support is required to complete this process and would encourage anyone to get in touch directly. NHS Sussex is keen that when patients and their families are

34   'Family win back £70,000 care home fees after NHS appeal.' *Western Morning News*, 3 May 2012.

35   Magill, P. 'Haslingden dementia patient was overcharged by £90,000.' *Lancashire Telegraph*, 16 April 2012.

eligible for funding they receive all the money they are entitled to, without having to spend some of it on legal fees paid to solicitors.[36]

In the author's view, the abusive aspects of NHS continuing health care include not just the actual cavalier approach to older people's money and the law but also the misleading and disingenuous representations and statements made about it. In this particular case, for instance, the family only went to lawyers because they had run into such obstructive bureaucracy.[37]

Even the belated concession by government, some years ago, that the NHS would at least contribute something financially to people's nursing needs in care homes was also disingenuous. Many of those residents should have had all their needs met and paid for by the NHS; and, in any case, the weekly hundred pounds or so barely makes inroads into the huge weekly fees payable for nursing home care. Disingenuousness is too kind a word. As Claire Rayner, health campaigner, put it: they said they would make people's nursing care free in future; they were lying.[38]

36   Ryan, S. 'Family win battle with NHS over dementia bill.' *The Argus*, 20 April 2012.
37   Williams, B. 'Continuing Healthcare: deadline looms for "secret" care fund.' *The Guardian*, 18 August 2012.
38   Rayner, C. 'Claire Rayner: I'm leaving the Labour Party after 50 faithful years.' *The Independent*, 26 September 2001.

The National Health Service: systemic poor care and neglect

Key points
    Nature of poor care and neglect
Main factors underpinning systemic neglect in the NHS
    Evidence of systemic nature of poor care and neglect
    Mismatch between the model of care and the needs of older people
    Persistence of poor care made possible by denial, disingenuousness
        and doublespeak
    Lack of accountability for poor care and neglect
    Fear, bullying and whistleblowing
Evidence of systemic poor care and neglect in hospitals
    Overview of the evidence of poor care and neglect
    Sample list of evidence of poor care and neglect within the NHS
Perpetration and persistence of systemic poor care and neglect
    Unevidenced and harmful reduction of hospital beds
    Rehabilitation and intermediate care
    Care pathways, payment by results and patients as market commodities
Lack of transparency
    Meaningless language, doublespeak and undermining of clinical integrity
    Manipulating information and statistics
    Pay rises for self-assessed good care, whilst patients die
    Denial and concealment by politicians and the Department of Health
    Department of Health's indifference to poor care and neglect: from
        chief executive downward
Lack of responsibility and accountability
    Lack of accountability within the senior management caste
    Accountability and law
Whistleblowing in the NHS
Corruption of public institutions and undermining of trust
    Corruption of public life, morals and trust in the context of the NHS
    Pervasiveness of corruption of integrity
    Plain cheating
    Transparency and accountability for those in positions of power
    Typical examples in the NHS of corruption of public life
    Moral corruption and where it leads
    Fiction, fear, doublethink – and enemies of the State

KEY POINTS

In order to understand what it is that safeguarding is up against, we need to understand the nature of the poor care and neglect that is all too often under the noses, daily, of health and social care practitioners in hospitals. Poor care and neglect about which, persistently, not enough is done and safeguarding is not invoked.

In summary, this chapter shows a clear nexus between (a) the overwhelming evidence of systemic failings, (b) an inappropriate model of care being increasingly applied to older people, (c) denial that anything is amiss, (d) lack of accountability, and (e) a culture of fear and bullying within the NHS, emanating from the top of the Department of Health and resulting in the savage treatment of whistleblowers.

It points out that if this is happening in a State-run institution, the moral, legal and political stakes are greatly raised. And that the widespread denial, lying and lack of accountability, together with the persecution of those within the NHS who raise concerns about patient care, represents a significant corruption of public life.

Note. It must be emphasised that the point of this chapter is not to condemn the NHS. First, because there remains a great deal of good care, even for older people, although this is being fast eroded. Second, because the NHS is such a venerated and fine institution and needs saving from a new generation of managers and from politicians who are steadily but surely destroying an ethos of public service, care, compassion and dedication – and thereby cranking up levels of poor care and neglect for the most vulnerable of patients.

NATURE OF POOR CARE AND NEGLECT

By way introduction to this chapter, poor care and neglect includes patients not being helped to eat and drink and suffering severe dehydration and malnutrition, patients drinking out of flower vases in desperation, and hospital doctors resorting to prescribing tap water in patients' notes, in order to ensure they are given something to drink.

Or patients who do not receive adequate care to prevent painful and lethal pressure sores down to the bone, who are left in agony and denied pain relief, or who are told to defecate and urinate in bed and left lying in that bodily waste for hours. Or allowed to fall, fall and fall again with finally fatal results, without a risk assessment – or with one, which has been ignored in practice.

Patients are moved from ward to ward for non-clinical reasons, leading to an undermining of continuity of care, of clinical effectiveness and of care and safety. Patients are deprived of help to bathe, to shower or to otherwise wash. They are deprived of care of hair, nails and teeth – and left in filthy sheets.

They might simply not be spoken to. They might be left naked in bed, covered from head to foot in dried faeces – in full view of others. Or, confused due to infection, they are left standing on the ward, naked from the waist down, in front of other visitors and patients – with nurses simply taking no notice and surprised when a relative asks that something be done about this.

Men with dementia might be dressed by nurses in women's frilly pink nightwear – the patients' own clothes having been lost or continually soiled, which, in turn, is because the ward has run out of appropriate continence aids. Older patients with complex needs might not receive appropriate assessments by doctors and nurses with the relevant skills and fail to receive adequate, or even any, rehabilitation from therapists.

Patients – confused or ill (or even dying) – risk being discharged, unplanned, in the middle of the night. Or forced to wait from 9am to 9pm in the hospital discharge lounge, without food or drink – finally arriving at the care home or back at their own home, dehydrated, wrapped in blankets – naked underneath, with soiled incontinence pads, full of dried faeces.

MAIN FACTORS UNDERPINNING SYSTEMIC NEGLECT IN THE NHS

A number of points can be linked together to explain what is going on, why and what safeguarding, as an activity, is up against.

There is a clear link between (a) the overwhelming evidence of systemic failings, (b) an inappropriate model of care for older people, (c) denial that anything is amiss, (d) lack of accountability, (e) a culture of fear and bullying within the NHS, emanating from the top of the Department of Health and resulting in the savage treatment of whistleblowers.

EVIDENCE OF SYSTEMIC NATURE OF POOR CARE AND NEGLECT

First, the evidence of the past 15 years shows, without doubt, that poor care and neglect are systemic within NHS hospitals. This does not mean, either logically or in practice, that there is not plenty of good practice as well. All it means is that poor care and neglect are sufficiently widespread, across many hospitals, to count as systemic. And it is this widespread poor care, particularly of older people with complex needs, that, at its worst, provides a fertile soil for outright neglect.

There is thus an all-important logical error to avoid. It is a trap laid frequently by the Department of Health and other deniers of, or apologists for, unacceptable and inhumane care. The error is to suppose that the existence of significant levels of good practice means that bad practice either does not exist or is isolated.

For those involved in safeguarding, and the priorities they should be making, some clear thinking on this issue is needed.

It has been pointed out that if only 2 per cent of inpatients receive poor care, this is still a lot of people.

In order to gauge seriousness, we have to factor in not just the incidence of poor care but also the consequences. It has been asked how many times is it acceptable to leave patients in urine or faeces – ten times a month or 20? Likewise, how often is it all right for staff to squeal, giggle and ignore confused and semi-naked patients wandering the corridors at night?[1]

In any case, once you start to narrow down the group of patients involved to the more vulnerable, the statistics might look far worse. For instance, many patients who might have suffered poor care would be unable to participate in such a survey, for the good reason that they have died soon after or otherwise lack the ability or capacity to participate.

Thus, when relatives of 1000 patients were asked about inpatient care, only 23 per cent were satisfied with the help given to patients with food and drink, 30 per cent with bowel and bladder care, and 32 per cent with assistance with personal hygiene.[2]

A further example of such an approach is the work carried out by the National Confidential Enquiry into Patient Outcome and Death. It looked at 800 older people who had received surgery and died within 30 days. Its conclusion was that only 36 per cent of those patients had received acceptable care.[3]

The Department of Health continues to ignore such serious statistics, to ignore their implications or to ignore both.

MISMATCH BETWEEN THE MODEL OF CARE AND THE NEEDS OF OLDER PEOPLE

Second, the poor care exists and persists because of a refusal of politicians, the Department of Health and NHS trust chief executives to heed, and to act on, the evidence about the needs of older people in hospital. They continue to plan and organise hospital services as though older people with complex needs barely existed. The consequence is that the type, quantity and quality of beds, assessment, treatment and care available are inadequate.

PERSISTENCE OF POOR CARE MADE POSSIBLE BY DENIAL, DISINGENUOUSNESS AND DOUBLESPEAK

Third, the only reason this state of affairs persists is because of widespread denial, disingenuousness, concealment and lies on the part of those running the health service at senior levels, nationally and locally. Flowing from this is an all-pervasive culture of doublespeak and deceit which is forced on to the NHS workforce, both lower-level management and frontline staff, and on to patients.

---

1   Ken Jarrold, quoted in: Patients' Association. *Listen to patients, speak up for change.* London: Patients' Association, 2010, p.3.

2   Alzheimer's Society. *Counting the cost: caring for people with dementia on hospital wards.* London: Alzheimer's Society, 2009.

3   Wilkinson, K., Martin, I.C., Gough, M.J. *et al. An age old problem: a review of the care received by elderly patients undergoing surgery.* London: National Confidential Enquiry into Patient Outcome and Death, 2010, p.5.

The extent of this web of disingenuousness, and the size of the problem it is covering up, is not commonly appreciated.

LACK OF ACCOUNTABILITY FOR POOR CARE AND NEGLECT
Fourth, with this denial and deceit comes a lack of accountability. This means that what should be regarded as monstrous deeds and omissions becomes the norm.

FEAR, BULLYING AND WHISTLEBLOWING
Fifth, closely linked to denial and lack of accountability is the extraordinary culture within the NHS of fear, bullying and anxiety which leads too often to the ruthless and savage treatment of those NHS staff who do try responsibly to raise concerns about poor care and neglect. This culture is perpetrated directly from the centre – from the Department of Health – downward.

PERPETRATION BY THE STATE: RAISED MORAL, LEGAL AND POLITICAL STAKES
Sixth, and following on from these points, what makes the above so striking is that this systemic poor care and neglect is State-perpetrated. This means two things. That the moral, legal and political stakes are greatly raised. But also that something can be done: it means poor care and neglect are not part of an inexorable law of physics but man-made and something within our control.

Which is where safeguarding should come into play. Somehow, it has to try to do what it can in tackling what has become a problem – monstrous and unconscionable – integral to NHS care.

EVIDENCE OF SYSTEMIC POOR CARE AND NEGLECT IN HOSPITALS
The problem of neglect, in terms of the care provided in its hospitals – particularly for older people – is of an order of magnitude. The evidence of this, stretching over at least the past 15 years, is overwhelming. In quantity, nature and gravity, it is astonishing. Astonishing that we should have allowed this to happen and equally so that we done little effective about it. The evidence suggests things are getting worse.

The important point to understand seems to be that systemic neglect in the NHS arises not from individual, maverick practices but from a soil of widespread poor care afforded to mainly, but not only, older people. And it is from this poor care that cultures of neglect grow rapidly in particular hospitals as a whole or in particular wards.

The poor care has taken such root because of political and management failure to acknowledge – let alone face up to – the needs of elderly patients with underlying multiple pathology, admitted to hospital following an acute episode. The fiction that beds and staff (numbers and competencies) can be continually reduced – because somehow elderly people with acute and complex needs can be treated 'in the community' – is precisely that. It is not grounded on the evidence or in reality.

First, many do need to be in hospital. Second, to the extent that some needs could be managed – or, of course, prevented – in the community, the community services and facilities are underfunded and too often not in place.

The evidence points to widespread and systemic poor care and neglect of patients within our hospitals, in particular of elderly patients. It is systemic in the sense that it is routine and widespread; this does not, of course, mean that there is not plenty of good practice remaining in the NHS. But it is a fundamental logical, as well as empirical, error to suppose that the existence of the good precludes necessarily the bad.

The reason for summarising the evidence in some detail is to make quite clear two points about safeguarding. First, it is not open to central government, local NHS trusts and local authorities to plead ignorance and to excuse their inaction. Second, the evidence shows that, over this 15-year period, the safeguarding of vulnerable adults in the care of the health service from institutional neglect has been ineffective.

Furthermore, the predisposing factors that have come to light in the evidence tend to be common across the NHS. In part, they seem to be an unintended, though not unpredictable, consequence of central government policy which continues to place a greater priority on financial, performance and political targets – delivered in the form of computer tick boxes – than on humane and dignified care. This is not idle contention. It has been pointed out by the House of Commons Health Committee that government policy has contributed to 'appalling care':

> Government policy has too often given the impression that there are priorities, notably hitting targets (particularly for waiting lists, and Accident and Emergency waiting), achieving financial balance and attaining Foundation Trust status, which are more important than patient safety. This has undoubtedly, in a number of well documented cases, been a contributory factor in making services unsafe.[4]

OVERVIEW OF THE EVIDENCE OF POOR CARE AND NEGLECT
The evidence is incontrovertible and raises serious doubts as to whether safeguarding policies and practice, both national and locally, have come anywhere near to treating it seriously, let alone making inroads.

A book published in 2011 considered in detail the evidence for poor care and neglect, particularly of older people, since 1997. In particular, it brought together different types of source. These included the reports of regulatory bodies, independent inquiries, parliamentary committees, voluntary bodies, National Audit Office, individual press accounts, coroners' findings and the many comments and

---

4   House of Commons Health Committee. *Patient safety: sixth report of Session 2008–09.* HC 151-I. London: TSO, 2009, pp.7, 10.

accounts now posted on the internet on sites such as NHS Choices or Patient Opinion.

The book also considers the implications of each of these types of evidence, in terms of reliability and how widespread a problem is revealed. In particular, it notes that we have no reassurance that the reported scandals are anything like the whole picture, and that it is more by chance than through any safeguards in the system that we know the details of the terrible care provided at the Mid Staffordshire NHS Foundation Trust.

Which may well mean that the situation is worse than even the reported evidence suggests. After all, it was only determined relatives, a group called Cure the NHS, who forced the government to appoint an independent inquiry into Staffordshire, the greatest scandal of them all. Without the group, the details of the inhumane and lethal care at the hospital would never have become known. And, in 2012, over half of NHS Trust chief executives believed that the regulatory system would not identify another scandal, even on the scale of Mid Staffordshire.[5]

The book concludes that a compelling picture emerges. The different sources of evidence tie up and are corroborative of one another. It draws these conclusions about the evidence:

> The question that needs answering is twofold: how serious, and how widespread, is the poor and neglectful care depicted within this body of evidence? The seriousness of what occurs is not in dispute; the sticking point is the prevalence. The rest of the answer seems to be that, taken on their own, none of these sources would be enough to point conclusively to a systemic issue. Taken together, however, they make a powerful argument, not least because they corroborate one another. It is a bit like verifying an observation, by making it from more than one angle and using different instruments...
>
> The combination accords with the thesis of this book; there is plenty of good care provided in our health services, as well as an unacceptable and substantial stratum of bad...
>
> In summary, this is about joining up the dots. They are scattered, as evidence, all over the sheet of paper. As always, care must be taken not to link them in the wrong way and end up with a misleading image. But there are so many points, forming such a salient pattern, that the picture emerging is only too clear.[6]

---

5   'Trust chiefs fear regulators would not spot scandal.' *Health Service Journal*, 26 July 2012.
6   Mandelstam, M. *How we treat the sick: neglect and abuse in our health services.* London: Jessica Kingsley Publishers, 2011, pp.46, 57, 58.

SAMPLE LIST OF EVIDENCE OF POOR CARE AND NEGLECT WITHIN THE NHS
A summary of the evidence includes the following. It is by no means exhaustive; even so, it is a lengthy list, to help dispel any doubts that might linger about whether there is a hidden safeguarding scandal in our hospitals.

2000: Not because they are old. In 2000, the Health Advisory Service published *Not because they are old*. It highlighted a string of failings in the hospital care of older people. These comprised deficiencies in the physical fabric of wards, shortage of basic supplies and technical equipment, staff shortages, lack of assistance in helping people to eat and drink, diminution of dignity (related to personal hygiene and dressing) because of the physical environment but also staff attitudes, inadequate communication with patients and relatives because of time pressures on staff – and so on.[7]

2000: North Lakeland NHS Trust: tying people up on commodes. Also in 2000, at the North Lakeland NHS Trust, practices reported on by the Commission for Health Improvement included the following: a patient being restrained by being tied to a commode, patients being denied ordinary food, patients being fed while sitting on commodes and patients being deliberately deprived of clothing and blankets. An external review had already concluded that the occupational therapy department had made a wooden board and harness for use as a restraint device.[8]

2001: Standing Nursing and Midwifery Advisory Committee: dignity not being preserved. Already by 2001 the Department of Health's own Standing Nursing and Midwifery Advisory Committee advised that a 'large critical literature has been amassed which shows that current standards of care often fail to preserve older people's dignity, privacy, autonomy and independence'. The Committee went on to point out that hospital nurses had, in principle, to attend not just to acute symptoms but also to the needs of the whole person including nutrition, tissue viability and promotion of independent activity. Yet it reported that the nursing care of older people was in practice deficient in such very fundamental aspects including the need for food, fluid, rest, activity and elimination, and recognition of people's psychological, mental health and rehabilitation needs. The Committee identified widespread problems in practice with:

- respect for older people's dignity
- promotion of choice, involvement and independence
- communication with older people and their carers
- individualised care and its management
- continence
- dementia
- mental health
- mobility
- nutrition and hydration
- pain management

---

7   Health Advisory Service. *Not because they are old: an independent inquiry into the care of older people on acute wards in general hospitals.* London: HAS, 2000, pp.iii–iv.

8   Commission for Health Improvement. *Investigation into the North Lakeland NHS Trust, November.* London: CHI, 2000, p.29.

- palliative care
- pressure damage prevention and management.[9]

2002: East Kent Hospitals NHS Trust: overcrowding and poor care. Reporting on East Kent Hospitals NHS Trust, the Commission for Health Improvement found that overcrowding in the hospital's accident and emergency department put patients at clinical risk and staff under unremitting pressure. Patients were simply admitted to any bed, 'causing staff to care for patients they may not have the skills or training to care for and forcing doctors to seek out their patients throughout the hospital'.

The overcrowding and pressure resulted in other compromises in care. Trays regularly came to the ward with dirty cutlery. Food was often cold. There were insufficient toilets and washing facilities for the number of patients, who were sometimes physically examined in open areas. Patients might be left in corridors for days rather than hours. It was difficult for doctors to get to outlying wards; this caused delays in ordering treatments, obtaining drugs and discharging patients; one patient waited over 14 hours to have a cannula replaced because of difficulty getting in touch with the responsible doctor.[10]

2002: Gosport War Memorial Hospital: undignified care and reckless administration of palliative care medication for people who were not dying. Likewise, in 2002, the Commission for Health Improvement found inadequate safeguards in Portsmouth for the prescribing of medicines for older people, such that concerns had arisen about the deaths of a number of patients. There was no evidence of a policy to ensure appropriate prescription and dose escalation of powerful pain-relieving drugs. Experts commissioned by the police had serious concerns about anticipatory prescribing. There was inappropriate combined subcutaneous administration of diamorphine, midazolam and haloperidol which risked excessive sedation and respiratory depression leading to death. No clear guidelines were available for staff to guard against their making assumptions that patients had been admitted for palliative rather than rehabilitative care. In other words, there was a danger of unnecessarily killing off patients.

Staff failed to recognise potential adverse effects of prescribed medicines. Clinical managers failed routinely to monitor and supervise care on the ward. Wider concerns about care included continence management and claims by relatives that patients were automatically catheterised to save nursing time, patients not being dressed in their own clothes (despite these having been clearly labelled) and physical transfers from one hospital to another involving lengthy waits, inadequate clothing and cover during the journey, and one patient being carried on nothing more than a sheet.[11]

2003: Rowan Ward, Manchester: abuse of elderly people with dementia. In 2003, it was revealed how staff had strayed far from the path of good care on Rowan Ward, part of the Manchester Mental Health and Social Care NHS Trust. Initial enquiries suggested that abuse of elderly people with dementia, over a period of several years, included hitting, slapping, stamping on feet, thumb twisting, intimidatory language and emotional abuse in the form of restricting food and playing on known anxieties of patients. The Commission

9   Standing Nursing and Midwifery Advisory Committee. *Caring for older people – a nursing priority: integrating knowledge, practice and values.* London: Department of Health, 2001, pp.17–18, 29.

10 Commission for Health Improvement. *Clinical performance review: East Kent Hospitals NHS Trust.* London: CHI, 2002, pp.5–10.

11 Commission for Healthcare Improvement. *Investigation into the Portsmouth Healthcare NHS Trust: Gosport War Memorial Hospital, July 2002.* London: CHI, 2002, pp.12–13, 22–23.

for Health Improvement was called in and confirmed that such practices had been taking place.[12]

2004: National Audit Office, reckless approach to infection control. The National Audit Office issued a report on patient safety and infection. It accurately drew attention to the fact that NHS trusts had taken their eye off the ball, and in effect anticipated precisely the scandals to come at Stoke Mandeville Hospital and at Maidstone and Tunbridge Wells NHS Trust.[13]

2006: Age Concern England on malnourishment and dehydration in hospitals. The report *Hungry to be heard* highlighted the fact that significant numbers of older people were suffering from malnourishment and dehydration in NHS hospitals.[14]

2006: Healthcare Commission: poor standards of care. The Healthcare Commission, Audit Commission and Commission for Social Care Inspection published a report called *Living well in later life*. Amongst its findings was evidence of ageism towards older people across all services. This included 'patronising and thoughtless treatment from staff', failure to take needs and aspirations of older people seriously, lack of dignity, lack of respect, poor standards of care on general hospital wards, being repeatedly moved between wards for non-clinical reasons, being cared for in mixed-sex bays or wards, having meals taken away before they could be eaten due to a lack of assistance, abuse and neglect. And so on. In addition, older people were concerned about access to health services in rural areas.[15]

2006: Cornwall Partnership NHS Trust: abuse of people with learning disabilities. The Healthcare Commission, together with the Commission for Social Care Inspection, reported on the Cornwall Partnership NHS Trust. A catalogue of poor and abusive care had come to light, which the NHS Trust itself had belatedly ascertained from members of staff, who reported having witnessed 64 incidents over a five-year period.

They included: staff hitting, pushing, shoving, dragging, kicking, secluding, belittling, mocking and goading people who used the Trust's services, withholding food, giving cold showers, over-zealous or premature use of restraint, poor attitude towards people who used services, poor atmosphere, roughness, care not being provided, a lack of dignity and respect, no privacy.[16]

2006: Mid Cheshire Hospitals NHS Trust: targets and culture undermining basic standards of care. The Healthcare Commission published its findings on the Mid Cheshire Hospitals NHS Trust. This included the fact that medication and pain relief were inadequate, and staff shortages affected adversely patient care which was described as generally sloppy. The management of beds focused primarily on the hitting of government-set targets, the system was not working in the interests of patients, and patients were moved to inappropriate wards to their clinical detriment. It was a culture of 'nurses who were rushed, short-staffed, stretched and not delivering basic standards of care'.

12   Commission for Health Improvement. *Investigation into matters arising from care on Rowan Ward, Manchester Mental Health and Social Care Trust, September 2003*. London: CHI, 2003, p.8.

13   National Audit Office. *Improving patient care by reducing the risk of hospital acquired infection: a progress report*. London: NAO, 2004.

14   Age Concern England. *Hungry to be heard: the scandal of malnourished older people in hospital*. London: ACE, 2006.

15   Healthcare Commission; Audit Commission; Commission for Social Care Inspection. *Living well in later life*. London: HC/AC/CSCI, 2006, Summary.

16   Commission for Social Care Inspection; Healthcare Commission. *Joint investigation into the provision of services for people with learning disabilities at Cornwall Partnership NHS Trust, July 2006*. London: HC/CSCI, 2006, p.31.

Drug rounds might be two hours late because of staff shortage, and medication simply left at patients' bedsides where it was either not taken or taken late. Nutritional drinks were likewise left, becoming warm and undrinkable. Crash trolleys were not properly stocked; even after the Healthcare Commission had raised this issue, the problem persisted seven weeks later.

Assistance with eating and drinking was provided only 50 per cent of the time it was needed. Call bells would be out of reach or not answered by staff. Patients could not get to the bathroom, commode or bedpan in time. Only about half of patients were cared for on appropriate wards; those on the wrong wards would be called 'outliers'. Patients were being moved throughout the evening, sometimes after midnight. These movements, for non-clinical reasons, contributed to the spread of infection, in the form of MRSA and *Clostridium difficile*.[17]

2006: Stoke Mandeville; 2007: Maidstone and Tunbridge Wells NHS Trust: pursuit of performance and financial targets, together with concealment of the problems, leads to scores of deaths from infection. In 2006 and 2007, the Healthcare Commission issued two reports concerning outbreaks of the bacterium *Clostridium difficile* in Buckinghamshire (Stoke Mandeville Hospital) and in Kent (Maidstone and Tunbridge Wells NHS Trust). In the former, poor infection control was associated with nearly 40 deaths; in the latter, with nearly 90 deaths.

What concerned the Healthcare Commission was that in both NHS trusts it appeared that, at board and chief executive level, the preoccupation was with finance and performance rather than infection control. This led to tardy and ineffective measures to control the infection once it had taken hold – including explicit disregarding of the advice offered by the infection control team.

More generally, this preoccupation with performance and finance led also to the factors that laid the ground for the infection to take such hold. These factors included running the hospitals with very high bed occupancy, moving patients from ward to ward for non-clinical reasons in order to meet accident and emergency targets (such moves spread infection and are clinically counter-indicated), reduced staffing levels, an autocratic style of management, staff frightened to speak out, stressed staff and managers, staff shortages, broken cleaning equipment, contaminated bedpans and commodes, lack of time to clean beds and mattresses, not taking patients to the lavatory, leaving patients in wet and soiled bedding for hours.[18]

2007: Help the Aged: absence of care and dignity for older people. In 2007, Help the Aged identified a number of factors contributing to dignity, including personal hygiene, eating and nutrition, privacy, communication, pain, autonomy, personal care, end of life, and social inclusion. It pointed out that ten years before, it had:

> uncovered a quiet outrage, of modern hospitals delivering archaic care, of professional care workers acting in an uncaring and inhuman way, of sophisticated health services not even delivering on the basics of toileting, mealtimes and communication… So now, after ten years of initiatives, plans, targets and frameworks, where do we stand…surely we have moved beyond the basics, the mere minimum entitlement in any decent society. Too often the answer is no…[19]

---

17   Healthcare Commission. *Investigation into Mid Cheshire Hospitals NHS Trust, January 2006*. London: HC, 2006, p.30.

18   See generally: Healthcare Commission. *Investigation into outbreaks of* Clostridium difficile *at Stoke Mandeville Hospital, Buckinghamshire Hospitals NHS Trust, July 2006*. London: HC, 2006. Also: Healthcare Commission. *Investigation into outbreaks of* Clostridium difficile *at Maidstone and Tunbridge Wells NHS Trust, October 2007*. London: HC, 2007.

19   Levenson, R. *The challenge of dignity in care: upholding the rights of the individual*. London: Help the Aged, 2007, p.4.

2007: Healthcare Commission: degrading treatment of patients. The Healthcare Commission highlighted common examples relating to dignity generally, on the basis of complaints received. These included patients not being spoken to in an appropriate manner, not being given proper information, consent not being sought, being left in soiled clothes, being exposed in an embarrassing manner, not being given appropriate food or help with eating and drinking, being placed in mixed-sex accommodation, being left in pain, being in a noisy nocturnal environment causing lack of sleep, using premises that are unclean and noisome (toilets and wards), suffering lack of protection of personal property including personal aids (hearing and visual), being subjected to abuse and violent behaviour.[20]

2007: Tameside Hospital, independent review: failures in most basic care. An independent review of care at Tameside Hospital was published, detailing a long list of failings collated by the Tameside Hospital Action Group. These included basic failures in nutrition, hydration, continence, personal hygiene, care of skin pressure areas, management of infection, nurses' competence. This is not to mention, also, intimidation by staff, dirty wards, alteration of patients' notes by staff, lack of communication from staff, shortage of staff, rudeness of staff, call bells out of reach, patients left to wet their beds and then being left in them – and so on.[21]

2007: Sutton and Merton NHS Primary Care Trust. The Healthcare Commission published its findings into events in the Sutton and Merton NHS Primary Care Trust. It found that the way in which people were cared for reflected convenience for the service providers rather than the needs of individual service users. This included regimented mealtimes, unsuitable accommodation and equipment, inappropriate restraint, inappropriate staff behaviour, serious incidents including incidents of assault and sexual offences, inadequate staffing (levels, training, risk management).[22]

2007: Mencap on treatment of people with learning disabilities in hospitals. The report *Death by indifference* highlights six patients with learning disabilities and the substandard treatment they received in hospital. Mencap argues that these cases indicate institutional discrimination against people with learning disabilities in the health service.[23]

2008: Mental Health Act Commission: basic evils relating to dignity and safety. The Mental Health Act Commission produced its biennial report of 2008. It felt impelled to make comparisons with the *Parliamentary Inquiry into Madhouses of 1815/6*. This had identified a number of 'basic evils' which the Commission had found alive and well and undermining people's dignity, privacy and safety. For instance, restrictions on bathing because of staff shortages, inappropriate restraint, a dying man being nursed in the dining room while other patients were having lunch (again, because of lack of staff), vulnerable women housed with predatory men, blinds to patients' rooms being kept open permanently for staff convenience, seclusion rooms with no privacy to use the toilet, new acute wards being run at *135 per cent* bed occupancy, with patients sleeping in day rooms and staff run off their feet, inappropriate use of closed circuit television, and a woman in seclusion deprived of sanitary protection whilst menstruating.[24]

---

20   Healthcare Commission. *Caring for dignity*. London: HC, 2007, p.14.
21   Fielding, F. (Professor Dame). *Independent review of older people's care at Tameside General Hospital*. Manchester: NHS North West, 2007, p.5.
22   Healthcare Commission. *Investigation into the service for people with learning disabilities provided by Sutton and Merton Primary Care Trust*. London: HC, 2007.
23   Mencap. *Death by indifference*. London: Mencap, 2007, p.2
24   Mental Health Act Commission. *Risk, rights, recovery: twelfth biennial report, 2005–2007*. London: MHAC, 2008, pp.10–11, 17–29.

2008: Independent inquiry into health care for people with learning disabilities. An independent inquiry, set up by the government following Mencap's report *Death by indifference*, points to people with learning disabilities receiving less effective health care treatment than others and to appalling examples of discrimination, abuse and neglect.[25]

2009: Nutrition Action Plan Delivery Board: continuing problems with basic nutrition in hospitals. The Board, a government quango, produced its annual and final report. It advised that there was a significant and continuing problem of malnutrition and help with eating and that official figures underestimated the prevalence of malnutrition in hospitals and care settings.[26]

2009: House of Commons Health Committee: report on patient safety and care. That same year saw the publication of a House of Commons Health Committee report on patient safety, drawing attention to what it considered to be widespread defects in the approach to patient safety and welfare in NHS trusts.[27]

2009: Patients' Association: more accounts of hospital neglect. The Association published *Patients not numbers, people not statistics*. It contained a number of accounts of neglectful patient care, drawn from the large number of accounts given to them by patients and relatives.

Claire Rayner, then President of the Association, summarised thus:

> For far too long now, the Patients' Association has been receiving calls on our Helpline from people wanting to talk about the dreadful, neglectful, demeaning, painful and sometimes downright cruel treatment their elderly relatives had experienced at the hands of NHS nurses. Some found it helped to talk to us, for they had had scant comfort from trying to make complaints or even seek explanations about what had happened to the people they loved, never mind the supportive counselling they should have done... The personal accounts given here are just a few of those brought to us. Some cannot be reported now because the surviving relatives have chosen to go to law, so are *sub judice* and some are frankly too distressing – even worse than those on which we have based our report.[28]

2009: Healthcare Commission: more degrading and harmful care. The Commission published a report based on the consistent complaints it was receiving about the following matters:

- patients addressed in an inappropriate manner or being spoken about as if they were not there
- patients not given proper information
- patients' consent not sought or their wishes considered
- patients left in soiled clothes or exposed in an embarrassing manner
- patients not given appropriate food or help with eating or drinking
- patients placed in mixed-sex accommodation

25 Michael, J. *Healthcare for all: report of the independent inquiry into access to healthcare for people with learning disabilities.* London: Department of Health, 2008, p.7.

26 Lishman, G. (Chair). *Nutrition Action Plan Delivery Board end of year progress report.* London: Department of Health, 2009, p.5.

27 House of Commons Health Committee. *Patient safety: sixth report of Session 2008–09.* HC 151-I. London: TSO, 2009, p.87.

28 Patients' Association. *Patients not numbers, people not statistics.* London: PA, 2009, p.3.

- patients left in pain
- a noisy environment at night causing a lack of sleep
- wards and toilets unclean and smelly
- lack of protection of personal property including hearing or sight aids
- patients subjected to abuse and violent behaviour.[29]

2009: Mid Staffordshire NHS Foundation Trust: shocking care standards and hundreds of deaths. The Commission reported multiple failures in care that compromised the dignity of patients. These included *not* doing the following things: answering call bells, assisting people to the toilet or commode, respecting privacy and dignity, giving medication promptly and appropriately and making sure it was taken, helping with food and drink, completing charts accurately, paying attention to skin and avoiding pressure sores.[30] The Commission's draft report originally referred to the number of 'excess' deaths being between 400 and 1200; the author of the report was forced to remove this figure.

2009: Mid Stafford, Thomé and Alberti reports. The Department of Health then published two reports, by Professor Alberti and Dr Thomé.[31]

2010: Mid Stafford independent inquiry: horrifying care over three- to four-year period. The subsequent independent inquiry into Mid Staffordshire NHS Foundation Trust, which reported in 2010, focused explicitly at the outset on the headings in the Department of Health's document *Essence of care*, nine years after the latter's original publication date and seven since its revision.

It found deficiencies in continence and bladder and bowel care, safety, personal and oral hygiene, nutrition and hydration, pressure area care, cleanliness and infection control, privacy and dignity, record keeping, diagnosis and treatment, communication, and the management of discharge from hospital. These were the very types of defect that the Standing Nursing and Midwifery Advisory Committee had so aptly stressed no fewer than nine years before.

Under the heading 'privacy and dignity' in particular, the inquiry referred to incontinent patients left in degrading conditions; patients left inadequately dressed in full view of passers-by; patients moved and handled in unsympathetic and unskilled ways, causing pain and distress; failures to talk to patients by name or by their preferred name; rudeness or hostility. The inquiry stated that there could be no excuse for such treatment and that respect for dignity should be a priority.

In fact, the priority had been financial and performance targets — so that foundation trust status could be achieved. Standards of care had been pared to the bone; this resulted in poor and degrading care, suffering and death.[32]

2010: Age UK: continuing malnutrition in hospitals. In 2010, Age UK followed up Age Concern's 2006 report on malnutrition in hospitals with *Still hungry to be heard*.

2010: National Confidential Enquiry into Patient Outcome and Death: poor care, pressures sores, lack of pain relief for older surgical patients. This was

---

29   Healthcare Commission. *State of healthcare 2008*. London: HC, 2008, p.107.

30   Healthcare Commission. *Investigation into Mid Staffordshire NHS Foundation Trust, March 2009*. London: HC, 2009.

31   Alberti, G. (Professor Sir). *Mid Staffordshire NHS Foundation Trust: a review of the procedures for emergency admissions and treatment, and progress against the recommendation of the March Healthcare Commission report*. London: Department of Health, 2009. Also: Thomé, D.C. (Dr), *Mid Staffordshire NHS Foundation Trust: a review of lessons learnt for commissioners and performance managers following the Healthcare Commission investigation*. London: Department of Health, 2009.

32   Francis, R. (Chair). *Independent inquiry into care provided by Mid Staffordshire NHS Foundation Trust January 2005–March 2009*. London: TSO, 2010.

an observational study of 800 elderly patients who had all died within 30 days of surgery. It was entitled *An age old problem*. Its findings included the fact that underlying problems beyond the surgical were not diagnosed or understood, and competent input by hospital consultants with expertise in care of the elderly was often lacking. This meant that recovery from surgery could be jeopardised, always supposing the surgery was performed in a timely manner, which in nearly 30 per cent of cases it was not.

Compared to a typical younger adult, an older person with a fractured hip was more likely to be already dehydrated, have nutritional problems, have thrombotic (blood coagulation) complications, experience slower healing, and be at risk of tissue breakdown (pressure sores). Some singularly damning findings emerged. Only 36 per cent of patients received 'good care'; and even this did not mean 'exceptionally brilliant' but merely 'appropriate'. This was particularly troubling because the patients considered in the study were of the type that will become more prevalent as the population of people aged over 85 doubles within the next 25 years.

The study did not even find that, whether or not they were receiving appropriate medical diagnosis and intervention, patients received adequate pain relief. This, in the enquiry's view, indicated 'what must sometimes be an organisational failure to respond to suffering'.[33]

2010: Patients' Association: patient and relative accounts of continuing neglect in hospitals. By November 2010, the Association issued another report called *Listen to patients, speak up for change*. Like its 2009 predecessor, it drew on case studies to illustrate the type of account given them by patients and relatives of extremely poor and neglectful care.[34]

2011: health service ombudsman report: lack of care and compassion in hospitals. This was a report to Parliament, called *Care and compassion*, produced by the health service ombudsman, Ann Abraham. It draws on ten complaints from the many hundreds her office receives annually about elderly care and is unequivocal about the failure of the NHS to provide dignity, compassion and basic care.

The report acknowledged the question of extra resources required in hospitals but stresses the dismissive attitude and indifference of staff. It then describes neglect. It describes tongues like dried leather, nutrition and hydration ignored, patients squealing with unmanaged pain, pressure sores thriving, call bells out of reach, lack of cleanliness and comfort, multiple unrecorded falls, bathing or showering unavailable, weeping wounds not dressed and an absence of patient monitoring.[35]

2011: Care Quality Commission, 100 dignity and nutrition inspections: widespread breaches of the regulations. Later that year, in October 2011, the Care Quality Commission published an overview report of 100 hospital inspections carried out in 2011 – two wards in each hospital – on the theme of nutrition and dignity. It found 20 per cent of hospitals not complying with legal regulations and 50 per cent giving cause for concern. The Commission noted:

> Time and time again, we found cases where patients were treated by staff in a way that stripped them of their dignity and respect. People were spoken over, and not

33   Wilkinson, K., Martin, I.C., Gough, M.J. *et al. An age old problem: a review of the care received by elderly patients undergoing surgery*. London: National Confidential Enquiry into Patient Outcome and Death, 2010, pp.4–7.

34   Patients' Association. *Listen to patients, speak up for change*. London: PA, 2010, p.3.

35   Parliamentary and Health Service Ombudsman. *Care and compassion? Report of the Health Service Ombudsman on ten investigations into NHS care of older people*. HC 778. London: TSO, 2011.

spoken to; people were left without call bells, ignored for hours on end, or not given assistance to do the basics of life – to eat, drink, or go to the toilet.[36]

2011: Action on Elder Abuse: 55 per cent of hospitals non-compliant with dignity and nutrition legal standards. This analysis of the 100 inspection reports from the Care Quality Commission on dignity and nutrition in hospital claimed that 55 per cent of hospitals were in fact non-compliant (not the 20 per cent reported by the Commission). This was based on the serious lapses in patient care reported in the individual inspection reports, of even those hospitals deemed to be compliant but a cause for concern.[37]

2011: Patients' Association: yet more patient and relative accounts of poor care and neglect. The Association returned to the fray with *We've been listening, have you been learning?* It noted that it felt impelled to produce this further report 'because it needs to be understood that that these stories are not isolated incidents, but represent a systemic problem within the National Health Service'.

It concluded:

> In the 21st century, in one of the most developed countries and health systems in the world, patients should not be left starving or thirsty, they shouldn't be left in pain and they shouldn't be forced to urinate or defecate in their bed because the nurse designated to them says it's easier for them to change the sheets later than to help them to the toilet now. Yet this is what is happening around the country every day.[38]

2012: patients discharged in middle of night. A Freedom of Information Act request was sent to 170 NHS hospital trusts. Replies came from 100. They revealed that 239,233 patients had been sent home during the night during the previous year. If representative of all trusts, this would mean 400,000 discharges of this type each year, some 8000 per week.

Such discharges can be without warning, be distressing and result in harm to patient and be followed by death shortly after.[39]

2012: Leeds General Infirmary. Inspectors from the Care Quality Commission had to help distressed patients during their inspection. Basic failings included patients banging on tables for attention, pleading with staff not to be so rough, waiting for 30 minutes to be taken to the lavatory, not being helped at mealtimes, having requests for help ignored, being laid in undignified or uncomfortable positions. Staffing levels were of concern – for example, one qualified nurse to cover a 30-bed ward at night. The CQC found a lack of safe and effective care.[40]

2012: King's Fund, Sir Roger Banister Health Summit: model of acute care inappropriate for older people with complex needs; care pathways and performance targets irrelevant or obstructive to high-quality care. This identified a number of problems with the care of older patients with complex needs: 'the great urgency is to turn the guidance and rhetoric of personalised care into a reality of everyday care and practice'. It noted that:

---

36   Care Quality Commission. *Dignity and nutrition inspection programme: national overview.* London: CQC, 2011, p.4.

37   Action on Elder Abuse. *Regulatory activity in hospital settings: a critical analysis of the Care Quality Commission's Dignity and Nutrition Inspection of 100 English hospitals.* London: AEA, 2011, p.79.

38   Patients' Association. *We've been listening, have you been learning?* London: PA, 2011, pp.5–7.

39   Bates, C. 'Scandal of NHS patients sent home in the middle of the night to "free up hospital beds".' *Daily Mail,* 12 April 2012.

40   Care Quality Commission. *Review of compliance: Leeds Teaching Hospitals NHS Trust, Leeds General Infirmary.* London: CQC, 2012. And: Ward, V. 'Hospital criticised by watchdog due to staff shortages.' *Daily Telegraph,* 19 April 2012.

the physical environment, working practices and care processes of acute hospitals geared to the model of acute medical care presuppose that the main task of the hospital is treatment and cure. However, care pathways and performance targets for waiting times and access to elective procedures are either irrelevant or actively obstructive to high-quality care for patients with complex conditions. These patients need reliable holistic (bio-psychosocial) assessment; multi-disciplinary care planning; advance planning to avoid predictable emergencies; care co-ordination; excellent nursing; excellent communication and collaborative relationships between staff, patients and carers. Too often what they get is: late and missed diagnosis; no care planning; unpredicted (but eminently predictable and therefore avoidable) events followed by unplanned interventions; lack of access to specialists and diagnostics; sometimes lack of access to generalists; lack of information; poor communication; lack of continuity, and poorly informed and sometimes unsympathetic interactions with professional staff.[41]

2012: University Hospitals of Morecambe Bay NHS Foundation Trust and Royal Lancaster Infirmary, Furness General Hospital: belated concerns of the Care Quality Commission result in report, published in July 2012, of serious failings. These repeated similar types of failing identified at Mid Staffordshire NHS Foundation Trust. They included a chronic shortage of nurses, doctors and even porters. One in four accident and emergency staff were agency or casual employees. Security guards were asked to carry out caring duties including helping patients at risk of falling. Patients at risk of falls were not being assessed or cared for appropriately.

Emergency patients waited in accident and emergency for up to seven hours. Patients were left unattended in corridors and left without pain relief. A suicidal patient was left to wander alone. Staff were reported by patients and relatives as laughing, taunting or being rude. Staff were bullying and aggressive amongst themselves. There was a staff culture of 'shared helplessness'. Seven whistleblowers contacted the CQC, too afraid to report concerns to their own managers.

There were bed shortages and poor community services. Owing to equipment that was old, broken, out of date and not fit for purpose, operations did not take place, blood pressures were not taken and patients were left to sleep on condemned mattresses.[42]

2012: Royal College of Physicians: inability of hospitals to treat, decently, older people with complex needs. A report in September 2012 identified acute hospitals as being on the edge, in terms of their ability to treat older people with complex needs. It makes a direct link between the resulting poor care and neglect, such as that uncovered at Stafford Hospital. Amongst its findings was a serious shortage of beds, with a 33 per cent drop in numbers over a decade but a 37 per cent rise in emergency admissions. Nearly 66 per cent of hospital admissions were of elderly patients, increasingly with frailty and/or dementia. To their detriment, older patients were frequently moved up to four or five times during their stay, with no formal handover and often with incomplete notes.

It noted the myth and discriminatory attitude that older people should not be in hospital and are in the 'wrong place'. Instead, it stated that:

41   Cornwell, J. *The care of frail older people with complex needs: time for a revolution.* Sir Roger Banister Health Summit, Leeds Castle. London: King's Fund, 2012, pp.1–3.

42   Lakhani, N. 'Damning state of care found at "safe" NHS trust.' *The Independent,* 14 July 2012. And: Care Quality Commission. *University Hospitals of Morecambe Bay NHS Foundation Trust and Royal Lancaster Infirmary, Furness General Hospital: investigation report.* London: CQC, 2012.

Older people must have equal access to healthcare services; it is not acceptable to view older people in hospital as being in the 'wrong place'. Hospital services must adapt to ensure that older patients, including those who are frail and have a diagnosis of dementia, have access to safe, high-quality care in settings that meet their needs.[43]

2012: Patients' Association: another report. Accounts from patients and relatives about hospital neglect and problems with surrounding communication, toileting, accessing effective pain relief and nutrition.[44]

2012: Secretary of State for Health's recognition of cruelty and contempt. In November 2012, Jeremy Hunt, the Secretary of State for Health, referred to NHS patients' experience of 'coldness, resentment, indifference...contempt'. He talked of 'a kind of normalisation of cruelty' – and to managers 'buried in spreadsheets'. He noted that he was not talking about isolated incidents but about practices that had become 'part of the fabric'.[45]

2012: Ann Clwyd, MP: death of husband in hospital, treated like a battery hen. In December 2012, Ann Clwyd, Member of Parliament, recounted how her husband had died in hospital – and of the 'callous lack of care...coldness, resentment, indifference and even contempt'. She related how he lay crushed 'like a battery hen' against the bars of his hospital bed – with an oxygen mask so small it cut into his face and pumped cold air into his infected eye.[46]

2013: Mid Stafford public inquiry: systemic failure underpinning large scale failure in patient care. Following the independent inquiry published in 2010, the coalition government appointed the same chairman, Robert Francis QC, to chair a second – this time a statutory, public inquiry. The remit of this second inquiry was to seek and analyse the wider causes of the neglectful and inhumane treatment of patients, which had been exposed and harrowingly documented in the report of the first inquiry.

Many hopes were pinned on the public inquiry, to the effect that if it could report clearly and cogently, overwhelming pressure would be put on central government to act. In the event, something went badly wrong – and not just the publication of the report some 18 months later than originally planned.[47]

On the positive side, the report of the public inquiry was painstakingly thorough, yet is readable and coherent through all of its three volumes and their 2000 pages – not to mention the executive summary of a mere 125 pages. Thorough but also devastating in its exposure of calamitous failures involving just about everybody connected with the hospital in some way: the Department of Health, strategic health authority, the primary care trust, the Care Quality Commission, Monitor, Health and Safety Executive, Royal College of Nursing, the General Medical Council, Nursing and Midwifery Council, local health overview and scrutiny committee of the local authority, the Trust Board, chief executive, managers, doctors, nurses.

The report also returned, time and again, to the denials from those who should have known better, the lack of transparency, disingenuousness, reckless optimism, targets,

43   Royal College of Physicians. *Hospitals on the edge: the time for action.* London: RCP, 2012, pp.2–3.

44   Patients' Association. Stories from the present: lessons for the future. London: PA, 2012.

45   Hunt, J. 28 November 2012, Jeremy Hunt, Kings Fund – quality of care. Accessed on 17 January 2013 at: http://mediacentre.dh.gov.uk/2012/11/28/28-november-2012-jeremy-hunt-kings-fund-quality-of-care.

46   Hill, A. 'Ann Clwyd: my husband died like a battery hen in hospital.' *The Guardian,* 4 December 2012.

47   Francis, R. (Chair). *Report of the Mid Staffordshire NHS Foundation Trust Public Inquiry.* Executive Summary and three volumes. HC 898. London: TSO, 2013.

finance, defensiveness – and the almost total ineffectiveness of whistleblowing procedures and practice.

It also set out five key things that were needed: (a) fundamental standards complied with and enforced, (b) openness, transparency and candour, (c) compassionate caring and committed nursing care, (d) patient centred leadership, (e) accurate, useful and relevant information.[48]

However, most unfortunately, the report – in particular its overall conclusions and recommendations – arguably fell at the final hurdle.

First, it failed to recommend that blame be apportioned to any individual, high or low – from nurses on the wards right up to the chief executive of the NHS. (The latter had at the relevant time been driving policy at the strategic health authority whilst people were dying. He had been, by his own admission, obsessed with targets and finance but not the quality of patient care. He had also operated at the centre of, and overseen, a culture of fear and bullying within the NHS.) The report's explanation was that the failure was systemic and that it would be a mistake to pick on individuals by way of scapegoats.

This was a very dangerous conclusion for the report to have reached. Dangerous because it sent a message that no matter how much needless suffering and avoidable deaths occur, nobody will in reality be held accountable. The system at Mid Staffordshire was driven by a number of 'leaders' (at Trust Board, primary care trust, strategic health authority and Department of Health level) determined to hit political, performance and financial targets. These leaders enjoyed status, power and salary. They took a reckless approach to hundreds of lives and to the care of often helpless patients.

To conclude that such leaders should not be held accountable in any way is extraordinary. It also makes the job of trying to safeguard vulnerable adults in hospital an even more difficult and thankless task if accountability is removed from the lexicon.

The culture of an organisation is down to its leaders. If they are not held accountable, then there is no justice of any sort either for those who were subjected to inhumane and fatal care – or for their relatives. This is something of an irony given that the chairman of the inquiry was a lawyer, but appeared to have a 'distressing lack of understanding of the difference between scapegoating and demanding personal responsibility'.[49]

Indeed, by February 2013 when the inquiry report was published (four years after the events at Mid Stafford were exposed, and nearly eight years since they began to take place), nobody – at a higher or a lower level – has been held accountable in terms of civil or criminal law, or even in respect of dismissal from their jobs. (The chief executive and chairman of Mid Staffordshire NHS Foundation Trust had long since disappeared off the scene, without in any formal way being held to account.)

The second main problem is that the report makes 290 recommendations – required to bring about the five main changes needed (see six paragraphs above). Paradoxically, this is an invitation to do nothing. The NHS, in the midst of a hugely disruptive restructuring in 2013, is already a sea of disorganised, shifting, costly and insecure bureaucracy. Such a large number of action points is overkill, almost certainly unrealistic and risks diluting effective change.

At the time of writing this book, the report has only just been published. It may be that the recommendations will be acted on, and effectively. However, given the enormity of the

48   Francis, R. (Chair). *Report of the Mid Staffordshire NHS Foundation Trust Public Inquiry*. Press statement, 6 February 2013. Accessed on 6 February 2013 at: http://cdn.midstaffspublicinquiry.com/sites/default/files/report/Chairman%27s%20statement.pdf.

49   Hammond, P. 'The boss must go. NHS staff must step up.' *The Times*, 7 February 2013.

change required, the author is not optimistic. There is a mountain to climb. In particular: (a) the challenges of providing good hospital care for older people with acute needs underlain by multiple pathology, (b) pressing financial restrictions which have implications for quality of care, required hospital bed numbers, staffing numbers and staffing competencies, (c) a deeply embedded culture at the Department of Health and in the NHS hierarchy of disingenuousness, lack of transparency, bullying – and, ultimately, what can amount to a contempt for patients (especially the elderly) and staff, and (d) an increasingly demoralised, oppressed and de-skilled work force.

Third, the inquiry declined to set Mid Staffordshire in a wider context. In fairness, the chairman was constrained by his remit and the focus on one hospital, on one NHS trust. Any conscientious and transparent government would have set up an inquiry not into Stafford Hospital alone, but into the hospital care generally of older people in England. The evidence over the last 15 years about the poor treatment of elderly people in hospitals is overwhelming; Stafford Hospital represented a logical progression. To isolate Stafford was always going to make it easier for government to fudge effective action – on the grounds that Stafford was exceptional and to some degree isolated. And easier to avoid the much bigger and ever pressing question about how society should face up to treating older people and their complex health needs.

So, to an extent, the chairman's hands were indeed tied. However, to have made sense of and to analyse what happened at Stafford, the wider context and evidence (readily available) of the last 15 years arguably needed to be considered and made prominent in the report. It would not only have been legitimate to do this, even within the inquiry's remit, but surely essential. It is a matter of enormous regret that the chairman felt unable to do so.

PERPETRATION AND PERSISTENCE OF SYSTEMIC POOR CARE AND NEGLECT

The reason why poor care and neglect persist is surprisingly simple. Despite the evidence, outlined above, the health service continues to ignore the plight of older people with complex needs. It continues to plan, commission and run the service as if they didn't exist.

UNEVIDENCED AND HARMFUL REDUCTION OF HOSPITAL BEDS

The reduction of hospital beds for older people, together with reductions in quantity and quality of staff, is an obvious example. The closure of large numbers of acute and non-acute hospital beds during the last 12 years was born of wishful, unevidenced and irresponsible thinking about what could be achieved in the community instead, of a denial about the complexity of older people's needs, and of the desire to save money, instead of paying attention to the evidence of what was needed. This has led to overcrowding, understaffing (numbers and competency) and sometimes very poor levels of care.

The scale of the cuts was out of sync both with the demand for beds and with the ability or appropriateness of community services coping with people's acute needs out of hospital. By 2008, it had become clear that instead of an increase in NHS beds, as promised in 2000, there had in fact been a huge decrease. The statistics revealed a loss of 32,000 NHS hospital beds – one in six – in the ten-year period between 1997 and 2007. In 2007 alone, 8400 beds were lost. In 1997, there were nearly 190,000 NHS beds in England; by 2007, this figure had dropped to 160,000.[50]

Contrast this – a loss of some 30,000 beds in a decade – with what the NHS Plan of 2000 had stated was actually needed in that decade: 7000 additional beds – 5000 in acute hospitals and 2000 for intermediate care.[51]

Despite the obvious fact that older people with acute medical needs, underlain by a range of chronic multiple pathology, need to be in hospital receiving expert care, elements within the NHS continue to refer to them pejoratively as bed blockers and as the reason for hospital crises – or alternatively blame local authority social services for not doing more.[52]

REHABILITATION AND INTERMEDIATE CARE

Rehabilitation, too, has suffered greatly, with intensive, skilled and complex rehabilitation – particularly for older people – rapidly becoming a thing of the past.

The policy of intermediate care was meant to enhance rehabilitation – adding another level of complex service – but has had the effect of diminishing rehabilitation. This was warned against over ten years ago when intermediate care was introduced. And there is a link between this occurrence and poor care and neglect.

Professors Grimley Evans and Tallis, eminent geriatricians both, foresaw in 2001 what would happen. They understood that intermediate care was being introduced as part of a long-standing political and managerial agenda to keep old people out of hospital, even if they needed to be there. This was in the hope that 'somehow they would disappear from the system'.

They noted how convenient it was for the caste of management to confuse convalescence out of hospital with a need for rehabilitation within. They also foresaw, correctly, the premature discharge of people from hospital direct to intermediate care, 'bypassing the skilled diagnostic evaluation that the complexities of disease and disability in old age require'. The trouble was, of course, that specialist rehabilitation was expensive. Nobody was owning up to all this, but, as they noted, 'practice is substance, policy mere spin'.[53]

A year before, the Audit Commission had warned about the same thing: the danger of intermediate care displacing specialist rehabilitation and the danger of bundling older people out of hospital without having provided proper assessment, diagnosis, treatment and care.[54]

50   Donnelly, L. 'NHS hospitals lose 32,000 beds in a decade.' *Daily Telegraph*, 24 May 2008.

51   Department of Health. *Implementing the NHS Plan: developing services following the National Beds Inquiry.* Health Service Circular 2001/03. London: DH, 2001, para 7.

52   NHS Confederation. *Papering over the cracks: the impact of social care funding on the NHS.* London: NHS Confederation, 2012.

53   Grimley Evans, J. and Tallis, R. 'A new beginning for care for elderly people? Not if the psychopathology of this new national framework gets in the way.' *British Medical Journal 7*, April 2001, pp.807–8.

54   Audit Commission. *The way to go home: rehabilitation and remedial services for older people.* London: AC, 2000, pp.9, 21.

Once you start treating people as unwanted in hospital and pretend that they don't really have any needs, rehabilitation or otherwise, you are well on the way to treating them poorly, as second-class citizens or worse.

CARE PATHWAYS, PAYMENT BY RESULTS AND PATIENTS AS MARKET COMMODITIES

Since 2000, the NHS has been subject to a period of grooming. This has been about beating a path to opening up health care to the markets.

One way of doing this has been to cease to regard hospitals as part of a true National Health Service. Instead, they have individually to take responsibility increasingly for breaking even, making a profit and competing for contracts and patient care – competing against other NHS hospitals or against private sector providers. If they don't do this, they stand to be taken over by private sector companies, as has happened at Hinchingbrooke Hospital.

This has involved increased use of a system of payment by results and 'care pathways', to price up the care provided, with a view to contracting it out to private providers. It has involved hospitals becoming 'foundation trusts', a cornerstone of which is financial breaking even and profitability. It was this aim that led Stafford Hospital to make such drastic cuts to the quality and quantity of care, which in turn led to disastrous care standards and to many deaths.

The result of all this – in public and private sectors – has, arguably, been to exacerbate (if not to create) the problem of inhumane, undignified and unprofessional care for those in most need.

People with multiple pathology, particularly the elderly, have complex needs and are not readily transmuted into easily quantifiable business commodities. Too often, they do not fit into the inevitably relatively crude pathways.[55] And to the extent they could be, there is no will to do it. Because a proper valuation of complex needs would result in expensive commodities. But older people are not valued; nobody wants to pay for them.

There is a much simpler way of understanding this. In 1997, a journalist called Martin Bright helped kickstart the Dignity on the Ward campaign, outraged at the way his grandmother was treated. Four years later, he pointed out that the need for a model of care attuned to older people is not 'far removed from telling those who run Disneyland that it would be good if they catered for the needs of children'.[56]

The short point is that the model of health care being remorselessly applied by the Department of Health leads to poor care taking root, flourishing, being concealed and inexorably leading to neglect.

---

55   Cornwell, J. *The care of frail older people with complex needs: time for a revolution.* Sir Roger Banister Health Summit, Leeds Castle. London: King's Fund, 2012, pp.1–3. See also: O'Connor, R. and Neumann, V. 'Payment by results or payment by outcome? The history of measuring medicine.' *Journal of the Royal Society of Medicine 99,* 2006, 226–31.

56   Bright, M. 'A blow struck for dignity.' *Society Guardian,* 1 April 2001.

LACK OF TRANSPARENCY

Poor care, neglect and lack of accountability have become entrenched only because of the lack of transparency and concealment that is commonplace within the NHS. But for this, we would never stand for what has been going on. Denial, disingenuousness, doublespeak, manipulation of information and statistics, lies and deceit are rife.

This lack of transparency exacerbates greatly the harm being perpetrated because it undermines the possibility of recognition and prevention. It is so prevalent that a few examples will have to suffice.

Concealment of infection and death at Stoke Mandeville. At Stoke Mandeville Hospital, the Healthcare Commission found that, despite the two very serious outbreaks of *Clostridium difficile*, the NHS Trust Board had consistently resisted the recommendations of its infection control team and had not publicly owned up to what was going on. The Commission found that the Trust changed its approach only when the Department of Health found out and, more particularly, following a leak to the press.[57]

Incomplete, misleading information in Kent: infection, poor care and many deaths. In Maidstone and Tunbridge, the Healthcare Commission uncovered a catalogue of incomplete, misleading and belated information given by the Trust and, in particular, the chief executive – to the public, the press and to the Commission itself. This was while very poor care practices and *Clostridium difficile* were running unchecked and killing scores of patients at the Trust. The chief executive even deprived her own Trust Board of relevant information. The Commission also found that while the Board was making statements about how patient safety was a priority, the Trust's actual practice was almost diametrically opposed to this. The statement was meaningless. Managers referred to the 'positive spin' employed by the chief executive.[58]

MEANINGLESS LANGUAGE, DOUBLESPEAK AND UNDERMINING OF CLINICAL INTEGRITY

Thus, in the last example, the make-believe world that NHS trusts set up for themselves and inhabit was illustrated at Maidstone and Tunbridge Wells NHS Trust. The culture of disingenuousness and corruption of judgement had infected clinicians as well. In the midst of scores of avoidable deaths, chaos, overcrowding, filth, infection, lack of basic care and dignity, a nursing report was submitted to the Board of the Maidstone and Tunbridge Wells NHS Trust.

The report assured the Board that every patient had received 'the best care in the best place on the ward' – a claim dismissed as pure fabrication by the Healthcare Commission.[59]

---

57   Healthcare Commission. *Investigation into outbreaks of* Clostridium difficile *at Stoke Mandeville Hospital, Buckinghamshire Hospitals NHS Trust, July 2006.* London: HC, 2006, pp.7, 63.

58   Healthcare Commission. *Investigation into outbreaks of* Clostridium difficile *at Maidstone and Tunbridge Wells NHS Trust, October 2007.* London: HC, 2007, p.94.

59   Healthcare Commission. *Investigation into outbreaks of* Clostridium difficile *at Maidstone and Tunbridge Wells NHS Trust, October 2007.* London: HC, 2007, p.94.

Leaving aside the departure from the facts, this claim is in any case absurd. Because of the superlative nature of the word 'best', at the top of the comparative scale running 'good', 'better', 'best', it is arguably not possible, logically let alone practical, that every patient would receive the 'best' care.

However, this type of phrase is used within the health service by managers, taking their cue from a phrase used in *The NHS Plan*. This was that the patient should 'receive the right care at the right time in the right place'.[60] The phrase is pernicious and has been used extensively to justify harmful changes within the NHS over the past decade. It is a meaningless and otiose; why would you want to provide anything other? In practice, it came to mean whatever NHS chief executives wanted it to mean.

In the following example, the NHS trust concerned was determined not to concede that anything might be wrong.

Waking people up and sending them home, unplanned, in the middle of the night. At Ipswich Hospital, a state of blue alert had been declared at the hospital shortly before Christmas. The crisis was such that patients were being woken up and discharged, unplanned, in the middle of the night. Given that the hospital had anyway been on black alert for some while, and so would not have retained patients who did not need to be there, the statement from the hospital is inexplicable: 'Some of the patients had to be woken up so they could be discharged, but there were very sick people who needed to come in. Those who went home were all ready and happy to leave and we organised transport for them.'[61]

Discharging vulnerable, older patients – unplanned – in the middle of the night is clearly, potentially, an adult protection and safeguarding issue. Euphemistic statements made by hospitals make it even more so because they represent a denial that anything is wrong. As one hospital did when it discharged an 89-year-old patient with dementia, unplanned, at 2 o'clock in the morning, claiming it was in her best interests. She had been admitted after a fall in her care home. The hospital concerned, Warrington, had already been reported as having one of the highest rates of night-time discharges in the country.[62]

MANIPULATING INFORMATION AND STATISTICS

In Stafford Hospital, even after four reports, all concurring in their view of the terrible events, denial was still the order of the day. At one point, the Trust had put the fuss all down to problems with 'data capture' of mortality rates, ignoring the point (even had this contention been true, which it wasn't): the standards of care which, incontrovertibly, prevailed at the hospital (whether or not they killed people).[63]

---

60   Secretary of State for Health. *The NHS Plan: a plan for investment, a plan for reform.* Cm 4818-I. London: TSO, 2000, p.71.

61   Bond, A. 'Hospital hit by bed crisis.' *East Anglian Daily Times*, 22 December 2007.

62   Narain, J. 'Family's fury as hospital releases dementia patient, 89, at 2am and claims it was "in her BEST INTERESTS".' *Daily Mail*, 26 April 2012.

63   Healthcare Commission. *Investigation into Mid Staffordshire NHS Foundation Trust, March 2009.* London: HC, 2009, pp.10, 109–10.

Clearly, for the chief executive and the NHS Trust Board, it was all a game of numbers and statistics. The real sin, within many NHS circles, is not whether patients suffer or die, but whether the NHS trust gets publicly caught out on the figures.

PAY RISES FOR SELF-ASSESSED GOOD CARE, WHILST PATIENTS DIE

For those involved in safeguarding who seem to be under the spell of supposing that NHS senior management is well-meaning, honourable and should not be held to account, they might wish to consider the following.

Whilst hundreds of people were dying and many more subjected to utterly degrading care at Stafford Hospital, the chief executive and Board reported to the regulatory body, Monitor, that the hospital was providing good care. On that basis, the Trust was awarded foundation status by Monitor, and pay rises were awarded to members of the Board – by those very same members.[64]

Nor, despite a decade and more of scandal, are there any signs of chronic concealment and disingenuousness abating.

In 2010, it emerged that University Hospitals of Morecambe Bay NHS Foundation Trust had concealed, for a year, a highly critical report (the Fielding report), which it had commissioned about the safety of its maternity services. The regulator, the Care Quality Commission, had, during this time, not seen the report and failed to take decisive action against the Trust. Instead, the Commission had relied on assurances given by the Trust.[65] By 2012, the Commission belatedly launched a full-scale investigation which uncovered very serious concerns relating not just to maternity services but also to emergency services.[66]

DENIAL AND CONCEALMENT BY POLITICIANS
AND THE DEPARTMENT OF HEALTH

Denial and attempt to conceal is not limited to NHS trust chief executives and boards. When patients and relatives demanded a public inquiry into events at Stafford Hospital, the government refused; it only acceded, in the end, to an independent inquiry when threatened with judicial review by Cure the NHS, a group of relatives of dead patients.[67] There can be no more blatant and damning example of a government, for all the usual protestations about wanting transparency, wishing to spare itself embarrassment and to cover up.

---

64 Evans, M. 'Failed hospital bosses given pay rises while crisis unfolded: senior managers who oversaw one of the worst scandals in the history of the NHS awarded themselves bumper pay increases at the same time as hundreds of patients were needlessly dying, it can be disclosed.' *Daily Telegraph*, 26 February 2010.

65 Smith R. 'Morecambe Bay hospitals: regulator should have acted sooner.' *Daily Telegraph*, 14 July 2012.

66 Care Quality Commission. *University Hospitals of Morecambe Bay NHS Foundation Trust and Royal Lancaster Infirmary Furness General Hospital: investigation report.* London: CQC, 2012.

67 Leigh Day & Co. 'Judicial reviews and the Mid Staffordshire inquiries.' *News*, 12 May 2010. Accessed on 5 August 2010 at: www.leighday.co.uk/Our-expertise/human-rights/Mid-Staffordshire-Inquiry/Judicial-reviews-and-the-Mid-Staffordshire-inquiri.

So it is important to stress that culpability is to be found at the very top, in understanding how the culture of denial and concealment finds its way down the rigid and unforgiving hierarchy that is the NHS.

DEPARTMENT OF HEALTH'S INDIFFERENCE TO POOR CARE AND NEGLECT: FROM CHIEF EXECUTIVE DOWNWARD

In September 2011, Sir David Nicholson gave evidence to the public inquiry into Stafford Hospital. Back in 2005, both Stafford Hospital and the Primary Care Trust (which commissioned local services) were under the supervision and direction, particularly financial, of the West Midlands Strategic Health Authority – which reported to the Department of Health.

The Authority, which was formed of a merger in 2005, was overseen by David Nicholson at the time. The concern was money, not care, as he conceded to the inquiry. At the time, he was quite prepared to act ruthlessly; if trusts did not slash their deficits, then boards were sacked, or forced to resign – as happened at the time to the University Hospital of North Staffordshire.[68]

However, in front of the inquiry, he claimed that everybody had learnt from the events at Stafford and that it had had a profound effect on the health service. The emptiness of such words and sentiments, however, had already been revealed a few months earlier.[69]

Earlier in 2011, the health service ombudsman published a report with a sample of complaints she had received about neglectful care in the NHS.[70] On the day of publication, the response of Sir David Nicholson, now chief executive of the whole NHS as well as a knight, speaks volumes – albeit in a short missive. On that day, 15th February 2011, he sent a letter to NHS trust chairmen.

Exhibiting neither urgency nor explicit condemnation, it mentions 'important issues' and urges chairmen to read the report (as a 'learning tool'). It also does refer to the report as a 'reality check' but then, extraordinarily, suggests the answer may lie in consulting an 'on-line Patient Experience Network'. The complacency and detachment evident in this letter are arguably indicative of how the elderly, and reports about their neglect, are regarded as a fly in the official ointment, to which lip service must be paid. There is no reference to Stafford Hospital, no reference to the 15 years of overwhelming evidence which the ombudsman was merely corroborating and no instructions to chairmen to make sure their patients were treated decently and humanely – or else lose their jobs. This is a chief executive,

---

68   'Stafford Hospital gave "no cause for concern".' *BBC News*, 27 September 2011. Accessed on 12 January 2012 at: www.bbc.co.uk/news/uk-england-stoke-staffordshire-15078033.

69   'Stafford Hospital gave "no cause for concern".' *BBC News*, 27 September 2011. Accessed on 12 January 2012 at: www.bbc.co.uk/news/uk-england-stoke-staffordshire-15078033.

70   Parliamentary and Health Service Ombudsman. *Care and compassion? Report of the Health Service Ombudsman on ten investigations into NHS care of older people.* HC 778. London: TSO, 2011.

mind, who, as we already have noted, is quite prepared to dismiss whole boards on financial grounds.[71]

It got worse. Under his auspices, too, NHS Choices, the public face of the NHS on the internet, made clear the Department's disregard for the ombudsman's report. The NHS Choices website noted that it was not scientific, not a reliable indicator about NHS care, and was selective in highlighting the most serious cases in such 'fine detail'. It quoted the NHS Confederation to the effect that such care was not typical.[72]

It is evident that, despite over 15 years of solid evidence about poor care for the elderly, the Department of Health is not minded to do anything about it – other than to continue (a) to promote policies and ways of working inimical to the needs of the elderly with complex needs, and (b) worse, absurdly to deny there is a serious problem.

LOCAL CHIEF EXECUTIVES TAKE THEIR CUE FROM THE CENTRE IN DISINGENUOUSNESS WHILST INFLICTING PATIENT SUFFERING

It is from such irresponsibility and lack of accountability at the top that local chief executives and other senior managers take their cue. They do what they are told without question, knowingly or recklessly undermining the humane care of the most vulnerable of patients – and then disingenuously claiming to be doing the opposite. As when an NHS trust chief executive, hastily closing beds, reducing staff and diminishing competencies, states airily – with no evidence whatsoever – that it is all for the best and that patient care will not suffer.

This is not idle accusation. So many examples could be given. Two will have to suffice.

Chief executive: cutting staff and hospital beds would be exciting and good for patients. When large hospital staff and bed cuts were announced for Southampton in June 2006, following similar cuts the year before, the chief executive stated that not only was it all about improving services for patients but that it would be 'exciting' for staff.[73] By 2010, it was reported that transfers of patients for non-clinical reasons in Southampton were high, with the clear potential for clinical detriment (whether infection or other matters).

Patients being transferred from ward to ward for non-clinical reasons. For instance, between July 2008 and July 2010, an average of 5922 patients were admitted monthly, and, of these, 703 would be transferred for non-clinical reasons – that is, 12 per cent of admitted patients.[74]

71   Nicholson, D. *Care and compassion? Report of the health service ombudsman on ten investigations into NHS care of older people.* Dear Chair letter. London: Department of Health, 15 February 2011.

72   NHS Choices. *NHS failures in elderly care 'not typical'.* Accessed on 15 February 2011 at: www.nhs.uk/news/2011/02February/Pages/health-service-ombudsman-report-on-care-of-the-elderly.aspx.

73   Makin, J. 'Job cuts will lead to a better service.' *Southern Daily Echo,* 28 June 2006.

74   West, D. 'Hospital bed transfers put thousands of patients at risk of infection.' *Nursing Times,* 5 October 2010.

Example of individual patient suffering and dying. And to bring it all down to an individual in Southampton General Hospital, moved from ward to ward only to develop pressure sores and MRSA and then to die in a nursing home from the latter, a relative explained. In 2009, her mother was admitted following a fall. She recovered from the fall with no injuries within 24 hours but was kept in the hospital because of a urine infection. She was moved to four different wards for no obvious reason. She then developed pressure sores which became infected with MRSA. This was not diagnosed by the hospital while she was in their care. After eight weeks in hospital, she was declared medically fit and released to a care home where she died six weeks later. The principal cause of death on her death certificate was MRSA.[75]

In 2008, a war veteran died a painful death from pressure sores at the Queen's Hospital, Romford. In 2009, the coroner held that neglect had contributed to his death. The pressure sores were due to two separate 12-hour waits on trolleys in the hospital because of a shortage of beds.[76] In 2006, the chief executive of the newly built hospital announced the closure of 190 beds and the cutting of 650 staff. But he noted that patient care would not suffer because these reductions were 'clinically sustainable'.[77]

Such chief executives bear a heavy responsibility and should be held accountable for their servility and ruthlessness. But this is not happening. And that is why, from top to bottom of the NHS, the conspiracy (not used lightly) continues; senior managers know that they will not be held to account because they are part of a collective fiction about health care for the elderly which loudly, brazenly and falsely drums out the reality.

LACK OF RESPONSIBILITY AND ACCOUNTABILITY

Self-evidently, lack of transparency, concealment and cover-up results in a failure to hold individuals to account.

It is true that many contributory factors, explanations and possible remedies are put forward for poor care and neglect in hospitals. People talk of too few nurses, too few competencies, too few beds, nurses who are too posh to wash, problems in nurse education, too many health care assistants, discriminatory frames of mind in relation to the elderly. And no doubt all are relevant to a greater or lesser extent. But none of them is remediable overnight. And this is why such solace is taken in them. Continued referral to them is like kicking the issue into the long grass.

But there is one key factor that seems continually to be overlooked. Nobody is going to implement, effectively and decisively, any of the remedies – long- or short-term – unless there is responsibility and accountability for the neglect and abuse that is going on.

---

75   *Patient Opinion.* Accessed on 20 October 2010 at: www.patientopinion.org.uk/opinions/14654.

76   Schlesinger, F. 'Coroner's fury as great-grandfather, 86, dies after being dumped on A&E trolley for 19 hours TWICE.' *Daily Mail*, 22 May 2009.

77   '£24 million debt NHS trust cuts 650 jobs: up to 650 jobs are to be cut and 190 beds closed by an NHS trust that is trying to tackle debts.' *BBC News*, 28 April 2006. Accessed on 20 July 2010 at: http://news.bbc.co.uk/1/hi/england/london/4954818.stm.

It is these last that are missing. Because, at heart, if you are a chief executive of an organisation, on the board or part of senior management, what happens in that organisation should be your responsibility and you should be held accountable. Not just for the finances (for which chief executives and boards do get sacked) but for the standard of care (for which, by and large, they do not).

Yet accountability is largely missing. First, because there is widespread concealment achieved by widespread denial, doublespeak, disingenuousness and bullying of whistleblowers. Second, even when, in spite of the concealment, a scandal does emerge, accountability remains in short supply.

Clearly, from the point of view of an overall solution, there is complexity in the above factors underlying poor care and neglect. But taking refuge in the complexity is a way of doing nothing. Safeguarding is about protecting people from neglect and abuse at the hands of other people. And what is certain is that poor and neglectful care is not some inexorable law of physics, such as gravity, which we can do nothing about; rather, it is man-made.

LACK OF ACCOUNTABILITY WITHIN THE SENIOR MANAGEMENT CASTE

Poor care and neglect are being delivered, managed and directed by real people. And the way safeguarding normally works, in other contexts, is to hold somebody accountable. But not, by and large, in the case of the NHS.

For instance, when a chief executive oversaw very poor care standards, 90 arguably avoidable deaths from infection and the concealment of what was happening, she stepped down and successfully pursued, through the courts, a payoff of more than £200,000.[78]

After the chief executive of the Mid Staffordshire NHS Foundation Trust had to step down after inhumane treatment and death of patients on a large scale, he received a £400,000 payoff and had a £1 million pension. But he successfully avoided giving evidence not just to the independent inquiry but to the public inquiry as well. This was on the grounds of ill health – post-traumatic stress disorder. Instead of giving evidence to the inquiries, he went on a skiing holiday in Switzerland. At the same time that he avoided giving evidence, he was also offering his services to NHS trusts as an adviser – despite the fact that his lawyer had a year previously said that he would never be able to work again.[79]

Stafford Hospital and the Primary Care Trust (which commissioned local services) were, at the relevant time, under the orders and direction of the West Midlands Strategic Health Authority, which reported to the Department of Health. The Authority, which was formed of a merger in 2005, was headed up for nearly a year between 2005 and 2006 by David Nicholson (see above). The concern was money, not care, as he much later conceded to the public inquiry. At the time, he was quite prepared to act ruthlessly; if trusts did not slash their deficits, then boards

---

78   *Rose Gibb v Maidstone and Tunbridge Wells NHS Trust* [2010] EWCA Civ 678.
79   'Stafford Hospital chief "too ill" to attend inquiries went on skiing trip.' *Daily Telegraph*, 27 November 2011.

were sacked or forced to resign – as happened at the time at the University Hospital of North Staffordshire.[80] His reward for pursuing targets and finance at the expense of patients' dignity and lives was to receive a knighthood and to be made chief executive of the whole of the NHS.

Cynthia Bower took over as head of the West Midlands Strategic Health Authority. She, too, oversaw the catastrophic events at Stafford Hospital, pursuing local NHS trusts concerning finance but not quality of care. Her reward was to be made chief executive of the Care Quality Commission in 2009.

Andy Burnham was the Health Secretary when the Stafford scandal broke, although not during the years of shocking care. However, without sufficient information, he had approved the NHS Trust's gaining foundation status, on the pretence that it was providing good care and on the fact that it had balanced its books (the very reason people were dying). Following the Healthcare Commission's report, he wasted no time in trying to cover it up in order to protect his party and government politically. He refused to order a public inquiry and only set up an independent inquiry when threatened with judicial review by relatives of dead patients.[81] He, too, has not been held to account for such irresponsibility.

ACCOUNTABILITY AND LAW

So, expectations that the NHS will sort it all out itself are, so far, wide of the mark. And whilst one would not wish to over-legalise health care, nonetheless the time has surely come to start to deploy criminal law.

The one thing that might make managers (at whatever level) and professionals pause before supporting policies and practices that result in degradation, suffering, neglect and death – and then concealing the fact, as well as bullying, threatening and victimising those who wish to speak out – would be a threat of losing their jobs and their financial perks, or criminal conviction – of themselves or their organisation (e.g. corporate manslaughter or health and safety at work breaches).

From an organisational point of view, in this ideological health care market, to which central government (of whatever hue) is increasingly committed, criminal convictions are bad publicity and therefore bad commercially. In fact, bad news all round.

WHISTLEBLOWING IN THE NHS

Occasionally, there is a danger that, despite the prevailing disingenuousness and lack of accountability, the truth may out. This happens when staff and sometimes managers are prepared to raise the issue, usually within the organisation.

---

80   'Stafford Hospital gave "no cause for concern".' *BBC News*, 27 September 2011. Accessed on 12 January 2012 at: www.bbc.co.uk/news/uk-england-stoke-staffordshire-15078033.

81   Leigh Day & Co. 'Judicial reviews and the Mid Staffordshire inquiries.' *News*, 12 May 2010. Accessed on 23 November 2012 at: www.leighday.co.uk/Our-expertise/human-rights/Mid-Staffordshire-Inquiry/Judicial-reviews-and-the-Mid-Staffordshire-inquiri.

Despite an official policy of encouraging whistleblowing, the NHS tends to treat whistleblowers with a ruthlessness, ferocity and cowardliness that is breathtaking. This is particularly so if the whistleblowing is about institutional and systemic problems. The suppression of whistleblowers is the last bastion, the ultimate defence used to maintain the fiction that systemic poor care and neglect does not exist within the NHS. It is effective and pernicious.

Whistleblowing in the NHS is considered in detail in Chapter 12.

CORRUPTION OF PUBLIC INSTITUTIONS AND UNDERMINING OF TRUST

In September 2012, a culture of systematic concealment was exposed within the South Yorkshire Police and beyond. This related to events immediately after 96 Liverpool supporters had died at a football match in 1989. When it became clear, 23 years later, that ambulance records and over a hundred police eyewitness accounts had been altered – and that a black propaganda campaign had been run to smear the dead and deflect blame – two points were made.[82]

First, there was talk of criminal prosecution, including for manslaughter and perverting the course of justice. Second, that such concealment and dishonesty – as opposed to the original mistakes made by the police – represent corruption not just in a narrow but also a wider sense. Dr John Ashton, who tried to help the dying on the pitch at Hillsborough, put it this way: 'What happened at Hillsborough is a symptom of the corruption in public life that is endemic now. At stake is the vitality of our democracy.'[83]

Such a corruption of morals and of public life comes not with the tragedy itself but precisely with the cover-up that followed. So it is with the NHS. It is not the poor care that represents a corruption – although it is truly shocking – but an all-pervasive culture of denial and disingenuousness. Made worse by the resulting lack of accountability and ruthless treatment meted out to whistleblowers.

CORRUPTION OF PUBLIC LIFE, MORALS AND TRUST IN THE CONTEXT OF THE NHS

At Mid Staffordshire Foundation Trust, greater numbers died than at Hillsborough during a three- to four-year period of systemic inhumane care being given to significant numbers of patients. And concealment and disingenuousness were rife – just as they were at Stoke Mandeville Hospital where 38 died, and Maidstone and Tunbridge Wells NHS Trust where there were 90 deaths. These three examples are the tip of a large iceberg, revealed by the compelling evidence of the past 15 years, as summarised above.

---

82   Hillsborough Independent Panel (Chairman: Right Reverend James Jones, Bishop of Liverpool). *Hillsborough: the report of the Hillsborough Independent Panel*. HC 581. London: TSO, 2012, pp.22–26.

83   Owen, J., Lott-Lavigna, R. and Mahony, H. 'Hillsborough: ten testimonies – "Indescribable scenes of chaos in a theatre of death".' *The Independent*, 16 September 2012.

What makes the corruption still worse is that those clinicians, and sometimes managers, who seek to dispel the fiction that all is well by raising concern face vilification, persecution and the loss of their job, reputation and mental well-being. It is a system that too often brooks no argument, dissent or discordant voice, even if fundamental patient safety is in issue.

Even highly competent chief executives and chairmen are hounded out of their jobs if they wish to put patient safety before finance, performance and political targets. What hope for frontline staff who raise awkward questions about patient care and safety?

One reason why this is happening is that we do not wish to believe it. And this is not for want of evidence but (a) because of the very size of the problem which is difficult to grasp, and (b) because of the built-in deference and trust we have in a fine State-run system of health care.

Of course, disingenuousness, cover-up and corruption of morals are not peculiar to a State-run service. But they are more significant since we look to the State to set an example, moral and political.

PERVASIVENESS OF CORRUPTION OF INTEGRITY

The corruption of people's integrity comes from the very top, at the Department of Health, and seeps right down through higher layers of local NHS management to lower management and frontline staff.

It does so in different forms. Some people lie and dissemble to gain or retain power, salary, position and ambition. Others genuinely convince themselves about what they are saying or doing by suspending all critical judgement and ignoring the evidence and reality in front of their eyes. Others still retain integrity of judgement but are too fearful of saying anything and so remain silent.

One journalist has referred to the timeless issues of how good people can be corrupted, how cheating can be concealed and how secrets can be kept for so long. He was referring to systemic corruption not in health care but in cycling and the astonishing evidence about the widespread doping, drugs and cheating in world cycling, epitomised by Lance Armstrong, seven times 'winner' of the Tour de France.[84]

But the question applies exactly to health care: how can so many people have been sucked into a form of corruption that covers up the most miserable and unforgivable treatment of highly vulnerable, elderly people?

PLAIN CHEATING

In issue are not just untruths but, as in the cycling scandal, plain cheating. Cheating, when facts are misrepresented and when targets and statistics are cynically

---

84   Dickinson, M. 'Greatest fraud in sport is laid bare in black and white.' *The Times*, 11 October 2012.

manipulated and misreported. When 20 per cent of ambulance trusts misreport statistics.[85] With ambulances arriving, according to returns, in less than one minute or even breaking the law of physics by arriving in less than zero seconds.[86]

In 2012, such practices are alive and well, only now transferring also to the private sector, to which NHS services are increasingly being contracted out. As happened in Cornwall, when Serco admitted falsifying over 250 records so as to present a fictional picture of how quickly it was responding to calls as part of its out-of-hours GP service. Of course, the records did not amend themselves; the amendments were carried out by staff.[87] The Chair of the Public Accounts Committee raised the question of whether this was fraud.[88]

The cheating is made worse by the fact that it is in reality welcomed by central government if the consequence is political mileage. It is only if the cheating becomes public that government becomes uncomfortable and utters sanctimonious condemnation.

But the cheating gets worse still, even if financial and performance targets have genuinely been met without fixing and manipulation. This is because the achievement of narrow performance and financial targets has often been achieved only through the distortion of clinical priorities – and at catastrophic cost to care of elderly people across NHS hospitals generally. This was epitomised at Stoke Mandeville Hospital where, in order to hit targets, the hospital management refused to treat a significant outbreak of infection seriously. In order to safeguard those targets, 38 people died avoidably.[89]

TRANSPARENCY AND ACCOUNTABILITY FOR THOSE IN POSITIONS OF POWER

The chairman of the Hillsborough inquiry, the Bishop of Liverpool (Rt Rev James Jones), stated:

> It is timely for us to reconsider how people in positions of power, whoever they may be, behave in a transparent and accountable manner because to do so will then win back the trust which is so vulnerable at the moment in our society... We need a new standard of transparency and accountability.[90]

These comments would apply tenfold to the NHS, to whom transparency and accountability are alien concepts.

85   Hawkes, N. 'Ambulance trusts "fiddled statistics to meet targets".' *The Times*, 15 August 2006.
86   House of Commons Public Administration Committee. *On target? Government by measurement*. HC 61-I. London: TSO, 2003, paras 59–60.
87   'Serco admits staff falsified records.' *Health Service Journal*, 21 September 2012.
88   Lawrence, F. 'Serco gave NHS false data about its GP service 252 times: private firm admits altering data about out-of-hours doctor service in Cornwall, prompting call for review of contract.' *The Guardian*, 20 September 2012.
89   Healthcare Commission. *Investigation into outbreaks of* Clostridium difficile *at Stoke Mandeville Hospital, Buckinghamshire Hospitals NHS Trust, July 2006*. London: HC, 2006.
90   Gledhill, R. 'Liverpool bishop calls for new rules to control the powerful.' *The Times*, 22 September 2012.

TYPICAL EXAMPLES IN THE NHS OF CORRUPTION OF PUBLIC LIFE

The following are a set of random examples, to give a sketch of just how far corruption of morals and integrity has advanced in the NHS. Although the corruption has set in at all levels, there can be no doubt at all that its progress has been greatly aided in particular by two things.

First, by the determination at the Department of Health to cost up and treat patients as commodities, without properly assessing and valuing older people's complex needs – whether they are to be met by the NHS or by independent providers under contract to the NHS.

Second, by a new generation of NHS chief executives and chairmen, who, since 2000, have shown unrivalled servility to their political masters, sheer ruthlessness, cynical disingenuousness and indifference to the health care needs of elderly people.

The effect of this approach has been to corrupt morality within the NHS, in terms of a loss of honesty, transparency and integrity – in the exercise of naked abuse of power. The author has elsewhere, at great length and exhaustively, documented this.[91]

So, the following are a very few examples, selected at random and from many happening day in, day out, within the NHS. They are not reported anywhere; they are just everyday fare.

Senior clinician warned off talking to health scrutiny committee. A chief executive has a word in the ear of senior clinician who is about to speak to the local authority health scrutiny committee about concerns regarding cuts to elderly care services. She is told that she will not have a job if she does. On the day of the committee hearing, the clinician's name-labelled chair is empty; she has a mortgage and two children to bring up.

Doctor on Trust Board publicly supports what he knows is clinically harmful. A senior medical doctor sits on the local NHS trust's board. He attends a public meeting attended by hundreds. In reply to a local person who has spoken at the meeting about his fears concerning reduction of elderly care services, the doctor speaks eloquently in favour of the cuts, as a respected doctor. On his way out of the church, he bends down and whispers in the ear of the speaker whose concerns he has ridiculed publicly, 'I agree with every word you said.'

Outstanding senior therapist threatened with dismissal, on grounds of having done unpaid overtime, for raising concerns. A senior therapist at annual appraisal is assessed as being an expert practitioner, providing a high standard of treatment for patients, and a role model for the whole team. Because of staff shortages and inexperience, he had even been doing some unpaid overtime to help out.

Having raised concerns about patient safety and quality of care informally for over a year, he then sends an email to management, formally setting out these concerns. His manager (responsible for the appraisal) initially supports the therapist but immediately comes under pressure from her manager.

91   Mandelstam, M. *How we treat the sick: neglect and abuse in our health services.* London: Jessica Kingsley Publishers, 2011.

Instead of continuing the support, she now sends a letter to the therapist, threatening him with the capability process (applied in cases of lack of competence) and possible dismissal. When he queries the grounds of the process – since he had just been judged to be an expert practitioner – he is informed that the process is being invoked because he had done unpaid overtime. The fact that the overtime was not due to incompetence but was an effort to make up shortfalls in staffing levels is ignored.

The stress is such that the therapist decides to fall silent about his concerns; the threat is then withdrawn.

NHS trust chief executive admitting political and financial role and imperative. A chief executive of an NHS trust, in a meeting, candidly asks those who are querying her decisions why they are talking to her about health care and clinical consequences of her decision, since her true role is purely financial and political.

Hospital transport system: suffering of patients, undermining of dignity; dissenting voices silenced, concerns ignored. A hospital has contracted out its hospital transport to the private sector, to 'improve' the service. Consequent on this, hospital discharge coordinators have been filing 'hospital discharge alerts' for two years. Nothing is done because the alerts are fed back to the managers responsible for operating the new, cut-price, transport.

Elderly patients are taken down to the discharge lounge at 9am. They wait all day long, with nothing to eat and drink. They dare not leave the lounge in case the transport arrives. It finally comes at 9pm. They arrive at the care home at 10pm, parched, dehydrated, hungry and distressed. Sometimes, they arrive at the care home wrapped in blankets, naked underneath with faeces-soiled pads, long since dried.

When the coordinator raises these issues in a meeting, including the lack of action on the discharge alerts, she is shouted down aggressively by the manager chairing the meeting.

The erosion of integrity goes further. Care home managers say nothing about the state in which patients are arriving because, under contract to the NHS and local authorities, they are fearful of upsetting those organisations, fearing they might lose their contracts.

MORAL CORRUPTION AND WHERE IT LEADS

Parallels must be made with caution but can be very useful in understanding the significance of systemic poor care and neglect. A combination of how older people are treated in hospital and the denial, recklessness as to their treatment and indifference shown invite serious observations.

In 1997, Professor Grimley Evans, a distinguished geriatrician, warned of the danger of creating a class – the elderly – 'of *Untermenschen* whose lives and well-being are deemed not worth spending money on'. He maintained that we should not discriminate against older people but instead should base treatment on a person's physiological condition and ability to benefit.[92] This is not happening.

---

92   Grimley Evans, J. (Professor). 'Rationing health care by age: the case against.' *British Medical Journal 314*, 1997, p.822.

CREATING AN UNDERCLASS IN HEALTH CARE AND SOCIETY

Use of the German word *Untermensch* was chosen carefully by that writer. It was used 60 years earlier in Nazi Germany to refer to inferior races. It can be translated as meaning a subhuman. There is no doubt that, reading the care afforded to some older people in hospital, one can conclude they have been treated as subhuman.

If you do not give sick people food and drink, if you leave them in dried faeces, do not talk to them and allow them to die in agony from pressure sores, you are indeed treating them as subhuman. It really is as simple as that.

Of course, we are not living in Nazi Germany or anything like it. But to suggest we have nothing to learn would be complacent.

It is well documented how ordinary people went along with Nazi policies and indeed ended up being functionaries in that system. And how many fell into the ideology and regarded it as normal, respectable, rational and for the greater good. And looked the other way, or simply chose not to believe what was happening to their Jewish neighbours. Chose not to, or could not, bring themselves to believe, because of the enormity of it all.[93]

If one looks in detail at the evidence of the last 15 years,[94] it is clear that some in the Department of Health and within the NHS have displayed a willingness to impose, or allow, suffering and inhumane treatment on a significant scale – and yet, at the same time, they have denied it, even when the evidence was glaring. Or looked the other way.

In 2011, the BBC screened a science fiction series of *Torchwood,* sometimes described as 'Doctor Who for adults'. It was called *Miracle Day.* In this series, there were simply too many people (particularly the elderly) alive because of 'miracle day' on which people had stopped dying. Finding it increasingly difficult to cope, the government announced to the public that the NHS was setting up specialist care centres. In fact, those centres were for the incineration of still-living patients. Health care professionals are shown going along with it. It was sanctioned by their managers and politicians; it was indeed for the greater good. They were doing their best.

Given an ageing population, increased longevity, inhumane care and neglect of elderly people in our hospitals, involving sometimes suffering and death on a significant scale, this story repays closer attention. It is not as far-fetched as might appear at first glance.

Writing in November 2012, Lord Lipsey (a member of the 1999 Royal Commission on Long Term Care for the Elderly), reminded us of a 19th-century novel called *The fixed period.* At the age of 67, everybody goes to a 'college' where

---

93   Moorhouse, R. 'Beyond belief: Berliners and the Holocaust.' *History Today 60*, 9, 2010. Accessed on 22 November 2012 at: www.historytoday.com/roger-moorhouse/berliners-holocaust.

94   Mandelstam, M. *How we treat the sick: neglect and abuse in our health services.* London: Jessica Kingsley Publishers, 2011.

they are well-treated and spend a year reflecting on their life. They are then placed in a warm bath and their veins opened.[95]

First, given the extreme inhumaneness, suffering, misery and sometimes death inflicted on a significant number of patients in hospital, we would have to ask the question, which David Lipsey half raises, as to whether 'the college' might come to seem preferable to such neglect prior to death. At least you would be treated well before being killed.

Second, the book is a disturbing read. It describes imprisonment followed by murder, although neither of these words is used. It is organised euthanasia by the State. Euphemism comes to the rescue. Imprisonment becomes 'deposition'. And murder becomes 'mode of transition' or 'act of grace'. And a son would lead his father to the college with pride, honour and affection.[96]

Euphemism, in the midst of suffering and death, is no stranger in the NHS, as a nurse at the Department of Health conceded. We have 'sub-optimal care' instead of neglect, 'systems failure' instead of recklessness, 'clinical error' instead of clinical incompetence, 'busy ward' instead of dangerous practice, 'learning collective lessons' instead of acceptance of personal responsibility and 'isolated incident' instead of pattern of behaviour.[97]

Not to mention storerooms or cupboards, reportedly utilised routinely for patients under the nomenclature of 'treatment rooms'.[98] And, as noted elsewhere in this book, when 90 patients were dying at an NHS trust, in circumstances of poor, inhumane care and neglect, a nursing report stated that every patient was receiving 'the best care in the best place on the ward'.[99] Whilst a Prime Minister, in response to an MP's description of her husband dying in hospital with all the dignity of a 'battery hen' in 2012, manages to concede only that some elderly patients did not receive 'appropriate' care.[100]

FICTION, FEAR, DOUBLETHINK – AND ENEMIES OF THE STATE

Perhaps the more apt comparison is with Stalin's Russia. Again, great caution must be taken. We live in a social democracy, not a totalitarian state. Even so, we should not be complacent about certain behaviours and ways of thinking that have more in common with totalitarian regimes than we might wish to admit.

Whisperers in the health service. First, in Stalin's Russia, if people said the wrong thing or indeed posed the most reasonable question about aspects of the regime's policy,

95   Lipsey, D. 'Read Trollope. We cannot afford to cut social services: you cannot improve productivity in care as easily as in other areas.' *The Times*, 29 November 2012.

96   Trollope, A. *The fixed period.* Oxford: Oxford University Press, 1993, pp.9, 21, 33.

97   Phair, L. 'The Vetting and Barring Scheme and its role in safeguarding.' Presentation notes at a 'Safeguarding vulnerable adults: empowerment through Implementation of "No secrets"' conference, 17 March 2010, London.

98   Hope, J. 'Shocking picture shows how elderly patient was abandoned for two days in hospital store cupboard with little food or medication.' *Daily Mail*, 14 February 2010.

99   Healthcare Commission. *Investigation into outbreaks of* Clostridium difficile *at Maidstone and Tunbridge Wells NHS Trust, October 2007.* London: HC, 2007, p.94.

100 Hill, A. 'Ann Clwyd: my husband died like a battery hen in hospital.' *The Guardian*, 4 December 2012.

they faced loss of their job, their housing and, in many cases, their freedom and lives. They became enemies of the state. This resulted in a great fear amongst many about expressing their doubts about the regime – to anybody at all. It was a generation of 'whisperers': whispering for fear of being overheard, or whispering behind people's backs and informing on them.[101]

Now, in the NHS, if practitioners (or indeed managers with a conscience) speak out, they may not risk loss of their freedom, but they do face loss of job, salary and sometimes mental health. There is a great fear in the NHS; were this not so, systemic neglect could not survive.

Misuse and misreporting of quotas (targets). Second, Stalin's Russia ran on targets: agricultural, industrial and sometimes virtually homicidal (quotas were imposed as to the number of 'kulaks' from each area or village who had to be dispossessed and deported to camps, where many died). As result, local officials would manipulate statistics and returns, just as happens in the NHS. Central government welcomed inflated returns, since it was political good news. But, on the back of that fiction, would then demand greater returns, placing even more impossible pressure on those local managers.

Quotas achieved at catastrophic effect to some. Third, the targets for grain output from the countryside in Russia were to support an increasing industrial workforce in the towns. Notwithstanding famine, inefficiencies created by 'collectivisation' of farms and unrealistic targets, the demand for grain was insatiable. The consequence was that the peasants were sacrificed, literally, in their millions – in favour of the growing urban population and the imperative of rapid industrialisation.

The NHS parallel is a model of care slanted toward adults (mainly younger) with single health conditions requiring treatment – at the expense and welfare of older people with complex needs.

Doublethink. Fourth, Stalin's Russia created a form of doublethink, in which slogans and policies in fact were often the reverse of reality. As portrayed and caricatured so famously by George Orwell in *1984*. That is, the ability to play tricks with reality, to do it consciously enough so as to succeed with the chicanery, but also sufficiently unconsciously so as to avoid feelings of guilt and to believe genuinely that reality has not been compromised. At its very heart, it is about marrying conscious deception to strength of purpose normally associated with total honesty. In essence, a monstrous system of mental cheating.[102]

There is no question at all that the NHS frequently employs every conceivable euphemism to distort the picture of what is really going on. Black is white, less is more, and – when patient services are cut, beds reduced, and staff made redundant, downgraded and demoralised – it is all about improvement, development and world-class standards of care.

When (already detailed above) patients are suffering, in pain and dying on the wards, as happened at Stafford Hospital, the official line was that good care was being provided. So much so that the Board congratulated itself with pay rises. And when 90 people were receiving substandard care and dying in the Maidstone and Tunbridge Wells NHS Trust, a nursing report stated that all patients were receiving the best possible care.

Are such comparisons purely fanciful? When a doctor's mental health was questioned by the General Medical Council following her exposure of poor care of elderly

---

101 Figes, O. *The whisperers: private life in Stalin's Russia.* London: Penguin, 2008, p.xxxii.

102 Orwell, G. (2003) *1984.* London: Penguin Books, p.244. (First published in 1949.)

hospital patients, a High Court judge thought not. He referred to her treatment being akin to totalitarianism in Russia: toe the party line or be deemed mentally ill.[103] An enemy of the State.

And if we doubt the doublethink, consider the following. The official line, according to the NHS Constitution, is:

> We respond with humanity and kindness to each person's pain, distress, anxiety or need. We search for things we can do, however small, to give comfort and relieve suffering... We do not wait to be asked because we care.[104]

The reality, arguably a direct result of the real – as opposed to the pretended – policy in the NHS, which disregards the elderly with complex needs, can be as follows:

> We got there about 10 o'clock and I could not believe my eyes. The door was wide open. There were people walking past. Mum was in bed with the cot sides up and she hadn't got a stitch of clothing on. I mean, she would have been horrified. She was completely naked and if I said covered in faeces, she was. It was everywhere. It was in her hair, her eyes, her nails, her hands and on all the cot side, so she had obviously been trying to lift herself up or move about, because the bed was covered and it was literally everywhere and it was dried. It would have been there a long time, it wasn't new.[105]

103 Transcript, day 2: *Dr Rita Pal v General Medical Council* [2004] EWHC 1485 (QB).

104 Department of Health. *NHS Constitution*. London: DH, 2012, p.14.

105 Quoted in: Francis, R. (Chair). *Independent inquiry into care provided by Mid Staffordshire NHS Foundation Trust January 2005–March 2009*. London: TSO, 2010, p.55.

8

Regulation of health and social care providers

KEY POINTS

Health and social care providers are regulated and inspected by the Care Quality Commission (CQC) under the Health and Social Care Act 2008.

Regulations set out what providers should be doing by way of providing care. The CQC is meant to prevent poor and neglectful care. Not totally, because there are always liable to be pockets of bad practice, which even an excellent regulator would not be able necessarily to root out. But poor care and neglect in health and social care, in State and private sectors, particularly of older people, is systemic, has been so for many years, and promises to remain and get worse. The Care Quality Commission and its predecessors have failed to prevent this happening.

In place since April 2009, the CQC is in fact an amalgam of the Healthcare Commission, the Commission for Social Care Inspection (CSCI) (previously responsible for regulating social care providers) and the Mental Health Act Commission. It is worth summarising the Commission's functions and powers. Its ineffectiveness is not because it lacks power, but it has lacked resources and the will to take a stronger lead and is subject to constant political pressure from the Department of Health.

SUMMARY OF CARE QUALITY COMMISSION'S ROLE

The CQC's role under the Health and Social Care Act 2008 is to register, review and investigate health (and social) care providers. It has the power to issue statutory warning notices, impose, vary or remove registration conditions, issue financial penalty notices, suspend or cancel registration, prosecute specified offences and issue simple cautions. Urgent cancellation orders can be sought from a justice of the peace if there is a serious risk to a person's life, health or well-being.

The Commission can prosecute in some circumstances, including for breach of specific regulations. These regulations cover neglectful and abusive health care and specifically mention dignity, nutrition, hydration and infection control. They also place a duty on care providers to operate systems to assess the risks of infection and to prevent, detect, treat and control its spread. Likewise, standards of design, cleanliness and hygiene in relation to equipment and premises must be adhered to.

Providers must make arrangements to ensure people's dignity, privacy and independence. There must be a proper system of record keeping, in order to protect service users against the risk of inappropriate care or treatment; there must also be sufficient numbers of suitably qualified, skilled and experienced staff. And service users must also be protected against the risks of unsuitable or unsafe premises and against the risks of unsafe, unsuitable or lack of equipment.[1]

In addition, there must be a complaints system geared toward assessing, preventing or reducing the impact of inappropriate care or treatment. It is a duty for care providers to report certain types of harm to the CQC (or NHS Commissioning Board), including certain types of patient death, harm, injuries, abuse and police involvement.

Overall, it is important to make this distinction between theory and practice. On the one hand, the Care Quality Commission has plenty of legal power to inspect, monitor and intervene, drastically if need be, in order to ensure that neglect and abuse are rooted out. On the other, it – like its predecessors – has failed to do this on anything like the scale arguably required.

---

1   SI 2010/781. The Health and Social Care Act 2008 (Regulated Activities) Regulations 2010.

REGULATION OF HEALTH AND SOCIAL CARE PROVIDERS: THE BASIC FRAMEWORK

The Health and Social Care Act 2008 created the Care Quality Commission.

The Commission has functions of registration, review, investigation in relation to health and social care, and functions under the Mental Health Act 1983. Health care is defined widely, as is social care.[2] The Act covers the NHS and local authorities, as well as independent providers of health and social care. The Commission replaced three previous regulators: the Healthcare Commission, the Commission for Social Care Inspection and the Mental Health Commission.

REGISTRATION

Anybody carrying on a regulated activity – that is, the provision of health and social care – must be registered with the CQC. Such provision includes the supply of staff, the provision of transport or accommodation for people requiring care, and the provision of advice in respect of care.[3]

HEALTH AND SOCIAL CARE DEFINITIONS

Health care includes all forms of health care provided for people, whether relating to physical or mental health, and also includes procedures that are similar to forms of medical or surgical care but are not provided in connection with a medical condition.

Social care includes all forms of personal care and other practical assistance provided for individuals who, by reason of age, illness, disability, pregnancy, childbirth, dependence on alcohol or drugs, or any other similar circumstances, are in need of such care or other assistance.[4]

REGISTRATION, CONDITIONS, SUSPENSION, CANCELLATION

It is an offence for a service provider not to be registered for a regulated activity.[5] Registration can be granted unconditionally or with conditions attached. Registration must be granted if the Commission is satisfied that the requirements have been met of regulations made under s.20 by the Secretary of State.[6] Managers must also apply for registration as prescribed.[7]

The Commission can cancel registration on a number of specified grounds; it can also suspend registration.[8]

The Act provides for regulations to be made in relation to the quality of services provided, health, safety, welfare, fitness of persons to carry on a regulated activity,

---

2   Health and Social Care Act 2008, s.2.
3   Health and Social Care Act 2008, s.8.
4   Health and Social Care Act 2008, s.9.
5   Health and Social Care Act 2008, s.10.
6   Health and Social Care Act 2008, s.12.
7   Health and Social Care Act 2008, s.13.
8   Health and Social Care Act 2008, ss.17–18.

management, training, premises, records, financial information and accounts, information about charges for services, requirements for review of the quality of services and for reports, handling of complaints and disputes. Regulations may also be made about preventing health care associated infections.[9] These regulations are summarised below.

CODE OF PRACTICE AND GUIDANCE

The Secretary of State may issue a code of practice about compliance with regulations;[10] and the Commission must issue compliance guidance in respect of the regulations.[11] The Commission must take account of both the code of practice and the guidance in reaching decisions, and both would be admissible in civil and criminal proceedings; non-compliance would not be decisive in liability.[12]

WARNING NOTICES, CANCELLATION, OFFENCES

The Commission can give statutory warning notices.[13] It can seek an order from a justice of the peace for urgent cancellation if there is a serious risk to a person's life, health or well-being.[14] There is also an urgent procedure for variation or suspension of registration.[15] Appeals lie to the Care Standards Tribunal.[16]

It is an offence for providers to fail to comply, without reasonable excuse, with conditions set by the Commission.[17] It is an offence to carry on regulated activity following suspension or cancellation of registration.[18] Regulations may specify that it is an offence to contravene them.[19] It is an offence to give a false description of a concern or of premises; likewise, to make false statements in applications for registration.[20]

The Act gives the Secretary of State power to publish statements of standards relating to health care.[21] The Commission must carry out periodic reviews of NHS bodies and local authorities. It can conduct special reviews and investigations.[22] It must recommend special measures to the Secretary of State in the case of failing local authorities.[23] The Commission has powers of entry and inspection and power to

---

9   Health and Social Care Act 2008, s.20.
10   Health and Social Care Act 2008, s.21.
11   Health and Social Care Act 2008, s.23.
12   Health and Social Care Act 2008, s.25.
13   Health and Social Care Act 2008, s.29.
14   Health and Social Care Act 2008, s.30.
15   Health and Social Care Act 2008, s.31.
16   Health and Social Care Act 2008, s.32.
17   Health and Social Care Act 2008, s.33.
18   Health and Social Care Act 2008, s.34.
19   Health and Social Care Act 2008, s.35.
20   Health and Social Care Act 2008, ss.36–37.
21   Health and Social Care Act 2008, s.45.
22   Health and Social Care Act 2008, s.46.
23   Health and Social Care Act 2008, s.50.

require information, documents and records it considers are necessary or expedient for any of its regulatory functions.[24]

The Act places restrictions on the disclosure of personal information that the Commission has obtained, but then provides an extensive list of permitted disclosures.[25]

REGULATIONS ABOUT QUALITY OF SERVICES, NEGLECT AND ABUSE

Regulations lay down more detailed rules about the quality of services, including protection from abuse and basic, essential standards of care.[26]

ARRANGEMENTS TO PREVENT AND RESPOND TO ABUSE

There must be suitable arrangements to ensure that service users are safeguarded against the risk of abuse.

Abuse is defined as: sexual abuse; physical or psychological ill-treatment; theft, misuse or misappropriation of money or property; or neglect and acts of omission which cause harm or place at risk of harm. Reference to neglect and acts of omission means that this aspect of the regulations overlaps with other aspects – concerning basic care – outlined below.

The provider must (a) take reasonable steps to identify the possibility of abuse and to prevent it, and (b) respond appropriately to any allegation of abuse.

Where any form of control or restraint is used in the carrying on of the regulated activity, the registered person must have suitable arrangements to protect service users against the risk of such control or restraint being unlawful or otherwise excessive.[27]

The Care Quality Commission has published, under s.23 of the Health and Social Care Act 2008, a guide to compliance called *Essential standards of quality and safety*.[28] The standards are a tool to aid judgement about compliance with the legislation.

One section covers abuse in particular, stating that providers should (bracketed headings added):

> [prevention] take action to identify and prevent abuse from happening in a service.

> [appropriate response] respond appropriately when it is suspected that abuse has occurred or is at risk of occurring.

> [guidance] ensure that Government and local guidance about safeguarding people from abuse is accessible to all staff and put into practice.

---

24   Health and Social Care Act 2008, ss.60–64.
25   Health and Social Care Act 2008, ss.76–80.
26   SI 2010/781. The Health and Social Care Act 2008 (Regulated Activities) Regulations 2010.
27   SI 2010/781. The Health and Social Care Act 2008 (Regulated Activities) Regulations 2010.
28   Care Quality Commission. *Essential standards of quality and safety*. London: CQC, 2009.

[restraint] make sure that the use of restraint is always appropriate, reasonable, proportionate and justifiable to that individual.

[de-escalation] only use de-escalation or restraint in a way that respects dignity and protects human rights, and where possible respects the preferences of people who use services.

[diversity and safeguarding] understand how diversity, beliefs and values of people who use services may influence the identification, prevention and response to safeguarding concerns.

[protection of other people] protect others from the negative effect of any behaviour by people who use services.

[deprivation of liberty] where applicable, only use Deprivation of Liberty Safeguards when it is in the best interests of the person who uses the service and in accordance with the Mental Capacity Act 2005.[29]

In addition, the guidance states that, in order to safeguard people, providers need to consider effective leadership, personalised care, promotion of rights and choices.[30]

UNSAFE CARE, NUTRITION, INFECTION, DIGNITY

Under the regulations, providers are obliged to protect service users from inappropriate or unsafe care or treatment, from health care associated infection, from the risks of unsafe use and management of medicines and from inadequate nutrition and hydration. And they must protect people's dignity.[31]

NUTRITION AND HYDRATION

There should be: (a) a choice of suitable and nutritious food and hydration, in sufficient quantities to meet service users' needs; (b) food and hydration that meet any reasonable requirements arising from a service user's religious or cultural background; and (c) support, where necessary, for the purposes of enabling service users to eat and drink sufficient amounts for their needs.[32]

INFECTION CONTROL

Inadequate infection control, linked to poor standards of care, has been implicated in avoidable patient deaths – sometimes running to scores of deaths in just one hospital. As a result, the regulations place a duty on care providers to operate systems to assess the risks of infection and to prevent, detect, treat and control the spread of infection.

---

29   Quoted from: Care Quality Commission. *Essential standards of quality and safety*, London: CQC, 2009, Outcome 7.
30   Care Quality Commission. *Essential standards of quality and safety*, London: CQC, 2009, Outcome 7.
31   SI 2010/781. The Health and Social Care Act 2008 (Regulated Activities) Regulations 2010.
32   SI 2010/781. The Health and Social Care Act 2008 (Regulated Activities) Regulations 2010.

In addition, providers must maintain appropriate standards of design, cleanliness and hygiene in relation to premises and equipment. This includes vehicles used for transporting patients for treatment – and also materials used to treat patients. It is an offence not to comply with these rules.[33]

A code of practice concerning infection control has been published under the Health and Social Care Act 2008. Breach of it may indicate a breach of the regulations. The Code covers a number of matters, including, in summary:

- implement systems to manage and monitor the prevention and control of infection

- provide and maintain a clean and appropriate environment

- provide suitable accurate information on infections to service users and their visitors

- provide suitable accurate information on infections to anybody concerned with providing further support or nursing/medical care

- ensure that people who have or develop an infection are identified promptly and receive the appropriate treatment and care to reduce the risk of passing on the infection to other people

- ensure that all staff and those employed to provide care in all settings are fully involved in the process of preventing and controlling infection

- provide or secure adequate isolation facilities

- secure adequate access to laboratory support

- have and adhere to policies that will help to prevent and control infections

- ensure, so far as is reasonably practicable, that care workers are free of and are protected from exposure to infections that can be caught at work and that all staff are suitably educated in the prevention and control of infection associated with the provision of health and social care.[34]

DIGNITY

The registered person must, so far as reasonably practicable, make suitable arrangements to ensure (a) the dignity, privacy and independence of service users, and (b) that service users are enabled to make, or participate in making, decisions relating to their care or treatment.

---

33   SI 2010/781. The Health and Social Care Act 2008 (Regulated Activities) Regulations 2010.
34   Department of Health. *The Health and Social Care Act 2008 code of practice for health and adult social care on the prevention and control of infections and related guidance.* London: DH, 2011, p.13.

The registered person must have in place arrangements for obtaining and acting on the consent of service users in relation to care and treatment provided. There must be a proper system of record keeping to protect service users against the risk of inappropriate care or treatment.[35]

All these are, of course, also important elements in the safeguarding of vulnerable adults; not talking to people, not consulting with them and not gaining their consent can too often be a slippery slope to harming them in one way or another. Likewise, the absence of recording – leading to an absence of monitoring, for example, nutrition, body weight, tissue viability, continence and bowel movements – can all too easily lead to neglectful care.

SUITABLE AND SUFFICIENT STAFF, EQUIPMENT AND PREMISES

In order to safeguard the health, safety and welfare of service users, the registered person must take appropriate steps to ensure that, at all times, there are sufficient numbers of suitably qualified, skilled and experienced staff. Service users must also be protected against the risks of unsuitable or unsafe premises, and against the risks of unsafe, unsuitable or lack of equipment.[36]

FITNESS OF PROVIDERS, MANAGERS AND STAFF

The regulations stipulate that – in relation to regulated activity – a person registered as a service provider, a registered manager or a worker must be fit to carry out that activity. He or she will not be fit unless he or she is of good character, physically and mentally fit to carry out the regulated activity and has the necessary qualifications, skills and experience to do so.[37]

For instance, according to equivalent rules under the Care Standards Act 2000 (preceding the Health and Social Care Act 2008), the Care Standards Tribunal found the following care home manager unfit.

Fitness of manager: death of resident. A resident died at 3.30am in a bath of scalding water. There were no thermostatic mixing valves. There had been no adequate risk assessment. There were also dangerously hot radiators. Parts of the home were badly stained and smelt badly. Residents were taken to the bathroom and brought back without their spectacles. The tribunal upheld the Commission for Social Care Inspection's finding that the manager of this home was unfit.[38]

INFORMATION ABOUT MANAGERS AND STAFF

Specified information must be available about managers and staff. This includes: proof of identity; criminal record certificate; evidence of conduct in previous employment (involving health or social care, or work with vulnerable adults or

---

35   SI 2010/781. The Health and Social Care Act 2008 (Regulated Activities) Regulations 2010.
36   SI 2010/781. The Health and Social Care Act 2008 (Regulated Activities) Regulations 2010.
37   SI 2010/781. The Health and Social Care Act 2008 (Regulated Activities) Regulations 2010.
38   *Hillier v Commission for Social Care Inspection* [2003] EWCST 0187 (NC).

children); where previous work involved vulnerable adults or children, satisfactory evidence about how that employment ended; satisfactory documentary evidence of any relevant qualification; full employment history; satisfactory evidence about physical or mental health conditions relevant to the work.

The registered person must operate effective recruitment procedures and also ensure that staff are registered, where necessary, with the appropriate professional body. If the person is no longer fit to undertake the work, the registered person should take appropriate steps. These would include informing the relevant professional body.[39]

COMPLAINTS SYSTEM

There must be a complaints system for the overall purpose of assessing, preventing or reducing the impact of inappropriate care or treatment.[40]

REPORTING HARM TO THE CARE QUALITY COMMISSION OR NHS COMMISSIONING BOARD

Regulations state that the registered person must inform the Care Quality Commission of certain types of harm suffered by a service user.[41]

NHS bodies need not report to the Commission if they have instead reported the incident to the National Health Service Commissioning Board.[42]

Health service reporting in this context was previously to the National Patient Safety Agency (NPSA, now abolished). This was with a view to there being 'national learning'.[43] And this was exactly the point. The NPSA gathered information and statistics and issued guidance. It didn't investigate. This separate system of reporting effectively meant that problems in the NHS were concealed. Reporting to the NHS Commissioning Board is likely to be with same end in mind: of controlling and concealing bad news.

DEATH OF A SERVICE USER

Matters that have to be reported without delay include the death of a service user (and the circumstances of it) whilst services were being provided or as a result of their being provided.

In the case of a health service body, the same obligation applies but only if the death cannot be reasonably attributed to the course of the service user's illness or medical condition (assuming he or she had been receiving appropriate care or treatment). The death or unauthorised absence of a service user detained (or liable

39   SI 2010/781. The Health and Social Care Act 2008 (Regulated Activities) Regulations 2010.
40   SI 2010/781. The Health and Social Care Act 2008 (Regulated Activities) Regulations 2010, r.19.
41   SI 2009/3112. Care Quality Commission (Registration) Regulations 2009.
42   SI 2009/3112. Care Quality Commission (Registration) Regulations 2009, r.16.
43   SI 2009/3112. Care Quality Commission (Registration) Regulations 2009.

to be detained) under the Mental Health Act 1983 must also be notified without undue delay.[44]

REPORTING INJURY, ABUSE, DEPRIVATION OF LIBERTY, POLICE INVOLVEMENT

In addition, a range of other incidents must be reported without delay. These include injury, deprivation of liberty, abuse, police involvement, safety of service including adequacy of staff. In summary:

(a) **injury** to the service user which a health professional reasonably believes has resulted in (i) an impairment of the sensory, motor or intellectual functions of the service user which is not likely to be temporary, (ii) changes to the structure of a service user's body, (iii) the service user experiencing prolonged pain or prolonged psychological harm, or (iv) the shortening of the life expectancy of the service user

(b) **injury** to a service user which a health professional reasonably believes requires treatment to prevent death or an injury which, if left untreated, would lead to one or more of the outcomes outlined immediately above

(c) **deprivation of liberty:** request to a local authority or primary care trust for a standard authorisation to deprive a person lacking capacity of his or her liberty, or application to a court for the same purpose

(d) **abuse:** any abuse or allegation of abuse in relation to a service user

(e) **police:** any incident which is reported to, or investigated by, the police (this does not apply to an NHS body)

(f) **safety:** anything that may prevent the safe provision of services or adherence to registration requirements, including insufficient number of qualified, skilled and experienced staff – and other issues affecting the provision of services.[45]

EFFECTIVENESS OF REGULATORS

Central government has, for well over a decade, made great play of regulation and continues to chop and change the legislation, apparently to try to get it right.

However, this continual tampering is suggestive of just how political the issue of regulation has become. And the motives of central government are, it must be concluded, opaque and mixed – for political reasons.

The Department of Health is presumably keen, on the one hand, to avoid political scandal and probably hopes that the Care Quality Commission will detect and prevent catastrophes.

---

44   SI 2009/3112. Care Quality Commission (Registration) Regulations 2009, r.17.
45   SI 2009/3112. Care Quality Commission (Registration) Regulations 2009, r.18.

But, equally, it seems that government does not want truly independent and thorough regulation. It appears not to want evidence coming to light of serious problems because of the political embarrassment that ensues. As pointed out in Chapter 7, government and the NHS go to enormous lengths to suppress knowledge of poor care, neglect, suffering and death.

In addition, government wishes to promote the advancement of independent health and social providers – those providing services both under contract to the NHS and local authorities and in their own right direct to people privately. Efficient and firm – some might say heavy-handed – regulation could be seen as commercially unattractive. So, from government's point of view, it tries to walk a tightrope.

There is no doubt that the Care Quality Commission has the requisite powers. It sometimes removes registration status from care homes. And, even short of deregistration and closure, it can prosecute. For instance:

Prosecution of care home. The Care Quality Commission had visited a care home. It requested that the home review various arrangements to rectify failings that had been identified. Two months later, the home had still not rectified these. The Commission prosecuted the home for failing to comply with care homes regulations requiring them to make arrangements for the recording, handling, safe keeping, safe administration and disposal of medicines, and failing to ensure that care plans properly reflected how residents' needs were to be met. The care home was fined £1600 on each charge and had to cover the Commission's legal costs of nearly £800.[46]

The problem is that, in the case of care homes, the Care Quality Commission has been unable to enforce reasonable standards across the board. And, in the case of the NHS, it has simply declined to exercise its powers effectively, for what are probably largely political reasons.

REGULATORY APPROVAL DOES NOT GUARANTEE ABSENCE OF ABUSE AND NEGLECT

Repeatedly, scandals have occurred, involving providers who have been approved by the relevant regulatory body.

There is frequently a disconnection between a care provider's quality, according to the regulator, and its actual performance. Because it must be remembered that health and social care providers, in order to operate at all, must be registered by the Care Quality Commission as fit to do so.

This concern applies, twofold, to both the CQC as well its predecessors. First, the ratings given to providers are exposed with some frequency as being unreliable. Second, these ratings have been based in the past, and continue to rely (though not wholly), on self-assessment and self-reporting.[47]

The following are merely a few examples, chosen from many.

---

46   Care Quality Commission. *CQC prosecutes care home for breaches in regulations. News, 15 February 2010*. London: CQC.
47   'Spot-checks reveal mistakes when hospitals self-certify.' *BBC News*, 8 March 2010. Accessed on 5 August 2010 at: http://news.bbc.co.uk/1/hi/uk/8551668.stm.

Abuse at care home undetected for years: Health and Safety Executive step in, in the absence of action from the regulator. Physical abuse at a care home in Hull had gone effectively undetected for a period of three years; eventually, several care workers were sent to prison and health and safety prosecutions were brought as well.[48] Yet, during this period, the home was registered and must have been inspected on a number of occasions.

Newspaper, not regulator, exposing neglect in a care home. After a newspaper undercover report revealed evidence of abuse and neglect in a care home run by Southern Cross, the CSCI inspected the home and found 'inadequate' standards shortly afterwards. However, the home had been inspected on a number of previous occasions and received 'poor' inspection reports, which included details about complaints concerning the mistreatment of residents. Yet it seemed that the newspaper's investigations were required to bring things to a head and for CSCI now to issue statutory notices.

Incontinence pads not changed and full of flies; carers who could not communicate with residents. The reporter wrote about residents waiting for hours before incontinence pads were changed; flies crawling inside one pad when it was removed; manual handling techniques employed persistently in a way that could harm residents; care assistants unable to communicate with residents because of poor English; residents pulled across beds instead of slide sheets being used; stone cold food; inadequate numbers of staff to help people eat and drink; poor staff hygiene with carers not washing their hands, changing gloves or aprons between handling each resident; unavailability of clean clothes; shortages of sheets and towels; broken washing machine.

Italian wallpaper but 'no bloody sheets'. The manager had called a meeting about turning the care home into a five-star hotel; one of the staff had commented to the reporter that while management talked of posh Italian wallpaper and flat-screen televisions, there were 'no bloody sheets'.[49]

Excessive deaths, poor hygiene despite high score on hygiene. When Basildon and Thurrock University Hospitals NHS Foundation Trust was investigated by the CQC because of apparently excessive death rates, very poor standards of hygiene were found. The Trust was served with a warning notice. And yet it had recently scored 13 out of 14 for cleanliness.[50]

High-quality care declared in the middle of degrading care and death. The Mid Staffordshire NHS Foundation Trust had received a 'fair' rating for some years from the Healthcare Commission despite its high rates of mortality.[51] In its successful attempt to gain elite foundation trust status in February 2008, it had declared to the regulating body Monitor that it was delivering high-quality care to patients – even though it was doing precisely the opposite.[52]

Mice and cockroach infestations despite self-assessed good hygiene standards. The Mental Health Act Commission reported a patient's evidence of infestations of mice and cockroaches, despite the Trust's own declared approval of its standards of hygiene:

48   Mark, D. 'Care home firm which failed to act on abuse claims is fined £100,000.' *Yorkshire Post*, 28 October 2005.
49   Newell, C. 'Exposed: filth and abuse in care home.' *Sunday Times*, 4 November, 2007.
50   Bowcott, O. 'Hygiene inquiry into deaths at Essex NHS trust.' *The Guardian*, 26 November, 2009.
51   Healthcare Commission (2009) *Investigation into Mid Staffordshire NHS Foundation Trust, March 2009*. London: HC, p.17.
52   Francis, R. (Chair). *Independent inquiry into care provided by Mid Staffordshire NHS Foundation Trust January 2005–March 2009*. London: TSO, 2010, p.182.

'…there are mice everywhere on the ward; in the bedroom, dining room, day room. They sometimes crawl up on the table when we have our meals.' Although we had raised the issue of cleanliness and vermin infestation with the Trust, the hospital concerned had self-assessed itself as compliant with Healthcare Commission hygiene standards throughout this reporting period. Were it not for our visits to the hospital concerned this disparity would not have been evident.[53]

Deaths of several residents from pressure sores in highly praised care home. At the Briars care home in Southampton, the owner and manager were convicted of wilful neglect after the deaths of a number of residents between January 2007 and August 2008. Suspicion first arose in August 2007 following one resident's death in hospital from a large pressure sore. And yet, no more than a few months earlier in May 2007, the CSCI – then regulatory body for social care, now part of the CQC – had referred to the home as well maintained, bright and comfortable, as well as praising the commitment, attitude and professionalism of staff.[54] (The convictions were subsequently overturned because of failings in the way the prosecution case was put and the judge's summing up.)

Neglect, screaming with pain, death: regulator arrives too late. In February 2009, an 85-year-old man was admitted from the Eltandia Hall nursing home to hospital, screaming with the pain of pressure sores and gangrene. The inquest found he died of heart failure precipitated by neglect. The coroner said it was one of the worst cases of nursing home care she had seen. The Inspectorate (then the Commission for Social Care Inspection) went in and began to enforce higher standards but only *after* the event, in April 2009.[55]

Care agency with highest rating from the regulator employs ill-qualified staff member who causes severe brain damage to service user. In 2009, a 37-year-old man with tetraplegia was living in his own home, where he received care and was dependent on a life support machine. Though physically paralysed, he could talk, use a wheelchair and operate a computer by means of voice activation. Responsibility for his care lay with Wiltshire NHS Primary Care Trust (PCT).

The Trust contracted out his care to an agency. He was concerned about the standard of care, so much so that he complained by email to the NHS; he received no answer. He had a web camera installed. The camera then caught a nurse switching off his life support machine inadvertently and failing to switch it back on. The man was aware of what was happening and urgently clicked his tongue, before he lost consciousness. Deprived of oxygen for 20 minutes, he suffered brain damage which reduced his intellectual abilities to that of a young child.

Highest rating but systemic failings in the provider. The agency concerned, Ambition 24hours, to which the care had been contracted out and for whom the nurse worked, had received the highest rating from the CSCI but three months before the incident. Furthermore, at the end of 2009, the CQC also gave it the maximum rating. However, the PCT's investigation revealed that the nurse involved was not qualified in the use of such ventilators, even though this was a requirement of the job. Furthermore, Ambition 24hours

---

53   Mental Health Act Commission. *Risk, rights, recovery: twelfth biennial report, 2005–2007.* London: MHAC, 2008, p.55.

54   Martin, A. 'Everybody makes mistakes: care home owner denies neglect following suspicious deaths of six elderly residents.' *Daily Mail*, 25 September 2008.

55   Burnett, C. 'Norbury Eltandia care home resident died after neglect, coroner finds.' *Streatham Guardian*, 25 November 2009.

had inadequate systems for checking the training their staff had received.[56] The nurse was subsequently struck off the nursing register, since she had undertaken to provide care on that shift which she was not competent to provide.[57]

Lack of communication by Care Quality Commission: contributing factor in death of five care home residents from pressure sores and malnutrition. In 2009, five residents at the Parkside Nursing Home, Northampton, died within the same week of what appeared to be self-neglect, including severe pressure sores. The subsequent serious case review noted that, although the CQC had judged the home's adequate rating to be marginal, nonetheless it had not then consulted with professionals to gain further information about what was going on. Conversely, the individual professionals from social services and the NHS involved with the home did not identify or do anything about what should have been obvious: that the home was not caring adequately for some of its residents.[58]

Death of two care home residents from falls: failure of Care Quality Commission to identify risks and dangers at the home. A serious case review was conducted by the Devon Adults Safeguarding Board into care and safety at a care home, including two fatal incidents involving falls. It noted that the home had received an adequate, then a good, rating from the Commission for Social Care Inspection (CQC's predecessor), but that the Commission had, in effect, failed to identify some of the most serious environmental risks and dangers to the elderly vulnerable residents of the care home.[59]

Winterbourne View and abuse of people with learning disabilities: acceptable rating by the Care Quality Commission and failure to act on whistleblowing. In 2011, the CQC's inability to intervene effectively was highlighted in a *Panorama* programme about abuse and neglect of people with learning disabilities at Winterbourne View private hospital in Bristol, run by Castlebeck Ltd. Previously, the home had received an acceptable rating by the regulator. Worse, when a senior nurse contacted the CQC several times prior to the *Panorama* programme, he was largely ignored.[60]

Care Quality Commission: relative inaction following findings that 55 per cent of 100 hospitals inspected were breaking the law or nearly doing so on dignity and nutrition. Perhaps most worrying is the 100 dignity and nutrition inspections carried out by CQC during 2011 at the instigation of Paul Burstow, the Care Services Minister at the time. The Commission found that some 20 per cent were breaking the law and that another 35 per cent constituted a cause for concern.[61]

Lack of urgency on the CQC's part to safeguard individual patients subject to neglect. In their analysis Action on Elder Abuse pointed out the complete lack of urgency and effectiveness of the CQC in doing anything about the appalling state of affairs it had uncovered:

> Additionally, these inspections suggest CQC has little or no sense of urgency in terms of its regulatory activity, often leaving very vulnerable people in neglectful and

56   Lister, S. and de Bruxelles, S. 'Nurse switched off life support by accident.' *The Times*, 26 October 2010.

57   'Agency nurse struck off for switching off ventilator.' *Nursing Times*, 16 March 2012.

58   Sloper, G. *Serious case review, Executive Summary: Parkside House, 49–53 St Matthews Parade, Northampton NN2 7HE.* Northampton: Northamptonshire Safeguarding Adults Board, 2010, paras a, 1, 5.

59   Devon Safeguarding Adults Board. *Serious case review (B): following concerns over care and safety standards in a care home and two fatal incidents.* Exeter: DSAB, 2001, para 4.9.

60   BBC *Panorama*. 'Undercover care: the abuse exposed.' First broadcast 31 May 2011.

61   Care Quality Commission. *Dignity and nutrition inspection programme: national overview.* London: CQC, 2011, p.6.

abusive settings while waiting for 'action plans' to be delivered by a care provider. In our view this is a major failing in its 'duty of care' and could leave CQC open to legal action by patients and their families, particularly where it has failed to respond to section 44 of the Mental Capacity Act 2005 in relation to the neglect of patients without capacity.[62]

Inaction of the Department of Health. Action on Elder Abuse went on:

And the Department of Health cannot stand back as yet another impartial observer of life. If the systems are not working they must act. And at least two reports this year told them the system was not working. The CQC reports scream it at them. They must do more than just ask for views and opinions, and talk about independent regulation, and consider their position against a back drop of political change. They too must act with urgency and immediacy.[63]

These are but a few examples. In fact, in every instance of 'scandal', of shocking care, of neglect, the Commission has almost by definition come on the scene too late. Up to that point, regulated and approved by the Commission, the provider would have been suitable, ready and open for business. To be fair, the odd case is inevitable, but what calls into question the regulator's effectiveness is the sheer number of instances in which systemic poor care has gone undetected.

This does mean that commissioners of care, service users and their families cannot, without more information, put store by the judgements of CQC. And those involved in safeguarding should not be lulled into a false sense of security by the actions, judgements and ratings of the Commission.

62   Action on Elder Abuse. *Regulatory activity in hospital settings: a critical analysis of the Care Quality Commission's Dignity and Nutrition Inspection of 100 English Hospitals.* London: AEA, 2011, p.12.

63   Action on Elder Abuse. *Regulatory activity in hospital settings: a critical analysis of the Care Quality Commission's Dignity and Nutrition Inspection of 100 English Hospitals.* London: AEA, 2011, p.5.

9

Regulation of health and social care professionals

Key points
    Professional codes state that service users should not be harmed
        and that professionals should speak up if they see harm happening
General Medical Council
    General Medical Council guidance: confidentiality, neglect and abuse
    Nursing and Midwifery Council
    Health and Care Professions Council
Professional regulation of poor, neglectful and abusive practice
Systemic failings in health and social care
    Systemic failures in nursing care

KEY POINTS

The second main area of regulation, aside from the regulation of providers by the Care Quality Commission, is the registration of health and social care professionals. They are regulated under legislation by statutory bodies.

The four main bodies have in the past been the General Medical Council (GMC), Nursing and Midwifery Council (NMC), Health Professions Council and General Social Care Council.[1] In the summer of 2012, the latter two merged to become the Health and Care Professions Council.

These regulatory bodies have the power to impose sanctions including suspension, conditions of practice and striking-off. To the extent that these councils have been successful in their role, they have been conspicuously more so in the case of the individual rogues, as it were, than in the case of those professionals caught up in widespread and systemic neglect. To date, where numbers of professionals have been involved in gross organisational and professional failures, they tend to be left to get on with it by the regulatory councils.

This chapter sets out the legal framework, key points from codes of practice and a selection of illustrative professional conduct cases. In particular, it also explores, using case law, how the Nursing and Midwifery Council could tackle poor care that is typical of systemic, rather than isolated, poor treatment and neglect.

---

1   Medical Act 1983 (doctors), SI 2002/253. Nursing and Midwifery Order (for nurses). And: SI 2002/254. Health and Social Work Professions Order (for allied health professionals and social workers). The latter two orders are made under the Health Act 1999.

PROFESSIONAL CODES STATE THAT SERVICE USERS SHOULD NOT BE HARMED AND THAT PROFESSIONALS SHOULD SPEAK UP IF THEY SEE HARM HAPPENING

The three main professional codes state two important and obvious things. First, professionals should not be harming service users. Second, if they see harm coming to service users, then they should say something about it.

These are very simple principles, yet they are clearly being ignored by many professionals. The reported scale of neglect in, for example, hospitals and care homes is such that not only must it be the case that significant numbers of professionals are involved, but also that many more have witnessed this happening without formally raising their concerns.

GENERAL MEDICAL COUNCIL

The General Medical Council's *Good medical practice* states:

> Doctors should treat patients with dignity, treat each patient as an individual, support patients.

It goes on to state, unequivocally, that this is not just a matter of not directly harming patients but is also about speaking out:

> If patient safety is seriously compromised by inadequate premises, equipment, resources, policies or systems, the doctor should put the matter right. Otherwise the doctor should tell the employer. If they take inadequate action, the doctor should take independent advice on how to take the matter further – and record the concerns and steps taken.[2]

Such is the concern that medical doctors are not speaking out about the poor or neglectful care that they witness, the General Medical Council issued further guidance in 2012. It emphasises, bluntly, that doctors have a professional duty to put patients' interests first, even if they are anxious that by speaking out 'nothing will be done or that raising your concern may cause problems for colleagues; have a negative effect on working relationships; have a negative effect on your career; or result in a complaint about you'. Thus:

- You have a duty to put patients' interests first and act to protect them, which overrides personal and professional loyalties.

- The law provides legal protection against victimisation or dismissal for individuals who reveal information to raise genuine concerns and expose malpractice in the workplace.

---

2   General Medical Council. *Good medical practice.* London: GMC, 2006, pp.9, 11.

- You do not need to wait for proof – you will be able to justify raising a concern if you do so honestly, on the basis of reasonable belief and through appropriate channels, even if you are mistaken.[3]

The British Medical Association also has issued specific guidance on whistleblowing, which points out that raising concerns may not be a matter just of personal conscience but of professional obligation.[4]

GENERAL MEDICAL COUNCIL GUIDANCE: CONFIDENTIALITY, NEGLECT AND ABUSE

The General Medical Council comes at the same issue in yet further guidance, this time on confidentiality.

It makes three key points. First, doctors should avoid disclosure without patient consent if the only risk arising is to the patient themselves. However, disclosure could be 'justified in the public interest if failure to disclose may expose others to a risk of death or serious harm. You should still seek the patient's consent to disclosure if practicable and consider any reasons given for refusal.'[5]

It goes on to consider neglect and abuse in the context of people lacking capacity to consent to disclosure:

If you believe that a patient may be a victim of neglect or physical, sexual or emotional abuse, and that they lack capacity to consent to disclosure, you must give information promptly to an appropriate responsible person or authority, if you believe that the disclosure is in the patient's best interests or necessary to protect others from a risk of serious harm. If, for any reason, you believe that disclosure of information is not in the best interests of a neglected or abused patient, you should discuss the issues with an experienced colleague. If you decide not to disclose information, you should document in the patient's record your discussions and the reasons for deciding not to disclose. You should be prepared to justify your decision.[6]

NURSING AND MIDWIFERY COUNCIL

The Nursing and Midwifery Council's code of conduct states:

You must treat people as individuals and respect their dignity. You must not discriminate in any way against those in your care. You must treat people kindly and considerately.

---

3   Quoted from: General Medical Council. *Raising and acting on concerns about patient safety.* London: GMC, 2012, paras 7–10.

4   British Medical Association. *Whistleblowing. Advice for BMA members working in NHS secondary care about raising concerns in the workplace.* London: BMA, 2009, p.4.

5   General Medical Council. *Confidentiality.* London: GMC, 2009, paras 51–53.

6   General Medical Council. *Confidentiality.* London: GMC, 2009, para 63.

And goes on to discuss disclosure of information if a patient is at risk of harm or standards of care are falling:

- You must disclose information if you believe someone may be at risk of harm...

- You must act without delay if you believe that you, a colleague or anyone else may be putting someone at risk.

- You must inform someone in authority if you experience problems that prevent you working within this Code or other nationally agreed standards.

- You must report your concerns in writing if problems in the environment of care are putting people at risk.[7]

HEALTH AND CARE PROFESSIONS COUNCIL

The Health and Care Professions Council regulates various health professionals including art therapists, biomedical scientists, chiropodists and podiatrists, clinical scientists, dieticians, hearing aid dispensers, occupational therapists, operating department practitioners, orthoptists, paramedics, physiotherapists, practitioner psychologists, prosthetists and orthotists, radiographers, and speech and language therapists.

From August 2012, it has also regulated social workers in England. This came about when the General Social Care Council was abolished and the register of social workers was transferred to the Health Professions Council – which, in turn, changed its name to become the Health and Care Professions Council.[8]

The code of conduct states simply:

You must treat service users with respect and dignity.

And:

You must protect service users if you believe that any situation puts them in danger. This includes the conduct, performance or health of a colleague. The safety of service users must come before any personal or professional loyalties at all times. As soon as you become aware of a situation that puts a service user in danger, you should discuss the matter with a senior colleague or another appropriate person.[9]

---

7   Quoted from: Nursing and Midwifery Council. *The Code: standards of conduct, performance and ethics for nurses and midwives.* London: NMC, 2008, pp.2–3.

8   SI 2012/1479. The Health and Social Care Act 2012 (Consequential Provision – Social Workers) Order 2012.

9   Health Professions Council. *Standards of conduct, performance and ethics.* London: HPC, 2008, p.8.

PROFESSIONAL REGULATION OF POOR, NEGLECTFUL AND ABUSIVE PRACTICE

The following examples are drawn from Nursing and Midwifery Council cases and relate to action taken against nurses, acting individually, in a clearly unacceptable manner. They form a small selection, to give just a flavour of the relevance to safeguarding.

Not reporting harm perpetrated by others. A nurse who witnessed a care assistant roughly handling a resident failed to stop it, failed to report it and advised another colleague not to report it. A caution was placed against the nurse's entry in the register. She had a good history, it was an isolated incident, she admitted and regretted it, and had provided good testimonials.[10]

Mocking patients. A nurse put a patient's glass eye in a ward sister's drink, painted a smiley face on a patient's fist-sized hernia and falsified patient records with a magic pen. She was struck off by the NMC.[11]

Financial abuse of patients. Following conviction in the Crown Court on six counts of theft, five of false accounting and 13 of obtaining property by deception, a nurse was sentenced to 18 months in prison. The Council struck her off the register, given the gross abuse of trust of the vulnerable people from whom she had dishonestly obtained property.[12]

Physical abuse, unacceptable restraint and violence. A nurse, working in a nursing home, was struck off following a number of allegations including leaving a patient with learning disabilities lying in his own vomit, dragging a patient by his collar, slamming a door in his face, stamping on his foot and calling him a 'thieving bastard'.[13]

Likewise, a nurse was struck off for, amongst other things, rough handling of patients, which represented a failure to treat the patients with dignity and respect.[14]

Striking-off befell a nurse in respect of various failures including assaulting a resident (for which she had been convicted in court), rough handling of a resident, slapping the resident's hand and telling the resident that he was a 'naughty boy'.[15]

Striking-off followed for a nurse who had spoken inappropriately to a patient by telling him to shut up and had roughly handled him by pinning his arm to the bed and putting his hand around his neck – this was 'wholly unnecessary physical restraint'.[16]

A nurse in a care home was issued with a caution order, having taken hold of a resident's hand, put his arm up his back, marched him to his room and pushed him on to the bed. The Council was concerned at this treatment of a vulnerable elderly resident but took into account that it was not done maliciously, that it was a one-off incident and that there were no other concerns about the nurse's practice.[17]

A caution order followed also when a nurse slapped a patient's leg, pulled and yanked it. The nurse nearly suffered removal from the register because physical abuse of an elderly and demented patient was a very serious matter. But she had a 36-year unblemished work

10   Nursing and Midwifery Council: Case 01G20690, 4 October 2007.
11   Ward, D. 'Nurse who put patient's glass eye in drink is struck off.' *The Guardian*, 17 February 2006.
12   Nursing and Midwifery Council: Case 712h2138E, 28 March 2008.
13   'Nurse who left man lying in own vomit is struck off.' *South Manchester Reporter*, 29 January 2004.
14   Nursing and Midwifery Council: Case 83Y0105W, 6 March 2008.
15   Nursing and Midwifery Council: Case 02H12440, 8 January 2008.
16   Nursing and Midwifery Council: Case 87H01616E, 26 July 2007.
17   Nursing and Midwifery Council: Case L71Y1288E, 12 July 2007.

record, it was an isolated incident and she had impressive references and testimonials. A caution order was the proportionate response.[18]

Verbal abuse. Striking-off from the register followed findings that a nurse, amongst other things, had said to a patient, 'If you were a dog you would have been put down, instead I'll smack your arse.'[19]

And a nurse was struck off for, amongst other things, slapping a resident, verbal abuse to residents ('get your fucking legs off the lift', 'you can't fucking hear anyway', 'talk to the hand because the face ain't listening') and rough handling of a resident after failing to warn the resident that she was about to move her.[20]

Neglect and emotional harm. A nurse working in a care home with people with learning disabilities forced a resident out of a chair, inappropriately requested he remove his crockery without assistance (this was not part of his routine, it put him at physical risk, added to his mental and emotional distress, and was not part of his formal or informal care plan), saw him fall but failed to provide or allow appropriate assistance to be given, and failed to report the fall. In respect of the latter, he was in a state of shock and disarray; the nurse went on hovering around him. The nurse was struck off.[21]

Inappropriate personal relationships. A nurse was struck off for developing an inappropriate relationship with a patient who was vulnerable and required care at a time of major crisis in her life; this represented a total abuse of his professional status.[22]

SYSTEMIC FAILINGS IN HEALTH AND SOCIAL CARE

The regulatory councils have generally found it a challenge to act against individuals caught up in systemic failings in health and social care. There are at least three reasons for this.

First, it is more difficult to locate professional and moral responsibility blame when the matter is institutional.

Second, even if responsibility is identified, there might be resistance to blaming an individual.

Third, the prospect of acting against numbers of professionals within one large workplace, such as a hospital, might be singularly unappealing to the regulatory body. It would involve considerable work and also diminish the reputation of the profession as a whole.

That said, there are two further considerations to bear in mind. First, it is easier to tackle a systemic problem in a smaller institution – and one that is not protected by a large bureaucracy (such as the NHS), evincing defensiveness and practising concealment.

And, second, it is open to the regulatory body to argue that the individual retains professional responsibility even in the face of institutional failure. The Nursing and Midwifery Council's code of conduct states:

18   Nursing and Midwifery Council: Case 68IO223N, 10 October 2007.
19   Nursing and Midwifery Council: Case 83A0008E, 27 March 2008.
20   Nursing and Midwifery Council: Case 8711737E, 17 October 2007.
21   Nursing and Midwifery Council: Case 79K0365E, 16 July 2007.
22   Nursing and Midwifery Council: Case 89H0066H, 12 September 2007.

> As a professional, you are personally accountable for actions and omissions in your practice and must always be able to justify your decisions.[23]

The Council seems, in the past, for whatever reasons, to have taken this principle sometimes to heart in the case of the independent care sector but not in the case of the National Health Service.

A further obstacle, however, is the extreme slowness with which regulatory bodies sometimes act. For instance, in 2012, the Nursing and Midwifery Council applied to the High Court to extend the interim suspensions against nurses allegedly involved in the deaths, through pressure sores and malnutrition, of five elderly people in 2009. The High Court warned the Council that it could not extend its investigations forever. The Council had claimed the case was the biggest and most complex it had ever been faced with.[24]

Yet, even more remarkably, in 2012, the Council concluded a case against two nurses that had taken 11 years. It revolved around Lynde House Care Home in Twickenham and allegations that residents were neglected – for example, having faeces under their fingernails, not being washed and not having water to drink. The Council eventually found misconduct proved but decided to take no further action against the two nurses.[25]

This does not bode well for the Council ever getting to grips with the large scale of neglect that sometimes occurs in hospitals.

SYSTEMIC FAILURES IN NURSING CARE

The following example involved systemic failings in a care home.

Multiple failings in care. The registered manager of a care home was struck off on a whole host of grounds. These included the finding of a resident sitting in a darkened room with a mattress on the floor and faecal matter on the bedding, and a number of residents with their mattress on the floor. However, wider failings, too many to list, included, for example, missing toilet seats, showers not working, dirty fridges, malodorous rooms, incontinence pads in waste bins in toilets, call bells missing, fluid intake charts not completed, pressure sore wound assessment and management not recorded.[26]

One case stands out, in which a director of nursing was, very unusually, held to account (at least on an interim basis) at a large acute hospital.

Director of nursing suspended for implementing cuts to standards of care. Following the revelations of the independent inquiry into patient care at Stafford Hospital, the Nursing and Midwifery Council, unusually if not uniquely, raised its sights to a director of nursing and imposed an 18-month interim suspension order, pending further enquiries.

23   Nursing and Midwifery Council. *The Code: standards of conduct, performance and ethics for nurses and midwives.* London: NMC, 2008, p.1.

24   Spoors, N. 'Top judge criticises investigation delays into misconduct of nurses at Northampton care home.' *Northampton Chronicle & Echo,* 2 April 2012.

25   Bishop, R. 'Longest case ends with two Twickenham nursing home workers guilty.' *Richmond & Twickenham Times,* 22 December 2011.

26   Nursing and Midwifery Council: Case 75U6681E, 27–28 March 2008.

The grounds related to allegations about the failure to maintain safe levels of nursing practice, infection control and patient care. The case against her was that they were serious allegations, there was a risk of repetition if she took on a similar, senior role elsewhere, and she evinced both denial and lack of insight into the alleged failings. An interim suspension order was justifiable for general protection of the public and also of the reputation of the profession and the Council.[27]

Nonetheless, this last case is an exception. It is more usual for the NMC to look into systemic failures in care homes, rather than the NHS, and sometimes hold individuals to account, even if they were merely part of a wider system of poor care.

In the following case, both the NMC and the GMC took action against professionals at a care home in Birmingham.

Systemic failure in care home in Birmingham. In 2002, a 77-year-old war veteran, Mr Leslie Vines, entered the Maypole Nursing Home. He suffered from Alzheimer's disease and Parkinson's disease, but was otherwise considered to be physically fit. Ten days later he was dead, having been sedated and placed in a bucket chair, which effectively immobilised him and may have restricted his ability to breathe when he contracted a chest infection. The inquest returned a verdict of death from natural causes.

This verdict did not mean that all had been well at the care home. By 2003, the home had been closed down because of concerns about the death of 15 other residents as well. As a result, in June 2008, three nurses – including a manager – responsible for the care of patients were struck off the nursing register by the NMC. Their professional misconduct included incorrect medication, inappropriate restraint, and hygiene and personal care failings. All this had led to a lack of dignity for the elderly and vulnerable residents. In addition, the two general practitioners (GPs) who owned the home, husband and wife, were struck off the medical register by the GMC.[28]

In the next case, the list of failures for which the nurse was struck off come up time and again in the evidence, over the past 15 years, in relation to poor care and neglect in NHS hospitals. If the NMC applied a similar approach as it did to this nurse working in a care home, there would have been sanctions against large numbers of hospital nurses. She had covertly administered medication in a resident's beaker and allowed medication to be stored in an unlocked bathroom. In addition, she had failed to ensure, in summary:

- the room was kept clean
- oral swabs were disposed of
- there were bumpers on the bed rails
- fresh drinks
- the resident was offered fluids from 6.30 to 8.45am

27   Nursing and Midwifery Council. *Interim suspension order decision: Janice Margaret Harry*, PIN 70I1747E, 25 October 2010. London: NMC.

28   Mitchell, I. 'Inquest returns verdict of natural causes in Maypole Nursing Home death.' *News*, 15 March 2010. Accessed on 20 September 2010 at: www.irwinmitchell.com/news/Pages/Inquestreturnsverdict ofnaturalcausesinMaypoleNursingHomedeath.aspx.

- fluids were recorded

- the care plan was kept up to date

- a pain assessment

- a pressure-relieving care plan

- instructions given to her were followed (she didn't ensure the resident was offered fluids every 15 minutes and did not make sure fluids offered were recorded)

- another resident's care plan was kept up to date

- a referral to a dietician.[29]

In 2004, three nurses were struck off for their part in what must have been a systemic breakdown of care, in 2000, at the Wells Spring Nursing Home in Bradford. A fourth nurse received a caution.

Pressure sores: nurses held accountable. A man was admitted to the home just for a week while his wife underwent cataract surgery. He had long-standing Parkinson's disease but was otherwise described as strong and healthy. By the end of the week, he had developed multiple pressure sores so painful he cried if they were touched; he was admitted to hospital where he died three months later of bronchopneumonia. His wife had repeatedly asked the home that a pressure-relief mattress be supplied for her husband; it was not. In reaching its decision, the NMC's professional conduct committee stressed personal, professional responsibility: 'Each individual nurse had an obligation to champion the care of this patient, and failed.'[30]

In another case, an argument put forward by a nurse, that her failure to attend to patients was part of the accepted system at the Parkside House care home where five people died from pressure sores, failed.

Poor pressure sore care practices part of the system of work at the care home. The allegation was that she had been the nurse in charge of three shifts in the working week over a long period of time and had been negligent in her duty towards the residents in the care home. During these shifts, she did not care for all the needs of the patients but referred pressure sore issues to the deputy manager. She explained that this was in accordance with an instruction from the management system in the home.

However, the NMC decided that, irrespective of this point, she was responsible for meeting the care needs of the residents; they clearly had such needs because a number of them had severe pressure sores. The NMC decided to impose interim conditions of practice and then subsequently suspended her from the profession.[31]

29   Clark, L. 'Retired care home nurse struck off by Nursing and Midwifery Council.' *The Courier* (Tayside and Fife), 20 August 2012.

30   Patty, A. 'Nurses whose lack of care led to pensioner's death struck off.' *The Times*, 30 November 2004.

31   Nursing and Midwifery Council. *Interim order decision: Girlie Franklin*, PIN 73D0633E, 5 October 2010. London: NMC. Also: 'Nurse suspended following neglect of residents with dementia.' *Northampton Chronicle and Echo*, 6 August 2012.

Nurse failing to seek assistance but systemic failings at care home. At a care home, in 2006, a nurse failed to seek assistance from a doctor, another nurse or ambulance when a resident's behaviour changed, a bruise appeared on her leg and she screamed in pain. The nurse did not assess properly the manual handling technique to be used after the resident had fallen, and did not, on a subsequent occasion, seek help when the resident fell, sustained bruising and complained of pain. The panel noted that practice in the care home was lax, with little supervision or training; in fact, a former manager described it as horrific. Nonetheless, the nurse had to retain responsibility for her own professional conduct within the team. A suspension order was imposed.[32]

ACTION AGAINST NURSES FOR FAILURES ASSOCIATED WITH SYSTEMIC PROBLEMS

The remaining selection of cases involving the NMC may or may not – it is not always easy to tell from the reports – have actually involved systemic failures. Some of them may have been particular lapses by individuals, unrepresentative of the institution. Either way, they are about aspects of care that typically do surface in accounts of systemic failures in care.

At the very least, therefore, these cases indicate that the regulatory body can, and sometimes will, take action in such circumstances. It is just that in the case of the NHS, in particular, it seems to do so relatively infrequently and ineffectively.

Not washing hands. A care home nurse was struck off in 2007 for failing to wash her hands for the purpose of infection control. She was reported as being the first nurse to have suffered such a fate for this misdemeanour.[33] This is notable since, throughout the 2000s, shortcuts in infection control, including handwashing, were rife within the NHS. It is curious, therefore, that the first nurse to be struck off did not work in the NHS.

Not tending to patients. In September 2010, a nurse working at the Queen Mary's Hospital, Sidcup, Kent, was struck off the nursing register. The patient was Mr Derek Sauter, a retired administrator from the Healthcare Commission. He had been admitted ostensibly for treatment of a chest infection requiring antibiotics but died of pneumonia. His telephone was taken away from him, his condition not checked in the night, even though his oxygen levels dropped, and his wife was not contacted until after he had died.[34]

Not answering call bells. Call bells are a recurring matter in the neglect by nurses of patients' needs. In September 2010, a nurse working at West Suffolk Hospital in Bury St Edmunds had conditions placed on his work and registration. This was in relation to an incident in 2006 when, having connected antibiotics direct to a patient's heart, he failed to seek help for 20 minutes when the flat-line alarm sounded.[35]

Another case relating to call bells involved a nurse working at Darent Valley Hospital, Dartford. In 2005 and 2006, she silenced ventilator alarms on several occasions without investigating why the alarms were sounding and without calling for help. She also suctioned

32   Nursing and Midwifery Council. *Suspension order: Meundju Hungi*, PIN 03J0092O, 21–23 April 2010. London: NMC.

33   'Nurse struck off for MRSA failure.' *BBC News*, 23 November 2007. Accessed on 13 August 2012 at: http://news.bbc.co.uk/1/hi/england/7108925.stm.

34   Fagge, N. 'Nurse refused dying man glass of water then took his mobile phone when he tried to call for help.' *Daily Mail*, 16 September 2010. Also: Randhawa, K. 'Nurse who denied dying patient water is struck off.' *London Evening Standard*, 17 September 2010.

35   Thewlis, J. 'Nurse banned from critical care.' *Ipswich Evening Star*, 1 October 2010.

a patient's mouth instead of the lungs when it was the latter that required the process, and failed to give prescribed drugs to a patient. The nurse was consequently struck off the register.[36]

A nurse was suspended for 18 months following other misconduct, which included issues related to call bells. This followed events at Stanley House care home in Herefordshire. On several occasions, she placed a call bell out of reach of an extremely vulnerable resident, who tended to use it a lot and disturb other residents. After he had settled down, she would return the bell to him. There were some mitigating circumstances because the nurse did not conceal her actions and recorded them in her nursing notes. In addition, management did not take steps to change her approach, nor did it consider a better solution to the particular resident's behaviour. Nevertheless, the nurse's actions constituted misconduct.[37]

In another such case, a nurse at Burton Hospital NHS Trust did not attend the patient until later one evening, during which time the patient had been left in pain. The nurse told the patient not to use the call bell, failed to check the notes to see what pain relief could be administered, did not realise until early the next morning that oramorph could be administered, and did not seek help from a doctor. Because of her hip and problems in moving, the patient was variously in discomfort, pain and complete agony. A suspension order was imposed.[38]

Humiliating and insulting patients. A general disregard of patients' needs, including bladder and bowel, can spill over into blatantly abusive treatment. As happened in the case of a nurse, working in a care home, who received a striking-off order for various forms of misconduct, including shouting at a resident with words to the effect of 'disgusting woman pissing all over the floor, I am not here to wipe up piss'.[39]

In 2007, at the Worcestershire Royal Hospital, an elderly woman had wet herself. The nurse then shouted at her, stripped her naked in front of other patients and pushed her on to a commode, on which she was left sitting in full view whilst the nurse went to fetch a mop and bucket. When the woman asked to be washed before being given a clean nightdress, the nurse refused. The woman was left crying inconsolably.[40] The nurse was struck off.[41]

Leaving patients lying in their own bodily waste. In principle, it is misconduct on the part of nurses to leave their patients lying in their own bodily waste. In May 2010, for example, a suspension order was imposed on a senior nurse responsible for provision of care on a night shift. Another member of staff had discovered patients lying in their own excrement.[42]

---

36   Nursing and Midwifery Council. 'Nurse struck off for putting patients at risk.' *News*, 30 March 2009. Accessed on 20 September 2010 at: www.nmc-uk.org/Press-and-media/News-archive/Nurse-struck-off-for-putting-patients-at-risk.

37   Nursing and Midwifery Council. *Suspension order: Nicola Edwards*, PIN 04L0490E, 5–7 October 2010. London: NMC.

38   Nursing and Midwifery Council. *Suspension order: Susan Lesley Bloore*, PIN 88A0628E, 26 May 2010. London: NMC.

39   Nursing and Midwifery Council. *Striking off order: Kanthee Devi Ramdhunee*, PIN 68A0094W, 18–19 October 2010. London: NMC.

40   'Nurse "shouted at elderly woman and stripped her naked in full view of other patients because she'd wet herself".' *Daily Mail*, 25 June 2009.

41   'UK discharge heartless Zimbabwe nurse.' *Zimdiaspora*, 26 June 2009. Accessed on 20 September 2010 at: www.zimdiaspora.com/index.php?option=com_content&view=article&id=1466:a-zimbabwe-nurse-struck-off-register-in-uk&catid=38:travel-tips&Itemid=293.

42   Nursing and Midwifery Council. *Suspension order: Karen Louise Weatherhogg*, PIN0011772E, 21 May 2010. London: NMC.

Not recording and monitoring patient condition. Another theme in the case of systemic failures in basic care is the lack of monitoring and recording of patients' conditions.

At Paignton Hospital, a nurse was struck off after a number of allegations were made against her in relation to the care she provided for a dying woman in 2006. In addition to giving antibiotics without medical authorisation, she did not carry out blood pressure and oxygen level observations, did not note the patient's deterioration and did not keep records (such as fluid balance charts). Nor did she instigate a medication review, despite the cocktail of drugs the woman was taking, which might have been responsible for the patient's renal failure and also lowered her blood pressure.[43]

A nurse at Leeds General Infirmary, in 2005, failed to record blood pressure, oxygen saturation, fluid balance and to ensure that a turning chart was kept. Following this, when the patient was found unresponsive, she then failed to sound the emergency alarm, to apply basic airway management and to start basic life support. The nurse was a staff nurse, in charge of the ward on the night in question and with specific responsibility for the particular patient. This patient had supra-nuclear palsy, required monitoring and observation, was fed through a naso-gastric tube, could not move independently, needed regular turning in bed and had been subject to low oxygen saturation levels. The faults of the nurse amounted to misconduct and a three-year caution order was imposed.[44]

Falls. Failure to assess for the risk of falls in hospitals, and to record and act on falls once they have happened, also forms a pattern that can be indicative of systemic poor care and neglect.

In 2008, at Tor-Na-Dee nursing home in Aberdeen, a patient fell, but the nurse neither assessed the patient's condition nor completed the appropriate paperwork. She then denied the resident had fallen; this dishonesty was fatal to her career and she was struck off the register of nurses, following an NMC hearing.[45]

At the Crown Nursing Home, Oxford, a nurse found a resident at the foot of the stairs with a cut head and bruised face. The resident was elderly, frail, suffering from Alzheimer's disease, with a tendency to 'wander'. The nurse failed to call the emergency services, to record neurological observations and to assess (both before and after she was moved) whether an internal head injury might have been sustained. The resident was taken back to her room. A few hours later, her head was bleeding profusely; she was taken to hospital where she died of a subarachnoid haemorrhage. A suspension order was imposed by the Council.[46]

The following case, too, resulted in the striking from the register of a nurse for multiple individual failings in care, in 2005, at the University Hospital of Wales, Cardiff. They included failure to take and to record a patient's blood pressure and oxygen levels, to record that a patient had sustained an injury falling from a commode, and to update that patient's risk assessment and care plan following the fall. In addition, whilst about to wash a patient who was in the bath, she received a call on her mobile phone; she turned away from the patient to take the call, leaving the patient lying there naked.[47]

43   Pope, S. 'Nurse struck off for care of patient.' *Express and Echo* (Exeter), 9 December 2008.
44   Nursing and Midwifery Council. *Caution order: Helen Garrand,* PIN 86J049E, 14 April 2010. London: NMC.
45   Davidson, R. 'Nurse struck off after lying about fall.' *The Press and Journal* (Aberdeen), 9 June 2010.
46   Nursing and Midwifery Council. *Suspension order: Nonhlanhla Kubheka,* PIN 04A0789O, 20 July 2010. London: NMC.
47   'Nurse watched porn on duty and put patients at risk.' *Wales on Sunday,* 11 November 2007.

In 2012, a nurse working in a care home was struck off for failing to report a fall that resulted in a broken hip and subsequent death of a resident.[48]

Keeping people warm, clean and well-groomed. Failing to keep people warm, well-groomed and clean can be misconduct.

At Drey House nursing home, a nurse acting as clinical manager was found guilty in these respects and given a caution order to last for five years. Particular misconduct included failure to keep the temperature at an appropriate level in a resident's room, to ensure the resident was dressed appropriately in relation to the temperature (the resident was cold to the touch on some occasions), to change the resident's clothes regularly and to ensure that the resident's fingernails were properly or regularly cleaned.[49]

Communication and talking to patients. Lack of communication with patients – a frequent criticism made by health service patients – is also capable of founding misconduct. When a nurse checked patients for the infusions they were having in cubicles at the Royal Victoria Hospital, Newcastle-upon-Tyne, she did so without talking to the patients. She also did not check that patients understood their care plans. This was misconduct and, together with other failings, resulted in a suspension order of 12 months.[50]

48   Robertson, C. 'Nurse struck off for failed to report care home resident's fall.' *Galloway News*, 19 January 2012.
49   Nursing and Midwifery Council. *Caution order: John Mitchell-Whiteford*, PIN87A1871E, 17 February 2010. London: NMC.
50   Nursing and Midwifery Council. *Suspension order: Morag Isobel Robson*, PIN 9013697E, 29 March 2010. London: NMC.

10

Barring workers: the Disclosure and Barring Service

Upper Tribunal limited to questioning factual or legal issues, not
the merits of the overall decision
Appeals: facts, law, weighting and merits of decisions
Barring decisions and appeals: examples
Barring people for financial abuse
Physical and other neglect or mistreatment cases
Management failings
Barring and link with other remedies

KEY POINTS

A third branch of regulation is designed to protect vulnerable adults by barring certain people from working with them.

The Independent Safeguarding Authority (ISA) has maintained a barred list for this purpose and also a separate barred list in respect of working with children. These lists replaced two previous lists – the POVA (Protection of Vulnerable Adults) and POCA (Protection of Children Act) lists, held by the Secretary of State.

Under s.88 of the Protection of Freedoms Act 2012, the ISA ceased to exist and was subsumed (along with the Criminal Records Bureau) under the Disclosure and Barring Service (DBS), in December 2012. Any references to the Independent Safeguarding Authority, below, should therefore be read with this change in mind.

If a person is placed on this barred list, then he or she is unable, lawfully, to work with vulnerable adults.

Central government has had considerable trouble setting out criteria for barring that strike the right balance between protecting vulnerable adults (and children) and treating workers fairly (by not barring them unfairly). Case law continues to explore how this balance should be struck.

As well as setting out the legal framework and rules, this chapter digests a considerable quantity of case law in order to give a flavour of the process of barring and the questions of appropriateness and fairness of barring.

SAFEGUARDING VULNERABLE ADULTS ACT 2006

From October 2009, the barred list replaced the Protection of Vulnerable Adults (POVA) list scheme which had been maintained by the Secretary of State for Health under the Care Standards Act 2000. People placed on the POVA list were unable, legally, to work with vulnerable adults.

The barred list is underpinned by the Safeguarding Vulnerable Groups Act 2006 (SVGA) and associated regulations. Inclusion on the list means that a person is prohibited from working with vulnerable adults if that work involves 'regulated activity'.

The Act also provided for a monitoring list. This was going to be the converse of the barred list; unless a person was on the list, and therefore subject to monitoring, they would have been unable to work with vulnerable adults (or children).

As originally conceived, the monitoring list would have covered 11 million people who had contact in various capacities (not just working) with vulnerable adults and children. The Coalition government decided to abandon the monitoring list before it had even begun, as a disproportionate and excessive way of trying to protect vulnerable adults and children.

The 2006 Act applies to England and Wales and, by extension, to Northern Ireland. It does not apply to Scotland. However, it contains a provision, in s.54, to give effect to the corresponding Scottish legislation, the Protection of Vulnerable Groups (Scotland) Act 2007. The latter has an equivalent provision, in s.87, to give effect in Scotland to the 2006 Act.

DISCLOSURE AND BARRING SERVICE (DBS) FUNCTIONS

In brief, the DBS has a duty to establish an 'adults' barred list' (and a children's list also). If a person is included in this adults' barred list, he or she is barred from engaging in a 'regulated activity' with vulnerable adults.[1] A person might be placed on one or both lists.

It is an offence for a barred person to seek, to offer to or actually to engage in regulated activity. The offence carries a maximum sentence of five years in prison. There are two main defences: the person could not reasonably have known that he or she was on the barred list, or the person thought it was necessary to engage in that activity to prevent harm to a vulnerable adult.[2]

DEFINITION OF VULNERABLE ADULT

The definition of vulnerable adult was changed and simplified by the Protection of Freedoms Act 2012. A vulnerable adult is now defined in s.60 of the SVGA 2006 as being 18 years or more and means any person 'to whom an activity which is a regulated activity relating to vulnerable adults…is provided'.

INFORMATION ABOUT A PERSON HELD ON THE BARRED LIST

Regulations prescribe the information about a person that is to be held on the barred list.

The information includes, for example, any alternative names and aliases, address, information submitted by the individual in any monitoring application, information relevant to the barring decision, information from relevant registers (kept by a professional body) or supervisory authorities (regulatory body), relevant police information provided to the ISA, reasons for barring, information (including representations from the individual) relevant to any subsequent appeal or review, outcome of any such appeal or review.[3]

---

1   Safeguarding Vulnerable Groups Act 2006, ss.2–3.
2   Safeguarding Vulnerable Groups Act 2006, s.7.
3   SI 2008/16. The Safeguarding Vulnerable Groups Act 2006 (Barred List Prescribed Information) Regulations 2008.

DEFINITIONS: REGULATED ACTIVITY, HEALTH CARE, PERSONAL CARE, REGULATED ACTIVITY PROVIDER

Regulated activity, the key focus of the Act, is defined as follows. This definition, in turn, spawns a number of others.

a. the provision to an adult of health care by, or under the direction or supervision of, a health care professional,

b. the provision to an adult of relevant personal care,

c. the provision by a social care worker of relevant social work to an adult who is a client or potential client,

d. the provision of assistance in relation to general household matters to an adult who is in need of it by reason of age, illness or disability,

e. any relevant assistance in the conduct of an adult's own affairs,

f. the conveying by persons of a prescribed description in such circumstances as may be prescribed of adults who need to be conveyed by reason of age, illness or disability,

g. such activities –

(a) involving, or connected with, the provision of health care or relevant personal care to adults, and

(b) not falling within any of the above paragraphs, as are of a prescribed description.[4]

HEALTH CARE

Health care is defined to include all forms of health care provided for individuals, whether relating to physical or mental health and also includes palliative care and procedures that are similar to forms of medical or surgical care but are not provided in connection with a medical condition.[5]

PERSONAL CARE

Relevant personal care means:

a. physical assistance, given to a person who is in need of it by reason of age, illness or disability, in connection with –

(a) eating or drinking (including the administration of parenteral nutrition),

(b) toileting (including in relation to the process of menstruation),

---

4   Quoted from: Safeguarding Vulnerable Groups Act 2006, schedule 4, para 7.
5   Safeguarding Vulnerable Groups Act 2006, schedule 4, para 7.

(c) washing or bathing,

(d) dressing,

(e) oral care, or

(f) the care of skin, hair or nails,

b. the prompting, together with supervision, of a person who is in need of it by reason of age, illness or disability in relation to the performance of any of the activities listed in paragraph (a) where the person is unable to make a decision in relation to performing such an activity without such prompting and supervision, or

c. any form of training, instruction, advice or guidance which –

(a) relates to the performance of any of the activities listed in paragraph (a),

(b) is given to a person who is in need of it by reason of age, illness or disability, and

(c) does not fall within paragraph (b).[6]

Assistance in relation to general household matters is day-to-day assistance in relation to the running of the household of the person concerned where the assistance is the carrying out of one or more of the following activities on behalf of that person:

a. managing the person's cash,

b. paying the person's bills,

c. shopping.[7]

Relevant assistance in the conduct of a person's own affairs is anything done on behalf of the person by virtue of:

a. a lasting power of attorney created in respect of the person in accordance with section 9 of the Mental Capacity Act 2005,

b. an enduring power of attorney (within the meaning of Schedule 4 to that Act) in respect of the person which is –

(a) registered in accordance with that Schedule, or

(b) the subject of an application to be so registered,

(c) an order made under section 16 of that Act by the Court of Protection in relation to the making of decisions on the person's behalf,

6   Quoted from: Safeguarding Vulnerable Groups Act 2006, schedule 4, para 7.
7   Quoted from: Safeguarding Vulnerable Groups Act 2006, schedule 4, para 7.

(d) the appointment of an independent mental health advocate or (as the case may be) an independent mental capacity advocate in respect of the person in pursuance of arrangements under section 130A of the Mental Health Act 1983 or section 35 of the Mental Capacity Act 2005,

c. the provision of independent advocacy services (within the meaning of section 248 of the National Health Service Act 2006 or section 187 of the National Health Service (Wales) Act 2006) in respect of the person, or

d. the appointment of a representative to receive payments on behalf of the person in pursuance of regulations made under the Social Security Administration Act 1992.[8]

Day-to-day supervision or management of any of the above regulated activities, as defined above, is defined as regulated activity.[9]

FAMILY OR PERSONAL RELATIONSHIPS

The Act does not apply to activity carried out in the course of a family or personal relationship.[10]

REGULATED ACTIVITY PROVIDERS

A regulated activity provider is defined as a person responsible for the management or control of a regulated activity.

If the regulated activity is carried on for the purposes of an organisation, a person is responsible if he or she is not subject to supervision or direction. Likewise, a person is a regulated activity provider if he or she makes or authorises arrangements for somebody else to engage in the activity.

A person is such a provider if he or she carries on a scheme where an individual agrees to provide care or support to an adult in need of it (i.e. adult placement) and if there is a requirement to register under s.10 of the Health and Social Care Act 2008.

However, a person is not defined as a regulated activity provider if he or she is an individual and the arrangements made are private arrangements. The arrangements are private if the regulated activity is for the person himself or herself; likewise, if they are for a vulnerable adult who is a member of the person's family or a friend of the person.[11]

The recipient of a community care direct payment, under the Health and Social Care Act 2001, is not a regulated activity provider for the purposes of the Act. However, if that recipient receives a direct payment on behalf of a person lacking

8   Quoted from: Safeguarding Vulnerable Groups Act 2006, schedule 4, para 7.
9   Safeguarding Vulnerable Groups Act 2006, schedule 4, para 7.
10   Safeguarding Vulnerable Groups Act 2006, s.58.
11   Safeguarding Vulnerable Groups Act 2006, s.6.

capacity, and the recipient is not a close relative or friend of the person, then that person does count as a regulated activity provider.[12]

DUTY OF REGULATORY PROVIDER TO CHECK IF A PERSON IS BARRED

Regulated activity providers have a duty to check whether a person is barred before they permit a person to engage in regulated activity. Likewise, personnel suppliers.

The duty to check is discharged if the provider has (a) obtained information as to whether the person is barred from the DBS, (b) obtained an enhanced criminal record certificate (under the Police Act 1997, which will indicate whether a person is barred), or (c) checked such a certificate and received up-to-date information about it under s.116A of the Police Act.[13]

In the future, certain persons[14] – for example, regulated activity providers – will be able to register an interest in persons engaged in regulated activity. They will then be notified should an individual become barred from regulated activity. However, such registration will require the consent of the individual concerned.[15]

It is also an offence for a person to allow an individual barred from regulated activity to engage in that activity if the person knows or has reason to believe the individual is barred and if the individual engages in the activity.

Similarly, if a personnel supplier supplies such an individual to somebody else with a view to the individual engaging in regulated activity from which the individual is barred. The maximum penalty is five years in prison.

There are defences based on lack of knowledge or on necessity to prevent harm.[16]

REGULATED ACTIVITY PROVIDERS: DUTY TO REFER PERSON TO THE ISA

Regulated activity providers have a duty to provide information to the ISA.

The duty is triggered if the provider or person has withdrawn permission for the individual to engage in regulated activity, or would have done so if the individual had not already ceased to engage in that activity. This must have been for the reasons that (a) the provider thinks the individual falls into the category of person where placing on the barring list is automatic, or (b) the person has engaged in 'relevant conduct'.

Alternatively, the reason could be that the 'harm test' is satisfied in relation to the individual. The harm test is that the individual may harm a child or vulnerable adult, cause a child or vulnerable adult to be harmed, put a child or vulnerable adult

---

12   Department of Health. *Guidance on direct payments for community care, services for carers and children's services, England 2009.* London: DH, 2009, para 154.

13   Safeguarding Vulnerable Groups Act 2006, s.34ZA.

14   Safeguarding Vulnerable Groups Act 2006, schedule 7.

15   Safeguarding Vulnerable Groups Act 2006, s.30B.

16   Safeguarding Vulnerable Groups Act 2006, s.9.

at risk of harm, attempt to harm a child or vulnerable adult, or incite another to harm a child or vulnerable adult.

A comparable duty applies to personnel suppliers.[17]

It is an offence if providers or personnel suppliers, without reasonable excuse, fail to make the referral to the ISA.[18]

INCENTIVES FOR AN EMPLOYER NOT TO DISMISS WORKERS AND NOT TO REFER TO THE ISA

The main duty to refer workers therefore rests on the employer. It is an offence for the employer not to do this if the grounds for referral are evident.

However, there may be a practical incentive for an employer not to refer. This incentive may become particularly sharp if the poor practices, for which it should be removing staff and referring to the ISA, are institutional in nature and closely connected with policies and resources of the organisation.

For instance, guidance from the Disclosure and Barring Service (formerly the ISA) states that harm that could be grounds for a referral to the Authority would include the following:

> Untreated weight loss, failing to administer reasonable care resulting in pressure sores or uncharacteristic problems with continence. Poor hygiene, soiled clothes not changed, insufficient food or drink, ignoring resident's requests, unmet social or care needs.[19]

Using this quotation, an example of a possibly reluctant employer springs to mind. It has been explained elsewhere in this book how systemic and extensive poor practice and neglect have been in health service hospitals. If NHS employers took their duties seriously, they would have been referring significant numbers of staff. The reason they have not done so is that systemic poor practice often flows from the policies, priorities, targets and limited resources of the employer. And if they are not dismissing these staff, or at least removing them from patient care, the duty of the referral to the DBS will not be triggered.

The following case resulted in a senior care assistant in a care home being barred from working with vulnerable adults. However, if one reads the background to this and compares this with what has been repeatedly reported of the NHS over the last decade and more, it is difficult to reconcile the fate of care home workers and that of NHS staff.

Example of barring: failing to check a patient during the night. A man had a qualification from Bulgaria as a doctor's or physician's assistant. He was working in a care home as senior night care assistant. He was dismissed for gross misconduct. The incident involved a man who had suffered a stroke, was doubly incontinent, had restricted mobility and problems communicating. When the day shift took over, he was found to be heavily

---

17   Safeguarding Vulnerable Groups Act 2006, ss.35–36.
18   Safeguarding Vulnerable Groups Act 2006, s.38.
19   Independent Safeguarding Authority. *ISA referral guidance*. London: ISA, 2009, p.12.

soiled, distressed, with his scrotum red and bleeding. The evidence showed that he must have been in a soiled state for several hours; the regular checking that the assistant should have carried out must have involved no more than putting his head round the door. This failure to check was misconduct that harmed a vulnerable adult. The tribunal concluded he was unsuitable to work with vulnerable adults, not least because public confidence – a relevant and important consideration – demanded this.[20]

In 2011, an audit was published querying why referral rates from the NHS were so low. It gave a number of reasons as to why this might be so. Amongst them was the factor that the NHS is uninterested in safeguarding.[21]

MISUSE OF THE BARRING SYSTEM BY AN EMPLOYER

Conversely, an employer might perform its duty of referral for all the wrong reasons, in order to victimise a member of staff who has whistleblown to the regulator about poor practice.

Employer victimising worker by making unwarranted referral to the ISA. A Somerset care worker was employed at the Moorlands care home in 2008. The employer sacked the care worker. She went to an employment tribunal and won; he then referred her to the ISA to try to get her banned from working in the care sector. A further tribunal found 'that the giving of the anonymous information and then the formal referral were malicious and an attempt to get back at the claimant with the respondent believing that it would never come to light that it was him because of data protection'. The care worker succeeded in gaining further damages for this ill-founded disclosure to the ISA.[22]

BALANCING THE DUTY TO SUSPEND, DISMISS AND REFER WITH THE PRINCIPLE OF GOOD FAITH IN EMPLOYMENT CONTRACTS

More generally, when suspending and dismissing employees (and then coming under a duty to refer to the ISA), employers should bear in mind the implied duty and principle of good faith in employment contracts.

In 2012, this was remarked upon by the Court of Appeal in a case in which it found that an NHS trust had overreacted to a restraint issue in respect of two nurses with long unblemished work records. It had suspended and then dismissed both nurses. It referred to the duty of trust and confidence an employer has towards an employee, stating that knee-jerk reactions, by over-eager suspension and dismissal, breach this duty.[23]

The Court of Appeal referred to an older case, which also showed the potential human and legal consequences of what the court regarded as an overreaction, leading to breach of the principle of good faith in employment contracts and to

---

20   *Kostadinov v Secretary of State for Health* [2009] UKFTT 157 (HESC).

21   Phair, L. *An audit of disciplinary outcomes and incident reporting and the relationship with the vetting and barring scheme in the NHS.* London: Social Care Workforce Research Unit, King's College London, 2011, pp.11–12.

22   'Somerset care home worker wins further damages.' *BBC News,* 30 May 2012. Accessed on 13 August 2012 at: www.bbc.co.uk/news/uk-england-somerset-18264272.

23   *Crawford v Suffolk Mental Health Partnership NHS Trust* [2012] EWCA Civ 138.

financial compensation payable for psychiatric personal injury to the member of staff concerned who had effectively been wrongly accused of abuse.

Premature suspension, employer thereby breaching employment contract. A residential social worker was suspended following potential allegations made by a child with learning and communication difficulties. Following a 'strategy meeting', a decision was taken to hold an investigation under s.47 of the Children Act 1989.

The investigation concluded that the child had never disclosed any abuse in relation to any member of staff and, while in therapy, had never said anything that could be construed as an allegation of abuse. The social worker was immediately reinstated, but by then she was ill and had by and large not worked since the suspension. She claimed loss of earnings and damages for personal injury caused by breach of contract; she now suffered from clinical depression caused by the suspension.

Suspension of member of staff must be reasonable and proper. The court held that it was quite proper for the local authority to investigate and make enquiries, but it did not necessarily follow that a member of staff, who may have been implicated in the risk to the vulnerable person, had to be suspended. The question should be whether, in the individual circumstances, it was reasonable and proper to do so. The court thought not. The strategy meeting had itself recognised that the information was 'difficult to evaluate', and to describe it as an allegation of abuse was putting it 'far too high'.

Knee-jerk reaction damaging relationship of trust and confidence with employee. The court also asked whether there were not other alternatives, such as a short period of leave or a transfer to other useful work. Instead, there had been a 'knee-jerk' reaction. The local authority had seriously damaged the relationship of trust and confidence between employee and employer – a relationship implied into contracts of employment. The claimant was entitled to damages.[24]

SHARING OF INFORMATION BETWEEN ORGANISATIONS

A detailed set of provisions governs information disclosure, obliging or permitting various bodies and the ISA to share information. Some of these are as follows.

DBS: POWERS AND DUTIES TO OBTAIN OR PROVIDE INFORMATION

The DBS has the power to obtain certain police information relating to cautions and convictions.[25] And has a duty to provide information to the police.[26]

The DBS can require regulated activity providers and personnel suppliers to provide it with prescribed information relating to an individual whom it is considering for inclusion in, or removal from, the barred list. It is an offence not to supply the information, without reasonable excuse.[27]

LOCAL AUTHORITIES: POWER TO REFER PEOPLE TO THE DBS

A local authority has the power to provide the DBS with information if two conditions are satisfied. First, that it believes that any of the four statutory grounds

---

24   *Gogay v Hertfordshire County Council* [2001] 1 FLR 280 (Court of Appeal).
25   Safeguarding Vulnerable Groups Act 2006, schedule 3, para 13.
26   Safeguarding Vulnerable Groups Act 2006, s.50A.
27   Safeguarding Vulnerable Groups Act 2006, s.37.

of referral (explained above) apply. Second, that the local authority thinks the person is engaged, or may engage, in regulated activity and that the DBS may consider it appropriate to include the person on a barred list.

The DBS may also require local authorities to provide it with prescribed information, and the local authority must comply with the request.[28]

(If the local authority itself is a regulated activity provider, then, in the relevant circumstances, it will be under a duty to refer.)

PROFESSIONAL BODIES

Various professional bodies (e.g. the Health and Care Professions Council, the General Medical Council, the Nursing and Midwifery Council) that keep 'relevant registers' may provide the DBS with information if they believe that any of the referral grounds (see above) apply.[29] The DBS can demand prescribed information from these bodies.[30]

Conversely, the DBS must share information with the keeper of the register if the individual is newly barred. The DBS also has a power to provide certain information to the professional bodies (or, as the Act puts it, the keepers of these registers).[31] The keeper of the relevant register can apply to the DBS for certain information relating to barring and monitoring.[32] The DBS does not have to provide the information if it believes the professional body has the information already.

REGULATORY BODIES

'Supervisory' authorities (a regulatory body such as the Care Quality Commission) may refer an individual to the DBS if any of the referral grounds (see above) apply.[33] They must also provide information to the DBS on request and have a power to apply for information from the DBS about an individual and whether he or she is barred.[34]

The DBS must, in turn, inform supervisory authorities about an individual who is barred, unless he or she believes the supervisory authority already has the information.[35] The DBS may also provide information to supervisory authorities if it thinks it is relevant.[36]

LIABILITY FOR MISTAKES

No claims for damages are possible in respect of an individual being included, or not included, on a barred list, or in respect of the provision of information, unless

28   Safeguarding Vulnerable Groups Act 2006, ss.39–40.
29   Safeguarding Vulnerable Groups Act 2006, s.41.
30   Safeguarding Vulnerable Groups Act 2006, s.42.
31   Safeguarding Vulnerable Groups Act 2006, s.43.
32   Safeguarding Vulnerable Groups Act 2006, s.44.
33   Safeguarding Vulnerable Groups Act 2006, s.45.
34   Safeguarding Vulnerable Groups Act 2006, ss.46–47.
35   Safeguarding Vulnerable Groups Act 2006, s.49.
36   Safeguarding Vulnerable Groups Act 2006, s.50.

the provider knew the information was untrue. However, this does not affect the power of the courts to award damages under the Human Rights Act 1998 against a public authority.[37]

PLACING PEOPLE ON THE BARRED LIST

There should be no doubt about the seriousness, for the worker, of being placed on the barred list. As the courts put it (commenting on the barred list's similar predecessor, the POVA list):

> The scope of the ban is very wide... The ban is also likely to have an effect in practice going beyond its effect in law. Even though the lists are not made public, the fact is likely to get about and the stigma will be considerable. The scheme must therefore be devised in such a way as to prevent possible breaches of the article 8 rights.[38]

The DBS places an individual on the barred list in four main ways.

AUTOMATIC BARRING WITH NO REPRESENTATIONS ALLOWED

First, if certain prescribed criteria – relating to particular criminal offences – apply to the individual, barring by the DBS is automatic, without the right to make representations.[39] Regulations stipulate that the offences in this category are those sexual offences contained in ss.30–41 of the Sexual Offences Act 2003, involving victims with a mental disorder.[40]

'AUTOMATIC' BARRING; BUT REPRESENTATIONS ALLOWED BEFORE PERSON IS PLACED ON LIST

Second, if certain other prescribed criteria apply, the person will be in line for barring. But only if the criteria apply for barring under this section – namely, certain convictions or cautions – and the person has been, or might in future be, engaged in regulated activity with vulnerable adults.

The DBS must then give the person the opportunity to make representations within a prescribed time. If representations are not received within a set period of time, then the person will be added to the list. If representations are received in time, then the DBS must place the person on the barred list if:

- it is satisfied that the criteria (certain convictions or cautions) apply

- it has reason to believe that the person is or has been, or might in future be, engaged in regulated activity relating to vulnerable adults, and

37   Safeguarding Vulnerable Groups Act 2006, s.57.
38   *R(on the application of Wright and others) v Secretary of State for Health and another* [2009] UKHL 3.
39   Safeguarding Vulnerable Groups Act 2006, schedule 3, para 7.
40   SI 2009/37. The Safeguarding Vulnerable Groups Act 2006 (Prescribed Criteria and Miscellaneous Provisions) Regulations 2009.

- is satisfied that it is appropriate to include the person in the adults' barred list.[41]

Inclusion for this category of person was originally automatic, but the individual was then allowed subsequently to make representations as to why he or she should be removed from the list. If the DBS considered that it was not appropriate to include the individual on the list in the light of such representations, then it had to remove him or her.

However, this rule was successfully challenged in the courts, and the government had to amend the legislation in 2012 to allow prior representations.

Regulations state that a person comes under this category where he or she is the subject of a risk of sexual harm order under the Sexual Offences Act 2003 or the Protection of Children and Prevention of Sexual Offences (Scotland) Act 2005, or has been convicted of, or cautioned in relation to, a specified offence.

Specified offences include, for example, murder, kidnapping, false imprisonment, infanticide, rape, a range of other sexual offences, offences against the person, ill-treatment or wilful neglect, causing or allowing the death of a vulnerable adult.[42]

GIVING WORKERS A FAIR HEARING BEFORE THEY ARE BARRED

This provision was always going to prove controversial in its original form. Already, central government had lost a case under the old POVA list rules, under the Care Standards Act 2000.

The courts had stated that placing people on the POVA list without giving them the ability to make representations first was contrary to the balance required by the Human Rights Act 1998. The Court of Appeal held that article 6 (right to a fair hearing) of the European Convention on Human Rights had been breached; it did not rule on article 8 (right to respect for private and family life), although the High Court had found a breach of article 8.[43]

An example under the old POVA list rules came in the guise of the example of a psychiatric nurse (not one of the claimants in the actual case) who had won an award for innovation and excellence in dementia care. After she was provisionally included on the list in February 2006, she launched judicial review proceedings in June 2006 and in the same month won an employment tribunal case for unfair dismissal. In July 2006, she was removed from the list. However, by this time she had been unable to work and keep up her mortgage payments, with the result that she had lost her home.[44]

So, when the Safeguarding Vulnerable Groups Act 2006 was in its draft stage, the government was warned against making the same mistake twice, on this very

---

41   Safeguarding Vulnerable Groups Act 2006, schedule 3, para 8, as amended by s.67 of the Protection of Freedoms Act 2012.

42   SI 2009/37. The Safeguarding Vulnerable Groups Act 2006 (Prescribed Criteria and Miscellaneous Provisions) Regulations 2009.

43   *R(Wright) v Secretary of State for Health* [2006] EWHC 2886 (Admin); [2007] EWCA 999 Civ (Court of Appeal).

44   *R(Wright) v Secretary of State for Health* [2006] EWHC 2886 (Admin); [2007] EWCA Civ 999 (Court of Appeal).

issue of allowing representations before a person is placed on the list. Unaccountably, it didn't listen.

Predictably, in 2010, a case reached the courts about this second category of barred list placements under the new 2006 Act. And the main ground of challenge was indeed the fact that representations were allowed, but only after the person had been placed on the barred list. This meant that a person might remain on the list for many weeks or months, only to be removed when representations had been considered. However, by that time, his or her livelihood and reputation might have suffered severe damage.

Barring of nurse for dubious caution. One claimant was a staff nurse on an acute hospital ward. He accepted a police caution for an act of cruelty towards a child, under s.1 of the Children and Young Persons Act 1933. During the evening in question, in May 2009, his wife had left their children alone at home. He was at work; there was no suggestion that he knew his wife intended to leave the children alone or that he had expected her to do so. The court queried why the caution had been given at all.

Following these events, social services concluded that the children were well cared for and thriving at school and that there was no cause for concern for their welfare. The episode had been an isolated incident. On 28 May 2009, the claimant's employer concluded that he posed no risk to patients and that he should continue in his employment. However, the ISA was informed by the claimant about the caution in September 2009. In March 2010, the ISA placed him on the barred lists. There was no explanation given for the delay of seven months.

The Royal College of Nursing sent representations to the ISA in May 2010. In July, the ISA removed him from the lists and he resumed his normal duties. Whilst he had been on the lists, he was prevented from carrying out nursing tasks but had been transferred to office duties. As a result, he had lost wages of nearly £5000.

A second claimant in the case had also lost earnings, following provisional listing and before being cleared and removed from the list.

Provisional barring for nurse. Another claimant was also a nurse who had accepted a caution for leaving her son, aged 11 years, at home alone whilst she went shopping. She was referred to the Nursing and Midwifery Council but was placed on the barred list before any hearing could take place. The Royal College of Nursing made representations on her behalf and she was removed from the list, about ten weeks after having been placed on it. In the meantime, she had been unable to work as a nurse or in any other capacity. She suffered a loss of earnings of £3267.23 in the relevant period.

The challenge in this case comprised four main grounds.

First, it was wrong that the scheme required the ISA to place individuals who have been convicted or cautioned for a wide range of offences on the barred lists, without the right to make representations prior to listing contrary to articles 6 and 8 of the European Convention. Second, the scheme did not allow individuals who are given a right to make representations to do so orally rather than solely in writing, contrary to article 6 of the Convention. Third, the scheme did not give individuals placed on a barred list the opportunity of a full merits review on appeal, contrary to article 6. Fourth, the minimum barring period of ten years for a person aged 25 or over was disproportionate and a breach of article 8.

The judge could not accept that placing the claimants on the barred list before receiving representations was a legitimate and proportionate holding exercise. Noting the very significant delay before their names appeared on the barred lists, he went on to say that the 'holding' measure of placing somebody on the barred list prior to representations would have the worst effect on those convicted or cautioned for more minor offences, because more serious offenders would be in prison:

> Yet it seems to me that automatic barring is bound to have the greatest adverse effect upon those cautioned or convicted for offences at the less serious end of the scale, however efficiently their cases are considered. It is persons convicted or cautioned for comparatively minor specified offences that suffer most from automatic barring and have most to gain if they are permitted to make representations about whether they should be barred in advance of barring taking place...
>
> I cannot conclude, however, that the automatic inclusion of all persons convicted or cautioned of specified offences can be justified simply to cater for what must be a very small number of truly urgent cases.

In short, the judge found that the scheme gave rise to potential breaches of human rights and was incompatible with article 8 of the European Convention (right to respect for private life).

On the other points – no right to an oral hearing before the ISA, no full merits based appeal to the tribunal and a barring period of ten years – the judge found no breach of human rights.[45]

RELEVANT CONDUCT TRIGGERING REFERRAL TO THE ISA

Third, if it appears to the DBS that the person has engaged in 'relevant conduct' (see below) and it proposes to include the individual on the list, it must give the person the opportunity to make representations as to why he or she should not be included. If the DBS is satisfied that the person has engaged in the relevant conduct, and that it appears to the DBS that it is appropriate to include him or her on the list, then it must do so. But only if, in addition, it has reason to believe that the person is or has been, or might in future be, engaged in regulated activity relating to vulnerable adults.

Relevant conduct is, in summary:

- conduct endangering, or likely to endanger, a vulnerable adult
- conduct which, if repeated, would endanger, or be likely to endanger, a vulnerable adult

---

45   R(Royal College of Nursing) v Secretary of State for the Home Department and the Independent Safeguarding Authority [2010] EWHC 2761 (Admin).

- conduct involving sexual material relating to children

- inappropriate conduct involving sexually explicit images depicting violence against human beings

- inappropriate conduct of a sexual nature involving a vulnerable adult.[46]

Endangering a vulnerable adult occurs when the worker harms, causes to be harmed, puts at risk of harm, attempts to harm, or incites somebody else to harm a vulnerable adult.[47]

RELEVANT CONDUCT: EXAMPLE OF STRICT AND AUTHORITARIAN BEHAVIOUR

One case about the meaning of relevant conduct considered whether strictness and authoritarianism could amount to relevant conduct.

It involved a staff nurse, predominantly on night duty at an elderly care unit. Allegations, on the basis of which he had been placed on the barred list, were that he: (a) deliberately inflicted pain on a patient, CW, by pinching his nipples on the night of 3 February 2008 and at least one previous occasion; (b) deliberately inflicted pain on DM by pinching his nipples on a number of occasions; (c) behaved in a strict and authoritarian manner with patients and staff.

Part of the appeal rested on the reference to 'strict and authoritarian', which, it was argued, could not amount to 'relevant conduct'. The Upper Tribunal stated that it could if it intimidated or put patients in fear:

> It is our view that an allegation that a person is strict and authoritarian to staff and/or to patients by itself would not normally amount to 'relevant conduct' so as to engage the protective measures of the SVGA 2006. The issue is whether this behaviour 'intimidates patients or puts them in fear'. If it does do so, then it falls within the definition of 'relevant conduct'.[48]

The allegations were made out, including the ground of strict and authoritarian behaviour:

> He came over as a man who was firm in his view that his approach was the correct one. We can well see patients saying that he liked to show his authority and wanting to give the impression that he is boss, and that his attitudes were heavy handed (CW) or that he was pompous, and that there was a mild sense of dread when he came on duty (DM).
>
> Staff refer to him as intimidating (Miss P) and very strict with staff and patients (BW). Ms Davies accepts that some staff members have positive things to say about him (in his heart, he is not bad: JM). He may well have behaved in a strict and authoritarian manner with other members of staff. However, we have reservations that there is sufficient evidence in relation to

46   Safeguarding Vulnerable Groups Act 2006, schedule 3, para 10.
47   Safeguarding Vulnerable Groups Act 2006, schedule 3, para 10.
48   *KS v Independent Safeguarding Authority* [2011] UKUT 426 (AAC).

his behaviour with other members of staff to demonstrate that this behaviour amounted to placing patients in fear. These reservations however in no way persuade us that there has been a mistake of material fact on which the decision has been made.

There is more than sufficient evidence in the documents that we have seen to arrive at the conclusion that the ISA have not made a mistake of fact on which the decision was made relating to the Appellant's general attitude to patients (acting in a strict and authoritarian manner) of such a degree that it intimidated patients.[49]

RISK OF DOING HARM: TRIGGERING REFERRAL TO THE ISA

Fourth, and last, is the 'risk of harm' test. If it appears to the DBS that a person may harm a vulnerable adult, cause a vulnerable adult to be harmed, put a vulnerable adult at risk of harm, attempt to harm a vulnerable adult, or incite another person to harm a vulnerable adult, then the DBS must give the person an opportunity to make representations as to why he or she should not be barred. If it appears appropriate to include the person on the barred list, the DBS must do so. But only if it has reason to believe that the person is or has been, or might in future be, engaged in regulated activity relating to vulnerable adults.[50]

TRANSFER FROM POVA LIST TO BARRED LIST

When the legislation changed, the ISA had to transfer a person already on the POVA list under the Care Standards Act 2000 to the adults' barred list under the 2006 Act.

It had to give any such person an opportunity to make representations as to why he or she should be removed from the barred list, and had to consider those representations, unless, under the 2006 Act, the person fell under the category of person to whom no right of representation is extended (i.e. first category of automatic inclusion: see above).[51]

MINIMUM BARRED PERIODS AND TIMING OF REVIEWS

Regulations set out minimum periods of barring to be applied to people on the barred list.

If a person was already subject to restriction (under the POVA list) and was 18 at the time of the decision, then the period is ten years, less the time the person was already on the POVA list before being transferred to the barred list.

Where there were no previous restrictions, the minimum barring period is one year for a person under 18, five years for a person aged between 18 and 25, and ten years for those 25 or over.

---

49   *KS v Independent Safeguarding Authority* [2011] UKUT 426 (AAC).
50   Safeguarding Vulnerable Groups Act 2006, schedule 3, para 11.
51   SI 2008/473. Safeguarding Vulnerable Groups Act 2006 (Transitional Provisions) Order.

The regulations also govern how much time must elapse before the person can seek a review. Generally, the period is one year for people under 18, five years for people aged between 18 and 25, and ten years in any other case.[52]

REVIEW OF INCLUSION ON THE LIST

As originally drafted, the Act allowed a person, with permission from the ISA, to seek a review with the ISA of his or her inclusion on the barred list. However, application could only be made at the end of the minimum barred period and if he or she has made no other such application.

The ISA could not grant permission unless it thought that the person's circumstances had changed since inclusion on the list or the last application, and that the change is such that permission should be given.[53]

The Act was subsequently amended to allow what is now the DBS to exercise a wider discretion in deciding to review an inclusion. The DBS may, at any time, review the person's inclusion in the list and remove the person from the list. However, it has to be satisfied that it is not appropriate for the person to be included in the list, in the light of (a) information that it did not have at the time of the person's inclusion in the list, (b) any change of circumstances relating to the person concerned, or (c) any error by the DBS.[54]

The Upper Tribunal, which hears appeals against inclusion on the barred list, has referred to the potential value of the Tribunal being able to exercise this wider discretion.[55]

APPEAL AGAINST INCLUSION ON THE LIST

Appeals lie to the Upper Tribunal against the decision of the DBS to include a person on the list or not to remove him or her from the list.

Appeals to the Tribunal can only be made on grounds that a mistake has been made on a point of law or on a finding of fact. However, the decision made by the DBS as to whether it is 'appropriate' to bar a person is a question of neither law nor fact, and so cannot be appealed to the Tribunal. If the Tribunal finds no mistake of fact or law, then it must confirm the DBS's decision. Appeals can only be made with permission of the Tribunal.

Beyond the Tribunal, an appeal to the Court of Appeal on a point of law may be made, with that Court's permission.[56]

---

52   SI 2008/474. The Safeguarding Vulnerable Groups Act 2006 (Barring Procedure) Regulations 2008.
53   Safeguarding Vulnerable Groups Act 2006, schedule 3, para 18.
54   Safeguarding Vulnerable Groups Act 2006, s.18A, as amended by s.71 of the Protection of Freedoms Act 2012.
55   *VW v Independent Safeguarding Authority* [2011] UKUT 435 (AAC). See also: *SJB v Independent Safeguarding Authority* [2011] UKUT 286 (AAC).
56   Safeguarding Vulnerable Groups Act 2006, s.4.

UPPER TRIBUNAL LIMITED TO QUESTIONING FACTUAL OR LEGAL ISSUES, NOT THE MERITS OF THE OVERALL DECISION

On its face, the Act significantly restricts the role of the Upper Tribunal by its apparent ability to consider only factual or legal issues, rather than consider overall whether it is appropriate to bar a person. In other words, the Act appears to warn the Tribunal off from making its own judgments about appropriateness to bar.

The issue is clearly one of importance. The predecessor to the Upper Tribunal, the Care Standards Tribunal (CST) operating under the Care Standards Act 2000, was explicitly charged in the statute with considering whether a person was unsuitable to work with vulnerable adults. In some of the case examples, set out below, the CST clearly gave its own view about whether a person should be on the POVA list or not – without necessarily giving grounds of fact or law for its decision. The way in which the 2006 Act reads is such as to suggest that some of the successful appeals under the old POVA list system would not now succeed.

A number of cases have confirmed that there is indeed such a restriction, although it is arguable that a backdoor remains slightly ajar, enabling the Tribunal to interfere with the decisions of the DBS about appropriateness to bar (by citing legal grounds of 'proportionality' rather than dwelling on 'appropriateness'). The position is as follows.

The High Court has stated that:

> the decision whether or not it is appropriate for an individual to be included in a barred list is not a question of law or fact. In these circumstances it cannot be said that the individual has a full merits based right of appeal.[57]

On any view, then, the appeal would appear to have to be based on arguments about the law or fact, not on appropriateness. However, boundaries blur.

For instance, grounds such as unreasonableness, irrationality and disproportionality are concepts that are part of public law in terms of traditional judicial review and human rights. Clearly, the question of whether it is appropriate to bar somebody on the facts could easily involve consideration of whether a proportionate response to those facts should be barring. So the courts have held that an appeal would not be precluded on such grounds.[58]

Once proportionality comes into the picture, the Tribunal is able, as a matter of law, to question the weight the DBS has given to certain facts about the case, even if there is no dispute about the bare facts themselves.

Consequently, the Upper Tribunal has explored fully, in a number of cases, the grounds on which the decisions of the DBS can be challenged and the remit of the Tribunal itself. Some of these cases have involved consideration of the decision

---

57 *R(Royal College of Nursing) v Secretary of State for the Home Department and the Independent Safeguarding Authority* [2010] EWHC 2761 (Admin).

58 *R(Royal College of Nursing) v Secretary of State for the Home Department and the Independent Safeguarding Authority* [2010] EWHC 2761 (Admin).

making of the DBS in the context of guidance, called *Guidance notes for the barring decision making process.*[59]

APPEALS: FACTS, LAW, WEIGHTING AND MERITS OF DECISIONS

It is worth setting out the wording of the Act, so as to understand better the rulings of the Upper Tribunal on its meaning (italics added):

(2) *An appeal under subsection (1) may be made only on the grounds that ISA [DBS] has made a mistake –*

(a) *on any point of law;*

(b) *in any finding of fact which it has made and on which the decision mentioned in that subsection was based.*

(3) For the purposes of subsection (2), *the decision whether or not it is appropriate for an individual to be included in a barred list is not a question of law or fact.*

(4) An appeal under subsection (1) may be made only with the permission of the Upper Tribunal.

(5) Unless the Upper Tribunal finds that ISA [DBS] has made a mistake of law or fact, it must confirm the decision of ISA [DBS].

(6) If the Upper Tribunal finds that ISA [DBS] has made such a mistake it must –

(a) direct ISA [DBS] to remove the person from the list, or

(b) remit the matter to ISA [DBS] for a new decision.

(7) If the Upper Tribunal remits a matter to ISA[DBS] under subsection (6)(b) –

(a) the Upper Tribunal may set out any findings of fact which it has made (on which ISA[DBS] must base its new decision); and

(b) the person must be removed from the list until ISA [DBS] makes its new decision, unless the Upper Tribunal directs otherwise.[60]

WEIGHTING GIVEN TO THE EVIDENCE: A MATTER FOR THE DBS OR THE TRIBUNAL?

In one case, the argument was put to a Tribunal that the 'weighting' given to the evidence was solely a matter for the ISA and part of the decision about whether it was appropriate to bar – in which case there would be no role for the Tribunal.

First, in response, the Tribunal noted the High Court's view that unreasonable or irrational decisions would amount to an error of *law*:

---

59   Independent Safeguarding Authority. *Guidance notes for the barring decision making process.* London: ISA, 2009.

60   Quoted from: Safeguarding Vulnerable Groups Act 2006, s.4.

... If [ISA] reached a decision that it was appropriate for an individual to be included in a barred list or appropriate to refuse to remove an individual from a barred list yet that conclusion was unreasonable or irrational that would constitute an error of law. I do not read section 4(3) of the Act as precluding a challenge to the ultimate decision on grounds that a decision to include an individual upon a barred list or to refuse to remove him from a list was unreasonable or irrational or...disproportionate. In my judgment all that section 4(3) precludes is an appeal against the ultimate decision when that decision is not flawed by any error of law or fact.[61]

Second was the issue of proportionality. The ISA argued that this went to weighting and appropriateness, not to law. The Tribunal disagreed, stating that decisions taking a disproportionate approach to the evidence are challengeable as an error of law:

[The ISA] submitted, however, that section 4(3) prevents the Tribunal from considering issues relating to the *weight* that ISA attached to individual issues...[and] submitted that the amount of *weight* the Respondent attached to a particular issue is not for the Tribunal to re-determine, and that when one particular issue is one of many factors, this goes to 'appropriateness' expressly excluded by s 4(3).

We are not able to agree with this submission. We are mindful that we must read section 4(3) in a way that is compatible with the Human Rights Act 1998... If a decision taken by ISA to place a person on a list, or not to remove him from the list, is *disproportionate* to the facts as presented to the Respondent, then there is an error of law, and the Tribunal on appeal is entitled, indeed obliged, to direct ISA to remove the person from the list, or remit the matter to ISA for a new decision.[62]

So the Tribunal can at least challenge more closely the way in which the DBS takes decisions, enabling it to consider the weighting given to facts and evidence, as a matter of law:

The only way in which a Tribunal can form a view as to whether a decision of the Respondent [the ISA] is disproportionate is to engage in 'a weighing of evidence exercise', not so as to ascertain whether the decision is or is not appropriate (that is a matter solely for the [ISA]) but so as to ascertain whether it is disproportionate and therefore outwith the lawful decision making exercise of the [ISA]. It is therefore the totality of the evidence that the Tribunal must concern itself with. In considering the totality of the evidence, it is in our view necessary to look carefully at individual aspects to

---

61   R(Royal College of Nursing) v Secretary of State for the Home Department and the Independent Safeguarding Authority [2010] EWHC 2761 (Admin).

62   SB v Independent Safeguarding Authority [2011] UKUT 404 (AAC).

> that evidence and to form a view whether the conclusion that the [ISA] has placed on the totality of the evidence is disproportionate.[63]

But a Tribunal still has to show that the decision of the DBS was not reasonable or proportionate, thus constituting an error of law:

> The approach that we take is to look at all of this evidence and see whether the decision taken by the Respondent, in the light of this evidence, is disproportionate. This is not the same as asking ourselves the question whether we would have arrived at the same decision. Only if we are to decide that the decision taken cannot be justified by the evidence available to the decision maker can we conclude that the decision is disproportionate and therefore constitutes an error of law.[64]

DISPROPORTIONALITY AND INTERFERENCE BY TRIBUNAL, IF THE DBS SIGNIFICANTLY MISCONSTRUES THE EVIDENCE

The matter of proportionality arose as a matter of law, in a case involving a school teacher who, under some stress, had assaulted a pupil in the classroom – an excessive response to abuse, misbehaviour and rank disobedience. He was convicted in the Crown Court and given a community service order, having already spent eight months on remand. He was placed on the children's barred list but also on the adults' barred list. It was the latter against which he appealed. The Upper Tribunal found in his favour on the grounds of disproportionality. Part of this was due to the misconstruction that the ISA had placed on a doctor's report:

> The ISA has not given any detailed thought to the reasons for placing PH on the Vulnerable Adults' List. Indeed, we are inclined to adopt the phrase used…that in this case ISA has been 'worryingly myopic'. This is particularly the case because it has adopted the various safeguards identified as prudent by [a doctor]…as a reason for the Barring on the Vulnerable Adults' List. These safeguards are suggested by [the doctor] for a different reason, namely to support his opinion that PH represents a low risk. Given that these safeguards will be in place, an absolute bar is in our view disproportionate.

The Tribunal characterised, therefore, the (mis)interpretation of the doctor's report not as a question of appropriateness but as an error of law:

> [It was submitted] that ISA conducted a detailed balancing exercise, considered all of the evidence, and made a decision that was proportionate. We are unable to agree… The exercise ISA conducted was not a balancing exercise, and in particular ISA misconstrued the evidence of [the doctor], the only medical evidence that was before them. The decision that they made

63   *SB v Independent Safeguarding Authority* [2011] UKUT 404 (AAC).
64   *SB v Independent Safeguarding Authority* [2011] UKUT 404 (AAC).

was disproportionate, and accordingly constituted an error of law, and must be quashed.[65]

ONCE AN APPEAL HAS BEEN MADE ON GROUNDS OF A MISTAKE OF FACT OR LAW, CAN THE TRIBUNAL GO FURTHER AND DECIDE FOR ITSELF THE APPROPRIATENESS OF BARRING A PERSON?

In the *VT* case, the Tribunal seemed to go further. It maintained that although the appeal had to be on the grounds of a mistake of fact or law, once the appeal was made, the Tribunal could in fact decide, overall, on the appropriateness (and thus merits) of barring. It made five key points justifying this approach.[66]

The Tribunal effectively argued, in the *VT* case, that once an appeal had been made on the grounds of mistake of fact or law, the only grounds permissible, then the Tribunal could – at the appeal – rule not just on any factual or legal matters but on appropriateness and 'merits' issues. This was undoubtedly an argument to circumvent the restrictions placed by the legislation on the Tribunal, which it felt were not consistent with human rights law, given how important barring decisions are.

The *SB* case (see immediately below), heard by the Court of Appeal, seems to have rejected the lawfulness of this approach by the Tribunal and to have emphasised the statutory limitations imposed on the latter.

COURT OF APPEAL CONFIRMS RESTRICTIONS ON THE REMIT OF THE UPPER TRIBUNAL

In 2012, the Court of Appeal considered, in the *SB* case, the extent and restrictions on the powers of the Tribunal. It effectively closed the backdoor that the Tribunal had attempted to open up. It did not refer to the *VT* case, but it would appear to have ruled out the Tribunal's contention that once an appeal has been made on factual or legal issues, the Tribunal then has a free hand to deal with appropriateness to bar issues.

In this case (*SB*), the key challenge by the ISA against the original decision of the Tribunal was that consideration of weighting given by the ISA to facts and evidence was beyond the remit of the Tribunal – because it was about the 'appropriateness to bar' question (the ISA's remit) rather than law (the court's province).[67]

In answering this question, the Court of Appeal made these points.

First, it was clearly open to the Tribunal to consider matters of proportionality and rationality, not least because of the requirements of article 8 of the European Convention, which required that interference by the State (e.g. in barring a worker) be 'necessary' and therefore proportionate.

---

65   *PH v Independent Safeguarding Authority* [2012] UKUT 91 (AAC).
66   *VT v Independent Safeguarding Authority* [2011] UKUT 427 (AAC).
67   *SB v Independent Safeguarding Authority* [2012] EWCA Civ 977.

Second, this would involve looking at weighting issues. But this could only go so far. In the case under consideration, the Court felt that the Tribunal took little notice of how and what the ISA had decided, and simply got on and made its own decision – not least because it based its decision not just on the documentation (as the ISA had) but also by taking the worker's oral evidence (something the ISA never does, as a matter of policy).

Third, the Court of Appeal confirmed that the Tribunal 'is statutorily disabled from revisiting the appropriateness of an individual being included in a Barred List, *simpliciter*'. It went on to state a rationale for this:

> I intend no disrespect to the judicial or non-legal members of the UT in the present or any other case when I say that, by necessary statutory qualification, the ISA is particularly equipped to make safeguarding decisions of this kind, whereas the UT is designed not to consider the appropriateness of listing but more to adjudicate upon 'mistakes' on points of law or findings of fact.[68]

It did, however, acknowledge the strange position in which the legislation has placed the Tribunal:

> Finally, I acknowledge the difficulty faced by the UT in a case such as this. I can think of no other statutory regime in which a tribunal is expressly prohibited from revisiting 'appropriateness' but is obliged to address proportionality. However, the lines have been drawn and, as I have said, they are different lines from those which governed the jurisdiction of the Care Standards Tribunal under the previous legislation.[69]

IMPLICATIONS OF RESTRICTED ROLE OF THE UPPER TRIBUNAL

This whole issue is one of concern. The legislation has curbed the role of the Tribunal, the Tribunal has tried to find a way around those curbs, and the Court of Appeal has now, at least in part, reminded the Tribunal of just how limited its role is. There is still scope for the Tribunal to interfere with judgements being made by the DBS on grounds of proportionality.

Nonetheless, the general position is that we are left with a quango, the DBS, that (a) as a matter of policy doesn't afford workers an oral hearing, (b) wishes to prove itself, as it were, and so will be at risk of being over-enthusiastic in tending to bar people, and (c) might, quite understandably, be risk averse and so, again, tend to bar people, rather than face the music if a person who is not barred goes on to harm a vulnerable adult or child. In addition is the danger of the DBS going along with making scapegoats of workers, who are offered up by their employer as sacrifices, in order to avoid owning up to systemic failures.

---

68   *SB v Independent Safeguarding Authority* [2012] EWCA Civ 977.
69   *SB v Independent Safeguarding Authority* [2012] EWCA Civ 977.

Two well-known examples of such scapegoats were Lisa Arthurworrey and Angella Mairs, latterly the former's manager before the death of Victoria Climbié in Haringey. Both were placed on the POVA list at the time by the Secretary of State; both won their appeals before the Care Standards Tribunal, which, legally, unlike the current Tribunal, had a wider remit.[70] Sometimes, the determination to make a scapegoat is considerable; the Secretary of State appealed to the High Court against the Tribunal's decision to remove the bar on Angella Mairs. The judge upheld the Tribunal's decision.[71]

If the Upper Tribunal had the normal powers of a tribunal, then this would represent a reasonable counterbalance to the potential excesses of a body such as the ISA. But it does not.

DECISION LETTERS

If the DBS writes a decision letter, which appears to indicate an error of law in the decision-making process, the Tribunal will look at the substance of the decision lying behind the letter before deciding whether the letter represents a true of error of law.

For example, when a music teacher was sent a barring letter, it stated that the ISA did not find 'that the evidence provided by you in your representations is sufficient to disprove the allegations made against you'. Had this been a true reflection of the ISA's decision making, it would have been an error of law because it would have been a reversal of the burden of proof.[72]

In the same vein, unhelpfully brief decision letters might fail to reflect the more complex decision that has taken place, and so be criticised by the Tribunal; nonetheless, it remains the substance of the decision that has to be examined.[73]

STANDARD OF PROOF

Proceedings before the DBS and the Upper Tribunal are civil in nature. The standard of proof is therefore not the high (beyond reasonable doubt) level applied in criminal proceedings. The Tribunal has pointed out that:

> One argument is that ISA is an independent public body that accepts referrals from e.g. employers and other bodies which 'think' that an individual has engaged in 'relevant conduct', or poses a risk of harm, and which then makes factual findings in the context of an overall assessment as to future risk. In that context, formal legal notions such as the 'burden of proof' may not be apposite.[74]

---

70   *Mairs v Secretary of State for Education and Skills* [2004] 269 (PC). And: *Lisa Arthurworrey v Secretary of State for Education and Skills* [2004] 268 (PC).

71   *Secretary of State for Education and Skills v Mairs* [2005] EWHC 996 (Admin).

72   *XY v Independent Safeguarding Authority* [2011] UKUT 289 (AAC).

73   *VW v Independent Safeguarding Authority* [2011] UKUT 435 (AAC).

74   *XY v Independent Safeguarding Authority* [2011] UKUT 289 (AAC).

Therefore:

> a criminal prosecution may not succeed, for any number of reasons, but there may still be sufficient evidence to conclude on the balance of probabilities that the alleged abuser has engaged in 'relevant conduct' with children and should be prevented from working with children.[75]

ORAL HEARINGS

The legislation does not demand that the DBS grant oral hearings to those it is minded to bar; equally, this is not prohibited.

The Upper Tribunal has noted that the Supreme Court has cast some doubt on the value of oral hearings; the latter quoted Lord Bingham: 'the current tendency is (I think) on the whole to distrust the demeanour of a witness as a reliable pointer to his honesty'.[76]

However, the Tribunal has also noted the High Court's view that:

> a failure or refusal to conduct an oral hearing in circumstances which would allow of an argument that the failure or refusal was unreasonable or irrational would itself raise the prospect of an appeal to the Upper Tribunal on a point of law.[77]

Thus, whilst the Tribunal has accepted that there is no automatic right to an oral hearing, it has put the position as follows:

> However, with respect, and notwithstanding both the powerful points made by the majority of the Supreme Court, and our own conclusions on the relevant law, we would encourage ISA to consider the circumstances in which it would be appropriate to hold an oral hearing. There may well be circumstances in which the common law duty of procedural fairness may point to the need for an oral hearing.[78]

Troubling is the fact, as a Tribunal noted in 2011, that so far the ISA had granted no oral hearings at all in a single case.[79] The Court of Appeal, in 2012, noted that the ISA seemed to have a policy of granting no oral hearings at all, but made no comment on the legal soundness of the policy.[80]

There is little doubt that the Tribunal, in its former guise under the Care Standards Act 2000 (and the POVA list) and in its present form, has sometimes put store by hearing from 'accused' people themselves. In one case, it believed that an oral hearing before the Tribunal was part of the process enabling it to

---

75 *XY v Independent Safeguarding Authority* [2011] UKUT 289 (AAC).

76 *R(G) v The Governors of X School* [2011] UKSC 30.

77 *R(Royal College of Nursing) v Secretary of State for the Home Department and the Independent Safeguarding Authority* [2010] EWHC 2761 (Admin).

78 *XY v Independent Safeguarding Authority* [2011] UKUT 289 (AAC).

79 *SB v Independent Safeguarding Authority* [2011] UKUT 404 (AAC).

80 *SB v Independent Safeguarding Authority* [2012] EWCA Civ 977.

consider the worker 'as a person'. However, it was in that case that the Court of Appeal subsequently held that the Tribunal had gone too far in challenging the ISA's reasoning.[81]

In another case, involving a teacher who, provoked, had assaulted a boy in the classroom, the Tribunal noted that both it and a doctor who had judged the man to be a low risk to vulnerable adults, had had the advantage of questioning him and analysing his answers. Whereas the ISA worker had relied solely on paperwork.[82]

BEING BARRED IS NOT A PUNISHMENT

The Upper Tribunal has noted that being placed on the list is not a punishment; it is a protection for vulnerable adults (or children):

> Being placed on a Children's Barred List is not a punishment. The Appellant has been punished by the Court. Being placed on the Children's Barred List is to provide protection for children. The legislation establishes a delicate balance between protecting rights of children (and vulnerable adults) and protecting the rights of those who wish to work, either as employed or as volunteers, with them.[83]

IRRATIONALITY, PERVERSITY, DISPROPORTIONALITY

The Tribunal can interfere with DBS decisions on these grounds, which constitute an error of law. The ground of perversity would require that 'a claim that a decision is perverse should only succeed where an overwhelming case is made out that the Tribunal reached a decision which no reasonable tribunal, on a proper appreciation of the evidence and the law, would have reached'.[84]

Proportionality has been considered at some length above.

CONSIDERING RELEVANT INFORMATION

A failure to obtain and to consider relevant information can amount to an error of law.

In one case, for example, the ISA failed to make efforts to get hold of an up-to-date probation service report. The ISA claimed that it was not 'charged with an investigative function'. The Tribunal disagreed, quoting from the ISA's own guidance for its staff: "'The second stage is information gathering. The ISA considers all the facts it has on the case and may seek additional material from a range of other sources to ensure it has all known relevant information.'"

The Tribunal went on to say the guidance was 'unsurprising and accurate as a statement of law'.[85]

---

81   *SB v Independent Safeguarding Authority* [2012] EWCA Civ 977.
82   *PH v Independent Safeguarding Authority* [2012] UKUT 91 (AAC).
83   *SB v Independent Safeguarding Authority* [2011] UKUT 404 (AAC).
84   *XY v Independent Safeguarding Authority* [2011] UKUT 289 (AAC).
85   *VW v Independent Safeguarding Authority* [2011] UKUT 435 (AAC).

Furthermore, the failure to obtain the probation service report meant that a conflict of evidence was not solved and irrational weight was given to a police report which, far from containing facts, in substantial measure comprised non-factual material.[86]

REACHING CONCLUSION NOT SUPPORTED BY THE EVIDENCE: ERROR OF FACT AND LAW

The DBS might make material errors of fact and law in one and the same breath.

For instance, in considering testimonials put forward on a person's behalf in one case, the ISA had given them little weight. This was partly on the basis that, of seven testimonial writers, the ISA concluded that only two were aware of the person's criminal conviction. In fact, at least three had stated explicitly their awareness, and awareness could be inferred in the other four. The Tribunal noted:

> The appellant had asserted that each was aware and invited the ISA to get in contact with them if it wished. Instead the ISA has concluded that only two were aware. That in our view is a finding of fact (even if its purpose was to assist the respondent in evaluating the evidence) and as such incorrect, but it is also an error of law as being a position which no reasonable decision maker could adopt on the evidence before it.[87]

In another case, the ISA claimed to have evaluated the evidence, but the Tribunal held that the ISA clearly had not done this. The ISA had stated that the person:

> was formerly of good standing in his community and was involved in numerous voluntary and community matters. He expresses a fervent wish to continue helping others. Whilst his offending and risk factors indicate an unacceptable risk to children...there is insufficient information to indicate he has harmed or poses a risk of harm to vulnerable adults.[88]

The Tribunal pointed out that:

> It is the first clause in the final sentence which has caused us to conclude that the [ISA] has arrived at a decision which is disproportionate to the evidence and accordingly that it has made an error of law. When the [ISA] considers whether to remove a person from the Register, it must consider all of the risk factors in order to reach a decision. It is said that the risk factors indicated an unacceptable risk to children. It is our view that this conclusion cannot be justified by the evidence, and that it is a decision which goes beyond a conclusion that falls within the definition of a proportionate decision. There

86   *VW v Independent Safeguarding Authority* [2011] UKUT 435 (AAC).
87   *VW v Independent Safeguarding Authority* [2011] UKUT 435 (AAC).
88   *SB v Independent Safeguarding Authority* [2011] UKUT 404 (AAC).

is a failure to take account of the wealth of evidence which supports the approach of the Probation Service that he poses a low risk of reoffending.[89]

Nonetheless, in this second case, the Court of Appeal stated that the Tribunal had itself taken a lopsided approach to the ISA's decision making and interfered excessively with the judgement the ISA had made. The ISA's original barring was restored by the Court.[90] This was despite the apparently compelling reasoning of the Tribunal. (The Court of Appeal's decision does not read quite so compellingly; it possibly suggests that the Court was using the case to put the Tribunal in its place, to remind it of the statutory restrictions placed on it.)

NOT PUTTING INFORMATION TO THE PERSON: ERROR OF LAW

Failing to put certain material to the person, resulting in a mistaken view of the facts, might also be a material error of law. For instance, a Criminal Records Bureau (CRB) report relied on by the ISA stated the person was seeking a job involving contact with children. This point was not put to the person. In fact, the sports organisation involved provided a letter (to the Tribunal) stating that the work would have involved largely adults and that in any case no trainees were allowed to work unsupervised.[91]

DBS NOT FOLLOWING ITS OWN GUIDANCE: ERROR OF LAW

In one case, the ISA had barred a person without following the procedures about taking certain cases to line management and the ISA Board, laid down in the ISA's structured judgement procedure (SJP) to be used by staff:

> ISA had a clearly stated policy expressed in mandatory terms that was contained in both guidance published to the world at large and in internal protocols. The guidance was that normally a decision to bar would require definite concerns across at least two areas of the SJP. In the absence of such a profile, the decision to bar could be maintained but only if the case was taken to line management and then to the Board for a final decision. In VT's case the presumption did not apply, the case was not escalated to the Board as required and no adequate explanation was given for that departure from published guidance. In our view, this failure alone amounts to a clear error of law on the part of ISA.[92]

PUBLIC CONFIDENCE

The Tribunal has acknowledged the relevance, albeit limited, of public confidence and decisions to bar:

89   *SB v Independent Safeguarding Authority* [2011] UKUT 404 (AAC).
90   *SB v Independent Safeguarding Authority* [2012] EWCA Civ 977.
91   *VW v Independent Safeguarding Authority* [2011] UKUT 435 (AAC).
92   *VT v Independent Safeguarding Authority* [2011] UKUT 427 (AAC).

We naturally recognise the harm and abuse involved in accessing child pornography on the internet, as did the former Care Standards Tribunal in its case law. We have also had regard to the need for public confidence in the listing regime. In our judgement, given our finding that VT does not himself represent a risk of harm to children, the only possible reason for maintaining his inclusion on the list is the question of public confidence. However, in that context we note the observation in ISA's Guidance Notes that 'issues of public confidence will more likely play a useful supportive role alongside other significant factors in marginal barring decisions. It would certainly be a rare and highly exceptional case where public confidence is the main reason for a barring decision in the absence of other significant factors'... We agree with that proposition.[93]

However, that does not mean that public confidence should not be considered as a reason for barring. The Court of Appeal found fault with the Upper Tribunal in another case, for failing to consider this ground in terms of a person being barred. The Court noted that 'public confidence is not an inevitable trump card. However, it is something which must be placed in the scales when consideration is being given to the personal characteristics and interests of an appellant.'[94] It approved the approach outlined in a previous case, which recognised the vital importance of public confidence, without giving in to the baying of the mob:

The tribunal, in my judgment, is plainly right, and for the reasons it has given, in stressing the vital importance of the issue of public confidence. This does not mean, of course, that the tribunal is simply to pander to the unreasoned baying of the mob; but it does mean that it is entitled to have regard to matters which are likely to be of concern to ordinary sensible people. For my part I would not wish to question the tribunal's jurisprudence. In my judgment it is quite plainly correct.[95]

BARRING DECISIONS AND APPEALS: EXAMPLES

Under the old POVA list, a significant number of people appealed to the Care Standards Tribunal against their inclusion. The Tribunal's decisions were on the record and gave a flavour of the type of person being placed on the list and why.

Some of these cases remain a useful guide as to the types of matter that is likely to come before DBS under the new system of barring.

However, the important distinction to bear in mind is that – as outlined above – the Upper Tribunal's remit is more circumscribed than that of the former Care Standards Tribunal. Which means that the following examples are not a precise guide to the success of appeals under the current scheme.

---

93   *VT v Independent Safeguarding Authority* [2011] UKUT 427 (AAC).
94   *SB v Independent Safeguarding Authority* [2012] EWCA Civ 977.
95   *Secretary of State for Children v BP* [2009] EWHC 866 (Admin).

BARRING PEOPLE FOR FINANCIAL ABUSE

Not being a 'bad person' did not necessarily mean that a person was suitable to work with vulnerable adults, having stolen money from an 88-year-old woman.

Stealing money, not a 'bad person' but not suitable to work with vulnerable adults. Allegations were made that money had been stolen from a resident in a care home. The police were informed and they installed a covert camera. The care worker concerned eventually pleaded guilty to theft and received a community punishment order. She was referred to the POVA list. The resident concerned was 88 years of age. The theft had a huge impact on her, and she no longer trusted her carers. The care worker argued that her name should be removed from the POVA list because she had, as she explained, 'put her hands up to that, walked out on her job, paid the lady back, did some community service and hung her head in shame for years'.

The Tribunal concluded that:

> although we warmed to her as an individual and have some empathy with her, her lack of insight of the effect of her actions on the victim and the failure to understand that her integrity has been affected, do not help us conclude she is now suitable... We do appreciate that, in her words, she is 'not a bad person' but, again, that does not mean she is suitable to work with vulnerable adults.[96]

In another case, a depressed local authority care worker stole a sum of money, returned it anonymously and expressed deep regret.

Care worker with mental health problems stealing money, returning it, expressing deep regret: but might do it again. A care worker stole a sum of £240 from the home of a service user. Some months later, an envelope was found at the service user's home with the same amount of money and an anonymous note apologising for the theft. The carer was taking medication for depression and for schizophrenia. The Tribunal found both misconduct and actual harm, since the theft would have had an effect on the woman's well-being and have caused anxiety, as well undermining confidence in services provided by the local authority. The Tribunal accepted that the carer deeply regretted her actions, but was not satisfied she would not do the same again. Her rationalisation of why she committed the theft, together with her failure to disclose past theft and fraud offences, meant she was unsuitable to work with vulnerable adults.[97]

More straightforwardly, another case about money involved an agency care worker in a person's own home who, having fraudulently written out a cheque to herself, then tried to make the service user feel guilty. The Tribunal confirmed that she was unsuitable to work with vulnerable adults, but also took a side swipe at the agency that employed her, in relation to its failure to visit and apologise to the woman and to its recruiting and training procedures.

Fraudulent use of cheque made out for £2500. The service user, who was severely disabled through multiple sclerosis, paid the agency using direct payments received from the local authority. The carer told the woman that she had lost her glasses; the woman wrote out a blank cheque so the carer could buy some new ones. The carer made out the cheque to herself for £2500. She subsequently apologised, paid back £2000 with a

---

96   *DG v Secretary of State* [2006] 824 (PVA).

97   *SM v Secretary of State* [2007] 1006 (PVA).

promise of repaying the rest. Nobody from the agency ever visited the woman, even after the misconduct had come to light (something the Tribunal subsequently criticised).

The Tribunal took the view that the carer had not lost her glasses, the plan was premeditated, and she only apologised after the fraud came to light when the bank phoned to say that the woman had become overdrawn (the carer had miscalculated how much money was in the account). Even then, the carer had persuaded the woman not to report it.

The Tribunal noted that the woman was 'trapped in her house at the mercy of a live-in carer. She must have felt very frightened and angry.' It was surprised that the agency had not visited and apologised, wondered what checks had been carried out and hoped that the agency had significantly improved its recruiting and training procedures. The carer had had a five-minute interview before being taken on by the agency. She was clearly unsuitable to work with vulnerable adults.[98]

Other cases have been more opaque. For instance, suspicion is one thing, proof and evidence quite another. This is so even though, in such tribunal proceedings, the standard of proof is the lower, civil, standard. In the following case, involving a domiciliary care worker, there were 12 alleged incidents of theft; ten were discounted, and although the other two involved taking money, the Tribunal found they did not amount to theft.

Twelve incidents of alleged theft: smoke did not necessarily mean fire – no misconduct. A domiciliary care worker had been included on the POVA list as result of allegations of theft on 12 occasions. The Tribunal responded as follows.

Missing money, handbag, purse. An allegation about missing money from a man's flat was dismissed, since there was no evidence that money was in fact missing. In another instance, a woman had been unable to find her handbag and purse, but no specific allegation was made that the care worker had taken it. A third allegation was made to a neighbour about theft of a purse, but considerable doubt was cast on whether it was stolen (as opposed to mislaid) by the woman's godson, and there was no evidence of its having been stolen by the care worker.

Missing money, missing watch, borrowing money. In another instance of alleged missing money, there was insufficient evidence; it was unclear when the money went missing, and other carers visited as well as the care worker in question. Another allegation was withdrawn concerning pound coins going missing from a couple's house; it transpired that a carer had made this observation, but no accusation had been made against the care worker. The next allegation involved the taking of a watch; the care worker said she had taken it for mending. There was no evidence that she had intended to take the watch permanently. It was further alleged that the care worker had borrowed £135 (there was no evidence for this) and that her husband had decorated the service user's house and been paid £100 (the care worker stated this had been requested of her husband by a mutual friend of his and of the service user).

Money missing from purse, theft of duvet, toilet rolls. Another service user alleged the theft of £60 from her purse. This was investigated by the police, who had noted that she had numerous carers visiting her and there was no evidence that the care worker was responsible. Another allegation, that the care worker had retained for herself a duvet she was meant to take to a charity shop, was not made out. The care worker should have obtained a receipt, but at that time her employer's procedures and policies did not specify

---

98   *Nkala v Secretary of State for Health* [2007] 1015 (PVA).

the obtaining of receipts for goods. Yet another allegation, concerning the theft of toilet rolls and sums of £10 and £30, was discounted; there was no direct evidence and up to ten other carers were also visiting the service user at the relevant time.

Cashing pension of sister of service user. The two allegations of most potential substance were as follows. The care worker took the sister of a service user (they lived together) to the Post Office to cash her pension, which produced a sum of over £1000. The care worker reported this to the office and also that she had been given a plant by the service user. Subsequently, a large proportion of this money went missing. The care worker was a suspect because she knew the money was in the house. The Tribunal noted that the care worker had gone beyond what was expected of her, but the company manager did state that it was not unusual for carers to look out for the interests of the partners of service users. The care worker faced criminal charges on this allegation but was acquitted.

Although the Tribunal worked to a lower standard of proof (balance of probability only), it was not minded to find this allegation proven. The time the money went missing was unknown and there were other visitors to the house. Furthermore, reporting to her employer about the cashing of the pension and the large sum of money in the house seemed inconsistent with an intention to steal. At a later date, the care worker was found with the sister's (who was herself now a service user as well as the first sister) pension book in her possession (without a receipt having been given), but there was no evidence that she intended to retain it and obtain cash for herself.

Entrapment of care worker. Last was the allegation that she had taken £10 from a service user's house, money that had been planted by the company to entrap the care worker. She had been found with it on the dashboard of her car; she argued that she had taken it to buy food for the service user. The Tribunal did not accept that she intended to steal the money, but felt the matter came to a failure to give a receipt – which she had not given because, on the evidence, she was in a rush.

No misconduct. The Tribunal concluded that there was no misconduct that harmed or placed at risk of harm a vulnerable adult; thus it did not have to consider whether the care worker was unsuitable to work with vulnerable adults. Her appeal succeeded.[99]

Similarly, in another case the Tribunal decided that the allegations against the care worker were not made out, despite a damning list of accusations. These included:

- force-feeding of tablets and liquids (no reliable recording and probable exaggerated accounts of what happened)

- placing call bells out of reach (no evidence that she had removed them)

- leaving a service user on a commode for too long (nothing wrong with leaving resident for certain amount of time on the commode in her room; in fact, part of privacy)

- rough turning of service users (no evidence of rough turning or that a resident's screams were connected to the turning)

- rough and unprofessional catheterisation of a service user (carer acted properly and promptly to relieve suffering)

---

99   *Pain v Secretary of State* [2006] 636 (PVA).

- casual and excessive administration of Lactulose (unclear evidence)

- carelessly causing or permitting scalding with hot drinks (not clear that a hot drink had been spilt, or that it would have been misconduct)

- failing to disclose convictions for dishonesty in relation to benefits (misconduct, but did not harm residents, and the allegations did not concern dishonesty).

The Tribunal noted that one of the witnesses supporting the allegation was young and inexperienced and that the 'events were seen through the eyes of a then new and very inexperienced care assistant, whose interpretation of what she saw may not have been wholly correct'.[100]

PHYSICAL AND OTHER NEGLECT OR MISTREATMENT CASES

Tribunal decisions might be relatively straightforward, as in the case of proven allegations of sexual assault on clients with mental disabilities in residential settings – and non-disclosure of previous convictions.[101]

Similarly, the taking of objectively obscene photographs of elderly residents by a care worker, apparently formerly a medical doctor in Bulgaria – compounded by disingenuousness and the fact that he was an intelligent man with professional medical training – meant this was misconduct and he was unsuitable to work with vulnerable adults or children.[102]

A Bulgarian physician's assistant was working as a senior care worker in a care home. Following a night shift, a resident was discovered in the morning heavily soiled and wet, distressed and with a bleeding scrotum from the urine. The care worker was dismissed and placed on the POVA list. He lost his appeal. He had argued that he needed the man's consent and he could not gain this because the man was asleep. The Tribunal noted that the care plan laid down two-hourly checks, given that the resident was doubly incontinent.[103]

It might simply be assault.

Bending back the thumbs of residents. A care assistant working in a nursing home had been found guilty of assault, following allegations that she had bent back the thumbs of residents. Aggravating features were that the actions had been premeditated against elderly, mentally ill residents. She had not appealed against her inclusion on the POVA list, but contested her inclusion on the POCA list. The Tribunal rejected her appeal.[104]

The fact that a care worker had spent most of her life caring and had troubled to improve her skills to achieve senior status was not enough to excuse reckless care of residents.

---

100   *Wright v Secretary of State for Health* [2006] 655 (PVA).

101   *McNish v Secretary of State for Health* [2006] 0646 (PVA).

102   *Kalchev v Secretary of State for Education and Skills* [2005] 589 (PVA)/590 (PC).

103   *Kostadinov v Secretary of State for Health* [2008] 1418 (PVA).

104   *Mwaura v Secretary of State for Health* [2006] 687 (PVA)/688 (PC).

Force-feeding by senior care worker. A senior carer had tried to force food into elderly residents' mouths. One was able to say whether she had had enough; the other had a poor swallow reflex and could have choked if the food had been pushed in any further. Despite the fact that the care worker had spent most of her life working in the care sector, had gone to the trouble of getting qualifications and had achieved senior care status, the Tribunal found both misconduct and unsuitability to work with vulnerable adults or children.[105]

The issue might simply be evidential, one person's word against another.

Knocking a resident to the floor: misconduct but not unsuitable to work with vulnerable adults. At a care home, it was alleged by one care assistant that, during the night, another (senior) care worker slapped a service user against a wall and then pushed her in the back, forcing her to the floor.

The resident had been heading for the smokers' lounge, although claimed to be going to the toilet. The senior care worker stated that the resident had struck out at her and she had raised her hands to block the blow. In so doing, however, she had hit the resident on the shoulder, who then fell to the floor. She was 'mortified' at what had happened. She apologised and checked on the resident through the night. She did not, however, report the incident. When it came to light, she did nothing to defend her job; she knew she was going to be sacked but did not feel she could have done anything differently.

The tribunal was impressed by her evidence and her approach. Her failure to report the incident amounted to misconduct. However, it noted that prior to her disciplinary hearing she had been given no opportunity to explain her actions and she had herself 'on all accounts been the victim of an assault…and been offered no support by her employers'. The tribunal concluded that, notwithstanding the misconduct, she was not unsuitable to work with vulnerable adults or children. The care assistant's appeal succeeded.[106]

The evidence might alternatively be overwhelming, involving the death of a service user and abuse of others.

Sleeping on duty, taunting, flicking water, distressing residents. A 40-year-old carer worked at a care home for adults with learning disabilities. One night, she slept and during this time one of the residents trapped his head between the headboard and bed rails. He suffered brain damage and subsequently died. The carer subsequently attempted to persuade another member of staff (young and inexperienced) to change a detail in the records, saying that she had turned the man 16 times during the night rather than just six. This would have given the impression that she had been providing care rather than sleeping. The Tribunal noted that this attempt was a 'flagrant piece of improper conduct'. In addition, the Tribunal found that she had flicked water over another resident who particularly disliked water on her body, distressed a second by threatening to wash her clothes even though she had a propensity to become distressed at such laundering, and had taunted a third resident and mimicked her self-harming actions. The Tribunal found misconduct and unsuitability to work with vulnerable adults (and children). She had started as a very good carer but had become a poor one with an attitude that was dangerous to service users.[107]

---

105 *Jackson v Secretary of State for Health* [2005] 623 (PVA)/624 (PC).
106 *Dixon v Secretary of State for Health* [2005] 621 (PVA).
107 *Close v Secretary of State for Health* [2006] 852 (PVA).

Care workers might react to considerable provocation, but the Tribunal would still bear in mind that dealing with challenging behaviour is part of the job.

Reacting to being spat at: no excuse. A domiciliary support worker had, in his own words, 'lost it' when a man with challenging behaviour struck out and spat at the worker in the shower. The worker first pushed the man's head hard to the side, then subsequently raised his hand in front of the man's face and caught him on the forehead, pushing him backwards. The worker was convicted of assault. He submitted to the Tribunal that he had a phobia about spitting and that he would not react in such a way again. The Tribunal was not convinced and concluded that he was unsuitable to work with vulnerable adults.[108]

Manual handling is by no means always a straightforward issue, but the following case illustrates an unacceptable extreme, when poor practice becomes the criminal offence of assault, as well as a barring matter.

Dragging 20-stone resident across the floor by his underpants. A senior carer in a care home had manoeuvred a fallen resident, weighing 20 stone (127 kg), by holding and pulling his underpants. He denied dragging the man across the floor in this manner (the Tribunal found this allegation unproven). He received a caution from the police for assault. Initially, he had lied about what had occurred. Although he had not received all planning manual handling training, he was an experienced care worker, had received manual handling training in Singapore and had a nursing degree from the Philippines. The incident was misconduct, and he was unfit to work with vulnerable adults because he failed to recognise the high risk he took with the resident and because he had denied what had actually happened.[109]

In the following case, a strict and inflexible regime led to a range of unacceptable treatment of service users.

Strict and inflexible regime, leading to lack of tolerance of people with learning disabilities. A care worker was part of a team supporting three service users with learning disabilities, living in a supported living tenancy. Various allegations were made. On one occasion, a service user dropped his comfort stick; another carer picked it up, but the care worker told the latter to put it back on the floor: the man should pick it up himself. On another occasion, he dropped it into the toilet; the carer told him to put his hand into the toilet to retrieve it. The carer referred to another service user as a 'slaughtered pig' when she was menstruating. In addition was a failure to help service users out of bed. There was also falsification of records. All this was misconduct harming, or placing at risk of harm, vulnerable adults. Overall, the carer had operated a strict and inflexible regime, leading to a lack of tolerance. The carer was unsuitable to work with vulnerable adults.[110]

The evidence might simply not hold up and a care worker might win an appeal, apparently against all the odds, even after the care worker had been dismissed and lost hearings both before an employment tribunal and an employment appeal tribunal. (The Care Standards Tribunal explained the discrepancy between its findings and

108   *SP v Secretary of State* [2006] 725 (PVA)/726 (PC).
109   *Del Mundo v Secretary of State for Health* [2005] 557 (PVA)/558 (PC).
110   *Johnston v Secretary of State for Health* [2007] 1064 (PC).

that of the employment tribunals. It was that employment law demanded a lower standard of proof than the civil standard applied by the Care Standards Tribunal.)

Unfounded allegations of sexual misconduct. In a small home for four people with learning disabilities, one of the residents made certain signs which were interpreted as an allegation of sexual, anal penetration by a member of staff. The member of staff was a care worker with an unblemished work record of 30 years as a nurse and a carer. He was suspended and never returned to the home. He was then dismissed, lost an appeal against it, lost his appeal before an Employment Tribunal and lost his appeal against that decision – and was then placed on the POVA list.

The Care Standards Tribunal now doubted whether there had been anal penetration; the police surgeon had found no evidence of it. If there had been, the Care Standards Tribunal could not identify why the staff member should have been the perpetrator. Furthermore, there was doubt about what the man had been trying to communicate that day; it seemed most likely it was all about a broken lunch box. This case demanded the 'heightened' standard of proof, but, even on the lower civil standard, the Tribunal could not be satisfied that there was any misconduct.

The reason for the difference between this Tribunal's finding and that of the Employment Appeal Tribunal was that employment law demanded only that the employer have reasonable suspicion of misconduct – a lower standard of proof than the civil standard of proof involving balance of probability.[111]

Falsifying log books led to a care worker being placed on the POVA list. She was a domiciliary care worker who filled in a client log of her visits ahead of the visit and then didn't turn up. The Care Standards Tribunal, to which she appealed, was in no doubt that she had placed vulnerable adults at risk of harm. She had displayed a cavalier attitude to a fundamental part of her job, the keeping of records. Cutting corners with vulnerable people was unacceptable.[112]

MANAGEMENT FAILINGS

A background of management failing all too often surfaces in tribunal hearings, as mitigation for the individual who is appealing against being barred. But acknowledgement of this has not necessarily saved the person appealing against being barred.

Controlled drugs: poor management but misconduct and unsuitability of nurse confirmed. Incorrect administration of a controlled drug by a registered mental health nurse – even when under pressure – constituted misconduct, following a failure to check the drugs chart and the controlled drugs register. Likewise, the failure to dispose of controlled drugs that a resident had not taken and to record what had happened. This was notwithstanding woefully inadequate training, support and supervision, and that the nurse appeared to have become a scapegoat for poor practice generally in the nursing home. The misconduct was made out, and the Tribunal held also that he was unsuitable to work with vulnerable adults or children. His appeal failed.[113]

---

111   *NJ v Secretary of State for Health* [2006] 727 (PVA).

112   *VP v Secretary of State for Health* [2008] 1251 (PVA).

113   *EK v Secretary of State* [2006] 0716 (PVA)/0717 (PC).

Conversely, management-related failings might be a significant factor in a care worker's favour – as in the following case which essentially was about crossing the boundary between paid carer and friend.

Care worker crossing the line between paid carer and friend; risk of financial harm; failures of the domiciliary care agency. The appellant was employed as a cleaner for a woman in her own home. She had a good relationship with the woman, who was of low intellect, housebound, partially sighted and had insulin-dependent diabetes. At some point she became her carer, still in her employed role. The woman then alleged she had been exploited by the care worker.

Going on holiday, buying and cleaning carpets, doing the gardening, redecorating the house, putting money into a Christmas club – all outside the care plan. The care worker conceded that she had been on holiday twice with the woman (but the woman had paid only for herself), bought a new carpet with the woman's money which was laid in the woman's house by the carer's husband, bought two new armchairs and a bed for her, arranged for her husband to do the gardening for £10 an hour, arranged via the social worker for her husband to redecorate the house at a cost of £400, arranged for her husband to clean the carpets monthly (due to incontinence), and took up to £35 a week to put into a Christmas club for the service user (all this money was properly accounted for).

Lack of training, guidance, support, supervision. The Tribunal found that when her role changed from cleaner to carer, the care worker had received no training, guidance, support or supervision. She had never been given a cash book or received guidance on the handling of money. She had a close relationship with the woman. She came across as straightforward and uncomplicated. The decoration by the husband was done to a high standard at a commercial rate. The social worker's sanctioning of this arrangement was bad practice. The woman appeared to have had a good time on holiday and had paid only for herself, and the motive on the part of the care worker was one of fondness for the woman, rather than a desire to swindle her. The care worker had made a number of withdrawals from the woman's bank account over the years, but these were authorised by the woman and were consistent with the woman's expenditure patterns. There was no element in all of this of dishonesty or financial exploitation.

Overstepping the bounds of good practice. The care worker had clearly overstepped the bounds of good practice, but the Tribunal found that the blame for this fell squarely on the agency because of the lack of training, supervision or even basic management. The Tribunal took the woman's allegations seriously, but noted that the woman had a history of making such allegations, that she could be very 'difficult', that there was evidence that she had struck the care worker twice, and that a neighbour, who had previously been banned from the house because of her malign influence, was not only present when the allegations were made but was actively prompting the woman.

Misconduct and risk of harm, but suitable to work with vulnerable adults. The Tribunal held that the care worker was guilty of misconduct because, by crossing the dividing line between carer and friend, she had placed the woman at risk of harm of financial exploitation (although no such harm occurred). However, the Tribunal found that she had been 'left to her own devices, received little training, no supervision and no management. She accepts her failings and is willing to be supervised. Above all she presents as a caring person and we have little doubt that provided she is properly trained, managed and supervised she will provide good quality care in the future.'

The Tribunal also noted the virtue of oral hearings. The papers had presented a damning picture; it was only through seeing and hearing witnesses that a different picture emerged.[114]

In another case, a care worker at a residential home had clearly left residents at risk of harm, but the root of the problem seemed to lie with management, rather than the unsuitability of the care worker.

Care worker topping up her mobile phone leaving residents unattended in the dark at a care home. A care home worker left residents unattended in order to go to a local shop to top up her mobile phone so that she could make an urgent phone call. She had understood that she was not allowed to use the telephones in the care home itself. She had left one resident, bathed and dressed, in the lounge downstairs, in the dark. She left the backdoor propped open. Although no residents came to any actual harm, the Tribunal was in no doubt that they had been put at risk of harm through misconduct. However, the tribunal noted that the care worker had considerable family difficulties at the time and had believed she was not allowed to use the phones in the home, even though management denied there was any such ban.

Brisk expedition of management, lack of pastoral approach, quiet reticence of care worker, misunderstanding. The Tribunal found that the root of the problem appeared to lie between 'the brisk expedition…and loquacious exuberance' of the managers on the one hand and the 'quiet reticence' of the care worker on the other. Had management been a 'little more pastoral and pro-active in their staff management', the problem might have been avoided. Indeed, the documentary evidence showed that the care worker had been pursuing her career with 'diligence and enthusiasm', and management at the home had previously been satisfied with her work and personality. The Tribunal was unable to find that the care worker was unsuitable to work with vulnerable adults.[115]

A somewhat similar case involved a teacher who was also a part-time support worker at a care home for nine people with learning disabilities. He did two hours' induction training, could not attend other training but was given two DVDs instead. He did a weekend night shift twice a month. He used his own bed linen to sleep over. One day, he had forgotten to bring it with him and he left the home for 15 minutes. He was suspended and dismissed for gross misconduct and referred to the Secretary of State. As a result, he was placed on both the Protection of Children Act (POCA) and POVA lists. He lost his job as a teacher. The Tribunal allowed his appeal.

Night support worker: going home to get bed linen, leaving residents for 15 minutes.

The only reliable evidence of misconduct is the single incident of 17th June 2006, which the Appellant himself has admitted. We do not regard this as sufficient to show unsuitability. The Appellant was entirely new to the field of care and this job was not his profession or calling: the situation might well have been different if he had been a manager or a professional or member of staff with long experience.

As to the Appellant's future suitability, we note the clear indications that he needs more understanding of the needs of service users, how best to provide for

114 *Mrs P v Secretary of State for Education and Skills* [2005] 562 (PVA)/563 (PC).
115 *Matswairo v Secretary of State for Health* [2007] 0937 (PVA).

them and of the importance of care plans. Nevertheless, he has undoubtedly learned and suffered extensive consequences from this experience, including the loss of his principal teaching job. If Mrs M and he are to pursue their stated intention of opening a home together either here or abroad, the Appellant will need to address his lack of specific training.

In conclusion, we find the Appellant guilty of a single incident of misconduct but not unsuitable to work with vulnerable adults. It follows that his appeal against his inclusion on the POVA list is upheld.[116]

The Tribunal then turned its attention to the process by which he had been barred in the first place. At the employer's end, it flagged up the very poor investigating process that had taken place. It also criticised the Secretary of State's POVA staff for accepting such a substandard referral and acting on it. The result had been unfair and disastrous.[117]

It might be a catalogue of poor professional practice on the part of a manager herself.

Multiple failings in care. A registered mental health nurse, acting as manager in a nursing home, lost her appeal after the Tribunal found proven allegations which included (a) lack of staff supervision, monitoring and training, (b) failure to check staff references, (c) failure to keep service user files up to date with relevant information, (d) failure to provide adequate wound care and pressure sore care, (e) failure to monitor the weight of residents, and (f) failure to provide adequate care and neglecting residents.[118]

In the following case, the Tribunal did find a number of failings in the actions of a nurse working in nursing home. However, it noted that although he failed to keep fluid charts and made no tissue viability care plan, nobody else did either, and the Tribunal felt it was unfair to blame one individual worker.

Nurse dismissed for gross misconduct. A nurse working in a nursing home was dismissed for gross misconduct. He had been in charge of a particular shift. The allegations were that he failed to (a) do a risk assessment in relation to a resident operating the controls of an electric bed, (b) monitor his blood sugar levels for diabetes, (c) review his nutrition care plan having identified potential malnutrition associated with weight loss and reduced appetite, (d) implement appropriate monitoring in relation to turning the resident and to fluid intake, (e) update the tissue viability care plan, given identified bruising or wound on return from hospital, and take photographs and keep wound charts.

The Tribunal did not find misconduct. Failing to risk-assess the bed was an oversight but not misconduct (there was in reality no risk). Second, in an ideal world, blood sugar levels would be taken twice a day, but the system was once a week in the absence of specific concerns – and the patient often refused in any case. Third, the resident's weight had been 'all over the place' – he had just come back from hospital – and a record was kept of what he did and didn't eat. Fourth, there was a failure to keep fluid charts, but nobody else did, and this collective failure should not be visited on one person. As to turning, there was no need or point in trying to keep a turning chart if the person could turn himself. Fifth, there

---

116 *TM v Secretary of State for Health* [2007] 1118 (PVA).
117 *TM v Secretary of State for Health* [2007] 1118 (PVA).
118 *JF v Secretary of State* [2005] 591 (PVA)/592 (PC).

was no tissue viability care plan, but this, too, was a collective responsibility, and the nurse did not have sole responsibility for this. Even the hospital staff had made no record of the pressure sore.

Overall, there were clearly failures in the system of work in the care home, but it was not fair to blame one individual worker. His appeal was allowed.[119]

MEDICATION, NURSING CARE AND GENERAL CARE CASES

An easy and thoughtful manner might be insufficient to remedy serious lapses in the giving of medication.

Not giving residents their medication. A senior care assistant in a care home had a thoughtful, easy manner with service users, a caring concern for them and a practical interest in their well-being. His demeanour and attitude were those of somebody who could easily get on with people of different backgrounds – an important quality. However, none of this saved him from a finding by the Tribunal of unsuitability to work with vulnerable adults, after he failed to check on the medication required for a new resident and overlooked one area of the care home on his rounds and so had not given residents their medication.[120]

Conversely, when a senior care worker failed to sign certain medication sheets immediately and to give medication to a resident who was drowsy, no misconduct was found. The prescribing doctor confirmed that the latter decision was not improper. On the former issue, it was not, in all the circumstances, misconduct; it had been a difficult and stressful day, with residents restless and difficult. No misconduct was established.[121]

Likewise, even when a nurse had been struck off the nursing register for a lapse in the care of a diabetic resident, she was not found to be unsuitable to work with vulnerable adults.

Failure to monitor diabetic resident; mitigating factors: isolated incident, updating of skills, remorse, undoubted skills. When a nurse failed to monitor a resident in a care home properly, he lapsed into a hypoglycaemic coma and had to be taken to hospital for treatment. This was clearly misconduct which placed a vulnerable adult at risk of harm. She had been struck off the nursing register by the Nursing and Midwifery Council but now wished to work as a carer.

Yet the Tribunal did not hold that she was unsuitable to work with vulnerable adults, finding mitigating factors. The incident had occurred four years previous to the hearing; the nurse was remorseful, had never denied her error and had made genuine attempts to update her knowledge; the misconduct was an isolated incident, a one-off event, in a nursing career spanning 14 years; she clearly had learnt from her mistake and wanted to use her undoubted skills in the caring profession.[122]

SLEEPING ON DUTY

Not every lapse resulted in a finding of unsuitability.

119 Gedara v Secretary of State [2009] UKFTT 20 (HESC).
120 *Rathbone v Secretary of State* [2007] 975 (PVA).
121 *PHH v Secretary of State for Education and Skills* [2006] 876 (PVA).
122 *LLM v Secretary of State* [2006] 832 (PVA).

Sleeping on the job. Sleeping on duty in a residential complex with 20 flats for elderly, vulnerable people amounted to misconduct but, in all the circumstances, did not mean that vulnerable adults would be at significant risk of harm. Furthermore, any such risk as did exist was as much the responsibility of the employer as the care assistant. The care assistant was therefore not unsuitable to work with vulnerable adults. Her appeal succeeded.[123]

In another case concerning sleeping on duty, the Tribunal likewise found that the two care workers concerned – in a care home of 42 residents, some requiring nursing and some with dementia – were not unsuitable to work with vulnerable adults. The Tribunal rejected allegations that the sleeping was deliberately planned on the night in question. Although it found that there was some falsification of records by the care workers, the evidence showed that it was routine practice in the home to complete fluid and turning charts in advance and to amend them later if necessary, and that the care workers had received little training or guidance.

Contrary to the evidence of the manager, who had maintained the training was of an extremely high standard, it turned out that, at the relevant time, all training had been suspended within the company's homes. The care workers also showed genuine remorse and realised the gravity of their misconduct; they would be unlikely ever to do it again.[124]

In yet another case, the evidence stacked up against the care worker accused of sleeping on duty. The allegations, and grounds for her inclusion on the POVA list, were formidable. It is a reminder of how apparently overwhelming accusations, sometimes thrown into a case to make it more convincing, may lack substance – and so it is worth setting out the accusations in detail:

(1) The Appellant took her shoes off, put her feet up, covered herself with her cardigan, put a blanket over her legs and went to sleep on two chairs, with her colleague, in the lounge of the Home, leaving the residents of the Home uncared for and neglected and rendering her unable to immediately respond to any of the residents' needs or any emergencies;

(2) The Appellant failed to untie and/or unblock the doors to the lounge from the main corridor, resulting in the barring of that exit route to the three residents inside the lounge and the barring of that entry route to the residents outside the lounge;

(3) The Appellant failed to unblock the alternative doors to the lounge from the back corridor, resulting in the barring of that exit route to the three residents inside the lounge and the barring of that entry route to the residents outside the lounge;

123 *Brown v Secretary of State for Health* [2005] 580 (PVA)/581 (PC).
124 *LU and DH v Secretary of State for Health* [2007] 1092 (PVA).

(4) The Appellant failed to secure medication (an Imodium tablet), leaving it on a shelf in the lounge of the Home where it was accessible to other residents and endangering those who could have taken the medication;

(5) The Appellant failed to secure the security door to the dementia unit, thereby endangering the lives of the residents who may have left the unit by this door; and

(6) The Appellant failed to ensure that the unit was maintained in a state complying with the requisite standards of health and hygiene, as demonstrated by the fact that:

(a) the lounge was in an untidy state;

(b) an incontinence pad was present on the dining room floor;

(c) the small tables in the lounge were not wiped down; and

(d) a chair had been left outside and was soaked with rain water.[125]

Yet, on examination, the other allegations melted away, and the serious ground left in play was sleeping on duty. However, the Tribunal found that this had been associated with the calming of a disturbed resident, and that, in calming her down, the care worker had in fact done the right thing. Furthermore, it accepted that she had not been told that it was BUPA policy that she could take a break during the night shift. The Tribunal found in her favour:

> It may indeed be the case that it is BUPA policy to allow breaks on a night shift as required by law, but the Tribunal accepted that the Appellant had not been made aware of that. In addition. Three residents were refusing to go to bed and GH was displaying particularly challenging behaviour. In an attempt to calm her down and encourage her to fall asleep, the Appellant dimmed the lights in the lounge and sat with GH, holding her hand. The Appellant accepts that she fell asleep. In the majority of cases, falling asleep on duty will amount to misconduct, but the Tribunal considers that, in the Appellant's case, it was concomitant with her attempts to calm and soothe GH rather than a deliberate intention on her part to sleep. In the light of what had gone on before, the behaviour of GH and the lack of a break to take a drink and some food to revive herself, the Tribunal does not find, on balance, that this amounted to misconduct.[126]

In another sleeping case, the Tribunal upheld the barring of the care worker who was found sleeping, and photographed doing so, by a manager who visited the home in the middle of the night. The care worker was of Vietnamese origin, and the Tribunal made some observations about the market for care workers. It noted

---

125 Quoted from: *Joyce v Secretary of State for Health* [2006] 813 (PVA).
126 *Joyce v Secretary of State for Health* [2006] 813 (PVA).

the linguistic limitations of the worker, and the fact that this would have been a hindrance, as well as low pay and low skills. It noted:

> ...the over-riding need for providers to pay particular attention and rigour in terms of suitability in recruitment, to avoid setting up individuals for failure at worst or, compromising aspects of care at best...

> The Tribunal is mindful that within the caring services, both in public, private and voluntary sectors, it is still the case that the overwhelming majority of workers are women, of non-white racial and ethnic group, relatively unqualified in health and social care and comparatively low paid and to a visible extent, candidates fitting the general profile of the Appellant fit the specification recruited within the sectors.

> At its worst case, poor practice and quality of care can result if providers do not urgently invest in the necessary skills uplift made more difficult by the continuing depleted state of the care staff resources market.[127]

BARRING AND LINK WITH OTHER REMEDIES

Barring might go hand in hand with other civil sanctions – for example, with deregistration by a professional body – or with criminal sanctions – for example, the offence of wilful neglect.

Referral of care home staff to the ISA and the Nursing and Midwifery Council. For instance, at a care home where five elderly people had suffered severe neglect and died, staff were referred to the Independent Safeguarding Authority and some also to the Nursing and Midwifery Council.[128]

In such types of case, staff might find themselves also facing prosecution under s.44 of the Mental Capacity Act 2005 for the offences of ill-treatment or wilful neglect.

If, for whatever reason, a person is struck off a professional register but not barred by the ISA, that person can still work with vulnerable adults, in a non-professional capacity.

Nurse struck off but working in non-nursing capacity. When a nurse was struck off the nursing register by the Nursing and Midwifery Council, she was not barred from working in a care home in a non-nursing capacity. She had lost her registered status for various failings, including not informing authorities about the deaths of six elderly residents, not keeping proper drugs records and failing to ensure a resident received the drugs he needed (he was subsequently rushed to hospital). She later worked at another care home working as a care manager, but not involving medication or nursing tasks.[129]

So, sanctions might not be applied uniformly.

---

127 *Phan v Secretary of State for Health* [2008] UKFTT 1 (HESC).

128 Ellicott, C. and Fernandez, C. '"Severe neglect" of staff blamed for appalling deaths of five elderly care home residents in just two weeks.' *Daily Mail*, 6 October 2010.

129 'Struck-off nurse is working as manager in Bristol nursing home.' *Bristol Evening Post*, 29 February 2012.

Convicted for wilful neglect, but neither struck off by professional body nor barred from working with vulnerable adults. In a case heard by a Tribunal, a nurse had been convicted of the criminal offence of wilful neglect of a resident who had died, unsupervised and untended, during the night (although the lack of continual attention was not the cause of death). The fault of the senior nurse had been to fail to ensure that other staff kept to the agreed rota that night. Yet the Nursing and Midwifery Council subsequently found that he had no case to answer. However, he had been barred, under the (now superseded) Protection of Vulnerable Adults List by the Secretary of State for Health. He appealed against his inclusion and the Tribunal upheld his appeal. It also noted that even the trial judge had noted the qualities of the nurse and imposed a conditional discharge.[130]

But if one route fails, another might succeed.

Worker barred despite no criminal conviction. When a domiciliary care worker had used the bank card of a woman with physical and mental health problems to steal over £4000, the criminal case could not proceed. This was because, despite arranging for special measures – a video link to the court – the woman's health was too poor even for this. Her doctors said she would be unable to give evidence. However, the care worker was placed on the POVA list and barred from working with vulnerable adults. On appeal, the Care Standards Tribunal dismissed her argument that she had not been convicted and therefore done nothing wrong.[131]

130 *Salisu v Secretary of State for Health* [2011] UKFTT 1 (HESC).
131 *Burman v Secretary of State for Health* [2007] 1182 (PVA).

11

Regulating workers: criminal record certificates

KEY POINTS

A fourth form of regulation comes in the form of criminal record certificates.

Regulations made under the Health and Social Care Act 2008 stipulate that providers must obtain criminal record certificates from the Disclosure and Barring Service for certain types of worker – including those working with vulnerable adults.

Under the Protection of Freedoms Act 2012, the Criminal Records Bureau (CRB) was dissolved and subsumed under a new body, the Disclosure and Barring Service (DBS), at the end of 2012. References below to the CRB should therefore be read with this in mind.

The certificates themselves are provided under the Police Act 1997.

The overall purpose of the criminal record certificate scheme is to put the potential employer in possession of both conviction and sometimes non-conviction information about the potential employee, to assist the former in deciding whether to employ the latter to work with vulnerable adults.

Ongoing legal cases highlight the difficulty of striking the right balance in deciding what information should appear in a criminal record certificate and in what circumstances. The Human Rights Act 1998 lies at the heart of the legal imperative that disclosure of information on a criminal record certificate be proportionate in relation to aim and purpose.

APPLICATION FOR CERTIFICATES

In the past, an application for a standard or enhanced disclosure had to be countersigned by a person registered with the CRB.[1]

Changes introduced by the Protection of Freedoms Act 2012, expected to come into force sometime in 2013, will mean that it is the worker who receives the certificate for passing on to the employer. This means that the worker will have the opportunity to make representations to, or challenge, the DBS about any content before the employer sees the certificate.[2]

LEVELS OF DISCLOSURE

The Police Act 1997 provides for three different levels of disclosure.

BASIC DISCLOSURE

The first is basic disclosure, which contains details of convictions held in central police records that are not 'spent' under the Rehabilitation of Offenders Act 1974. However, the DBS does not, at the time of writing, issue such disclosures.

STANDARD DISCLOSURE

The second is standard disclosure, containing details of spent and unspent convictions but also cautions, reprimands and warnings recorded centrally by the police. The disclosure will also indicate whether the person is on the barred list held by the Disclosure and Barring Service and thus unsuitable to work with vulnerable adults.[3]

Certain convictions do not become spent under the provisions of the 1974 Act – for example, in relation to the provision of care services to vulnerable adults, representation or advocacy services for vulnerable adults (approved by the Secretary of State or under statute) or health services.[4] Such convictions continue to be disclosed for the purpose of standard and enhanced certificates.

ENHANCED DISCLOSURE

The third level is enhanced disclosure, which contains the same information as a standard disclosure but can also contain additional 'soft', local non-conviction information held on the Police National Database, but not on the Police National Computer (PNC). In the past, the test of whether to include such information was

1   Police Act 1997, s.120. And: SI 2006/750. Police Act 1997 (Criminal Records) (Registration) Regulations.
2   Police Act 1997, s.113; and see Protection of Freedoms Act 2012, Explanatory Notes, section 79.
3   Police Act 1997, s.113A.
4   SI 1975/1023. Rehabilitation of Offenders Act 1974 (Exceptions) Order 1975, schedule 1, paras 12–13.

whether, in the opinion of the chief police officer, such information 'might be relevant' and ought to be included in the certificate.

In the light of various case law and concerns that the police were too readily disclosing information, the test has now changed. Introduced by the Protection of Freedoms Act 2012, the test is now about information the chief officer 'reasonably believes to be relevant' and which, in his or her opinion, ought to be included in the certificate.[5] This is explained further below.

In addition, the Police Act 1997 stated previously that the CRB (now the DBS) had to ask the chief police officer to provide any information relevant as to the person's suitability.[6] That is, information that the chief police officer thought ought to be provided, ought not to be included in the certificate in the interests of the prevention or detection of crime, but which could nevertheless still be disclosed to the registered body. This rule has now been removed; so-called 'brown envelope' information will no longer be provided.

Explanatory notes to the Protection of Freedoms Act 2012 explain that this means there is no longer:

> a statutory obligation to disclose the relevant information to the registered body in these circumstances. However, it would remain open to the police, using their common law powers to prevent crime and protect the public, to pass such information to a potential employer where they considered it justified and proportionate.[7]

DISPUTE PROCESS ABOUT INFORMATION INCLUDED IN ENHANCED CERTIFICATE

There is a dispute process, introduced by the Protection of Freedoms Act 2012, in relation to soft, non-conviction information supplied by the police.[8]

This allows the person to apply to an independent monitor (appointed under section 119B of the 1997 Act), for the latter to decide whether such information is relevant and should be included in the certificate. The independent monitor has then to ask the police to review whether the information concerned is relevant and ought to be included on the certificate.

If, following that review, the independent monitor decides that the information either is not relevant or should not be included in the certificate, the independent monitor must inform the DBS, who must issue a new certificate excluding that information.[9]

---

5   Police Act 1997, s.113B.
6   Police Act 1997, s.113B(4).
7   Protection of Freedoms Act 2012, Explanatory Notes, para 331.
8   Police Act 1997, s.117A.
9   Protection of Freedoms Act 2012, Explanatory Notes, para 341.

CASE LAW ABOUT REPRESENTATIONS BEFORE DISCLOSURE OF SOFT INFORMATION TO EMPLOYER

This introduction in law of a dispute process, brought about by the Protection of Freedoms Act 2012, has put on a statutory footing the principle that the courts had anyway begun to develop – about fairness demanding that a person be able to make representations before such information was disclosed:

> In cases of doubt, especially where it is unclear whether the position for which the applicant is applying really does require the disclosure of sensitive information, where there is room for doubt as to whether an allegation of a sensitive kind could be substantiated or where the information may indicate a state of affairs that is out of date or no longer true, chief constables should offer the applicant an opportunity of making representations before the information is released.[10]

Thus, in one case involving a man applying to be college lecturer in welding, the Manchester police supplied information about an allegation, never substantiated, about historic sex abuse dating back 15 years. The result of the disclosure was that he had found it impossible to get the job. The court was clear that fairness demanded that he should be able to make representations first. Not least because there 'did not appear to have been any detailed consideration of what the risk was that C, as a welding lecturer in a further education college, would come into contact with a child'. Disclosure had been a breach of his rights under article 8 of the European Convention; it had been disproportionate.[11]

VULNERABLE ADULTS

Enhanced disclosure applies to workers who are working with vulnerable adults. 'Vulnerable adult' is defined under the Safeguarding Vulnerable Groups Act 2006 (see Chapter 10).

When enhanced disclosure is made, 'suitability' information must be included. This is: (a) whether the applicant is barred from regulated activity; (b) if the applicant is barred, certain details about the circumstances; (c) whether the DBS is considering whether to include the applicant in the adults' barred list.[12]

PRESUMPTION OF DISCLOSURE OF 'SOFT' INFORMATION DISPLACED BY MORE BALANCED APPROACH TO DISCLOSURE

In the past few years, and notwithstanding this clear statutory authority for disclosure of information, the question has arisen in the courts as to what extent a presumption of disclosure now applies to the police when providing soft

---

10   *R(L) v Commissioner of Police for the Metropolis, Michaelmas Term* [2009] UKSC 3.

11   *R(C) v Secretary of State for the Home Department* [2011] EWCA Civ 175.

12   Police Act 1997, s.113BB.

information (non-conviction information, not centrally held) and how this relates to the common law of confidentiality and human rights.

OLDER CASES: PRESUMPTION OF DISCLOSURE

To begin with, some years ago, the courts, in effect, gave carte blanche to the police to disclose, if not anything and everything, then pretty much what they wanted. They held that the duty to disclose, under s.115 (as it was then) of the Police Act 1997, had effectively displaced the common law presumption of non-disclosure. These older cases are included in this book by way of examples of the sort of information that might come into question and in what circumstances.

Older case: enhanced criminal record certificate and soft information: presumption of disclosure. An enhanced criminal record certificate was issued under s.115 of the Police Act 1997 concerning an African-Caribbean social worker with no convictions. Certain 'soft' information was included, provided by the relevant local police force. This stated that it had been alleged that, in December 2001, the social worker indecently exposed himself to a female petrol station attendant. It was alleged that he repeated the offence in May 2002. He was arrested and interviewed; he stated that he did not think he had committed the offence but he was suffering from stress and anxiety at the time.

> **Charge of indecent exposure fails for want of identification of suspect.** At that time, he was employed by a child care company and was charged with two counts of indecent exposure. However, the alleged victim failed to identify the suspect during a covert identification parade. The case was subsequently discontinued.

In the High Court, the chief constable's decision to provide this information in the certificate was found to be unlawful, essentially on the grounds that the balance in favour of disclosure had been wrongly struck.

> **Presumption of disclosure and no right to make representations.** The High Court decision was subsequently overturned in the Court of Appeal. In particular, the latter found that the common law principle of confidentiality, though generally entailing a presumption of non-disclosure, did not apply to the present case. The statutory framework created by the Police Act 1997 meant that the position was more positively in favour of disclosure – which had to be made unless there was a good reason for not doing so. Furthermore, the judge had also been wrong in stating that the police should have informed the man before disclosure and given him an opportunity to make representations. This would place too heavy a burden on the police. As the information was being made available in accordance with the law, there was no breach of article 8 (right to respect for privacy) of the European Convention on Human Rights.[13]

Following this case, the courts adhered to a firm line.

Older case: inclusion in certificate of information not relating to a criminal offence: headmistress of special school. The headmistress of a special school for children with disabilities had been prosecuted for manslaughter. This was after a child wandered out and was killed by a passing lorry. He had got out through fire doors (which the Fire Service had said could not have locks on them) and then through the school gates

---

13   *R(X) v Chief Constable of West Midlands Police* [2004] EWHC 61 (Admin); [2004] EWCA Civ 1068 (Court of Appeal).

which had been left open by a contractor, contrary to a notice at the gates. It seemed also that the senior member of staff in charge of the child had left him for some minutes without informing any other member of staff.

No criminality but possible civil negligence. The judge had withdrawn the manslaughter case from the jury, stating that, on the evidence, there was no chance of a conviction that she had been grossly negligent (required for manslaughter). However, he had left open the possibility that she might have been ordinarily, rather than grossly, negligent in civil law.

Disclosure justifiable. Subsequently, information about the whole episode was included in an enhanced criminal record certificate. The woman now challenged this in a judicial review case, arguing that it should not have been included because, at most, it related to a possible civil wrong, not to a criminal offence. The judge in the present case stated that the question was whether this information 'might be relevant' to a prospective employer in considering her suitability for a position involving work with children. He concluded that there could only be one answer, and that the decision to disclose the information was not irrational.[14]

The Court of Appeal then confirmed in a further case that the 'common law presumption against disclosure of relevant information had been turned on its head'. In addition, it stated that relevant information in relation to an enhanced certificate can cover past conduct which, even if proved, would neither constitute a criminal offence nor even reveal a risk that a criminal offence would be committed in the future.[15]

The theme continued in more case law, despite the admitted weaknesses in the following case of the allegations of sexual abuse.

Older case: doubtful allegations of sexual abuse based on facilitated communication included in criminal record certificate. The case involved the deputy principal of a college for young autistic adults. Following reorganisation at work, his employment had been transferred to a national charity and he was required to obtain a criminal record certificate. It contained details, supplied on behalf of the assistant chief constable, of three allegations made against him of sexual abuse of three autistic young adults on a trip to Wales. No criminal charges were ever brought.

Evidence based on facilitated communication. On being threatened with a legal challenge against the certificate, the police had revised the information, still referring to the allegations but containing more detail and noting that they had all been made by 'facilitated communication'. This is a process by which the facilitator supports the hand or arm of somebody with impaired communication ability, while the person uses a keyboard or typing device. The courts have, in the past, referred to the dangers of relying on evidence obtained in this way in Re D.[16]

Weakness of allegations. The court noted various weaknesses in the allegations, including in one case the failure to confirm the allegations by using a second 'clean' facilitator, in another the withdrawal at one point of the allegations and failure to make an allegation when an independent facilitator was used, and the upholding, by the police and the Police Complaints Authority, of some of the complaints made by the person about the police

---

14   *R(G) v Chief Constable of Staffordshire* [2006] EWHC 482 (Admin).

15   *R(L) v Commissioner of Police for the Metropolis* [2007] EWCA Civ 168.

16   *Re D (Evidence: facilitated communication)* [2001] 1 FLR.

investigation. However, the court held that the question for the chief constable had been whether the information 'might be relevant', and whether the allegations might be true. Although strong doubt was cast on the allegations, they were not negated, and were not 'so devoid of substance so as to make it unreasonable to conclude that they might be true'. The court therefore found in favour of the chief constable, although it noted how damaging all this could be to the person.[17]

COURTS CHANGE APPROACH AND COME OUT AGAINST PRESUMPTION OF DISCLOSURE

The worm then finally turned. The Supreme Court was appealed to in the case of *R(L) v Commissioner of Police for the Metropolis*, already referred to immediately above at the Court of Appeal stage. The case concerned a woman who was working as a midday assistant at a secondary school.

It involved her supervising children in the lunchtime break, both in the canteen and in the playground. The enhanced criminal record certificate stated that there were no convictions or cautions. However, the additional, soft, information provided stated that her 13-year-old son had been placed on the child protection register for neglect. The woman lost her job. She also lost her appeal to the Supreme Court, which felt that the facts justified disclosure.

The court now adjusted the legal test for disclosure that should be applied under the Act. This was in the light of article 8 of the European Convention on Human Rights, which required a balance to be struck between protection of children and the right to respect for private life of the worker. This balance meant that a presumption of disclosure was not the correct legal position. Instead, there should be no precedence and no presumption either way.

> The correct approach, as in other cases where competing Convention rights are in issue, is that neither consideration has precedence over the other... The rating table in MP9 should be restructured so that the precedence that is given to the risk that failure to disclose would cause to the vulnerable group is removed. It should indicate that careful consideration is required in all cases where the disruption to the private life of anyone is judged to be as great, or more so, as the risk of non-disclosure to the vulnerable group. The advice that, where careful consideration is required, the rationale for disclosure should make it very clear why the human rights infringement outweighs the risk posed to the vulnerable group also needs to be reworded. It should no longer be assumed that the presumption is for disclosure unless there is a good reason for not doing so.[18]

So, in the following case, the court found that inclusion of allegations of ill-treatment of vulnerable adults, made against a registered nurse, was not justified. This was despite her previous caution for child cruelty, and four allegations against

---

17   *R(Pinnington) v Chief Constable of Thames Valley* [2008] EWHC 1870 (Admin).
18   *R(L) v Commissioner of Police for the Metropolis*, Michaelmas Term [2009] UKSC 3.

her by older people in care homes. The case shows, if nothing else, that assumptions should not be made simply on the basis of allegations – and that it is simply not about throwing everything into the criminal record certificate 'just in case'.

Allegations against nurse should not have been included in criminal record certificate. In 2005, a registered nurse had received a police caution for child cruelty against her own child – for leaving him on his own for longer than was acceptable. In 2011, she applied for two nursing positions. The criminal record certificate issued contained not just reference to this caution, but also to two separate allegations made against her – one in 2007, the other in 2011.

First allegation. The first related to a complaint made to the police that the resident of a care home had been assaulted by the nurse. In fact she claimed that the nurse had been too severe and heavy-handed – although the nurse had apologised to her at the time. She did not wish to make an official complaint; the police took no further action.

Second allegation. The second, in 2011, was an allegation that in another care home, for blind people, the nurse had grabbed a resident by the head and pulled her up. The police had wanted to interview the resident, but she was very ill and dying and could not be interviewed. (It turned out that two other residents at the home had also complained about mistreatment; however, the police regarded them as unreliable witnesses on account of their dementia.)

Denial of allegations by nurse. The nurse was not given a chance by the police to comment on the allegations before they were included in the criminal record certificate. The Royal College of Nursing argued that the first allegation involved an error and inadvertent hurting of the resident, and that the second appeared to have been fabricated by an unwell patient. It argued that inclusion of the information was disproportionate (and therefore a breach of article 8 of the European Convention). However, the police refused to amend the criminal record certificate.

Nurse should have been given opportunity to make representations. The case ended up in court. The judge held that the nurse should have been given the opportunity to make representations before the information was included.

Findings on allegations. The judge held that the 2007 incident was, at heart, about poor manual handling technique and did not warrant inclusion in the certificate. About the main complaint in 2011, the judge held that without substantial support from other sources no adverse conclusion could be formed – given the state of health and awareness of the resident concerned.

(As to the other two 2011 complaints, one was from a woman with dementia who was also significantly visually impaired, who claimed that the nurse had entered her room, without identifying herself, and had felt something hard and heavy on her chest. The second, a man, also suffering from dementia, alleged forcefulness by the nurse when she was giving him his medication for Parkinson's disease. The judge noted that the police found neither of these residents to be credible witnesses.)

Heavy-handedness by nurse did not justify inclusion of allegations in certificate. Overall the judge concluded that, even cumulatively, the allegations pointed at most to occasional heavy-handedness by the nurse. But that the risks posed by this did not outweigh the nurse's right to respect for private life under the Convention. As such, the inclusion of these allegations in the certificate, by the police, was not lawful.[19]

---

19   *R(J) v Chief Constable of Devon and Cornwall* [2012] EWHC 2996 (Admin).

This turnabout by the courts has now been subsequently strengthened by a change in the wording of legislation, already alluded to above. It is not now a question of whether the chief constable believes that soft information 'might be relevant', but whether he or she reasonably believes it to be relevant.[20]

INFORMATION HELD BY POLICE

Of course, a decision to disclose information, soft or otherwise, presupposes that the police have retained the relevant information and thus have it still to divulge.

In the Soham case, involving the murder of two schoolgirls by a school caretaker, it transpired that the police had failed to keep details of various complaints that had been made about him over the years in relation to alleged sexual offences. This was partly because of an incoherent policy on weeding, reviewing and deleting records and because of concerns about the Data Protection Act. As it turned out, the Bichard inquiry exonerated the Act itself; the loss of intelligence was due to failings in the record-keeping systems of the police.[21]

INFORMATION HELD ON THE POLICE NATIONAL COMPUTER

For enhanced criminal record certificates, as explained above, there is a discretion and judgement to be applied about 'soft information'. However, no such discretion or judgement exists in relation to information held centrally on the Police National Computer. Such information must be disclosed for both standard and enhanced criminal record certificates.

The Police and Criminal Evidence Act 1984 now states that not just convictions but also cautions, reprimands and warnings should be held on the Police National Computer.[22] Additional, soft, information is not.

The police operate to guidelines published by the Association of Chief Police Officers. The guidelines state that records on the Police National Computer will be deleted only when a person reaches 100 years of age. Some offences will be 'stepped down' after shorter periods and then become 'for police eyes only'.[23] However, even stepped-down information has to be provided for the purposes of a criminal record certificate (standard or enhanced).

RETENTION OF RECORDS OF MINOR MISDEMEANOURS

The police were reported in 2007 as still holding information relating to the theft of a packet of meat worth 99 pence in 1984 by a 16-year-old. Likewise, a 19-year-old woman in Stafford had wanted to become a carer. However, a reprimand she

20   Police Act 1997, s.113B.
21   Bichard, M. *The Bichard inquiry report*. London: TSO, 2004, pp.86, 127.
22   Police and Criminal Evidence Act 1984, s.27.
23   Association of Chief Police Officers. *Retention guidelines: incorporating the step down model*. London: ACPO, 2006, para 3 and Appendix 1.

had received as a 12-year-old for minor assault was still coming up on criminal record checks.

The Information Commissioner's Office commented on such cases that some of the incidents dating back 30 years were non-custodial offences (some had not even led to convictions) and that there was no justification for such blanket retention. It ordered that the information be destroyed.[24] The police appealed the case to the Information Tribunal which upheld the Information Commissioner's decision. However, a further appeal to the Court of Appeal brought success for the police in the *Humberside* case.

Justifiable purpose of the police keeping old information about even minor convictions. Details of old, minor criminal convictions were stored on the Police National Database. Five individuals had complained about this:

1. A 40-year-old man had received a £15 fine for theft from Marks and Spencer when he was 15.

2. A woman, now aged 20, wanted to train as a carer, but at the age of 13 had been reprimanded for common assault against a 15-year-old girl – and had now been told by the police that her reprimand had not been deleted from the records, as originally promised.

3. A 48-year-old man had, aged 21, been convicted of deception in obtaining electrical goods and was fined £250.

4. A 46-year-old man had, aged 15, been convicted of two offences of attempted theft and been fined £25. He had inserted metal blanks into a roulette machine in an amusement arcade.

5. A 44-year-old woman had, aged 18, been convicted of theft using a cashpoint card belonging to somebody else; she was given a suspended prison sentence and fined £185.

This meant that when these individuals required a criminal record certificate (standard or enhanced), these details emerged. The Information Commissioner and then the Information Tribunal held that such retention could not be justified under the Data Protection Act in relation to a legitimate purpose.

The Court of Appeal disagreed, stating that if the police stated rationally and reasonably that convictions, however old or minor, had a value in the work they do, then that should be end of the matter.[25]

ARGUMENT ABOUT UNSATISFACTORY RETENTION BY POLICE OF RECORDS OF MINOR OFFENCES FOR A PERSON'S LIFETIME

A review carried out by the government in 2011 recommended that retention and use of information needs to be balanced and proportionate to the seriousness and risks involved. It recommended that a filter should be introduced to remove, where appropriate, old and minor conviction information from criminal record checks (if

24 Ford, R. 'Police told to erase irrelevant crime records.' *The Times*, 1 November 2007, p.14. And: Information Commissioner's Office. *Police told to delete old criminal conviction records.* Press release, 1 November 2007. Wilmslow: ICO.

25 *Chief Constable of Humberside Police v Information Commissioner* [2009] EWCA Civ 1079.

not from the PNC itself). The government has said it will look into this but so far has done nothing:

> The Government will continue to consider this proposal, part of which means trying to identify an appropriate and workable filtering mechanism. It is important that old and minor disposals should not unreasonably compromise employment prospects, but equally important that potentially relevant information should be available to those employing people in sensitive positions.[26]

The consequence of government inaction and the Court of Appeal decision in the *Humberside* case is continuing disquiet, and not just on the part of Sunita Mason, who carried out the review for the government, but also the judiciary, as in the following case.

The claimant was a 20-year-old student. He was applying for admission to a sports studies degree course and had applied for an enhanced criminal record certificate to facilitate his entry. The certificate was duly issued but contained details of a warning for theft of two bicycles issued to him in 2002, when he was 11 years old, by the Greater Manchester Police.

The judge felt constrained by the Court of Appeal decision in the *Humberside* case to say that the inclusion of such information, as demanded by the Police Act 1997 (convictions, cautions, warnings – as opposed to soft information, about which there is some discretion), was indeed consistent with human rights, in particular article 8 of the European Convention. But it was clear that the judge did not consider justice had been served by the decision he had felt bound to come to:

> The issue is one of general importance that fully deserves to be considered by a higher court, and I had already indicated that I would give permission to the unsuccessful party to appeal to the Court of Appeal.[27]

The case was subsequently appealed. There were three appellants. First was the man who had stolen the two bicycles as a child. The second was a woman who had as an adult received a caution when she paid for moisturiser in a shop, but walked out without paying for a packet of false nails under her arm (which action she claimed had been inadvertent). The third, also a woman, had as a 16-year-old been involved in perpetrating a violent car-jacking and been sentenced to a five-year period of detention.

Rehabilitation of Offenders Act and Order: incompatibility with human rights. The Court of Appeal held that the Rehabilitation of Offenders Act 1974 and, more specifically, the Rehabilitation of Offenders Act 1974 (Exceptions) Order 1975 were not compatible with article 8 of the European Convention on Human Rights. This was because, without exception, they provided for convictions and cautions – as well as reprimands and warnings (which for those under 18 years old replace cautions) – to be excepted from the

---

26   Home Office. *Independent review of the criminal records regime – Government response.* London: HO, 2011, p.3.
27   *R(T) v Chief Constable of Greater Manchester Police* [2012] EWHC 147 (Admin).

'spent conviction' rule if the job being applied for involved children or vulnerable adults. Hence the appearance on criminal record certificates of convictions, cautions, reprimands or warnings, which would otherwise be spent.

Disproportionality. The reason for the incompatibility was that the blanket rule about disclosure on a criminal record certificate could result in disproportionate interference by the State even when the matter was minor. Thus, the first two appellants succeeded in their case; the third did not because of the seriousness of her offence.

Police Act 1997. The link between the Police Act 1997 and the Rehabilitation of Offenders Act 1974 was close; it was the asking of otherwise 'exempt questions' under the 1997 Act with reference to the exceptions contained in the 1974 Act, which had led to the incompatibility. If the 1974 Act was undermined in this respect, so too would the criminal record certificate system be under the 1997 Act. This being so, the Court of Appeal ruled that its judgment should not come into force, pending an appeal by the Home Office to the Supreme Court.[28]

EFFECT OF ADVERSE INFORMATION COMING TO LIGHT IN CRIMINAL RECORD CERTIFICATE

Inclusion on the barred list held by the Disclosure and Barring Service (see Chapter 10) legally precludes a person working with vulnerable adults, but this is not the legal effect of information disclosed in connection with a criminal record certificate. It is simply for the prospective employer to judge whether any adverse information is relevant to the prospective employee's being taken on.

For instance, in the following case, the registered nurse would have a 'formidable hurdle' to overcome, given the content of the criminal record certificate, but this did not mean she should not be given the chance to do so.

Enhanced criminal record certificate detailing criminal charges being brought against a nurse. A registered nurse wanted to appeal to the Care Standards Tribunal against a decision by Welsh Ministers not to register her as a manager of a care home. She was on police bail at the time, having been charged with wilful neglect. This was for allegedly failing to ensure that junior staff knew what was required of them, following the death of a resident with senile dementia. A decision had been made not to register her, partly (there were other reasons) with reference to the contents of an enhanced criminal record certificate, which outlined a police investigation into a number of deaths.

By the time the court considered the issue, the position had moved from a police investigation to actual criminal charges. However, the court stated that she was still entitled to have her case considered by the tribunal, even though she would have a formidable hurdle to overcome.[29]

Although employers should have a balanced and fair policy about employing ex-offenders,[30] and some will have this, others may, in practice, simply rule people out, without fair consideration.

---

28   *R(T) v Chief Constable of Greater Manchester* [2013] EWCA Civ 25.

29   *Welsh Ministers v Care Standards Tribunal* [2008] EWHC 49 (Admin).

30   Chartered Institute of Personnel and Development (CIPD). *Employing ex-offenders: a practical guide.* London: Criminal Records Bureau (undated).

Thus, in one case, three weeks after having received a police caution for assaulting a vulnerable 69-year-old patient with dementia, a care worker was employed in another nursing home. His new employer explained that it was fully aware of his history and had carried out the necessary criminal record and POVA checks. It regarded him as a hard-working and respected employee.[31]

That said, it can all turn out badly. In one case, a carer with a drugs problem had been convicted previously of stealing his father's cheque book. The care agency with which he had now started work carried out a criminal record check but decided to employ him even so. Within six weeks of starting his new job as a home carer, he had stolen money from clients in their own homes, was prosecuted and admitted four charges of burglary. The employer said after the case that it would in future 'blacklist' carers known to have a criminal record.[32]

In the legal case, already outlined above in this chapter, about disclosure of the allegations of sexual abuse made against a deputy principal of a college for young autistic adults, the court upheld the decision of the police to supply details of the allegations in a criminal record certificate. As a consequence of disclosure, the man had been instantly dismissed because his employer had a blanket policy of insisting on a 'clean certificate'.

The court was troubled by this because the law imposed a relatively low threshold for disclosure (the case was before the courts changed tack and the government changed the wording in the legislation) and employers needed to understand this; a properly formed decision by the employer would take account of other information or explanation provided by the employee, additional to what appeared in the certificate. But a blanket policy did not allow for this to happen. The court suggested that the person might therefore have a reasonable prospect of contesting his dismissal before an employment tribunal.[33]

31   'Care home employs nurse cautioned for patient attack.' *This is Cornwall,* 23 October, Accessed on 23 October 2008 at: www.thisiscornwall.co.uk.

32   Hudson, C. 'Carer stole from patients.' *Macclesfield Express,* 22 November 2006.

33   *R(Pinnington) v Chief Constable of Thames Valley* [2008] EWHC 1870 (Admin).

12

Irregular regulation: whistleblowing

Key points
Protected and qualifying disclosures
    Disclosure to the employer
    Disclosure to regulatory body
    Wider disclosure
Examples of whistleblowing and the legal consequences
Whistleblowing in the National Health Service
    Range of typical reactions of the NHS to whistleblowing staff
    Examples of whistleblowing in the NHS
    Gagging clauses
    NHS whistleblowing: continuing lack of political will to resolve
        the problems

KEY POINTS

The fifth and final – albeit informal, irregular and unreliable – form of regulation, often not welcomed by employers, comes in the form of whistleblowing.

The legal rule is meant to be that if employees have serious concerns about matters at work, they are protected if, in certain circumstances, they 'whistleblow'. This comes under the Employment Rights Act 1996, as amended by the Public Interest Disclosure Act 1998. In summary, the Act provides for a hierarchy of reasonable actions for the concerned employee to take. These are summarised below.

Whistleblowing might, of course, be crucial to adult protection and the safeguarding of adults – when it works. For instance, the mistreatment and abuse of patients at the North Lakeland NHS Trust was identified only after two student nurses, bravely, had raised their concerns.[1]

In principle, whistleblowing is all-important and many organisations pay considerable lip service to it. It is the politically correct thing to encourage.

However, in practice, it is fraught with complication, and many organisations in reality not only do not welcome it but also proceed to victimise the whistleblower. This is especially so if the whistleblower is raising organisational issues. This makes it particularly difficult to tackle systemic neglect accorded to older people within health and social care.

---

1   Commission for Health Improvement. *Investigation into the North Lakeland* NHS *Trust*. London: CHI, 2000.

For professionals, a dilemma is created. Their codes of practice state that they should raise concerns if patients or clients are suffering harm and that they should persist in raising them if nothing is done. However, if they have a mortgage, family and career hopes, they would be better advised to keep quiet.

PROTECTED AND QUALIFYING DISCLOSURES

For an employee to be protected from detriment, at the hands of an employer retaliating to the disclosure, there needs to be a 'protected disclosure'. A protected disclosure has to (a) be a 'qualifying' disclosure, and (b) comply with various requirements relating to whom the disclosure was made.

A qualifying disclosure means the 'disclosure of information which, in the reasonable belief of the worker making the disclosure' is about a criminal offence, breach of a legal obligation, miscarriage of justice, health and safety, damage to the environment, or is about any of these matters being deliberately concealed.[2]

The protection afforded the person who is making the qualifying disclosure is on a sliding scale, depending on the identity of the person to whom the disclosure is made.

DISCLOSURE TO THE EMPLOYER

First, protection arises if the disclosure is made to the employer, or to somebody else, when the failure relates to the conduct of that other person or where legal responsibility is held by that other person rather than the employer. Likewise, if the disclosure is made to somebody else in accordance with the employer's own procedure.[3]

DISCLOSURE TO REGULATORY BODY

Second, protection is given to a person who makes a qualifying disclosure (a) in good faith, (b) to a person 'prescribed by the Secretary of State', and (c) where she or he reasonably believes that the failure is relevant to the prescribed functions of that person – and that the information and allegation are substantially true.[4]

The persons in this category, to whom disclosure might be made, include regulatory bodies such as the Healthcare Commission, Care Quality Commission, Health and Safety Executive, local authorities with health and safety enforcement functions, the Information Commissioner.[5]

WIDER DISCLOSURE

Third, there comes wider disclosure beyond the employer or relevant regulatory body – for instance, to the press. Protection arises if a qualifying disclosure is made

---

2   Employment Rights Act 1998, s.43B.
3   Employment Rights Act 1998, s.43C.
4   Employment Rights Act 1998, s.43F.
5   SI 1999/1549. Public Interest Disclosure (Prescribed Persons) Order 1999.

(a) in good faith or (b) in the reasonable belief that the information disclosed, and any allegation made, are substantially true; (c) if the disclosure is not made for personal gain, and (d) in all the circumstances of the case, it is reasonable to make the disclosure.

In addition, the worker must reasonably believe (a) that he or she would be subjected to detriment if the disclosure were made instead either to the employer or to the relevant regulatory body, or (b) that, if there is no relevant (regulatory) body, evidence about the failure will be concealed if disclosure is made to the employer, or (c) the worker had previously made a disclosure of substantially the same information to the employer or to a regulatory body.[6]

EXAMPLES OF WHISTLEBLOWING AND THE LEGAL CONSEQUENCES

Theoretical protection does not stop employers victimising whistleblowers in the real world. And workers who raise their concerns may have to resort to an employment tribunal in order to gain compensation for being sacked. Which is all too late.

In the following employment tribunal case, wider disclosure in the form of a satirical letter was protected. It was about the atrocious standards of care suffered by elderly hospital patients at Christmas time:

> So Prime Minister, Mr Health Secretary and NHS Management Executive, as you return bleary-eyed from your Christmas break (no doubt well rested and well fed) spare a thought for the poor, sickly old patient lying hurting and exhausted on an NHS trolley…hang on a minute, we can't let patients lie around on trolleys, that would muck up the waiting time statistics. Quick, shove her into any bed you can find. What? We haven't got any beds. Well MAKE SOME. How about shoving those patients from the Elderly Ward into that old shed at the back – the one with the crib and baby in it? Yes I know it's the Obs and Gynae Ward. They'll be fine there, even if they don't get any physiotherapy and the staff there haven't a clue about caring for elderly people. The old gerries won't complain; half of them are deaf and demented anyway. Tomorrow we can move them somewhere else – the laundry perhaps – with a bit of luck some of them might catch pneumonia there and create a few more beds. Happy New Year by the way. That new patient doesn't look too well, does she? No, poor old sod. Good job she's got the NHS to fall back on.[7]

It was published by *The Journal* newspaper in 2000, having been submitted by Mr Kay, a highly qualified ward manager at Wansbeck Hospital. His employer,

---

6   Employment Rights Act 1998, s.43G.

7   *Kay v Northumbria Healthcare NHS Trust.* Employment Tribunal case no. 6405617/00, 29 November 2001 (Newcastle upon Tyne). From: Bowers, J., Fodder, M., Lewis, J. and Mitchell, J. *Whistleblowing: law and practice.* Oxford: Oxford University Press, 2007, pp.575–577.

Northumbria Healthcare NHS Trust, took both a dim view and disciplinary action against him; consequently, he went to an employment tribunal in 2001 and won his case.

It came within the third category of wider disclosure. The manager had been disciplined and issued with a final written warning that he had acted in an unprofessional and totally unacceptable manner. The employment tribunal reached the conclusion that it was a protected disclosure: he had a reasonable belief that it was substantially true, it was not made for personal gain, and he had previously made a disclosure of substantially the same information to his employer. He was not aware of any other route by which he could raise the matter. The tribunal found in the ward manager's favour.[8]

The Trust commented that 'at all times, [it] had acted in the best interests of patients'. The Royal College of Nursing's regional officer's understanding was a little different, noting that staff were frightened to say anything, knowing that failure to toe the party line meant that they were finished.[9]

Other examples include the following, just to give a flavour.

Failures at children's home. When six employees spoke to the press about failures in a children's home, they were sacked, but subsequently were compensated by the council in advance of an employment tribunal. The settlement was reportedly in the region of £1 million.[10]

Employer victimising whistleblowing nurse with referral to Nursing and Midwifery Council. When a nurse alerted the police to the standard of care in a care home, an adult protection investigation was launched. The Commission for Social Care Inspection visited the home and produced a confidential report. The nurse used the Freedom of Information Act 2000 to bring about its publication. It noted, amongst other things, faeces on beds in empty rooms, unkempt residents, broken showers and toilets, pressure sores covered in faeces, emaciation – and the fact that the inspectors were shocked. The nurse was reported by the home to the Nursing and Midwifery Council for aggression toward a resident, but the hearing went in his favour.[11]

President of the Nepalese Nurses Association UK: sacked for whistleblowing. A nurse, president of this association, was sacked by the owners of a care home. She had raised concerns about abuse of elderly residents by colleagues and poor administration of medicines. For example, one care home resident was allegedly left outside in hot sunshine as a punishment and threatened with having water poured over his head when he refused medication. The nurse subsequently won an employment tribunal case, winning £15,000.

The tribunal noted:

> The respondent company had created an environment where there was an atmosphere that was not conducive to complaints being made by staff to the management about the care of residents. On the contrary…there was an atmosphere where it was

8   *Kay v Northumbria Healthcare NHS Trust.* Employment Tribunal case no. 6405617/00, 29 November 2001 (Newcastle upon Tyne).

9   'Trust action to silence whistleblower nurse seen as sign of culture "uncomfortable with debate".' *Health Service Journal,* 6 December 2001.

10   'Whistleblowers win payout.' *Community Care,* 23 August 2007, p.7.

11   'Act used to show "shocking" care.' *Nursing Standard,* 13 April 2005.

difficult, if not impossible, for such allegations to be made without the complainant running some risk of their employment being jeopardised.[12]

Carer forced out of her job by domiciliary care agency. A carer contacted the Care Quality Commission, concerned about practices by a domiciliary care agency for which she worked. She reported medication running out for a stroke victim, bed sheets unchanged for six weeks (including for an incontinent resident), inadequate diet for a diabetic patient, charges of £10 an hour being levied on patients for a free medication collection service, out-of-date care plans and risk assessments. She claimed she was forced out of her job, through constructive dismissal, went to an employment tribunal and won her case. She accused senior staff of lying when they denied that she had reported concerns to them. The Care Quality Commission had subsequently investigated and confirmed her concerns, producing a critical report.[13]

WHISTLEBLOWING IN THE NATIONAL HEALTH SERVICE

A climate of fear and bullying is prevalent in the NHS, is a cultural phenomenon and is driven from the top. The examples below, a tip of an iceberg, leave little room for doubt.

It runs from Ministers, through the chief executive of the NHS, right down to chief executives of NHS trusts and layers of local senior management. And the way it works is extremely simple. Each layer of management is fearful of admitting problems to the next layer up. So fearful are they that the only solution to frontline staff who are raising serious issues is to persecute those staff to shut them up.

That this pervasive and corrosive culture does come from the top can be seen in the example of the chairman and chief executive of the United Lincolnshire NHS Trust. Having turned the Trust's finances and performance around in the past couple of years, they explained one particular winter to the strategic health authority (under the control of the Department of Health) that they could not both hit targets and maintain patient safety. They were told to worry about the targets but not patient safety. They both protested and ultimately lost their jobs (see below).

This is not only a question of non-clinicians bullying and silencing clinicians. It was a former general practitioner, who had become chief executive of the strategic health authority, who demanded targets ahead of patient safety in Lincolnshire. And who, in 2012, was referred for investigation to the General Medical Council as a result of her actions.[14] But it is not just clinicians at the top; any clinicians in a management position are prey to the fear and anxiety that lead to the suppression of concerns about patient care.

Of course, whistleblowing does work sometimes, without reported victimisation of the staff, but the examples of victimisation are significant and numerous enough to suggest there is a serious problem. And not just in relation to what happens to

---

12 'Whistleblowing nurse wins £15,000 payout after unfair dismissal.' *Nursing Times*, 6 October 2011.

13 'Justice for Birmingham carer sacked by Care4U for reporting neglect.' *The Midlands Times*, 3 April 2012.

14 Lintern, S. 'GMC investigates complaint against Dame Barbara Hakin.' *Health Service Journal*, 25 September 2012.

those who do whistleblow, but also to the fact that many stay silent because of the climate of fear prevailing in too many NHS bodies.

RANGE OF TYPICAL REACTIONS OF THE NHS TO WHISTLEBLOWING STAFF

In summary, typical reactions within the NHS to staff who raise concerns about care include the following. They are drawn from an article in *Private Eye*, which was shortlisted in 2011 for the Martha Gellhorn Prize for Journalism. The article cited Dr Peter Gooderham who had put his finger on the following:

(a) Subtle sanctions, such as reducing secretarial help, cutting teaching budgets, blocking appointments and merit awards, adverse but informal briefing against the whistleblower

(b) Inflict reprisals by searching out misdemeanours, real or imagined

(c) Allege that the whistleblower is mentally ill

(d) Refuse to disclose incriminating documents, making use of the Data Protection and Freedom of Information Acts

(e) Threaten colleagues who support the whistleblower

(f) Threaten the whistleblower (Dr Peter Brambleby, formerly of Norwich Primary Care Trust, was warned he might end up in the woods like David Kelly)

(g) Accuse the whistleblower of raising concerns belatedly

(h) Claim the matter is an employment one and that public interest disclosure protection does not apply

(i) Pay off and gag the whistleblower

(j) Concoct complaints about the whistleblower to his or her professional, regulatory body

(k) Saddle the whistleblower with crippling employment tribunal costs, even if the whistleblower wins

(l) Arrange sham, internal investigations

(m) Hold an external investigation, but recruit the panel, control the terms of reference, hold it in secret, and keep much of the final report back from the public

(n) Gain succour from public inquiries which come too late, and are typically dismissed as dealing only with historical matters.[15]

---

15   Quoted from: Hammond, P. and Bousfield, A. 'Shoot the messenger: how NHS whistleblowers are silenced and sacked.' *Private Eye*, 22 July 2011.

EXAMPLES OF WHISTLEBLOWING IN THE NHS

The following are summaries of a number of cases, illustrating the response of the NHS to staff raising concerns in good faith.

Student nurses whistleblowing: North Lakelands. In the late 1990s, at North Lakeland NHS Trust, it took two sets of student whistleblowers – subsequently praised for their bravery – to raise the alarm about the shocking treatment of elderly patients. However, in contrast, the hospital consultant in charge of the patients who had been abused denied all knowledge, saying that he had felt he was a stranger on the ward. The Commission for Healthcare Improvement (CHI) expressed itself greatly disturbed at his passive role, compounded by the fact that he was associate medical director of the Trust with joint responsibility for clinical governance.

Whistleblowing nurses intimidated and pilloried. Nonetheless, the whistleblowers were subsequently intimidated and pilloried by other staff, and things had only got a little better when an external review was published. Even then, they still experienced hostility.

Regulator not confident that abuse would be reported, or acted on, in future. So, if other staff members do not recognise that something is awry, the whistleblower is not only up against it, but obstacles to change will be all the greater. The CHI had reported on 'unprofessional, counter therapeutic and degrading, even cruel, practices' relating to elderly patients. It noted, however, that even during its investigation, following the external review, some staff still failed to recognise that abuse had taken place and that it represented unacceptable practice. The Commission had no confidence that further abuse would be reported or that the Trust would respond to it.[16]

Rowan Ward, Manchester. On Rowan Ward in Manchester, the ball only got rolling, culminating in a CHI report, through whistleblowing. Concerns had grown about the care and abuse – including potential criminal offences – of elderly patients suffering from dementia. During a training event, staff had expressed their disquiet. One nurse agreed to use the whistleblowing procedure; other staff later supported the allegations the nurse had made.[17]

Stoke Mandeville: collective whistleblowing via the Royal College of Nursing unsuccessful, followed by effective, anonymous leak to the press. At Stoke Mandeville Hospital, nurses were extremely worried and reported their concerns about infection control and the deaths occurring from *Clostridium difficile*. These were not, however, acted on. The nurses then contacted (three times) the RCN, which took a grievance against the Trust, but even this led to no real or sustained improvement.

Likewise, clinical staff at the hospital, including doctors, were worried about patient movement between wards, failure to isolate patients, number of patients on inappropriate wards and the consequent degree of clinical risk. Many senior staff wrote to the executive team; the response was that nothing would change unless a disaster occurred. Which it subsequently did. The nurses felt professionally compromised and helpless. In the end, Buckinghamshire Hospitals NHS Trust only took action when details of the infection outbreak and deaths were leaked to the national press.[18]

---

16   Commission for Health Improvement. *Investigation into the North Lakeland NHS Trust, November*. London: CHI, 2000, p.1.

17   Commission for Health Improvement. *Investigation into matters arising from care on Rowan Ward, Manchester Mental Health and Social Care Trust, September 2003*. London: CHI, 2003, p.8.

18   Healthcare Commission. *Investigation into outbreaks of* Clostridium difficile *at Stoke Mandeville Hospital, Buckinghamshire Hospitals NHS Trust, July 2006*. London: Healthcare Commission, 2006, p.28.

Mid Staffordshire NHS Foundation Trust: dearth of whistleblowing. Leaking, anonymously or otherwise, is a big step to take, particularly if staff know that even ordinary reporting within the organisation – without the added embarrassment of publicity – is not welcome. For instance, the Mid Staffordshire independent inquiry recognised that, amidst the suffering and dying that took place in Stafford Hospital, the whistleblowing procedure was barely used: 'Many staff members did raise concerns, individually and collectively, but none experienced a satisfactory response. This discouraged persistent reporting of concerns. In the case of the medical staff, many appear to have been disengaged from the management process.'[19]

    Nurse ordered to lie. One nurse did raise concerns, to little effect, with senior managers in 2007. A woman with a bowel condition had been brought into accident and emergency (A&E) with acute abdominal pain. A junior doctor wished to examine her but was told to get on and discharge her. She waited seven hours for an ambulance to take her home; she died the next day of a perforated bowel. The nurse recounted also how she had been ordered to lie about how long people had waited in the A&E department and how:

> Patients were left for hours, unable to reach the buzzer, shouting for help, medication, soiling themselves because no one would assist them. It was completely horrific… I kept thinking what if that patient was my mother, or my grandmother? The way people were being treated was shocking.[20]

Dr Ramon Niekrash, Queen Elizabeth Hospital, Woolwich: bullying and harassment. In 2010, in what was regarded as a perhaps unusual and even landmark case, a hospital consultant, Dr Ramon Niekrash, won damages in an employment tribunal case for the bullying and harassment he suffered from his employer. He had criticised the Queen Elizabeth Hospital in Woolwich for reducing the number of specialist nurses and closing a specialist urology ward, both of which he argued were detrimental to patients. The hospital responded by excluding him from the hospital and suspending him.

    The judge noted that there was a clear nexus between the consultant's actions and political and financial stipulations made by the Department of Health:

> What is immediately apparent is that there has been a tension between the professional desire of the claimant and his consultant colleagues to provide a good quality urology service for the patients and the requirement of management to reduce or limit costs and also comply with varying targets laid down by the Department of Health from time to time.[21]

Ruinous cost to whistleblower even when successful in employment tribunal. However, though winning £17,500 in damages, he had to pay his own legal costs of £160,000.[22]

Dr Rita Pal, City General Hospital, Stoke-on-Trent: attacked by General Medical Council for speaking out. In 2000, a junior doctor, Dr Rita Pal, decided to raise issues with the GMC and the press about what she considered to be neglectful

19   Francis, R. (Chair). *Independent inquiry into care provided by Mid Staffordshire NHS Foundation Trust January 2005–March 2009.* London: TSO, pp.186, 281.

20   Donnelly, L. 'Nurse warned about Stafford scandal: a nurse warned managers about the abuse and neglect of patients at Stafford Hospital more than a year before one of the worst scandals in NHS history was publically exposed, it can be revealed.' *Daily Telegraph,* 16 May 2009.

21   Verkaik, R. 'Damages win for consultant who criticised cost-cutting.' *The Independent,* 3 February 2010.

22   'Woolwich march in support of whistleblower Ramon Niekrash.' *EDP 24,* 9 March 2011. Accessed on 5 January 2013 at: www.edp24.co.uk/news/health/woolwich_march_in_support_of_whistleblower_ramon_niekrash_1_824045.

treatment of elderly patients on Ward 87 at the City General Hospital in Stoke-on-Trent, North Staffordshire. She had originally raised these matters within the hospital in 1998. Her concerns included lack of basic equipment such as drip sets, lack of support for junior doctors, lack of basic care for patients, inappropriate use of 'do not resuscitate' instructions and gross staffing shortages.[23]

Internal report backs up whistleblower's concerns. An internal report produced in 2001 for the NHS Trust found a substantial core of Dr Pal's concerns justified. Failings within the hospital identified by this investigation related to, for example, patient care, nursing, monitoring, care plans, adequate equipment, induction, supervision, staffing levels and allocation of patients to appropriate wards. There was also an inappropriate response to Dr Pal's concerns; the report noted that, although other medical and nursing staff were worried, only Dr Pal spoke up. This seemed to be because either they had become accepting of what was happening or they felt unable to raise their concerns.[24]

Whistleblower's mental stability and fitness to practise questioned by General Medical Council. By 2003, she discovered that the GMC was investigating her, rather than her allegations, and was questioning her mental stability and fitness to practise. She eventually took it to court, alleging breaches of data protection law, human rights breaches and defamation. The GMC attempted to have the case dismissed early, by arguing that summary judgment should be given in its favour. The judge refused, holding that a defamation case could succeed. Before the case went to full hearing, the GMC settled out of court.[25]

Court refers to the General Medical Council's approach as symptomatic of a totalitarian regime such as Stalin's Russia. During the course of this hearing, the judge linked the GMC's reaction to that of a totalitarian state:

> For myself I don't really see why somebody complaining about the behaviour of doctors or the GMC, if that is what they are doing, why that should raise a question about their mental stability, unless anybody who wishes to criticise 'the party' is automatically showing themselves to be mentally unstable because they don't agree with the point of view put forward on behalf of the GMC or the party... It is like a totalitarian regime: anybody who criticises it is said to be prima facie mentally ill – what used to happen in Russia.[26]

Kay Sheldon, whistleblower and member of the Care Quality Commission's board; mental health questioned. After Kay Sheldon had spoken out at the Mid Staffordshire public inquiry about serious problems at the Commission relating to patient safety, the chairman of the Commission (Dame Jo Williams) resorted to a typical tactic within the NHS: she questioned the whistleblower's mental health. The chairman asked the Secretary of State to dismiss the whistleblower; the Secretary of State refused. The chairman subsequently apologised to the Health Select Committee and resigned from the Commission.[27]

23   See: Marsh, P. 'Doctor quit nightmare of the ward; people put their trust in hospitals and that trust is sometimes being abused.' *Birmingham Post*, 18 February 2000. Also: *North Staffordshire NHS Trust Ward 87: the evidence.* Accessed on 20 October 2010 at: http://sites.google.com/site/ward87whistleblower/home.

24   North Staffordshire Hospital NHS Trust. *Report of the extended investigation into the allegations made by Dr R. Pal in November 1998. June 2001, 4th Draft,* 2010. Accessed on 20 October 2010 at: http://sites.google.com/site/ward87whistleblower/home.

25   Wells, T. 'Pay-out victory for doc.' *Sunday Mercury,* 2 October 2005. See also: *Dr Rita Pal v General Medical Council* [2004] EWHC 1485 (QB).

26   Transcript, day 2: *Dr Rita Pal v General Medical Council* [2004] EWHC 1485 (QB).

27   Cassidy, S. 'Former chief "sorry" for attack on whistleblower: Dame Jo Williams tells MPs she was wrong to cast doubt on board member's mental health.' *The Independent,* 12 September 2012.

Margaret Haywood: attacked by the Nursing and Midwifery Council for speaking out against poor care. The Nursing and Midwifery Council, too, is just as inclined to attack whistleblowers, as the well-publicised case of a nurse, Margaret Haywood, illustrated.

BBC Panorama programme. In 2005, she participated in a BBC *Panorama* programme about care at the Royal Sussex Hospital. Undercover filming took place. It revealed dreadful care for which Sussex University Hospitals NHS Trust apologised, admitting to serious lapses in the quality of care.[28] Patients were not helped to the toilet and nurses were filmed eating patients' food.[29]

Suffering of patients. In particular, the programme showed a woman literally gasping with thirst, cancer patients not receiving their pain relief medication in time and crying out in pain, a patient waiting two hours to be helped to the toilet, a nurse speaking harshly to a patient who had called for help, people not getting help with food and drink (including a blind woman), staff eating food intended for patients, fluid and food and weight charts not being kept, missing care plans, medication not being given, a low-grade albeit experienced nurse being left in charge of a ward, and patients wearing split-back gowns for ease of nursing and so losing dignity.[30]

Nursing and Midwifery Council strikes whistleblower from register of nurses. Margaret Haywood received no thanks, from her employer or her regulatory body, for the public service she had performed. By 2009, she was working in a nursing home; then, in April of that year, the Nursing and Midwifery Council (NMC) struck her off the nursing register. This was for the breach of patient confidentiality that occurred in the filming of the programme, although no patients or relatives complained about *this*. In fact, they had been complaining, previously and without success, about something else: the poor care being provided.

The NMC stated that what she had done was fundamentally incompatible with being a nurse, as she had filmed elderly, vulnerable patients in the last stages of their lives who could not meaningfully give consent 'in circumstances where their dignity was most compromised'.[31] The NMC appeared unconcerned about all those nurses involved in depriving those patients of that dignity.

Legal challenge results in reinstatement of whistleblower. Within a month, a petition launched by the RCN attracted 40,000 signatures.[32] Later that year, she won the *Nursing Standard*'s nurse of the year award.[33] In October 2009, the High Court overturned her striking-off; she received a one-year caution instead.[34]

Disingenuousness of Department of Health. Lurking in the background, the Department of Health had responded in the most disingenuous and irresponsible fashion by effectively condoning her striking-off, implying she should simply have talked to her managers: 'We expect that any member of staff who reports concerns about the safety

28   Rose, D. '"Whistleblower" nurse Margaret Haywood struck off over Panorama film.' *The Times*, 17 April, 2009.

29   'Whistleblower nurse charges dropped.' *BBC News*, 27 November 2008. Accessed on 5 August 2010 at: http://news.bbc.co.uk/1/hi/programmes/panorama/7752691.stm.

30   'Margaret Haywood interview.' *BBC News*, 20 July 2005. Accessed on 5 August 2010 at: http://news.bbc.co.uk/1/hi/programmes/panorama/4701521.stm. Also: 'Interview with Peter Coles.' *BBC News*, 20 July 2005. Accessed on 20 August 2010 at: http://news.bbc.co.uk/1/hi/programmes/panorama/4701921.stm.

31   Plunkett, J. 'Nurse who secretly filmed for Panorama is struck off the Register.' *The Guardian*, 16 April 2009.

32   Laurance, J. '40,000 names on petition for sacked NHS whistle blower.' *The Independent*, 11 May 2009.

33   'Whistleblowing nurse Margaret Haywood wins patient award.' *Nursingtimes.net*, 10 November 2009. Accessed on 5 August at: www.nursingtimes.net/whats-new-in-nursing/news-topics/whistleblowing/whistleblowing-nurse-margaret-haywood-wins-patient-award/5008374.article.

34   Smith, L. 'High Court reinstates nurse who exposed neglect.' *The Independent*, 13 October 2009.

or quality of care to be listened to by their managers and action taken to address their concerns.'[35]

Dr Steve Bolsin, Bristol Royal Infirmary, children's heart surgery: hounded out of medicine in this country. In 1999, by the time Dr (later Professor) Steve Bolsin was giving evidence to the public inquiry into children's heart surgery in Bristol, he had been reportedly hounded out of medicine in this country and was working in Australia.[36] He had whistleblown and his concerns were fully vindicated, but the public inquiry noted that he had not been heeded and that the 'difficulties he encountered reveal both the territorial loyalties and boundaries within the culture of medicine and of the NHS, and also the realities of power and influence'.[37]

Dr Kim Holt, predicting child protection failure at Great Ormond Street Hospital: vilified and excluded. Dr Kim Holt, together with three other consultants, raised concerns, in 2006, with her NHS Trust employer about cuts to paediatric services at St Anne's Hospital in Haringey and about the implications for child protection. Unfortunately, her concerns were vindicated; by the time 'Baby P' died in 2007 and a locum paediatrician at the hospital had missed life-threatening injuries, there were no experienced consultant paediatricians working there.

After she had taken leave in 2006, partly related to an excessive workload, the Great Ormond Street Hospital for Children NHS Trust apparently obstructed her return to work. Between 2007 and 2010, it seems that, though she was fit to return to work, she was not supported to return to her post and remained on authorised, paid leave.[38]

One view is that Dr Holt was 'subjected to the rage of a managerial machine that tolerates no dissent'.[39] Another was that of a report commissioned by NHS London, which studiously avoided getting to the heart of the matter and instead stated that nobody was to blame. The report went only so far as to suggest that the Trust might have handled things better, but that it had not targeted Dr Holt. It did, tellingly, concede, however, that it disagreed with the lead clinician for the Trust; he had maintained that increased waiting times through excessive workload, lack of follow-up appointments and the unavailability of notes did not affect patient safety.[40] The report noted that Dr Holt was highly intelligent and committed. In September 2010, she announced her intention to sue the Trust.[41]

John Watkinson: victimised and sacked for insisting that the law be adhered to. John Watkinson, the chief executive of Royal Cornwall Hospital NHS Trust, won an employment tribunal case. The tribunal ruled that he had been dismissed from his post by the Trust Board because of pressure placed on the Trust from the strategic health authority (SHA). The chief executive and chairman of the SHA refused to give evidence at the tribunal. But it appears that the SHA was irritated that he had insisted on a public

35   'Secret filming nurse struck off.' *BBC News*, 16 April 2009. Accessed on 30 July 2010 at: http://news.bbc. co.uk/1/hi/england/sussex/8002559.stm.

36   'Bolsin: the Bristol whistleblower.' BBC News, 22 November 1999. Accessed on 20 September 2010 at: http:// news.bbc.co.uk/1/hi/health/532006.stm.

37   Kennedy, I. (Chair). *Learning from Bristol. The report of the public inquiry into children's heart surgery at the Bristol Royal Infirmary 1984–1995.* Cm 5207(1). London: TSO, 2001, p.161.

38   Rose, D. 'Doctor who raised alarm at Baby P clinic sues Great Ormond St. to get her job back.' *The Times*, 20 September 2010.

39   Campbell, B. 'The persecution of NHS whistleblowers.' *The Guardian*, 11 December 2009.

40   Widdowson, D. and Persaud, N. *Report on an investigation into allegations made by Dr. Kim Holt, consultant community paediatrician.* London: NHS London, 2009, pp.5, 12, 44.

41   Rose, D. 'Doctor who raised alarm at Baby P clinic sues Great Ormond St. to get her job back.' *The Times*, 20 September 2010.

consultation exercise – as, in fact, the law demanded – before local cancer services were removed. The tribunal ruled that his dismissal flew in the face of fairness. The new Secretary of State for Health promptly ordered an inquiry.[42]

David Bowles, raising concerns about patient safety in Lincolnshire: bullied and resigned. Allegations were made by David Bowles, chairman of the United Lincolnshire Hospitals NHS Trust, who resigned in 2009. He cited bullying by the East Midlands Strategic Health Authority in relation to the hitting of targets. He was supported by other non-executive members of the Trust's Board, in not being prepared to guarantee the hitting of non-urgent targets at a time when emergency admissions were very high. He wanted to know from the chief executive of the NHS (David Nicholson) 'whether he thinks it is fair and reasonable to ask for that guarantee… I would like to know whether this is a renegade SHA or do ministers agree with unconditional guarantees on non-urgent targets.' His stance was that, were he to offer such a guarantee, this would be at the expense of patient safety.[43]

David Nicholson then set up an inquiry, chaired by an independent consultant, a former SHA chief executive. The report's findings bore the hallmarks of a whitewash, exonerating the East Midlands SHA of harassment and bullying. However, it did note that 'Given the increasing pressures on NHS leadership and management that will result from the impact of the economic downturn on public services there is the possibility of firm performance management being interpreted as bullying or harassment'. It refers also to the importance of good relationships and collaborative behaviour.[44]

Gary Walker: sacked for raising patient safety concerns in Lincolnshire and gagged. Chief executive of United Lincolnshire Hospitals NHS Trust, Gary Walker had, in a two-year tenure, turned around both financial deficits and missed targets. However, by the winter of 2008, he was concerned – like his chairman, David Bowles – about patient safety because of increased accident and emergency admissions. His view was that adhering to targets, which included non-emergency care, would undermine the safety of patients in urgent and emergency need. He was told by the strategic health authority that he had to meet targets, come what may. The SHA then started publicly to cast doubts on governance at the Trust, and Gary Walker was told that if he did not leave, his career would be in ruins. He refused to resign after he had been offered £43,000 to sign a compromise agreement. So he was sacked, on the grounds that he swore nine times at meetings over a two-year period(!).[45]

He then claimed unfair dismissal. However, he dropped this in favour of a severance deal. This involved payment to him of £500,000 but crucially, also, a compromise agreement, whereby he was not allowed to talk about the reasons for his dismissal or patient safety: a gagging clause. Extraordinarily, other witnesses who would have appeared at the employment tribunal, including David Bowles (the former Trust chairman) also received gagging letters as part of the agreement. The Trust described the severance deal as amicable; Mr Walker's supporters said if he had not signed it, he might well have lost his house.[46]

42   Lakhani, N. 'Top-level review ordered into sacking of whistle-blower.' *Independent on Sunday*, 16 May 2010.

43   Moore, A. 'Resigning trust chair calls for David Nicholson to investigate "SHA pressure".' *Health Service Journal*, 27 July 2009.

44   Department of Health. *Review of allegations of bullying and harassment of the United Lincolnshire Hospitals NHS Trust by the East Midlands Strategic Health Authority: summary of findings, 28th October 2009.* London: DH, 2009.

45   Hammond, P. and Bousfield, A. 'Shoot the messenger: how NHS whistleblowers are silenced and sacked.' *Private Eye*, 22 July 2011.

46   'Ex-NHS chief Gary Walker "being gagged".' *BBC News*, 29 June 2012. Accessed on 8 August 2012 at www.bbc. co.uk/news/uk-18639088.

Dr Antoinette Geoghegan: treated with contempt, impatience and vitriol.
A consultant psychiatrist (who suffered with depression and, later, work-related stress) raised concerns in 2007 about management changes to working practices in her child and adolescent mental health department at the Northumberland Tyne and Wear NHS Mental Health Trust. She referred to excessive workload, bullying and intimidation, inadequate staff numbers, poor communication and high use of agency workers (putting patients at risk). The raising of these concerns led to subsequent discriminatory treatment.

In 2009, she had intervened after a young girl was, in the consultant's view, prematurely discharged. She was right; the girl was being sexually abused. The NHS trust raised a 'serious untoward incident', not about the premature discharge but instead about the consultant's intervention.

The employment tribunal later referred to this as 'malicious and capricious', and an example of 'oppressive and unjustified' criticism of her by the Trust.

The consultant then complained that her health was being jeopardised by the way the Trust was treating her. It banned her from contact. She became stressed and unfit for work.

The employment tribunal found that at no time did the Trust show concern or compassion for her welfare, that there was a direct link between her complaints and the discriminatory treatment she suffered, and that she was treated with 'little more than contempt, impatience and vitriol'.[47]

Sharmila Chowdhury: blew the whistle, subjected to false counter-allegation of fraud and marched off the premises. A radiology manager at a London district general hospital, at Ealing Hospital NHS Trust, alleged that medical colleagues were claiming, wrongly, thousands of pounds of public money every month for patient sessions they were not present at. The doctors and Trust denied this.

Having made these allegations, she was subject to an unfounded counter-allegation of fraud by a junior colleague whom she had previously reported for breaching safety procedures. She was then marched off the premises.

The NHS Trust spent hundreds of thousands of pounds trying to get rid of her, leaving her depressed, unemployed and without income. She expected to lose her home. She won an employment tribunal case. The tribunal had ordered her reinstated, but she was then made redundant, with a severance package to be agreed. However, she had incurred legal costs of £100,000 in bringing the case. She had an unblemished work record of 20 years.[48]

GAGGING CLAUSES

Another feature of the NHS attempting to cover up and suppress stories of poor, unsafe and neglectful care comes in the form of gagging clauses. These are imposed sometimes in contracts from the outset, sometimes in agreements when a whistleblower reaches a settlement with his or her NHS employer. A gagging clause might, for example, state that the clinician is never allowed to talk about the circumstances and reasons for his or her leaving the trust's employment.

This is despite the fact that guidance issued by the Department of Health was clear that gagging clauses in employment contracts and severance agreements,

47   'Tyne and Wear NHS: trust them.' *Private Eye*, 19 October 2012, p.31.
48   Lakhani, N. 'Hung out to dry: scandal of the abandoned NHS whistleblowers.' *The Independent*, 4 July 2012.

conflicting with the protection afforded by the Public Interest Disclosure Act 1998, were void.[49]

Further guidance maintained this stance by stating:

> Any confidentiality clause in a contract between an employee or ex-employee and his/her employer or ex-employer which seeks to prevent the employee making a 'protected' disclosure in accordance with the Public Interest Disclosure Act 1998 read with the Employment Rights Act 1996 (hereinafter referred to as the 'Public Interest Disclosure Act 1998') is void and ineffective.[50]

However, it then muddied the waters by going on to state about severance agreements:

> Subject to the above, it is not contrary to the Department of Health's policy for confidentiality clauses to be contained in severance agreements. However, employers must consider with their legal advisers whether a confidentiality clause is necessary in the particular circumstances of each case. Further, if it is decided that a clause is appropriate, then its terms should go no further than is necessary to protect the NHS Body's legitimate interests.[51]

It would appear in practice that the NHS sometimes falls into the trap of considering preservation of its reputation to be a legitimate interest, which trumps everything else, including patients' welfare and even their very lives.

In 2001, the National Audit Office published a report about the manipulation of waiting list statistics, and also referred to the inappropriate use of gagging clauses on those managers who subsequently were suspended, retired or resigned, sometimes with compensation payments.[52]

In addition to the Department of Health, it transpired that the Care Quality Commission, too, has been using gagging clauses to silence staff from expressing concerns about standards of care within the NHS. The House of Commons Public Accounts Committee was highly critical of this practice:

> The Commission has been criticised for being overly concerned with reputation management at the expense of transparency and accountability. Staff leaving the Commission have been made to sign compromise agreements containing confidentiality clauses, tantamount to gagging clauses. This Committee has expressed concern on previous occasions about the use of such clauses. The Department confirmed that confidentiality clauses are not in themselves prohibited, but its guidance makes clear that clauses that seek

---

49 HSC 1999/198. *Public Interest Disclosure Act 1998: whistleblowing in the NHS.* London: Department of Health, 1999.

50 HSC 2004/001. *Use of confidentiality and clawback clauses in connection with termination of a contract of employment.* London: Department of Health, 2004, para 10.

51 HSC 2004/001. *Use of confidentiality and clawback clauses in connection with termination of a contract of employment.* London: Department of Health, 2004, para 13.

52 National Audit Office. *Inappropriate adjustments to NHS waiting lists.* London: NAO, 2001, para 3.

to prevent the disclosure of information in the public interest should not be allowed. We are concerned, however, that the use of confidentiality clauses makes people reluctant to speak out, even though their whistleblowing rights may be legally protected.[53]

In fact, not only was the Care Quality Commission attempting to suppress whistleblowing from within but it seemed unconcerned if it came from without. When the BBC broadcast a programme about the persistent abuse of people with learning disabilities at a private hospital, called Winterbourne View, it transpired that a whistleblower, a senior nurse from the hospital, had contacted the Care Quality Commission twice – without the Commission taking action, other than passing on concerns to the local authority.[54]

Gagging appears to continue and to be in good health. And yet it is contrary to professional conduct laid down by the General Medical Council for any doctor to sign, or impose, a gagging clause about patient safety:

> You must not enter into contracts or agreements with your employing or contracting body that seek to prevent you from or restrict you in raising concerns about patient safety. Contracts or agreements are void if they intend to stop an employee from making a protected disclosure…
>
> If you have a management role or responsibility, you must make sure that…you do not try to prevent employees or former employees raising concerns about patient safety – for example, you must not propose or condone contracts or agreements that seek to restrict or remove the contractor's freedom to disclose information relevant to their concerns.[55]

NHS WHISTLEBLOWING: CONTINUING LACK OF POLITICAL WILL TO RESOLVE THE PROBLEMS

The House of Commons Health Committee concluded, in 2009, that NHS workers were fearful of being blamed or victimised if they blew the whistle, that the NHS generally was unsupportive of whistleblowing and that the Department of Health should develop proposals to improve the situation.[56]

The NHS Constitution now does contain a pledge 'to support all staff in raising concerns at the earliest reasonable opportunity about safety, malpractice or wrongdoing at work, responding to and, where necessary, investigating the concerns raised and acting consistently with the Public Interest Disclosure Act 1998'.[57]

---

53   House of Commons Public Accounts Committee. *The Care Quality Commission: regulating the quality and safety of health and adult social care.* London: TSO, 2012, p.8.

54   House of Commons Public Accounts Committee. *The Care Quality Commission: regulating the quality and safety of health and adult social care.* London: TSO, 2012, para 24.

55   General Medical Council. *Raising and acting on concerns about patient safety.* London: GMC, 2012, paras 8, 22.

56   House of Commons Health Committee. *Patient safety: Sixth report of Session 2008–09.* HC 151-I. London: TSO, 2009, p.92.

57   Department of Health. *NHS Constitution.* London: DH, 2012, p.11.

But legal substance is there none, and no such verbiage in the NHS Constitution will prevent frightened, weak and bullying managers from stamping on staff who raise awkward concerns.

It is of some interest to note that proposals made by the Welsh Government in 2012 suggest that staff working with vulnerable adults in any setting would have a duty to report if they are aware of those adults being at risk of abuse.[58] In principle, one assumes this could have a significantly beneficial effect, so long as the sanctions for not doing so – and for obstructive employers – were to be likewise significant. The Stafford public inquiry also recommended, in early 2013, that a statutory duty of candour be placed on health care staff.[59]

Finally, the can of worms, which whistleblowing and gagging clauses had become, was opened up barely a week after the Stafford public inquiry had been published. It concerned Gary Walker, the chief executive of an NHS trust who, as already described above, had argued that patient safety should take precedence over targets. He was consequently dismissed on apparently trumped up grounds and gagged in 2009 with a payout, to avoid employment tribunal proceedings. He finally decided to discard the gag and speak on the *BBC Radio 4 Today* programme on 14th February 2013.[60]

The Stafford inquiry had been clear that a culture of transparency and of putting patient safety first was required in the NHS. Yet Mr Walker's former employer, the United Lincolnshire Hospitals NHS Trust, seemed not to have received the message. It immediately threatened to take legal proceedings against him as a result of his speaking out (and thus potentially to ruin him financially), notwithstanding gags about patient safety arguably being unlawful under the Public Interest Disclosure Act 1998. The chairman of the House of Commons Health Committee then stepped in, asking Jeremy Hunt, the Secretary of State for Health, to intervene.[61]

The irony, apparently lost on the Trust, was this. It had spent £500,000 of public money on gagging its former chief executive. It was now threatening to spend more public money pursuing him through the courts. Yet, only three days previously, on 11th February, the medical director of the NHS had announced that 14 hospitals were now under investigation for their high mortality rates – the very indicator that had led to Stafford being uncovered. The United Lincolnshire Hospitals NHS Trust was one of those hospitals.[62]

58   Welsh Government. *Social Services (Wales) Bill: consultation document.* Cardiff: WG, 2012, p.66.

59   Francis, R. (Chair). *Report of the Mid Staffordshire NHS Foundation Trust Public Inquiry.* Executive summary and three volumes. HC 898. London: TSO, 2013.

60   Hosken, A. 'NHS chief "stopped from speaking on patient safety".' *BBC News,* 14 February 2013. Accessed on 14 February 2013 at: www.bbc.co.uk/news/health-21444058.

61   'Jeremy Hunt: gagging order for NHS whistleblower unacceptable.' *Daily Telegraph,* 15 February 2013.

62   Smith, R. 'Mid Staffs: 14 hospitals under investigation: A further 2,800 patients may have died needlessly as nine more hospitals were identified as having worrying mortality rates over the last two years.' *Daily Telegraph,* 11 February 2013.

Mental capacity

Power to instruct IMCA in case of abuse or neglect
Offences of ill-treatment or wilful neglect
Office of the Public Guardian
Appointees
Mental Capacity Act application to children and young people

KEY POINTS

Almost by definition, a person who is deemed to lack capacity to make significant decisions about aspects of his or her life becomes potentially a vulnerable adult for obvious reasons. For example, he or she might be unable to decide what medical treatment to have, where to live, with whom to have contact, how to manage his or her money and property, when to wash, what to eat, what to wear, what to do each day – and so on.

The Mental Capacity Act 2005 (MCA 2005) operates on two different principles: empowerment and protection.

It empowers people by enshrining the principles that incapacity should not be assumed, that people should be assisted to make decisions for themselves, that unwise decisions do not necessarily mean incapacity and that, even with incapacity, people should still be involved in decisions as far as possible. All this protects people from having a fundamental right – to make decisions – being taken inappropriately away from them. In another way, protection comes in the form of actions and decisions taken by other people in the person's best interests, when he or she clearly lacks the capacity to take a particular decision.

However, this dual function of the Act sometimes results in tension when it comes to protecting and safeguarding vulnerable adults. This happens particularly when an adult with capacity to make certain decisions is making those decisions in such a way as to render himself or herself vulnerable to significant harm.

It is beyond the scope of this book to set out the Mental Capacity Act 2005 in detail. Instead, it highlights key points and provides practical examples of how the Act is particularly relevant to adult protection and safeguarding adults.

BACKGROUND BEFORE THE MENTAL CAPACITY ACT

Most of the Mental Capacity Act 2005 came into force in October 2007. Prior to the passing of this Act, the position with regard to decision-making capacity was as follows.

As far as finance and property were concerned, a person as donor could make an enduring power of attorney, authorising the attorney (typically a family member) to take decisions on behalf of the donor, in case of the donor losing capacity to manage such affairs. This was under the Enduring Powers of Attorney Act 1985.

In the absence of such a power of attorney, the Court of Protection could intervene in such matters under the Mental Health Act 1983, making orders or appointing a receiver for ongoing management of a person's affairs. If the only finance to be dealt with was in the form of social security benefits, then somebody could be appointed by the Benefits Agency under different legislation. The law remains the same in this latter respect.

If health or welfare decisions had to be made, the law did not allow anybody directly to consent or make decisions on behalf of the person lacking capacity. However, it did allow 'necessity' and 'best interests' interventions, which could range from deciding about what somebody should eat, what clothes they should wear and when they should get washed to major medical interventions or decisions about where somebody should live. When significant issues were in question, resort had to be made to the Family Division of the High Court in case of uncertainty, of dispute or of some very serious interventions.

The court would then exercise its own powers, called the 'inherent jurisdiction', by making a declaration or order as to what should happen in a person's best interests. Sometimes, the court was called on to decide whether a person himself or herself had capacity to decide the issue in question. Through this legal case law, the court developed a set of rules about decision-making capacity. Many of these rules have found their way into the Mental Capacity Act 2005, which is a tribute to the quality of the decision making evolved under the inherent jurisdiction.

Note. A number of cases heard previous to the coming into force of the Mental Capacity Act 2005 are included in this chapter, when the principles involved are consistent with those under the Act and when the examples are useful.

SUMMARY OF THE MENTAL CAPACITY ACT

In summary, the 2005 Act sets out a number of key principles that run throughout the Act and which should govern decisions and interventions in relation to people lacking capacity.

These are that capacity should be assumed unless otherwise shown, that people should be helped to take decisions for themselves and that unwise decisions do not necessarily mean that a person lacks capacity. The Act defines lack of capacity and states that interventions have to be in people's 'best interests', which should be achieved in a less or least restrictive manner.

The Act provides legal protection for people who provide care and treatment for a person lacking capacity, so long as they have done so reasonably. At the same time, the Act prohibits excessive restraint of a person.

It contains separate rules about going beyond restraint and instead depriving a person, lacking capacity, of his or her liberty. These rules have given rise to considerable difficulty as to when and how they should be applied.

A major change introduced by the Act was to replace enduring powers of attorney with lasting powers of attorney. This means that a donor, with capacity, can create such a power authorising the attorney to take not only financial decisions but also health and welfare decisions for the donor, when the latter loses capacity to take those decisions. Attorneys should act in a person's best interests but do not always do so. This can then give rise to safeguarding concerns.

Parallel with this change in the law, the Act created a new Court of Protection which can intervene not only in financial but also in health and welfare matters. This contrasts with the previous position, in which the Court of Protection (under the Mental Health Act 1983) was limited to interventions relating to finance, business and property only.

The Act clarified the law about advance decisions, or 'living wills' as they are sometimes called. They involve a person with capacity stipulating in advance his or her refusal of specified medical treatment, in case at the relevant time he or she lacks the capacity to do so directly.

A statutory independent mental capacity advocacy (IMCA) service was created by the Act. This means that in certain circumstances, related to the provision of care home and hospital accommodation or of serious medical treatment, local authorities and NHS bodies have an obligation to instruct an advocate before a decision is made. There is also a power, though not a duty, to instruct such an advocate where an adult protection issue has arisen.

The Act also contains the (separate) offences of wilful neglect and ill-treatment of a person lacking capacity. These mirror the same offences contained in the Mental Health Act 1983 in respect of people with a mental disorder.

CORE PRINCIPLES

Certain core principles apply throughout the Act. These directly impact on how decisions about welfare, health and finance are made in relation to a person who lacks, or may lack, capacity. The application of these principles is fundamental in judging, and getting right, safeguarding and protective interventions.

ASSUMPTION OF CAPACITY (PRINCIPLE 1)

A person is assumed to have capacity to take a decision unless it is established otherwise.[1] The effect of this principle is that whoever is seeking to show lack of capacity has to work all the harder in doing so. In case of doubt, one must lean towards capacity rather than incapacity.

The principle in common law was that, once capacity has been shown to have been lost, there is a presumption of continuance of that loss. However, the Court of Appeal rejected this approach in the case, for example, of head injury, from which there might be recovery. One reason for taking this approach is because of the drastic consequences of being judged to lack capacity: a person is deprived of important civil rights.[2]

---

1   Mental Capacity Act 2005, s.1.
2   *Masterman-Lister v Brutton* [2002] EWHC 417 (QB); [2002] EWCA Civ 1889 (Court of Appeal).

In another case, in which a man with learning disabilities clearly lacked the capacity to consent to marriage, the court noted that the possibility of future improvement in his capacity had to be borne in mind.[3]

Under the Mental Capacity Act 2005, the courts continue to remind that a regaining of capacity over time must be borne in mind. This is particularly apt under the Act because, as explained below, the Act makes quite clear that questions of capacity are not only issue-specific but also time-specific.

ALL PRACTICABLE STEPS TO HELP PERSON TAKE DECISION (PRINCIPLE 2)

The next core principle is that all practicable steps should be taken to help a person take the decision.[4] So this second principle, too, is of the empowering type.

Such practicable steps could be various. The code of practice refers to the importance of relevant information, avoidance of excessive detail, outlining risks and benefits, explanation of the effects of the decision, balanced presentation and consideration of obtaining specialist advice.

In terms of communication, 'all possible and appropriate means of communication should be tried'. This may include finding out the best means of communication, using simple language, pictures, objects, illustrations, picture boards, hearing interpreter, mechanical or electronic communication aids, interpreting behaviour that is indicative of feelings, speaking at the right volume and speed with appropriate sentence structure and vocabulary, breaking down information into smaller bits, allowing the person time to understand each bit of information, repeating information, getting help from people the person trusts, awareness of cultural, ethical or religious factors, using a professional language interpreter, using an advocate.

Location might be decisive – for instance, a quiet one free of background noise or other distractions, and one where privacy and dignity is respected; perhaps taking a person to the relevant location (such as a hospital) may assist him or her to understand what is in issue and to make the decision.

Likewise, timing may be decisive; a person may be more alert in the morning, less alert immediately after taking drowsiness-inducing medication, and become tired or confused if asked to decide too much in one go. Simply delaying the decision may help, so that more steps can be taken to assist the person to take the decision. Support from other people may be of benefit; the presence of a relative or a friend may (or may not be) reassuring and reduce anxiety.[5]

Both practitioners and the courts recognise the temptation – to be resisted – to blur the question of best interests with capacity; that is, to err towards a judgement

---

3   *X City Council v MB & Ors* [2006] EWHC 168 (Fam).
4   Mental Capacity Act 2005, s.1.
5   Lord Chancellor. *Mental Capacity Act 2005: code of practice.* London: TSO, 2007, paras 3.9–3.15.

that a person lacks capacity because he or she is taking what the professional believes to be an unwise decision.[6]

However, some practitioners concede – in safeguarding situations – that this consideration can, almost unnoticed, creep into the giving of assistance to people to take a decision for themselves. If the person is likely to make what practitioners view as a catastrophic decision, then they may be tempted not to give quite as much assistance as they might otherwise have given. This would not, of course, be in accordance with the provisions or the spirit of the Act.

In the following example, it was perhaps understandable why the local authority was arguing that a woman with learning disabilities lacked capacity to decide about contraception. It wanted to stop her having another baby; two previous babies had been taken away from her because she lacked the ability to cope. But the judge was not minded so readily to conclude that she lacked capacity to decide.

Efforts to be made to help a woman take a capacitated decision about contraception. In one case, for example, the local authority had gone to court, arguing that a woman lacked capacity to understand about contraception; this being the case, the authority wanted a court order allowing it forcibly to remove the woman to hospital and forcibly to administer contraception. The judge, in effect, told the local authority not to go too fast. The judge stated that, before reaching this conclusion, professionals needed to work with the woman to try to help her understand. It also required an effort from her husband who had hitherto been obstructive; he agreed to stand back and give the professionals better access to his wife.

> In such a sensitive area, it is difficult if not impossible to envisage any acceptable way forward on these particular facts, other than by an attempt to achieve a capacitated decision from Mrs A, through 'ability-appropriate' help and discussion without undue contrary pressure from Mr A.[7]

UNWISE DECISION DOES NOT NECESSARILY INDICATE LACK OF CAPACITY (PRINCIPLE 3)

The third core principle is that just because a person with a disorder or disability of mind takes what is considered to be an unwise decision, it does not necessarily mean that he or she lacks capacity.[8]

This is a key principle, which will frequently arise when local authorities and others consider how to safeguard and protect vulnerable adults. It recognises the fact that everybody makes unwise decisions. It does also mean that protecting a vulnerable adult might not be possible (at least under the 2005 Act), even if he or she is at risk of harm or exploitation. As the courts put it in an older case, decided under the common law: 'It is not the task of the courts to prevent those who have the mental capacity to make rational decisions from making decisions which

---

6   *CC v KK* [2012] EWHC 2136 (COP).

7   *A Local Authority v Mrs. A* [2010] EWHC 1549 (Fam).

8   Mental Capacity Act 2005, s.1.

others may regard as rash or irresponsible.' After all, many people 'make rash and irresponsible decisions, but are of full capacity'.[9]

The question is thus not whether the person is making a rational decision but whether he or she has the capacity to make a rational decision.[10] Nonetheless, this does not mean that vulnerability to exploitation is not relevant to the question of capacity. The courts have stated in the past that outcomes can often 'cast a flood of light on capacity' and are likely to be important, though not conclusive, indicators.[11]

In the following case, under the inherent jurisdiction before the coming of the Mental Capacity Act, the local authority probably viewed such legal issues as an impediment in their attempt to protect a person whom they clearly regarded as highly vulnerable. It wanted to stop her marrying; the court pointed out that the issue was not to do with the wisdom of the marriage.

Marriage between a woman with learning disabilities and a convicted sex offender. A 23-year-old woman with learning disabilities wished to marry a 37-year-old man with a substantial history of sexually violent crimes; the court was called on to consider whether or not she had capacity to marry. It made the following point:

> The question of whether E has capacity to marry is quite distinct from the question of whether E is wise to marry; either wise to marry at all, or wise to marry X rather than Y, or wise to marry S. In relation to her marriage the only question for the court is whether E has capacity to marry. The court has no jurisdiction to consider whether it is in E's best interests to marry or to marry S. It is not concerned with the wisdom of her marriage in general or her marriage to S in particular.[12]

The consequence is that, up to a point at least, the risk of – or vulnerability to – making a mistake or being exploited will not in itself indicate a lack of capacity.

For instance, in the older case immediately below, the judge stated that on the evidence the person was not 'sufficiently vulnerable to the risk of unwise decisions, bad advice or self-interested and manipulative persons to justify the inroads upon his personal freedoms', were he now to be declared incapable of managing his property and affairs. Yet this was not to say he was not still vulnerable in some degree to exploitation.

Dysexecutive syndrome and distinction between lack of capacity and vulnerability: brain injury. A challenge was made as to whether or not a person who had suffered a head injury – when a milk float hit his motor cycle – had been capable of managing his property and affairs (for the purpose of Part 7 of the Mental Health Act 1983) when he had previously made a settlement in respect of his personal injury. The court's decision now would affect the validity of that personal injury settlement.

Obsessionality, immaturity, rigidity, eccentricity, emotionality. The dysexecutive syndrome that the man suffered from as a consequence of the accident resulted in changes such as obsessionality, immaturity, rigidity of thinking, eccentricity and emotional outbursts. This impaired his ability to organise his life and to plan. However, his pre-accident level of

9   *Masterman-Lister v Brutton* [2002] EWHC 417 (QB); [2002] EWCA Civ 1889 (Court of Appeal).
10   *Lindsay v Wood* [2006] EWHC 2895 (QB).
11   *Masterman-Lister v Brutton* [2002] EWHC 417 (QB); [2002] EWCA Civ 1889 (Court of Appeal).
12   *Sheffield CC v E* [2004] EWHC 2808 (Fam).

intelligence was largely unchanged. This meant that his relationships with other people and with the problems of life did not always quite 'mesh'. There were conflicting medical views as to his capacity to conduct litigation.

Difference between wisdom and understanding. The court made a distinction between wisdom in transactions and understanding; the former was not relevant to capacity. He had perhaps been overly generous to girlfriends, to the Vegan Society and to anti-hunt protestors, caused trouble to some builders, broken a cooker valve and lost the replacement, and overstocked his fridge. But the judge concluded that the evidence of the last 20 years (since the accident) showed that the man was, by and large, perfectly capable of looking after himself. Indeed, there was various evidence of highly responsible actions, such as advising friends on how to maximise social security benefits or avoid sexual harassment at work, alerting the police to the possible exposure of three young girls to sexual abuse at a naturist swimming pool, and writing impressive letters of advice to his nephew who was away at boarding school.

When greater problems arose, he recognised the need to seek assistance. The mental disorders identified in the medical reports were capable of leading to a finding of incapacity, if present to a sufficiently severe degree, but they were not of that degree in this case.

Differentiate capacity from outcomes. The Court of Appeal agreed, pointing out that the judge rightly distinguished between capacity and outcomes and between everyday matters and the management of more serious problems. In reaching his decision, the judge had considered all the relevant evidence, both medical and lay. He had also considered the man's diaries and letters. Matters such as losing a pressure cooker valve and overstocking the fridge may have been symptomatic of memory loss, but they were mishaps that could occur to those without the claimant's disabilities.[13]

More recent cases have thrown up similar issues. Sometimes what practitioners deem to be quite obviously unwise, detrimental and harmful decisions are in issue.

For example, in one case, a local authority was adamant that, one way or another, a woman with mental health problems should be prevented from engaging in harmful sexual relationships with men. In order to protect the woman from these unwise decisions she was taking, the local authority sought to set a higher bar for the understanding of sex. The judge was having none of it.[14]

In another case, despite being subjected to a degree of what could be termed domestic violence, the court held that the local authority had no legal power to prevent a young woman with serious mental health problems from having a relationship with her boyfriend.

Capacity to engage in sexual relationship disapproved of by the local authority.
A woman suffered from schizophrenia, characterised by prominent visual, auditory and tactile somatic hallucinations, made worse by stress. She had a moderate learning disability and had poor cognitive functioning. She had significantly impaired or non-existent verbal recall and was functionally illiterate. She lacked the capacity to litigate, decide where and with whom to live, to determine with whom she should have contact, to manage her own financial arrangements and to marry. But, legally, she had the capacity to consent to sexual relations.

---

13   *Masterman-Lister v Brutton* [2002] EWHC 417 (QB); [2002] EWCA Civ 1889 (Court of Appeal).
14   *Ealing London Borough Council v KS* [2008] EWHC 636 (Fam).

For 15 years, she had conducted a personal, sexual relationship with a man who himself had a psychopathic personality disorder and misused alcohol. He led an unstable and nomadic life; he had been violent towards the woman and was alleged to have used her benefit money to buy alcohol. He had previously encouraged her to follow him, which, according to the local authority, led to deterioration in her mental health. However, equally, it was clear that the relationship was all-important to the woman and that she derived considerable benefit from it in terms of positive emotional feelings. Also, she was more than capable of expressing her wishes and feelings 'as her oral evidence and the manner in which she gave it so vividly demonstrated'.[15]

Likewise, in a further case, the courts contemplated a woman with learning disabilities – if she was shown to have the capacity to decide about contraception – making the decision to have another baby. This was even though two babies had already been removed at birth, on the grounds that she had no concept of what was involved in motherhood. It was all a question of whether she had capacity or not.[16]

The financial ombudsman has had to adjudicate on unwise financial transactions. In the first case, the unwise transaction was associated with lack of capacity to enter into it. The second case, however, turned out differently, the man with learning disabilities and autism being held to have had capacity to enter into a loan agreement.

Credit card and loan to person with mental disorder: not liable to repayment.
A man with a mental disorder, and observed by several shops in the morning to be unwell and not behaving normally, was given a loan and credit card by the local branch of a 'firm' that same morning, together with a large amount of cash on credit. The shops had refused to do business with him. Later that day, someone took advantage of his confused condition and stole the cash. The father complained to the financial ombudsman who judged not only that the man lacked capacity at the time but that the firm should have known this by paying as much attention to his manner and appearance as the other shops had done. The ombudsman told the firm that the man was not bound by the loan and credit agreements and was not liable for the debt.[17]

Loan to person with learning disabilities: liable to repayment. When a man with learning disabilities and autism was liable for repayment of a loan from a firm, his mother complained to the financial ombudsman that her son had been taken advantage of, because he could not have understood the nature of the loan or his legal obligation. The ombudsman found otherwise, pointing out that an assumption of lack of capacity should not be made and that, on the evidence, the man's learning difficulties did not prevent him from understanding how ordinary banking products worked and understanding the particular transaction. Furthermore, he had been employed in a steady job for many years, during which time he had been a customer of the firm and managed his finances without difficulty.[18]

---

15 *Local Authority X v MM* [2007] EWHC 2003 (Fam).
16 *A Local Authority v Mrs. A* [2010] EWHC 1549 (Fam).
17 *Financial Ombudsman News*, Issue 50, November/December 2005, case 50/5.
18 *Financial Ombudsman News*, Issue 50, November/December 2005, case 50/4.

INTERVENTIONS MUST BE IN A PERSON'S BEST INTERESTS (PRINCIPLE 4)

The fourth principle in s.1 of the Act is that acts done or decisions made for people lacking capacity must be in their best interests. Best interests are defined in section 4 of the Act and are covered later in this chapter.

LESS OR LEAST RESTRICTIVE INTERVENTION (PRINCIPLE 5)

The fifth and last core principle of the Act is as follows. Before an act is done for a person lacking capacity, regard must be had to whether the purpose of the act can be as effectively achieved in a way that is less restrictive of the person's rights and freedom of action.[19]

Intervention in the case of a person lacking capacity is a major intrusion because, by definition, it is effected without the person's consent. Therefore, the Act makes clear that it should be no more restrictive than necessary.

Restrictive interventions might be various in nature and give rise to adult protection concerns. Restraint is one obvious example, and section 6 of the Act elaborates specifically on restraint and how it must be a proportionate response to the risk of harm. Another, highly topical, example of a restrictive intervention is deprivation of liberty, whereby the restrictions placed on a person are so great that they cross a certain threshold and engage article 5 of the European Convention on Human Rights. Under the principle of best interests, such restrictions should therefore be a last resort.

However, there are other interventions that could equally fall foul of this principle of less or least restriction. For instance, the Healthcare Commission found a universal teapot – ready milked and sugared – being used at mealtimes for people with learning disabilities.[20] On the assumption, for illustrative purposes, that those around the table lacked capacity to choose, this could be characterised as an over-restrictive way of acting in those persons' best interests.

It is worth pointing out, however, that least restrictive does not necessarily mean safest. Thus, the courts have pointed out that best interests decisions must take account of psychological and emotional issues (such as happiness), not just physical health and safety: see below in this chapter.

LACK OF CAPACITY

Section 2 of the Act states that:

> ...a person lacks capacity in relation to a matter if at the material time he is unable to make a decision for himself in relation to the matter because of an impairment of, or a disturbance in the functioning of, the mind or brain.

---

19   Mental Capacity Act 2005, s.1.
20   Healthcare Commission. *Investigation into the service for people with learning disabilities provided by Sutton and Merton Primary Care Trust.* London: HC, 2007, p.33.

The test is therefore twofold, concerning (a) whether there is a disturbance in the functioning of mind or brain affecting a particular decision at a particular time, *and* (b) whether there is an inability to take a decision.

Without the first – the diagnostic – part of the test being satisfied, the second is irrelevant.

DISTURBANCE IN THE FUNCTIONING OF THE MIND OR BRAIN

The first part of the test relates to an impairment or disturbance in the functioning of the mind or brain. This may be permanent or temporary. The code of practice states that examples of impairment or disturbance in the functioning of the mind or brain might include:

- conditions associated with some types of mental illness

- dementia

- significant learning disabilities

- brain damage

- physical or mental conditions causing confusion, drowsiness or loss of consciousness

- delirium

- concussion following head injury

- symptoms of alcohol or drug abuse.[21]

The impairment or disturbance must relate to a particular decision at a particular time. Thus, capacity is not all or nothing; it is both issue- and time-specific.

The issue-specific nature of decision making may well be relevant in situations potentially linked to safeguarding. For instance:

Issue specificity of decision: for example, ability to understand power of attorney but not financial affairs. The court held that a person had the capacity to make an enduring power of attorney in respect of the management of her affairs – if she understood the nature and effect of the power – even if, at the same time, she lacked the capacity to manage those affairs.[22] Such a situation might at first glance raise safeguarding concerns, but in this particular case the court held there was nothing untoward.

A comparable distinction, but in respect of time, between making a will and signing it, was drawn in the following court case (not under the Mental Capacity Act, but illustrating the point).

Time specificity of decision: making of a will. A woman was terminally ill. She made her final will in March, two days before she died. The medical evidence suggested that on that day she lacked the testamentary capacity (i.e. the capacity to make a will). However,

---

21   Quoted from: Lord Chancellor. *Mental Capacity Act 2005: code of practice.* London: TSO, 2007, para 4.12.

22   *Re K* [1988] 2 FLR 15.

the will had been prepared in accordance with instructions she had given in December when she did have undisputed testamentary capacity. In March, she was able to understand that the document she was signing had been in accordance with those instructions, even if she no longer understood the detail. The will was therefore valid.[23]

In the following case also (not a Mental Capacity Act case), the court had to consider instead the question of time and whether there had been a lucid interval in relation to what otherwise were suspicious circumstances.

Time specificity of decision: making of will and lucid interval. An 84-year-old woman lived with her sister. On 8 April, she was admitted to hospital, suffering from various conditions including uncontrolled diabetes and dehydration. Her medical notes indicated she had been increasingly confused a few days before this admission. A care plan was set up by social services and she was discharged home on 26 April.

A friend whom she had known for 20 years then suggested that she make a will, making the friend sole executrix and beneficiary. The will was drawn up by the friend's brother-in-law who was a solicitor and to whom the friend communicated the woman's instructions. The draft will was returned to the friend who made arrangements for its execution when the sister was out of the house, on the afternoon of 13 May. That morning, a GP specialising in geriatric medicine had visited and found the woman confused; towards the end of the day, a neighbour had visited and found the same. However, the friend maintained at the time of the will's execution that the woman had not been confused.

The judge stated that the burden of showing testamentary capacity lay on the friend since she had procured the execution of the will and was the beneficiary. He concluded that the woman's confusion was the product of her diabetes and drug regime, and, on all the evidence, it was not credible that she had had a period of lucidity on the day in question in between the earlier and later periods of confusion on that same day.[24]

Nonetheless, the fact that capacity is issue-specific can complicate matters when a local authority is seeking to safeguard and protect an adult. In one case, the understandable anxiety of the local authority to protect a highly vulnerable woman was complicated by this variable capacity. The anxiety led it to an unbalanced decision to which the courts objected.

Unable to take most decisions, but with capacity to consent to sexual relations. A woman suffered from schizophrenia, characterised by prominent visual, auditory and tactile somatic hallucinations, made worse by stress. She had a moderate learning disability and had poor cognitive functioning. She had significantly impaired or non-existent verbal recall and was functionally illiterate. She lacked the capacity to litigate, decide where and with whom to live, to determine with whom she should have contact, to manage her own financial arrangements and to marry. But, legally, she had the capacity to consent to sexual relations.[25]

The complexity of judging capacity about different issues was illustrated in a case in which the court decided that a woman with mild learning disabilities (a) had had the capacity to marry her husband, (b) still understood the obligations of marriage,

---

23   *Clancy v Clancy* [2003] EWHC 1885.
24   *Richards v Allan* [2000] unreported (Chancery).
25   *Local Authority X v MM* [2007] EWHC 2003 (Fam).

(c) lacked the capacity to litigate, (d) lacked also the capacity to understand the threat her husband potentially posed to her following his release from prison – and to decide whether to resume cohabitation with him. Nonetheless, the court held that, despite all these circumstances, it was still in her best interests to resume cohabitation.[26]

Similarly, but involving instead specificity of *time* rather than *issue*, another case centred on the capacity of a woman with a schizo-affective disorder. The matters to be decided included her capacity to marry (she had already had a number of husbands), to decide where to live, to decide about contact with her mother and sisters, and to consent to sexual relations. In respect of the last matter, the evidence had already established that at times she had capacity, at other times not. The capacity was fluctuating. This, in turn, gave rise to a concern within the local authority about how it could protect her from harmful sexual activity at times when she did have capacity.[27]

INABILITY TO TAKE A DECISION

The second part of the test of mental capacity is the so-called functional approach, as opposed to a status or outcome approach, to capacity.[28] The status approach would be based on a person's medical diagnosis or condition, the outcome approach on the consequences of a person's decision. Both have made way for the functional approach.

Section 3 of the 2005 Act states, in summary, that:

- a person is unable to take a decision if he or she is unable to understand the relevant information, or to retain it, or to use or weigh it as part of the decision-making process, or to communicate it

- however, the person is not to be regarded as unable to take the decisions if he or she can understand an explanation in a way appropriate to his or her circumstances (e.g. using simple language, visual aids or any other means)

- if the person can retain the information relevant to the decision for a short time only, this does not necessarily mean the person cannot make decisions

- information relevant to a decision includes information about the reasonably foreseeable consequences of deciding one way or another, or of failing to make the decision.

The following example is an older landmark case, decided under the inherent jurisdiction, some years before the advent of the Mental Capacity Act. It illustrates the court's rejection of the status and outcome approach, in favour of the functional approach. The outcome of the person's decision was that he might well die; the

---

26   *CYC v PC* [2012] UZ0120352 COP No. 12015615.

27   *Ealing London Borough Council v KS* [2008] EWHC 636 (Fam).

28   Law Commission. *Mental Incapacity Law.* Law Com. no. 231. London: HMSO, 1995, para 3.3.

status issue was that he was a mental health patient in a special hospital. However, neither fact meant that he necessarily lacked the requisite decision-making capacity, which overrode the doctors' wish to protect him.

Amputation of gangrenous leg. A patient detained in a special secure hospital suffered from chronic paranoid schizophrenia. He was found to be suffering from an ulcerated, gangrenous foot and transferred to a general hospital, where the surgeon recommended amputation. The patient refused but agreed to conservative treatment; he sought an injunction to stop amputation unless he consented in writing. The court held that his schizophrenia did not mean that he could not understand the nature, purpose and effects of the treatment. He understood the relevant information, believed it and arrived at a clear choice. The court granted the injunction.[29]

This case illustrates the potential tension between empowering a person to take his or her own decisions and the wishes of others to protect the person. Similarly:

Prisoner able to weigh up risk of septicaemia and death. The courts held that a prisoner had the capacity to refuse medical treatment, which, accordingly, could not be given. It was medically required because he was at risk of death from septicaemia, after he had cut open his right leg and kept it open by forcing foreign objects into it.[30]

However, another court case, also concerning a detained mental health patient, had a different result.

Mental health patient unable to weigh up information about CT scan and cancer. An elderly woman, detained under s.3 of the Mental Health Act 1983, refused to accept medical treatment because she regarded it as part of a plot against her. The hospital sought the court's declaration that it was in the woman's best interests to have a general anaesthetic and CT scan, in order to investigate a suspected renal carcinoma. They gave the hospital permission to carry out the procedures, since the woman was clearly unable to believe the relevant information and weigh up the benefits; she appeared to have no insight into her condition.[31]

So, in line with this functional approach, the fact that a person has learning disabilities and severe behavioural disturbance will not necessarily mean that he or she lacks capacity to take a decision about vital medical intervention.

Not treating renal failure. A 25-year-old woman had learning disabilities and severe behavioural problems. Suffering from renal failure, she nevertheless resisted attempts to administer dialysis treatment. The court held that on the evidence she had capacity to make this decision, and that the dialysis could not be provided compulsorily against her will as treatment for mental disorder under the Mental Health Act 1983. Therefore, provision of the treatment without her consent would amount to both a criminal assault and a civil wrong.[32]

Similarly, age, medication or dementia will not necessarily be legally decisive as to incapacity.

29   *Re C (Adult: refusal of treatment)* [1994] 1 WLR 290.
30   *Re W (Adult: refusal of treatment)* [2002] EWHC 901 (Fam).
31   *Doncaster & Bassetlaw Hospitals NHS Trust & Anor v C* [2004] EWHC 1657 (Fam).
32   *JT (Adult: refusal of medical treatment)* [1998] FLR 48.

Cocktail of drugs: woman still had wits about her. A 79-year-old woman made a will in hospital five days before she died, leaving her entire estate to her brother. Her son contested the will, mainly on the grounds that the cocktail of drugs his mother was receiving must have meant that she lacked testamentary capacity. However, the court accepted that it was not a foregone conclusion that the drugs would have had this effect and that evidence from medical witnesses suggested that she had had her wits about her.[33]

In line with the issue-specific nature of decision-making capacity, delusions in themselves will not necessarily render a will invalid. In a 19th-century case, the testator had been in the county lunatic asylum. He had delusions that he was pursued and molested by a certain man and by devils or evil spirits. The jury nonetheless found that he had the capacity to make his will.[34]

Similarly, moderately advanced dementia will not necessarily deprive a person of capacity.

Making of a valid will by a woman with mild to moderate dementia. A woman made a new will in 1994, which changed the terms of her previous will made in 1987; beneficiaries under the 1987 will were displaced by the 1994 will and were aggrieved. At the time she made the second will, the woman suffered at least mild to moderate Alzheimer-type dementia. However, the court found that, on the balance of probabilities, she understood the claims of the former beneficiaries, and was capable of understanding without further explanation, and knew and approved, the contents of the will.[35]

(The courts have sometimes referred to a 'golden rule', to the effect that if a solicitor is drawing up a will for an aged or seriously ill person, it should be witnessed or approved by a medical practitioner.[36])

The above examples demonstrate how this functional approach to capacity dovetails with the principle in s.1 of the Mental Capacity Act 2005 – that unwise decisions do not necessarily indicate a lack of capacity.

COMMON LAW TESTS OF CAPACITY

Tests of capacity for some particular types of decision have developed their own common law rules. It is expected that the courts will, over time, consider these rules in the light of the general test of capacity in the 2005 Act. However, these particular tests remain applicable and a number are relevant to safeguarding and adult protection issues – such as capacity to make a will, make a gift, consent to medical treatment, get married, engage in sexual activity. The tests for gifts and wills are outlined in Chapter 24. Those for marriage and sexual activity are covered below in this chapter.

The common law test of capacity to litigate has in the past (prior to the Mental Capacity Act) been characterised as follows:

---

33   *Barrett v Kasprzyk* [2000] unreported, High Court (Chancery). (Not a Mental Capacity Act case.)
34   *Banks v Goodfellow* (1870) LR 5 QB 549. (Not a Mental Capacity Act case.)
35   *Hoff, Beagan, Wiechulla v Atherton* [2004] EWHC 177 (Chancery); [2004] EWCA Civ 1554 (Court of Appeal). (Not a Mental Capacity Act case.)
36   *Kenward v Adams* [1975]. *The Times Law Reports*, 28 November 1975.

The mental abilities required include the ability to recognise a problem, obtain and receive, understand and retain relevant information, including advice; the ability to weigh the information (including that derived from advice) in the balance in reaching a decision, and the ability to communicate that decision.[37]

The courts in the past have held that the test of capacity to consent to medical treatment is as follows:

A person lacks capacity if some impairment or disturbance of mental functioning renders the person unable to make a decision whether to consent to or to refuse treatment. That inability to make a decision will occur when: (a) the patient is unable to comprehend and retain the information which is material to the decision, especially as to the likely consequences of having or not having the treatment in question; (b) the patient is unable to use the information and weigh it in the balance as part of the process of arriving at the decision.[38]

This test has now blended with the principles of the Mental Capacity Act.

ASCERTAINING INABILITY TO TAKE A DECISION

Ultimately, the question of capacity is a legal not a medical one. Indeed, the Mental Capacity Act and the accompanying code of practice envisage that all manner of person may be taking this decision.

The onus of taking reasonable steps to make this decision lies on the person – who may be a professional, but who may alternatively be a family member, for example – proposing to act in somebody else's best interests.

Code of practice: reasonable steps in deciding capacity. The code of practice states that the person who assesses capacity will usually be the person directly concerned with the decision that has to be made. This means, for 'most day-to-day' decisions, the immediate carer. For acts of care or treatment, the assessor must, under s.5 of the Act, have a reasonable belief that the person lacks capacity. More complex decisions are likely to need more formal assessments, but the final decision is to be made by the person intending to make the intervention in terms of care or treatment. Of course, professionals such as doctors or solicitors will have to assess capacity in relation to proposed medical treatment or legal transactions respectively.

The code goes on to state that carers, including family carers, do not have to be expert assessors, but must be able to explain the reasonable steps they have taken to ascertain the lack of capacity. Thus, reasonable steps will depend on individual circumstances and the urgency of the decision; professionals would normally be expected to undertake a fuller assessment than family members without formal qualifications. However, a professional opinion may be required when a complex or major decision has to be made. This might

---

37   *Masterman-Lister v Brutton* [2002] EWHC 417 (QB); [2002] EWCA Civ 1889 (Court of Appeal).
38   *Re MB (Adult: caesarian section)* [1997] 2 FCR 541.

be from a general practitioner or, for example and depending on the condition or disorder, consultant psychiatrist, psychologist or speech and language therapist.[39]

In a case involving a woman with fluctuating capacity to consent to sexual relations, the court emphasised that neither it nor the local authority could prevent her having such relations at times when she had capacity. However, it agreed with the local authority that her carers should be given a clear list of indicators of possible loss of capacity to consent to sexual intercourse or other sexual contacts.[40]

There is thus no rule that the evidence about capacity can only be medical, but, in case of doubt, medical doctors may be substantially relied upon, including by the courts. In a case involving the validity of an advance decision made by an anorexic woman in danger of death, the judge held the absence of a medical assessment of her capacity (at the time she made the decision) crucial to its invalidity, despite the fact that other people, including a solicitor and advocate, had judged that she had capacity to make it.[41]

In contrast, when an elderly woman wanted to return to her village home, all the professionals, including medical doctors, lined up against her and stated that she lacked the capacity to decide this. The judge disagreed with all of them, stating that they had allowed their concerns about physical risk to cloud their examination of the true legal question. He held that she had the capacity to take the decision.[42]

The lack of medical evidence in the following case, which 'bristled with suspicion', told against the son who was the main beneficiary of a new will.

Failure to obtain medical evidence. A woman had a stroke, lacked the ability to communicate, was deteriorating and had suffered a fall. She made a new will under pressure from her family. The will was drafted by one of her sons, the main beneficiary of the new will. He was advised by solicitors that an expert medical opinion be obtained concerning his mother's capacity. He ignored this advice. The judges found the circumstances 'bristled with suspicion', in which case the son had to prove that his mother had testamentary capacity. He came nowhere near this; the will was set aside because of grave suspicion not only about her knowledge and approval of the contents but also about her capacity.[43]

On the other hand, in coming to the conclusion in one case that a person, arguably vulnerable to financial exploitation, did not lack capacity to manage his financial affairs, the court took particular account of the person's diary entries made over a period of many years. The medical experts giving evidence in the case had not reached a consensus, and so the judge had to look particularly hard at non-medical evidence.[44]

39   Lord Chancellor. *Mental Capacity Act 2005: code of practice.* London: TSO, 2007, paras 4.38–4.51.
40   *Ealing London Borough Council v KS* [2008] EWHC 636 (Fam).
41   *A Local Authority v E* [2012] EWHC 1639 (COP).
42   *CC v KK* [2012] EWHC 2136 (COP).
43   *Vaughan v Vaughan* [2002] EWHC 699 (Chancery).
44   *Masterman-Lister v Brutton* [2002] EWHC 417 (QB); [2002] EWCA Civ 1889 (Court of Appeal).

In a more recent case, about the validity of a lasting power of attorney, the court preferred the evidence of a solicitor to that of a medical doctor for the following reasons:

> Essentially, the issue is whether I prefer the evidence of the certificate provider [the solicitor] that [the person] had the capacity to create the LPA to that of [the doctor], the Court of Protection Special Visitor, who hazarded a guess that he may have lacked such capacity at the requisite time.
>
> In my judgment, the best evidence in this case is [the solicitor's]. I have described it as the 'best' evidence, not because it is of superlative quality (which it isn't), but simply because it is the best evidence that the circumstances of this case will allow. It is the only evidence that is both issue-specific and time-specific, insofar as it addresses [the person's] specific ability to create an LPA, at a specific time, namely on 3 June 2010 and 9 June 2010.
>
> [The solicitor] is an experienced solicitor of ten years' admission, and is familiar with the professional and ethical standards and safeguards that one needs to take into account when assessing whether an elderly person is capable of entering into a transaction of this kind. Her opinion is neither woolly nor equivocal. She was satisfied that [the person] understood the nature and effect of the LPA when he signed it. [The doctor's] opinion has the major disadvantage of being retrospective, and is thus neither time-specific nor issue-specific.[45]

In Scotland (governed by different capacity legislation but to roughly the same effect), the Mental Welfare Commission reported on a failure to protect a 67-year-old woman from a series of serious sexual assaults over a prolonged period of time. She had been in the care of the local authority since she was eight years old. It underlined the limitations of relying only on medical views as to capacity. Contributing to this failure was the judgement that she lacked competence as a witness in any criminal proceedings. This judgement had been made by psychiatrists and psychologists; but the Commission thought that the 'assessment of an individual's capacity to be a reliable witness is far too complex an issue to undertake without the involvement of those who are closely involved in his/her ongoing care'. Furthermore, there was no clear evidence that the professionals involved had considered how support might have been given to help the woman act as a witness.[46]

In another case (though not a Mental Capacity Act case), involving serious financial abuse by carers from a neighbouring village, the evidence to the court was from many quarters including, but not just, medical.

---

45   *In the matter of Collis*, October 2010, Court of Protection.
46   Mental Welfare Commission for Scotland. *Summary of our investigation into the care and treatment of Ms A.* Edinburgh: MHWC, 2008, p.2.

Sources of evidence about a woman's mental capacity to consent to transferring her home (in circumstances of gross exploitation). In a case concerning exploitation by carers of an elderly woman (now dead, found strangled by her clothing on a stairlift) and whether the transfer of her home to the carers should be set aside, the court heard evidence from a whole range of people. These included three general practitioners, a hospital senior house officer, a pathologist and another hospital consultant who had examined histological slides of the woman's brain, a chiropodist, friends, neighbours, a social worker, a retired Methodist minister, a solicitors' clerk and a borough council emergency contact service supervisor.[47]

Likewise, the following decision in a case about a disputed will was not based solely on the medical evidence.

Evidence to establish capacity. In a dispute about the validity of a will, the court concluded that the woman who made it (the testatrix) lacked testamentary capacity. This was in the light of the medical evidence that cast doubt on such capacity both before and after the signing of the will, a solicitor's assessment that lucidity was present only in intervals at the relevant time, her wandering off and her inability to understand that her husband had died and her failure to recognise close members of her family.[48]

In a well-publicised case – which involved suggestions of impropriety – an elderly woman had become close friends with a Chinese family which ran a select Chinese restaurant in Witham, Essex.

Conflicting medical views and non-medical evidence. The woman died, aged 89 years old, leaving property worth £10 million to the family. Her nieces and nephews disputed the will, claiming that when it was made their aunt had lacked capacity. Not only did the medical evidence conflict, but none of the doctors, 'however eminent', had actually seen the woman; they were basing their evidence on inferences – which, ultimately, it was for the court, and not expert witnesses, to make. She had made the will in 1994 and by December 1993 had mild dementia. However, the judge concluded, weighing up various factors including non-medical evidence, that she had capacity at the relevant time.[49]

REFUSAL OF ASSESSMENT OF CAPACITY

Some people might refuse or object to an assessment of mental capacity.

The code of practice states that nobody 'can be forced to undergo an assessment of capacity. If someone refuses to open the door to their home, it cannot be forced.' It points out that if there were serious concerns about a person's mental health, it may be possible to obtain a warrant and force entry under s.135 of the Mental Health Act 1983. However, the code underlines that 'simply refusing an assessment of capacity is in no way sufficient grounds for an assessment' under the 1983 Act.[50]

Section 15 of the Mental Capacity Act 2005 empowers the Court of Protection to make a declaration about a person's capacity. However, where there are significant

---

47   *Special Trustees of Great Ormond Street Hospital v Rushin* [1997] unreported (Chancery).
48   *Brown v Mott* [2002] unreported, High Court (Chancery). (Not a Mental Capacity Act case.)
49   *Blackman v Kim Sing Man* [2007] Case no. HC050C01190, 7 December 2007, High Court (Chancery). (Not a Mental Capacity Act case.)
50   Lord Chancellor. *Mental Capacity Act 2005: code of practice.* London: TSO, 2007, para 4.59.

doubts or uncertainties in the way of such an order, section 48 of the Act enables the court to make an interim order. This may be useful when there is some doubt about capacity and a need for an assessment (see below).

BEST INTERESTS

In protecting and safeguarding an adult who lacks capacity to take a particular decision, the person intervening must decide and act in the person's best interests. This is the fourth core principle in s.1 of the Act. Section 4 sets out in detail what is involved (bracketed headings added):

- **[best interests]** any act done or decision taken, for or on behalf of a person lacking capacity, must be in that person's best interests

- **[avoiding unjustified assumptions]** in determining best interests, the person making the determination must not make it merely on the basis of the person's age or appearance or a condition or aspect of behaviour, which might lead others to make unjustified assumptions about what might be in his best interests

- **[considerations]** best interests involve the decision-maker in:

  - **[regaining of capacity]** considering whether it is likely that the person will at some time have capacity and, if so, when that is likely to be

  - **[participation of person]** permitting and encouraging the person to participate as fully as possible in the decision and any decision affecting him

  - **[not desiring to bring about death]** where life-sustaining treatment is in issue, the decision-maker must not be motivated by a desire to bring about the person's death

  - **[past and present wishes, etc.]** considering, if reasonably ascertainable, the person's past and present wishes and feelings (and, in particular, any relevant written statement made by the person when he or she had capacity), beliefs and values, other factors

  - **[consulting others]** taking into account, where consultation is appropriate and practicable, the views of anyone named by the person, any person caring for the person or interested in the person's welfare, any donee of a lasting power of attorney, any Court of Protection appointed deputy.

- **[reasonable belief]** this section of the Act is complied with if the person doing the act or making the decision reasonably believes that the act or decision is in the best interests of the person concerned.[51]

---

51   Quoted from: Mental Capacity Act 2005, s.4.

The person making the decision or intervention ultimately has to decide about the best interests, after applying the above test. There is no indication in the Act as to which, if any, of these factors should take precedence in the reaching of a best interests decision.

The code of practice states that, for example, a person's wishes and feelings, values and beliefs 'will not necessarily be the deciding factor in working out their best interests'. Yet the code notes the legal requirement to pay special attention to any written statements the person may have made before losing capacity.[52]

LESS CAPACITY, LESS AUTONOMY

The courts have stated in this respect, that the 'further capacity is reduced, the lighter autonomy weighs'.[53] So, conversely:

> The nearer to the borderline the particular adult, even if she falls on the wrong side of the line, the more weight must in principle be attached to her wishes and feelings, because the greater distress, the humiliation and indeed it may even be the anger she is likely to feel the better she is able to appreciate that others are taking on her behalf decisions which vitally affect her – matters, it may be, as here [a personal, sexual relationship], of an intensely private and personal nature.[54]

BREADTH OF BEST INTERESTS

Although it is the decision maker who has to decide about best interests, nonetheless those best interests are not confined to issues within the expertise of that decision maker.

For instance, a decision about a medical intervention would encompass not just medical but also emotional and all other welfare issues. Furthermore, deciding about a person's best interests is not just about identifying a range of acceptable options, but instead is about identifying the 'best', a superlative term. This does not therefore equate with the common law duty of care owed by professionals, which is at least to adopt a reasonable course of action, but not necessarily the best.[55]

BEST INTERESTS: OF THE PERSON LACKING CAPACITY, NOT OF OTHER PEOPLE

The courts have also made clear that the best interests in issue are those of the person lacking capacity – even if, for example, the decision in question affects the life or death of a close family member.[56]

---

52   Lord Chancellor. *Mental Capacity Act 2005: code of practice.* London: TSO, 2007, paras 5.38–5.42.

53   *Re C (Adult: refusal of treatment)* [1994] 1 WLR 290.

54   *Local Authority X v MM* [2007] EWHC 2003 (Fam).

55   *SL v SL* (2000) 3 WLR 1288 (Court of Appeal).

56   *Re Y (Mental incapacity: bone marrow transplant)* [1996] 2 FLR 787.

BEST INTERESTS: NOT SUBSTITUTED DECISION AND RARELY, IF EVER, UNWISE

But it is all-important to recognise that a best interests decision is not a simple substituted decision – that is, an informed guess at what the person would have decided had they retained capacity. Certainly, it is possible that the best interests decision will coincide with what the person probably would have decided; but it may not do.

One way of explaining this is to point out that, with capacity, we are free to make unwise decisions, whereas a best interests decision will rarely, if ever, be unwise:

> I would add that although the fact that P makes an unwise decision does not on its own give rise to any inference of incapacity…once the decision making power shifts to a third party (whether carer, deputy or the court) I cannot see that it would be a proper exercise for a third party decision maker consciously to make an unwise decision merely because P would have done so. A consciously unwise decision will rarely if ever be made in P's best interests.[57]

Although even that principle begs the question of how one decides what is 'unwise' in any particular case.

BEST INTERESTS: DRAWING UP THE BALANCE SHEET

Over a number of years, even before the Mental Capacity Act arrived, the courts were being increasingly called on to make important welfare decisions about best interests, often involving potential or actual safeguarding issues – for example, about whether a woman with learning disabilities should be sterilised for non-therapeutic reasons,[58] where people with learning disabilities should live,[59] whether they have capacity to marry or have sexual relations,[60] or whether elderly people with dementia should remain at home, cared for by a spouse, or be admitted to hospital or care home.[61]

Both then and since, with the advent of the Act, the courts have often referred to what they call the balance sheet approach. That is, weighing up the pros and cons of a particular course of action. There are many cases in which this approach has been applied. Of course, drawing up such a balance sheet is not simply for the courts; it should be treated as a useful blueprint to be used by decision makers, such as local authorities and the NHS, to arrive at a defensible best interests decision.

In a recent case, treated as safeguarding, the local authority was determined not to allow a woman in her eighties to return from hospital to the care of her husband. The judge concluded the case by drawing up two columns, one of factors in favour

---

57   *In the matter of P* [2009] EWHC 163 (Chancery).
58   *SL v SL* [2000] 3 WLR 1288 (Court of Appeal).
59   *Newham London Borough Council v BS* [2003] EWHC 1909 (Fam).
60   *Sheffield CC v E* [2004] EWHC 2808 (Fam).
61   *B Borough Council v Mrs S* [2006] EWHC 2584 (Fam).

of her being deprived of her liberty in a nursing home, the other in favour of her returning home. Once the two columns were complete, the task was to consider which column was the weightier.[62]

BEST INTERESTS AND LESS OR LEAST RESTRICTIVE OPTION

A number of matters have been considered by the courts concerning best interests, the taking of a less restrictive approach and pitfalls to be avoided.

DANGERS OF DRASTIC INTERVENTIONS BY THE STATE

First, and generally, the courts have pointed out that, no matter how well intentioned, there are real dangers in drastic interventions by State bodies. And that the State should be wary of embarking upon social engineering and should not lightly interfere with family life, for fear the intervention itself may become abusive. In sum:

> At the end of the day, the simple point, surely, is this: the quality of public care must be at least as good as that from which the child or vulnerable adult has been rescued. Indeed that sets the requirement too low. If the State is to justify removing children from their parents or vulnerable adults from their relatives, partners, friends or carers it can only be on the basis that the State is going to provide a better quality of care than that which they have hitherto been receiving...
>
> The fact is that in this type of case the court is exercising an essentially protective jurisdiction. The court should intervene only where there is a need to protect a vulnerable adult from abuse or the real possibility of abuse... The jurisdiction is to be invoked if, but only if, there is a demonstrated need to protect a vulnerable adult. And the court must be careful to ensure that in rescuing a vulnerable adult from one type of abuse it does not expose her to the risk of treatment at the hands of the State which, however well intentioned, can itself end up being abusive of her dignity, her happiness and indeed of her human rights.
>
> That said, the law must always be astute to protect the weak and helpless, not least in circumstances where, as often happens in such cases, the very people they need to be protected from are their own relatives, partners or friends.[63]

COURTS REJECT STARTING POINT OF PEOPLE BEING BETTER OFF WITH THEIR FAMILIES

Second, it follows that, before deciding on a drastic course of intervention, the local authority should have drawn up the balance sheet (discussed above) and identified

---

62   *A London Local Authority v JH* [2011] EWHC 2420 (COP).
63   *Local Authority X v MM* [2007] EWHC 2003 (Fam).

weighty reasons why, for example, a person should be removed from his or her family home.

This approach led to the suggestion that there should be a 'starting point' that people are better off with their families. It seemed an intuitively correct approach, as set out by Mr Justice Munby in 2003, although it has since been rejected:

> I am not saying that there is in law any presumption that mentally incapacitated adults are better off with their families: often they will be; sometimes they will not be. But respect for our human condition, regard for the realities of our society and…common sense…surely indicate that the starting point should be the normal assumption that mentally incapacitated adults will be better off if they live with a family rather than in an institution – however benign and enlightened the institution may be, and however well integrated into the community – and that mentally incapacitated adults who have been looked after within their family will be better off if they continue to be looked after within the family rather than by the State.[64]

With this came a warning against the State embarking on social engineering:

> We have to be conscious of the limited ability of public authorities to improve on nature. We need to be careful…not to embark upon 'social engineering'… Other things being equal, the parent, if he is willing and able, is the most appropriate person to look after a mentally incapacitated adult; not some public authority, however well meaning and seemingly well equipped to do so… This is not to ignore or devalue the welfare principle; this common sense approach is in no way inconsistent with proper adherence to the unqualified principle that the welfare of the incapacitated person is, from beginning to end, the paramount consideration.[65]

However, the idea of such a starting point was later considered and rejected by the Court of Appeal in 2012, finding that it did not follow from article 8 of the European Convention (right to respect for family and private life). The argument in the case was that there was, currently, a normalisation agenda: 'that is to say intervention by professionals who promise to make the life of the incapacitated adult like other people's lives'. And that a corrective to such social engineering was to have a starting point or assumption that people lacking capacity were better off with their family. The court reacted strongly against this, pointing out that there was no such starting point or presumption in the Mental Capacity Act:

> Judges who try family cases of all types know how infinitely variable are the considerations that may need to be considered in determining what is in someone's best interests. The norms and values of society change over time, as do the ways available to attempt to meet people's needs. There

---

64   *Re S* [2003] 1 FLR 292.
65   *Re S* [2003] 1 FLR 292.

can be no substitute for a careful analysis of the evidence in the particular case. Factual disputes have to be determined and the recommendations and opinions of professionals evaluated in order to arrive at a conclusion. This is the everyday work of those who try cases involving children and, increasingly, it is becoming a routine exercise for those who sit in the Court of Protection. I would not wish to impose upon that exercise a structure which is not contained within the Act which confers the various powers and duties and dictates how they should be exercised.

It is, of course, of great importance that regard should be had to Article 8 when making decisions on behalf of an adult who lacks capacity. Article 8 declares a right to respect for private and family life, home and correspondence. Courts and local authorities are both public authorities and must not interfere with the exercise of that right except as Article 8(2) provides. It does not require a prescribed starting point to achieve compliance with that.[66]

Therefore, in short, the role of the court was to stick to the best interests test as set out in the Mental Capacity Act (which does not set out a presumption that people are better off with their families):

I conclude that the safe approach of the trial judge in Mental Capacity Act cases is to ascertain the best interests of the incapacitated adult on the application of the section 4 checklist. The judge should then ask whether the resulting conclusion amounts to a violation of Article 8 rights and whether that violation is nonetheless necessary and proportionate.[67]

In an earlier case, involving a woman with learning disabilities, the local authority wanted her to remain living at a residential unit where she enjoyed substantial social activities and opportunities. Her parents wanted her to live at home with them; otherwise, they threatened to sever contact altogether. The judge accepted that it was in her best interests for a shared care scheme to operate, but this was not at present possible because of the uncompromising stance of the parents. The parents currently lacked the ability to bring the best out of their daughter. Thus, her best interests would be served by full-time placement at the unit, but attempts should continue to be made to implement a shared care arrangement if the parents relented from their present position.[68]

None of this, however, has stopped the courts, in a number of cases involving older people, stressing the importance of a person's home. As the judge put it in one, when disagreeing with the local authority and a number of experts who had conducted assessments: 'There is, truly, no place like home, and the emotional

---

66   *K v LBX* [2012] EWCA Civ 79.
67   *K v LBX* [2012] EWCA Civ 79.
68   *A Local Authority v E* [2007] EWHC 2396 (Fam).

strength and succour which an elderly person derives from being at home, surrounded by familiar reminders of past life, must not be underestimated.'[69]

AVOIDING ASSUMPTIONS

Third, the courts will wish to ensure that, as section 4 of the Act states, assumptions about a person's best interests are not made on the basis of a person's condition.

AVOIDING TICK-BOX OR SUPERFICIAL APPROACHES TO BEST INTERESTS

Fourth, when the Act states that the decision maker has to consult with other relevant people – including, of course, the person lacking capacity – this is not to invite a tick-box approach, given the importance of getting things right when a person lacks capacity to take a major decision. In addition, of course, considering options, and in particular less or least restrictive options, may also take time and effort.

An example of how not to do this came in a much reported case involving the London Borough of Hillingdon, which had attempted to prevent a young man with learning disabilities from returning to live with his father. The judge criticised a series of best interests assessments which had taken place during the course of the year when the son had been deprived of his liberty. For instance, the following assessment had been completed on the basis of a communication of the greatest brevity with the father:

> On 21 June, the second DOL standard authorisation was granted. A different best interests assessor (BIA2) consulted Mr Neary. He describes her telephoning him at lunchtime for 10 minutes, saying that she had to file her report by 3 p.m. He says that to every point he raised she replied 'but Hillingdon say this…' He did not consider that she was carrying out a proper or independent assessment and lodged a complaint about her.[70]

Likewise, there was but cursory communication with the son:

> I have not heard evidence from BIA2, but I have read her assessment. She recommends a three-month period for deprivation of liberty. Substantial parts of her short report are cut and pasted from the previous best interests report. She appears to have had cursory contact with Steven on 21 June, the date her report was filed (even though it is unaccountably signed on 18 June). No reference is made to his wishes and feelings. No reference is made to Mr Neary's opposition to the placement. On the contrary, the following appears: 'I understand from my conversation with Mr M Neary that he believes the current care plan is positively supporting his son and his transitional programme.'[71]

---

69   *CC v KK* [2012] EWHC 2136 (COP).
70   *London Borough of Hillingdon v Neary* [2011] EWHC 1377 (COP).
71   *London Borough of Hillingdon v Neary* [2011] EWHC 1377 (COP).

And no consideration of a return home, which would have constituted a less restrictive option:

> No reference is made to the possibility of a placement at home alleviating the need for a deprivation of liberty. The recommendation is made for two conditions to be attached, one of which suggests that the three outstanding risk assessments for Steven's activities should be completed within eight weeks (in the context of a three-month deprivation recommendation). No reference is made to the absence of an IMCA, despite the condition in the previous standard authorisation, nor to the Court of Protection, despite the references in the previous assessment. I regret to say that the report has all the hallmarks of a document completed in a hurry.[72]

To cap it all, the granting of a further period of deprivation of liberty perpetuated the fiction that a proper and lawful assessment of best interests had been performed. The authorisation had in fact merely been a rubber stamping of a flawed best interests assessment:

> On the same day, when drafting reasons why the standard authorisation was in Steven's best interests, proportionate and necessary, the service manager wrote: *'Evidence exists of the managing authority's efforts to evaluate and manage the risks involved in the least restrictive way. The management strategy arrived at is proportionate and, at this time, represents the best approach to preventing harm.'* Again, the standard authorisation gives no clue to the real issue in this situation, even though it was well known to senior management by this time, and it was signed off by the Director on that day.[73]

EMOTIONAL AND PSYCHOLOGICAL FACTORS IN DECIDING BEST INTERESTS

Fifth, the courts have begun to query local authority decisions that they believe have placed an excessive emphasis on mechanistic, physical health and safety and failed to consider matters such as emotional and psychological welfare including happiness. Although balancing these can be genuinely difficult, local authorities have not helped themselves when a poor quality of decision making is added to the mix.

A cue has been taken from a judgment given under the inherent jurisdiction, prior to the Mental Capacity Act, in which Mr Justice Munby (as he then was) drew attention to the futility of making people safe but miserable:

> A great judge once said, 'all life is an experiment,' adding that 'every year if not every day we have to wager our salvation upon some prophecy based upon imperfect knowledge' (see Holmes J in *Abrams v United States* (1919) 250 US 616 at pages 624, 630). The fact is that all life involves risk, and the

---

72   *London Borough of Hillingdon v Neary* [2011] EWHC 1377 (COP).
73   *London Borough of Hillingdon v Neary* [2011] EWHC 1377 (COP).

young, the elderly and the vulnerable are exposed to additional risks and to risks they are less well equipped than others to cope with. But just as wise parents resist the temptation to keep their children metaphorically wrapped up in cotton wool, so too we must avoid the temptation always to put the physical health and safety of the elderly and the vulnerable before everything else. Often it will be appropriate to do so, but not always.

Physical health and safety can sometimes be bought at too high a price in happiness and emotional welfare. The emphasis must be on sensible risk appraisal, not striving to avoid all risk, whatever the price, but instead seeking a proper balance and being willing to tolerate manageable or acceptable risks as the price appropriately to be paid in order to achieve some other good in particular to achieve the vital good of the elderly or vulnerable person's happiness. What good is it making someone safer if it merely makes them miserable?[74]

More recently, a judge considered whether a woman in her eighties, having suffered two strokes and dementia, should return home to her husband. The balance sheet appraisal concluded overall that the physical standard of care would probably have been higher in a nursing home; but the emotional and psychological issues outweighed this factor and pointed to her best interests being in her own home:

In my view, the appropriate interim decision is that Mrs H returns home with a package of care of the kind summarised below. In coming to my decision, I have given consideration to all of the factors which I have referred to and analysed. The quality of Mrs H's relationship with her husband, the strength of their marriage, and the fundamental importance of that relationship to her happiness and indeed her care, have deserved considerable weight.[75]

The judge acknowledged the risks of her being cared for at home because the husband might struggle to manage sometimes and not always carry out tasks in line with good professional practice. However, he found that the benefits of being at home outweighed these risks:

I have tried to apply a 'pragmatic, common sense and robust approach to the identification, evaluation and management of perceived risk'. Having done so, I believe the risks associated with residence in a nursing home outweigh the risks involved in a return home, that the benefits of being at home are greater than the risks involved in being cared for there, and that these benefits are considerably more significant for Mrs H than the benefits of a nursing home. In both settings it is likely that she will receive less than optimal care, at home because realistically not all of the past disagreements

---

74   *Local Authority X v MM* [2007] EWHC 2003 (Fam).
75   *A London Local Authority v JH* [2011] EWHC 2420 (COP).

will be resolved overnight and simply evaporate into thin air, at the nursing home because she will resist and resent care and the disagreements remain.[76]

In reaching this decision, the judge also drew attention to a moving statement made by the husband. If nothing else, it highlights the difficulty in such cases for the local authority in trying to balance concerns about physical risk with deep-seated emotional factors. It is worth reproducing, *verbatim*, at some length:

What I will say is that I have been married to JH for over thirty years and during that time we have been devoted to one another. I do not consider it to be an understatement to say that we cannot live without each other and if the court went against my wife, mine and the wishes of her family and placed her in a nursing home I believe it would be the end of us. I do not say this lightly and I do not want this to be interpreted as a threat, it is a simple fact.

One thing I would wish to make clear is that this is our life, [JH] and mine, we have lived together happily for over thirty years and are still devoted to one another. The professionals involved have come into our lives and instead of trying to understand us they have tried to impose their thoughts about JH's care on us. These people will come and go, there will be different carers, social workers and district nurses that will come and go from our lives, but we are each other's constants. We are husband and wife and this is our life, this is not work, not something we will be involved in for a few months here and there before we move onto a new client but it is our life and the outcome of these proceedings have the ability to break up a loving family because we are considered to be difficult. I am made out to be causing harm to my wife, this is simply not true. The care I provide to my wife stems from the love and respect I have for her and the wish for her to be happy. The care I give her is not because I am being paid to do it. When I give her care I am not restrained in the time I can dedicate to her because I have several other service users that need my attention as would be the case if she were placed in a nursing home. The level of care I can provide for my wife will always be superior to that provided by people employed to provide it.

It can be seen that from the evidence of the local authority there has been no reference to any criticism of the care I have provided to her.

I know that I may come across as being difficult and that I may appear to be a stubborn man, but everything I have ever done has always been with the belief that I am doing in her best interests.[77]

Another case involved an 80-year-old man who had suffered from vascular dementia for 17 years brought on by alcohol damage. He had been living with a woman and her adult son who had at times both struggled to cope with caring for him; there had been compulsory hospital detention under both the Mental Health Act and the Mental Capacity Act. The hospital wanted him admitted to a care home and for the legal deprivation of his liberty to continue; his carers wanted him home. The judge

76   *A London Local Authority v JH* [2011] EWHC 2420 (COP).
77   *A London Local Authority v JH* [2011] EWHC 2420 (COP).

acknowledged that the physical care in the care home would be of a reasonable standard; refreshingly, however, he referred to the transitory, low-paid staff in care homes and how this was not conducive to the meeting of emotional needs:

> Very often in these Court of Protection cases those two matters pull in opposite directions, and this case is no exception. On the one hand, if the court goes down the line of authorising an admission to a care home, the court can be reasonably confident that all GM's physical and medical needs will be sufficiently and properly attended to. On the other hand, he will be one of several, many perhaps, depending upon the home, who are cared for by a staff which is not necessarily consistent in its personnel. It is well-known that care staff can often be quite transitory, coming, as they do, all too often, and no doubt regrettably, at the lower end of pay scales generally available, so that the emotional component, although not ignored, cannot begin to be met in the same way that it can if you achieve a placement within a family setting.[78]

The judge took all this into account, as well as the fact that the man was not expected to live very long. He noted the huge emotional significance of the decision:

> On the other hand, in the history of this case, such a placement contains a formidable emotional component which GM for over 20 years has clearly regarded as being of profound importance to him. These are the single most important relationships in his life. This is the place where he belongs, and where he matters in a sense that he could never matter in an institutional care setting. So in this case, as in many others, the court has this difficult balance to strike, difficult because you cannot compare like with like. This is very much a comparison of apples and pears and trying in the context of it to strike the best interests with as broad a view of those interests as it is possible to do.[79]

He went on to ask the stark question as to the starting point of why the man should not return home, before pointing out that if he were to go to a care home now, he would never return home, and nobody would ever know whether going home might have worked. Whereas if he returned home, at least then it would have been tried, even if it failed:

> If there is a placement in a care home, we will probably never know whether that was right or not. If there is a placement at home, we most certainly will discover whether it was right or wrong, and I specifically acknowledge that the court may be shown to have been wrong in the decision that it takes.[80]

---

78   *FP v GH and a Health Board*, January 2011, Liverpool Civil and Family Courts, case no.1193196.
79   *FP v GH and a Health Board*, January 2011, Liverpool Civil and Family Courts, case no.1193196.
80   *FP v GH and a Health Board*, January 2011, Liverpool Civil and Family Courts, case no.1193196.

What is of note is the last comment: it might not work. The court conceded that there was no way of guaranteeing 'success' in these types of case; there is no perfect solution.

A similar comment was made in the *JH* case, detailed above, when the judge said of the choice – between depriving the wife of her liberty in a care home and allowing her to return home to her husband – that there was 'no solution', in the sense of perfect solution:

> There is, of course, no solution. None of the options canvassed with the court will provide Mrs H with security, safety, liberty, happiness, an absence of suffering and an unrestricted home and family life. These different considerations cannot all be reconciled and promoted within a single setting, and the realisation of some of them must inevitably involve the sacrifice of others. The task is to choose which of these legitimate values and aims to compromise and which to give expression to, in Mrs H's best interests.[81]

Likewise, in another case of this type involving an elderly person, the court found that it would be in the best interests for a placement back at home to be tried, despite past difficulties which had included a pendant alarm going off accidentally, the police attending and their concern being such that both person and carer were admitted to hospital. It was noted by the judge that the return should be tried, even though it would be attended by 'a degree of pessimism', was contrary to the professional advice and might fail. The court also noted that paying heed to the least restrictive intervention involved an escalation of risk, to the extent of setting a 'lower standard in relation to the acceptability or manageability of risk and quality of care'.[82]

DANGER OF CONCERNS ABOUT RISK UNDERMINING PRINCIPLES OF MENTAL CAPACITY ACT

A further case concerned a woman (paralysed at the age of three, down one side, after a diphtheria inoculation) who wished to continue living in her village home.

She had rented it following the death of her husband. She was attached to her bungalow, the view (of village, church and tower) and to her porcelain dolls. The local authority was adamant that she should instead reside in a care home. The professional experts all judged that she lacked the capacity to make a decision. Yet she had provided the court with an articulate explanation of her wishes and her understanding of the risks involved.

The judge decided against the local authority and in the woman's favour; namely, that she had capacity to take the decision herself. The judge noted, in particular, that the local authority was concerned about her excessive use of an emergency

---

81   *FP v GH and a Health Board*, January 2011, Liverpool Civil and Family Courts, case no.1193196.
82   *Re GC* [2008] EWHC 3402 (COP).

lifeline contact number and also her failure always to eat and drink adequately. Yet neither was indicative of a lack of capacity:

> Ultimately, however, I am not persuaded that calling an emergency service because one feels the need to speak to someone in the middle of the night, without fully understanding that one has that need or the full implications of making the call, is indicative of a lack of capacity to decide where one lives.
>
> Another factor which features strongly in the local authority's thinking is KK's failure to eat and drink. Here again, however, I conclude that more could be done to address this issue by written notes and reminders, and by paying greater attention to KK's likes and dislikes. KK is not the only older person who is fussy about what she eats and drinks.

The judge pointed out the danger of professionals consciously or subconsciously attaching excessive weight to their own views about protecting her physical safety, without giving sufficient weight to her (in fact, capacitated) views of how her emotional needs should be met.[83]

MOTIVATION TO BRING ABOUT DEATH

The code of practice explains that in case of deciding about best interests and life-sustaining treatment, the decision maker must not be motivated to bring about the death of the person. However, if treatment is futile, overly burdensome or there is no prospect of recovery, a decision may sometimes be made that further life-sustaining treatment is not in the person's best interests. However, this would not be the same as being motivated to bring about the person's death, even if this is from a sense of compassion. By the same token, this rule cannot be interpreted to mean that doctors are obliged to provide life-sustaining treatment where this is not in the person's best interests.[84]

DEPRIVATION OF LIBERTY

The question about deprivation of liberty of people lacking the capacity to consent has been pronounced for over ten years, since a major legal case in the mid-1990s. Following an extended legal saga, the government amended the Mental Capacity Act 2005, so as to put in place safeguards.

Such safeguards can cut two ways. First, depriving a person of liberty, when he or she lacks the capacity to decide, is a major intervention but may be the only realistic means of protecting a person. Equally, however, drastic interventions can go wrong. In which case, the local authority or NHS body may believe that it is protecting a person from harm, but in fact ends up subjecting the person to greater harm.

---

83   *CC v KK* [2012] EWHC 2136 (COP).
84   Lord Chancellor. *Mental Capacity Act 2005: code of practice.* London: TSO, 2007, paras 5.31–5.33.

BACKGROUND TO DEPRIVATION OF LIBERTY AND THE LAW

In the mid-1990s, the English courts held that in the case of a mentally incapable, but compliant, person, it was not necessary that he or she be formally sectioned under the 1983 Act in order to effect a deprivation of liberty. The common law of best interests and necessity sufficed, making lawful what would otherwise be unlawful. The courts decided this, though, with some unease because of the absence of formal safeguards.

Removal to hospital. A 48-year-old man had been autistic since birth. He was unable to speak, required 24-hour care and was unable to go outside alone. He had no ability to communicate consent or dissent to treatment or to express preferences as to where he should live. He was frequently agitated, had no sense of danger and had a history of self-harm. From the age of 13, for over 30 years, he was resident at a hospital. He was then discharged on a trial basis into the community, going to live with paid carers.

Taken to hospital, compliant but mentally incapacited. One day, he was attending a day centre and became agitated and was banging his head against a wall and hitting his head with his fists. The day centre got in touch with a local doctor who came and administered a sedative; the social worker with overall responsibility for him was contacted and recommended that he be taken by ambulance to accident and emergency. There, after further agitation, a psychiatrist assessed that he needed inpatient treatment. However, it was decided that he could be admitted informally, rather than making use of s.2 or s.3 of the 1983 Act, because he appeared to be fully compliant and did not resist admission. He subsequently remained in hospital for several months on this informal basis, before eventually being formally detained (after the Court of Appeal had ruled his informal detention to be unlawful) and then discharged a few weeks later.

A fairy tale. The House of Lords, overruling the Court of Appeal, held that it was permissible to admit informally to hospital (s.131 of the Mental Health Act 1983) patients who lacked the capacity to consent but who did not positively object. The court stated that the removal, care and treatment of the person had been in his best interests and was justified by the common law doctrine of necessity, which was not excluded by the provisions of the 1983 Act. Nevertheless, one of the law lords pointed out that this conclusion was not wholly satisfactory, since it meant that the formal safeguards contained in the Mental Health Act did not apply to this particular class of vulnerable informal patient. In addition, although the majority of the court ruled that he had not in fact been detained, the minority pointed out that to suggest the man had been free to leave was a 'fairy tale'.[85]

The case was then taken to the European Court of Human Rights, which found that the man had been deprived of his liberty in breach of article 5 of the European Convention on Human Rights because of the lack of legal safeguards – that is, the deprivation had not been in accordance with an adequate procedure prescribed by law, since the common law doctrine of necessity lacked fair and proper procedures.[86]

Between the European Court ruling in *HL v UK* and the coming into force of the 'authorisation' legal rules (see below), the courts made clear that – in this interim period – a court order, with built-in reviews, represented the necessary

---

85   *R v Bournewood Community and Mental Health NHS Trust, ex p L* [1998] 1 CCLR 390 (House of Lords).
86   *HL v United Kingdom* [2004] 40 EHRR 761 (European Court of Human Rights).

safeguard to prevent human rights being breached.[87] Such an order could authorise proportionate restraint where necessary – for example, in the context of an order providing for the assessment in hospital of a person with severe, complex and uncontrolled epilepsy.[88]

DEPRIVATION OF LIBERTY: PERMITTED UNDER THE MENTAL CAPACITY ACT 2005

The Mental Capacity Act 2005 does not authorise any person to deprive any other person of his or her liberty, subject to certain exceptions, in which case the Act applies specific safeguards. These safeguards were added by the Mental Health Act 2007, which amended the 2005 Act.

Deprivation of liberty is defined in the MCA 2005 with reference to article 5 of the European Convention on Human Rights and applies whether the deprivation is publicly or privately funded.[89] The only lawful way to deprive a person of his or her liberty is either through an authorisation procedure contained within the Act and applied by local authorities or the NHS, or by a court order, normally from the Court of Protection.

Both the European Court and the English courts, have found it hard to define and apply the concept of deprivation of liberty. The difference between deprivation of and restriction of liberty is one of degree or intensity, not one of nature or substance. Relevant issues include type, duration, effects and manner of implementation.[90]

Inevitably, practitioners and lawyers look for clear rules of thumb to determine whether a person is being deprived of his or her liberty. To date, those rules have been elusive.

The following paragraphs try to encapsulate the issues. The legal picture is fuzzy. The law continues to develop.

DEPRIVATION MUST, BY DEFINITION, BE IN A PERSON'S BEST INTERESTS

The significance of depriving a person of his or liberty is that, if legally sanctioned, it allows very significant curtailment of a person's autonomy and freedom of movement. In proportion to such a curtailment, legal safeguards are triggered over and above the application of the best interests test, together with the less or least restrictive option test under s.1 of the Mental Capacity Act. The safeguards are contained either within the authorisation procedure operated by local authorities and NHS bodies under the MCA, or by means of a court order under the Act.

---

87   *City of Sunderland v PS* [2007] EWHC 623 (Fam).

88   *A Primary Care Trust v P* [2008] EWHC 1403 (Fam).

89   Mental Capacity Act 2005, s.64.

90   *Engel v Netherlands* [1979–80] 1 EHRR 647. And: *Guzzardi v Italy* [1981] 3 EHRR 333.

In sum, a deprivation of liberty must be in a person's best interests; it also follows that it will not be in the person's best interests if consideration has not been given to a less restrictive option.

THE FACT THAT A DEPRIVATION IS IN A PERSON'S BEST INTERESTS DOES NOT MAKE IT ANY LESS A DEPRIVATION

By definition, deprivation of liberty must be in a person's best interests. So too must restriction (i.e. falling short of deprivation) of liberty. To suggest, therefore, that a care regime would not be a deprivation of liberty if it were in a person's best interests is quite wrong. It would make no sense logically or legally. Because if either deprivation or restriction is not in a person's best interests, then it is not consistent with the Mental Capacity Act.

This might seem obvious, but even the courts sometimes seem to become ensnared. For instance, in a case concerning a woman with learning disabilities who required surgery for cancer, the question arose of using force and sedating her in order to convey her to hospital, followed by the need 'to detain' her post-operatively to ensure recovery. The judge, the President of the Family Division of the High Court, stated that all this would not give rise to a deprivation of liberty. On the face of it, the reasoning as to why there was no deprivation is difficult if not impossible to understand: 'If it is in P's interests (as it plainly is) to have the operation, it is plainly in her interests to recover appropriately from it.'[91]

IMPORTANCE OF BEST INTERESTS AND LESS RESTRICTIVE OPTIONS

As already stated, given the sometimes fine line between deprivation and restriction, the crucial issue is that (a) decisions are made in a person's best interests, and (b) consideration has been given to less restrictive options.

This is because these two considerations apply whether or not the person is being deprived of liberty.[92]

Furthermore, these are the most substantial considerations relating to the welfare of the person; if a local authority, for example, has got these right but got the label wrong – by treating the situation as deprivation when it isn't or vice versa – the courts are unlikely to be unduly critical.

In one case, for example, a High Court judge decided there was a deprivation of liberty; then the Court of Appeal decided there was not. But, notably, the actual restrictions contained in the person's care plan were criticised by neither court because they could be shown to be in the person's interests.[93]

This was in contrast to the *Hillingdon* case discussed above, when the local authority not only got the label wrong but the substantive care was wrong as well. First, for some four months, it deprived the man concerned of his liberty but did

91   *DH NHS Foundation Trust v PS* [2010] EWHC 1217 (Fam).

92   *A Local Authority v PB* [2011] EWHC 2675 (COP).

93   *Chester West and Chester Council v P* [2011] EWCA Civ 1257.

not call it deprivation and so did not attempt to follow the legal rules. Second, for the next seven months, it continued to deprive of him his liberty; this time, it recognised that this was what it was doing. It invoked the deprivation of liberty legal safeguards but did not apply them properly. Third, and crucially, in both periods, the substantive care plan was not in his best interests and proper consideration had not been given to the less restrictive option of trying to get him back to his father.[94]

The courts have also suggested, in cases of uncertainty, that a standard authorisation should be granted. This would authorise – but not necessitate – deprivation as and when and if needed.[95]

OBJECTIVE ELEMENT, SUBJECTIVE ELEMENT AND AGENCY OF THE STATE REQUIRED IF HUMAN RIGHTS ARE TO BE ENGAGED

The courts have pointed to a threefold requirement for deprivation of liberty under the Mental Capacity Act. The Act defines deprivation of liberty as having the same meaning as in article 5 of the European Convention on Human Rights. So, for there to be deprivation of liberty under the Act, there must be:

- an objective element of a person's confinement in a restricted space for a not negligible length of time

- a subjective element, in that the person has not validly consented

- the deprivation must be imputable to the State.[96]

OBJECTIVE ELEMENT OF DEPRIVATION

Each individual situation needs to be considered as to whether a person is being deprived of liberty:

> In order to determine whether someone has been 'deprived of his liberty' within the meaning of Article 5, the starting point must be his concrete situation and account must be taken of a whole range of criteria such as the type, duration, effects and manner of implementation of the measure in question.[97]

Whether doors are locked, or even lockable, is not decisive.[98] In one case, a local authority had threatened to call the police if a person tried to leave a care home, but later argued that it was an empty threat. The judge maintained that the threat, empty or otherwise, pointed to deprivation of liberty:

> These threats, whether or not they were as devoid of legal content as [Surrey County Council] would now have us believe, were intended to achieve and,

94   *London Borough of Hillingdon v Neary* [2011] EWHC 1377 (COP).
95   *A Local Authority v PB* [2011] EWHC 2675 (COP).
96   *JE v DE and Surrey CC* [2006] EWHC 3459 (Fam).
97   *Guzzardi v Italy* [1981] 3 EHRR 333.
98   *HL v United Kingdom* [2004] 40 EHRR 761.

as it seems to me, did achieve, the desired objective of preventing DE's removal first from the X home and then from the Y home. A person can be as effectively 'deprived of his liberty' by the misuse or misrepresentation of even non-existent authority as by locked doors and physical barriers.[99]

Yet, in a different case, a locked door every night in the family home did not constitute a deprivation of liberty.[100] The context was entirely different.

RESTRICTIONS ON ALL FREEDOM OF MOVEMENT OR CONTACT

Objective confinement does not necessarily mean that all freedom of movement or social contact is restricted. A man in a care home could see his wife in the care home and could also go out. But he could not, and was not allowed to, do the one thing that he and his wife wanted, which was for him to return home. This was deprivation of liberty.[101]

ORDINARY HEALTH AND SAFETY MEASURES IN A CARE HOME

Ordinary health and safety measures will not necessarily amount to a deprivation of liberty.

In one case, the judge concluded that a man who had been placed in a care home may have had his liberty restricted but he had not been deprived of it. Restriction, as opposed to deprivation, of liberty does not amount to a breach of article 5 of the European Convention. Some of the relevant factors the court took into account were that:

> (a) the care home was an ordinary care home where only ordinary restrictions of liberty applied; (b) the family was able to visit on a largely unrestricted basis and could take him on outings; (c) the man was personally compliant and expressed himself happy; (d) there was no occasion on which he was objectively deprived of his liberty.[102]

HAPPINESS

Happiness cannot by itself mean that a deprivation is not taking place: 'a person's happiness, as such, is not relevant to whether she is deprived of her liberty'.

But, equally, signs of unhappiness might indicate a deprivation, if only because the more unhappy and opposed a person is to the care regime being imposed, the more likely is conflict to arise – including physical restraint and tussles. And such conflict would be an indicator of a deprivation of liberty, in the objective sense.[103]

---

99 *JE v DE and Surrey CC* [2006] EWHC 3459 (Fam).
100 *A Local Authority v A and B* [2010] EWHC 978 (Fam).
101 *JE v DE and Surrey CC* [2006] EWHC 3459 (Fam).
102 *LLBC v TG* [2007] EWHC 2640 (Fam).
103 *P & Q v Surrey CC* [2011] EWCA Civ 190.

MEDICATION

Administration of medication may indicate deprivation:

> In my view the administration to a person of medication, at any rate of antipsychotic drugs and other tranquilisers, is always a pointer towards the existence of the objective element: for it suppresses her liberty to express herself as she would otherwise wish. Indeed, if the administration of it is attended by force, its relevance is increased. Furthermore, in that objections may be highly relevant, medication which has the effect of suppressing them may be relevant to an equally high degree. But again, conversely, the absence of medication is a pointer in the other direction.[104]

CONTINUOUS SUPERVISION AND CONTROL

This may indicate deprivation of liberty, as occurred on a hospital ward in the well-known *Bournewood* case:

> ...between 22 July to 29 October 1997, the applicant was under continuous supervision and control and was not free to leave. It made no difference whether the ward in which he was being treated was locked or lockable. The Court therefore concluded that the applicant was 'deprived of his liberty', within the meaning of Article 5.1, during this period.[105]

However, that case was in the context of not being free to leave and being subject to severe restrictions. It is by no means clear that continuous supervision and control, alone, is necessarily deprivation. There are some situations in which such supervision and control may be allowing the person freedom of movement and the ability to engage in everyday activities – as was the case of a young man with learning disabilities. He required a very high level of supervision and control, but could wander freely in the bungalow and gardens, attended a day centre regularly and went on outings.[106]

PURPOSE AND REASONS

Cautiously, the courts have allowed that the objective purpose of care arrangements may be relevant as to whether there is a deprivation of liberty. However, at the time of writing, there is legal uncertainty about this question (see discussion immediately below about motive, context and circumstances).

In one case, involving two women, one living in a family home, the other in a small home with three other residents, the High Court considered there was no deprivation because the purpose of the arrangements was not to treat but to receive care:

---

104   *P & Q v Surrey CC* [2011] EWCA Civ 190.
105   *HL v United Kingdom* (2004) 40 EHRR 761 (European Court of Human Rights).
106   *Chester West and Chester Council v P* [2011] EWCA Civ 1257.

I treat with extreme caution the suggestion that purpose is relevant in this type of case, save that it does seem to me to be realistic to put into the equation when trying to discern the factual matrix and whether these girls are objectively deprived of their liberty, that both girls were placed in their respective placements as children in need, because they need homes, rather than because they require restraint, or treatment. It is also relevant in my view to consider the reasons why they are under continuous supervision and control.[107]

The Court of Appeal linked this to the normality of the living arrangements in question.

In another Court of Appeal case, objective purpose and reasons were allowed as relevant as to whether there is deprivation. For example, if a husband restricts the movements of his wife in the marital home because she has dementia (the reason) and for her safety (the purpose), this will not be a deprivation. If he confines her (as happened in an older court case), however, because she is denying him what he perceived to be his conjugal rights (the reason), in order to enforce those perceived rights (the purpose), then there would be a deprivation.[108]

MOTIVE

Motives are generally not relevant. So a good motive does not mean that a deprivation is not taking place, but a bad motive may be enough to create deprivation of liberty:

An improper motive or intention may have the effect that what would otherwise not be is in fact, and for that very reason, a deprivation of liberty. But a good motive or intention cannot render innocuous what would otherwise be a deprivation of liberty. Putting the same point another way, good intentions are essentially neutral. At most they merely negative the existence of some improper motive or intention. That is all.[109]

In a 2012 case about police, demonstrators and 'kettling' (penning of the demonstrators by the police), the European Court stated that motive was irrelevant as to whether deprivation of liberty was taking place:

Indeed, it is clear from the Court's case-law that an underlying public interest motive, for example to protect the community against a perceived threat emanating from an individual, has no bearing on the question whether that person has been deprived of his liberty, although it might be relevant to the subsequent inquiry whether the deprivation of liberty was justified under one of the subparagraphs of Article 5.1.[110]

---

107 *P & Q v Surrey CC* [2011] EWCA Civ 190.
108 *Chester West and Chester Council v P* [2011] EWCA Civ 1257.
109 *Chester West and Chester Council v P* [2011] EWCA Civ 1257.
110 *Austin v United Kingdom*, March 2012, European Court of Human Rights, case nos. 39692/09, 40713/09 and 41008/09.

TYPE OF RESTRICTION, MANNER OF IMPLEMENTATION, SPECIFIC CONTEXT AND SURROUNDING CIRCUMSTANCES

The European Court, in the same kettling case about public order, went on to state, however, that type of restriction, manner of implementation, specific context and surrounding circumstances were all relevant as to whether there is a deprivation of liberty – *at least in public order situations.*

These four characteristics could, via the backdoor as it were, allow purpose and motivation back into the picture, even though, in principle, motive is irrelevant. More difficult is to know how the English courts and European Court would apply these considerations to deprivation of liberty in health and social care.

> However, the Court is of the view that the requirement to take account of the 'type' and 'manner of implementation' of the measure in question...enables it to have regard to the specific context and circumstances surrounding types of restriction other than the paradigm of confinement in a cell... Indeed, the context in which action is taken is an important factor to be taken into account, since situations commonly occur in modern society where the public may be called on to endure restrictions on freedom of movement or liberty in the interests of the common good. As the judges in the Court of Appeal and House of Lords observed, members of the public generally accept that temporary restrictions may be placed on their freedom of movement in certain contexts, such as travel by public transport or on the motorway, or attendance at a football match... The Court does not consider that such commonly occurring restrictions on movement, so long as they are rendered unavoidable as a result of circumstances beyond the control of the authorities and are necessary to avert a real risk of serious injury or damage, and are kept to the minimum required for that purpose, can properly be described as 'deprivations of liberty' within the meaning of Article 5.1.[111]

SETTING: NORMALITY, HOMELINESS

The courts have steered towards saying that the more normal, and homely, the setting, the less likely will there be a deprivation of liberty. At one end of the spectrum, the family home, small children's home or nursing home, and, at the other, a hospital designed for compulsory detention:

> For, by her reference to the provision for the girls of *care* in a *home*, the judge was by implication stressing the relative normality of the living arrangements under scrutiny. If the person is living with her parents or other members of his natural family in their home, she is living – in that respect – the most normal life possible. Typically – but sadly not always – there will be no deprivation of liberty in such circumstances... Not much less normal for this

---

111 *Austin v United Kingdom*, March 2012, European Court of Human Rights, case nos. 39692/09, 40713/09 and 41008/09.

purpose is the life of a child in the home of foster parents or of an adult, such as Mr HL, in the home of carers... But, even when the person lives in an institution rather than in a family home, there is a wide spectrum between the small children's home or nursing home, on the one hand, and a hospital designed for compulsory detentions like *Bournewood*; and it is in my view necessary to place each case along it.[112]

The courts have reviewed the settings that would tend less to result in deprivation of liberty and those that would tend more. But, clearly, even then, setting is not absolutely determinative. The following is extracted from the Court of Appeal's judgment in the *Chester* case, and Lord Justice Munby's encapsulation of the spectrum of settings for deprivation of liberty:

The family home: *Re A and C (Equality and Human Rights Commission Intervening)*...concerned two young, unrelated, women, one still a child, the other an adult, both of whom suffered from Smith Magenis Syndrome. Each lived at home with her family. I held that neither was deprived of her liberty.

Foster and analogous placements: *Re MIG and MEG*...concerned two young sisters, MIG (P), who was 18 at the time of the hearing before Parker J, and MEG (Q), who was 17. Both suffered from learning disabilities. At the time of the hearing before Parker J, MIG was living in foster care. Parker J held that she was not deprived of her liberty. This court upheld her decision.

Sheltered accommodation: I have already summarised the circumstances in *Re MIG and MEG*. At the time of the hearing before Parker J, MEG was living in a small specialist home for adolescents of which she was one of four residents. Parker J held that she was not deprived of her liberty. This court upheld her decision.

A children's home: In *Re RK (Minor: Deprivation of Liberty)*...a 17½ year old girl suffering from autism, ADHD and severe learning difficulties was placed in a children's home which...did not involve a deprivation of liberty.

An 'ordinary' care home: In *LLBC v TG, JG and KR*...TG, an elderly man of 78 suffering from dementia and cognitive impairment, had been placed in...'an ordinary care home where only ordinary restrictions of liberty applied'. He held that there was no deprivation of liberty, although adding... that the circumstances 'may be near the borderline'. It may be noted that TG was described by the judge as being 'personally compliant' and 'objectively content with his situation there'.

A residential special school: In *C (by his litigation friend the Official Solicitor) v A Local Authority and LM, LPM*...a child, now 18, with severe autism, severe learning difficulties and extreme challenging behaviours, had been placed in

---

a residential special school under a regime which Ryder J held…involved a deprivation of liberty.

A support unit: In *London Borough of Hillingdon v Neary*…a man of 21 with childhood autism and a severe learning disability was placed in a support unit which Peter Jackson J found to involve a deprivation of liberty. 'Key features', according to the judge, were…'his objection to being at the support unit, the objection of his father, and the total effective control of [his] every waking moment in an environment that was not his home'.

Two cases lie towards the other end of the spectrum: The first is *HL v United Kingdom*, the original *Bournewood* case. The facts are too familiar to require elaboration. HL was an informal patient in a mental hospital. The Strasbourg court held that he had been deprived of his liberty. The central core of its reasoning is…: 'the key factor in the present case [is] that the health care professionals treating and managing the applicant exercised complete and effective control over his care and movements… The…applicant would only be released from the hospital to the care of Mr and Mrs E as and when those professionals considered it appropriate… Accordingly, the concrete situation was that the applicant was under continuous supervision and control and was not free to leave.'

The other case is *DE v JE and Surrey County Council*…where I was concerned with DE, an elderly man of 75 who, following a stroke, suffered from short term memory loss and dementia and had been placed in a residential care home. I identified the crucial issue as follows…'the crucial question in this case…is not so much whether (and, if so, to what extent) DE's freedom or liberty was or is curtailed within the institutional setting. The fundamental issue…is whether DE…has been and is deprived of his liberty to leave the Y home…in the sense of removing himself permanently in order to live where and with whom he chooses, specifically removing himself to live at home with [his wife].'

I continued…'he is being "deprived of his liberty" by being prevented from returning to live where *he* wants and with those *he* chooses to live with, in other words at home and with [his wife]… Just as HL was, in the view of the Strasbourg court, deprived of his liberty…so in very much the same way DE…is being deprived of his liberty. The simple reality is that DE will be permitted to leave the institution in which [the local authority] has placed him and be released to the care of [his wife] only as and when…[the local authority] considers it appropriate.'[113]

---

113 *Chester West and Chester Council v P* [2011] EWCA Civ 1257.

NORMALITY AND COMPARATOR

So, linked to the question of setting are the questions of 'normality' and also 'comparator'. On normality:

> Of course the enquiry into normality transcends an enquiry into the residential arrangements. Of potentially great relevance in the case of children or young adults is whether, as would be normal almost irrespective of the degree of any disability, they go out to some sort of school or college; and, in the case of other adults, whether they go out to college or to a day centre or indeed in order to pursue some form of occupation… Furthermore, as I have shown, stress was laid in the cases both of *HL* and of *Storck* on the restrictions placed on outside social contact, i.e., another major aspect of normal life.[114]

The courts have now gone further, in what, for some, is a controversial direction, by stating that normality is to be measured in the context of a person's disability. So that what would be deprivation for one person might not be for another:

> In determining whether or not there is a deprivation of liberty, it is always relevant to evaluate and assess the 'relative normality' (or otherwise) of the concrete situation. But the assessment must take account of the particular capabilities of the person concerned. What may be a deprivation of liberty for one person may not be for another. In most contexts (as, for example, in the control order cases) the relevant comparator is the ordinary adult going about the kind of life which the able-bodied man or woman on the Clapham omnibus would normally expect to lead.
>
> But not in the kind of cases that come before the Family Division or the Court of Protection. A child is not an adult. Some adults are inherently restricted by their circumstances. The Court of Protection is dealing with adults with disabilities, often, as in the present case, adults with significant physical and learning disabilities, whose lives are dictated by their own cognitive and other limitations.
>
> In such cases the contrast is not with the previous life led by X (nor with some future life that X might lead), nor with the life of the able-bodied man or woman on the Clapham omnibus. The contrast is with the kind of lives that people like X would normally expect to lead. The comparator is an adult of similar age with the same capabilities as X, affected by the same condition or suffering the same inherent mental and physical disabilities and limitations as X. Likewise, in the case of a child the comparator is a child of the same age and development as X.[115]

---

114 *P & Q v Surrey CC* [2011] EWCA Civ 190.
115 *Chester West and Chester Council v P* [2011] EWCA Civ 1257.

RESTRICTIONS TO PREVENT HARM, AND NOWHERE ELSE REALISTIC TO LIVE

The courts have suggested also that restrictions to keep a person safe (e.g. in relation to epileptic fits) might not amount to deprivation, especially if there is nowhere else realistic for him or her to live.

Thus, despite a man's violent attempts to kick his way out of a care home, the court felt that the restrictive care regime was normal for somebody like him, and so did not constitute a deprivation of liberty. He had been placed in the care home, subject to a guardianship order under the Mental Health Act 1983 and also a standard authorisation of deprivation of liberty under the Mental Capacity Act 2005. He was near to the border of having capacity; in fact, he had a janitorial role in the care home. To give a flavour:

> In January 2011, the police were called after Mr C had kicked down a door when trying to leave the care home. As a result, assessments were carried out and a standard DOLS authorisation was issued on 23 January 2011 for 12 months. This was reviewed in May 2011, and some less stringent controls on Mr C's visits to his family were substituted. In the same month there was an incident of aggression by Mr C towards a female staff member.
>
> As Mr C's guardian, the LA has required him to live at the care home, which has locked doors. Mr C has 1:1 supervision inside and outside the home, including when on trips to his family (this at their request). Such trips out of the home are frequent, nearly daily, but are limited by the availability of the supervising staff, who have other responsibilities. When Mr C tries to leave unsupervised, distraction techniques are employed. His mood is controlled by antipsychotic medication.

The man wanted both the guardianship and deprivation of liberty orders lifted. An independent social worker had concluded that, in his best interests, he should be in a different environment, which would include rehabilitation and ultimately being supported to live in the community again. The judge concluded that there was in fact no deprivation, only a restriction, of liberty. This was on the basis that the restrictions were for his own safety and that realistically there was nowhere else for him to go.

The problem with this judgment is that it is no longer clear just what circumstances would constitute a deprivation of liberty:

> I accept that Mr C is acutely anxious about the restraints upon him, being more aware of his predicament than the subjects of previous reported cases. On the other hand, the restraints upon him within and outside the care home are relatively lighter. The existence of locked doors and a requirement of supervision are not in themselves a deprivation of liberty, where their purpose is to protect a resident from the consequence of an epileptic fit, or harm caused by a lack of awareness of risk, or from self-harm. The limit on the number of outings as a consequence of staffing levels does not tip the

balance, when Mr C in fact has quite regular access to the community and to his family.

I reach this conclusion after consideration of Mr C's particular circumstances and the guidance given in the Cheshire case. One feature mentioned in that decision…is the difference it makes if a person has somewhere else to go and wants to live there. In the present case Mr C undoubtedly wants to live somewhere else, but this is a reflection of his unhappiness with the care home. He would like to be able to live an unconfined life in the community, but this is not realistically possible due to the extent of his difficulties. I distinguish his situation from those where a person has been removed from a home that is still realistically available. While Mr W's suggestion of another unit is consistent with Mr C's wish to leave the care home, it does not represent an actual alternative at the present time.[116]

NORMALITY AND INVOLVEMENT IN THE COMMUNITY

The idea of normality is reinforced if there is interaction of the person within the wider community, which may then be a further counter-indicator of deprivation of liberty.[117] So the restrictions, including close supervision imposed on a person, may actually be empowering if they enable him or her to participate in the community:

> Of course, the enquiry into normality transcends an enquiry into the domestic arrangements. A vital aspect is the nature and extent of P's participation in and interaction with the wider community outside Z House [local authority bungalow for four residents], whether in terms of education or occupation, social contact, sport or other outdoor activities. But the evidence in relation to this is clear. Not merely is P, when he is at Z House, living a life which is as normal as it can be for someone in his situation, his life outside Z House is as normal as it can be for someone, to use Smith LJ's phrase, with his capabilities.[118]

SUBJECTIVE ELEMENT OF DEPRIVATION

Consent or compliance by a person in giving up himself or herself for detention is not determinative; there could still be a deprivation of liberty.[119] But, clearly and in any case, a person who lacks capacity to consent or to comply cannot do so in a legally meaningful way.[120]

The courts will sometimes take objections to the deprivation as indicator that a deprivation of liberty is required, especially when there is somewhere else realistic

116 *C v Blackburn with Darwen Borough Council* [2011] EWHC 3321 (COP).

117 *P & Q v Surrey CC* [2011] EWCA Civ 190.

118 *Chester West and Chester Council v P* [2011] EWCA Civ 1257.

119 *HL v United Kingdom* [2004] 40 EHRR 761.

120 *Storck v Germany* [2005] ECHR 406.

for the person to live. In a case involving where an elderly woman should live, a care home or her own home, the judge noted:

> Her physical and mental state, on the information I have read, are and have been deteriorating. She is also clearly at risk of falls and of causing herself physical harm. She has been expressing and continues to express a wish that she wishes to go home and live in her house in Loughborough... The most recent report before me, for reasons which I regard as compelling internally to it, indicates that HA does not have capacity to make decisions as to where she should live, as to her medical care, as to her property and affairs and relating to litigation... Notwithstanding that report, the continuing expression by HA of a wish to go home is a major factor in the argument that by being prevented from leaving the care home for her safety and the safety of others she is or may be being deprived of her liberty.[121]

USE OF DOLS AUTHORISATION BY LOCAL AUTHORITIES: NOT TO BE USED TO OVERRULE FAMILY MEMBERS

The deprivation of liberty safeguards contained within the Act, and exercisable by local authorities or the NHS, should not be used simply to overrule, for example, family members who are opposed to the care regime being proposed or implemented. Where there is such a conflict, then an application should be made to the Court of Protection:

> Significant welfare issues that cannot be resolved by discussion should be placed before the Court of Protection, where decisions can be taken as a matter of urgency where necessary. The DOL scheme is an important safeguard against arbitrary detention. Where stringent conditions are met, it allows a managing authority to deprive a person of liberty at a particular place. It is *not* to be used by a local authority as a means of getting its own way on the question of whether it is in the person's best interests to be in the place at all. Using the DOL regime in that way turns the spirit of the Mental Capacity Act 2005 on its head, with a code designed to protect the liberty of vulnerable people being used instead as an instrument of confinement. In this case, far from being a safeguard, the way in which the DOL process was used masked the real deprivation of liberty, which was the refusal to allow Steven to go home.[122]

REASONABLE FORCE

Reasonable force can be used in terms of reasonable and proportionate measures.[123]

---

121 *Re HA* [2012] EWHC 1068 (COP).
122 *London Borough of Hillingdon v Neary* [2011] EWHC 1377 (COP).
123 *City of Sunderland v PS* [2007] EWHC 623 (Fam).

DEPRIVATION OF LIBERTY SAFEGUARDS IN THE MENTAL CAPACITY ACT

These apply only to care homes and hospitals. Deprivation elsewhere has to be authorised by the courts.

DEPRIVATION MUST BE IMPUTABLE TO THE STATE

Where a local authority or NHS body places a person in some sort of accommodation, hospital, care home or supported living, then obviously the State is involved.

However, if the deprivation is occurring, for example, in a family setting, what is the role of the State and what are the human rights implications? The courts have put it this way:

> Where the State – here, a local authority – knows or ought to know that a vulnerable child or adult is subject to restrictions on their liberty by a private individual that arguably give rise to a deprivation of liberty, then its positive obligations under Article 5 will be triggered.[124]

DEPRIVATION OF LIBERTY SAFEGUARDS: RULES FOR AUTHORISATION

The Mental Capacity Act 2005 stipulates that a person lacking capacity can only be deprived of his or her liberty in limited circumstances.

Such rules are all about making sure that people are not arbitrarily deprived of a fundamental right of autonomy and freedom to make choices. Arbitrary detention and its consequences themselves are safeguarding matters. The circumstances are as follows.

First, if the Court of Protection has made an order (for deprivation in a hospital, a care home or anywhere else).

Second, if the deprivation in a hospital or care home has been 'authorised' by a local authority (or, hitherto, an NHS primary care trust) under the deprivation of liberty safeguards (DOLS) set out in the Act.

Third, if the deprivation relates to life-sustaining treatment or a vital act, whilst a decision is being sought from the Court of Protection. A vital act is defined as doing anything which the person doing it reasonably believes to be necessary to prevent a serious deterioration in the person's condition.[125]

These rules means that if a person is being deprived of his or her liberty somewhere other than a care home or hospital (e.g. in family home or in supported living), then it will be anyway necessary to seek a Court of Protection order because authorisation applies only to deprivation in hospitals or care homes.

Department of Health guidance is clear that if there are long-term issues about contact between the person lacking capacity and other people, probably an

---

124 *A Local Authority v A and B* [2010] EWHC 978 (Fam).
125 Mental Capacity Act 2005, ss.4A–4B.

application should be made to the Court of Protection. It notes that, in any case, restrictions on contact would not necessarily constitute a deprivation of liberty.[126]

STANDARD AUTHORISATION BY LOCAL AUTHORITIES OR THE NHS

A 'supervisory body' is defined as a local authority or NHS primary care trust (but only until PCTs are abolished, probably in April 2013). It can authorise the deprivation of a person's liberty in a hospital or care home – but only if certain 'qualifying requirements' are met. This is called 'standard authorisation'.[127]

The qualifying requirements for such a deprivation are defined in terms of a number of assessments. These assessments relate to the person's age, mental health, mental capacity, best interests, 'eligibility' and 'no refusals'. In summary:

(a) **Age:** The person must be at least 18 years old.

(b) **Mental health:** The person must be suffering from a mental disorder as defined in the Mental Health Act 1983. However, the exclusions in the Mental Health Act 1983 for people with learning disabilities do not apply. (The 1983 Act excludes, for certain purposes, people with learning disabilities from the definition of mental disorder, unless their disability is associated with abnormally aggressive or seriously irresponsible conduct.)

(c) **Mental capacity:** Lack of mental capacity must relate to the person's incapacity to decide whether to be accommodated in a hospital or care home in order to receive care or treatment.

(d) **Best interests:** To establish whether it is in the person's best interests to be detained, the detention is required to prevent harm to the person, and the detention is a proportionate response to the risk of harm (in terms of seriousness and likelihood of that harm).

(e) **Eligibility:** This is to do with whether authorisation is prohibited under the Mental Capacity Act 2005 because the Mental Health Act 1983 must be used instead to detain the person. This is summarised below.

(f) **No refusals:** This concerns whether the person has made a valid 'advance decision' (see below) which is applicable to some or all of the relevant treatment. Alternatively, it is about whether receiving care or treatment in a care home or hospital would conflict with a valid decision made by the donee of a lasting power of attorney or a deputy appointed by the Court of Protection. In either case, deprivation of liberty would not be possible under the Act.[128]

---

126 Department of Health. *The Mental Capacity Act 2005 Deprivation of Liberty Safeguards – the early picture.* London: DH, 2010, paras 19–22.

127 Mental Capacity Act 2005, schedule A1.

128 Mental Capacity Act 2005, schedule A1, paras 12–20.

DEPRIVATION OF LIBERTY: MENTAL HEALTH ACT 1983

It is not legally possible to deprive a person of liberty under the Mental Capacity Act 2005 if, instead, the Mental Health Act 1983 must be used to effect such a deprivation. Whether this is the case is assessed under the 'eligibility' qualifying requirement which has to be assessed by the supervisory body.

This rule applies also to any order made by the Court of Protection.

A person is not eligible to be deprived of his or her liberty under the Mental Capacity Act 2005 if any of the following applies. The rules are complicated. In summary, they are:

(a) **Detention:** He or she is subject to detention under the Mental Health Act (under ss.2, 3, 4, 17, 35, 36, 37, 38, 44, 45A, 47, 48, 51).

(b) **Not detained:** He or she is subject to the hospital treatment regime but not detained. This means on leave of absence from detention (s.17) or conditionally discharged (ss.42, 73), *and* (i) the action to be authorised under the 2005 Act is inconsistent with a requirement in place under the 1983 Act, or (ii) the care or treatment required consists in whole or in part of medical treatment for mental disorder in a hospital.

(c) **Community treatment order:** He or she is subject to supervised community treatment (s.17A) or subject to a community treatment order, *and* (i) the action to be authorised under the 2005 Act is inconsistent with a requirement in place under the 1983 Act, or (ii) the care or treatment required consists in whole or in part of medical treatment for mental disorder in a hospital.

(d) **Guardianship:** He or she is subject to guardianship and (i) the action to be authorised under the 2005 Act is inconsistent with a requirement in place under the 1983 Act, or (ii) the authorisation under 2005 Act would mean the person becoming a mental health patient in hospital for medical treatment for mental disorder, *and* the person objects to being a mental health patient or to being given some or all of the mental health treatment, *and* no valid consent has been given by a person with a lasting power of attorney or a deputy appointed by the Court of Protection.

(e) **Within the scope of the Mental Health Act:** He or she is within the scope of the 1983 Act (i.e. would meet the criteria for detention under s.2 or s.3), *and* the authorised action under the 2005 Act would make him or her a mental health patient in hospital for treatment for mental disorder, *and* the person objects to being a mental health patient or to being given some or all of the mental health treatment, *and* no valid consent has been given by a person with a lasting power of attorney or a deputy appointed by the Court of Protection.[129]

---

129 Mental Capacity Act 2005, schedule A1.

In determining whether the person objects, his or her behaviour, wishes, feelings, views, beliefs and values must be considered. Past circumstances are only to be had regard to insofar as it is still appropriate to do so. But any such objection can be overridden (and the 2005 Act still be used) if a donee of a lasting power of attorney or a deputy has validly consented to the detention and treatment.

All this is complex. It is beyond the scope of this book to go into detail, but the following examples give a flavour. In one case, a woman required a neuropsychiatric assessment and treatment but was objecting. However, the deprivation of liberty was to take place in a care home, rather than a hospital. This meant the deprivation would be under the Mental Capacity Act rather than the Mental Health Act.

Deprivation of liberty in a care home for assessment and treatment. A woman with a very rare bone disorder and a brain injury needed a neuropsychiatric assessment and treatment. She objected to being at the institution in question, which was a care home rather than a hospital. The question was whether she should therefore be deprived of her liberty under the Mental Capacity Act or the Mental Health Act 1983. She appeared to come within category (e) above. However, that refers to her being a mental health patient – and that in turn requires being accommodated in a hospital. The care home was not a hospital, so (e) did not apply, and it was the Mental Capacity Act 2005 that should apply, the woman's objections to being at the care home notwithstanding.[130]

In a further case, the question arose whether a man with a mental disorder, requiring hospital treatment for his diabetes, should be deprived of his liberty under mental health or mental capacity legislation. The court held that the physical condition did not flow from the mental disorder and that treatment for it would not directly affect the mental disorder. Therefore, the detention and treatment for it in hospital lay under the Mental Capacity Act 2005.[131]

TREATMENT FOR A PHYSICAL DISORDER

The eligibility rules above concern *deprivation of liberty*. But a separate question arises about *treatment* of a person lacking capacity. First is the question of treatment for physical disorder.

If a person lacks capacity and requires treatment for a physical disorder, the general rule is that the treatment must be given under the Mental Capacity Act 2005, even if, for example, the person is already detained in hospital under the Mental Health Act 1983.

However, even this may not always be straightforward. If physical treatment flows from or will directly affect the mental disorder – for which a person is, or could be, detained under the Mental Health Act 1983 – then the detention and treatment might come under the 1983 Act rather than the Mental Capacity Act 2005.

---

130 *W PCT v TB* [2009] EWHC 1737 (Fam).
131 *GJ v The Foundation Trust* [2009] EWHC 2972 (Fam).

In one case, a caesarean section could come within the Mental Health Act 1983 because it was viewed as part of the treatment of the person's mental disorder.[132] Equally, in other cases, such an intervention would most definitely not come under the Mental Health Act.[133] Likewise, nasogastric tube feeding to avert starvation flowing from self-harm (associated with a borderline personality disorder) amounted to treatment for the person's mental disorder under the 1983 Act.[134]

On the other hand, proposed amputation of the leg of a schizophrenic man was not treatment for mental disorder and could not come under the 1983 Act. In fact, it could not be carried out at all because he had mental capacity to take the decision about his leg.[135]

In more recent case, a man was detained in hospital. He suffered from diagnosis of vascular dementia, Korsakoff's syndrome and amnestic disease due to alcohol. He also had diabetes. He lacked the capacity to take a decision about treatment for the latter. The judge posited the question as to why, fundamentally, did he need to be in hospital. The answer was the diabetes. And because the diabetes was not caused by the mental disorder and because treatment for the diabetes would not alleviate the mental disorder, both the detention and treatment fell under the Mental Capacity Act.[136]

TREATMENT FOR MENTAL DISORDER: WHICH ACT?

Next is the question about treatment for a mental disorder and which Act should be used.

The short answer is that patients cannot be given treatment for mental disorder under the Mental Capacity Act if their treatment is regulated by Part 4 of the Mental Health Act – that is, they are liable to be detained under the 1983 Act or are under a community treatment order.[137] This includes patients on leave of absence. However, it does not include emergency, very short-term detention provisions or conditional discharge under the 1983 Act; people under these provisions would be subject to treatment under the 2005 Act. People under guardianship may be treated under the 2005 Act.

There are one or two provisos. For all patients, certain highly invasive treatments cannot in any case be given under the 2005 Act; they are subject to the safeguards of s.57 of the 1983 Act. Section 57 covers surgical operation for destroying (the functioning of) brain tissue.

And, under s.58A of the 1983 Act, electroconvulsive therapy can only be given to a person lacking capacity (even if the other conditions under s.58A for treatment

132 *Tameside and Glossop Acute Services Trust v CH* [1996] 1 FLR 762.
133 *R v Collins, Pathfinder Mental Health Services NHS Trust and St George's Healthcare NHS Trust, ex p S* [1998] 1 CCLR 578 (Court of Appeal).
134 *B v Croydon Health Authority* [1995] WLR 294.
135 *Re C (Adult: Refusal of Treatment)* [1994] 1 WLR. 290.
136 *GJ v The Foundation Trust* [2009] EWHC 2972 (Fam).
137 Mental Capacity Act 2005, ss.28–28(1A).

are met) if the treatment does not conflict with a valid and applicable advance decision made by the person (under the 2005 Act) or with a decision made by a donee of a lasting power of attorney or a deputy appointed by the Court of Protection.

PROCEDURAL RULES FOR STANDARD AUTHORISATIONS DEPRIVING A PERSON OF LIBERTY

If the qualifying requirements are met, deprivation of liberty may follow if the 'supervisory body' (local authority or NHS) has given a standard authorisation. A 'managing authority' will request that the supervisory body grant an authorisation.

At the time of writing, in the case of a hospital, the PCT will be identified as supervisory body if it is commissioning the relevant care or treatment, or if it is the PCT for the area in which the hospital is situated. In the case of a care home, the local authority will be identified as supervisory body according to where the relevant person is ordinarily resident. If the person is not ordinarily resident within a local authority, then it is the local authority for the area in which the care home is situated.

However, when changes in the Health and Social Care Act 2012 come into force, the local authority will be the supervisory body even in the case of hospitals.[138]

A managing authority, in respect of a hospital, is the NHS body with responsibility for the administration of the hospital – for example, an NHS trust or NHS foundation trust. In the case of an independent hospital, the managing authority is the person registered under the Health and Social Care Act 2008.

Managing authority in respect of a care home means the person registered under the Health and Social Care Act 2008.[139]

REQUEST FOR STANDARD AUTHORISATION

A supervisory body cannot give a standard authorisation unless requested by the managing authority of the relevant hospital or care home, or asked by a third party. A managing authority must request a standard authorisation if it appears to it that the person is already being detained or likely to be so within the next 28 days:

- is not yet accommodated in the relevant hospital or care home but is likely to be a detained resident within the next 28 days and meet the qualifying requirements, or

- is already accommodated in the relevant hospital or care home, is likely to be detained within the next 28 days and is likely to meet the qualifying requirements, or

---

138 Health and Social Care Act 2012, s.136, as it amends para 180 of schedule A1 of the Mental Capacity Act 2005.
139 Mental Capacity Act 2005, schedule A1, paras 175–182.

- is already a detained resident and meets the qualifying requirements or is likely to in the next 28 days. Likewise, a request must be made if an authorisation already exists but there is to be change in the place of detention.

A request to the supervisory body is not necessary if a court order authorises detention of the person. But if a Court of Protection order authorising deprivation of liberty is about to expire, then a request must be made by the managing authority before the expiry.[140]

CARRYING OUT ASSESSMENTS FOR STANDARD AUTHORISATION

The supervisory body must ensure that assessments are carried out in relation to all the qualifying requirements.[141]

The Act sets out in detail what the best interests assessor must do. This includes consulting the relevant managing authority, and having regard to (a) the mental health assessor's conclusions, (b) any relevant needs assessment, and (c) any relevant care plan. He or she must also state the maximum authorisation period (which can be no more than one year).[142]

However, if there are existing (no older than 12 months) assessments which meet all the requirements, and there is no reason to doubt their accuracy, then the supervisory body does not have to ensure that new assessments are carried out. In deciding the question of continuing accuracy in respect of best interests assessment, information provided by the person's personal representative (or independent mental capacity advocate (IMCA) specially appointed for the purpose) must be taken into account.[143]

ASSESSORS FOR STANDARD AUTHORISATIONS AND REVIEWS

It is for the supervisory body to select a person to carry out an assessment in connection with a request for a standard authorisation or a review. Regulations carry details about the suitability and eligibility of people to carry out assessments. The same person must not be selected to carry out both the mental health and best interests assessments.[144]

Regulations state that supervisory bodies have to be satisfied about the skills and experience of assessors. Mental health assessors must be approved under s.12 of the Mental Health Act 1983 or be a registered medical practitioner, with (to the satisfaction of the supervisory body) special experience in the diagnosis and treatment of mental disorder.

Best interests assessments can be carried out by approved mental health professionals (under s.114 of the Mental Health Act 1983), registered social

---

140 Mental Capacity Act 2005, schedule A1, paras 21–27.
141 Mental Capacity Act 2005, schedule A1, para 33.
142 Mental Capacity Act 2005, schedule A1, paras 38–45.
143 Mental Capacity Act 2005, schedule A1, para 49.
144 Mental Capacity Act 2005, schedule A1, paras 126–136.

workers, first-level nurses in mental health or learning disabilities, occupational therapists or chartered psychologists.

Mental capacity assessments can be carried out by anybody eligible to carry out a mental health or best interests assessment. The supervisory body cannot appoint certain people as assessors – for example, those with a financial interest in the care of the person (any close relative or somebody with such a financial interest). There are further restrictions on who can be best interests assessors; they may not be involved with the care of the person or employed in the care home or hospital where the detention takes place.[145]

ASSESSMENTS: TIME AND INFORMATION

Regulations also set out timeframes. Assessments must be completed within 21 days of the supervisory body receiving a request for a standard authorisation. If the managing authority has given an urgent authorisation, and a standard authorisation is now sought, the assessments must be completed during the period of the urgent authorisation.

Requests for a standard authorisation must contain the information set out in the regulations. If a question arises about the ordinary residence of the person, and thus about responsibility for authorisation, the local authority body receiving the request should act as supervisory body until the question is resolved, unless the other authority agrees to do this.[146]

GIVING A STANDARD AUTHORISATION

If all the assessments are positive and written copies are in the hands of the supervisory body, it must give a standard authorisation.

Such authorisation must be in writing, stating the name of the relevant person, the name of the hospital or care home, the period of the authorisation, the purpose, any conditions, the reason why each qualifying requirement is met. A copy must be given to the relevant person's personal representative (or IMCA), the managing authority, the person themselves and every interested person consulted by the best interests assessor. Likewise, if an authorisation is not granted.[147]

Although the Act states that the supervisory body must make the authorisation if all the assessments are positive, there is a proviso. In the *Hillingdon* case, the judge was at pains to point out how the best interests assessment was the cornerstone of the whole process and that supervisory bodies should not be rubber-stamping such assessments but scrutinising them for thoroughness. So it by no means follows that authorisation must be granted if the best interests assessment is shoddy:

---

145 SI 2008/1858. Mental Capacity (Deprivation of Liberty: Standard Authorisations, Assessments and Ordinary Residence) Regulations 2008.

146 SI 2008/1858. Mental Capacity (Deprivation of Liberty: Standard Authorisations, Assessments and Ordinary Residence) Regulations 2008.

147 Mental Capacity Act 2005, schedule A1, paras 50–58.

Although the framework of the Act requires the supervising body to commission a number of paper assessments before granting a standard authorisation, the best interests assessment is anything but a routine piece of paperwork. Properly viewed, it should be seen as a cornerstone of the protection that the DOL safeguards offer to people facing deprivation of liberty if they are to be effective as safeguards at all.

The corollary of this, in my view, is that the supervisory body that receives the best interests assessment must actively *supervise* the process by scrutinising the assessment with independence and with a degree of care that is appropriate to the seriousness of the decision and the circumstances of the individual case that are or should be known to it.

Paragraph 50 provides that a supervisory body must give a standard authorisation if all assessments are positive. This obligation must be read in the light of the overall scheme of the schedule, which cannot be to require the supervisory body to grant an authorisation where it is not or should not be satisfied that the best interests assessment is a thorough piece of work that adequately analyses the four necessary conditions.[148]

EFFECT OF STANDARD AUTHORISATION

If an authorisation is granted, a number of rules then come into play concerning, in summary:

- the managing authority ensuring the person understands (if practicable) his or her right to make a court application, to request a review or to have an IMCA appointed

- the supervisory body keeping a written record

- restrictions on variation of the authorisation

- the seeking of a new standard authorisation

- coming into force and cessation of a standard authorisation.[149]

UNAUTHORISED DEPRIVATION OF LIBERTY

If it appears that a person is being deprived of his or her liberty without authorisation as set out in s.4A of the Act, an 'eligible person' (anybody other than the relevant managing authority and with an interest in the person's welfare) may request that the supervisory body decide whether there is an unauthorised deprivation of liberty. A number of conditions attach to such a request. The supervisory body has to appoint somebody to assess, unless the request appears vexatious or frivolous, or the issue has previously been decided and there has been no change of circumstance.[150]

---

148 *London Borough of Hillingdon v Neary* [2011] EWHC 1377 (COP).
149 Mental Capacity Act 2005, schedule A1, paras 59–65.
150 Mental Capacity Act 2005, schedule A1, paras 67–69.

URGENT AUTHORISATION

In addition to standard authorisations are 'urgent authorisations'. These may be given by a managing authority (hospital or care home) if the need is so urgent that there is no time to request, or at least to obtain, a standard authorisation. The maximum period of an urgent authorisation is seven days.

A number of rules apply: the authorisation must be in writing, certain details must be included, certain people must be notified. Extension of an urgent authorisation – up to a further seven days – can be requested of the supervisory body by the managing authority. The supervisory body may grant this extension if it appears that the management authority has requested a standard authorisation, there are exceptional reasons why no decision has yet been reached, and it is essential for the existing detention to continue.[151]

SUSPENSION AND REACTIVATION OF STANDARD AUTHORISATION

If a person ceases to meet a qualifying requirement, provision is made for a standard authorisation to be suspended – and to be reactivated if the person becomes eligible once again within 28 days.[152]

REVIEWING A STANDARD AUTHORISATION

Review of a standard authorisation may be made at any time by the supervisory body. However, it must conduct a review if requested by the person themselves, their representative or the managing authority of the relevant hospital or care home. These can ask for a review at any time. Managing authorities are under a duty to make such a request if any of the qualifying requirements appear to be reviewable (age, mental health, mental capacity, best interests, no refusals).

Qualifying requirements are reviewable on the grounds that the person no longer meets any one of them. This might be because the actual reason as to why the person meets the requirement is not the reason stated in the standard authorisation; or because there has been a change in the person's case and it would be appropriate to vary the conditions to which the authorisation is subject.[153]

RELEVANT PERSON'S REPRESENTATIVE AND INDEPENDENT MENTAL CAPACITY ADVOCATES

First, the supervisory body must appoint a person to be the 'relevant person's representative' as soon as practicable after a standard authorisation is given – if it appears that the representative would maintain contact with, represent and support the person. The functions of any such representative do not affect the authority of any donee, deputy or powers of the court. The functions of the representative are to maintain contact with, represent and support the person lacking capacity. They

151 Mental Capacity Act 2005, schedule A1, para 84.
152 Mental Capacity Act 2005, schedule A1, paras 91–97.
153 Mental Capacity Act 2005, schedule A1, paras 101–107.

are additional to, and do not affect, the appointment and functions of a donee of a lasting power of attorney and do not affect the powers of the court.[154]

SECTION 39A IMCA

Second, if a person becomes subject to the authorisation provisions, and the managing authority is satisfied that there is nobody (other than a person engaged in providing care or treatment for the person in a professional capacity or for remuneration) appropriate to consult about the person's best interests, then it must notify the supervisory authority. The latter must then instruct an independent mental capacity advocate (IMCA). A person becomes 'subject' to the authorisation provisions if an urgent authorisation is given or a request for standard authorisation is made.[155]

SECTION 39C IMCA

Third, if an authorisation is in force, and the appointment of a representative ends, or the managing authority is satisfied that there is nobody (other than a person engaged in providing care or treatment for the person in a professional capacity or for remuneration) appropriate to consult about the person's best interests, it must notify the supervisory body. The latter must then instruct an independent mental capacity advocate (IMCA) to represent the person. This appointment ends when a new representative is appointed.[156]

SECTION 39D IMCA

Lastly, an IMCA must be appointed if an authorisation of deprivation of liberty is in force under schedule A1, there is an appointed representative, that representative is not being paid and the following applies. First, the person lacking capacity or the representative requests an advocate, or, second, the supervisory body has reason to believe (a) that without the help of an advocate, the person and the representative would be unable to exercise their right to apply to court or right of review, or (b) that the person and the representative have failed, or are unlikely to exercise such rights, when it would have been (or would be) reasonable to exercise them.[157]

It was the failure to appoint a section 39D IMCA, when the father and son were struggling to deal with the latter's deprivation of liberty by the London Borough of Hillingdon, that contributed to the local authority's legal downfall in that case.[158]

---

154 Mental Capacity Act 2005, schedule A1, paras 137–141.
155 Mental Capacity Act 2005, ss.39A–39B.
156 Mental Capacity Act 2005, s.39C.
157 Mental Capacity Act 2005, s.39D.
158 *London Borough of Hillingdon v Neary* [2011] EWHC 1377 (COP).

RULES ABOUT APPOINTMENT OF PERSONAL REPRESENTATIVE

Regulations prescribe eligibility conditions and procedure for the appointment of a representative. For example, the representative must be 18 years or over, be able to keep in contact with the person, be willing, not be financially interested in the managing authority (or not be related to somebody who is so financially interested), not be linked through work to the managing authority.

If the person is judged by the best interests assessor to have the capacity, the person can select a family member, friend or carer as his or her representative. In case of lack of capacity, a donee or deputy with relevant powers can select. If the person, or the donee or the deputy, does not want to select somebody, then the best interests assessor can do so, but this is subject to the objection of the person, donee or deputy. Failing all this, the supervisory body may select a representative to perform the role in a professional capacity, with satisfactory skills and experience, who is not a family member, friend or carer, and who is not employed to work in the managing authority or supervisory body.

Procedural matters are also covered in the draft regulations, including a number of grounds for termination.[159]

MONITORING OF THE SAFEGUARDS

The Act allows for regulations to be made giving a monitoring body, the Care Quality Commission, the power to report generally on the operation of the deprivation of liberty safeguards, to visit hospitals and care homes, to visit and interview people accommodated in hospitals and care homes, and to require the production of, and to inspect, records.[160]

ACTS IN CONNECTION WITH CARE OR TREATMENT

Section 5 of the Mental Capacity Act provides a general defence for people providing care or treatment for a person lacking capacity. This might be an important safeguard if, for example, in a safeguarding context, somebody had to act in haste to protect a person, and did so reasonably, but hindsight revealed an error about either the person's capacity or his or her best interests.

A person is protected from liability if he or she does an act in connection with care or treatment, and he or she took reasonable steps to establish that the person lacked capacity in respect of the matter in question and reasonably believed that the person lacked that capacity and that it was in his or her own best interests that the act be done.

---

159 SI 2008/1315. Mental Capacity (Deprivation of Liberty: Appointment of Relevant Person's Representative) Regulations.

160 Mental Capacity Act 2005, schedule A1, para 162.

However, this does not exclude civil liability for loss or damage, or criminal liability arising from negligence in doing the act.

And section 5 does not provide protection to the extent of overriding an advance decision or a decision made by a person with lasting power of attorney or by a deputy appointed by the Court of Protection.

The code of practice points out that simply because somebody has come to an incorrect conclusion about a person's capacity or best interests does not mean that he or she will not be protected from liability. But they must 'be able to show that it was reasonable for them to think that the person lacked capacity and that they were acting in the person's best interests at the time they made their decision or took action'.[161]

As a consultant psychiatrist has put it, decisions regarding mental capacity and best interests should be carefully documented, not least because there may be, in many cases, no 'right answer', and good documentation will go a long way in protecting both patient and doctor.[162]

The protection from liability is in respect of both civil and criminal liability that could otherwise arise from doing things for or to a person without his or her consent. For instance, as the code of practice points out, a carer dressing a person without the latter's consent could theoretically be prosecuted for assault. A neighbour entering and cleaning the house of a person lacking capacity to give permission could be trespassing on the person's property.[163]

The code gives a non-exhaustive list of the sort of actions that are covered by way of care under s.5. These include help with washing, dressing, personal hygiene, eating, drinking, communication, mobility, and with a person's taking part in education, social or leisure activities. Also included are going to a person's house to see if they are all right, doing the shopping with the person's money, arranging household services, providing home help services, undertaking actions related to community care services (e.g. day care, care home accommodation, nursing care) and helping a person move home.

Health care and treatment might include diagnostic examinations and tests, medical or dental treatment, medication, taking a person to hospital for assessment or treatment, nursing care, other procedures or therapies (e.g. physiotherapy or chiropody), emergency care.[164]

Wide as section 5 goes, there are limits. When police removed a person with a mental disorder from her home, under what should have been s.135 of the Mental Health Act 1983, they purported to act under ss.5 and 6 of the Mental Capacity Act 2005. When the woman got to hospital, she was placed in the s.136 suite, and staff

---

161 Lord Chancellor. *Mental Capacity Act 2005: code of practice*. London: TSO, 2007, para 5.59.
162 Hotopf, M. 'The assessment of mental capacity.' *Clinical Medicine*, November/December 2005, p.580.
163 Lord Chancellor. *Mental Capacity Act 2005: code of practice*. London: TSO, 2007, para 6.2.
164 Lord Chancellor. *Mental Capacity Act 2005: code of practice*. London: TSO, 2007, para 6.5.

understood s.136 of the 1983 Act to be the basis of the detention. The court noted that ss.5 and 6 of the Mental Capacity Act 2005 could not be used, alternatively as it were, for the purposes of ss.135 and 136 of the Mental Health Act.[165]

LIMITATIONS ON RESTRAINT AND ON SECTION 5

The Act permits restraint of a person lacking capacity, but only if certain conditions are met. As already explained, a legal distinction needs to be made between a restriction of liberty, which comes under s.6 of the MCA, and deprivation of liberty and the specific rules attaching to it.

It is particularly important that practitioners understand the rules about restraint and that it is permitted in certain circumstances. A failure to understand this led local authority staff in one case to tamper with the notes of a resident of who was subject to restraint when required – for example, to excavate bits of incontinence pad and faeces, which he was in the habit of eating, from his mouth. The irony was that the staff interfered with the recorded care plan because of their apparent misunderstanding about the law and lost their jobs. Yet, ultimately, the courts – both the High Court and Court of Appeal – found no fault with the care plan, including the restraint for which it provided.[166]

Section 6 of the MCA states that (bracketed headings added):

- **[prevention of harm]** to restrain a person and be protected under s.5, the person (the restrainer) must reasonably believe it is necessary to prevent harm to the person lacking capacity

- **[proportionality]** the response must be proportionate in relation to the likelihood of the person suffering harm and the seriousness of that harm

- **[definition]** restraint involves use or threats to use force to secure the doing of an act which the person resists – or restriction of liberty of the person's movement whether or not the person resists

- **[conflict with attorney's or deputy's decision]** section 5 does not authorise an act which conflicts with a decision made, by a donee of a lasting power of attorney or a court-appointed deputy (within the scope of the donee's or deputy's authority). But this does not stop a person providing life-sustaining treatment, or doing any act·which he or she believes necessary to prevent a serious deterioration in the person's condition – while a decision about any relevant issue is sought from the court.[167]

165   *R(Sessay) v South London and Maudsley NHS Foundation Trust* [2011] EWHC 2617 (Admin).
166   *Chester West and Chester Council* [2011] EWHC 1330 (Fam). And: *Chester West and Chester Council v P* [2011] EWCA Civ 1257 (Court of Appeal).
167   Quoted from: Mental Capacity Act 2005, s.6.

The code of practice points out that the common law also imposes a duty of care on health care and social care staff to take appropriate and necessary action to restrain or remove a person – with challenging behaviour or who is in the acute stages of illness – who may cause harm to themselves or other people.[168]

Past cases, when the court applied the common law along similar lines, involved just such a weighing up of factors and justification for the proposed restraint. For instance, it might be lawful to impose treatment and overcome resistance by sedation and reasonable use of restraint if the treatment (a total hysterectomy) was in the patient's best interests. Nonetheless, a careful balancing of benefit and disadvantage had to take place, and care needed to be taken that the patient's human right (under article 3 of the European Convention on Human Rights) was not thereby infringed.[169]

Similarly, the court accepted that the administering of a general anaesthetic, in order to carry out a CT scan on an uncooperative patient lacking capacity, was permissible and would be compliant with human rights, given the doctor's evidence that the nurses were trained in safe restraint techniques and that this usually led to uneventful anaesthesia.[170]

As already indicated above, the line between deprivation of liberty and restraint may be a fine one.

Restraint cases are summarised and discussed in Chapter 26.

PAYMENT FOR NECESSARY GOODS AND SERVICES (SECTION 7)

Section 7 of the Mental Capacity Act is about a person entering into a contract for goods or services, even though he or she lacks the capacity to do so.

It states that if necessary goods or services are supplied to a person lacking capacity to contract for them, the person must nevertheless pay a reasonable price for them. 'Necessary' means suitable to a person's condition in life and to his or her actual requirements at the time when goods or services are supplied.

The code of practice explains that, in general, a contract entered into by a person lacking capacity cannot be enforced if the other person knows, or should have known, about the lack of capacity. The Act modifies this rule by stating that such a contract is anyway enforceable if the goods or services contracted for are 'necessary'.[171]

A Tribunal has held that a tenancy could legally qualify as a necessary service under s.7 of the Act; if it was wrong about that, then a tenancy could fall into the common law definition of a 'necessary' – the common law rule surviving in case the MCA rule did not stretch that far. The Tribunal referred to an old Court of Appeal case from 1890:

---

168 Lord Chancellor. *Mental Capacity Act 2005: code of practice*. London: TSO, 2007, para 6.43.

169 *Trust A v H (An Adult Patient)* [2006] EWHC 1230 (Fam).

170 *Doncaster & Bassetlaw Hospitals NHS Trust & Anor v C* [2004] EWHC 1657 (Fam).

171 Lord Chancellor. *Mental Capacity Act 2005: code of practice*. London: TSO, 2007, para 6.57.

The Court of Appeal concluded that the provision of the accommodation in the asylum was a necessary and that in appropriate circumstances the lady could have come under an obligation implied by law to repay the balance... The members of the Court of Appeal all emphasised that the obligation to repay did not arise by way of implied contract. As put by Cotton LJ at p.105 'whenever necessaries are supplied to a person who by reason of disability cannot himself contract, the law implies an obligation on the part of such person to pay for such necessaries out of his own property... But, then, although there may be an implied obligation on the part of the lunatic, the necessaries must be supplied under circumstances which would justify the Court in implying an obligation to repay the money spent upon them.'[172]

EXPENDITURE: PLEDGE OF PERSON'S EXPENDITURE (SECTION 8)

Under s.8 of the Mental Capacity Act, in relation to section 5 (care or treatment), it is lawful for the carer to pledge the person's (who lacks capacity) credit for the purpose of expenditure or to use money in the person's possession. The carer can reimburse himself or herself from money in the person's possession or be otherwise indemnified by the second person. The code of practice explains that the carer could use cash that the person lacking capacity may have, or use his or her own money with a view to being paid back by the person lacking capacity.[173]

LASTING POWER OF ATTORNEY (SECTIONS 9–14)

A donee of a lasting power of attorney is able to take various decisions for a person (the donor) lacking capacity. These decisions can include a range of finance and welfare matters. Some attorneys will abuse their power and this may give rise to safeguarding and protection concerns. So it is worth setting out some of the key legal points below. And it seems to be not uncommon, even if there are not clear safeguarding issues, for attorneys to misunderstand the scope of their legal power and to seek to take decisions that they have no legal power to take.

A number of conditions must be fulfilled for such a power to valid. In addition, the power can be revoked by the Court of Protection on a number of grounds, including the situation where the power is being misused.

Sections 9–14 of the Mental Capacity Act cover lasting power of attorney, in summary:

(a) **Capacity and age of donor:** A person, the donor, is able to create a lasting power of attorney, whilst he or she retains the capacity to do so, and must be at least 18 years old.

172 *Wychavon District Council v EM*, Upper Tribunal, January 2012, CH/171/2011.
173 Lord Chancellor. *Mental Capacity Act 2005: code of practice.* London: TSO, 2007, para 6.61.

(b) **Scope of power:** Such a lasting power can give the attorney authorisation to deal with property and financial affairs, as well as personal welfare matters (including health care decisions) when the donor no longer has capacity.

(c) **Prescribed form:** The power must be contained in an instrument of a certain form and must be registered with the Public Guardian; otherwise, it is not effective.

(d) **Principles of Act apply:** A lasting power of attorney is subject to the provisions of the Act, in particular the principles in s.1 of the Act, as well as any conditions or restrictions specified in the instrument (s.9).

(e) **Age of donee:** A donee must be at least 18 years old.

(f) **Attorneys acting jointly or severally:** Attorneys may be appointed to act jointly, jointly and severally – or jointly in respect of some matters and jointly and severally in respect of others (s.10).

(g) **Restraint:** The use of the power to restrain the donor is restricted to where it is necessary and proportionate (to the likelihood of the person suffering harm), and the person lacks capacity or the attorney reasonably believes that the person lacks capacity in relation to the matter.

(h) **Welfare powers useable only on loss of capacity:** The personal welfare powers cannot be used unless the donor lacks capacity or the attorney reasonably believes that the donor lacks capacity.

(i) **Relation to advance decisions:** The personal welfare power is subject to any advance decisions on treatment made by the donor, and does not cover decisions about life-sustaining treatment, unless this has been expressly included by the donor in the lasting power of attorney.

(j) **Health care treatment:** The personal welfare power can be specified so as to include consent, or refusal of consent, to health care treatment (s.11).

(k) **Restrictions on gifts:** There are restrictions on gifts, other than on customary gifts or charities to whom the donor might have made gifts, insofar as the value of any such gift is reasonable in respect of the donor's estate.

(l) **Prescribed information:** The document must include prescribed information.

(m) **donor signature:** the donor must sign a statement that they have read the information and want the power to apply when they have lost capacity.

(n) **Named people to be informed:** The document must name people who should be informed when an application is made to register the power.

(o) **Attorneys' signature:** The attorneys must sign to say they have read the information and understand their duties, including the duty to act in the person's best interests.

(p) **Certification by third party of donor's understanding:** The document must include a certificate completed by an independent third party to the effect that, in their view, the donor understands the power being created, no undue pressure of fraud has been used and there is nothing to stop the power being created (schedule 1).

(q) **Identity of certifying third party:** The independent third party (not a family member) can be someone who has known the donor personally for two years, or a person chosen by the donor on account of their professional skills and expertise, and whom the donor reasonably considers to be competent to certify the relevant matters.[174]

(r) **Public Guardian and registration:** The Public Guardian charges registration fees.

(s) **Separate forms and fees for welfare and finance:** There are separate forms, and fee payable, for a welfare power and a finance power.[175]

In short, a person aged 18 years or over, with capacity to do so, can make what is called a lasting power of attorney. This authorises the attorney to deal with property and financial affairs and/or welfare matters when the donor loses capacity to take such decisions. Welfare decisions can include matters such as health care, place of residence, contact. More than one attorney can be appointed. There is a choice of appointing the attorneys to act jointly, or jointly and severally. Acting jointly is clearly a safeguard but could be more cumbersome. There are restrictions on gifts that can be made; otherwise, application must be made to the Court of Protection.

LASTING POWER OF ATTORNEY: FINANCE, HEALTH AND WELFARE

The Act allows a donor of a lasting power of attorney to specify not just finance, business and property issues but also health or welfare matters. However, the power does not have to cover all these things. The donor can specify. It is not all or nothing. Equally, the donor might appoint one attorney to deal with finance and another to deal with welfare. Up to five attorneys may be appointed. Joint attorneys must always act together; joint and several attorneys can act either together or independently. The donor could even specify that some matters could be dealt with severally but others jointly.

The distinction between finance and welfare issues will usually be clear enough. There will nevertheless be a grey area in which a decision concerning property or

---

174 SI 2007/1253. Lasting Powers of Attorney, Enduring Powers of Attorney and Public Guardian Regulations 2007.
175 SI 2007/1253. Lasting Powers of Attorney, Enduring Powers of Attorney and Public Guardian Regulations 2007.
      And: SI 2007/2051. Public Guardian (Fees, etc.) Regulations 2007.

finance will overlap with welfare matters. For instance, a decision about whether to enter a care home is, strictly speaking, a welfare decision, but deciding how much to spend on the care placement is a financial one.

Lasting powers of attorney can be registered with the Office of the Public Guardian at any time and cannot be used until registered. A finance, property and business power can be used by the attorney before the donor loses capacity, but a welfare power can be used only when the donor lacks the capacity to take a relevant welfare decision.[176]

COMMON LAW DUTY OF CARE OF ATTORNEYS

The code of practice spells out that attorneys must follow the principles of the Act, make decisions in the donor's best interests, have regard to the code and remain within the authority contained in the power of attorney. In addition, as agent of the person lacking capacity, the attorney has a common law duty of care to apply reasonable standards of care and skill, a fiduciary duty (including principles such as trust, good faith, honesty, not taking advantage of the position and acting so as to benefit the donor, not him- or herself), should not delegate his or her authority, has a duty of confidentiality, a duty to comply with Court of Protection directions, a duty not to give up the role without notifying the donor and the Office of the Public Guardian, a duty to keep accounts, a duty to keep the donor's money and property separate from his or her own.[177]

ABUSE OF POWERS OF ATTORNEY

Enduring powers of attorney were the legal predecessors of lasting powers of attorney, up to October 2007 (see below), although such powers made before that date remain valid.

It has been recognised that a proportion of enduring powers of attorney are abused, perhaps some 10 to 15 per cent. There is little reason to suppose that this pattern will not be continued with lasting powers of attorney.

The extent of abuse ranges from the making of unauthorised gifts at one extreme to criminal fraud at the other. For instance, one fraud involved about £2 million, siphoned from a spinster over 90 years old, living in a care home, with no known relatives, and involving an attorney who had not registered the power and was proprietor of the care home.[178]

Abuse of enduring power of attorney by niece. A spinster in her eighties suffered two strokes and three serious falls. She lost her hearing and ability to write. She entered a nursing home in 1996. Her niece, who was the donee of an enduring power of attorney, operated the power and in March 1997 sold shares worth over £23,000; the next year she sold more shares worth over £72,000. Both sums were placed in her bank account; some

176 Mental Capacity Act 2005, ss.9, 11.
177 Lord Chancellor. *Mental Capacity Act 2005: code of practice.* London: TSO, 2007, paras 7.52–7.68.
178 Cretney, S. and Lush, D. *Cretney and Lush on enduring powers of attorney* (5th edition). Bristol: Jordan, 2001, p.133.

of the money was lent to her husband's companies. The courts found that she had abused the power of attorney.[179]

In the following case, the son, with an enduring power of attorney for his mother, was in clear breach of his fiduciary duty.

Son with enduring power of attorney in clear breach of fiduciary duty towards mother. When the son of an elderly woman had an enduring power of attorney, he used her assets to place a new house in his name, but not his mother's, bought a sports car and power boat, moved large sums of money into a company account owned by his wife, and sold shares and paid the proceeds into another account to be drawn on by his wife. The mother was left with no assets, nothing to pass on to her grandchildren, nothing to use to provide for her own needs at the end of her life. She obtained no benefits from the transfers. The court noted that the law imposed 'rigorous and inflexible duties on fiduciaries who enter into transactions with the person to whom the duty is owed' – that is, where the mother's assets were flowing directly into the son's possession. This meant justifying the transaction and proving affirmatively that the transaction was fair and entered into on the basis of proper and independent advice. The son and his wife were in clear breach of their fiduciary duty.[180]

On the other hand, it might not be straightforward to identify breach of fiduciary duty.

Making gifts without the Court of Protection's authorisation. The donor of an enduring power of attorney was a 90-year-old woman living in a nursing home. There were three siblings between whom there had been a history of hostility. The eldest had been granted the power.

The making of £20,000 of gifts by the donee from the donor's estate, even-handedly to herself and siblings, for estate planning purposes, did not necessarily make the attorney unsuitable, even though she should have sought the Court of Protection's authorisation (because the attorney's power to make gifts was extremely limited). However, at worst, she 'ought to have known the law if she was to take on the responsibility of such an important fiduciary position'. But what had occurred did not portray a picture of greed. Furthermore, the other siblings, who had now brought the case to displace the third sibling, had not complained at the time. It was also possible that, at the time the gifts were made, only shortly after the power had been executed, the donee was acting under the instructions of the donor, since the latter might have had capacity to direct that the gifts were made.

In addition, the fact of hostility between the three siblings did not automatically make the donee unsuitable. In this case, it did not. In other circumstances, it might have done so – for instance, if the donor's estate had been complex and required strategic decision making requiring consultation and work with the other siblings.[181]

In the following two cases, dishonesty was abundantly clear. In the first, a woman stole from her husband's uncle, even though she was (unknown to her) in his will.

Woman with power of attorney for husband's uncle: convicted of theft. A 60-year-old woman had an enduring power of attorney on behalf of her former husband's uncle. When his mental health deteriorated, he entered a care home and she then managed

---

179 *Jennings and Lewis v Cairns* [2003] EWCA Civ 1935.
180 *Hodson v Hodson* [2006] EWHC 2878 (Chancery).
181 *Re a power given by Mrs W, a donor* [1999] Chancery (Court of Protection).

his finances. She made cash withdrawals for herself from his building society account, making out cheques to pay off her own overdraft and to buy Christmas presents. He had wanted her to buy a car and authorised £5000 for this, but she bought one for £4400 and kept the rest. With the money she stole, she funded family holidays as well as her gambling habit. In total, she was charged with, and pleaded guilty to, theft of £17,500. She was sentenced to nine months' imprisonment, as the judge put it, having taken advantage of an elderly and vulnerable victim. The irony, which she was not aware of at the time, was that much of the money she had stolen was from her own inheritance, detailed in the man's will.[182]

In the second, a local authority social worker had been advised to make an application for a Court of Protection order for a 79-year-old client. Instead, she obtained enduring power of attorney for herself and proceeded to steal nearly £65,000.

Social worker failing to seek Court of Protection order for client, instead obtaining enduring power of attorney for herself and attempting to steal tens of thousands of pounds. A local authority social worker was convicted of theft, after receiving a referral in respect of a 79-year-old woman with no known relatives. She had dementia, £25,000 in cash and owned her own home. The social worker helped the woman go into a care home. A consultant psychiatrist recommended that a Court of Protection order be sought because of the woman's lack of capacity to manage her affairs. The social worker took no steps to do this. Instead, she started to steal money and obtained an enduring power of attorney, even though the woman lacked the capacity to make it. The power was not registered with the Court of Protection.

Regular bank withdrawals, selling of house: cheque for £42,000. She then started to make cash withdrawals. She withdrew £8180 from cash machines, followed by other withdrawals at about £250 per week. She eventually sold the woman's house for some £87,000. She then began to write cheques out to herself, including one for £42,000. A further banker's draft for £5000 was made payable to Age Concern – the social worker's husband was the regional manager of that charity.

Another local authority officer was asked to reassess the woman, now in the care home. This social worker became suspicious when she found out that the social worker was still visiting. It transpired that the social worker had asked the care home to remove the woman's name from the records and the woman's social services file was missing.

Deliberation, cynicism, most serious breach of trust. She was sentenced to three and a half years in prison, having stolen nearly £65,000. The judge referred to the deliberate plan to take advantage of an old lady who could not look after herself, describing it as deliberate, cynical and a gross breach of trust. The social worker knew perfectly well that the victim would not be able to do anything about it. He described it as the most serious breach of trust by a social worker that he had come across in 20 years on the bench. For sentence, the judge took a starting point of five years. After considering the mitigation (guilty plea, good references, high standard of behaviour in prison, low risk of reoffending), he arrived at three and a half years, which was upheld on appeal.[183]

Similarly, a solicitor with a position of professional responsibility.

Solicitor defrauding 84-year-old woman who treated him like a son and had made him beneficiary of her will. A solicitor gained an enduring power of attorney

182 'Carer jailed for theft from elderly widower.' *Wiltshire Gazette and Herald*, 24 March 2005.
183 *R v Hardwick* [2006] EWCA Crim 969.

for an 84-year-old woman who treated him like a son. He had known her for 30 years. He was sent to prison for 26 months, for fraud, having stolen £51,000 after she had entered a care home and developed dementia. He withdrew the money from three building society accounts and a Post Office account before building society staff became suspicious. The irony was that, under the terms of her will (drawn up via another solicitor), he was beneficiary to 50 per cent of the woman's estate.[184]

In a further case, a man with power of attorney for his mother was sent to prison for stealing over £80,000, representing money that was meant to pay for her nursing home fees. Instead, he used it to solve his own money problems. The judge stated that he had plundered his mother's assets almost to extinction.[185]

After his deaf and blind mother-in-law had to go into a care home, a man obtained power of attorney. He abused it, stealing nearly £250,000 for a luxury lifestyle. The money should have been used to pay for his mother-in-law's care home fees but instead went on his business, top-of-the range cars and expensive holidays. He was sentenced to three years in prison.[186]

In the following case, a woman abused a power of attorney for her uncle-in-law.

Abuse of enduring power of attorney amounting to theft. For instance, a 60-year-old woman, niece-in-law of an 86-year-old man, had enduring power of attorney and was executor of his will. She was convicted of theft of £17,500. She had full access to his bank accounts, in order that she might spend money in his best interests. Instead, she purchased for herself a car, washing machine, tumble dryer and two holidays. She also gambled money. Of previous good character, she was sentenced to nine months in prison and ordered to repay £17,500 within 28 days.[187]

A purported rather than actual power of attorney might be abused.

Nephew using power of attorney that had never been registered or agreed. A power of attorney that had never been registered or agreed was used by a man to steal £75,000 from his elderly aunt with dementia. He drafted it himself and, after his aunt was admitted to a care home, he used it to sell her house for £124,000, of which he appropriated £75,000 for himself. He was sent to prison for nine rather than 18 months. In mitigation, he was a hard-working family man, had a mother with mental health problems, had found his father dead aged 14, was close to his aunt and was ashamed of what he had done. A Proceeds of Crime confiscation hearing would be held at a later date.[188]

---

184 Blake, M. 'Solicitor jailed for stealing over £50,000 from elderly dementia sufferer who treated him "like a son".' *Daily Mail*, 23 March 2012.

185 'Bankrupt man stole £80,000 from mother.' *Suffolk Free Press*, 20 January 2009.

186 '"Walter Mitty" conman who fleeced his mother-in-law of £250,000 is jailed for three years.' *Daily Mail*, 2 July 2012. (Not clear from report what sort of power of attorney it was.)

187 *R v Carter* [2005] reported in 'Chippenham woman sentenced for theft from elderly male relative.' *Wiltshire Police News*, 2005. Accessed on 20 October 2007 at: http://wiltshire.police.uk/news/newsview.asp?id=644.

188 'Bristol man jailed for stealing £75,000 from his elderly aunt.' *Bristol Evening Post*, 28 October 2011.

REVOCATION OF LASTING POWER OF ATTORNEY, INCLUDING IN CIRCUMSTANCES OF FRAUD, UNDUE PRESSURE, NOT ACTING IN BEST INTERESTS

Lasting powers of attorney may be subject to revocation in a number of situations. One of these is where the donor, at any time he or she has capacity, decides on revocation.[189]

Section 22 of the Act sets out the power of the Court of Protection to intervene and determine whether the requirements for creation of a lasting power of attorney have been met, whether the power has been revoked, whether fraud or undue pressure was exercised, whether the donee is behaving inconsistently with the authority given by the power or not behaving in the donor's best interests. The court has the power to prevent registration of the power.[190]

In the following case, the Court of Protection revoked an enduring power of attorney because of the way in which the attorney was using his mother's money. The local authority had become involved because of a dispute with the attorney about unpaid care home fees.

Son using mother's money to buy a house and a pick-up vehicle and to give his daughter rent-free accommodation: revocation of power of attorney. The Office of the Public Guardian applied to the court for the enduring power of attorney for his mother to be revoked.

This was on the grounds that he had mixed his own and his mother's monies, bought a new property registered in his name (with the unrealistic claim that his mother could live there even though she needed to be in a care home), had bought a pick-up truck for some £5000 to transfer belongings (although he could have hired one much more cheaply), had not paid care home fees (he claimed he would once it was established whether the local authority or the NHS should be responsible for the placement) and did not charge his daughter rent for living in the new property (claiming that his mother would not have wanted him to do so).

The court found against the attorney on all these points. It also departed from the normal rule on costs in such court cases and ordered that the son pay his own costs.[191]

In the next case, too, involving a woman (an auditor by occupation) acting with a lasting power of attorney for her mother, the court revoked the power.

Attorney not paying care home fees, and other unexplained transactions. A care home owner contacted the local authority, expressing concern that the mother's care home fees were not being paid and that she was being given very little pocket money by her daughter.

The owner was also concerned because the mother had received a letter from a bank, confirming a loan to her of £5000, and also other correspondence confirming that her credit card applications had been accepted. The daughter also visited only very sporadically, possibly once every two months.

---

189 Mental Capacity Act 2005, s.13.
190 Mental Capacity Act 2005, s.22.
191 *Re Stapleton* [2012] MHLO 72.

When the Office of the Public Guardian tried to investigate and obtain an explanation from the attorney, the latter persistently failed to cooperate, making a number of excuses. The court found the attorney to have been deliberately obstructive. It also noted that, as an auditor, a higher standard would be expected from the daughter in terms of managing and presenting her mother's accounts. The power was revoked; a deputy would be appointed instead.[192]

ENDURING POWERS OF ATTORNEY MADE BEFORE OCTOBER 2007

From October 2007, no new enduring powers of attorney could be made. Any made before that date remain valid, whether or not the donor has yet lost capacity and the power has been registered with the Court of Protection.[193]

COURT OF PROTECTION

Sections 15 to 20 of the Act outline the function of the Court of Protection. Some of the key points are as follows, in summary:

(a) **Declarations about capacity and interventions:** It has the power to make declarations about whether or not a person has capacity and about lawfulness of any act done or proposed to be done in relation to the person (s.15).

(b) **Making orders, appointing deputies:** It can make a decision (by making an order) or, alternatively, appoint a deputy, whose powers may extend to personal welfare, as well as to property and affairs.

(c) **Orders preferred to deputies:** A decision of the court is to be preferred to the appointment of a deputy. The powers conferred on a deputy should be as limited in scope and duration as is reasonably practicable.

(d) **Court subject to principles of Act:** The powers of the court are subject to the provisions of the Act, in particular the principles in s.1 and the test of best interests in s.4 (s.16).

(e) **Scope of welfare decisions:** Personal welfare decisions could include, in particular, where the incapacitated person is to live, with whom he or she should have contact, consent or refusal to health care treatment (s.17).

(f) **Age of deputy, joint or several:** A deputy must be at least 18 years old. Two more deputies may be appointed to act jointly or severally (s.19).

(g) **Restraint:** If a deputy restrains the person, such intervention must be within the scope of the deputy's authority, necessary and proportionate, and the person lack capacity or the deputy reasonably believe that the person lacks capacity in relation to the matter.

---

192 *Re Harcourt* [2012] MHLO 74.
193 Mental Capacity Act 2005, schedule 4.

(h) **Property, wills:** A deputy cannot be given power to settle any of the person's property, to execute the person's will or to exercise any power vested in the person (e.g. trusteeship).

(i) **Life-sustaining treatment:** A deputy cannot refuse consent to life-sustaining treatment.

(j) **Limit to authority:** A deputy cannot make a decision inconsistent with the scope of his or her authority or with a decision made by the donee of a lasting power of attorney.

(k) **Contact and health care:** A deputy cannot be given powers to prohibit a named person from having contact with the person lacking capacity, nor to direct a person responsible for the person's health care to allow somebody else to take over the responsibility (s.20).

(l) **Fees:** Where deputies are appointed, there are both appointment fees and supervision fees (specified at three levels) charged by the Public Guardian. There are exemptions in relation to receipt of benefits and also reduction and remission and fees in exceptional circumstances involving undue hardship.[194]

(m) **Deprivation of liberty:** In relation to standard authorisations concerning deprivation of liberty, the court can determine questions relating to whether the person meets the qualifying requirements, the period the authorisation is to be in force, the purpose of the authorisation, the conditions attached to the authorisation. It can vary or terminate the authorisation or direct that the supervisory body do so (s.21A).

Receiverships (dealing only with property, business, finance) previously put in place by the former Court of Protection under Part 7 of the Mental Health Act 1983 remain valid but are treated as equivalent to deputyship.[195]

In the absence of a more suitable person, the Court of Protection might indicate that it would be appropriate and desirable for a local authority – for example, in the form of the director of social services – to be appointed deputy. Were the local authority to refuse, a challenge to that refusal would need to be by means of a judicial review decision in order to scrutinise the rationality or lawfulness of that refusal.[196]

---

194 SI 2007/2051. Public Guardian (Fees, etc.) Regulations 2007.
195 Mental Capacity Act 2005, schedule 5.
196 *R(M) v Birmingham County Council* [2008] EWHC 949 (Admin).

COURT OF PROTECTION: INVOLVEMENT

For finance and property, a court order will usually be necessary unless the only income involved is from state benefits or an enduring or lasting power of attorney exists.

The code of practice states that the court may make a particular finance decision – for example, to terminate a tenancy or to make or amend a will. However, it may appoint a deputy for ongoing management of such affairs (a) for dealing with cash assets over a specified amount, (b) for selling a person's property, or (c) where the person has a level of income or capital that the court thinks a deputy needs to manage.[197]

COURT OF PROTECTION: WELFARE ISSUES

Court of Protection involvement is intended to be a last resort for welfare issues.

The code of practice states that, in a dispute about best interests (about welfare matters), a decision maker could be challenged through use of an advocate, getting a second opinion, holding a case conference, mediation or use of a complaints procedure. Only then, the code states, should application be made to the court.[198]

However, the code also states that application to the court about personal welfare, including health interventions, may be necessary in case of particularly difficult decisions, disagreements that cannot otherwise be resolved or situations where ongoing decisions may need to be made. The courts have in the past stated that certain serious medical interventions should always go to court, including decisions about artificial nutrition and hydration for patients in a persistent vegetative state,[199] bone marrow donation[200] and non-therapeutic sterilisation.[201]

The courts have held that in case of disagreements (e.g. between local authority and family) about deprivation of a person's liberty, an application to the court must be made. And that the onus is on the public body to make the application. When a local authority had taken the view that it was up to the father to take the matter to the court, rather than for it to do so, the judge was scathing:

> Lastly, I have already indicated that the protracted delay in applying to court in this case was highly unfortunate. There are repeated references, particularly by the service manager, to the burden being on Mr Neary to take the matter to court if he wished to challenge what was happening. That approach cannot be right. I have already referred to the decision in *Re S*, which rightly observes that the practical and evidential burden is on a local authority to demonstrate that its arrangements are better than those that can be achieved within the family. It will discharge the practical burden

---

197 Lord Chancellor. *Mental Capacity Act 2005: code of practice*. London: TSO, 2007, paras 8.27–8.35.
198 Lord Chancellor. *Mental Capacity Act 2005: code of practice*. London: TSO, 2007, para 5.68.
199 *Airedale Trust v Bland* [1993] AC 789 (House of Lords).
200 *Re Y (Mental incapacity: bone marrow transplant)* [1996] 2 FLR 787.
201 *SL v SL* [2000] 3 WLR 1288 (Court of Appeal).

by ensuring that there is a proper forum for decision. It will not do so by allowing the situation it has brought about to continue by default. Nor is it an answer to say, as Hillingdon has done, that Mr Neary could always have gone to court himself, and that it had told him so. It was Steven's rights, and not those of his father, that were in issue. Moreover, local authorities have the advantage over individuals both in terms of experience and, even nowadays, depth of pocket. The fact that an individual does not bring a matter to court does not relieve the local authority of the obligation to act, it redoubles it.[202]

On the welfare side, the court might be dealing with, for example, issues concerning medical treatment, where a person with learning disabilities should live, marriage of a person with learning disabilities, where older people should live and be cared for. Prior to October 2007, the High Court was dealing with just such matters by exercising its inherent jurisdiction. Many of the principles it applied are now embodied in the Mental Capacity Act 2005, so these cases remain, to some extent, relevant to the working of the Act.

DISCRETION TO MAKE AN ORDER

Orders are at the discretion of the Court of Protection.

For instance, the court may be called on to confirm a lack of capacity and make an order – as in one case about preventing a woman's parents (motivated by strong cultural and religious influences) from entering into a contract of marriage for her, and forbidding them to take her abroad (to Pakistan) without permission from the court.[203]

Alternatively, it might decide not to make an order. In another case concerning a possible marriage in Pakistan for a man with learning disabilities who clearly lacked capacity to marry, the court refrained from such an order on the grounds that his parents were honourable people and the court would accept their undertakings not to contract a marriage or take him to Pakistan without application to the court.[204]

INTERIM ORDERS

The Mental Capacity Act 2005 empowers the Court of Protection to make an interim order under s.48 of the Act. It states that the court may make an order or give directions on any matter if:

(a) there is reason to believe that P [the person] lacks capacity in relation to the matter,

(b) the matter is one to which its powers under this Act extend, and

---

202 *London Borough of Hillingdon v Neary* [2011] EWHC 1377 (COP).

203 *M v B* [2005] EWHC 1681 (Fam).

204 *X City Council v MB & Ors* [2006] EWHC 168 (Fam).

(c)   it is in P's best interests to make the order, or give the directions, without delay.[205]

For such an order to be given, there must be reason to believe that a person may lack capacity. However, this is not the same as requiring that lack of capacity be established on the balance of probability, which is the higher test needed for the court to make an ordinary (rather than an interim) order.

Thus, sometimes a vulnerable person may be refusing assistance, serious matters are at stake and there is some question about the person's capacity. One possibility might be to apply for an interim order.

Question of capacity to refuse or not to cooperate with services. A 52-year-old woman had a dissociative disorder of movement and a somatisation disorder. This had, for a long time, left her in pain, bed-bound and largely unable to move. The local authority found her behaviour antagonistic and uncooperative, making it impossible to provide appropriate care for her. Consequently, only minimum nursing care was provided; she was left for long periods with her physical needs unattended. However, the local authority had concerns about her mental condition.

The question of capacity arose. Hitherto, she had been treated as having capacity to accept or reject care services. The local authority was not sure whether this was still correct. If it was not, the court could make a declaration under s.15 of the Act and then decide on her best interests.

The court recognised that the test of incapacity, for the court to proceed under s.15 or s.16, is whether, on the balance of probability, a person lacked capacity. But that could sometimes take time to establish, and sometimes things needed to be done quickly. Under s.48 of the Act, the court could make an interim order, for which the threshold was lower. It required only that there was reason to believe that the person lacks capacity.[206]

Given a question about a person's capacity, an interim order from the court could cover matters such as taking immediate safeguarding steps, or giving directions to resolve the issue of capacity quickly. But the steps to be taken under the interim order would depend on the individual facts and circumstances of the case, the urgency involved and the principle that the person's autonomy should be restricted as little as is consistent with his or her best interests. Possibly, even the only direction by the court, were capacity still uncertain, would be to obtain the evidence to enable capacity reliably to be determined.[207]

In another case, an interim order was associated not only with the person's probable lack of capacity but also with achieving a proper overall assessment and treatment of his condition, with a degree of force to be used *if necessary*.

Interim order concerning capacity, assessment and treatment. A 22-year-old man had severe, complex and currently uncontrolled epilepsy. He lived with his adoptive mother. Secure, adequate medical assessment and treatment were required as he was not complying with the treatment being provided. On the basis of medical evidence, the court

---

205 Quoted from: Mental Capacity Act 2005, s.48
206 *Re F*, Court of Protection (case no. 11649371), 28 May 2009.
207 *Re F*, Court of Protection (case no. 11649371), 28 May 2009.

had previously granted an interim declaration of incapacity in relation to decisions about his health and social care. The PCT then put forward two options for assessment and treatment, the first being community-based, the second residential. Everybody, it seems, was in favour of the latter, but the arrangements for the place broke down. Various options then were discussed; in the end, the court stated that something had to be done to sort out proper assessment and treatment. Because the man was generally compliant, force would probably not have to be used, but a proportionate degree of force could be used if necessary.[208]

STATUTORY WILLS

The Court of Protection has the power to make a statutory will.[209] It must be in a person's best interests. So a person's past or present wishes will not necessarily be decisive. In the following case, the court authorised such a will, effectively to keep a woman's assets out of the hands of the person who had exploited her.

Making a statutory will overriding a previous valid one: in a person's best interests. A woman had lived with a man and his family who cared for her. She had previously made a will leaving money to nine charities. She then revoked this will. The new one left her entire state to the man, who also had power of attorney.

She then lost capacity to take various decisions and, at the direction of the court, was now living in a care home. There was a question about whether she had had capacity when she changed her will or whether she had been unduly influenced in changing it. Either way, the Court of Protection had no jurisdiction, under the Mental Capacity Act 2005, to rule on the validity of the will. But what it could do now was to authorise – in her best interests – the making of a statutory will (thus superseding the previous one) which harked back to her original intention of leaving her money to the charities.[210]

The court in this last case also pointed out that the woman's best interests were relevant not only in life but also in death, in terms of funeral arrangements but also how she would be remembered.

Nonetheless, this does not mean that the Court of Protection will simply step in, as a matter of course, to mollify matters and ensure that people without capacity are seen, after their death, to have done the right thing. In another case, the judge pointed out that the person in question had 'an appalling track record'. He had spent his life doing the wrong thing by other people. His 'malevolence was such that he would probably relish the prospect of thwarting his children's designs on his estate and would rejoice at being remembered by them with disaffection'. In such circumstances, the court was prepared to authorise a statutory will in his best interests, so that the estate could be sorted out, but not so that he would be remembered fondly or for having done the right thing.[211]

---

208 *A Primary Care Trust v P* [2008] EWHC 1403 (Fam).
209 Mental Capacity Act 2005, s.18.
210 *ITW v Z* [2009] EWHC 2525 (Fam).
211 *D v JC* [2012] MHLO 35 (COP).

APPLICATIONS TO THE COURT OF PROTECTION

Permission is not needed to make an application to the court by a person lacking, or alleged to lack, capacity, by a person with a parental responsibility for a person under 18 years old, by a donor or donee of a lasting power of attorney, by a court-appointed deputy or by a person named in an existing court order (with which the application is concerned).

Otherwise, permission is required.[212] Applications to the court are governed by detailed rules.[213] Fees are charged, but there are exemptions in relation to receipt of benefits and also reduction and remission of fees in exceptional circumstances involving undue hardship.[214]

ADVANCE DECISIONS

Sections 24–26 of the Mental Capacity Act 2005 set out the rules about advance decisions or 'living wills' as they have commonly been known. These are about people's refusal of medical treatment in advance of loss of capacity. Knowledge of the rules may be crucial both in raising or allaying – depending on the circumstances – suspicions about what is happening to a vulnerable adult. The crucial point is that if all rules are complied with and conditions met, then an advance decision is legally binding.

The rules are as follows, in summary:

(a) **Age and capacity to specify refusal of medical treatment:** A person aged 18 or over, with the capacity to do so, may specify the circumstances in which at a future date, if he or she lacks capacity, specified treatment is not to be given.

(b) **Withdrawal:** The person may withdraw or alter an advance decision: a withdrawal need not be in writing.

(c) **Alteration:** An alteration need not be in writing, unless it relates to life-sustaining treatment (s.24).

(d) **Treatment:** Treatment is defined to include a 'diagnostic or other procedure'.

(e) **Invalidity:** The advance decision is not valid if the person has withdrawn it, subsequently conferred authority for the making of such a decision through a lasting power of attorney, or done anything inconsistent with the advance decision.

(f) **Non-applicability:** The advance decision is not applicable to the particular treatment in issue if at the time the person has capacity to refuse or to consent to the treatment, or if the treatment in question is not specified in the advance decision, or if the circumstances specified in the advance statement have not

---

212 Mental Capacity Act 2005, s.50.
213 SI 2007/1744. Court of Protection Rules.
214 SI 2007/1745. Court of Protection Fees Order.

arisen, or if there are reasonable grounds for believing that circumstances now exist that the person did not anticipate at the time of the advance decision, but which would have affected that decision had they been anticipated.

(g) **Life-sustaining treatment, must be in writing and witnessed:** The advance decision is not applicable to life-sustaining treatment unless the decision is verified by the person that it is to apply to that treatment even if life is at risk, and is in writing, signed by the person or by somebody else in the presence of, and by the direction of, the person, the signature is made or acknowledged by the person in the presence of a witness, and the witness signs it or acknowledges his/her signature in the person's presence.

(h) **Effect of valid and applicable decision:** Otherwise, an advance decision that is both valid and applicable to the treatment in question has effect as if the person had made it (and had the capacity to do so) at the time when the question arises about whether to carry out the treatment.

(i) **Liability:** A person does not incur liability for providing treatment unless he or she knows there was a valid and applicable advance decision.

(j) **Court of Protection:** The Court of Protection can make a declaration about the existence, validity or applicability of an advance decision.

(k) **Interim treatment:** Nothing in an apparent advance decision stops the provision of life-sustaining treatment or the prevention of serious deterioration in the person's condition, while a decision is sought from the court.

Under the Act, an advance decision about life-sustaining treatment must be in writing, but not necessarily written by the person making the decision. For instance, somebody else can sign at the direction of the person making the decision and in the presence of a witness.

In the following case (prior to the Mental Capacity Act), the person making the decision could not have written and signed anything, but somebody else could have signed, at his direction, in the presence of a witness.

Advance decision by means of slight eyelash movement. A man with motor neurone disease had slight eyelash movement as his only means of communication to express his wishes. By this means, he stated that when he lost this last means of communication, he wished the artificial ventilation to cease. The court stated that such a valid advance indication would be effective and that doctors would not be entitled to act inconsistently with it, so long as he did not subsequently indicate that his wishes had changed.[215]

In a more recent case, a similar advance decision, to withdraw life-prolonging treatment once he had lost ability to communicate, was made by a person also with motor neurone disease. However, by the time of the court hearing, he had lost capacity, because he had lost the ability to communicate in any way. Previous

---

215 *Re AK (Medical treatment: consent)* [2001] 1 FLR 129.

to that loss, he could communicate by moving his eyes to the right to indicate yes. The decision was agreed in the presence of his wife, his general practitioner and his mental capacity coordinator. The court upheld it as valid.[216]

CAPACITY TO MAKE AN ADVANCE DECISION

The person must have the requisite capacity at the time of making the statement. For instance, a person with borderline personality disorder, who self-harmed by cutting herself and by blood-letting, made such a statement refusing blood transfusions. She believed her blood was evil and that it also contaminated any blood being transfused. The evidence showed that she lacked capacity at the time of making the statement; it was therefore not legally effective.[217]

The courts have stated:

> that for an advance decision relating to life-sustaining treatment to be valid and applicable, there should be clear evidence establishing on the balance of probability that the maker had capacity at the relevant time. Where the evidence of capacity is doubtful or equivocal it is not appropriate to uphold the decision.[218]

This was in a case involving a woman suffering from anorexia and in an extremely weak physical and mental state, who was also sectioned under the Mental Health Act on the very day on which she signed, and had witnessed, an advance decision. There was some evidence suggesting capacity – for example, advice from her independent mental health advocate and from a solicitor, as well as the 'general medical view' at the time. But no formal capacity assessment was undertaken at the time.

> I find on the balance of probabilities that E did not have capacity at the time she signed the advance decision in October 2011. Against such an alerting background, a full, reasoned and contemporaneous assessment evidencing mental capacity to make such a momentous decision would in my view be necessary. No such assessment occurred in E's case and I think it at best doubtful that a thorough investigation at the time would have reached the conclusion that she had capacity.[219]

ADVANCE DECISIONS ARE ABOUT REFUSAL OF TREATMENT ONLY

Advance decisions concern refusal of treatment only. Any other advance statement – for example, about medical treatment desired or about location of care – would have to be taken account of in the best interests test applied under s.4 of the Act, but would not be legally binding.

---

216 *X Primary Care Trust v XB* [2012] EWHC 1390 (Fam).

217 *An NHS Trust v Ms T* [2004] EWHC 1279 (Fam).

218 *A Local Authority v E* [2012] EWHC 1639 (COP).

219 *A Local Authority v E* [2012] EWHC 1639 (COP).

The code of practice indicates that an advance decision could refuse artificial nutrition and hydration but not basic care:

> An advance decision cannot refuse actions that are needed to keep a person comfortable (sometimes called basic or essential care). Examples include warmth, shelter, actions to keep a person clean and the offer of food and water by mouth. Section 5 of the Act allows health care professionals to carry out these actions in the best interests of a person who lacks capacity to consent… An advance decision can refuse artificial nutrition and hydration.[220]

Nothing in the Act changes the law relating to murder, manslaughter or assisted suicide.[221]

VALIDITY AND APPLICABILITY OF ADVANCE DECISIONS

The following case, heard before the Mental Capacity Act 2005 was in force, well illustrates the two questions of whether an advance decision refusing medical treatment is both valid and applicable.

Religious beliefs and validity of advance decision in the light of mother's wish for her daughter to go without treatment and father's opposed wish. A 24-year-old woman had been born to Muslim parents. Her parents separated. Her mother became a Jehovah's Witness, as did her daughter. When she was 22 years old, she made an advance decision which expressly stated an absolute refusal to have a blood transfusion. She suffered from aortic valve disease. Two years later, she was taken seriously ill and was rushed to hospital, and needed a blood transfusion. She was unconscious. Her mother and other relatives were adamant that the advance directive should be observed. The situation became critical over the next couple of weeks.

Daughter's recent actions inconsistent with the advance decision. The matter was referred to the High Court. The father made a statement including the following points. First, for the past few months, his daughter had been betrothed to a Turkish Muslim man on condition she would revert back to being a Muslim. Second, following a promise to her fiancé, she had during this time not attended any Jehovah's Witness meetings, which she used to attend twice weekly. Third, prior to her collapse, she had admitted herself to hospital for two days, did not mention the advance directive and had said to her aunt and brother that she did not want to die. Fourth, she had announced to the family two months previously that she would not allow anything to get in the way of marrying her fiancé and that she would follow his Muslim faith.

Burden of proof on those who seek to establish validity, applicability. The judge set out certain principles. First, the burden of proof lies on those who seek to establish the existence, validity and applicability of an advance directive, because if there is doubt, that doubt should be resolved in favour of life. The proof needs to be clear and convincing, no more than the civil standard (balance of probability), but nonetheless stronger and more cogent in relation to the gravity of the issue.

He went on to point out that it is 'fundamental that an advance directive is, of its very essence and nature, inherently revocable'. Furthermore, such revocation need not be in

---

220 Lord Chancellor. *Mental Capacity Act 2005: code of practice.* London: TSO, 2007, para 9.28.
221 Mental Capacity Act 2005, s.62.

writing because, clearly, a 'patient who has changed his mind is not to be condemned to death because pen and ink are not readily to hand'.

Doubts should be resolved in favour of life. Ultimately, in this case, the judge found compelling the evidence of the father that his daughter had rejected her faith in the Jehovah's Witness religion, on which the advance directive was entirely founded. The directive was no longer valid. Even if he was wrong about this, the father's evidence – at the very lowest – threw 'considerable doubt' on the validity of the directive. And such doubt had to be resolved in favour of preservation of his daughter's life.[222]

On the other hand, in the following case, the coroner concluded there was nothing else the hospital and doctors could have done, other than to let the woman in question die.

Self-poisoning and advance decision. A woman had made an apparently valid and applicable advance decision under the Mental Capacity Act 2005. This stated that she did not want to be treated for self-poisoning. When she rang up the hospital so that she would not die alone and could receive pain relief, the doctors did not try to save her life. The woman died. This was because the doctors could otherwise have been liable (e.g. for trespass to the person) – or even criminally liable – had they intervened. The coroner did not blame the hospital for the woman's death.[223]

INVALIDITY NOT NECESSARILY FATAL TO OUTCOME DESIRED BY PERSON
The invalidity of an advance decision will not necessarily be fatal to achieving what the person wanted.

For instance, in a case where an operation had resulted in irrevocable brain damage and a persistent vegetative state, the person had declared his wishes in advance, refusing treatment to maintain a reduced quality of life, with little or no hope of recovery. But the signed letter had not been witnessed. However, the judge confirmed that it would anyway be in his best interests for active medical treatment to be withdrawn and that the best interests decision was heavily swayed by those wishes the man had expressed:

> Nevertheless, had there been anything to put in the balance against the other evidence, D's wishes would have carried very great weight with me. He was a very private man before his incapacity, who would have been horrified at the prospect of being kept alive in this condition, with the total loss of privacy that his dependency entails.[224]

OLDER ADVANCE DECISIONS
If an advance decision concerning life-sustaining treatment was made before the coming into force of the MCA (1 October 2007), it may still be valid and applicable in certain circumstances. These are, in summary:

---

222 *HE v A Hospital NHS Trust* [2003] EWHC 1017 (Fam).
223 Gabbatt, A. 'Doctors acted legally in living will suicide case.' *The Guardian*, 1 October 2009.
224 *Re D* [2012] EWHC 885 (COP).

- a person providing health care to the individual reasonably believes that such an advance decision had been made before 1 October 2007 and that since 1 October the individual has lacked the capacity (a) to verify by a statement that the advance decision is to apply to the treatment in question even if life is at risk, and (b) to carry out the requirement that the advance decision be signed and witnessed

- the advance decision is in writing

- the person did not withdraw the decision when he or she still had capacity to do so, and has not done anything else clearly inconsistent with the advance decision

- the person lacks the capacity to decide about the treatment in question at the material time

- the treatment in question is specified in the advance decision

- the circumstances specified in the advance decision are present

- there are no reasonable grounds for believing circumstances exist which the individual did not anticipate at the time of the advance decision and which would have affected that decision.[225]

The requirements that then do not have to be met are (a) the verifying statement that the decision is to apply to treatment even if life is at risk, and (b) the signing and witnessing of the decision.

BEST INTERESTS DECISIONS EXCLUDED FROM THE MENTAL CAPACITY ACT

Sections 27 and 29 set out a range of decisions that are not permitted to be taken in a person's best interests under the Act, when the person him- or herself lacks capacity to take the decision.

These exclusions include consent to marriage or civil partnership, consent to sexual relations, consent to divorce based on two years' separation, consent to a dissolution order in relation to civil partnership based on two years' separation, consent to child being placed for adoption, consent to making of an adoption order, discharging parental responsibilities in matters unrelated to child's property, giving consent under Human Fertilisation and Embryology Act 1990. Voting is also excluded.

The courts have pointed out that, in relation to such questions, best interests are simply irrelevant. If the person has capacity to take such a decision, then best interests have no part to play because the person can do as he or she likes. If there is lack of capacity, then likewise best interests are irrelevant because the person cannot take the decision anyway.

---

225 SI 2007/1898. The Mental Capacity Act 2005 (Transitional and Consequential Provisions) Order 2007.

In a case about whether a young woman had the capacity to marry, the court noted that there was significant confusion underlying an important part of the case. The local authority was asking the court to decide whether it was in the woman's best interests to marry. But the court had 'no business – in fact...no jurisdiction – to embark upon a determination of that question'.[226]

In that case, the judge pointed to the confusion on the part of the local authority. However, the point is worth reiterating because local authorities are not alone in getting confused. In a 2011 case, a judge set out the welfare questions that had to be answered, including 'whether it is in BB's best interests to be married'.[227]

Whilst best interests are not relevant to matters such as marriage and sexual activity, capacity clearly is. This has resulted in a large volume of case law devoted to trying to work out how to pinpoint capacity in these matters and in particular the capacity to engage in sexual activity.

Marriage and sexual relations may be key issues in respect of protection of a vulnerable adult. The courts considered the tests under the common law. Now, cases involving marriage and sexual relations are considered under the umbrella of the Mental Capacity Act 2005 but with reference to those previous tests.

MARRIAGE

In the case of marriage, the test has been characterised as follows:

> There are thus, in essence, two aspects to the inquiry whether someone has the capacity to marry. (1) Does he or she understand the nature of the marriage contract? (2) Does he or she understand the duties and responsibilities that normally attach to marriage? The duties and responsibilities that normally attach to marriage are as follows: marriage, whether civil or religious, is a contract, formally entered into. It confers on the parties the status of husband and wife, the essence of the contract being an agreement between a man and a woman to live together, and to love one another as husband and wife, to the exclusion of all others. It creates a relationship of mutual and reciprocal obligations, typically involving the sharing of a common home and a common domestic life and the right to enjoy each other's society, comfort and assistance.[228]

Setting the test of capacity for marriage too high could operate as an 'unfair, unnecessary and indeed discriminatory bar against the mentally disabled'. Furthermore, the test is whether the person understands the nature of marriage in general; it is not a test that is specific to a particular prospective spouse.[229]

---

226 *Sheffield CC v E* [2004] EWHC 2808 (Fam).
227 *London Borough of Tower Hamlets v BB* [2011] EWHC 2853 (Fam).
228 *Sheffield CC v E* [2004] EWHC 2808 (Fam).
229 *Sheffield CC v E* [2004] EWHC 2808 (Fam).

Capacity to understand and consent to marriage automatically embraces sexual activity. The converse is not so; therefore the test for marriage is higher and more complex than that for sexual activity.

SEXUAL ACTIVITY: NOT PERSON-SPECIFIC

The civil courts (Mr Justice Munby, as he was) have held that, just as for marriage, so too with sexual activity: capacity is not person-specific:

> The question is issue specific, both in the general sense and, as I have already pointed out, in the sense that capacity has to be assessed in relation to the particular kind of sexual activity in question. But capacity to consent to sexual relations is, in my judgment, a question directed to the nature of the activity rather than to the identity of the sexual partner. A woman either has capacity, for example, to consent to 'normal' penetrative vaginal intercourse, or she does not. It is difficult to see how it can sensibly be said that she has capacity to consent to a particular sexual act with Y whilst at the same time lacking capacity to consent to precisely the same sexual act with Z.[230]

However, the House of Lords, in a criminal case about the mentally disordered victim of a sexual offence, doubted the correctness of this. The court seemed to state that capacity issues about marriage and sexual relations were partner- and situation-specific, rather than a question of more general capacity status.[231]

It seems that the criminal court was considering a particular situation in which, irrespective of her general capacity to consent to sexual relations, the woman was in fear and panic, and so was deprived either of capacity or at least ability to communicate her wishes in that situation. Whereas, in mental capacity cases involving sexual relations or marriage, the civil court is having to take a general view about whether – all other things being equal – a person does or doesn't have capacity to marry to engage in sexual activity.

The best view therefore is that the House of Lords failed to outline the difference between a person having capacity generally (all other things being equal) and the exercise of that capacity in a particular situation. This was put forward as an explanation in the following case. Otherwise, a local authority would have to be vetting every potential suitor, or rather sexual partner, to see whether the vulnerable person had mental capacity to have sex with that particular partner:

> In my view the analogy drawn by Munby J with capacity to marry is faultless and is impossible to challenge successfully. Of course Lady Hale [in the criminal case] is right to say that 'it is difficult to think of an activity which is more person and situation specific than sexual relations', but the same is true (if not truer) of marriage. But it does not follow that capacity to marry is

---

230   *Local Authority X v MM* [2007] EWHC 2003 (Fam).
231   *R v C* [2009] UKHL 42.

spouse as opposed to status specific. Far from it. I do think, with the greatest possible respect, that there has been a conflation of capacity to consent to sex and the exercise of that capacity. There is also a very considerable practical problem in allowing a partner-specific dimension into the test. Consider this case. Is the local authority supposed to vet every proposed sexual partner to gauge if [the person] has the capacity to consent to sex with him or her?[232]

BASIC CAPACITY TEST FOR SEXUAL ACTIVITY

The test for sexual relations has been held to be as follows and is a much narrower and simpler test than for marriage:

> Does the person have sufficient knowledge and understanding of the nature and character – the sexual nature and character – of the act of sexual intercourse, and of the reasonably foreseeable consequences of sexual intercourse, to have the capacity to choose whether or not to engage in it, the capacity to decide whether to give or withhold consent to sexual intercourse (and, where relevant, to communicate their choice…)?[233]

In the same case, a sexual relationship was held generally to be implicit in any marriage. Thus, a person who lacked the capacity to consent to sexual relations would necessarily lack the capacity to marry, but the converse would not necessarily be true.

It was unsuccessfully argued in one case that understanding the 'reasonably foreseeable consequences' of sexual activity should be interpreted broadly in ascertaining capacity; this would have allowed the local authority to protect a vulnerable adult on grounds of incapacity. The court was having none of it and made clear that the fact the woman wrongly believed her sexual partners would marry her did not mean that she lacked capacity to engage in sexual activity.

Reasonably foreseeable consequences of sexual activity. The local authority maintained that understanding the 'reasonably foreseeable consequences' could include matters such as (a) the risk in deterioration in her mental state should she become pregnant or a romantic relationship collapse, (b) the social and emotional consequences of having sexual intercourse (whether or not it leads to pregnancy), (c) her beliefs about whether she would be allowed to keep any baby born to her, (d) her belief that any man who had sexual intercourse would marry her, and (e) her belief that she would only be happy when married and a mother.

The court stated that the local authority had blurred the line between capacity and best interests and that the law had 'not yet come to the stage, and I hope never will, that it will seek to intervene to prevent acts on the part of the citizen which it does not consider to be that citizen's best interests which are nevertheless lawful acts and which the citizen has the capacity to agree to'. The court was not prepared to consider and judge minutely the realism of the woman's beliefs. The local authority relied on the false beliefs of the

---

232 *D Borough Council v AB* [2011] EWHC 101 (COP).
233 *X City Council v MB & Ors* [2006] EWHC 168 (Fam).

woman to demonstrate incapacity; the court pointed out that 'sadly many young women in society who do not suffer from the particular afflictions of [the woman] similarly persuade themselves as to the attitude and intentions of their man towards them'.[234]

COMPLICATIONS WITH THE BASIC CAPACITY TEST FOR SEXUAL ACTIVITY

The courts have, however, acknowledged that even the apparently very basic test concerning the nature of the act and 'reasonably foreseeable consequences' is in fact not quite so straightforward.

For instance, in one case, the judge pointed out that, with sex between men, the issue of pregnancy did not arise, and in the case of non-penetrative sexual activity, understanding of health issues might not be required either. With some understatement, the judge referred to the 'serious management problems' of different kinds of sexual activity practised at different times:

> I therefore conclude that the capacity to consent to sex remains act-specific and requires an understanding and awareness of:
>
> - The mechanics of the act
>
> - That there are health risks involved, particularly the acquisition of sexually transmitted and sexually transmissible infections
>
> - That sex between a man and a woman may result in the woman becoming pregnant
>
> I would also make this observation. I am sure that the first and second of these criteria is needed to be able to consent to penetrative anal sex and oral sex. I doubt if the third is. And I doubt if either the second or third is needed to be able to consent to sexual activity such as mutual masturbation. This leads to potentially serious management problems where different kinds of sexual activities are practised at different times.[235]

And even if the courts are clear in a particular case about the lack of capacity, the management issues might remain significant.

In the following case, the judge referred to the highly restrictive care regime in place, involving a deprivation of liberty – a regime rooted in the woman's lack of capacity to consent to sexual activity and to keep her safe from exploitative and damaging activity:

> H lives in accommodation provided by a private agency in contract with the local authority. There are some three other residents living in the same building. At least 1:1 supervision is provided during the day and waking supervision is required overnight. H is supervised on a 1:1 basis at all times whether in or out of the property and she is not free to leave it on any

234 *Ealing London Borough Council v KS* [2008] EWHC 636 (Fam).
235 *D Borough Council v AB* [2011] EWHC 101 (COP).

other basis. Those who may enter the property are also carefully regulated. It is not that H does not have much to do, (she has a number of outside activities including two part time jobs) but that she cannot do it without 1:1 supervision.

This highly regulated regime evokes two observations: first, that it clearly constitutes a deprivation of liberty and indeed a DOLS standard authorisation under Schedule A1 of the Mental Capacity Act 2005 is in force and its renewal will be sought; and secondly, the purpose of these restrictions is to prevent H from engaging in sexual relations (which she would otherwise willingly do) because she does not have capacity to consent and they will be potentially exploitative and damaging.

These are considerable incursions into personal autonomy and freedom. They depend on a best interests judgment as to her needs and have their legal foundation in a finding of incapacity to consent to sexual relations.[236]

SEXUAL ACTIVITY AND MORAL OR EMOTIONAL UNDERSTANDING

Legal doubts continue, including whether the test for sexual activity should involve something by way of moral or emotional understanding.

In a case heard in early 2012, the court reiterated the necessity of understanding the nature of the physical act, pregnancy and health issues:

> Clearly a person must have a basic understanding of the mechanics of the physical act and clearly must have an understanding that vaginal intercourse may lead to pregnancy. Moreover it seems to me that capacity requires some grasp of issues of sexual health. However, given that that is linked to the knowledge of developments in medicine, it seems to me that the knowledge required is fairly rudimentary. In my view it should suffice if a person understands that sexual relations may lead to significant ill-health and that those risks can be reduced by precautions like a condom. I do not think more can be required.[237]

However, as to whether the capacity should include moral aspects, the answer was no:

> The greater problem for me is whether capacity needs in some way to reflect or encompass the moral and emotional aspect of human sexual relationships. I have reflected long and carefully on this... In relation to the moral aspect, I do not think it can be done. Of itself that does not alarm me for two reasons: first, I think the standard for capacity would be very modest not really going beyond an awareness of 'right' and 'wrong' behaviour as factors in making a choice; and secondly, the truly amoral human is a rarity and other issues

---

236 *A Local Authority v H* [2012] EWHC 49 (COP).
237 *A Local Authority v H* [2012] EWHC 49 (COP).

would then come into play. Accordingly, although in my judgment it is an important component in sexual relations it can have no specific role in a test of capacity.[238]

Likewise, for the emotional question:

And so one turns to the emotional component. It remains in my view an important, some might argue the most important, component; certainly it is the source of the greatest damage when sexual relations are abused. The act of intercourse is often understood as having an element of self-giving qualitatively different from any other human contact. Nevertheless, the challenge remains: can it be articulated into a workable test? Again I have thought long and hard about this and acknowledge the difficulty inherent in the task. In my judgment one can do no more than this: does the person whose capacity is in question understand that they do have a choice and that they can refuse? That seems to me an important aspect of capacity and is as far as it is really possible to go over and above an understanding of the physical component.[239]

CAPACITY AND CONTRACEPTION

Contraception has emerged as a separate issue. In one case, the local authority accepted that the woman in question had capacity to marry (she was indeed married) and therefore the capacity to engage in sexual activity, but it denied her ability to grasp contraception. The local authority wanted to include, in the test of capacity for contraception, an understanding of bringing up a child; the judge rejected this in favour of confining the test to proximate medical issues:

The test for capacity should be so applied as to ascertain the woman's ability to understand and weigh up the immediate medical issues surrounding contraceptive treatment ('the proximate medical issues'...), including:

(a) the reason for contraception and what it does (which includes the likelihood of pregnancy if it is not in use during sexual intercourse);

(b) the types available and how each is used;

(c) the advantages and disadvantages of each type;

(d) the possible side-effects of each and how they can be dealt with;

(e) how easily each type can be changed; and

(f) the generally accepted effectiveness of each.

I do not consider that questions need be asked as to the woman's understanding of what bringing up a child would be like in practice; nor any

238 *A Local Authority v H* [2012] EWHC 49 (COP).
239 *A Local Authority v H* [2012] EWHC 49 (COP).

opinion attempted as to how she would be likely to get on; nor whether any child would be likely to be removed from her care.[240]

CAPACITY, MARRIAGE, SEX AND CULTURAL MATTERS

The test of marriage and sexual relations might not set a high threshold, but the courts have adhered to it, even when cultural issues have arisen in relation to other countries which do not set such a threshold.

A number of cases have reached the courts. Typically, the parents see the prospective marriage as 'arranged' rather than 'forced' – even when their son or daughter lacks mental capacity – and in any case as being in their child's best interests. The courts will take a firm line; sometimes they will order that the person's passport be held by the court, so that the person lacking capacity cannot be taken abroad to marry.[241] Alternatively, they might simply accept undertakings by the parents not to take their son or daughter abroad.[242]

MENTAL CAPACITY, SEXUAL RELATIONS AND CRIMINAL OFFENCES

The spectre of criminal prosecution under the Sexual Offences Act 2003 is sometimes raised in the context of capacity and marriage if the rules about mental capacity and sexual relations are flouted – albeit for cultural reasons.

For instance, in one particular case, a man with learning disabilities – who lacked the capacity to understand the nature of marriage – was married, in a Muslim ceremony conducted on the telephone, to a woman in Bangladesh. The intention of the parents was clearly that the matrimonial home was to be in England. Accepting, in this particular case, that the marriage was indeed contracted in Bangladesh and that it was valid in that country, the Court of Appeal was emphatic that it would not be so in England. The court held that the man had to be protected from abuse permitted or encouraged by his parents.

Abusive and injurious marriage: person lacking capacity. The expert evidence suggested that;

> ...the marriage which his parents have arranged for him is potentially highly injurious. He has not the capacity to understand the introduction of NK into his life and that introduction would be likely to destroy his equilibrium or destabilize his emotional state... Were IC's parents to permit or encourage sexual intercourse...NK would be guilty of the crime of rape under the provisions of the Sexual Offences Act 2003. Physical intimacy which stops short of penetrative sex would constitute the crime of indecent assault... Their engineering of the telephonic marriage is potentially if not actually abusive of IC. It is the duty of the court to protect IC from that potential abuse. The refusal of recognition of the marriage is an essential foundation of that protection.[243]

---

240   *A Local Authority v Mrs A* [2010] EWHC 1549 (Fam).

241   *M v B* [2005] EWHC 1681 (Fam).

242   *X City Council v MAB* [2006] EWHC 168 (Fam).

243   *KC v City of Westminster Social and Community Services Department* [2008] EWCA Civ 198.

Note. A marriage generally is voidable if 'either party to the marriage did not validly consent to it, whether in consequence of duress, mistake, unsoundness of mind or otherwise'. This is under the Matrimonial Causes Act 1973, s.12c.

INDEPENDENT MENTAL CAPACITY ADVOCATES (IMCAS)

The Mental Capacity Act provides for independent mental capacity advocates (IMCAs) to be appointed. In particular, in addition to various duties, there is a power for NHS bodies or local authorities to appoint such an advocate where adult protection issues have arisen. In such circumstances, an IMCA could play a key role.

Additional functions are placed on IMCAs when authorisation of deprivation of liberty takes place: this has been covered above.

ROLE OF INDEPENDENT MENTAL CAPACITY ADVOCATE

Generally, section 35 places a duty on the Department of Health to make arrangements for independent mental capacity advocates. Local authorities are responsible for contracting locally with appropriate organisations. Such an advocate has the power to:

- interview the person whom he or she has been instructed to represent

- at all reasonable times examine and take copies of a health record, a local authority social services record or a record of a registered care provider which the holder of the record considers may be relevant to the advocate's investigation.

Section 36 details the advocate's core functions as being to provide support, obtain and evaluate relevant information, ascertain what the person's wishes, feelings, beliefs and values might be (if the person has capacity), ascertain alternative courses of action and obtain a further medical opinion where treatment is proposed (if the advocate thinks this should be obtained).

The advocate must prepare a report for the authorised person who instructed him or her. The advocate subsequently has the same rights to challenge the decision as if he or she were any other person engaged in caring for the person or interested in his or her welfare.[244]

DUTY TO APPOINT IMCA: ACCOMMODATION OR SERIOUS MEDICAL TREATMENT

Appointment of an IMCA may be a duty or power.

A duty arises (a) if the person lacking capacity is unbefriended – that is, if the local authority or NHS body is satisfied that there is no other person (other than one providing care or treatment in a professional capacity or for remuneration)

---

244 Mental Capacity Act 2005, s.36. And: SI 2006/1832 SI 2006/1832. The Mental Capacity Act 2005 (Independent Mental Capacity Advocates) (General) Regulations 2006.

whom it would be appropriate to consult about the person's best interests – and (b) if serious medical treatment or placement in a hospital or care home is in question.

In the case of a hospital, the placement must be likely to last longer than four weeks; in a care home, longer than eight weeks.

The code of practice makes clear that just because a 'family disagrees with the decision-maker's proposed action, this is not grounds for concluding that there is nobody whose views are relevant to the decision'.[245]

There is also no duty to appoint an advocate if there is another person, nominated by the person lacking capacity, to be consulted on matters to which the duty relates, if there is a donee of a lasting power of attorney authorised to make decisions on those welfare matters, or if there is a court-appointed deputy with the power to make decisions in relation to those welfare matters.[246]

Serious medical treatment involves providing, withdrawing or withholding treatment in the following circumstances:

- in the case of a single treatment, there is a fine balance between benefit, and burden and risk, to the patient

- where there is a choice of treatments, a decision as to which one to use is finely balanced; or

- what is proposed would be likely to involve serious consequences for the patient.[247]

The duty to appoint an IMCA falls either on the NHS body in the case of serious medical treatment or hospital or care home placement, or on the local authority in the case of a care home placement.

In addition, there are special IMCA provisions relating to authorisations to deprive a person of his or her liberty under schedule A1 of the MCA 2005. These have been detailed above.

In case of urgency, the rules are relaxed, and the IMCA should be subsequently appointed, in the case of provision of accommodation.[248]

POWER TO INSTRUCT IMCA IN CASE OF ABUSE OR NEGLECT

A power (rather than a duty) arises to appoint an IMCA in two circumstances. First, if adult protection measures are being or are going to be taken – whether or not there are family or friends appropriate to consult (see immediately below). Second, if the hospital or care home accommodation is being reviewed, where the person has been in the accommodation for at least 12 weeks continuously.[249]

---

245 Lord Chancellor. *Mental Capacity Act 2005: code of practice.* London: TSO, 2007, para 10.79.

246 Mental Capacity Act 2005, s.40.

247 Quoted from: SI 2006/1832. The Mental Capacity Act 2005 (Independent Mental Capacity Advocates) (General) Regulations 2006.

248 Mental Capacity Act 2007, ss.37–39.

249 Mental Capacity Act 2005, ss.36–39. And: SI 2006/2883. The Mental Capacity Act 2005 (Independent Mental Capacity Advocates) (Expansion of Role) Regulations 2006.

The power in relation to adult protection arises if the NHS body or local authority proposes to take, or has taken, protective measures for a person lacking capacity (a) following receipt of allegation of abuse or neglect (by another person), or (b) in accordance with arrangements made under adult protection guidance issued under s.7 Local Authority Social Services Act 1970.

The relevant guidance is the *No secrets* guidance issued in 2000 by the Department of Health.[250] Protective measures are defined to include measures to minimise risk of abuse or neglect.

The power is not dependent on the absence of another person, other than one providing care or treatment in a professional capacity or for remuneration, whom it would be appropriate to consult about the person's best interests.[251]

In spite of the fact that appointment of an IMCA is a power only, nonetheless a blanket policy not to appoint IMCAs in such circumstances would be a fettering of discretion and lay the local authority or NHS body open to legal challenge or complaint to the ombudsmen.

OFFENCES OF ILL-TREATMENT OR WILFUL NEGLECT

Section 44 creates offences of ill-treatment or wilful neglect by any person who has the care of another person who lacks, or who the first person reasonably believed to lack, capacity, or by any deputy or person with lasting power of attorney (s.44). These offences are dealt with in Chapter 21.

OFFICE OF THE PUBLIC GUARDIAN

The Mental Capacity Act created a new Public Guardian, supported by the Office of the Public Guardian.[252] The functions of the Public Guardian are to protect people lacking capacity and include, in summary:

- setting up and managing separate registers of lasting powers of attorney, of enduring powers of attorney, of court order appointed deputies

- supervising deputies

- sending Court of Protection visitors to visit people who may lack capacity and also those who have formal powers to act on their behalf

- receiving reports from attorneys acting under lasting powers of attorney and from deputies

- providing reports to the Court of Protection

---

250 Department of Health. *No secrets: guidance on developing and implementing multi-agency policies and procedures to protect vulnerable adults from abuse.* London: DH, 2000.

251 SI 2006/2883. The Mental Capacity Act 2005 (Independent Mental Capacity Advocates) (Expansion of Role) Regulations 2006.

252 Mental Capacity Act 2005, s.57.

- dealing with complaints about the way in which attorneys or deputies carry out their duties.[253]

The Office of the Public Guardian can investigate in the case of deputies or registered power of attorney, but not otherwise – for example, in the case of unregistered or fake powers of attorney.

APPOINTEES

The law relating to appointeeship remains outside of the Mental Capacity Act 2005.

If a person is receiving social security benefit but is 'for the time being unable to act', then someone may be appointed to manage the benefits, assuming that no deputy with the relevant power has been appointed by the Court of Protection.[254]

It is a matter of somebody applying to the Department of Work and Pensions to be appointee. If there is no one willing and able to take on the role, a local authority, for example, can take it on, with named officers signing the paperwork.

In the context of safeguarding, local authority staff often express uncertainty about what to do if they have concerns about the way an appointee is handling a person's social security benefits. Many believe that appointeeship comes under the MCA and assume serious abuse would be a matter ultimately for the Court of Protection. This is incorrect; the responsible organisation is the Department of Work and Pensions, and the relevant legislation, namely benefits regulations, does not come under the jurisdiction of the Court of Protection.

Guidance from the Department of Work and Pensions considers what 'unable to act' means:

> 3.80 Under the regulations, for a person to have an appointee they must be 'unable to act'.
>
> 3.81 Unable to act is not defined in the regulations but could mean that the person is be unable to manage their own affairs relating to Housing Benefit/ Council Tax Benefit (HB/CTB) because of incapacity which
>
> - can be physical or mental
>
> - does not have to be permanent providing they are unable to manage for the period they have an appointee. This means if the claimant recovers, you must cancel the appointee, see Review of appointeeship later in this chapter
>
> 3.82 It does not cover situations when a tenant
>
> - chooses not to claim despite being able to
>
> - does not claim because they
>
>   ○ cannot be bothered to, or
>
>   ○ are ignorant of the benefit system

253 Lord Chancellor. *Mental Capacity Act 2005: code of practice.* London: TSO, 2007, para 14.8.
254 SI 1987/1968. Social Security (Claims and Payments) Regulations 1987.

3.83 Whether a tenant is unable to act is a matter for the LA to decide after considering all the circumstances of the individual case.[255]

The guidance goes on to discuss who is suitable to be an appointee:

3.100 Appointees must be suitable to do the duties required of them. A suitable appointee is

- acceptable to the claimant

- capable of managing the claimant's affairs and can be trusted to do so in the interests of the claimant

- in regular contact with the claimant and has enough knowledge of the claimant's circumstances to notify the LA of relevant changes of circumstances and answer authority enquiries

- fully aware of the responsibilities of being an appointee, for example aware they are responsible for repaying overpaid benefit

3.101 Consider the suitability of a prospective appointee according to the circumstances of each case. Usually close members of the claimant's family would be the most suitable people to act as appointee. Ideally they would already be providing care and support for the claimant. However, in some cases close family friends may be best placed to act for the claimant.

3.102 In some cases it may not be immediately obvious there is anyone suitable to be the appointee. In these circumstances you may approach the appropriate social services department for advice. They may have family contacts who could be a suitable appointee who are unknown to the benefit section. If there is no close family or friends, you may need to consider if an officer from the LA should be appointed. If you decide this is appropriate, an officer from the social services or welfare department would be the most appropriate appointee in these circumstances.[256]

The guidance also considers who might be unsuitable:

3.130 There should be no potential for a conflict of interest, for example it might be inappropriate to make the claimant's landlord the appointee. However, in exceptional circumstances if no other appointee is available, you may consider a landlord providing they are suitable, see above for guidance on suitability.[257]

---

255 Department of Work and Pensions. *HB/CTB Guidance Manual, Amendment 15*. London: DWP, 2008.
256 Department of Work and Pensions. *HB/CTB Guidance Manual, Amendment 15*. London: DWP, 2008.
257 Department of Work and Pensions. *HB/CTB Guidance Manual, Amendment 15*. London: DWP, 2008.

MENTAL CAPACITY ACT APPLICATION TO CHILDREN AND YOUNG PEOPLE

The Act does not apply to people under 16 years old, unless the Court of Protection is making a decision about a child's (without capacity) property, if the child is likely still to lack capacity at age 18.[258]

The Act does apply to people aged 16 or 17 years, but (a) only people aged 18 or over can make a lasting power of attorney;[259] (b) only people aged 18 or over can make advance decisions;[260] and (c) the Court of Protection can only make a statutory will for a person aged 18 or over.[261]

Legal proceedings in respect of 16- or 17-year-olds who lack capacity to make the relevant decisions may be heard either by the Court of Protection or the family courts. Proceedings can be transferred between the two.[262]

The deprivation of liberty safeguards in relation to standard or urgent authorisations do not apply to people under 18 years old. The rules concerning the detention and treatment of children, particularly 16- and 17-year- olds, are complex as a result of these amendments to the Mental Capacity Act 2005 and amendments to the Mental Health Act 1983 (both sets of amendments being introduced by the Mental Health Act 2007).

---

258 Mental Capacity Act 2000, s.18.
259 Mental Capacity Act 2005, s.9.
260 Mental Capacity Act 2005, s.24.
261 Mental Capacity Act 2005, s.18.
262 Mental Capacity Act 2005, s.21. And SI 2007/1899. The Mental Capacity Act 2005 (Transfer of Proceedings) Order 2007.

Inherent jurisdiction of the High Court

Key points
Overbearing of a person's exercise of capacity
Inherent jurisdiction: constraint, undue influence, coercion
Inherent jurisdiction and vulnerable adults
Primary use of jurisdiction to facilitate, not dictate, decision making of adult
Granting a prohibitive order under the inherent jurisdiction
Use of the inherent jurisdiction in relation to an adult who lacks capacity
    Interventions under the inherent jurisdiction not necessarily
      restricted to best interests: and public policy also relevant

KEY POINTS

The inherent jurisdiction is a residual, common law power of the High Court to hear cases not coming under, or excluded by, legislation.

The Mental Capacity Act 2005 means that many decisions previously taken by the Family Division of the High Court under common law – the inherent jurisdiction – are now made by the Court of Protection. However, some issues may arise that fall outside the 2005 Act and so may still call for the exercise of the inherent jurisdiction.

The inherent jurisdiction comes into play either when a person effectively lacks capacity, but for some reason the matter in hand does not come under the rules of the Mental Capacity Act, or when a person has capacity to take a decision, but circumstances mean that he or she is being prevented from, or hindered in, exercising that capacity.

Use of the inherent jurisdiction for adults who are vulnerable but with capacity is a developing area of law and goes to the heart of a problem that so often troubles those involved in safeguarding: how to protect a vulnerable adult from unwise decisions. However, the jurisdiction by no means represents a magic wand, since it is exercised with caution and sparingly by the courts – for fear of undermining the principle of autonomy and the right of a person with capacity to take unwise decisions.

OVERBEARING OF A PERSON'S EXERCISE OF CAPACITY

In an older case involving a medical decision, the question arose whether a woman should have a blood transfusion. The court stated that it could intervene either on the ground of lack of capacity or if the woman's will had been overborne by outside influence.

Overbearing, by mother, of daughter's will in making a decision about life-saving treatment. A young woman, 34 weeks pregnant, had a car accident. Her parents were separated; her mother was a Jehovah's Witness, her father was not. She herself had held some Jehovah's Witness beliefs but had never formally been accepted into the faith. Before losing consciousness in the hospital, she had spent some time alone with her mother. Following this time, she said she did not want a blood transfusion; the doctors hesitated to give one. The case went urgently to the courts.

The Court of Appeal held that, in all the circumstances, she lacked capacity to take the decision that the transfusion could be given. The court would make a declaration to that effect. However, in addition, if she had capacity, it would also have found that the influence of her mother had vitiated her ability to make a decision. In this respect, it was one thing for a person to be persuaded, but another to have their will overborne. In such circumstances, doctors could take the view that the decision was not a true decision and apply to the courts for help.[1]

In another case, the High Court held that it can exercise the jurisdiction in respect of a competent adult whose capacity to consent to marriage is overborne by fear, duress or threat, such that she is deprived of the capacity to make relevant decisions.[2]

INHERENT JURISDICTION: CONSTRAINT, UNDUE INFLUENCE, COERCION

The courts have stated that the inherent jurisdiction is not confined only to cases involving lack of mental capacity or to cases where, although not lacking capacity, the adult is unable to communicate his or her decision.

In addition, it could extend to a vulnerable adult who:

> even if not incapacitated by mental disorder or mental illness, is, or is reasonably believed to be, either (i) under constraint, or (ii) subject to coercion or undue influence or (iii) for some other reason deprived of the capacity to make the relevant decision, or disabled from making a free choice, or incapacitated or disabled from giving or expressing real or genuine consent.[3]

Thus, in the same case, the court granted the order sought.

Protecting a person with the capacity to understand marriage. A woman was profoundly deaf. She had no speech and no oral communication. She had profound bilateral sensory neural loss and significant visual loss in one eye. She communicated in British Sign Language (BSL), which was based in English. Her ability to communicate with her parents was very limited because their first language was Punjabi. She had limited capacity to lip-read English. She could not understand, lip-read or sign in either Punjabi or Urdu. Neither of her parents could communicate with her using British Sign Language.

---

1   *Re T* [1992] 3 WLR 782.
2   *Re SK* [2004] EWHCD 3202 (Fam).
3   *Re SA* [2005] EWHC 2942 (Fam).

Understanding of marriage but risk of inability to communicate in Pakistan.
She had been assessed as having a rudimentary but clear and accurate understanding of the concept of marriage, the implications of a marriage contract, of a sexual relationship and its implications. However, the assessing doctor, a chartered forensic psychologist, was concerned that she might marry a person who could not communicate with her, especially outside the UK where she might be surrounded also by people with whom she could not communicate.

She had made it clear that although she wished to travel to Pakistan for an arranged marriage, she did not want to live there and wished to return to her home town. If this were not possible, she would rather not marry. However, she did not understand that any such husband might be prevented from returning with her by the immigration authorities. It had now come to the local authority's attention that a trip to Pakistan might be imminent.

Provision of court order to ensure informed consent of vulnerable adult. It was argued that the court should intervene, prohibiting her parents from threatening, intimidating and harassing her, using violence, preventing her communicating alone with her solicitor, applying for travel documents for her and removing her from England and Wales without express written consent, translated and explained in BSL and duly notarised. They would also be prohibited from making arrangements for her to be married unless they had her express written consent (as above), notarised consent of the bridegroom, allowed her to return to her home town within four months of the marriage ceremony, allowed her to reside in her home town, allowed a visit by a worker from the British High Commission in Islamabad four months after the ceremony to interview her alone as to whether she wished to return to England and Wales. A power of arrest was also sought, to be attached to any order made.

The court granted the order sought. In summary, the court stated that the person was:

> a vulnerable adult who there is every reason to believe may, by reason of her disabilities, and even in the absence of any undue influence or misinformation, be disabled from making a free choice and incapacitated or disabled from forming or expressing a real and genuine consent.[4]

INHERENT JURISDICTION AND VULNERABLE ADULTS

The courts have also considered who can be protected under the inherent jurisdiction and whether it applies to vulnerable adults only. The answer is not necessarily, but that the jurisdiction may be easier to invoke in the case of vulnerable adults:

> The inherent jurisdiction is not confined to those who are vulnerable adults, however that expression is understood, nor is a vulnerable adult amenable as such to the jurisdiction. The significance in this context of the concept of a vulnerable adult is pragmatic and evidential: it is simply that an adult who is vulnerable is more likely to fall into the category of the incapacitated in relation to whom the inherent jurisdiction is exercisable than an adult who is not vulnerable. So it is likely to be easier to persuade the court that there is a case calling for investigation where the adult is apparently vulnerable than where the adult is not on the face of it vulnerable.[5]

---

4   *Re SA* [2005] EWHC 2942 (Fam).
5   *Re SA (Vulnerable Adult with Capacity: Marriage)* [2005] EWHC 2942 (Fam).

PRIMARY USE OF JURISDICTION TO FACILITATE, NOT DICTATE, DECISION MAKING OF ADULT

The Court of Appeal has confirmed that the inherent jurisdiction survives the Mental Capacity Act 2005.[6]

However, the courts are understandably cautious about the inherent jurisdiction and have made clear that its primary use is precisely to enable free and informed decision making; it is not to be used simply to overrule the wishes of a person who has capacity. Apart from anything else, the latter type of usage would risk undermining the third main principle of the Mental Capacity Act 2005, that unwise decisions do not necessarily mean lack of capacity.

So the courts will draw a line, as they did in a case involving the fluctuating capacity of a mentally disordered woman to consent to sexual activity. The court accepted that the local authority could use the Mental Capacity Act 2005 to protect her when she lacked capacity. However, the court rejected the local authority's argument that it should exercise the inherent jurisdiction to make a protective order to apply at those times when she had capacity. The court concluded it had no legal power to do so.[7]

As things stand, the courts have been at pains therefore to emphasise that in such cases the inherent jurisdiction should be used not simply to overrule the wishes of a person with capacity wishing to take a decision; instead, the jurisdiction is about putting the person in a position whereby he or she can exercise free and informed choice and decision making about the matter in hand.

GRANTING A PROHIBITIVE ORDER UNDER THE INHERENT JURISDICTION

In 2011, the limits and scope of the jurisdiction were tested in a case where an elderly couple, both with the requisite mental capacity (at least at the outset of the case), lived with their son. He persistently mistreated them in a number of ways. The local authority had explored possible legal options but rejected them all: an application to the Court of Protection under the Mental Capacity Act, an application for an anti-social behaviour order under the Crime and Disorder Act 1998 and an application under section 153A of the Housing Act 1996 for an anti-social behaviour injunction. So the position was:

> The local authority acknowledges that, on the information currently available to it, neither Mr nor Mrs L lacks the capacity to take proceedings on behalf of themselves or each other by reason of any impairment of or disturbance in the functioning of the mind or brain. The local authority recognises that Mrs L, in particular, wishes to preserve her relationship with DL and does not want any proceedings taken against him. Furthermore, the local authority acknowledges that whilst Mr L is more critical of DL's behaviour, it remains

6   *KC v City of Westminster Social and Community Services Department* [2008] EWCA Civ 198.
7   *London Borough of Ealing v KS* [2008] EWHC 636 (Fam).

unclear as to whether he, Mr L, would wish to take steps in opposition to his wife's wishes.[8]

The order sought from the court was to try to prohibit the son from behaving in certain ways towards his parents:

(i)   assaulting or threatening to assault GRL or ML;

(ii)   preventing GRL [the husband] or ML [the mother] from having contact with friends and family members;

(iii)   seeking to persuade or coerce GRL into transferring ownership of the current family home;

(iv)   seeking to persuade or coerce ML into moving into a care home or nursing home;

(v)   engaging in behaviour towards GRL or ML that is otherwise degrading or coercive, including (but not limited to): stipulating which rooms in the house GRL or ML can use; preventing GRL or ML from using household appliances, including the washing-machine; 'punishing' GRL or ML, for example, by making GRL write 'lines'; shouting or otherwise behaving in an aggressive or intimidating manner towards them.

(vi)   giving orders to care staff;

(vii)   interfering in the provision of care and support to ML;

(viii)   refusing access to health and social care professionals;

(ix)   behaving in an aggressive and/or confrontational manner to care staff and care managers.[9]

The court granted the order.

It is noteworthy that the courts have referred to the Human Rights Act 1998 as a reason for retaining the inherent jurisdiction to be used to protect vulnerable adults. This, in turn, means that local authorities and NHS bodies must bear in mind that not to give consideration to the inherent jurisdiction could be inconsistent with their human rights obligations.

The courts emphasised in the *DL* case that, consistent with the demands of article 8 and the European Convention, the jurisdiction was to help people make decisions freely, rather than trample over their wishes – that is, 'facilitative rather than dictatorial' – and that 'its primary purpose is to create a situation where the person concerned can receive outside help free of coercion, to enable him or her to weigh things up and decide freely what he or she wishes to do'.[10]

---

8   *A Local Authority v DL* [2011] EWHC 1022 (Fam).
9   Quoted from: *A Local Authority v DL* [2011] EWHC 1022 (Fam).
10   *A Local Authority v DL* [2011] EWHC 1022 (Fam).

USE OF THE INHERENT JURISDICTION IN RELATION TO AN ADULT WHO LACKS CAPACITY

Use of the inherent jurisdiction has been described above as applicable to an adult with capacity to take a decision but unable to exercise that capacity in the particular circumstances – such as coercion, undue influence or threat.

However, the jurisdiction may arise in a different way. That is, where the requisite order cannot be made under the Mental Capacity Act 2005, despite the person lacking mental capacity, and so falls under the inherent jurisdiction instead.

For example, in a 2012 case the Court of Protection considered a woman living in England, lacking capacity to marry, who had been married in Bangladesh.

Her 'husband' then obtained a spouse's visa to enter the United Kingdom, which appears to have been his main motive for marrying. Her parents didn't think they had done anything wrong and couldn't understand the fuss being made. He shared a bedroom and a bed with her in her family home. Concerns about her welfare reached the local authority. The police obtained a forced marriage protection order. The Court of Protection warned the 'husband' that to have sexual relations with her would be a criminal offence. The court was now considering what to do about the marriage. The local authority, the Official Solicitor, the husband and the parents all urged the court not to make a declaration as to the non-validity of the marriage. Instead, prohibitions made by the court and assurances and undertakings should be relied on.

The court decided to go its own way. First, it was clear that marrying without capacity meant that the marriage was forced. Second, it wished to make a declaration that the Bangladeshi marriage was invalid in this country. But, looking at the range of declarations allowable under s.15 of the Mental Capacity Act, the court concluded that the required declaration could not be made under the Act:

> I could, I think, make a declaration pursuant to the MCA 2005 that it is unlawful for DD to be married in this jurisdiction. I do not think that I could make a declaration that it was or is unlawful for her to be married in Bangladesh. But even if I am wrong about this, there is no jurisdiction within the MCA 2005 to make a non-recognition declaration in respect of the marriage: and it is not a personal welfare decision.[11]

This meant that, although it could make other declarations and personal welfare decisions under the 2005 Act, it would have to use the inherent jurisdiction to declare the Bangladeshi marriage invalid in this country. The particular declaration did not fall into the 'repertoire of remedies' contained within the MCA.

In the same case, the judge made further comments about the nature of the inherent jurisdiction and in so doing attempted to give it more characteristics of its own and to distance it from being seen as a mere appendage to the Mental Capacity Act 2005.

---

11   *XCC v AA* [2012] EWHC 2183 (COP).

INTERVENTIONS UNDER THE INHERENT JURISDICTION NOT NECESSARILY RESTRICTED TO BEST INTERESTS: AND PUBLIC POLICY ALSO RELEVANT

In the case about the invalid marriage, *XCC v AA*, described immediately above, the judge explored further the nature of the inherent jurisdiction.

First, she noted that interventions under the inherent jurisdiction were not necessarily limited to the concept of best interests as set out in the MCA. However, she found that in any case best interests statements in this case pointed to a termination of marital relations, but she seemed to criticise the local authority and others: it was 'a remarkable feature of this case that the presentation of DD's welfare interests by those who have a duty to protect her welfare has focused on... the wishes and feelings of her family'.

The judge held also that the court did not strictly have to apply the least restrictive option principle found in s.1 of the MCA, although necessity and proportionality should still guide the court.

Second, she found that public policy (in this case, immigration considerations) could come into play when consideration is given to use of the inherent jurisdiction:

> The Court of Appeal in *KC v Westminster* held that 'the refusal of recognition of marriage is an essential foundation of the duty to protect the incapacitated adult'. The specific public policy considered by the Court of Appeal was that such a marriage is so offensive to the conscience of the court that it should not be recognised. I have said that to force a marriage on an incapacitous person is a gross interference with his or her autonomy. Its concomitants, sexual relations and, as a foreseeable consequence, pregnancy, constitute not only a breach of autonomy but also bodily integrity, perhaps one of the most severe that can be imagined, and the consequences may be lifelong.[12]

In this particular case, public policy was relevant because:

> The most important aspect of the immigration aspect of this case is that this non-consensual, forced marriage has been created in order to further the interests of others and not DD. That is a clear public policy consideration that affects DD. DD would not have been married to AA had he not wanted to come to England to live and work.[13]

---

12   *XCC v AA* [2012] EWHC 2183 (COP).
13   *XCC v AA* [2012] EWHC 2183 (COP).

Interventions and removal of people from their own homes (including in circumstances of self-neglect)

Key points
National Assistance Act 1948, section 47: removal of people from home
    Human rights
Protection of property: National Assistance Act 1948, section 48
Environmental health interventions
    Environmental Protection Act 1990
    Public Health Act 1936
Police powers of entry
    Entering and searching premises
    Entering and searching premises without warrant for indictable offence
    Arresting a person committing or about to commit an offence
Gas and electricity operators
Mental Health Act interventions
    Mental Health Act 1983: interventions and mental disorder
    Limited detention for assessment (and treatment) (section 2)
    Longer-term detention for treatment (section 3)
    Entry and inspection of premises (section 115)
    Warrant for search and removal from premises (section 135)
    Removal of a mentally disordered person from a public place (section 136)
    Guardianship (sections 7 and 8)
    Informal mental health patients (section 131)
Self-neglect
    Examples of self-neglect requiring more intervention
    Examples of self-neglect when nothing more could have been done
        to protect the person
    Diogenes syndrome (and manslaughter)

KEY POINTS

In order to protect vulnerable people in their own homes, often from themselves, a number of interventions are possible under various legislation, including the

National Assistance Act 1948, environmental health legislation, the Mental Health Act 1983 and the Mental Capacity Act 2005.

These interventions will sometimes be relevant to adult protection or safeguarding generally, and sometimes to self-neglect in particular.

The use of this legislation does not depend on whether a local authority or other body, such as an NHS trust, decides to categorise self-neglect as a safeguarding matter.

The Mental Capacity Act 2005 has already been covered in Chapter 13. It may well afford a ground for intervention in cases of self-neglect.

There are, however, other legal avenues. In the case of a person living neglected and in squalor, the National Assistance Act 1948 or environmental health legislation might also be relevant.

The Mental Health Act 1983 may also afford an intervention. For instance, guardianship allows a local authority to protect a person by determining where he or she should live, and s.135 allows for removing a person to a place of safety.

The Public Health Act 1936 and Environmental Protection Act 1990 provide, as a last resort, power of entry for environmental health officers to deal with public health hazards – for example, when a person is living in a state of squalor and self-neglect that has led to infestations or perhaps fire hazards.

Section 17 of the Police and Criminal Evidence Act 1984 provides for the police to exercise powers of entry – for instance, where there is believed to be risk to life and limb.

NATIONAL ASSISTANCE ACT 1948, SECTION 47: REMOVAL OF PEOPLE FROM HOME

In July 2012, the government stated that it intended to abolish s.47 of the National Assistance Act and to consult on whether any new provision, compliant with human rights, should replace it.[1] This proposal was based on the Law Commission's recommendations of the previous year.[2] Assuming the abolition takes place, this will probably happen by 2015. An equivalent power may or may not be included in new legislation.

Under s.47 of the National Assistance Act 1948, local authorities (district councils or borough councils) can, by magistrate's order, remove to institutional care people who:

- are suffering from grave chronic disease or, being aged, infirm or physically incapacitated, are living in insanitary conditions, and

- are unable to devote to themselves, and are not receiving from other persons, proper care and attention.[3]

1   Department of Health. *Reforming the law for adult care and support: the government's response to Law Commission report 326 on adult social care.* London: DH, 2012, para 9.17.
2   Law Commission. *Adult social care.* Law Com. no. 326. London: TSO, 2011, paras 9.60–9.96.
3   Quoted from: National Assistance Act 1948, s.47.

A medical officer of health (i.e. community physician) must certify to the authority that removal of the person is necessary either in his or her own best interests or for prevention of injury to the health of, or serious nuisance to, other people.

The authority can apply to a magistrates' court for an order that may authorise the person's detention for up to three months, although this may be extended by court order. Seven days' notice is required to be given to the person before a court can consider the application. The period of notice can be dispensed with under powers in the National Assistance (Amendment) Act 1951 if it is certified both by the medical officer of health and another registered medical practitioner that, in their opinion, it is necessary in the interests of the person that he or she be removed without delay.

HUMAN RIGHTS

However, the person does not have to be mentally incapacitated or mentally disordered for s.47 to operate. Thus, s.47 of the 1948 Act is probably contrary in principle to the Human Rights Act 1998. This would be on the basis that neglect alone is not a ground on which people may be deprived of their liberty under article 5 of the European Convention on Human Rights. The article refers to people of unsound mind, alcoholics, drug addicts or vagrants, but not to people who neglect themselves or are neglected, who have the mental capacity to decide where and how they want to live (and so are not of unsound mind) and who are not otherwise diagnosed as mentally disordered. And a person can scarcely be a vagrant in their own home.

In addition, even if a person were of unsound mind, the Law Commission believes that s.57 breaches article 5(4) of the European Convention, which demands a legal means of speedily reviewing the deprivation of liberty.[4]

It has long been accepted that there are human rights problems with s.47, although reference is still sometimes made to the case of *HM v Switzerland*, heard before the European Court of Human Rights (the United Kingdom courts must take account of, though not necessarily follow, the European Court's judgments). This case involved a s.47 type of situation, in which the Court found there had been no deprivation of liberty and hence no breach of article 5 of the Convention.

Removing a person from her own home. Under the Swiss Civil Code, a person can be deprived of liberty on grounds of mental weakness or neglect. A woman in her eighties was living at home, was fairly infirm and had leg sores, and was nearly blind but capable of making decisions for herself. She was receiving a home help service from a voluntary organisation. This service was withdrawn because of difficulties in the home – the son opening the door skimpily dressed and only after a delay, rubbish around the house impeding the home help workers, unheated rooms, chaos in the woman's bedroom. The family did not respond to a request to ameliorate these conditions.

---

4   Law Commission. *Adult social care.* Law Com. no. 326. London: TSO, 2011, para 9.94.

Woman removed against her will. The local authority ordered that the woman be removed, against her will, for an unlimited period to a nursing home on the grounds of serious neglect. She was not placed in the locked ward of the nursing home; she had freedom of movement and had social contacts with the outside world. The woman complained, arguing that she was able to wash and dress herself, that her son (also an invalid) could cook for her and that she did not want him left alone. The local authority disputed this. Both the Appeals Commission and Federal Court upheld the local authority's action.

No medical assessment of capacity. She was removed on grounds both of neglect and 'vagrancy' (an article 5 term) and unsoundness of mind. Yet she had never been examined by a medical expert in respect of the latter issue, although one of the members of the Appeals Commission was a medical expert.

The European Court held that article 5 was not engaged because she had not been deprived of her liberty. This conclusion was based on the fact that she had been placed in the home in her own interests in order to provide her with the necessary medical care, as well as satisfactory living conditions and hygiene.[5]

Nevertheless, one of the judges strongly dissented in *HM v Switzerland*. He believed that article 5 had been breached on various grounds. Most important, and decisive for this dissenting judge, was the fact that the finding by the Appeals Commission, that she effectively lacked capacity, had been challenged by the woman and never confirmed by a medical expert, whilst the Federal Court had declined to examine the issue on the grounds that serious neglect would anyway justify removal.

PROTECTION OF PROPERTY: NATIONAL ASSISTANCE ACT 1948, SECTION 48

Section 48 of the National Assistance Act is due to be revoked. However, the government has included an equivalent duty in its draft Care and Support Bill 2012.[6]

Currently, under s.48, a duty to protect a person's property arises for a local authority if:

- a person is admitted to hospital, admitted to residential accommodation under s.21 of the 1948 Act, or removed under s.47 of the 1948 Act

- it appears to the local social services authority that there is danger of loss of, or damage to, any of the person's movable property by reason of his or her temporary or permanent inability to protect or deal with the property

- no other suitable arrangements have been or are being made.[7]

If these conditions are satisfied, then the local authority must take reasonable steps to prevent or mitigate the loss or damage. The authority has the power, at all reasonable times, to enter the person's place of residence and to deal with any

---

5   *HM v Switzerland* [2002] Application 39187/98 (European Court of Human Rights).

6   See: Department of Health. *Reforming the law for adult care and support: the government's response to Law Commission report 326 on adult social care.* London: DH, 2012, para 9.20.

7   Quoted from: National Assistance Act 1948, s.48.

movable property in a reasonable way to prevent or mitigate loss or damage. The local authority can recover reasonable expenses either from the person concerned or anybody else liable to maintain him or her.

Examples of reasonable steps might include, for example, securing the premises, informing the police about an empty property, taking an inventory, turning off utilities, disposing of perishable food and arranging for pets to be cared for.[8]

ENVIRONMENTAL HEALTH INTERVENTIONS

In the context of safeguarding adults, gaining entry into domestic premises (via an appropriate legal channel) in cases of neglect is not necessarily easy if the person is not opening his or her door. However, local authority environmental health departments do have various statutory powers to enter premises to deal with public health problems.

ENVIRONMENTAL PROTECTION ACT 1990

Under the Environmental Protection Act 1990 (EPA), local authority powers of entry apply in respect of statutory nuisances. On the production of the requisite authority, an authorised person can enter premises at any reasonable time to ascertain whether a statutory nuisance exists, or to take action or execute work authorised under part 3 of the 1990 Act. In the case of residential property, 24 hours' notice is required, unless it is an emergency such as danger to life or health.[9]

Statutory nuisance is defined as including premises that are in a state prejudicial to health or nuisance; smoke, fumes or gases emitted from premises so as to be prejudicial to health or a nuisance; any accumulation or deposit prejudicial to health or a nuisance; any animal kept in such a place or manner as to be prejudicial to health or a nuisance; and noise emitted from premises so as to be prejudicial to health or a nuisance.[10]

These conditions, which could underpin an intervention, are expressed in quite wide terms. They could clearly be relevant, in some circumstances, to self-neglect.

A local authority has a duty to serve an abatement notice if a statutory nuisance exists. If the notice is not complied with, the local authority may itself abate the nuisance and recover expenses reasonably incurred.[11] As a last resort, the council has a power of entry to premises, using force if necessary. An order can be obtained from a magistrates' court.[12]

---

8   Jones, R. *Encyclopaedia of social services and child care law*. London: Sweet and Maxwell, 2004, para D1-088.

9   Environmental Protection Act 1990, schedule 3.

10   Environmental Protection Act 1990, s.79.

11   Environmental Protection Act 1990, ss.81–82.

12   Environmental Protection Act 1990, schedule 3, para 2.

PUBLIC HEALTH ACT 1936

Under the Public Health Act 1936, the local authority has powers in respect of certain public health issues referred to in the Act.

These include filthy, unwholesome, verminous premises; verminous persons or clothing (including removal of a person); and cleaning or destroying filthy or verminous articles.[13]

Also, there is a power to require vacation of premises during fumigation.[14] As a last resort, the council has a power of entry to premises, using force if necessary. An order can be obtained from a magistrates' court.[15]

The usefulness of such powers, but also the need to exercise them carefully, was demonstrated in the following local ombudsman case.

Cleaning of premises under the Public Health Act 1936. A man was in poor health with limited ability to care for himself. His home became dirty and cluttered to the point where it required thorough cleaning in order to prevent a health and safety risk to himself and his care workers. His sister got in touch with the local social services authority; it then liaised with the environmental health department. Under s.83 of the Public Health Act 1936, the latter proposed to clean the flat and explained to the sister that it would do the work and recover the cost from her brother. However, the council sent a very much larger bill (over £1100) than the cost the sister claimed originally to have been advised by the local authority (£300).

The ombudsman concluded that the council had not been clear enough in its explanation; the bill had also been wrongly calculated. It included VAT in error, and an inflated amount for environmental health officer time had been included. He recommended that the bill be corrected and then reduced by £300, that the sister receive £200 in recognition of her time and trouble, that the council review the wording of its letters about such work and charges for it, and that it check that all bills for such work carried out since January 2003 had been correctly calculated.[16]

POLICE POWERS OF ENTRY

Under the Police and Criminal Evidence Act 1984 (PACE 1984), the police have a number of powers of entry relevant to safeguarding adults.

ENTERING AND SEARCHING PREMISES

Section 17(1)(e) of the PACE 1984 gives the police a power to enter and search premises without a warrant, in order to save life or limb or prevent serious damage to property.

The term 'life and limb' clearly covers serious harm.

Police entry after report of a person going berserk with a knife. It was reported that a woman had gone berserk with a knife. Police entered the house and intended to search one of the women inside, but had not informed the person why they had entered.

---

13   Public Health Act 1936, ss.83–85.
14   Public Health Act 1936, s.36.
15   Public Health Act 1936, s.287.
16   Local Government Ombudsman Investigation: *Ealing London Borough Council 2004* (03/A/17640).

The court confirmed that the police could enter and search premises under s.17 without permission. Saving life and limb would cover saving a person from causing himself or herself, or a third party, serious harm. And although it is desirable for the police to explain why they are entering and searching, there is no hard and fast rule about this.[17]

However, it is not enough that the police are concerned more generally about somebody's welfare. This therefore places limits on the use to which s.17 can be legitimately put when safeguarding concerns have arisen.

Neighbours had telephoned the police, reporting a disturbance. The police went to the house explaining that they had power to enter in relation to a concern about a person's welfare. The occupants took a different view. There was no report of injury, no sign of damage, no indication that a criminal offence had been committed. One of the occupants explained there had been a verbal argument. The court held that concern about a person's welfare was not enough. Life and limb connotes something more serious. The court referred back to the *Baker* case (above), in which 'serious bodily injury' was referred to. Examples would be, though not limited to, knife or gunshot wounds.[18]

Clearly, therefore, thought must be given by the police to the legal basis for entry.

For instance, in a Court of Protection case, the judge heard how police, social workers and district nurses arrived at the door of an elderly couple. The police threatened to arrest the husband if he did not let them in to see his wife, for whom he cared. He had denied entry to the district nurses during the previous fortnight because of disagreement about the timing of their visits and the support package he and his wife were being given. The nurses were concerned about his wife's skin care and catheter care. He let them in and they found that both her skin and catheter were all right. The judge commented:

> The papers do not indicate on what legal basis the police claimed a right to enter the premises without a warrant, nor therefore (if they were seeking to trespass) on what basis they were empowered to arrest Mr H if he refused them entry. The court has not been told that a warrant was obtained under section 135 of the Mental Health Act 1983, or that the 'saving life or limb' provisions in section 17(1)(e) of the Police & Criminal Evidence Act 1984 applied.[19]

ENTERING AND SEARCHING PREMISES WITHOUT WARRANT FOR INDICTABLE OFFENCE

The police can enter and search premises without a warrant to effect arrest for an indictable offence (an offence that can be tried in the Crown Court – for example, theft, fraud or more serious physical harm).[20]

---

17   *Baker v Crown Prosecution Service* [2009] EWHC 299 (Admin).

18   *Syed v Director of Public Prosecutions* [2010] EWHC 81 (Admin).

19   *A London Local Authority v JH* [2011] EWHC 2420 (COP).

20   Police and Criminal Evidence Act 1984, s.17(1)(b).

They can enter and search premises in the course of recapturing somebody who is unlawfully at large and whom they are pursuing.[21] But there does have to be a pursuit first – for example, in the case of a person who has absconded from detention under the Mental Health Act 1983 and is therefore unlawfully at large.

Pursuing a mental health patient unlawfully at large. A woman had been detained under s.2 of the Mental Health Act 1983. Her husband visited her in hospital at 3.30pm three days later. Half an hour later she was back at home. Three hours later, the police went to the house believing the patient to be unlawfully at large, and thus they effected entry using reasonable force, purportedly under s.17. The court held that there was no pursuit or chase, however short in time or distance, and thus s.17 could not be used in this way.[22]

ARRESTING A PERSON COMMITTING OR ABOUT TO COMMIT AN OFFENCE

Under s.24 of the PACE 1984, the police can arrest, without a warrant, somebody who is committing, or is about to commit, an offence, or if there are reasonable grounds for suspecting this is about to happen. Likewise, if an offence has been committed or there are reasonable grounds for suspecting this.

However, this 'summary' power of arrest is dependent on the police believing that certain conditions are made out which necessitate the arrest. Amongst these grounds are that the arrest will prevent the person physically harming him- or herself or anybody else, causing loss of damage to property, or that it will protect a child or other vulnerable person.

There remains also a common law (i.e. not in legislation) power of entry to deal with a breach of the peace. The power arises in the case of behaviour that causes a constable to believe that a breach of the peace has occurred or will occur. It has to be related to violence. It occurs if harm is actually done or is likely to be done to a person or to his or her property. It also occurs if the person is put in fear of being harmed through an assault, affray, riot, unlawful assembly or other disturbance. In which case, the police can arrest the perpetrator without a warrant.[23]

GAS AND ELECTRICITY OPERATORS

There are powers of entry associated with utility companies. For instance, gas operators have such powers under the Gas Act 1986,[24] electricity operators under the Electricity Act 1989.[25]

Both of these powers of entry are underpinned by sections 1 and 2 of the Rights of Entry (Gas and Electricity Boards) Act 1954. The latter makes clear that entry has to be either with consent or with a warrant obtained from a justice of the peace (a magistrate).

---

21   Police and Criminal Evidence Act 1984, s.17(1)(d).
22   *D'Souza v Director Public Prosecutions* [1992] 1 WLR 1073.
23   *R v Howell* [1981] 3 WLR 501.
24   Gas Act 1986, schedule 2B, paras 23–28.
25   Electricity Act 1989, schedule 6, paras 7–10.

MENTAL HEALTH ACT INTERVENTIONS

Where mental disorder is an issue, adult protection and safeguarding may be served by certain interventions under the Mental Health Act 1983. These may break or prevent a cycle of abuse or neglect but can only be exercised if the relevant statutory grounds are made out. Compulsory interventions are a measure of last resort. It is beyond the scope of this book to consider the 1983 Act in any depth. However, guardianship is considered in a little more detail because it has arisen in a number of legal cases concerning adult protection and mental capacity.

MENTAL HEALTH ACT 1983: INTERVENTIONS AND MENTAL DISORDER

Mental disorder is defined as any disorder or disability of mind.

Learning disability is excluded from the definition of mental disorder unless it is associated with abnormally aggressive or seriously irresponsible conduct, and potentially longer-term detention under the Act is being considered.

However, this exclusion does not apply to short-term detention under s.2 of the Act, s.115 (entry by approved mental health professional), s.135 (search and removal) or s.136 (removal from public place). These sections of the Act can be used in respect of a person with learning disabilities, even if there is no abnormally aggressive or seriously irresponsible conduct – always supposing other relevant conditions are satisfied.

Learning disability is defined as a state of arrested or incomplete development of mind which includes significant impairment of intelligence and social functioning.

Under the Act, approved mental health professionals (AMHPs) have various functions.[26] These are social workers, first-level nurses practising in the mental health or learning disability fields, occupational therapists, chartered psychologists, with appropriate training and competencies.

LIMITED DETENTION FOR ASSESSMENT (AND TREATMENT) (SECTION 2)

Under s.2 of the 1983 Act, an application for admission for assessment is made on two grounds, both of which must be made out:

- The 'patient' is suffering from mental disorder of a nature or degree that warrants his or her detention in a hospital for assessment (or for assessment followed by medical treatment) for at least a limited period (up to 28 days).

- He or she ought to be detained in this way in the interests of his own health or safety or with a view to the protection of other persons.[27]

The breadth of s.2 (mental disorder including 'any other disorder or disability of mind') could allow detention of a person with a learning disability even in the

---

26   Mental Health Act 1983, s.114.
27   Quoted from: Mental Health Act 1983, s.2.

absence of abnormally aggressive or seriously irresponsible conduct – compared to s.3 (detention) or s.7 (guardianship), both of which require such conduct.

The following detention, although clearly designed for the protection of both mother and baby, was held to be unlawful and illustrates that good intentions and a concern to protect somebody are not enough.

Unlawful detention. A woman in the late stages of pregnancy was suffering from pre-eclampsia; there was a risk to the lives of both herself and the unborn baby. She fully understood the potential risks and clearly rejected medical intervention; she wanted the baby to be born 'naturally'. She was then sectioned (unlawfully as it turned out) under s.2 of the Mental Health Act 1983. It was unlawful because although mental disorder was present (depression), it was not of a type that warranted detention in hospital.[28]

The court was clear that the professionals in the case, the social worker and doctors, had all acted in good faith. But this did not make their actions any the less unlawful. This case was obviously not a safeguarding adults case. But it does serve as a reminder that compulsory interventions do need a legal underpinning: in adult safeguarding, there can be a tendency to intervene first and then worry about the law afterwards.

LONGER-TERM DETENTION FOR TREATMENT (SECTION 3)

Under s.3 of the 1983 Act, an application for admission for treatment is made on the following grounds, all of which must be made out in each case. In summary, they are:

- The patient is suffering from mental disorder of a nature or degree which makes it appropriate for him or her to receive medical treatment in a hospital.

- It is necessary for the health or safety of the patient or for the protection of other people that he should receive such treatment – and that it cannot be provided unless he is detained.

Under ss.64A-6K of the Mental Health Act 1983, patients who have been detained in hospital for treatment can be made subject to community treatment orders when they are discharged. This means that if they fail to comply with their treatment plan, they can be recalled to hospital.

ENTRY AND INSPECTION OF PREMISES (SECTION 115)

Under s.115 of the Mental Health Act 1983, an approved mental health professional may enter and inspect premises (not a hospital) in the area of that authority if he or she has reasonable cause to believe that a mentally disordered person is living there and is not 'under proper care'.

---

28   *R v Collins, Pathfinder Mental Health Services NHS Trust and St George's Healthcare NHS Trust, ex p S* [1998] 1 CCLR 578 (Court of Appeal). And: *R v Collins, Pathfinder Mental Health Services NHS Trust and St George's Healthcare NHS Trust, ex p S (no.2)* [1998] 3 WLR 936 (Court of Appeal).

This power to enter and inspect applies at all reasonable times after the social worker has produced, if asked to do so, some duly authenticated document showing that he or she is such a professional. Although s.115 does not allow for force to be used, obstruction could constitute an offence under s.129 of the 1983 Act.

WARRANT FOR SEARCH AND REMOVAL FROM PREMISES (SECTION 135)

Under s.135 of the Mental Health Act 1983, a justice of the peace may issue a warrant authorising a constable to enter premises, using force if necessary, in order, if it is thought fit, to remove a person to a place of safety for up to 72 hours.

This would be with a view to making an application under the Mental Health Act 1983 or other arrangements for care and treatment.

Such a warrant may be issued if it appears to the justice of the peace, from information received on oath by an approved mental health professional, that there is reasonable cause to suspect that a person believed to be suffering from mental disorder (a) has been, or is being, ill-treated, neglected or not kept under proper control, or (b) is unable to care for himself or herself and is living alone.

It is a potentially draconian power. It can, in principle, be used widely, not just in relation to a person who would typically be subject to formal detention under other parts of the Act.

The following case – as reported – illustrates, as well as any, the dilemma. The care workers and police were no doubt acting to the best of their ability, concerned about the care of an elderly, vulnerable woman. Equally, from the family's point of the view, the action taken by the authorities was extremely heavy-handed. First of all, a daughter had removed her mother from a care home, worried about her welfare.

Bringing an elderly person back home from a care home. An elderly woman with dementia was admitted to hospital for a minor ailment. She fell and broke her hip and so the stay was prolonged. She became increasingly confused. Social services suggested her care needs should be assessed. It was suggested that she go into a care home temporarily. The daughter observed that her mother was not happy.

Social services then visited the daughter and went through the adaptations that would be needed if her mother were to go back home. The mother then developed a mouth infection and was admitted to hospital, then sent back to the care home again. When the daughter visited her, she found her curled up, listless, her mouth black with dried blood and unable to eat the sandwich in front of her. The daughter and her sister (a qualified nurse) decided to take their mother back home; she appeared very happy to be home.[29]

It then seems that the local authority decided to use s.135 of the Mental Health Act 1983 in order to gain entry to the daughter's home and to remove the mother.

---

29   Craig O. 'Daughter of dementia sufferer says: "It's my mum's right to live – and die – with her family".' *Daily Telegraph*, 25 April 2009.

Use of the Mental Health Act to remove an elderly woman from the family home. Two days later, there was knock on the door. Outside were four policemen with a battering ram, social workers and doctors. They walked in and wheeled the mother out, having thrown a tea towel over her head, and took her back to the care home.

Some months later, it was reported that, after alterations had been made to the daughter's home, the mother had been allowed back into the care of her daughter.[30]

Allowing for any sensationalism in the reporting of this case, it is not difficult to understand why the daughter felt like an 'enemy of the people'. Yet, at the same time, the social workers and police would have been acting in absolute good faith.

REMOVAL OF A MENTALLY DISORDERED PERSON FROM A PUBLIC PLACE (SECTION 136)

Under s.136 of the Mental Act 1983, a constable may remove to a place of safety a person appearing to be suffering from mental disorder from a place to which members of the public have access. The constable may do this if (a) the person appears to be in immediate need of care and control; (b) the constable thinks it necessary in the interests of the person or other people.

The person may then be detained for up to 72 hours in the place of safety, so that he or she can be examined by a medical practitioner and interviewed by an approved mental health professional, and so that necessary arrangements for treatment or care can be made.

GUARDIANSHIP (SECTIONS 7 AND 8)

Guardianship can be used to specify where somebody should live. Under s.7 of the Mental Health Act 1983, a guardianship order can be made for a patient aged 16 years or over on the following grounds, in summary:

- that he or she is suffering from mental disorder

- that the mental disorder is of a nature or degree that warrants his or her reception into guardianship

- that this is necessary in the interests of the welfare of the patient, or for the protection of other persons, that the patient be so received.

Under s.8 of the Act, the guardian (either the local social services authority or other person) has the power, in summary:

- to require the patient to reside at a place specified by the authority or person named as guardian

- to require the patient to attend at specified places and times for medical treatment, occupation, education or training

---

30 Weathers, H. '"I was so numb I couldn't even cry": daughter blasts "Gestapo" social services as they bundle mother, 86, out of family home.' *Daily Mail*, 25 April 2009. Also: Johnston, L. 'Anger at "kidnap" of elderly patients.' *Sunday Express*, 16 August 2009.

- to require access to the patient to be given, at any place where the patient is residing, to any registered medical practitioner, approved social worker or other specified person.

A person subject to guardianship can be fetched back but also taken and conveyed to the required place of residence in the first place (Mental Health Act 1983, s.18).[31] However, in practice, persistent non-cooperation generally might render guardianship ineffective.

The question has arisen as to how far these powers may stretch. The courts have held that, up to a point, it is implicit that the guardian can promote the welfare of the person. For instance, this could be preventing the person seeing a sexually provocative magazine; it could also extend to limiting a person's contact, but would not allow the local authority to act in a totalitarian fashion.[32] However, a major contact issue, involving a person lacking capacity, might necessitate a separate court order under the Mental Capacity Act 2005.[33]

The Mental Health Act code of practice states that requiring a person under guardianship to live somewhere does not extend to depriving that person of his or her liberty. It states that this would only be possible (a) in the case of a person lacking capacity, and (b) only then if authorisation was obtained under the Mental Capacity Act 2005.[34] The courts have reiterated this point.[35]

GUARDIANSHIP UNAVAILABLE WITHOUT ABNORMALLY AGGRESSIVE OR SERIOUSLY IRRESPONSIBLE CONDUCT

For people with learning disabilities, for whom guardianship might be desirable, it is simply not available. This is because the definitions in the Act of impairment and severe mental impairment, which would apply to people with learning disabilities, include the requirement that the impairment be associated with abnormally aggressive or seriously irresponsible conduct.

This requirement is likely to exclude many people with learning disabilities from guardianship, since the courts have taken a restrictive approach to the term 'seriously irresponsible'.[36] Thus neither a young person's wish to go home against a background of possible sexual exploitation[37] nor a person's lack of road sense[38] constituted seriously irresponsible conduct.

On the other hand, historical conduct and the potential for aggressive or irresponsible behaviour to recur will be relevant and may mean that, even if there

---

31   Mental Health Act 1983, s.18.
32   *R v Kent County Council, ex p Marston* [1997], High Court, unreported.
33   *Lewis v Gibson* [2005] EWCA Civ 587.
34   Department of Health. *Code of practice: Mental Health Act 1983.* London: DH, 2008, para 26.3.
35   *C v Blackburn with Darwen Borough Council* [2011] EWHC 3321 (COP).
36   *Re F (Adult patient)* [2000] 3 CCLR 210 (Court of Appeal).
37   *Re F (A child)* [1999] 2 CCLR 445 (Court of Appeal).
38   *Newham London Borough Council v BS* [2003] EWHC 1909 (Fam).

has been amelioration in a person's condition, the conditions for guardianship will be made out.[39]

The courts have been increasingly asked to intervene in order to declare or order where the best interests of people with learning disabilities lie. The issue of guardianship has arisen on a number of occasions as an alternative to relying on mental capacity law. For instance:

Protecting a young woman with learning disabilities. A young woman, 18 years old, was in the care of the local authority. She had the level of intellectual functioning of a child aged five to eight years old. The local authority wished to control contact with her family and require her to live in local authority accommodation. The daughter had expressed a wish to return to her family. The local authority was concerned because its view of the home situation was one of chronic neglect, lack of minimum standards of hygiene and cleanliness in the home, serious lack of adequate parenting, and worrying exposure to those engaged in sexual exploitation and possible sexual abuse (seven other younger children are now in the care of the local authority). The mother opposed the local authority, arguing that it had no legal power to supervise and restrict contact, and was breaching human rights.

The court had already ruled, when the young woman was 17 years old, that guardianship under the Mental Health Act was not appropriate. This was because there was no abnormally aggressive or seriously irresponsible conduct; the local authority had argued the latter simply because the daughter wanted to return home to her mother. Yet the court could not characterise the wish of a child in care to return home as seriously irresponsible.[40]

On the assumption that the daughter lacked the capacity to decide the issue for herself, the court held that it had the inherent jurisdiction (the Mental Capacity Act did not yet exist) to make a declaration as to the daughter's best interests in the terms sought by the local authority. In addition, article 8 of the European Convention of Human Rights would not be breached, since it contained not a right to family life but a right to respect for family life. This meant an entitlement (within limits) to what was benign and positive in family life.[41]

The rules have not always been understood.

Inappropriate pursuit of guardianship to protect an adult. A complaint was made to the local ombudsman, following a protracted dispute between the local authority and the family of a man with learning disabilities about where he should live. The ombudsman criticised the local authority's persistent attempts to pursue guardianship. This was despite medical opinion each time that the conditions for guardianship were not met – in particular, the absence of abnormally aggressive or seriously irresponsible conduct.[42]

INFORMAL MENTAL HEALTH PATIENTS (SECTION 131)

There is nothing in the 1983 Act to prevent a person who needs treatment for mental disorder from being admitted to hospital without formal detention, or from remaining in hospital informally following any formal detention.[43] However, safeguards, under the Mental Capacity Act 2005, apply in the case of informal

---

39   *Lewis v Gibson* [2005] EWCA Civ 587.
40   *Re F (A child)* [1999] 2 CCLR 445 (Court of Appeal).
41   *Re F (Adult patient)* [2000] 3 CCLR 210 (Court of Appeal).
42   Bury Metropolitan Borough Council 2000 (97/C/3668).
43   Mental Health Act 1983, s.131.

patients who lack the capacity to make the decision about their care and treatment themselves.

SELF-NEGLECT

Generally, the issue of self-neglect has become a vexed one. Whether or not it is included within a local authority's definition of safeguarding activity is not the key question. More to the point is the question of what the legal response to it could or should be. Certainly, the legislation listed immediately above will sometimes be relevant, but applying it correctly in each case will not necessarily be straightforward.

EXAMPLES OF SELF-NEGLECT REQUIRING MORE INTERVENTION

The following examples are of situations in which the local authority or care agency involved should arguably have done more.

Man found dead in flat: self-neglect. A 59-year-old man with schizophrenia, living in Wandsworth, was found dead, having died of heart disease. Ulcers in his stomach were a sign of hypothermia. He lived in a dirty, damp and freezing flat, with mould growing on the floor and exposed electrical wires hanging off the walls. His boiler had broken, the bathroom ceiling had collapsed, and neighbours began to complain about the smell. The man had a loving family, a concerned landlord, and psychiatric nurses who visited him regularly to administer medication. He refused to move for cleaning and refurbishment work to be done. Health care professionals believed that to intervene would be a breach of human rights, since he had been judged to have the mental capacity to decide to live in that way.[44]

However, the coroner considered the Human Rights Act, Mental Capacity Act, Mental Health Act and National Assistance Act. He stated that the right to choose should be balanced with a duty of care and that the man could have been removed for 72 hours (under s.135 of the Mental Health Act, which requires mental disorder but not lack of mental capacity) to allow a blitz clean to take place. He noted:

> We all know about these people. They are all living in gradations of poverty, in unsanitary conditions. On the one hand, an elderly vulnerable awkward old lady may choose to live in a place that is dirtier than we would wish – an Englishman's home is his castle. On the other hand, when you have a place that is absolutely full of rubbish and vermin and smells…we have this difficulty. I would be very surprised if there weren't significant numbers of other similar cases.[45]

In the following case, too, the local authority was criticised, this time by the local government ombudsman who found maladministration when a local authority failed adequately to communicate to care workers the limited mental capacity of an elderly woman for whom they were providing care at home.

---

44   Harding, E. 'Intervening behind closed doors.' *The Guardian (Society)*, 31 March 2010.
45   Harding, E. 'Intervening behind closed doors.' *The Guardian (Society)*, 31 March 2010.

Failure of local authority staff to intervene and protect woman, in her best interests under the Mental Capacity Act, from overheating, serious dehydration and hospital admission. A woman with dementia lived at home alone. Over a period of a year, she was often left in a dirty house with bed linen and clothing left unwashed. Her personal hygiene, dress and food intake were not adequately monitored. The council also failed to carry out an assessment of need after she had been admitted to a residential home for such an assessment to be undertaken. There was no subsequent assessment of need or revision of the care package during the following month. This was during a spell of hot weather when the woman over-exercised and overdressed, unaware of the risks posed by this behaviour. This resulted in severe dehydration, deterioration in health and prolonged admission to hospital. She couldn't return home and entered residential care.

The local authority had failed to carry out adequate risk assessment or care planning. Crucially, it had failed to communicate to its care staff the limits of the woman's capacity. This had resulted, for example, in the care workers believing that they could not open a window, even on a hot day, in the woman's best interests (on grounds of limited capacity) or help her dress more appropriately. They had believed that they must adhere strictly to her every wish – as if she had full capacity, which she did not.[46]

In the following case, likewise, it was a case of standing back and doing nothing, as the person was dying.

Those charged with caring for a person should not simply stand back and do nothing. A man living on his own died of infection after he had been found lying on his sofa. He was cared for at home by workers from Allied Healthcare. Some weeks earlier, he had become too weak to move from the sofa and was refusing to be washed. The carers informed their manager and they were told not to wash him any more for safety reasons, but the family was not informed. He was apparently just left.

The coroner recorded a narrative verdict and stated that:

> It's a sorry state of affairs for a person to die in the circumstances that he did. Following concerns raised by carers there was a failure to organise an urgent review…and he was not promptly seen. There was a failure to provide a written care plan and proper communication.[47]

Similarly, a coroner criticised a domiciliary care company after a man with learning disabilities, epilepsy and scoliosis was found dead in his flat, covered in faeces and urine.

Care agency losing control of care of self-neglecting person: lack of experienced and knowledgeable staff. The dead man was underweight and surrounded by mouldy food and bags of soiled clothes. He had suffered diarrhoea for some five weeks before dying of dehydration. He lived in 24-hour supported accommodation but received only one-third of the care he should have been receiving – including cleaning, laundry and cooking. The flat had faulty wiring, a broken fridge and a damaged intercom. The coroner noted that he had not received the quality and quantity of care he should have; he clearly needed assistance before his death which he did not get; staff were well meaning but lacked experience and

---

46   Local Government Ombudsman Investigation: complaint no 09 013 172 against Worcestershire County Council, July 2011.

47   Smith, R. 'Northamptonshire man's care was "unacceptable", inquest hears.' *Northampton Chronicle & Echo*, 26 April 2012.

knowledge; the care agency's management had lost control; and the company's initial denial of its contribution to the death was 'woefully complacent'.[48]

But there were further ramifications because the care agency had been under contract to social services to care for the man.

Local authority to blame, as well as care agency, for losing control of situation. A subsequent serious case review found further fault and problems not only with the deficiencies of the care agency's management and staff but also with the failure of social services (Southampton City Council) to monitor his care. Furthermore, the local authority had lost control at the flats where the man lived in other respects as well. For instance, its staff rarely visited the flats, and yet a number of violent and unpleasant incidents had taken place there in the months leading up to the man's death. Indeed, the police had been called more than 50 times in 2010 alone and 20 times in the month before the man's death. There was also a lack of communication between staff and the different agencies involved.[49]

EXAMPLES OF SELF-NEGLECT WHEN NOTHING MORE COULD HAVE BEEN DONE TO PROTECT THE PERSON

The following examples are of cases in which it was concluded that little more could have been done.

Young man's death from self-neglect following Court of Protection ruling. In a 2011 case, a young man with learning disabilities died after the Court of Protection ruled that he could not be removed from his flat because he had capacity to take the decision himself about where to live. He died of a chest condition. The flat was in a filthy state, with dog mess in its carpets, mould in the sink and littered with empty takeaway boxes. This might have led to food poisoning and to the illness that killed him.[50]

In another case, a woman who had lived with her parents all her life was found dead after her father rang the emergency services.

40-year-old woman found dead from dehydration, ulceration (sepsis), breakdown of body tissue and other contributing factors. A serious case review summarised the isolation and rituals the woman engaged in:

> From an early age the subject experienced a number of different forms of fears and phobias, particularly regarding hygiene, germs and contamination. These manifested themselves in quite severe rituals and isolation. She described her own childhood at various times as 'terrifying', 'sad' and 'lonely'. She also suffered significant bereavements whilst still young; and as a teenager she became agoraphobic.
>
> The rituals and obsessions increased as the subject became older and they dominated the day to day life of her parents and herself, e.g. not entering certain rooms, internal doors locked, no one allowed upstairs, excessive washing and cleaning rituals, meals were taken in the middle of the night, very poor sleep patterns and virtually barricading herself in one small room.

Mental health needs, little contact with social services. For many years, she needed mental health services and had been detained twice under the Mental Health Act. There

---

48   Russell, T. 'Left to die in squalor.' *Daily Echo*, 7 March 2012.
49   Russell, T. 'Still no apology after failures led to death of Jonathan Ray.' *Daily Echo*, 30 August 2012.
50   'Coroner outraged as vulnerable man dies in filthy Mitcham flat.' *Wimbledon Guardian*, 24 March 2011.

was little contact with social services. She would often refuse services but was judged to have capacity to take such decisions and to have insight into her condition.

Limits to intervention of the State. The serious case review, following her death, concluded that the various agencies could not reasonably have done more at the time of the interventions and that the case raised important issues:

> This case raises interesting issues centring on the State and the individual. Society has to recognise that some adults will choose to remain living in risky situations and it is their right to make decisions, even unwise decisions. Sadly, we also have to conclude that the intervention of the services could not make a difference to the subject's life or ultimately to her death.[51]

In the following case also, blame was not attached by the coroner to the local authority.

Death of 82-year-old man who had refused help from social services. An 82-year-old man, with capacity to refuse help, did so, and as a result an inquest found that contributed to his own death. He lived with his cousin, aged 86, and with nine cats. He had refused a hip operation. His cousin looked after him and the cats. For about three years, both of them refused help from social services. By the time he was admitted to hospital, he was suffering from dehydration and hypothermia, was emaciated and showing signs of neglect. These included a 13-centimetre pressure sore down to the bone. He never recovered and died of bronchopneumonia contributed to by the sore.

Coroner's finding of neglect and that social services were not to blame. The coroner found death by natural causes but aggravated by both self-neglect and neglect. He expressed frustration that everything hinged on consent and capacity:

> I'm satisfied social services were not to blame. Not for the first time, I'm frustrated that an elderly person should have contributed and effectively caused their own death through an unwillingness to accept help. I do sometimes think the system is almost designed not to help, because everything depends on consent and capacity. If someone is deemed to have capacity, they are entitled to lead the lives they live, even if it leads to their own demise.[52]

DIOGENES SYNDROME (AND MANSLAUGHTER)

On the question of intervention via mental health or mental capacity legislation, medical opinion is sometimes divided in the case of people who suffer from so-called Diogenes syndrome. This is characterised by extreme self-neglect, domestic squalor, social withdrawal and apathy, and tendency to hoard rubbish. People with this syndrome often refuse assistance and have many physical problems, including nutritional deficiencies but may be content and survive without external support. Many might not be suffering from mental disorder but have rejected normal standards of behaviour.[53]

Yet, if statutory services do stand off, on legal grounds, there might still be legal consequences. For instance, in one case involving self-neglect, a daughter was

---

51   Sandwell Safeguarding Adults Board. *Serious case review, executive summary: female subject died aged 40 years.* Sandwell: SSAB, 2011.

52   'Independent OAP left help too late, inquest told.' *The Sentinel,* 21 April 2012.

53   Persaud, R. *From the edge of the couch.* London: Bantam Press, 2003, pp.304–306.

convicted of the manslaughter, through gross negligence, of her mother. She was sentenced to 30 months in prison. Yet the daughter's defence was that both she and her mother were suffering from Diogenes syndrome and also *folie à deux*, through which the daughter was in the shadow of her mother. Indeed, she had since moved out of the family home and her new dwelling was kept in good order. A summary of the case is as follows.

Woman with Diogenes syndrome, in the care of her daughter, found dead. The daughter was a civilian police worker living in Leeds. She failed to provide adequate food, nourishment and care for her mother. She didn't summon medical help. She finally drove her dead mother to hospital. Her mother had been confined to bed. Death was caused by a combination of malnutrition and infected pressure sores. Police found the property in an uninhabitable state. Rooms were piled high with discarded possessions, soiled clothes, soiled nappies, food waste, bottles filled with urine, human waste and decaying rubbish.

Daughter found guilty of manslaughter despite unusual home circumstances. The daughter argued she hadn't realised her mother was going to die. Yet the pressure sores were described by the judge as dreadful and shocking. Yet, outside of the home, the daughter was described as professional, diligent, articulate and capable in her work. She was also relatively wealthy. She loved her mother, whilst at the same time neglecting her. The daughter raised the issues of Diogenes syndrome and *folie à deux*. The judge acknowledged her unusual background. He found that mother and daughter were enmeshed and that the mother, but not the daughter, suffered from Diogenes syndrome. But the daughter had become accustomed to that way of life both as a child and adult. She was guilty of manslaughter.[54]

Of some note, given the legal quandary sometimes facing statutory services about intervening in such cases (assuming they get to know about them), are the comments of the senior police officer involved in the case. It was:

> an extremely sad case which will hopefully serve to remind people caring for elderly relatives, who may be experiencing difficulty, that there are a broad range of health and social care services available to provide support in such circumstances and the possible consequences of imprisonment in the most serious cases of neglect, where adequate care is not provided or sought.[55]

54   'Guiseley police worker jailed for letting mum, 82, starve to death.' *Yorkshire Post*, 11 July 2012.
55   'Guiseley police worker jailed for letting mum, 82, starve to death.' *Yorkshire Post*, 11 July 2012.

Civil orders and housing matters

Assured or secure tenancies
Other tenancies
Eviction of adults at risk of harm
Discrimination legislation

KEY POINTS

To protect a person from others, a range of legislation exists governing the making of civil orders.

Civil orders are sometimes an alternative to criminal justice. This might be for a number of reasons, including the victim's unwillingness to participate in criminal proceedings, a lack of evidence, a failed prosecution or simply that the behaviour in question does not constitute a criminal offence.

Orders relevant to safeguarding adults include protection from harassment injunctions, non-molestation orders, occupation orders, forced marriage protection orders, anti-social behaviour orders (ASBOs) and anti-social behaviour injunctions. In 2012, proposals were made to replace the latter two types of order with a new set of orders including criminal behaviour orders, crime prevention injunctions and community protection orders.

Although these orders are primarily civil in nature, it should be noted, for example, that the Protection from Harassment Act 1997 contains criminal offences as well, and that breach of a civil injunction under the Act can be a criminal offence. Likewise, breach of a non-molestation order. And penal notices and powers of arrest can be attached to occupation orders.

Another point of note is that non-molestation, occupation and forced marriage protection orders all come under the Family Law Act 1996. And, in the case of the last of these orders, provision is made for others (e.g. local authority or the police) to apply for an order, as well as the victim.

For non-molestation and occupation orders, however, the victim has to apply; there is a power in the Act under s.60 for others to apply, but this power has never been brought into force. The Law Commission queried, in 2011, whether it should now be.[1] The government has made no move to do so.

HARASSMENT

Guidance from the Association of Chief Police Officers notes that failure to deal with harassment might leave a victim or others at serious risk.

It also states that legal case law now suggests that the police force may be subject to legal challenge under the Human Rights Act if it does not respond reasonably in trying to protect people.[2] This point has been illustrated in European case law,

---

1   Law Commission. *Adult social care.* Law Com. no. 326. London: TSO, 2011, para 9.146.
2   Association of Police Chief Officers, National Policing Improvement Agency. *Practice Advice on Investigating Stalking and Harassment.* London: ACPO, NPIA, 2009.

involving the persistent harassment of adults with learning disabilities by school children and the inadequacy of response by the relevant State agencies.[3]

HARASSMENT AND CRIMINAL OFFENCES: OVERVIEW

The same guidance draws attention to some (not all) of the criminal offences that may apply to some form of harassment of a vulnerable adult – or anybody else, in summary:

(a) **Sending letters or other articles with intent to cause distress or anxiety:** Includes letter, electronic communication, phone call or other article (Malicious Communications Act 1988).

(b) **Harassment:** A course of conduct that causes harassment, alarm or distress (Protection from Harassment Act, s.2).

(c) **Putting people in fear of violence:** Conduct that causes another to fear on two or more occasions that violence will be used against them (Protection from Harassment Act, s.4).

(d) **Racially or religiously aggravated harassment or fear of violence:** A racially or religiously aggravated offence under s.2 or s.4 of the Protection from Harassment Act 1997 (Crime and Disorder Act 1998, s.32).

(e) **Improper use of public electronic communications system:** Sending, or causing to be sent, a message or other matter that is indecent, obscene, of menacing character or grossly offensive. For the purpose of causing annoyance, inconvenience or needless anxiety, causes a message to be sent or makes persistent use of a public electronic communications network or sends a message which he or she knows to be false (Communications Act 2003, s.127).

(f) **Fear or provocation of violence. Using threatening, abusive or insulting words or behaviour:** Or displaying or distributing threatening, abusive or insulting writing, signs or other visible representation. Intending to cause the victim to fear immediate unlawful violence against them or another, to provoke such violence, or where it is likely that a person will believe that such violence will be used, or where it is likely that such violence will be provoked. This offence does not apply if the people involved are all in a dwelling, not necessarily the same one (Public Order Act 1986. s.4).

(g) **Intentional harassment, harm or distress. Using threatening, abusive or insulting words or behaviour:** Or displaying or distributing threatening, abusive or insulting writing, signs or other visible representation. Intending to cause a person harassment, alarm or distress and actually causing this to

---

3   *Dordevic v Croatia.* European Court of Human Rights, case no. 41526/10, July 2012.

that person or another. This offence does not apply if the people involved are all in a dwelling, not necessarily the same one (Public Order Act 1986, s.4A).

(h) **Harassment, alarm or distress:** Using threatening, abusive or insulting words or behaviour, or distributing or displaying writing, signs or other visible representations that are threatening, abusive or insulting within the hearing or sight of a person likely to be caused harassment, alarm or distress by this conduct. This offence does not apply if the people involved are all in a dwelling, not necessarily the same one (Public Order Act 1986, s.5).

(i) **Threats to kill:** Threatening to kill any person with intent that the person to whom the threat is made will fear the threat would be carried out (Offences Against the Person Act 1861, s.16).

(j) **Witness/juror intimidation:** Intentionally intimidating a witness, victim or juror in an offence, intending to obstruct, pervert or interfere with the investigation or course of justice. Intentionally harming, or threatening harm, knowing that the person has been a victim, witness or juror in criminal proceedings (Criminal Justice and Public Order Act 1994, s.51).[4]

In addition to all of this, under s.149 of the Equality Act 2010, public bodies have a duty to have due regard to the need to eliminate harassment against disabled people.

The code of practice on this equality duty suggests that local authorities and the police could include, in their community safety strategy, a plan to reduce harassment of disabled people by, for example, working with local authority services, schools and transport operators.[5]

PROTECTION FROM HARASSMENT ACT 1997

The Protection from Harassment Act 1997 creates both civil and criminal remedies.

In summary, it states that a person must not pursue a course of conduct (a) which amounts to harassment of another, and (b) which he or she knows, or ought to know, amounts to harassment of the other.[6] Harassment is not defined in the Act, and is capable of being interpreted widely depending on the particular circumstances.

The Act contains a criminal offence of harassment, punishable by a fine or up to six months in prison,[7] and, more specifically, of putting a person in fear of violence on at least two occasions.[8] It also creates a civil right to claim damages and gives the courts the power to issue restraining orders in respect of a criminal offence,

4   Association of Police Chief Officers, National Policing Improvement Agency. *Practice Advice on Investigating Stalking and Harassment.* London: ACPO, NPIA, 2009.
5   Disability Rights Commission. *The duty to promote disability equality: statutory code of practice, England and Wales.* London: TSO, 2005, para 2.24.
6   Protection from Harassment Act 1997, s.1.
7   Protection from Harassment Act 1997, s.2.
8   Protection from Harassment Act 1997, s.4.

or a restraining injunction in respect of civil proceedings – breach of which is an offence, with a maximum sentence of five years in prison.[9]

PERSONS DO NOT HAVE TO BE ASSOCIATED FOR IT TO BE HARASSMENT

There is no need for the persons involved to be 'associated', as is the case with a non-molestation order under the Family Law Act 1996 (see below). However, there has to be a course of conduct – one act is not enough. Harassment can include alarming a person or causing distress.[10]

SIGNIFICANT MISCONDUCT

The courts have, however, held that irritations, annoyances and even upset are commonplace in everyday life. So, to become harassment – to go from the regrettable to the unacceptable – there has to be misconduct of an order that would sustain criminal liability under s.2, even if the case is about civil liability.[11] It needs to be oppressive and unacceptable.[12] However, the conduct has only to be proved to the civil standard in civil proceedings, even though a breach of an injunction could result in imprisonment.[13]

In the following case, a person was convicted on the basis of harassment by telephone calls, which amounted to a course of conduct, made by a service user to a social services manager.

Telephone harassment by service user of local authority manager. A man receiving social services from the local authority broke his foot and his care package was increased. On 8 November, he rang social services to complain about his care and left a message; the manager returned his call. He swore, shouted and verbally abused her. Later the same day, a similar thing occurred. On 9 November, he again rang; the manager again returned his call and again she was verbally abused. On 12 November, he was put through to her and again he was abusive; he promised he would not allow the manager to leave his house without an axe in her head.

The court found that these telephone calls did amount to a 'course of conduct'. The court also held that he either knew, or should have known, that what he was doing amounted to harassment. He was convicted of the offence.[14]

MENTAL DISORDER NOT IN ITSELF A DEFENCE AGAINST CRIMINAL CONVICTION

The fact that a person might have a mental disorder is not in itself a defence against conviction under s.2, since the courts have held that it was precisely the mischief of obsessive behaviour that the Act was there to deal with. In answer to the objection that the person might not have been aware of perpetrating the harassment, the Act

---

9   Protection from Harassment Act 1997, ss.3, 5.
10   Protection from Harassment Act 1997, s.7.
11   *Majrowski v Guy's and St Thomas' NHS Trust* [2006] UKHL 34.
12   *Conn v Sunderland CC* [2007] EWCA 1492.
13   *Hipgrave v Jones* [2004] EWHC 2901 (QB).
14   *James v CPS* [2009] EWHC 2925 (Admin).

states that it is about whether the person knew or ought to have known this. The latter is about what a reasonable person would have thought.[15]

Harassment by person with schizophrenia. A man with schizophrenia had written abusive letters to his Member of Parliament, who had felt threatened, suffered nightmares and had to alter family life as a result. The court held that conduct at which the Act was aimed included conduct likely to be pursued by those with obsessive or unusual psychological make-up – including those with an identifiable mental illness. The sentence – conviction under s.2 of the Act and the imposition of a restraining order – was upheld.[16]

NON-MOLESTATION ORDERS

Under the Family Law Act 1996, the court can issue civil non-molestation orders, breach of which is a criminal offence.

Molestation is not limited to violence or threats of violence. The word is not defined in the Act; it need not involve violence and could include pestering, annoying, inconvenience, harassing.

In relation to the adults concerned, there must be an association that in effect is a domestic connection. For a relevant association to apply, the adults must, in summary:

- be, or have been, married

- be, or have been, civil partners

- be cohabitants or former cohabitants, live or have lived in the same household (other than through one of them being the other's employee, tenant, lodger or boarder); this includes same sex co-habitants

- be people who have had an intimate personal relationship of significant duration who have not cohabited

- be relatives

- have agreed to marry (whether or not the agreement has since been terminated)

- in relation to a child, be the parents or have parental responsibility, be party to the same set of family proceedings.[17]

The court has discretion to make an order and must have regard to all the circumstances, including the health, safety and well-being of the applicant, the other party and any relevant child.[18] In the past, the court had the power to attach a power of arrest to an order. From July 2007, breach of an order without reasonable excuse became a criminal offence, with a maximum sentence of five years in prison.[19]

---

15   Protection from Harassment Act 1997, s.1.
16   *R v C* [2001] EWCA Crim 1251.
17   Family Law Act 1996, s.62.
18   Family Law Act 1996, s.42.
19   Family Law Act 1996, s.42A.

Non-molestation orders might sometimes be relevant in the context of safeguarding and protecting vulnerable adults. For instance, a non-molestation order, with a power of arrest, was granted against a son from going within 100 metres of his mother's home, where there had been a history of violence and threats of violence against his mother.[20]

MOLESTATION ORDERS AGAINST ADULTS WHO ARE THEMSELVES VULNERABLE

The following examples illustrate the care that needs to be taken in judging the appropriateness of a non-molestation order against a vulnerable adult.

Capacity to understand non-molestation order by man with mental disorder and abnormal jealousy. A man had become abnormally jealous of his wife, violent and abusive towards her, and had previously been detained under the Mental Health Act 1983. He was 82 years old and lived with a 62-year-old woman in the same house. They had previously divorced, although both continued to live in the matrimonial home. The woman had brought in a lodger with whom she ended up sharing her bedroom. The woman sought a non-molestation order on the grounds that her former husband had behaved improperly towards her. A social worker gave evidence that the man did not meet the criteria for residential care and that she had never found him to be aggressive. The man was having difficulty remembering things as he was suffering from the early stages of dementia.

Order should not be made against person lacking capacity to understand it. The court held that, on the evidence, this was a borderline case; that the judge in the original case was entitled to have made the non-molestation order, but that now the evidence suggested that the man's mental capacity was such that the order could not be continued. This was on the basis of a previous case,[21] in which it had been held that such an order should not be made against a person who was incapable of understanding its nature.[22]

Order could not be made against person whose abusive actions were a symptom of her mental disorder. The court held that a non-molestation order could not be made against a person previously detained under the Mental Health Act 1983, whose abuse towards her husband was a symptom of her mental condition and was such that she could not control it. Furthermore, although her verbal and physical aggression towards her husband put a strain on him, it did not significantly affect his health. A care regime, now in place, would ensure she was properly looked after and her husband relieved of the burden of care. In addition, the harm caused to the wife in making the order would be significantly greater than the harm to the husband if the order was not made.[23]

SOCIAL SERVICES INVOLVEMENT NEEDED WHEN THE VULNERABILITY CUTS BOTH WAYS

The vulnerability can clearly cut both ways and might require local authority social services intervention.

---

20   *Hutty v Hutty* [2005] EWCA Civ 1026.
21   *Wookey v Wookey* [1991] 3 WLR 135 (Court of Appeal).
22   *Harris v Harris* [1999] unreported (Court of Appeal).
23   *Banks v Banks* [1999] FLR 726.

Repeated breaches of non-molestation orders by vulnerable man: need for social services involvement. A 33-year-old man with a vulnerable personality, low intelligence and learning difficulties falling short of disability had been prohibited from using or threatening violence against his mother or returning to her house, where he had lived up to the age of 28. In fact, a series of such orders had been made, of which there had been 20 recorded breaches. He had now been sent to prison for 21 months for another breach that involved him going home, though not engaging in or threatening violence.

The Court of Appeal found the sentence to be excessive and reduced it to 12 months, meaning he would be due for release within two weeks of the court hearing. It was a 'most unfortunate case'. It called out for 'pro-active steps to be taken by...social services'. The man had great difficulty living independently and had never had permanent accommodation outside his mother's house. The court was 'of the very strong opinion that a plan must be formulated by [the man's] advisers in conjunction with...social services... Otherwise there is a very strong likelihood that he will be in breach again.'[24]

In the following case, the court referred to the implications of care in the community – namely, that vulnerable people needed support from social services, housing and the NHS, and that such support might be more effective than a judicial remedy in the form of injunctions. Implicitly, the court seemed to be suggesting that such support had not been forthcoming.

Support in the community may be more effective than injunction. An injunction was issued against a man with severe disabilities. He had Usher's syndrome, was deaf, dumb and had tunnel vision; his IQ was, however, average. He had separated from his wife. An injunction with a power of arrest had been made prohibiting him from going to the former matrimonial home. He breached it on numerous occasions. It appeared that he had the capacity to give instructions to solicitors and could understand the difference between right and wrong but did not have full capacity to understand the relevance of court proceedings and the implications of them. The judge decided that the man did have sufficient understanding in relation to the injunction and refused to discharge the injunction, but did not think he should go to prison.

Degree of understanding sufficient for issuing of injunction. The man appealed that the injunction should be discharged on the basis of his lack of understanding; it was argued that it was not so much a matter of him not retaining and understanding information as the fact that his disabilities meant he might not receive the information in the first place. The Court of Appeal also acknowledged the issue-specific nature of capacity generally, but that this would be unsatisfactory in the particular context. A degree of understanding might be sufficient for the issuing of the injunction. The court was not prepared to overturn the judge's original findings that the injunction should continue.

Balance between protecting victims and difficulty of restraining offenders with disability and mental disorder. However, the court noted that more people with disabilities or mental health problems were living in the community and that the courts had to balance the need to protect victims of violence or harassment against the difficulties of restraining offenders. The court faced the invidious choice between the compulsive behaviour of a most unfortunate individual and the safety and well-being of his family. Living in the community rather than an institution, he needed considerable support and protection in the community. Without such measures, his family remained at risk of harm, but they

---

24   *Gull v Gull* [2007] EWCA Civ 900.

were measures that lay outside the powers of the court. Social services, housing and mental health had an important part to play.[25]

OCCUPATION ORDERS

Under the Family Law Act 1996 (s.33 onward), the courts have a discretion, and sometimes a duty, to issue occupation orders. The precise rules vary, depending on the entitlement to occupy the dwelling of the applicant or of the respondent respectively. There needs to be an association or domestic connection between the applicant and the respondent, as for non-molestation orders.

The court can include a penal notice in the order and attach a power of arrest to the order.[26]

In summary, an order could allow the applicant – or forbid the respondent, the other person – to occupy the home or part of it, require the respondent to leave the home and not to return, prevent application of the applicant, require the party in occupation to take reasonable care of the home, regulate the use of furniture and chattels in the home, require either applicant or respondent to pay the mortgage.

APPLICANT WITH ENTITLEMENT TO OCCUPY DWELLING

If the applicant is entitled to occupy the dwelling house, then the order can cover a number of matters that could be relevant to safeguarding vulnerable adults. These are, in summary:

- entitlement to remain in occupation
- requiring the respondent to permit the applicant to enter and remain in the dwelling house or part of it
- regulating the occupation of the dwelling house by both parties
- prohibiting or suspending or restricting the right of the respondent to occupy the dwelling (if he or she is otherwise entitled to do so)
- if the respondent has matrimonial home rights, the restriction or termination of those rights
- requiring the respondent to leave the dwelling or part of it
- excluding the respondent from the specific area within which the dwelling lies.

The court has to have regard to the respective housing needs and resources of the parties and of any relevant child, the financial resources of the parties, the likely effect of any order or of any court decision not to exercise its powers on the health, safety and well-being of the parties and of any relevant child, and the conduct of parties to each other and otherwise.

---

25   *Page v Page* [1999] 2 FLR 897 (Fam) (Court of Appeal).
26   Family Law Act 1996, s.47.

The court's power turns into a duty if the applicant or any relevant child is likely to suffer significant harm. However, the order still need not be made if the respondent or relevant child is also likely to suffer significant harm if the order is made and that harm would be as great as, or greater than, the harm attributable to the conduct of the respondent and likely to be suffered by the applicant or child if the order is not made.[27]

OTHER CATEGORIES OF APPLICANT FOR AN OCCUPATION ORDER

The court also has a power to make many, but not all, of the orders listed immediately above, in relation to other categories of applicant. These are, namely, (a) former spouse or civil partner with no right to occupy the dwelling, (b) one cohabitant or former cohabitant with no existing right to occupy, (c) neither spouse or civil partner entitled to occupy, and (d) neither cohabitant or former cohabitant entitled to occupy.[28]

DOMESTIC VIOLENCE PROTECTION NOTICES AND ORDERS

The Crime and Security Act 2010 provides for the police to seek, from a magistrates' court, domestic violence protection notice orders. They are currently being piloted in a small number of areas. The background to the introduction of these orders is explained in guidance:

> It is not unusual for situations to arise in which a suspected offender, who is neither charged or otherwise on bail at the time of release from police custody, is free to return to the scene of abuse sometimes within hours of arrest. Research shows us that this is a time of increased risk to a victim. Where a risk assessment is undertaken it is frequently deemed necessary for the victim to consider leaving the address (with dependants where applicable) and/or for an injunction to be sought to prevent further abuse or harassment by the alleged perpetrator. Leaving home can have a negative impact on the victim's wellbeing and causes disruption to the victim's children and could well be another factor in the prosecution attrition rate.
>
> There is no readily available, consistent, affordable and timely access to civil court orders in the immediate aftermath of a domestic violence incident and therefore a gap exists between how the criminal justice system and civil law processes interact to provide immediate safety and a seamless service to victims at on-going risk of violence.[29]

In other words, they are intended to provide immediate protection for a victim of domestic violence. A notice can be issued by the police on the grounds that

---

27   Family Law Act 1996, s.33.
28   Family Law Act 1996, ss.35–38.
29   Ministry of Justice. *Domestic Violence Protection Notices (DVPNs) and Domestic Violence Protection Orders (DVPOs), sections 24–33 Crime and Security Act 2010: interim guidance document for Police Regional Pilot Schemes June 2011–June 2012.* London: MoJ, 2011, paras 1.4–1.5.

the perpetrator has been violent towards, or has threatened violence towards, an associated person, and that the notice is necessary to protect that person from violence or a threat of violence by the perpetrator. Once the police have issued a notice, they must apply for a domestic violence protection order, which application must be heard in a magistrates' court within 48 hours.

Notices and orders can stipulate non-molestation of the victim or prohibition of the perpetrator from premises shared with the victim (or coming within a certain distance of premises). Breach of an order allows a constable to arrest the perpetrator, to allow the latter to be brought before a magistrates' court for contempt of court.[30]

FORCED MARRIAGE PROTECTION ORDERS

Under the Family Law Act 1996, a court (county court or High Court) can grant orders protecting people from being forced into marriage.[31]

Such orders might be particularly relevant to the safeguarding of vulnerable adults, as defined in the *No secrets* guidance – for instance, where an adult lacking capacity to marry is subject to an arranged marriage, or where a vulnerable adult with capacity, but for some reason unable to give free and informed consent, is being subjected to marriage.

In addition to the Act itself, statutory guidance has been issued, obliging those to whom it is issued to have regard to it. This includes the police, local authorities and the NHS.[32]

The guidance points out that, quite apart from forced marriage protection orders, a range of criminal law may apply. For example, forced marriage might entail kidnap, false imprisonment, conspiracy, threatening behaviour, assault, abduction, theft (passport), imprisonment or murder. This is not to mention sexual offences, including rape.

In June 2012, the government announced that it would legislate to make forced marriage a criminal offence.

DEFINITION OF FORCED MARRIAGE AND CONSIDERING WHETHER TO MAKE AN ORDER

Legislation states that a person is forced into marriage by somebody else if they are not giving free and full consent. Force includes coercion by threats or other psychological means.

The court can make such an order to protect a person from being forced into marriage or to protect a person who has already been forced into one.

---

30 Crime and Security Act 2010, ss.24–31.
31 Family Law Act 1996, ss.63A–63S.
32 HM Government. *The right to choose: multi-agency statutory guidance for dealing with forced marriage.* London: Foreign and Commonwealth Office, 2009.

In deciding whether to make such an order, the court must consider all the circumstances – in particular, the need to secure the health, safety and well-being of the person to be protected.

Judging a person's well-being requires a consideration of the person's wishes and feelings, as is appropriate given the person's age and understanding.[33]

PROHIBITIONS, RESTRICTIONS, REQUIREMENTS IMPOSED BY AN ORDER

A forced marriage protection order may include prohibitions, restrictions or requirements and other terms as the court considers appropriate. The order may apply to conduct inside or outside England or Wales. It may apply to people who are, or who may in future become, involved in attempts to force a person into marriage.

It may also apply to other people who are, or who may become, involved in other respects (i.e. other than directly forcing the marriage). Examples of involvement in 'other respects' include aiding, abetting, counselling, procuring, encouraging or assisting another person to force, or to attempt to force, a person to enter into a marriage, or conspiring to force, or to attempt to force, a person to enter into a marriage.[34]

APPLICATION FOR AN ORDER BY THE VICTIM OR BY OTHER PEOPLE

Forced marriage protection orders can be sought in the following ways. The application can be made by the person who needs protecting or by a specified party. Local authorities are specified as such.[35]

In addition, if the court gives permission, an application can be made also by others. In deciding whether to give this permission, the court must consider all the circumstances, including the applicant's connection with the person to be protected, the applicant's knowledge of the person's circumstances, and the wishes and feelings of the person. It appears that, in the first year of the operation of the legislation, most such applications were being made by the police on behalf of victims.[36]

The victim's wishes are important but not necessarily decisive. The legislation states that the court must have regard to 'the wishes and feelings of the person to be protected so far as they are reasonably ascertainable and so far as the court considers it appropriate, in the light of the person's age and understanding, to have regard to them'.[37]

There are some circumstances, where family proceedings are already taking place, in which the court can make an order without an application being made.[38]

---

33   Family Law Act 1996, s.63A.
34   Family Law Act 1996, s.63B.
35   SI 2009/2023. The Family Law Act 1996 (Forced Marriage) (Relevant Third Party) Order 2009.
36   McCallum, L. 'A driving force.' *Solicitors' Journal*, 8 December 2009.
37   Family Law Act 1996, s.63C.
38   Family Law Act 1996, s.63C.

URGENT ORDERS

In some circumstances, the court can grant an urgent order ('*ex parte*') without first informing the respondent of the proceedings. The court can do this but must consider all the circumstances, including:

- the risk of significant harm to the person to be protected or somebody else

- whether the applicant will be deterred or prevented from applying if an order is not made immediately

- whether there is reason to believe that the respondent is deliberately avoiding participation in the proceedings and the person to be protected (or the applicant if not the same person) will be prejudiced by delay.

If the court does make such an order, it must give the perpetrator an opportunity to make representations at a full court hearing as soon as is just and convenient.[39]

ATTACHING A POWER OF ARREST TO THE FORCED MARRIAGE PROTECTION ORDER

The court can attach a power of arrest to the order and must do so if violence has been used or threatened, unless satisfied that in all the circumstances there will be adequate protection without it.

However, if the order is made without the perpetrator having been given notice, then a power of arrest can only be attached if, in addition to the (threatened) violence, there is also risk of significant harm if the power of arrest is not attached immediately.

If a power of arrest is attached, the police may arrest, without a warrant, a person whom they reasonably suspect of having breached a provision of the order, or who is otherwise in contempt of court.

If no power has been attached, but an interested person believes the order has been breached (or that the respondent is otherwise in contempt of court), an arrest warrant can be applied for.

If a person is arrested in either of these circumstances, he or she can be remanded; on release, on bail, the person can be required to comply with requirements imposed by the court.[40]

GIVING AN UNDERTAKING

Instead of an order, an undertaking can be accepted from the respondent, but not if a power of arrest would have been attached, had an order been made. The undertaking is, however, enforceable, to the extent that a breach of it is a contempt of court.[41]

---

39   Family Law Act 1996, s.63D.
40   Family Law Act 1996, s.63H.
41   Family Law Act 1996, s.63E.

VULNERABLE ADULTS FOR THE PURPOSE OF FORCED MARRIAGE: GUIDANCE

The guidance states that vulnerable adults are particularly at risk of forced marriage because they are often reliant on their families for care, may have communication difficulties and have less opportunity to tell anyone else what is happening.

If a person lacks mental capacity to take the decision to marry, it is a forced marriage by definition because the person is not consenting.

The guidance specifically addresses chief executives, directors and senior managers of various organisations, including schools, local authorities, police authorities and chief officers of police and youth offending teams. It states that they should ensure that vulnerable people are provided with additional assistance and support as needed. This would ideally include listening and making sure that vulnerable adults know how to raise concerns, meeting their support needs, ensuring access to adults outside the family, provision of speech and language therapists to facilitate communication, training staff, and providing independent mental capacity advocates in case of lack of mental capacity.

The guidance also emphasises the importance of a victim-based approach. This includes ensuring that victims are listened to, are able to communicate their needs and wishes, are given accurate information about rights and choices, and are respected about the level of intervention they require. It also means not using relatives, friends, community leaders or neighbours as interpreters or advocates; independent people should be used.[42]

The guidance states that organisations should ensure that staff understand their roles and responsibilities in relation to protecting people from forced marriage, clear lines of accountability, and effective inter-agency working and information sharing. It stresses the importance of sharing of information between agencies but also the dangers of breach of confidentiality: if family members become aware that the person has sought help, he or she may be in danger.[43]

INHERENT JURISDICTION OF THE HIGH COURT

The High Court has the power to exercise what is called its 'inherent jurisdiction' and make orders, including injunctions.

This jurisdiction means its common law powers; it does not have to refer to any legislation. Thus, if a vulnerable adult needs protection but has mental capacity so the Mental Capacity Act 2005 cannot be used, the courts will consider whether to use this jurisdiction. This has already been discussed in Chapter 14.

One recent example was the granting of an interim injunction to protect an elderly couple with mental capacity from the aggression, threats and sometimes

---

42   HM Government. *The right to choose: multi-agency statutory guidance for dealing with forced marriage.* London: Foreign and Commonwealth Office, 2009, paras 72–75, 57.

43   HM Government. *The right to choose: multi-agency statutory guidance for dealing with forced marriage.* London: Foreign and Commonwealth Office, 2009, para 62.

violence of their son. The court granted what was in effect a 'non-molestation' injunction under its inherent jurisdiction.[44]

COMMON LAW INJUNCTIONS

The county courts can issue common law injunctions, typically to stop a person coming on to another person's property or to stop them assaulting somebody else.

INJUNCTIONS UNDER THE LOCAL GOVERNMENT ACT 1972

A local authority can apply for injunctions (or conduct other legal proceedings) under s.222 of the Local Government Act 1972 when it believes this is expedient for the promotion or protection of the interests of the inhabitants of their area. A power of arrest can be attached if the injunction is aimed against behaviour capable of causing nuisance or annoyance.

If other legislation exists, then that should be used where it is obviously relevant. For instance, in an anti-social behaviour ('hoodies' and gangs) case, the local authority was directed to use legislation containing anti-social behaviour orders. Section 222 of the 1972 Act was not appropriate.[45]

However, in another case, a local authority wanted to protect an elderly couple from their son who lived with them. The couple had mental capacity to decide what they wanted. The local authority had both considered and rejected an application to the Court of Protection for an injunction and an anti-social behaviour order or injunction. The parents themselves would not take action against their son by, for example, themselves applying for a non-molestation order under the Family Law Act. In these circumstances, the court said an application for an injunction under s.222 would be possible, although it did in fact give the injunction under its 'inherent jurisdiction'.[46]

ANTI-SOCIAL BEHAVIOUR

Currently, anti-social behaviour orders may serve, amongst other things, to protect a vulnerable adult. For example, in hindsight, the much reported circumstances of Fiona Pilkington and her daughter were those in which use of anti-social behaviour orders or injunctions might have been used.

Anti-social behaviour, hate crime, possession proceedings. A woman killed herself and her disabled adult daughter by setting fire to the car they were in. She had been in despair at the persistent harassment received over a period of ten years from a group of local youths. However, when asked, she had chosen not to support criminal prosecution.

A serious case review concluded that the local authority and the police should have looked much harder at how to classify what was going on and what they could do about it. Three alternatives identified were anti-social behaviour (leading to voluntary good

---

44   *A Local Authority v DL* [2010] EWHC 2675 (Fam).

45   *Birmingham City Council v Shafi* [2008] EWCA Civ 1186.

46   *A Local Authority v DL* [2010] EWHC 2675 (Fam).

behaviour contracts or court injunctions), disability hate crime and possession proceedings against the perpetrators.[47]

At the same time, those classed as vulnerable adults might themselves sometimes be associated with anti-social behaviour. For example, the serious case review into the murder of a man with learning disabilities in Cornwall noted that he had been viewed by several agencies 'not primarily as a vulnerable adult to be protected from abuse and neglect but in terms of his own anti-social behaviour'. This complicated matters.[48]

ANTI-SOCIAL BEHAVIOUR: PROPOSALS FOR NEW LEGISLATION

At the time of writing, proposals have been made to replace anti-social behaviour injunctions and orders (explained below) with a new class of orders. These include the following, in summary, as set out in a White Paper of May 2012, *Putting victims first.*

Crime Prevention Injunction: civil orders through county court for adults and the Youth Court for ten- to 17-year-olds. This would replace anti-social behaviour orders on application, the anti-social behaviour injunctions (ASBI), the drinking banning order on application, intervention orders and individual support orders.

Such injunctions could be applied for by the police, local authorities, registered social housing providers, NHS Protect, Transport for London and the Environment Agency.

The test would be whether the person has engaged in conduct that is capable of causing nuisance or annoyance to any person and that it is just and convenient to grant the injunction. A power of arrest could be attached. Breach of the injunction by adults would be contempt of court, punishable in the usual way for the county court by up to two years in prison or an unlimited fine, as outlined in the Contempt of Court Act 1981. Breach by ten- to 17-year-olds would be a curfew, activity or supervision requirement, or, as a last resort, following repeated breach and serious harm, custody for up to three months for someone aged 14 to 17 years old.

The criminal behaviour order (CRIMBO). This would be a civil order. It would follow a conviction for any criminal offence in any criminal court. It would replace anti-social behaviour orders (ASBOs) on conviction and the drinking banning order on conviction. The order could be applied for by the prosecutor, either at the initiative of the prosecutor or following a request from the police or the relevant local authority.

The test would be that the order will assist in the prevention of harassment, alarm or distress being caused to any member of the public. There would be no need to prove specific past behaviour.

The minimum order would be one year for under-18s and two years for adults, and the maximum term would be three years for under-18s and indefinite for adults. Breach would be a criminal offence, with a maximum sentence of five years in prison. Because it is an order only on conviction, it would not criminalise someone for the first time merely for being in breach of a civil order.

---

47   Leicester, Leicestershire and Rutland Safeguarding Adults Board. *Executive Summary of Serious Case Review in relation to A and B,* 2008.

48   Cornwall County Council. *Findings of serious case review: Steven Hoskins.* Health and Adult Social Care Overview and Scrutiny Committee. Truro: Cornwall County Council, 2008, para 6.

Police directions power. This would enable the police to require a person who has committed, or is likely to commit, anti-social behaviour to leave a specified area and not return for a specified period of up to 48 hours. No advance designation or consultation would be required.

The test for use of the power would be whether the police have reasonable grounds for suspecting that the person's behaviour is contributing or is likely to contribute to anti-social behaviour or crime or disorder in the area and that the direction is necessary. Police officers would exercise the power fully, and community support officers could exercise elements of it. Failure to comply with the direction would be a criminal offence and would carry a maximum penalty of a fine and/or three months' imprisonment.

The community protection order (closure). This would consolidate various existing closure powers related to licensed and all other premises that are causing anti-social behaviour. The power to apply for the order would be available to the police and local authority.

The test for issuing an order will be that the police or local authority reasonably believes that there is a public nuisance or there is or is likely imminently to be disorder in the vicinity of and related to the premises and that the order is necessary to prevent occurrence or reoccurrence. The order has effect for up to 48 hours. The order has to state that access to the premises by any person other than someone who habitually resides in the premises or the owner of the premises is prohibited and that failure to comply is an offence.

The order could be extended up to three months by a magistrates' court if it is satisfied that: a person has engaged in disorder, anti-social or criminal behaviour on the premises; the use of the premises is associated with the occurrence of disorder or serious nuisance to members of the public; and that the order is necessary to prevent occurrence or reoccurrence. The order could be extended once more, but within the limitation the maximum length of the overall order would be six months.

There are also community protection orders (public spaces) envisaged and community protection notices.[49]

ANTI-SOCIAL BEHAVIOUR ORDERS

Currently, under s.1 of the Crime and Disorder Act 1998, an anti-social behaviour order (ASBO) can be applied for by a local authority, the police or a registered housing provider.

It can be sought against any person who is at least 10 years old on two grounds, both of which are required. First, that he or she has acted in a way that caused or was likely to cause harassment, alarm or distress to one or more people not within the same household as the perpetrator. Second, that such an order is necessary to protect relevant persons from further anti-social acts. A relevant person is, generally, anybody in the area of the council.

An order must be for at least two years. If the order is breached without a reasonable excuse, there is a maximum sentence of five years' imprisonment.

---

49   Secretary of State for the Home Department. *Putting victims first: more effective responses to anti social behaviour.* London: TSO, 2012, Annex C.

Application is to a magistrates' court. However, if other proceedings are taking place in a county court, an application can be made to the county court.

In addition, if a person is convicted of another criminal offence, the court can in certain circumstances make an anti-social behaviour order additional to any sentence for the original offence and to any conditional discharge order.[50] This is called an 'order on conviction' and is made at a separate civil hearing. It has been known as a CRASBO.

In the following case, an anti-social behaviour order was granted against a builder who exploited older people.

ASBO imposed on rogue builder targeting vulnerable people. A builder had targeted a 73-year-old woman, calling at her house and telling her that her roof needed repairing. Next day, he called back, telling her he had done the work and wanting payment. It turned out that he had done no work but had actually damaged the roof. He pleaded guilty to attempting to obtain property by deception and threatening to damage the woman's property.

The court sentenced him to 60 hours' unpaid community work and ordered him to pay his victim £450 compensation. In addition, an ASBO was imposed, prohibiting him from making unsolicited visits to dwelling houses for the purpose of obtaining building or gardening work for a period of five years.[51]

Similarly, the following case illustrates how an ASBO can be used to protect vulnerable people.

ASBO for teenager targeting vulnerable, elderly people. A teenager targeted vulnerable, elderly people with repeated verbal abuse, insults or homophobic language. He also took and damaged a wheelchair from an elderly resident. He was given an anti-social behaviour order to last for two years to prevent this behaviour.[52]

In another case, a 33-year-old woman was banned from visiting old people's housing complexes in Lincolnshire, from entering any house within the county without invitation of the occupier and from offering sex for money. A former heroin addict, she had a history of targeting elderly and vulnerable people, often posing as a care worker before stealing from them.[53]

STANDARD OF PROOF, SPECIAL MEASURES: ANTI-SOCIAL BEHAVIOUR ORDERS

Although ASBO proceedings are civil in nature, the standard of proof to be applied is the criminal standard.[54]

---

50   Crime and Disorder Act 1998, s.1C.
51   Cumbria County Council. 'ASBO for bogus builder.' *News*, 5 January 2007, www.cumbria.gov.uk/news/2007/january/05_01_2007-132919.asp.
52   Brown, C. 'A teenager who terrorised his neighbourhood has been given an Asbo to curb his ways.' *Liverpool Echo*, 27 January 2010.
53   '"Menace to elderly" gets 10-year ASBO.' *Skegness Standard*, 31 October 2011.
54   *R(McCann) v Manchester Crown Court* [2002] UKHL 39.

However, hearsay evidence is allowable.[55] This might be particularly useful. For instance, it means that a police officer could provide a statement on behalf of a witness or witnesses who wish to remain anonymous. Such evidence could relate, for instance, to dates, places, times, specific descriptions of actions, who was present and who said what.[56]

Also, vulnerable or intimidated witnesses can benefit from the 'special measures' available in criminal proceedings under the Youth Justice and Criminal Evidence Act 1999.[57] This would enable, for example, a witness to give evidence from behind a screen or by remote video link.

Sometimes a court makes an individual support order (for a child or young person). This will stipulate requirements aimed at avoiding breach of the anti-social behaviour order – for example, participating in specific activities or reporting to a certain place and person at particular times. Breach of such a support order attracts a fine.[58]

Similarly, intervention orders might be made on top of an anti-social behaviour order if the perpetrator misuses controlled drugs. The order will be aimed at preventing repetition of the behaviour in question and impose conditions such as participation in certain activities or reporting to a particular person at a given time. Breach of the order also attracts a fine.[59]

Interim orders, pending a court's final decision, are available.[60]

VULNERABILITY OF PERPETRATORS: ANTI-SOCIAL BEHAVIOUR

It is clear that perpetrators, against whom orders are sought, might themselves be vulnerable. Home Office guidance states that if the person against whom an order is sought may have drug, alcohol or mental health problems, or be on the autistic spectrum disorder, then support should be provided by social services. Social services have a duty to assess vulnerable adults under s.47 of the NHS and Community Care Act 1990 to find out whether they need community care services.

Home Office guidance states support should run parallel with the collection of evidence and application for the anti-social behaviour order (assuming application for such an order is deemed necessary). This will then give the court the material with which to balance the needs of the community with the needs of the alleged perpetrator.[61]

A person's vulnerability might mean that he or she cannot understand the order. In which case, it may not be appropriate to make the order because a lack of understanding would preclude ability to comply, as noted in the following case.

55   R(McCann) v Manchester Crown Court [2002] UKHL 39.
56   Home Office. A guide to anti-social behaviour orders. London: HO, 2006, p.26.
57   Crime and Disorder Act 1998, s.1I (as inserted by the Serious Organised Crime Act 2005).
58   Crime and Disorder Act 1998, ss.1AA–1AB.
59   Crime and Disorder Act 1998, ss.1G–1H.
60   Crime and Disorder Act 1998, ss.1D.
61   Home Office. A guide to anti-social behaviour orders. London: HO, 2006, p.21.

Question of whether person could understand simple order. The person concerned had a substantial criminal record. She had been convicted of 68 offences of affray and other public order offences, assaults on the police, criminal damage, theft, being drunk and disorderly, and breaches of a previous ASBO. She had been sentenced to community orders and to imprisonment, but these had not had a deterrent effect.

An ASBO, five years in duration, was now sought because of her regular attendance at a residential block of flats, where she was abusive, aggressive and drunk. The court concluded that the reports about the woman fell short of showing that she was incapable of understanding a simple instruction that she was not to do something.[62]

CLOSURE ORDERS FOR PREMISES USED FOR DRUGS

Under the Anti-Social Behaviour Act 2003, closure orders may be sought by the police for premises used in connection with the unlawful use, production or supply of a Class A controlled drug where this is associated with the occurrence of disorder or serious nuisance to the public. Application is to a magistrates' court. The order can last up to three months, but can be extended to a total of six months.[63]

The standard of proof required in considering closure orders is the civil standard. This is not set out in the legislation but has been decided by the courts. It is because the effects of a closure order on a person are less draconian than the effects of an anti-social behaviour order: it is shorter in duration, does not restrict liberty and stipulates a fine, rather than imprisonment, for a breach.[64]

All that said, such orders might mean that vulnerable adults lose their home, for example, after having been exploited by drug dealers. The courts have stated that the vulnerable adult may then qualify for housing under homelessness legislation, assuming he or she can convince a local authority that the homelessness is not intentional. But the courts have also conceded that 'some people who have done nothing wrong themselves will be displaced and will, at least for a period of time, suffer some hardship'.[65]

HOUSING-RELATED ANTI-SOCIAL BEHAVIOUR INJUNCTIONS

Under s.153A of the Housing Act 1996, certain landlords may seek anti-social behaviour injunctions from the county court or High Court.

The court can attach a power of arrest to an injunction if the conduct involves the use or threat of violence or if there is a significant risk of harm to the person in need of protection.[66] In some circumstances, a power of arrest can be attached to even a 'without notice' application – that is, where the perpetrator is not informed about the application.[67]

---

62   *Fairweather v Commissioner of Police for the Metropolis* [2008] EWHC 3073 (Admin).
63   Anti-Social Behaviour Act 2003, ss.1–5.
64   *Chief Constable of Merseyside v Harrison* [2006] EWHC 1106 (Admin).
65   *Chief Constable of Merseyside v Harrison* [2006] EWHC 1106 (Admin).
66   Housing Act 1996, ss.153C.
67   Housing Act 1996, s.154.

Anti-social behaviour is defined as conduct capable of causing nuisance to somebody else (who does not necessarily have to be identified) and which directly or indirectly relates to the housing management functions of the landlord.

The conduct must be capable of causing a nuisance or annoyance to (a) a person with a right to live in accommodation owned or managed by the landlord or in other housing vicinity, (b) a person with a right to live in other housing in the neighbourhood, (c) a person engaged in lawful activity in or in the vicinity of that accommodation, or (d) a person employed in connection with the landlord's management functions. A relevant landlord is a local authority or registered housing provider.[68]

A court can grant an anti-social behaviour injunction against a person who is engaging or threatening to engage in housing-related conduct. Furthermore, neither the perpetrator nor the victim(s) necessarily have to be tenants of the landlord.

Former tenant waging campaign against both local authority tenants and owner-occupiers in area. The perpetrator had been a secure tenant of the local authority. He had since been evicted as a result of his anti-social behaviour caused by alcohol. However, he kept on returning to the area and conducted a continuing campaign against his former neighbours. It was now argued that because he was no longer a local authority tenant, and the main victims were not local authority tenants either, his anti-social conduct was not housing-related. The court held that peace in the neighbourhood, whether for council tenants or owner-occupiers, was related to the housing management functions of the local authority.[69]

Injunctions are also available in respect of a person using or threatening to use the landlord's accommodation unlawfully.[70]

BREACH OF TENANCY CONDITIONS: ANTI-SOCIAL BEHAVIOUR INJUNCTIONS

Injunctions can be sought by landlords (local authority, registered housing provider) for breach (or anticipated breach) of a tenancy condition, where a person (a) is engaging or threatening to engage in conduct that is capable of causing nuisance or annoyance to any person, or (b) is allowing, inciting or encouraging any other person to engage or threaten to engage in such conduct.

The court can grant an injunction if it is satisfied that (a) the conduct includes the use or threatened use of violence, or (b) there is a significant risk of harm to any person. A power of arrest may be attached.[71] For example:

Vulnerable people put in fear: arrest and sentence for breach of injunction. An alcoholic man put in fear the residents of a block of flats who were mainly vulnerable by way of age, frailty or mental ability. He had the status of introductory tenant in the block. His behaviour included loud music, threats and abuse. He had been made subject to an

---

68   Housing Act 1996, s.153E.
69   *Swindon Borough Council v Redpath* [2009] EWCA Civ 943.
70   Housing Act 1996, s.153B.
71   Housing Act 1996, s.153D.

anti-social behaviour injunction under s.153D of the Housing Act 1996; a power of arrest was attached, but he did not adhere to its terms. He was sentenced to six months in prison; the sentence was upheld on appeal.[72]

DIFFERENCE BETWEEN ANTI-SOCIAL BEHAVIOUR INJUNCTIONS AND ANTI-SOCIAL BEHAVIOUR ORDERS

Anti-social behaviour injunctions (ASBIs) are available under the Housing Act 1996, anti-social behaviour orders (ASBOs) under the Crime and Disorder Act 1998. There are various differences, and it is clear that an ASBO is more drastic than an ASBI.[73] In summary:

- First, an ASBO can be obtained against anyone over the age of ten; an ASBI can be obtained against an adult only.

- Second, breach of an ASBO entails criminal sanctions, whereas an ASBI remains a civil remedy, even though a power of arrest is available.

- Third, an ASBO requires that the perpetrator 'has acted…in a manner that caused or was likely to cause harassment, alarm or distress', whereas an ASBI can be obtained where the behaviour is 'capable of causing a nuisance or annoyance'.

- Fourth, the standard of proof for ASBIs is civil, for ASBOs criminal.

- Fifth, an ASBI requires 'housing-related' conduct and specific classes of victim, whereas the only limitation on an ASBO is that the victim is not of the same household as the defendant.

ACCEPTABLE BEHAVIOUR CONTRACTS OR AGREEMENTS

Short of formal orders, the Home Office has encouraged the use of 'acceptable behaviour contracts'. They are not statutory, are not enforceable and are entered into voluntarily. Such a contract is a written agreement between the perpetrator and, for example, the local authority, landlord or police. They may act as a warning, with breach bringing the threat of an anti-social behaviour order or possession proceedings. Such contracts or agreements are not statutory.

The guidance suggests that, in the case of children under ten years old, parenting contracts might be preferred. These can be made under the Anti-Social Behaviour Act 2003 by youth offending teams, local authorities and registered housing providers.[74]

---

72   *Wear Valley District Council v Robson* [2008] EWCA Civ 1470.
73   *Swindon Borough Council v Redpath* [2009] EWCA Civ 943.
74   Home Office. *Acceptable behaviour contracts and agreements.* London: HO, 2007.

OTHER ACTIONS BY HOUSING PROVIDERS

The *No secrets* guidance refers to housing providers and providers of housing-related support services (including Supporting People providers) as integral to inter-agency working at local level. They are expected to have policies and procedures in relation to safeguarding.[75] But the guidance does not impose legal duties on housing providers. Confusingly, it does not even have the status of statutory (i.e. 'strong') guidance in respect of local authorities carrying out *housing* functions (as opposed to *social services* functions).

HOMELESSNESS

Under the Housing Act 1996, local authorities must give priority to certain groups when they provide accommodation for (unintentionally) homeless people. Several of these categories refer to groups of people who might be vulnerable adults. These include, in summary:

- people who are vulnerable as a result of old age, mental illness, learning disability, physical disability or for some other special reason

- people who, in the past, have been looked after by the local authority, accommodated or fostered (under the Children Act 1989) and are now aged 21 years or more

- people who have been in custody or detention

- people who are ceasing to occupy accommodation because of violence from another person or threats of violence from another person that are likely to be carried out.[76]

Vulnerability means when a homeless person is 'less able to fend for himself than an ordinary homeless person, so that injury or detriment to him will result when a less vulnerable man would be able to cope without harmful effects'.[77]

DOMESTIC VIOLENCE AS A PRIORITY CATEGORY FOR HOMELESSNESS

The legislation states that there are certain circumstances in which it is not reasonable for a person to go on occupying a property and that therefore the person is homeless. For example, it may not be reasonable for a person to continue to occupy accommodation if it is probable that this will lead to domestic or other types of violence against the person.

Violence means violence from another person or threats of violence that are likely to be carried out. For the behaviour to constitute domestic violence, there

---

75 Department of Health. *No secrets: guidance on developing and implementing multi-agency policies and procedures to protect vulnerable adults from abuse.* London: DH, 2000.

76 Housing Act 1996, s.189. And: SI 2002/2051. Homelessness (Priority Need for Accommodation) (England) Order.

77 *R v Camden LBC, ex p Pereira* [1998] 31 HLR 317.

needs to be a (defined) association between the perpetrator and victim. The domestic violence need not be within the dwelling; it can extend to outside the home.[78]

In housing guidance, the government has stated that, in this context, domestic violence should not be interpreted restrictively. It should be understood to include threatening behaviour, violence or abuse (psychological, physical, sexual, financial or emotional) between persons who are, or have been, intimate partners, family members or members of the same household, regardless of gender or sexuality.[79]

The courts, in the context of housing legislation about homelessness, have accepted that violence includes physical violence, threatening or intimidating behaviour and any other form of abuse which, directly or indirectly, may give rise to the risk of harm.[80]

HOUSING ALLOCATION

Under s.167 of the Housing Act 1996, local authorities must have a housing allocation scheme. They must operate the scheme so that 'reasonable preference' is given to certain groups of people. These include homeless people and also people who need to move on 'medical or welfare' grounds. Both categories could be relevant to safeguarding matters.

POSSESSION PROCEEDINGS TO PROTECT A VULNERABLE ADULT

There will be some circumstances in which a safeguarding issue has arisen, involving behaviour by a perpetrator who is also a tenant – behaviour that represents a clear breach of a condition of the tenancy.

Options, short of possession proceedings, include acceptable behaviour contracts, anti-social behaviour orders, injunctions and court action to enforce tenancy conditions.[81]

Local authorities and housing associations must also have a published policy on anti-social behaviour, explaining how the landlord will deal with it.[82]

MANAGEMENT TRANSFER

Some social landlords apply a 'management transfer' approach to neighbour disputes. However, this is open to criticism that it means 'nuisance pays', especially if it is the victim who is effectively forced to move. However, in England and Wales, this can only happen if the tenant consents. But landlords sometimes favour

---

78   Housing Act 1996, s.177.
79   Department of Education and Skills. *Homelessness code of guidance for local authorities.* London: Department for Communities and Local Government, 2008, para 8.21.
80   *Yemshaw v Hounslow London Borough Council* [2011] UKSC 3.
81   Office of the Deputy Prime Minister. *Possession proceedings.* London: ODPM, 2004, p.1.
82   Housing Act 1996, s.218A.

this approach because, compared to eviction proceedings, it is 'quick, cheap and produces a more predictable result than applying to court for an eviction order'.[83]

ASSURED OR SECURE TENANCIES

The rules for people with assured tenancies (not before 15 January 1989), including most housing association tenants and some private sector tenants, come under the Housing Act 1988.

Possession proceedings can be taken if the tenant or a person living there or visiting has been guilty of conduct causing or likely to cause a nuisance or annoyance to somebody living, visiting or 'otherwise engaging in a lawful activity in the locality'. Alternatively, that the tenant or person living there or visiting has been convicted of using the dwelling, or allowing it to be used, for immoral or illegal purposes, or has been convicted of an arrestable offence committed in, or in the locality of, the dwelling. Domestic violence also forms a ground.[84]

For secure tenants (local authority), the same grounds on which possession can be sought comes under the Housing Act 1985.[85]

When considering whether to grant possession, the courts must consider the effect of the nuisance or annoyance on other people and the continuing and likely effect of the nuisance. The court still does have to consider circumstances (such as mental health issues) that may have led to the anti-social behaviour but must bear in mind the effect on the victim and wider local community.[86]

OTHER TENANCIES

There are other tenancies in relation to which the landlord does not need to demonstrate to the court grounds for possession, although the notice to tenant must contain certain information and reasons.[87]

Introductory tenancies for local authorities are where the tenant is 'on probation', usually for 12 months. It is easier to evict tenants during this time. Tenants do, however, have a right to an internal review of the decision.[88] The introductory period can be extended for a further six months if there are problems.[89]

Starter tenancies, in relation to housing associations, are likewise probationary in nature for up to 12 months. Such tenants can be evicted in the same way as any other assured short-hold tenant, at any time after the first six months of the tenancy.

---

83   Wilson, W. *Anti-social behaviour in social housing*. Standard Note: SN/SP/264. London: House of Commons Library, 2012, para 3.2.
84   Housing Act 1988, schedule 2, grounds 14, 14A.
85   Housing Act 1985, schedule 2, grounds 2, 2A.
86   Housing Act 1985, s.85A; Housing Act 1988, s.9A. Also: Office of the Deputy Prime Minister. *Possession proceedings*. London: ODPM, 2004, pp.6–7.
87   Housing Act 1996, ss.124–128.
88   Housing Act 1996, ss.124–128.
89   Housing Act 2004, s.179.

Two months' notice is required, but the landlord does not have to prove grounds of fault on the part of the tenant.[90]

Secure tenants can be demoted by court order, on grounds of anti-social behaviour, to a less secure tenancy. The tenant will then have a status similar to an introductory tenancy.[91] A demotion and possession order may be sought; alternatively, a demotion, without possession proceedings, would serve as a warning to the tenant.[92] In case of eviction in relation to demoted tenancies, the courts have held that the tenant has a right for proportionality – that is, consistency with article 8 of the European Convention on Human Rights – to be assessed by a court.[93] The same principle may therefore apply to introductory and starter tenancies.

EVICTION OF ADULTS AT RISK OF HARM

Landlords sometimes take possession proceedings against a vulnerable adult. Vulnerable on one view; on another (e.g. held by neighbours), the person may be regarded as anti-social and a nuisance. In such circumstances, the landlord will need to weigh up competing considerations – the welfare of neighbours and other tenants against the needs and welfare of the vulnerable adult.

Government guidance talks of the need to try to deal with problems in other ways, before resorting to drastic interventions such as eviction. This includes giving support to perpetrators, in particular if they are vulnerable because of drug use, alcohol use, mental health or disability. It draws attention to the importance of multi-agency working, between the police, neighbourhood wardens, youth offending teams, schools, health services, drug action teams, social services and probation services.[94]

Local authorities must legally have regard to this guidance.[95] This means generally adhering to it, except where there is good reason not to. Thus, in the following case, the local authority was held by the court to have acted unreasonably by not considering such support.

Alternatives to possession in order to prevent anti-social behaviour. A local authority tenant had learning disabilities and a personality disorder. An incident arose, about the clearing-up of some broken glass, in which he assaulted the caretaker of the block of flats. The man accepted a caution from the police under s.4A of the Public Order Act 1986. The local authority then launched possession proceedings. The case went to court. There were two ways in which such possession proceedings could, in principle, be challenged. The first was on human rights grounds. The second was where the local authority was behaving in a legally unreasonable way.

---

90   Housing Act 1988, s.21.
91   Housing Act 1996, s.143.
92   Office of the Deputy Prime Minister. *Possession proceedings.* London: ODPM, 2004, p.7.
93   *Manchester City Council v Pinnock* [2010] UKSC 45.
94   Office of the Deputy Prime Minister. *Anti-social behaviour: policy and procedure. Code of guidance for local housing authorities and housing action trusts,* 2004, para 3.22.
95   Housing Act 1996, s.218A.

In this case, the court held that the local authority had behaved unreasonably in a legal sense. The court referred to the government's code of guidance for local authorities on anti-social behaviour. Furthermore, the local authority's own policy had stated that other alternatives to possession should first be explored in relation to vulnerable people. Yet, apparently, it had applied the policy in practice, without regard to the disability and mental health issues of the tenant.[96]

In the following case, the disability of the tenant was balanced against the nuisance to neighbours – and wish of the landlord to evict – by a compromise in the form of a suspended possession order.

Vulnerable tenant unable to control her adult son. The landlord sought possession because of the anti-social behaviour of the tenant's 20-year-old son. The tenant herself was described as immature and vulnerable, lacking assertiveness, unable to control her son and unable to throw him out of the house because of her emotional attachment to him and her need for help and support around the house. She could not read or write beyond the level of a nine-year-old. She was represented by the Official Solicitor.

A suspended possession order was granted by the court. Usually, such an order does not require that the landlord return to court before applying for a warrant in the event of a breach of the terms of the order. However, in this case, such a requirement was attached. One of the reasons for this was because, with her disability and with the involvement of the Official Solicitor, there was greater room for unfairness to her and of an administrative oversight than in the case of other tenants.[97]

DISCRIMINATION LEGISLATION

If a vulnerable adult is disabled, landlords will have to keep in mind the Equality Act 2010 when considering possession proceedings.

Under the Act, it is unlawful for a landlord to discriminate against disabled people in the selling, letting or management of residential premises.[98] This includes the taking of possession proceedings.

The Equality Act makes it unlawful to treat a disabled person unfavourably because of an issue arising from or as a consequence of a person's disability. It requires landlords to be able to demonstrate that possession proceedings against a disabled person are proportionate and that other options have been explored. This could include involving social services.

In one such case, under the Disability Discrimination Act 1995 (before it was subsumed under the Equality Act 2010), the courts did recognise the potential detriment to a mentally disordered person of losing his or her home and the importance of involving adult services to avert crises.

> This judgment shows that landlords whose tenants hold secure or assured tenancies must consider the position carefully before they decide to serve a notice seeking possession or to embark on possession proceedings against

---

96   *Barber v Croydon London Borough Council* [2010] EWCA Civ 51.
97   *Knowsley Housing Trust v McMullen* [2006] EWCA Civ 539.
98   Equality Act 2010, s.35.

a tenant who is or might be mentally impaired. This is likely to compel a local housing authority to liaise more closely with the local social services authority at an earlier stage of their consideration of a problem that might lead to an eviction than appears to be the case with many authorities, to judge from some of the papers the DRC [Disability Rights Commission] placed before the court. To remove someone from their home may be a traumatic thing to do in the case of many who are not mentally impaired. It may be even more traumatic for the mentally impaired.[99]

Social services involvement might not prevent a crisis, of course. For example, in the case of known and persistent disturbed, aggressive and anti-social behaviour from a psychotic tenant.[100]

Under the old Disability Discrimination Act 1995 (before being superseded by the Equality Act), there were three key questions. Presumably, they will remain relevant under the Equality Act as well.

First, it needed to be established whether the tenant was disabled within the meaning of the Act. Second, whether the reason for the anti-social behaviour or other breach of a tenancy condition was because of that person's disability. Third, whether the landlord knew, or should have known, of the disability.

If the answer to all those questions was yes, it meant the tenant was deemed to have been treated less favourably as a result of his or her disability. However, the landlord could still avoid a finding of discrimination if he or she could show that the less favourable treatment was justified.

Justification for less favourable treatment on health and safety grounds. A person with depressive mental illness was defined as being disabled for the purposes of the Disability Discrimination Act 1995 (now replaced by the Equality Act 2010). However, the court doubted whether the loud hammering and music played through the night was linked to the disability. Even had it been, less favourable treatment towards her, in terms of the possession proceedings, could be justified on health and safety grounds in respect of neighbours (a driving examiner becoming sleep-deprived). Likewise, a person with a personality disorder used abusive language towards a neighbour and her children. The behaviour was linked to the disability, but possession could be justified on health and safety grounds because of the effect on the neighbour.[101]

In another case, a man had got into rent arrears because the landlord had increased the rent. However, his disability (obsessive compulsive personality disorder) was unconnected to the reason for non-payment of rent. So there was no unlawful discrimination.[102]

---

99   *Manchester City Council v Romano* [2004] EWCA Civ 834.
100   *North Devon Homes v Brazier* [2003] EWHC 574 (QB).
101   *Manchester City Council v Romano; Manchester City Council v Samari* [2004] EWCA Civ 384.
102   *S v Floyd* [2008] EWCA Civ 201.

Sharing and disclosure of personal and other information

Key points
   Sharing information between agencies
   Requests for personal information
   Requests for non-personal information
   Other specific legislation affecting the disclosure of information
Common law of confidentiality and human rights
   Common law presumption of non-disclosure, and pressing need test
Data Protection Act 1998
   Data protection principles, schedule 1
   Adequacy, relevance, excessiveness, length of time
   Data protection principles, schedule 2
   Data protection principles, schedule 3: sensitive personal data
   Sharing information under the data protection principles
   Subject access to personal data
   Refusing subject access request on grounds relating to crime or harm
   Dead people not covered by Data Protection Act 1998
   People lacking capacity
Disclosure of non-personal information: freedom of information
   Freedom of Information Act: relevance to adult protection
   Exemptions from disclosure: absolute or qualified
   Exemption from disclosure: investigations and proceedings (section 30)
   Exemption from disclosure: prevention or detection of crime,
      administration of justice (section 31)
   Exemption from disclosure: prejudice to conduct of public affairs (section 36)
   Exemption from disclosure: personal information (section 40)
   Exemption from disclosure: breach of confidence actionable (section 41)
   Exemption from disclosure: legal privilege (section 42)
   Prohibition on disclosure under other legislation (section 44)
   Exemption from disclosure if compliance exceeds cost limit (section 12)
   Exemption from disclosure: information reasonably accessible by
      other means (section 21)
   Exemption from disclosure: vexatious requests (section 14)
Requests for minutes of safeguarding meetings
Processing personal information: Caldicott Guardians

KEY POINTS

The *No secrets* guidance refers to the importance of sharing personal information between agencies.[1]

In summary, the general law affecting the sharing and disclosure of personal information consists of the common law of confidentiality, the Data Protection Act 1998 and article 8 of the European Convention on Human Rights.

The Data Protection Act 1998 contains a number of specific rules relating to the processing of personal information.

In addition, the Freedom of Information Act 2000 is relevant to the disclosure of essentially non-personal information by public bodies.

A key issue is about striking the balance between the public and private interests of maintaining confidentiality and the public and private interests of disclosure.

Proportionality is the key in respect of relevant risks associated with disclosure or non-disclosure. From a legal point of view, an organisation's ability to justify its sharing of personal information is all-important.

In relation to safeguarding adults, information disclosure may arise in a number of different ways.

SHARING INFORMATION BETWEEN AGENCIES

First, sharing might sometimes need to be made within and between agencies, even if consent has not been, or cannot be, obtained from the person whose personal information is being shared.

Indeed, a vulnerable person might be inadequately protected from harm and abuse precisely because of a failure to share information. This might occur because of poor working arrangements between agencies and sometimes because of misplaced notions about the law and confidentiality.

For instance, the serious case review into the murder of a man with learning disabilities in Cornwall highlighted the fact that a number of agencies gathered extensive information about the problems building up but that cross-referral between those agencies did not occur. The agencies included the NHS, the police, the housing association and the local authority. Even within social services, adequate communication did not take place, with legal services not informing senior managers of a police request for information, and senior managers not even informing the director of adult social care of the man's murder.[2]

And, in Scotland, the Mental Welfare Commission reported on the failure by a local authority to protect a 67-year-old woman (in the care of the authority from the age of eight) from serious sexual assaults over a prolonged period of time. Contributory was the fact that the housing association, in whose property she lived,

1   Department of Health. *No secrets: guidance on developing and implementing multi-agency policies and procedures to protect vulnerable adults from abuse.* London: DH, 2000.

2   Cornwall County Council. *Findings of serious case review: Steven Hoskins.* Health and Adult Social Care Overview and Scrutiny Committee. Truro: Cornwall County Council, 2008.

had not been informed by the local authority of her vulnerability and the history of assaults.[3]

REQUESTS FOR PERSONAL INFORMATION

Second, a vulnerable adult, somebody acting on his or her behalf or perhaps a suspected perpetrator of harm or abuse might wish to see what personal data are being held about them. This might include the records and minutes of adult protection meetings. There are various rules under the Data Protection Act 1998 about such 'subject access' requests; disclosure can be refused on specific grounds.

REQUESTS FOR NON-PERSONAL INFORMATION

Third, access to non-personal information might also be directly relevant to the protection and safeguarding of vulnerable adults.

For instance, there have been examples of concealment by NHS trusts of facts concerning outbreaks of infection that arguably contributed to scores of deaths. Had these facts emerged earlier and been put in the public domain, some deaths might have been prevented. Such requests, involving non-personal information, come under the Freedom of Information Act 2000.

Equally, if a person asks for personal information about somebody else, the request also comes under the Freedom of Information Act (although, confusingly, the Data Protection Act principles will apply).

OTHER SPECIFIC LEGISLATION AFFECTING THE DISCLOSURE OF INFORMATION

There are other specific, relevant legislative provisions that govern the sharing or disclosure of information. All of which are covered elsewhere in this book.

These include, for example, information being disclosed by the police in the context of enhanced criminal record certificates under the Police Act 1997. Also the Safeguarding Vulnerable Groups Act 2006 specifically provides for extensive information sharing – duties and powers – in relation to the barring of people working with vulnerable adults.

Section 115 of the Crime and Disorder Act 1998 specifically confers additional legal power to share information. And section 325 of the Criminal Justice Act 2003 governs sharing of information for the purpose of multi-agency public protection arrangements (MAPPA).

Sometimes, legislation gives organisations a power – a discretion – to share information; sometimes, it demands it. For instance, health and social care providers have a duty to inform either the Care Quality Commission or the NHS Commissioning Board of certain occurrences.[4]

---

3   Mental Welfare Commission for Scotland. *Summary of our investigation into the care and treatment of Ms A*. Edinburgh: MHWC, 2008.

4   SI 2009/3112. Care Quality Commission (Registration) Regulations 2009, r.16.

COMMON LAW OF CONFIDENTIALITY AND HUMAN RIGHTS

A common law of confidentiality exists to the extent that any particular issue is not determined by other legislation.

In summary, confidential information disclosure is – in any particular circumstances – about balancing the private and public interests of confidentiality against the private and public interests of disclosure. The following are illustrations of such balancing exercises that the courts have had to perform.

Breaching confidentiality of mental health patient. A consultant psychiatrist prepared a report for a patient prior to a mental health review tribunal hearing. The report was unfavourable and the patient withdrew his application. However, the consultant was so concerned about the potential danger that the man represented that he sent the report to both the Home Office and the hospital where the man was detained. The court held that the breach of confidentiality was justified in the public interest.[5]

In the following case, the court found that the Data Protection Act 1998 did apply but was of limited assistance because of its generality. Instead, the judge turned to article 8 of the European Convention on Human Rights (right to respect for private life) and the common law of confidentiality. Both demanded that a balance be struck.

Disclosure of information to a mother. A mother was the nearest relative under the Mental Health Act 1983 of her adult son who was under the guardianship of the local authority. He lacked the capacity to take the relevant decisions for himself. She wished to gain access to her son's council files and his medical records. The council was prepared to let experts appointed by the mother have access and for them to communicate information as they thought fit to the mother and her solicitors. The mother challenged this.

Human rights and common law demanding balance. The court accepted that the Data Protection Act 1998 helped little; its generality meant that it did not prevent disclosure to the mother, but nor did it require the local authority positively to disclose. The judge turned to the common law of confidentiality and to human rights. Both required a balance to be struck between the 'public and private interests in maintaining the confidentiality of this information and the public and private interests in permitting, indeed requiring, its disclosure for certain purposes'.

The interests to be balanced consisted of the confidentiality of the information, the proper administration of justice and the mother's right of access to legal advice (relating to the guardianship, the mother's exercise of the nearest relative function and her possible displacement as nearest relative by the local authority), the rights of the mother and son to respect for their family life and adequate involvement in decision-making processes, the son's right to respect for his private life and the protection of the son's health and welfare.

The court held that the balance came down in favour of disclosure to the mother and her solicitors as well as the experts.[6]

In another case, the courts similarly found that disclosure would breach neither confidentiality nor human rights.

---

5   *W v Edgell* [1990] 1 All ER 835 (Court of Appeal).
6   *R v Plymouth City Council, ex p Stevens* [2002] EWCA Civ 388.

Disclosure by local authority of personal details of social work student to university. A woman was known to social services because of concerns and difficulties about the bringing up of her child. The woman subsequently wished to study to become a social worker. The local authority had concerns about her fitness for such a job; it disclosed its concerns to the university.

The court held that, in this instance, the local authority's disclosure was lawful, even though it had not maintained confidentiality. The matter was one of public interest. Good practice would have involved the council informing the woman first, so that she could seek an injunction to prevent disclosure; however, breach of good practice did not equate to a breach of the duty of confidence. Likewise, the claim failed under article 8 (right to respect for privacy); the means were proportionate and the purpose was to protect others from unsuitable social workers.[7]

Similarly, in a case concerning allegations surrounding the death of a resident in a nursing home, the courts found disclosure by the police to a regulatory body to be justified. Referring to article 8 of the European Convention on Human Rights, the court accepted the disclosure as necessary in a democratic society for the protection of health or morals or for the protection and rights of freedoms of others.

Nursing home death and disclosure. The matron of a nursing home was interviewed following the death of a resident alleged to have followed an overdose of diamorphine. The police concluded there was insufficient evidence to bring charges. The United Kingdom Central Council for Nursing, Midwifery and Health Visiting began an investigation. The police sought the matron's permission to disclose the statements she had made at police interview. The Royal College of Nursing, on behalf of the matron, refused that permission.

The court ruled in this case that the police could in such circumstances pass on such confidential information in the interests of public health or safety. Nevertheless, generally, a balance had to be struck between competing public interests in such circumstances; the individual should be notified about the proposed disclosure, and, in case of refusal, the court could be applied to.[8]

COMMON LAW PRESUMPTION OF NON-DISCLOSURE, AND PRESSING NEED TEST

In the past, the courts have pointed out that under the common law there is a presumption of non-disclosure, which can, of course, be displaced.

For example, even when there were suspicious deaths in a family and care proceedings under the Children Act 1989, the court cautioned against a presumption of disclosure to the police and instead insisted that a balancing act be carried out.[9] The courts have typically expected the disclosing organisation to carry out a 'pressing need' test before any disclosure is made. The disclosure might be justified.

Disclosure to caravan site owner of risk to children. A married couple were released from prison where they had served sentences for serious sexual offences against children. They went to live on a caravan site in the North of England. The local police asked

---

7   *Maddock v Devon County Council* [2003] unreported, case Ex190052, Exeter District Registry, High Court (QB).
8   *Woolgar v Chief Constable of Sussex Police* [2000] 1 WLR 25 (Court of Appeal).
9   *Chief Constable v A county council* [2002] EWHC 2198 (Fam).

them to move from the site before Easter, when many children would be visiting. The couple refused. The police disclosed their background to the caravan site owner. He asked them to leave. The couple claimed they had been treated unfairly and should have been shown the allegations.

The court held that they should have been informed of the gist of the information held by the police but that this would not have affected the conclusion. The police needed to apply a 'pressing need' test as to whether to disclose, on the basis of as much information as possible. The disclosure was lawful.[10]

So, disclosure might be unjustified in the absence of a pressing need test being applied.

Failure to apply pressing need test to the facts of the case: police disclosure to education department of a local authority. An uncorroborated allegation was made that a man had abused a child at a hostel for vulnerable children. A few years later, a further allegation that he had abused his daughter was made by the wife during acrimonious divorce proceedings. No action was taken, but the name of the family was placed on the child protection register. He then set up his own bus company with a contract to run school bus services. The police and social services disclosed his background to the education department of the local authority. The latter terminated the contract.

The court held that the disclosure by the police and by social services was unlawful because (a) disclosure should be the exception and not the rule, and (b) there was no evidence that either agency had applied the pressing need test in terms of considering the facts of the particular case.[11]

The pressing need test was brought into play concerning the issue of an NHS 'alert letter'[12] to ensure that all NHS bodies were aware of allegations made against a medical doctor.

NHS alert letter: justification by way of proportionality of disclosure and pressing need for it. An alert letter was issued containing details of allegations made about a medical doctor in relation to indecent assaults on female patients. Even after a decision had been taken that he would not be prosecuted, and the General Medical Council did not pursue the matter, the alert letter remained.

The Court of Appeal did not find this unlawful, noting that a balance had to be struck between the interests of the doctor and that of patients. The 'nature and strength of the allegations and the vulnerability of the class of persons to be protected are likely to be at the centre of the decision-maker's consideration'. In terms of human rights, under article 8 of the European Convention, the court accepted that the alert letter constituted an interference with respect for private life. But such interference could be justified if it was proportionate ('necessary in a democratic society'), with a legitimate aim in mind (protection of patients). The question was effectively the same as that posed by the common law – namely, whether there was a pressing need.

However, the court did emphasise that such alert letters needed to be reviewed at short intervals, with substantive consideration to be given to whether they should remain

---

10   *R v Chief Constable of North Wales, ex p AB* [1998] 3 WLR 57 (Court of Appeal).

11   *R v A local authority in the Midlands, ex p LM* [2000] 1 FLR 612.

12   HSC 2002/011. Department of Health. *Issue of Alert Letters for health professionals in England.* London: DH, 2002.

in circulation. This was because, in this particular case, a number of errors had been made, contrary to the Department of Health's guidance.[13]

The following case involved a local authority wishing to disclose information about a woman working in a care home in the area of a different local authority. The judge did approve disclosure but was meticulous in weighing up the relevant and competing factors before reaching a decision and insisting on the safeguards that would be required.

Disclosure of information, about assault by mother on child, to a care home for older people where the mother was working. A mother had assaulted her eight-year-old daughter, who was subsequently removed from the mother after the local authority had applied for and obtained a care order. The mother still worked at a care home for older people in the area of a second local authority. The first local authority wished to inform both the second local authority and the woman's employer about the background to the care proceedings. The judge referred to the *No secrets* guidance and its exhortation for inter-agency arrangements, as well as to the Protection of Vulnerable Adults list kept by the Secretary of State and the statutory duty of care on providers to refer care workers in case of misconduct causing harm (or risk of harm) to a vulnerable adult.

The first local authority believed that, whatever the Secretary of State decided, nonetheless the employer (and second local authority) needed to be able to discharge their statutory duties under the Care Standards Act 2000. They could only do that if the first local authority disclosed the information to them. The judge then set out the competing considerations.

Considerations against disclosure. Potentially militating against disclosure were: (a) the impact of disclosure on the child (there would be no benefit for the child in disclosure); (b) the consequences for the family (the woman might lose her job, she might not easily find other employment, the child might be upset if she became aware of the effect on her mother); (c) risk of publicity with potentially serious consequences for the child; and (d) importance of encouraging frankness in children's cases (fear of publicity may deter people revealing what is happening to children).

Considerations for disclosure. In favour of disclosure were: (a) the gravity of the conduct and risk to the public if there were no disclosure (serious assault on child meant that there was a real and potent risk to vulnerable adults); (b) evidence of a pressing need for disclosure (there was both a right and a duty to disclose); (c) interest of other bodies in receiving the information (significant obligations on second local authority and employer to carry out statutory duties); and (d) public interest in disclosure (strong and potent, with the need for public safety outweighing the mother's right to respect for her privacy, under article 8 of the European Convention on Human Rights).

Balance in favour of disclosure but with safeguards. The judge was quite clear that disclosure was the proper course but needed first to be satisfied that confidential discussions between the two local authorities and the employer could adequately address the question of avoiding publicity.[14]

---

13   *R(D) v Secretary of State for Health* [2006] EWCA 989.
14   *Brent LBC v SK* [2007] EWHC 1250 (Fam).

PRESSING NEED TEST EXAMPLE: UNLAWFUL, SCATTERGUN DISCLOSURE OF PAST SEXUAL OFFENCE AGAINST A CHILD

More recently, the pressing need test surfaced in a case involving direct payments made by the local authority to a disabled man (and to his disabled partner), who was active in the disability movement.

The authority had discovered, belatedly, that the man had been convicted, some years ago, of a sexual offence against a child. Having discovered this, the local authority set about doing the following.

First, it contacted nine organisations for whom the man provided services to inform them about the conviction. However, it did not establish that the work he provided for these nine organisations had anything to do with children; it did not. There was no pressing need demonstrated, since the pressing need, if any, was to protect children:

> The point, at the end of the day, is short and simple. Neither the local authority nor the judge engaged with the critically important fact that H and L [his partner] do not work with children. The local authority adopted a 'blanket' approach, its stance being that H should stand down from *all* the bodies and committees he was involved with and that it would make disclosure to *all* H's known contacts and, indeed, to any further contacts of which it became aware. This approach – in marked contrast with the approach the local authority adopted only six months later – was, in my judgment, neither fair nor balanced nor proportionate.

The second issue was that the local authority had noted that the contract the man and his partner had with their carers (employed through direct payments money provided by the council) had recently been amended to the effect that children were not to come to the house. The man had said he would abide by this condition. However, the local authority did not trust him, given a previous conviction for dishonesty. The local authority now wanted the man and his partner to provide each employee with a letter, setting out the view of the local authority that children should stay away.

The Court of Appeal agreed with the High Court's decision about this. It was unbalanced:

> The action proposed in relation to the personal assistants has to do with activities largely (exclusively, if H and L are correct when they say that they do not socialise with their carers) within the home of H and L. (2) The action must, of its nature, threaten to disrupt relationships which are of significance to H and L. (3) The action ignores the evidence from H and L as to two of the three long-term carers not having children and as to the recent insertion of a 'no children at work' provision in the relevant employment contracts. I

appreciate that ACC has reservations about the trustworthiness of H and L, but it does not follow that any evidence from them or any assurance they give as to their conduct should be wholly discounted. (4) The terms of the disclosure, which are perhaps inevitable, must raise in the minds of the carers suspicions as to their employers, which may (in the case of H) be more grave than his past conduct warrants and (in the case of L) be wholly unjustified.

Last, the local authority insisted that the direct payments should be paid through a managed account over which the local authority would have oversight and therefore be aware of each individual employee – with a view, therefore, of each of those employees receiving the letter about keeping children away. Just as with issue 2, the Court of Appeal found that this was not justified. Interestingly, it also found that the direct payments legislation anyway did not allow this.

The court relied both on article 8 of the European Convention (right to respect for private life) and the common law in reaching its conclusions in this case.[15]

DATA PROTECTION ACT 1998

The Data Protection Act 1998 contains a number of key points that are relevant to the holding, sharing and destruction of information in the context of safeguarding adults.

In particular, reference needs to be made to the data protection principles which include general rules and safeguards concerning the processing of information. There are various basic definitions contained within s.1 of the Data Protection Act 1998. In summary:

- **Personal data:** The Act applies to data controllers in respect of personal data. This means data relating to a living individual who can be identified from those data alone or from those data together with other information in the possession of, or likely to come into the possession of, the data controller. Personal data include any expression of opinion about the individual, as well as any indication of the intentions towards the individual of the data controller or any other person.

- **Sensitive personal data:** Sensitive personal data include information, among other things, about the person's racial or ethnic origin, physical or mental health or condition, sexual life, commission of an alleged offence, proceedings for any offence committed or allegedly committed and court sentence in any such proceedings.

- **Processing:** Processing of information is defined very widely. It means obtaining, recording or holding it or carrying out any operation on it, including (a) its organisation, adaptation or alteration; (b) retrieval,

---

15   *H and L v A City Council* [2011] EWCA Civ 403 (Court of Appeal). And: *H and L v A City Council* [2010] EWHC 466 (Admin).

consultation or use; (c) disclosure; and (d) alignment, combination, blocking, erasure or destruction.

- **Relevant filing system, manual information:** In addition to applying to automated, computerised information, the Act also applies to manual information held as part of a relevant filing system. This means a set of information structured so that specific information relating to a particular individual is readily accessible (s.1). From January 2005, the Freedom of Information Act 2000 amended the definition of data in the Data Protection Act 1998 so as to include, in effect, personal information held in unstructured manual filing systems by public authorities. However, personal health or social care information is anyway covered because it counts as an 'accessible record', which is a type of personal data also subject to the Act.

- **Accessible record:** This means a health record, educational record or accessible public record (s.68).[16]

- **Health record:** This means any record which '(a) consists of information relating to the physical or mental health or condition of an individual; and (b) has been made by or on behalf of a health professional in connection with the care of that individual' (s.68).

- **Accessible public record:** This means a record kept by housing and social services authorities for the purpose respectively of any of the authority's tenancies or 'for any purpose of the authority's social services functions'.[17]

DATA PROTECTION PRINCIPLES, SCHEDULE I

Data controllers must comply with data protection principles. All processing of personal data must comply with broad principles set out in schedule 1 of the Act. These include, in summary:

(a) **Fairness and lawfulness:** Personal data must be processed fairly and lawfully, and in particular the processing must meet (a) at least one condition in schedule 2, and (b), in the case of sensitive personal data, at least one condition in schedule 3.

(b) **Purpose:** The data must be obtained for one or more specified purposes and should not be processed for another, incompatible purpose.

(c) **Relevance:** The data must be adequate, relevant and not excessive for the purpose.

(d) **Length of time:** Data should be accurate and kept up to date, and not kept for longer than necessary for the purpose for which it had been processed.

---

16   Data Protection Act 1998, s.68.
17   Data Protection Act 1998, schedule 12.

(e) **Security:** Appropriate technical and organisational measures should be taken in relation to the security of the data.

ADEQUACY, RELEVANCE, EXCESSIVENESS, LENGTH OF TIME

Considerable latitude is given by the Act so that terms such as adequacy, relevance, excessiveness and length of time can be interpreted depending on context and circumstances. In the Soham murder case, police failed to retain information about the murderer. This seemed to be through misunderstanding the Act and not realising that a justification could have been given under schedule 1 for keeping the information, in terms of purpose and length of time.[18]

In contrast, the Court of Appeal considered, in 2009, the lawfulness of holding old minor conviction information on the Police National Computer. The records included the details of the theft in 1984 of a packet of meat valued at £0.99 with a fine of £15; of an offence of attempted theft committed 25 years ago and involving a fine of £25; and of a person under 14 years old who was cautioned for a minor assault, had been told that the information would be deleted when she reached 18, but had now been informed that it would not in fact be deleted for 100 years.[19]

The Court of Appeal held that the holding of such information was neither excessive for the purpose of police work nor longer than necessary.[20]

As to the purpose for which personal information is held, the Information Commissioner has issued a good practice note about the sharing of information between local authorities and local authority departments.

First, the sharing of such information between two separate local authorities is clearly subject to the Act.

Second, however, the sharing of personal information between two local authority departments is not subject to the Act, unless the second department will use the information for a different, 'secondary' purpose – in which case the principles of the Act do apply. In particular, under schedule 1, fair processing means that people must be informed about the purpose of processing the information, including any secondary uses. Personal information should be obtained only for one or more 'specified' purposes and should not be used for any other incompatible purpose.[21]

DATA PROTECTION PRINCIPLES, SCHEDULE 2

All personal data must be processed in accordance with at least one of the principles in schedule 2 of the Act. These entail either that the data subject has consented or that various principles are satisfied, including that the data processing is necessary – for example, because of, in summary:

18   Bichard, M. *The Bichard inquiry report*. London: TSO, 2004, pp.86, 127.
19   Information Commissioner's Office. *Police told to delete old criminal conviction records*. Press release, 1 November 2007. Wilmslow: ICO.
20   *Chief Constable of Humberside Police v Information Commissioner* [2009] EWCA Civ 1079.
21   Information Commissioner's Office. *Data sharing between different local authority departments*. Wilmslow: ICO.

- **legal obligation:** to comply with a legal obligation
- **vital interests:** to safeguard the vital interests of the data subject
- **justice:** for the administration of justice
- **legislation:** for the administration of justice, for the exercise of any functions conferred on any person by or under any enactment (i.e. legislation)
- **Crown functions:** for the exercise of any functions of the Crown, a Minister of the Crown or a government department
- **public interest:** for the exercise of any other functions of a public nature exercised in the public interest by any person
- **legitimate interests:** for the purposes of legitimate interests pursued by the data controller or by a third party seeking disclosure – unless the disclosure is unwarranted because of prejudice to the 'rights and freedoms or legitimate interests of the data subject'.

DATA PROTECTION PRINCIPLES, SCHEDULE 3: SENSITIVE PERSONAL DATA

In addition, in the case of sensitive personal data (particularly relevant to social care and health care), at least one of the principles in schedule 3 must be complied with. The person must have explicitly consented; otherwise, the principles include that the processing is necessary – for example, in summary:

- **right or obligation:** for the purpose of exercising or performing a right or obligation conferred by law on the data controller in connection with employment
- **inability to consent, protection of others:** to protect the vital interests of the data subject, where either consent cannot be given by or on behalf of the data subject and the data controller cannot reasonably be expected to obtain the consent of the data subject, or to protect the vital interests of someone else where consent by or on behalf of the data subject has been unreasonably withheld
- **public information:** the information contained in the personal data has been made public as a result of steps taken deliberately by the data subject
- **legal proceedings:** for the purpose of legal proceedings, obtaining legal advice, or otherwise in connection with establishing, exercising or defending legal rights
- **justice:** for the administration of justice

- **legislation:** for the exercise of any functions conferred on any person by or under any enactment

- **Crown functions:** for the exercise of any functions of the Crown, a Minister of the Crown or a government department

- **medical purposes:** for medical purposes and is undertaken by a health professional or by a person who, in the circumstances, owes a duty of confidentiality which is equivalent to that which would arise if that person were a health professional.

DISTINGUISHING BETWEEN HARM TO THE DATA SUBJECT AND OTHER PEOPLE

It will be noticed that under schedule 3, in the case of sensitive personal data, the fact that a person (with capacity) refuses consent to disclosure of personal information (second point above), such that he or she would thereby suffer harm, is not in itself sufficient to justify disclosure. Thus, Department of Health guidance notes:

> It is important to distinguish between serious harm to the individual to whom information relates and serious harm to others. Confidential information can be disclosed without consent to prevent serious harm or death to others. This is likely to be defensible in common law in the public interest.
>
> Where the patient is an adult lacking capacity, the Mental Capacity Act applies, and the best interests of the patient concerned can be sufficient to justify disclosure, i.e. information can be disclosed to prevent a patient who lacks capacity from being harmed.
>
> However, an individual's best interests are not sufficient to justify disclosure of confidential information where he/she has the capacity to decide for him/herself. There has to be an additional public interest justification, which may or may not be in the patient's best interests.[22]

Protection of the vital interests of somebody else will justify disclosure. Equally, disclosure may be justifiable under another point – for example, as part and parcel of the carrying out of statutory functions (e.g. social services functions, NHS functions, police functions, prevention of crime).

Thus, Department of Health guidance maintains that local social services authorities may disclose information in a number of circumstances in carrying out of their social services functions – without consent if necessary. For instance, information may be shared with line managers, other people caring for a client, such as a voluntary body or foster carers, and other departments or agencies, including health, education, child protection, inspection teams, legal advisers, finance staff, police.[23]

---

22   Department of Health. *Confidentiality: NHS code of practice: supplementary guidance: public interest disclosures*. London: DH, 2010, paras 7–9.

23   Department of Health. *Data Protection Act 1998: guidance to social services*. London: DH, 2000, para 6.18.

EXPLICIT CONSENT

Under schedule 3 also, in contrast to schedule 2, a person's consent must be explicit. Department of Health guidance states that the consent must therefore be absolutely clear and cover the specific detail of what is to be processed, as well as the purpose.[24]

PREVENTION OR DETECTION OF UNLAWFUL ACT

In addition, sensitive personal data can be processed if, amongst other things, the processing is in the substantial public interest, is necessary for the purposes of the prevention or detection of any unlawful act, and must necessarily be carried out without the explicit consent of the data subject being sought, so as not to prejudice those purposes. The schedule to the order refers to the processing being necessary for the exercise of any functions conferred on a constable by any rule of law.[25]

Information passed between police forces and then to education authority. Non-conviction information was passed from one police force to another; the latter then informed the education authority with whom the person concerned had applied for a job that involved working with children (headship of an infants' school). The job offer was withdrawn.

The court pointed out that the Data Protection Act 1998 was not breached either when the information passed between the police forces or when it passed from one police force to the education authority. This was because the information came under the 2000 order, which referred to the processing of sensitive personal data by a constable under any rule of law and to the prevention or detection of unlawful acts.[26]

In sum, it can be seen that the data protection principles are so broadly drawn that, in case of disclosure matters, the courts have sometimes held that the Act only gets one so far. It might justify both disclosure and non-disclosure. The balancing act has to be performed with reference to principles established in other areas of law such as human rights and the common law of confidentiality.[27]

SHARING INFORMATION UNDER THE DATA PROTECTION PRINCIPLES

The key point is that disclosure has to be justified; the Act by no means imports carte blanche for the sharing of information. Equally, it fully supports justified disclosure. It all depends.

AUTOMATIC BLANKET SHARING OF INFORMATION BY LOCAL AUTHORITY WITH THE POLICE

A query is sometimes raised about the automatic sharing of information, involving potential crime, by social services with the police. Indeed, the *No secrets* guidance appears to confirm that this should happen. It states:

---

24   Department of Health. *Data Protection Act 1998: guidance to social services.* London: DH, 2000, para 6.9.
25   SI 2000/417. Data Protection (Processing of Sensitive Personal Data) Order 2000.
26   *R v Chief Constables of C and D, ex p A* [2001] 2 FCR 431 (Admin) (High Court).
27   *R v Plymouth City Council, ex p Stevens* [2002] EWCA Civ 388.

Accordingly, when complaints about alleged abuse suggest that a criminal offence may have been committed it is imperative that reference should be made to the police as a matter of urgency. Criminal investigation by the police takes priority over all other lines of enquiry.[28]

Taken at face value, it must be doubted whether this can be right, given the courts' insistence that information sharing and disclosure between agencies, including the police, has to be justified against common law principles and human rights. In the absence of an explicit statutory duty compelling social services to share information about any possible crime (no matter how great or small) with the police, a public interest justification is surely required.

Separate Department of Health guidance to the NHS about confidentiality explores this a bit further. It is perhaps more helpful than the bald statement included in the *No secrets* guidance, introducing the important matter of proportionality into the decision:

> Confidential patient information can be disclosed in the public interest where that information can be used to prevent, detect, or prosecute, a serious crime. 'Serious crime' is not clearly defined in law but will include crimes that cause serious physical or psychological harm to individuals. This will certainly include murder, manslaughter, rape, treason, kidnapping, and child abuse or neglect causing significant harm and will likely include other crimes which carry a five-year minimum prison sentence but may also include other acts that have a high impact on the victim.
>
> On the other hand, theft, fraud or damage to property where loss or damage is not substantial are less likely to constitute a serious crime and as such may not warrant breach of confidential information, though proportionality is important here. It may, for example, be possible to disclose some information about an individual's involvement in crime without disclosing any clinical information.[29]

This does not suggest all crime, high or low, must automatically be reported to the police. In fact, to suggest that either the NHS or a local authority has an absolute duty to do so in every case would not only run up against legal principle but virtually make the NHS or social services an extension of the police force.

SUBJECT ACCESS TO PERSONAL DATA

Under the Data Protection Act 1998, people (data subjects) have a general right to find out about and receive copies of personal data of which they are the subject. However, there are some provisos to this right of access.

---

28   Department of Health. *No secrets: guidance on developing and implementing multi-agency policies and procedures to protect vulnerable adults from abuse.* London: DH, 2000, para 2.8.

29   Department of Health. *Confidentiality: NHS code of practice: supplementary guidance: public interest disclosures.* London: DH, 2010, paras 12–13.

One such is when complying with a request for information would also mean disclosing information relating to somebody else. In this case, the data controller is not obliged to disclose, unless (a) the other person has consented, (b) it is nevertheless reasonable in all the circumstances to disclose without that consent, or (c) the other individual referred to is either a health professional who has compiled or contributed to the information or has been involved in caring for the data subject, or is a 'relevant person' (such as a social worker) who has supplied the information in an official capacity or in connection with provision of a service.

However, the data controller could, in any case, communicate as much of the information as could be communicated without disclosing the identity of the other individual concerned.[30]

This rule, together with the possibility of independent review by the Information Commissioner or by the courts, is to remedy the problem identified in *Gaskin v United Kingdom* and which led to a breach of article 8 of the European Convention on Human Rights.[31] Under the earlier Data Protection Act 1984, no process was specified for such disclosure in case of lack of consent of a third party, nor the possibility of independent review. The European Court on Human Rights has accepted that this aspect of the 1998 Act cures the previous defect.[32]

REFUSING SUBJECT ACCESS REQUEST ON GROUNDS RELATING TO CRIME OR HARM

There are also specific exemptions relating to disclosure of data in response to a subject access request concerning the prevention or detection of crime, if these functions would be likely to be prejudiced by disclosure.[33]

Likewise, exemptions apply to information about a person's physical or mental health or condition or in relation to social services functions.

The exemption, in the case of information about a person's physical or mental health, is when access by the data subject to the information would be likely to cause serious harm to the physical or mental health or condition of the data subject or of any other person. If the data controller is not a health professional, then the data controller must consult the appropriate health professional about whether the exemption applies.[34]

In the case of information relating to social services functions, the exemption applies if disclosure would be likely to prejudice the carrying out of social work functions because serious harm would be caused to the physical or mental health or condition of the data subject or of any other person.[35]

---

30 Data Protection Act 1998, s.7. And: SI 2000/413. Data Protection (Subject Access Modification) (Health) Order 2000. And: SI 2000/415. Data Protection (Subject Access Modification) (Social Work) Order 2000.
31 *Gaskin v United Kingdom* [1989] 11 EHRR CD402.
32 *MG v United Kingdom* (2003) 36 EHRR 3.
33 Data Protection Act 1998, s.29.
34 Data Protection Act 1998, s.30. And: SI 2000/413. Data Protection (Subject Access Modification) (Health) Order 2000.
35 SI 2000/415. Data Protection (Subject Access Modification) (Social Work) Order 2000.

Department of Health guidance states that there is no general test of what constitutes serious harm but that restriction on the right of access should be exceptional and restricted to serious harm, such as risk of harm to a child to the extent that a child protection plan is in place.[36]

DEAD PEOPLE NOT COVERED BY DATA PROTECTION ACT 1998

The Data Protection Act 1998 does not apply to information relating to dead people since it covers personal data relating only to a living person.[37] Thus, a request for information about a deceased person will come under the Freedom of Information Act 2000. In some circumstances, it may come under the Access to Health Records Act 1990.

PEOPLE LACKING CAPACITY

The Mental Capacity Act 2005 code of practice states that, in the case of people lacking capacity, a person with a lasting power of attorney or enduring power of attorney or a court-appointed deputy could ask to see the information under the s.7 subject access provisions, so long as the information related to the decisions that the representative had the legal power to make.[38]

Regulations made under the Data Protection Act 1998 state that, in the case of information about the physical or mental health of the person lacking capacity, or information relating to social services functions, a person who has been appointed by the court to manage his or her affairs can make a subject access request under s.7 of the Act.

However, an exemption from disclosure would apply if (a) the information had been provided by the data subject in the expectation that it would not be disclosed to the person now making the request; (b) the information had been obtained as a result of any examination or investigation in the expectation that the information would not be disclosed; or (c) the data subject had expressly indicated that it should not be disclosed.[39]

Arguably, disclosure could still be made in a person's best interests in some other circumstances; in fact, the Mental Capacity Act 2005 code of practice points out that, in consulting about a person's best interests, health and social care staff may anyway need to disclose information about the person lacking capacity in order to make consultation meaningful.[40]

---

36   Department of Health. *Data Protection Act 1998: guidance to social services.* London: DH, 2000, para 5.37.

37   Data Protection Act 1998, s.1.

38   Lord Chancellor. *Mental Capacity Act 2005: code of practice.* London: TSO, 2007, chapter 16.

39   SI 2000/413. Data Protection (Subject Access Modification) (Health) Order 2000. And: SI 2000/415. Data Protection (Subject Access Modification) (Social Work) Order 2000.

40   Lord Chancellor. *Mental Capacity Act 2005: code of practice.* London: TSO, 2007, chapter 16.

DISCLOSURE OF NON-PERSONAL INFORMATION: FREEDOM OF INFORMATION

The Freedom of Information Act 2000 applies to public authorities including local authorities and the NHS. Public authorities must have a publication scheme (s.19) and provide information in response to requests (s.1). There are various exempted types of information, including the following that are relevant in the context of health and social care; in summary:

- information otherwise reasonably accessible to the applicant (s.21)
- information intended for future publication (s.22)
- information held in relation to:
  ○ security matters (s.23)
  ○ public authority investigations and proceedings (s.30)
  ○ law enforcement and related matters that would otherwise be prejudiced (s.31)
  ○ court records (s.32)
  ○ audit functions (s.33)
  ○ formulation of government policy (s.35)
  ○ conduct of public affairs that would otherwise be prejudiced (s.36)
  ○ health and safety (s.38)
  ○ personal information (s.40)
  ○ information provided in confidence (s.41)
  ○ legal professional privilege (s.42)
  ○ commercial interests (s.43)
- information, disclosure of which is prohibited by other legislation, is incompatible with any European Community obligation or would be a contempt of court (s.44).

Under s.50 of the Act, a complainant can apply to the Information Commissioner to make a decision about whether a request for information has been dealt with by a public body in accordance with the Act.

The Commissioner must make a decision unless (a) the complainant has not exhausted any complaints procedure provided by the public body in conformity with the code of practice made under the 2000 Act; (b) there has been undue delay making the application to the Commissioner; (c) the application is frivolous or vexatious; or (d) the application has been withdrawn or abandoned. Appeal lies, for the public body or the complainant, to the Information Tribunal.[41]

FREEDOM OF INFORMATION ACT: RELEVANCE TO ADULT PROTECTION

Requests are sometimes made to local authorities or the NHS to access information that may have a bearing on adult protection and safeguarding issues. Depending on who is asking for the information, and what information is being requested, the request will give rise to different applications of the Freedom of Information Act 2000.

For example, family members might be doing their own protection or safeguarding work, trying to find out what went wrong or what is going wrong in the health or social care of a relative. This might involve trying to get hold of investigations, reports, meeting minutes, care plans, evidence of how adult protection or safeguarding procedures were followed, details about staff involved.

In some circumstances, the request will in fact, legally, come to rest under the Data Protection Act 1998, even though the person has made the request under the 2000 Act. This might happen if it involves information about the requester. Alternatively, if it does involve somebody else's personal information, then the 2000 Act does apply, but reference to Data Protection Act principles must still be made. On occasion, the request might also come, legally, under other legislation altogether, such as the Access to Health Records Act 1990.

Alternatively, the information needed might be more general. For instance, in cases of systemic, institutional neglect, information about staffing levels and competencies, serious incidents, infection outbreaks, deaths, bed and ward closures (temporary or permanent), hospital discharge statistics might be all-important for safeguarding purposes.

For example, during 2012, it was a Freedom of Information Act request that exposed just how many NHS patients are sent home during the night.[42]

A major concern in health and social care is that independent care providers are not subject to the Freedom of Information Act 2000 because they are not public bodies. Yet ever more health and social care is being contracted out to such providers. Although requests could still be made, under the 2000 Act, to the commissioning NHS body or local authority, these are likely increasingly either to say they do not have the requested information (because they are no longer running the service) or that the information is commercially sensitive.

The following paragraphs consider in more detail some of the provisions of the Freedom of Information Act 2000 and illustrate them with examples explicitly linked to adult protection and safeguarding issues, or which at least involve relevant principles.

---

41   Freedom of Information Act 2000, s.57.
42   Bates, C. 'Scandal of NHS patients sent home in the middle of the night to "free up hospital beds".' *Daily Mail*, 12 April 2012.

EXEMPTIONS FROM DISCLOSURE: ABSOLUTE OR QUALIFIED

The Freedom of Information Act 2000 Act effectively creates an expectation that public bodies will confirm or deny that they hold the information sought and will disclose that information.[43]

This twofold duty is, however, subject to specified exemptions. Some of these exemptions are absolute, some are qualified. A qualified exemption means applying a test of whether, in all the circumstances of the case, the public interest in maintaining the exemption outweighs the public interest in disclosure.[44]

The presumption of disclosure in relation to qualified exemptions is the reverse of the test traditionally applied in the common law of confidentiality – namely, a presumption of non-disclosure which has to be outweighed by a public interest in disclosure.

EXEMPTION FROM DISCLOSURE: INVESTIGATIONS AND PROCEEDINGS (SECTION 30)

A qualified exemption (i.e. subject to the public interest test) applies to investigations carried out by public bodies (under a duty) and which may lead to a person being charged with an offence or to ascertaining whether the person is guilty of an offence already charged, or may lead to the public body instituting criminal proceedings.

Likewise, there is a qualified exemption in respect of information obtained from confidential sources in the course of such (and some other) investigations.

For instance, s.30 could apply to investigations by the Health and Safety Executive (HSE). In one Information Commissioner case, the HSE disclosed its factual report about a potentially fatal accident but not its analysis. In this particular case, the analysis did not contain obviously sensitive information, witness statements or information that would assist law breakers. The public interest in exemption was therefore outweighed by that of disclosure.[45]

EXEMPTION FROM DISCLOSURE: PREVENTION OR DETECTION OF CRIME, ADMINISTRATION OF JUSTICE (SECTION 31)

In addition, under s.31, qualified exemption applies for a variety of reasons. For instance, if disclosure would be likely to prejudice prevention or detection of crime, apprehension or prosecution of offenders or the administration of justice.

It applies also if a public authority is exercising various functions to determine failure to comply with the law, improper conduct or health and safety. Thus, a person requested details of records of a health and social services board investigation relating to the death of his mother. The board resisted disclosure under s.31 because the Northern Ireland ombudsman was investigating in response to separate complaints made. The Information Commissioner held that disclosure would

---

43   Freedom of Information Act 2000, s.1.
44   Freedom of Information Act 2000, s.2.
45   Information Commissioner Decision: *Health and Safety Executive* (2008), 18 February 2007.

prejudice the ombudsman's functions and that the public interest fell on the side of non-disclosure.[46]

EXEMPTION FROM DISCLOSURE: PREJUDICE TO CONDUCT OF PUBLIC AFFAIRS (SECTION 36)

A qualified exemption applies, under s.36 of the Act, if disclosure by a public body would prejudice the effective conduct of public affairs and would be likely to inhibit free and frank provision of advice or free and frank exchange of views for the purpose of deliberation.

Thus, in one case, a person sought information about adult protection procedures in respect of the death of his mother. The local authority put up various arguments, including one under s.36. This was that there was an expectation of confidence between a client and social services and that clients would be reluctant to provide appropriate information for fear of potential disclosure. This would arguably prejudice the conduct of public affairs. The Information Commissioner gave no view on this particular argument, finding instead that the information sought was anyway exempted from disclosure under ss.40 and 41 relating to personal information provided in confidence.[47]

In another case, an NHS primary care trust argued s.36 in relation to the medical records of a woman's father. The Information Commissioner was unable to reach a decision on this point because the PCT had destroyed the notes of a panel meeting at which the original non-disclosure decision in relation to s.36 was taken. The Commissioner did not find a breach of s.77 of the 2000 Act, which creates an offence of destroying or otherwise tampering with information with the intention of preventing disclosure – but came perilously close to it. He could not find sufficient evidence of deliberate intent.[48]

However, under s.36 also, the Information Commissioner clearly accepted that a 'part 8' serious case review by a local Area Child Protection Committee (ACPC) under the Children Act 1989 was exempt from disclosure.

Disclosure of child protection serious case review: prejudicial to the conduct of public affairs. The Information Commissioner found that disclosure would inhibit the participation of professionals; this would reduce the effectiveness of the review and in turn have a detrimental impact on child protection. So, whilst there was a high public interest in accountability and scrutiny, there were persuasive arguments for non-disclosure. Furthermore, the executive summary which was available provided a balanced and coherent overview, without disclosing sensitive information.

In addition, non-disclosure was justified under s.40 because of the personal information inextricably linked to the dead child and surviving members of the family; and the Commissioner could find no condition met in either schedule 2 or 3 of the Data Protection Act that would justify disclosure. In which case, the first data protection principle would be

46   Information Commissioner Decision: *Eastern Health and Social Services Board* (2006), 10 July 2006.
47   Information Commissioner Decision: *Trafford Metropolitan Borough Council* (2007), 27 November 2007.
48   Information Commissioner Decision: *Gloucestershire NHS Primary Care Trust* (2007), 12 November 2007.

breached (fairness and lawfulness). Likewise, the s.41 (duty of confidence) exemption would apply to the information about, or provided by, family members and their associates.[49]

EXEMPTION FROM DISCLOSURE: PERSONAL INFORMATION (SECTION 40)

An absolute exemption from disclosure under the 2000 Act applies to personal information on various grounds under section 40.

PERSONAL INFORMATION OF WHICH THE APPLICANT IS THE DATA SUBJECT

An absolute exemption applies to personal information, of which the applicant is the data subject. Such a request should be dealt with under the Data Protection Act 1998. For instance:

Family seeking information about complaint made against them. The parents of a baby asked to see details of a complaint made against them, with a view to identifying the hospital staff member who had made the complaint. The Information Commissioner held that the request fell under the Data Protection Act 1998 subject access provisions rather under than the 2000 Act.[50]

Thus, in terms of identification of the staff, the subject access rules under the 1998 Act, about third party information and about where that third party is a health professional, would apply (see above).

PERSONAL INFORMATION OF OTHER PEOPLE

If the request concerns the personal information of other people but not the data subject, then an absolute exemption applies in two cases.

First, the exemption applies if disclosure would contravene (a) any of the data protection principles under the Data Protection Act or (b) section 10 of the Data Protection Act.

Section 10 concerns notification by the data subject to the data controller, requesting non-disclosure of his or her personal information because of the substantial damage or distress that would be caused (to him or her or anybody else) and the response of the data controller as to whether it will comply with the request not to disclose.

Second, the exemption applies if any of the exemptions to subject access, under the Data Protection Act, apply.

The Information Commissioner has issued guidance about contravention of data protection principles under s.40. The guidance refers in particular to the principles of fairness and lawfulness, the first data protection principle. This states that at least one of the conditions in schedule 2 of the Act is met and, in the case of sensitive personal data, at least one in schedule 3.

---

49   Information Commissioner Decision: *Plymouth City Council* (2006), 23 August 2006.
50   Information Commissioner Investigation: *Southampton University Hospitals NHS Trust* (2007), 2 July 2007.

One of the conditions in schedule 2 refers to processing (including disclosure) being necessary for the purposes of legitimate interests pursued by the data controller or by a third party seeking disclosure, unless the disclosure is unwarranted because of prejudice to the 'rights and freedoms or legitimate interests of the data subject'.

In sum, the Information Tribunal has held that although s.40 represents an absolute exemption, this condition in schedule 2 of the 1998 Act actually imports a balance of competing interests comparable to that applied in the 2000 Act to qualified exemptions.[51] In other words, a public interest test by the backdoor.

Thus, according to the Information Commissioner's guidance, disclosure might concern personal health or social care information that was provided in confidence and so be likely to be exempt from disclosure. Fairness is referred to as harder to define and would involve questions about:

- the possible consequences of disclosure on the individual

- the reasonable expectations of the individual, taking into account expectations both at the time the information was collected and at the time of the request

- the nature of the information itself

- the circumstances in which the information was obtained

- whether the information has been or remains in the public domain

- the 'freedom of information' principles of transparency and accountability

- any legitimate interests in the public having access to the information relevant to the specific case.[52]

NON-DISCLOSURE: CONFIDENTIALITY OF PERSONAL INFORMATION ABOUT RELATIVES

In the following case, under s.40, a daughter was denied information about her mother's care because the information was personal and the mother had not given consent for her daughter to access it.

Daughter seeking information from local authority about her mother's care: exemption from disclosure under s.40. In relation to her mother's care, a woman wanted from the local authority copies of notes made by a social worker, written reports, copies of the minutes of a complaints panel meeting and information about a subsequent complaint about the 'shoddy, superficial and seriously deficient investigation'. The Information Commissioner held that the s.40 exemption applied. The information was personal and release of it without the data subject's (the mother's) consent would breach the data protection principle of fairness and lawfulness. There was no evidence that the

---

51   Information Tribunal: *House of Commons v Information Commissioner and Norman Baker, MP* (2007), 16 January 2007.

52   Information Commissioner's Office. *Freedom of Information Act, Environmental Information Regulations: the exemption for personal information.* London: ICO, 2011, p.2.

mother had given the daughter consent to access the information or that the daughter had any right to act on her mother's behalf.[53]

In another case, a woman sought information about what had happened to her mother and what adult protection procedures had been followed by the local authority. She found the information to be exempt from disclosure because it contained personal details of her mother's primary carer.

Information sought by daughter about adult protection procedures followed by a local authority in relation to care of her now dead mother: exemption from disclosure under section 40 (and s.41). A woman sought information concerning adult protection matters and the course of action the local authority took following notification by a GP of injuries sustained by her now deceased mother whilst in the care of a third party. In particular, she wanted to know how the vulnerable adult protection pathway procedure had been followed in this particular case, as well as the outcome of the enquiry and the documentation concerning the directions given by the GP. The local authority resisted disclosure under s.41 (information given in confidence), s.44 (prohibitions on disclosure because of human rights), s.36 (prejudice to conduct of public affairs) and s.40 (personal information and data protection principles).

Exemption from disclosure under s.40: personal information of primary carer. Under s.40, the information included details about the woman's primary carer, who provided virtually 24-hour care, as well as other social services and NHS employees. The information included opinions about the primary carer and references to the carer's personal circumstances, health and financial arrangements.

The Information Commissioner accepted that disclosure of this information would be unfair under the data protection principles because the primary carer would have had a reasonable belief that her interaction with the council was confidential, and access to the information did not outweigh her rights, freedoms and legitimate interests (under schedule 2 of the Data Protection Act 1998).

Likewise, disclosure could be unlawful in terms of breach of confidence of the carer's personal information, some of it 'sensitive' (under the 1998 Act).

Exemption from disclosure under s.41 (duty of confidence). Under s.41, information had derived from the dead woman, the primary carer, the GP and the local health authority. The woman would have had an expectation of confidence, which was important if clients were to share private information with social services. The Information Commissioner held that the duty of confidence towards the deceased survived her death and that a breach would be actionable. Thus, the exemption under s.41 applied. The Commissioner disregarded the s.44 and human rights argument.[54]

In another case, information was sought from an NHS trust about five critical incident reports relating to the murder of a patient. The reports contained personal information about identifiable individuals – including patients or family members – who would not have expected that the information they provided be made public. This was particularly so because such an internal review, which gave rise to the reports, was classed as confidential. Thus, under s.40, the Information Commissioner

---

53   Information Commissioner Decision: *Worcestershire County Council* (2006), 31 May 2006.
54   Information Commissioner Decision: *Trafford Metropolitan Borough Council* (2007), 27 November 2007.

held it would be unfair, under the first data protection principle, for disclosure to take place.[55]

PERSONAL INFORMATION: NAMES OF STAFF AND CONFIDENTIAL STATEMENTS MADE BY STAFF

Sometimes, if things have gone wrong, a patient or family member might want the names of staff. Thus, when a woman wanted the names of a number of registrars who had worked for a particular hospital consultant, the NHS trust supplied her with the name of the registrar who had treated her but not others. The Information Commissioner found this justified under s.40 because, while registrars might expect their current position to be disclosed, disclosure of past positions would, to a small degree, represent an infringement of privacy.[56]

The Information Commissioner has stated that normally, therefore, releasing the names of staff undertaking professional duties would not breach data protection principles but would be unfair if the data subject (the staff member) were exposed to a risk of harassment as a result.[57]

In the following case, a woman wanted information about an untoward incident involving her husband, but confidential witness statements prevented disclosure.

Exemption from disclosure under section 40: witness statements about untoward incident involving a patient. A woman sought witness statements that had been made about a serious untoward incident involving her late husband. The statements were given in the course of an internal investigation and staff members were informed that their statements would be treated confidentially. The Information Commissioner held that disclosure would breach the first principle of the Data Protection Act – lawfulness and fairness – because of the expectations of the staff about confidentiality.[58]

However, another similar type of case was not so straightforward.

Information about care and death of mother and unexplained use of haloperidol. A man tried to obtain information concerning the death of his mother and her care at Warwick and Heathcote Hospitals. There clearly were some issues, given his mother's active life before she was admitted, unexplained use of haloperidol and the upholding of his complaint by the Healthcare Commission, which had provided him with a 15-page letter containing the results of its investigation.

Further request for medical records, complaints file and investigator's report. The son made a request for further information, including his mother's medical records, the complaints file and the investigator's report. The Trust resisted on s.40 grounds concerning protection of staff. The s.40 argument was not wholly upheld by the Information Tribunal. It held that where staff had already been identified, explicitly or impliedly in the Healthcare Commission report (and letter), then the s.40 exemption no longer applied.

Opinions and views expressed by staff were exempt from disclosure. However, other opinions and views expressed by staff were protected:

---

55   Information Commissioner Decision: *Mersey Care NHS Trust* (2008), 14 January 2008.
56   Information Commissioner Decision: *St George's Healthcare NHS Trust* (2008), 19 March 2008.
57   Information Commissioner Decision: *NHS Litigation Authority* (2006), 27 September 2006.
58   Information Commissioner Decision: *Central and North West London NHS Foundation Trust* (2008), 17 March 2008.

In relation to the specific comments and opinions as set out in Confidential Schedule 2 the Tribunal is satisfied that it would not be fair to disclose them. The identity of the maker of the statement and the subject of the statement cannot be redacted with the content remaining because they would remain identifiable from either the context or the subject matter. The Tribunal is satisfied that disclosure would cause some distress in the context of colleagues working in close proximity.

The Tribunal also observes that a personal opinion would attract some sensitivity. In this case the disputed information goes beyond information directly concerning the individuals' employment or roles or the decision making process; it relates to personal evaluations and opinions, and although it concerns the individuals' employment (in the sense that it arose in the context of a complaint relating to a patient), it is not information so directly connected with their public role that its disclosure would automatically be fair.[59]

PERSONAL INFORMATION: NON-DISCLOSURE TO THE VERY PERSON WHO BLOWS THE WHISTLE

Sometimes people may seek evidence of underpinning reasons for lapses in treatment or care. In the following case, even though it was her allegations that triggered an internal report, the person was unable subsequently to access the report of the investigation.

Exempt from disclosure under section 40: internal report into alleged deficiencies in care on a ward. A former employee of an NHS trust requested a copy of an internal report – which had been triggered by allegations originally made by that employee – concerning supervision, management of medical staff and resource levels on a particular ward. The trust refused disclosure under s.40.

The Information Commissioner upheld this decision; disclosure would have been unfair under the first data protection principle. This was because staff were likely to have expected confidentiality when interviewed as part of the investigation, and this had in fact been indicated to staff. Furthermore, critical comments made by the trust about individuals would have caused considerable distress and damaged their employment prospects if those comments entered the public domain. Undue inferences might be made even about those members of staff who were reluctant or unwilling to provide information during the investigation if their names were disclosed.[60]

FUTURE EMPLOYMENT PROSPECTS OF STAFF LEAVING AN ORGANISATION

The Information Commissioner held that an NHS trust could resist disclosure under s.40 of information concerning an internal investigation against two senior executives, which resulted in their departure. The disclosure of the information could have a harmful effect on the current and future employment prospects of both of them; they also had a reasonable expectation that the information would not be disclosed. Furthermore, the Commissioner was satisfied that the internal

---

59   *Johnston v Information Commissioner* [2011]. In the First-Tier Tribunal Case No. EA/2011/0055 General Regulatory Chamber Information Rights. (On Appeal from: Information Commissioner's Decision Notice No: Fs50297286, 31 January 2011.)

60   Information Commissioner Decision: *University Hospital of North Staffordshire NHS Trust* (2007), 30 August 2007.

investigation had been thorough and independently verified. Thus, the public interest had largely been satisfied.[61]

Similar considerations arose about the departure of a chief executive from a public authority, following suspension. The NHS trust and executive had reached a compromise agreement and not all the allegations were fully investigated. He would not have expected details to be disclosed and to do so would have been unfair.[62]

REFUSAL EVEN TO CONFIRM OR DENY EXISTENCE OF INFORMATION (SECTION 40)

There is a part of s.40 concerning a public body's refusal to confirm or deny that it holds the relevant information, irrespective of whether it will disclose the actual information. It states that confirmation or denial is not required if it would breach data protection principles.

In one case, a man and his partner sought the minutes of a meeting alleged to have taken place between the NHS, social services and the police. The NHS trust refused to confirm or deny that there were any such minutes; this was on the grounds that to do so would provide information about the individuals named in the request and that this would be contrary to the first data protection principle. The Information Commissioner disagreed, pointing out that he had been provided with no evidence that any individual would suffer unwarranted detriment; therefore, the local authority should confirm or deny the existence of the minutes.[63]

However, in another case, a woman wrote to the Nursing and Midwifery Council. She was seeking disclosure of a statement sent to the Council by a nurse who worked at Barnet and Chase Farm Hospitals NHS Trust. This was in relation to the death at the hospital of the woman's mother. The Council refused to confirm or deny that it held the information. Its decision was upheld by the Information Tribunal.

This was on the grounds that it would not be fair and lawful to disclose under schedule 1 of the Data Protection Act 1998. This in turn was because of prejudice to the rights and freedoms or legitimate interests of the data subject, as referred to in paragraph 6, schedule 2 of the 1998 Act. The substantial reason was that confirming or denying would be enough to create prejudice, even if the information was held in relation to a trivial or mischievous complaint. And if there was a case to answer and a hearing held, then it would anyway become a matter of public record.[64]

---

61   Information Commissioner Decision: *Nottinghamshire Healthcare Trust* (2007), 13 August 2007.
62   Information Commissioner Decision: *George Eliot Hospital NHS Trust* (2007), 7 June 2007.
63   Information Commissioner Decision: *Rotherham NHS Primary Care Trust* (2007), 23 April 2007.
64   *Butters v Information Commissioner* [2009]. Information Tribunal Appeal Number EA/2008/0088 (Information Commissioner's Ref: FS50180310).

The reasoning of the Information Commissioner was similar when it upheld an NHS trust's refusal to confirm or deny whether it was instigating disciplinary proceedings against a particular nurse.[65]

Gagging clauses have arisen in relation to section 40. The Information Tribunal has held that even confirmation or denial of such a gagging agreement might be exempt under s.40 because of the possible prejudice to the person identified, even by implication. It has also emphasised that the tribunal has no jurisdiction to decide whether any such gagging agreements contravene the Public Interest Disclosure Act (which could invalidate any agreement requiring confidentiality). This was a case in which the information seeker believed that gagging clauses were designed to save higher management from embarrassment.[66]

EXEMPTION FROM DISCLOSURE: BREACH OF CONFIDENCE ACTIONABLE (SECTION 41)

An absolute exemption from disclosure applies if the information requested was obtained by the public body from any other person and if disclosure of that information to the public would constitute a breach of confidence actionable by that person (from whom it was obtained) or by anybody else.

Although section 41 is an absolute exemption, the common law involving breach of confidence contains its own public interest test. This means that disclosure will not constitute an actionable breach of confidence if there is a public interest in disclosure outweighing the public interest in confidentiality. Under the common law, there would be a presumption of non-disclosure. This therefore is the reverse of the public interest test applied generally under the Act to qualified exemption from disclosure, which assumes disclosure unless the public interest in confidentiality can be shown to outweigh the public interest in disclosure.[67]

The following case concerned information about the death of a man in a nursing home.

Exempt from disclosure under section 41: information provided by GP in relation to care and death of a man in a nursing home. A man sought information from an NHS primary care trust about the care of his late father-in-law and issues concerning a nursing home. It included correspondence between the nursing home, a doctor, the police and a coroner. A particular issue arose about the confidentiality of this information provided to the PCT by a GP. The Information Commissioner held that the public interest in the GP discussing issues of performance, with confidentiality assured, outweighed the public interest in disclosure. Likewise, the PCT was justified in withholding – under s.42 (see below) – five pieces of legal advice, on the basis of legal professional privilege.

---

65   *Central and North West London NHS Foundation Trust (CNWL)*. Information Commissioner case: FS50391625, 10 October 2011.

66   *Bousfield v Information Commissioner and County Durham and Darlington NHS Foundation Trust, St George's Healthcare NHS Trust, Heart of England NHS Foundation Trust, Somerset Partnership NHS Foundation Trust, South Tees Hospitals NHS Trust, University Hospitals of Leicester NHS Trust* [2012]. Appeals EA/2011/0212, EA/2011/0213, EA/2011/0247, EA/2011/0250, EA/2011/0251, EA/2011/0252.

67   Information Commissioner Decision: *Hounslow Primary Care Trust* (2008), 19 March 2008.

In that case, the confidentiality attached to the information provided by the GP was upheld.

However, in another case, when a man sought information about the care and death of his mother – including unexplained use of the drug haloperidol – the confidentiality of information provided by staff was held not to be covered by the exemption. This was because the tribunal believed:

> that the majority of the disputed information does relate to the normal aspects of the employment of the persons concerned, namely their actions and that of their colleagues and the processes and systems utilized in relation to the case. Whilst there are some elements which amount to a private opinion or judgment, the Tribunal is not satisfied that this is sufficient to impute an expectation of confidence into what was otherwise a non-confidential process.[68]

CONFIDENTIALITY: INFORMATION CONCERNING DEAD PEOPLE

Sometimes, family members or other people might be conducting their own 'adult protection' investigations, albeit retrospectively, following a person's death in health or social care. The request for information does not come under the Data Protection Act because that Act applies only to living persons.

Consequently, the Information Commissioner has considered a number of cases relating to whether the confidentiality exemption applies under s.41 of the Freedom of Information Act 2000. One such case reached the Information Tribunal. In sum, a duty of confidence does survive death.

Mother seeking information about daughter's death in hospital: section 41. A dead woman's mother sought information about her daughter's death. The NHS trust was not prepared to share the information without the consent of her widower, as next of kin. That consent was not forthcoming. The trust had, five years previously, admitted liability and reached a settlement with the widower. The trust argued that the s.41 exemption applied. The tribunal established that the medical records had been compiled with information from somebody else, namely the dead woman. It then asked a number of key questions.

Would the NHS have a defence to a breach of confidence claim? The first was whether the trust would have a defence to a breach of confidence claim, were it to disclose the information, because the public interest in disclosure would outweigh the public interest in maintaining confidence. The tribunal stated that patient confidentiality outweighed by some distance the interests in disclosure.

Another was whether an action for breach of confidence would be defeated because neither the dead woman nor her estate would suffer detriment by disclosure. The tribunal concluded that it would not necessarily be defeated since there needed to be no detriment beyond an invasion of privacy, which there would be, given the private information involved.

Did the duty of confidence survive death? A third question was whether the duty of confidence survived the woman's death. The tribunal was in no doubt that it did. If it did

---

68   *Johnston v Information Commissioner* [2011]. In the First-Tier Tribunal Case No. EA/2011/0055 General Regulatory Chamber Information Rights. (On Appeal from: Information Commissioner's Decision Notice No: Fs50297286, 31 January 2011.)

not, doctor and patient trust would be undermined if patients believed that information would be disclosed after death.

Bringing a claim for breach of confidence. Fourth was whether the dead woman's personal representatives would be able to bring a claim for breach of confidence. The answer was yes; and the duty of confidence would last until either the information became public or the public interest in disclosure outweighed that of confidentiality.

Human rights. Fifth, the trust argued that s.44 of the Act (legal prohibitions), the Human Rights Act 1998 and European Convention on Human Rights (article 8 concerning the right to respect for privacy) prevented disclosure. The tribunal did not regard article 8 as a directly enforceable legal prohibition. But, if it was wrong about that, disclosure would not be consistent in this case with article 8 and so would be exempt under s.44.[69]

In another case, the applicant, a professional writer, sought information about a dead person who had been under the care and supervision of a hospital. He initially applied under the Access to Health Records Act 1990 – unsuccessfully because, under s.3 of that Act, he was not the patient's personal representative or any person who might have a claim arising out of the patient's death. He then applied under the Freedom of Information Act 2000; the primary care trust refused on the basis of survival of the duty of confidence and the possibility of an action for breach of confidence. Such an action would probably not result in damages, since there would be no obvious financial loss at stake, but might lead to an injunction preventing publication. Thus, the Information Commissioner found the information exempt from disclosure under s.41 of the Act.[70]

In the following case, the duty of confidence to a dead man and his family meant that the information about his death was exempt from disclosure.

Internal reports about death of patient: exempt from disclosure: section 41. A request was made for internal reports into the circumstances surrounding the death of a patient. The information had come from medical records and interviews with relevant health professionals, from the police and from the coroner. Thus, under s.41, it had been obtained by a public body from somebody else. The Information Commissioner noted that the duty of confidence to the patient survived death and that there was an obligation of confidence created by the patient/doctor relationship. A breach of confidence action would have been possible if disclosure took place.

The exemption applied under s.41, and no public interest outweighed the duty of confidentiality in terms of (a) the confider consenting, (b) disclosure required by law, or (c) a public interest in disclosure overriding the duty of confidence. Exemption was also justified under s.40 because in the reports there was a small amount of information comprising personal information about the man's family. Because of the sensitivity of the information and the subject, it would have been unfair under the first data protection principle to disclose.[71]

And when a daughter sought her late father's medical records under the 2000 Act, the Information Commissioner ascertained that she was entitled to access under the

---

69   Information Tribunal: *Bluck v Information Commissioner and Epsom and St Helier University NHS Trust* [2007], 17 September 2007.

70   Information Commissioner Decision: *Walsall NHS Teaching Primary Care Trust* (2007), 13 December 2007.

71   Information Commissioner Decision: *East London and the City Mental Health NHS Trust* (2007) 3 December 2007.

Access to Health Records Act 1990, in which case it was an exempt disclosure under another section – s.21 of the 2000 Act – because the information was otherwise reasonably accessible and held by a public authority that was obliged to provide it – under the 1990 Act.[72]

Likewise, a man sought a copy of a report by a hospital consultant about the care of his late mother. The trust stated it would disclose under the 1990 Act if he provided proof that he was his dead mother's personal representative; it asked to see a copy of his birth certificate as proof. He failed to produce this and gave no reasons for not doing so; he sought the information instead under the 2000 Act. The Information Commissioner held that the trust was exempt from disclosing under s.21. The request of proof by the trust, under the 1990 Act, was reasonable.[73]

When the family of a dead woman wanted to see her social services care records, the local authority cited its duty of confidence to the dead woman. The Commissioner understood the family's wish for disclosure, but upheld the authority's stance:

> In the Commissioner's view it is important that social services' clients have confidence that the professionals caring for them will not disclose to the public sensitive information about them after they have died as this may discourage them from making information available. He gives weight to the argument that this, in turn, could ultimately undermine the quality of care that social services are able to provide or may lead to some people not becoming involved with social services in the first place. The Commissioner considers that this potential for prejudice to the effective functioning of social services is counter to the public interest.[74]

Witness statements made by staff to the coroner about the care of a dead patient were similarly held by the Information Commissioner to be exempt from disclosure under s.41 of the Act. This was because they had given information that related to the dead patient and had been given in confidence by that patient. The Commissioner went on to consider whether the public interest outweighed this duty of confidentiality and decided it did not.[75]

EXEMPTION FROM DISCLOSURE: LEGAL PRIVILEGE (SECTION 42)

A qualified exemption applies, under s.42 of the Act, to information that is subject to legal professional privilege.

---

72   Information Commissioner Decision: *Gloucestershire NHS Primary Care Trust*, 12 November 2007.
73   Information Commissioner Decision: *Liverpool Women's NHS Foundation Trust*, 19 February 2007.
74   Information Commissioner Decision: *East Sussex County Council*. Case no. FS50346570, 21 August 2012.
75   Information Commissioner Decision: *Central and North West London NHS Foundation Trust*. Case no. FS50406744, 18 January 2012.

Although this is not absolute, the Information Tribunal has noted that there is a strong element of public interest built into the privilege and that an equally strong consideration would be required to override it.[76]

In a case involving social services and members of his family, the applicant sought disclosure records, transactions and memoranda. Following intervention by the Information Commissioner, these were disclosed, but not the barrister's advice given to the council. The Information Tribunal upheld this non-disclosure under s.42, noting that the powerful arguments in favour of legal privilege can be outweighed exceptionally in the public interest – but not in this case.[77]

However, identifying exactly to what the legal privilege attaches will not always be straightforward, as the following Information Tribunal case illustrates.

Solicitors' papers about suicide of an NHS patient: varied status. A woman sought information in relation to the death of her son after he had jumped from a fourth-floor window, having discharged himself from the care of an NHS trust earlier in the day. Amongst the information sought were papers lodged with three sets of solicitors. The trust resisted disclosure on the basis either of legal professional privilege or that the papers held by the legal firms were not owned by, and held on behalf of, the trust, but were owned by the solicitors. In which case, they would not come under the Freedom of Information Act at all.

Of the three sets of papers, the tribunal found that the first did not belong to the trust, the second was covered by legal professional privilege (the tribunal emphasised the strength and public importance of this exemption, even though it is qualified rather than absolute) and the third set of papers was not privileged (because the papers would have been made available to all parties at the inquest, in which case the privilege is waived), did belong to the trust and so should be disclosed.[78]

PROHIBITION ON DISCLOSURE UNDER OTHER LEGISLATION (SECTION 44)

Under s.44 of the 2000 Act, there is an absolute exemption on certain grounds, including prohibition by other legislation.

For example, in relation to a complaint about an NHS trust, information was sought from the health service ombudsman who had investigated the complaint – in particular, transcripts of certain interviews. However, s.15 of the Health Service Commissioners Act 1993 contains a statutory bar on disclosure by the health service ombudsman of information obtained in an investigation, except in limited situations. Thus, the Information Tribunal held that the information was exempt from disclosure under s.44 of the 2000 Act because of this prohibition in the 1993 Act.[79]

---

76   Information Tribunal: *Bellamy v Information Commissioner* [2006], 27 March 2006.
77   Information Tribunal: *Kitchener v Information Commissioner and Derby City Council* [2006], 20 December 2006.
78   Information Tribunal: *Francis v Information Commissioner* [2008], 21 July 2008.
79   Information Tribunal: *Parker v Information Commissioner and Health Service Ombudsman* [2007], 15 October 2007.

The Information Tribunal has held that this prohibition applies not just to full investigations by the health service ombudsman but also to preliminary enquiries as well.[80]

However, equally, the tribunal has held that the exemption does not apply necessarily to the organisations that have supplied information to the ombudsman in the first place. It decided this in a case involving the attempts of a son to find out, from an NHS trust, about the death of his mother. It noted that:

> We do not think that our conclusion undermines the conduct of the Ombudsman's investigation. It is required by HSCA section 11(2) to be conducted in private, which will result, directly or indirectly, in the imposition of an obligation on those contributing information or submissions to it to maintain the confidentiality of the process and not, for example, to disclose the lines of enquiry that the Ombudsman may be pursuing or the issues she is putting to those whose actions are being investigated. It does not follow that the basic information, detached from any indication of such lines of enquiries or issues, must remain secret, just because it has previously been made available to the Ombudsman as part of her investigation. And, once a report has been issued (or the Ombudsman has decided not to pursue an investigation – as she had done in this case, before the information request had been refused), the privacy of the investigation also falls away.[81]

EXEMPTION FROM DISCLOSURE IF COMPLIANCE EXCEEDS COST LIMIT (SECTION 12)

Under s.12 of the Freedom of Information Act 2000, a public body does not have to comply with a request to disclose if the cost of complying would exceed the appropriate cost limit, which is set in regulations.[82] Thus, the following request, relevant to adult protection and safeguarding matters, failed.

Mistreatment, abuse and neglect: compliance request for details of complaints made would exceed the appropriate cost limit. The information sought revolved around complaints of mistreatment, neglect and abuse on NHS trust premises. The request asked for details of complaints made by patients, relatives and staff involving such issues and, in particular, hydration, nutrition, inappropriate use of diamorphine or potassium chloride, 'do not resuscitate' and 'not for intensive therapy' instructions. The NHS trust declined to disclose, arguing that to do so would mean exceeding the appropriate limit under s.12 (£450). It explained that complaints records were indexed alphabetically by patient, not by the nature or type of the complaint. The request would involve combing each complaints file for its contents. The Information Commissioner accepted the trust's argument: there were some 10,000 complaints files.[83]

---

80   *Thompson v Information Commissioner* [2011]. In the First-Tier Tribunal Case No. EA/2011/0164 & 0165. General Regulatory Chamber, Information Rights.

81   *Cubells v Information Commissioner* [2012]. In the First-Tier Tribunal Case No. EA/2011/0183. General Regulatory Chamber, Information Rights.

82   SI 2004/3244. Freedom of Information and Data Protection (Appropriate Limit and Fees) Regulations 2004.

83   Information Commissioner Decision: *Swansea NHS Trust*, 5 December 2006.

An obvious refusal, upheld by the Information Commissioner, was that of the Care Quality Commission when it declined, on cost grounds, to supply details of all its enforcement decisions. However, the Commissioner did find that it failed to provide adequate advice and assistance instead, under s.16 of the Act.[84]

EXEMPTION FROM DISCLOSURE: INFORMATION REASONABLY ACCESSIBLE BY OTHER MEANS (SECTION 21)

Under s.21 of the 2000 Act, an exemption applies if the information sought is reasonably accessible by other means and from a public authority with an obligation to provide it. For instance, this exemption will sometimes apply to disclosure of medical records of deceased people under the Access to Health Records Act 1990.

It also applied when a man wanted to obtain the background, details and legal basis for removal of his mother from hospital to a residential home where she subsequently died. The local authority argued that it had already disclosed this information in previous correspondence and in reports produced in response to the man's complaints. Both the Information Commissioner and then, on appeal, the Information Tribunal agreed with the local authority and held that s.21 applied.[85]

EXEMPTION FROM DISCLOSURE: VEXATIOUS REQUESTS (SECTION 14)

Under s.14 of the Freedom of Information Act 2000, a public body does not have to comply with a vexatious request. Guidance from the Information Commissioner refers to the key question as to being whether the request is likely to cause unjustified distress, disruption or irritation. In addition:

- Could the request fairly be seen as obsessive?

- Is the request harassing the authority or causing distress to staff?

- Would complying with the request impose a significant burden in terms of expense and distraction?

- Is the request designed to cause disruption or annoyance?

- Does the request lack any serious purpose or value?[86]

Some of the examples below illustrate clearly vexatious pursuit of local authorities, NHS or other public bodies. It is worth remembering, though, that on some occasions public bodies are capable of cover-up and obstruction that would drive the most reasonable of enquirers to frustration and vexatiousness. Now and again, the apparently vexatious application for information might indeed be well founded. The difficulty is knowing when.

---

84   Information Commissioner Decision: *Care Quality Commission.* Case no. FS50393575, 25 October 2011.
85   Information Tribunal: *Prior v Information Commissioner* [2006], 27 April 2006.
86   Quoted from: Information Commissioner's Office. *When can a request be considered vexatious or repeated?* London: ICO, 2012, p.1.

For example, one request for information, below, involving the South Yorkshire Police, was deemed vexatious. Yet that organisation is not one that has excelled itself in terms of transparency.[87]

VEXATIOUS REQUESTS: EXAMPLES

When an Age Concern volunteer obsessively pursued information about a woman's care plan drawn up by a local authority and the charges she had paid for that care, the Information Commissioner held that the local authority had correctly refused on grounds of vexatiousness.[88] The Information Tribunal upheld the decision but gave a few pointers about vexatiousness.

Information about alleged overcharging in respect of community care services. At the outset, the matters raised by the volunteer did show that the elderly woman was being overcharged, and the matter was rectified by the council. However, the volunteer believed that there were further irregularities. Overall, he went on to write to the local authority 73 letters and 17 postcards, and made 20 freedom of information requests. The allegations were investigated by an independent complaints investigator and the Commission for Social Care Inspection; the volunteer did not believe the veracity of these investigations. The police had also advised Age Concern that there was no evidence of dishonesty. At this point, the Tribunal noted, the volunteer should have let the matter drop.

However, the tribunal did caution against over-simple application of the Information Commissioner's guidance on vexatiousness. For example, the tribunal could imagine circumstances in which a request creates a significant burden and indeed harasses a public body but nonetheless could have a serious and proper purpose and so should not be considered vexatious.[89]

When a man's wife died at a hospital, he subsequently made 56 requests for information under the Freedom of Information Act. Both the Information Commissioner and the Information Tribunal found in the NHS trust's favour that the request under consideration was vexatious. It is worth spelling out the Commissioner's original reasoning:

> The death of a close family member will always be traumatic and will often lead to questions about the quality of health care offered to the individual. It is not unreasonable that a member of the family should want to know more about the surrounding circumstances, and where applicable, to hold an authority to account. However, there must be a limit to such enquiries. Since July 2006, the Trust had fielded 56 separate requests from the Appellant;
>
> The underlying complaint had been considered by the Trust and by the HC. The Appellant had, in effect, used FOIA to force the Trust to revisit an issue which had already been considered. Since the Appellant had been

---

87   Hillsborough Independent Panel (Chairman: Right Reverend James Jones, Bishop of Liverpool). *Hillsborough: the report of the Hillsborough Independent Panel*. HC 581. London: TSO, 2012. And: Conn, D. 'Hillsborough investigation should be extended to Orgreave, says NUM leader.' *The Guardian*, 22 October 2012.

88   Information Commissioner Decision: *Norfolk County Council*, 7 November 2007.

89   Information Tribunal: *Coggins v Information Commissioner* [2008], 13 May 2008.

informed that he had the opportunity to pursue the underlying complaint further through the Parliamentary Health Service Ombudsman (the 'Ombudsman'), his reason for pursuing the request was, at least in part, to continue his campaign against the Trust;

From the provocative nature of some of the Appellant's comments aimed at staff within the Trust, it was reasonable to conclude that the effect of the request would have been to harass the Trust and its staff…

The Trust had conceded that complying with the request would not be resource-intensive. However, it was reasonable for the Trust to consider that compliance would simply trigger further correspondence and further requests, therefore imposing a significant burden; and

The effect of much of the Appellant's contact with the Trust, particularly the revisiting of issues examined by the HC, was to cause disruption and annoyance, even though this may not have been intended. In relation to this particular request, the Appellant had sought to foster the perception that the Trust had purposefully obstructed or impeded his enquiries.

The tribunal emphasised that Freedom of Information Act requests were not a panacea for problems that had not been resolved through other channels, such as the complaints procedure.[90]

In another case, the Commissioner understood the upset caused by the death of a relative and the wish to know more, but found that the requests for information by the dead man's daughter had slid into harassing and obsessive behaviour. (The latest request, in question, concerned details about the administration of morphine.) Particularly, since one answered request invariably led to another request, and the complainant had already taken the case to the health service ombudsman, the Healthcare Commission and the police.[91]

In perhaps a more extreme case still, a woman had pursued matters about the medical care and death of her father for seven years. She continued to be dissatisfied with investigations conducted by the South Yorkshire Police, the South Yorkshire Police Authority, the Independent Police Complaints Commission, Doncaster Primary Care Trust, South Yorkshire Coroner and West Yorkshire Police. She had placed many details on a website. The Information Commissioner agreed that her continued information requests were vexatious and referred to the volume, frequency, hostility and condemnatory character of the woman's communications.[92]

However, in another case, an NHS trust (which garnered notoriety in 2007 following scores of deaths from infection) wrongly dismissed as vexatious an information request concerning correspondence between the trust and the coroner,

---

90   *Rigby v Information Commissioner* [2009]. In the First-Tier Tribunal Case no. EA/2009/0103. General Regulatory Chamber. Information Rights.

91   Information Commissioner Decision: *Sheffield Teaching Hospitals NHS Foundation Trust*. Case no. FS50421679, 21 May 2012.

92   Information Commissioner Decision: *Chief Constable of South Yorkshire Police*. Case no. FS50387841, 17 November 2011.

about the death of a man's wife. The man had to make a significant number of requests, partly because the trust's responses were confusing. The Information Commissioner held that the requests were not vexatious. However, the particular request, for which the trust had wrongly argued s.14, was in relation the coroner's report; by virtue of s.32 of the Act (documents held by the public body deriving from a court or inquiry), such disclosure was exempt.[93]

REQUESTS FOR MINUTES OF SAFEGUARDING MEETINGS

Requests might be made for minutes of safeguarding meetings involving, for example, social services staff, NHS staff and the police. They might be made by alleged perpetrators, victims or third parties. Relevant legislation to consider would be the Human Rights Act 1998, the Data Protection Act 1998 when a person is requesting information about themselves (subject access rules), and the Freedom of Information Act 2000 when the information is non-personal or about other people. All of which have been considered above.

PROCESSING PERSONAL INFORMATION: CALDICOTT GUARDIANS

The Department of Health issued guidance to local social services authorities, expecting them to have appointed, by April 2002, a 'Caldicott Guardian'. The function of this person is to safeguard and govern the use made of confidential information, particularly in respect of the requirements of the Data Protection Act 1998, including the processing, sharing and security of confidential information.[94] Caldicott Guardians had already been introduced to the NHS at an earlier date. Six key principles were outlined:

Principle 1 – Justify the purpose(s) for using confidential information

Principle 2 – Only use it when absolutely necessary

Principle 3 – Use the minimum that is required

Principle 4 – Access should be on a strict need-to-know basis

Principle 5 – Everyone must understand his or her responsibilities

Principle 6 – Understand and comply with the law[95]

Subsequent guidance was issued and included within it the fact that staff should be advised to seek help from the Caldicott Guardian, for example, in response to a request from the police for access to patient information, requests from patients to delete their records, an actual or alleged breach of confidentiality.[96]

---

93   Information Commissioner Decision: *Maidstone and Tunbridge Wells NHS Trust,* 19 April 2007.
94   HSC 2002/003. Department of Health. *Implementing the Caldicott standard in social care: appointment of 'Caldicott Guardians'.* London: DH, 2002.
95   Quoted from: HSC 2002/003. Department of Health. *Implementing the Caldicott standard in social care: appointment of 'Caldicott Guardians'.* London: DH, 2002.
96   Department of Health. *Caldicott Guardian Manual 2010.* London: DH, 2010, para 3.5.

Criminal justice: prosecution, evidence, protecting victims, coroners

Key points
No secrets: police interventions
Crown Prosecution Service: prosecution policies
    Older people: prosecution policy
    Guidance on prosecution of crimes committed against people with
        mental health problems and people with learning disabilities
    Domestic violence: prosecution policy
    Multi-agency risk assessment conference (MARAC)
Support for victims and witnesses
Sentencing
    Sentencing: vulnerability of victim
    Sentencing: domestic violence
Multi-agency public protection arrangements
    Three levels of MAPPA
    MAPPA: sharing information
    Disclosure of information by MAPPA agencies to third parties
    Requests from third parties for minutes of MAPPA meetings
Crime and Disorder Act 1998, section 115: power to share information
    Crime and disorder strategies
Coroners
    Coroners: shedding light on neglect and deaths of vulnerable adults
    Production of formal reports by coroners requiring responses from
        other agencies

KEY POINTS

As stated in the Department of Health's *No secrets* guidance, vulnerable people should have access to criminal justice.[1]

The police, Crown Prosecution Service (CPS) and the courts are central to this. The police investigate and gather evidence. The CPS takes decisions about prosecution. The courts try cases and decide innocence, guilt and sentencing.

---

1   Department of Health. *No secrets: guidance on developing and implementing multi-agency policies and procedures to protect vulnerable adults from abuse.* London: DH, 2000, p.2.

There are sentencing rules and guidelines applicable to vulnerable adults – that is, when a criminal offence is aggravated because of the vulnerability or disability of the victim.

The CPS has issued extensive guidance in relation to victims of domestic violence, older people, people with mental health problems and people with learning disabilities.

For managing risks posed by offenders, multi-agency public protection arrangements (MAPPA) are based in statute, involving cooperation and information sharing. In relation to protecting victims of domestic violence, there are also non-statutory 'multi-agency risk assessment conferences' (MARACs).

Lastly, coroners' inquests also play a key role in establishing how people died in questionable circumstances. They are notable in relation to vulnerable adults, especially in the case of the plentiful deaths in hospitals and care homes involving suspicions of neglect. Coroners have a statutory power to produce reports, send them to relevant agencies and demand a response.

NO SECRETS: POLICE INTERVENTIONS

The *No secrets* guidance itself emphasises the importance of early police involvement.

First, it states that early referral or consultation with the police will enable them to establish whether a criminal act has been committed.

Second, early involvement of the police will help ensure that forensic evidence is not lost or contaminated.

A notable example of preservation of evidence and early police intervention was illustrated in the following case as reported.

Conviction through drop of sweat on wheelchair. A drug addict who tricked his way into the homes of elderly people was given a prison sentence of eight years. He was identified by a drop of sweat he had left behind on the wheelchair of one woman when he lifted her out of it in the sheltered housing she lived in and stole £400. She had, at the time, a broken leg and wrist.[2]

Third, *No secrets* points out that police officers have considerable skill in investigating and interviewing. Early police involvement may avoid the need for unnecessary subsequent interviewing.

Fourth, police investigations should proceed alongside those dealing with health and social care issues.

Fifth, some witnesses will need protection.[3]

---

2   'Sweat traps thief.' *The Times*, 22 July 2009.
3   Department of Health. *No secrets.* London: DH, 2000, para 6.7.

CROWN PROSECUTION SERVICE: PROSECUTION POLICIES

The CPS is responsible (in most cases) for taking the decision to prosecute; it is then responsible for conducting the prosecution. It must apply the *Code for Crown Prosecutors* when making prosecution decisions.

(The Health and Safety Executive can prosecute under health and safety at work legislation, and the Care Quality Commission can do so under the Health and Social Care Act 2008. Likewise, local authority trading standards officers.)

In deciding whether to prosecute, the CPS applies a two-stage test. The first is the evidential stage. It is about whether there is enough evidence to provide a realistic prospect of conviction. The evidence has to be capable of being used in court and be reliable. Among the questions to be asked is whether the evidence is admissable, reliable and credible.[4]

In one case, the courts found that the Crown Prosecution Service had acted irrationally in failing blatantly to adhere to the code, as well as being in breach of article 3 of the European Convention on Human Rights.

Failure to adhere to the code in a case involving a mentally disordered victim: irrationality and breach of human rights. The CPS had wrongly jumped to conclusions about the credibility of the victim. It was about a man who suffered from a history of psychotic illness, involving paranoid beliefs and auditory and visual hallucinations. On Boxing Day, part of his ear had been bitten off. On the basis of a doctor's report, to the effect that his mental condition might affect his perception and recollection of events, the CPS decided not to prosecute. The judge was scathing:

> In the present case, if the prosecutor had applied the merits based approach and asked himself whether he thought that it was more likely than not, or at least as likely as not, that FB's identification of HR as the ear biter was the result of an hallucination, I cannot see how merely on the strength of Dr C's report he could have answered that question in the affirmative. There was an opportunity to explore the matter further, because Dr C was due to be available to answer further questions, but the decision to offer no evidence forestalled that.
>
> The reasoning process...for concluding that FB could not be placed before the jury as a credible witness was irrational in the true sense of the term. It did not follow from Dr C's report that the jury could not properly be invited to regard FB as a true witness when he described the assault which he undoubtedly suffered. The conclusion that he could not be put forward as a credible witness, despite the apparent factual credibility of his account, suggests either a misreading of Dr C's report (as though it had said that FB was incapable of being regarded as a credible witness) or an unfounded stereotyping of FB as someone who was not to be regarded as credible on any matter because of his history of mental problems.[5]

If there is enough evidence, the second stage – the public interest stage – is about whether it is in the public interest to prosecute. The more serious the offence, the more likely will a prosecution be needed in the public interest.[6]

---

4   Crown Prosecution Service. *Code for Crown Prosecutors*. London: CPS, 2013, para 4.6.

5   *R(B) v Director of Public Prosecutions* [2009] EWHC 106 (Admin).

6   Crown Prosecution Service. *Code for Crown Prosecutors*. London: CPS, 2013, para 4.12

The code points out that the CPS prosecutes on behalf of the public and not just the victim; however, the consequences for the victim of a decision to prosecute or not should be taken into account, together with any views expressed by the victim or the victim's family.[7]

The following case shows the determined reluctance of an alleged victim to participate in the criminal justice process and his view of police involvement. It is an example of what is sometimes a difficult balance to strike between a victim's choice and wishes, the need for the police and Crown Prosecution Service to bear in mind wider public interest in prosecution, and the difficulties of prosecuting without the victim's cooperation.

Alleged victim refusing to answer questions, no prosecution brought. Statements were made by at least ten nurses or carers that a person with motor neurone disease had been treated cruelly by his wife. One of the allegations concerned his being left in the garden on the hottest day of the year and suffering severe heatstroke. The alleged victim persistently refused to answer any questions and even threatened to take legal action against the police under the Protection from Harassment Act 1997. Had medical evidence independently corroborated the allegations, consideration might have been given to mounting a prosecution and even compelling the victim to give evidence as a 'hostile witness'. In the event, the prosecution did not take place.[8]

OLDER PEOPLE: PROSECUTION POLICY

In 2008, the CPS published guidance specifically about prosecuting crimes against older people.[9] It stresses that it regards crime against older people as serious and that it is therefore likely that a prosecution will be needed in the public interest. It lists a number of factors making prosecution more likely. These include, in summary, that:

- the offence is serious

- the defendant was in a position of authority or trust

- there are grounds for believing that the offence is likely to be continued or repeated

- the victim is vulnerable

- the victim is injured

- the defendant was motivated by prejudice or discrimination

- a weapon was used

- the defendant made threats before or after the attack

---

7   Crown Prosecution Service. *Code for Crown Prosecutors*. London: CPS, 2013, para 4.12

8   Peek, L. 'Hawking assaulted by wife, claim nurses.' *The Times*, 23 January 2004. Also: Peek, L. 'Police drop Hawking assault case.' *The Times*, 30 March 2004. Also: Fresco, A. 'Hawking may be called as hostile witness in "brutality" case.' *The Times*, 4 February 2004.

9   Crown Prosecution Service. *Crimes against older people: prosecution policy*. London: CPS, 2008, para 4.8.

- the defendant planned the attack

- there is a continuing threat to the health and safety of the victim or anyone else who is, or may become, involved

- the defendant has a criminal history, particularly involving convictions for offences against older people.

The guidance matches up behaviour towards older people with possible criminal offences. The range of offences is considerable. In summary:

(a) **Hitting, slapping, pushing, kicking.** Common assault under s.39 Criminal Justice Act 1988; actual bodily harm under s.47 Offences Against the Person Act (OAPA) 1861; grievous bodily harm/with intent ss.20 and 18 OAPA 1861.

(b) **Misuse of medication to manage behaviour.** Assault, false imprisonment, application of stupefying overpowering drugs with intent to commit indictable offence under s.22 OAPA 1861; poisoning with intent to injure, aggrieve or annoy under ss.23, 24 OAPA 1861; unlawfully administering medication under s.58 Medicines Act 1968; failure to comply with conditions for medication under Care Standards Act 2000 (now, the Health and Social Care Act 2008).

(c) **Inappropriate restraint.** False imprisonment, common assault, aggravated or grievous bodily harm under the OAPA 1861; kidnapping, contravention of care standards regulations, choking under s.21 OAPA 1861.

(d) **Inappropriate sanctions.** False imprisonment, assault, ill-treatment/wilful neglect under s.44 Mental Capacity Act 2005 or s.127 Mental Health Act 1983; breach of care standards regulations.

(e) **Sexual offences.** Sexual Offences Act 2003.

(f) **Threats of harm or abandonment.** Threats to kill under s.16 OAPA 1861; blackmail under s.21 Theft Act 1968; common assault, ill-treatment/ wilful neglect under s.44 Mental Capacity Act 2005 or s.127 Mental Health Act 1983.

(g) **Deprivation of contact, isolation or withdrawal from services or supportive networks.** False imprisonment; ill-treatment/wilful neglect under s.44 Mental Capacity Act 2005 or s.127 Mental Health Act 1983; breach of care standards regulations.

(h) **Humiliation, intimidation, emotional blackmail, verbal abuse.** Being shouted or sworn at: fear of violence under s.4 Public Order Act (POA) 1986; intentional harassment or alarm or distress under s.4A POA 1986; harassment or alarm or distress under s.5 POA 1986; course of conduct amounting to harassment/causing another to fear under ss.1 and 4 Protection from Harassment Act 1997; harassment of a person in his home under s.42A Criminal Justice and Police Act 2001; blackmail under s.21 Theft Act 1968; common assault.

(i) **Theft, fraud, exploitation, pressure in connection with wills, powers of attorney, financial transactions, or the misuse or misappropriation of property, benefits or possessions.** Theft or robbery ss.1 and 8 under Theft Act 1968; blackmail under s.21 Theft Act; fraud under Fraud Act 2006; forgery under s.25 Identity Cards Act 2006 and Forgery and Counterfeiting Act 1981.

(j) **Ignoring medical or physical care needs.** Failure to provide access to appropriate health services, withholding medication, adequate nutrition or heating, unmet physical needs such as bedding or clothing soaked in urine or faeces, decaying teeth, overgrown nails. False imprisonment, wilful neglect or ill-treatment of a person lacking mental capacity under s.44 Mental Capacity Act 2005 or s.127 Mental Health Act 1983; breach of care standards regulations.

(k) **Impairment of, or an avoidable deterioration in, physical or mental health.** The impairment of physical, intellectual, emotional, social or behavioural development. Wilful neglect or ill-treatment of a person lacking mental capacity under s.44 Mental Capacity Act 2005 or s.127 Mental Health Act 1983; breach of care standards regulations.

(l) **Actions resulting in death.** Murder; manslaughter; corporate manslaughter; causing or allowing death of a vulnerable person in a domestic setting under the Domestic Violence, Crime and Victims Act 2004; aiding or abetting suicide under s.2 Suicide Act 1961; breach of care standards regulations.[10]

GUIDANCE ON PROSECUTION OF CRIMES COMMITTED AGAINST PEOPLE WITH MENTAL HEALTH PROBLEMS AND PEOPLE WITH LEARNING DISABILITIES

Two further guidance documents deal with prosecution when crimes are committed against people with mental health problems and people with learning disabilities. This guidance warns against making assumptions that people cannot give evidence. It emphasises that mental capacity is relevant to the competence of the witness, but only in terms of assessing the ability of the witness to understand questions and to give comprehensible replies.[11]

---

10   Crown Prosecution Service. *Crimes against older people: prosecution policy.* London: CPS, 2008, Annex A.
11   Crown Prosecution Service: *Supporting victims and witnesses with mental health issues.* London: CPS, 2009. And: *Supporting victims and witnesses with a learning disability.* London: CPS, 2009.

DOMESTIC VIOLENCE: PROSECUTION POLICY

Domestic violence, per se, is not necessarily a safeguarding issue, as defined by the *No secrets* guidance. However, if it involves a vulnerable adult, then it will be.

The CPS has published policy guidance on domestic violence and maintains that it regards domestic violence as particularly serious.[12] The guidance provides a wide definition to domestic violence, giving the issue wide application.

In 2012, central government announced an amended (non-statutory) definition of domestic violence, to be used by government departments from March 2013:

> Any incident or pattern of incidents of controlling, coercive or threatening behaviour, violence or abuse between those aged 16 or over who are or have been intimate partners or family members regardless of gender or sexuality. This can encompass but is not limited to the following types of abuse:
>
> - psychological
> - physical
> - sexual
> - financial
> - emotional
>
> Controlling behaviour is: a range of acts designed to make a person subordinate and/or dependent by isolating them from sources of support, exploiting their resources and capacities for personal gain, depriving them of the means needed for independence, resistance and escape and regulating their everyday behaviour.
>
> Coercive behaviour is: an act or a pattern of acts of assault, threats, humiliation and intimidation or other abuse that is used to harm, punish, or frighten their victim.[13]

MULTI-AGENCY RISK ASSESSMENT CONFERENCE (MARAC)

The Association of Chief Police Officers sets out the approach to risk assessment and management of risk, including keeping witnesses safe and the use of non-statutory multi-agency risk assessment conferences (commonly referred to as MARACs).[14]

A MARAC is about sharing information between agencies, risk management where there is high risk of domestic violence, and focus on and protection of the victim. Various organisations and individuals may be involved, including independent domestic violence advisers, NHS staff, victim support workers,

---

12   Crown Prosecution Service. *CPS policy for prosecuting cases of domestic violence.* London: CPS, 2009.

13   Home Office. *New definition of domestic violence.* News, 18 September 2012. Accessed on 15 October 2012 at: www.homeoffice.gov.uk/media-centre/news/domestic-violence-definition.

14   Association of Chief Police Officers, National Policing Improvement Agency. *Guidance on investigating domestic abuse.* London: ACPO, NPIA 2008, para 6.2.2.

Women's Aid, housing, children's services, adult services, substance misuse services, probation. The focus is on the victim and to ensure that there is a protective plan in place.[15]

SUPPORT FOR VICTIMS AND WITNESSES

Various forms of support are available for witnesses.

These include trained, independent domestic violence advisers and domestic violence support organisations (e.g. Women's Aid).

The CPS and the police run Witness Care Units, whose staff offer advice, support and information for witnesses.

The Witness Service, run by Victim Support, is available at magistrates' courts and Crown Courts. Its activities include, for instance, pre-trial visits for people to familiarise themselves with the court and providing a separate waiting area to ensure the witness does not meet the defendant. Subject to the agreement of the court, a volunteer can accompany the witness to provide emotional support when the latter gives evidence.

There is also a statutory *Code of practice for victims of crime*. It details what support victims should receive in the criminal justice system. It talks about identifying and supporting vulnerable or intimidated witnesses and keeping victims informed about police and CPS decisions.[16] If the code is not adhered to, a complaint can be made to the service involved and ultimately to the parliamentary ombudsman.[17]

SENTENCING

The Criminal Justice Act 2003, s.146, states that the court must treat it as an aggravating feature of an offence if the offender showed hostility towards the victim based on the latter's disability or if the offence was motivated by hostility towards people who have a disability. (This section covers sexual orientation as well, and s.145 covers racial or religious aggravation of the offence.)

Policy guidance from the Crown Prosecution Service stresses that this hostility is required for s.146 to apply. For instance, it would not be enough that the defendant picked on the disabled person because the latter was vulnerable and represented an easy target.[18] In that case, s.143 might be applicable (see immediately below). In the following, the alleged homophobic offence was not proved.

Gratuitous violence but evidence required to show aggravating feature of hostility. Violence occurred after the complainants had been to an Elton John concert in Watford with other members of their family. They had left the concert and were walking towards the town centre when they came across the accused and his friend. There was

15   Ministry of Justice, National Probation Service, HM Prison Service, Association of Chief Police Officers. *MAPPA guidance, version 3.0*. London: MoJ, NPS, HMPS, ACPO, 2009, paras 5.1–5.6.

16   Criminal Justice System. *Code of practice for victims of crime*. London: Office for Criminal Justice Reform, 2005.

17   Parliamentary Commissioner Act 1967, as amended by Schedule 7 to the Domestic Violence, Crime and Victims Act 2004.

18   Crown Prosecution Service. *Guidance on prosecuting cases of disability hate crime*. London: CPS, 2007.

an exchange of words. The appellant hit one of the complainants, who fell to the ground. There were further punches. The accused was convicted, and sentence passed on the basis of aggravation – namely, that comments had been made concerning the presumed, though mistaken, sexual orientation of the complainants. The Court of Appeal stated that it had been gratuitous and unprovoked violence, but there was no actual evidence that the motive was homophobia. The sentence was therefore reduced on appeal.[19]

Certainly, not all crimes against disabled people will involve hostility. For instance, the perpetrator may not be aware of the disability, or the offence may be unrelated to the disability (e.g. when a wheelchair user's cleaner steals from her handbag).

Although hostility is required, the offence may go wider than is commonly appreciated, as further guidance points out, in summary:

> First, the requirement is precisely hostility, not actual hatred; the former sets a lower threshold than the latter.
>
> Second, hostility should be given its ordinary dictionary definition, including ill-will, ill-feeling, spite, contempt, prejudice, unfriendliness, antagonism, resentment, and dislike.
>
> Third, prosecutors should examine all the surrounding circumstances. For instance, an incident not appearing to be based on hostility, might so appear if it is part of a pattern: for example, a disabled person's home being the only one in the street repeatedly targeted for vandalism.
>
> Fourth, hostility can still legally be shown, even if there are other factors at play. For instance, verbal abuse of a wheelchair passenger requiring ramps to get on the train, might be triggered by anger at the ensuing delay; but this could still be hostility under s.146 of the Act.
>
> Fifth, the hostility does not necessarily have to be evident at the actual time the offence is commissioned; because s.146 refers to hostility, during, or immediately before or after the offence.[20]

SENTENCING: VULNERABILITY OF VICTIM

Under s.143 of the Criminal Justice Act 2003, the court must – in considering the seriousness of any offence – assess the offender's culpability in committing the offence and any harm that the offence caused, was intended to cause or might foreseeably have caused.

The Sentencing Guidelines Council states that this culpability will be greater when a vulnerable victim has been targeted because of age, youth, disability or the job they do. Relevant factors would also include abuse of power and abuse of a position of trust.[21]

---

19   *R v Peters* [2007] EWCA Crim 435.
20   Crown Prosecution Service. *Disability hate crime: guidance on the distinction between vulnerability and hostility in the context of crimes committed against disabled people.* London: CPS, 2010.
21   Sentencing Guidelines Council. *Overarching principles: seriousness.* London: SGC, 2004, pp.5–6.

Where death has resulted, then, under schedule 21 of the Criminal Justice Act 2003, it is an aggravating factor if the victim was particularly vulnerable because of age or disability.

Age and vulnerability of victim: aggravating factor in sentence for murder. The victim was 89 years old and living alone. The offender had tricked his way into his home to steal money. He beat the man with his walking stick and stamped on his head at least twice. The victim died four weeks later. In mitigation, the offender was 20 years old, not a mature adult and suffering from mental disorders from use of crack cocaine; he did not intend to kill the victim.

On appeal, the sentence for murder was increased from 20 to 25 years, with reference to schedule 21 of the Criminal Justice Act 2003. The offender had a history of targeting elderly people. He had attacked the frail victim unrelentingly. At the very least, he intended to inflict grave injury and had acted recklessly. There was no evidence that his judgement was impaired by any mental disorder – and any self-inflicted mental disorder did not lower his culpability. He had shown no genuine remorse.[22]

SENTENCING: DOMESTIC VIOLENCE

Under s.143 of the Criminal Justice Act 2003, where an offender has previously been convicted of an offence involving domestic violence either against the same or a different partner, this is likely to be a statutory aggravating factor.

The Sentencing Guidelines Council makes a number of points about domestic violence and sentencing. It states unequivocally that, as a starting point for sentence, offences committed in a domestic context should be regarded as being no less serious than offences committed in a non-domestic context. It refers to abuse of trust and of power and to vulnerability. In summary:

(a) **Abuse of trust**, whether through direct violence or emotional abuse, represents a violation of this understanding.

(b) **An abuse of power** in a relationship involves restricting another individual's autonomy which is sometimes a specific characteristic of domestic violence. This involves the exercise of control over an individual by means which may be psychological, physical, sexual, financial or emotional.

(c) **Vulnerability.** For cultural, religious, language, financial or any other reasons, some victims of domestic violence may be more vulnerable than others, not least because these issues may make it almost impossible for the victim to leave a violent relationship.

The Sentencing Guidelines Council states that if vulnerability has been exploited, then a higher sentence is warranted. It also notes that one of the factors in domestic violence is sometimes the 'two personae' of the perpetrator – good character external to the home at variance with what goes on within. It also refers to the fact that, generally, the sentence should relate to the seriousness of the offence and not the expressed wishes of the victim. However, on some occasions, the victim's wishes

---

22   *Attorney General's Reference (no. 30 of 2009); R v Stevenson* [2009] EWCA Crim 2344.

may affect the sentence, although the wish needs to be genuine and the victim not exposed to harm as a result.[23]

The following case illustrates the victim's reluctance to give evidence and the perpetrator's outward appearance.

Outward appearance of perpetrator of domestic violence. The offender had been married to the victim for several years. The relationship was turbulent. The victim had made previous allegations of violence. There were visible injuries. But she always declined to give evidence. The offence in question involved holding a heated iron to the victim's face four or five times, for two or three seconds at a time. The victim tried to get away and was punched repeatedly. Despite her reluctance to say what had really happened, the case went to trial two years later and the perpetrator pleaded guilty on the day of the trial. He received positive references from a number of people as mitigation. His sentence was two and a half years in prison.

The sentence was appealed as too lenient. The court pointed out that it was not uncommon for someone who beat their partner to appear different to the rest of the public; such a person often had two personas. Although M had glowing references, which provided powerful mitigation, that mitigation had to be seen in light of the sustained and determined cruelty of the offence. The sentence was increased to five years.[24]

More generally, the court must – in considering the seriousness of any offence – assess the offender's culpability in committing the offence and any harm that the offence caused, was intended to cause or might foreseeably have caused.[25]

MULTI-AGENCY PUBLIC PROTECTION ARRANGEMENTS

The Criminal Justice Act 2003 places a duty on 'responsible authorities' to establish arrangements for assessing and managing risks in relation to certain high-risk offenders. They are known as multi-agency public protection arrangements (MAPPA). Apart from the provisions contained within the Act itself, the relevant agencies involved in MAPPA must have regard to guidance issued under s.325. The current guidance, issued by the Ministry of Justice, is entitled *MAPPA guidance 2012, version 4*.

The responsible authorities are defined as the chief of police, probation board and prison service.

The duty applies to specified categories of violent and sex offenders, as well as to other people who have committed offences and who a responsible authority considers pose a risk of serious harm to the public.

THREE LEVELS OF MAPPA

Arrangements function on three levels. The first is single agency (usually the probation service) where there is a lower level of risk. The second involves a higher

---

23   Sentencing Guidelines Council. *Overarching principles: domestic violence.* London: Sentencing Guidelines Secretariat, 2006.

24   *Attorney General's Reference (No.80 of 2009) Sub Nom R v Harpal Singh Moore* [2010]. Court of Appeal, Criminal Division, 24 February 2010.

25   Criminal Justice Act 2003, s.143.

risk but one not requiring complex management; normally, this will involve more than one agency. At the third level are critical cases involving high risk and/or difficult risk management issues. These require multi-agency public protection panel (MAPPP) meetings.[26]

Apart from the three responsible authorities, other named organisations are under a duty to cooperate in MAPPA insofar as such cooperation is compatible with their own statutory functions.[27] They include local social services authorities, primary care trusts, other NHS trusts, strategic health authorities, Jobcentres Plus, local youth offending teams, registered housing providers that accommodate MAPPA offenders, local housing authorities, local education authorities, electronic monitoring service providers, the Borders Agency.[28]

MAPPA offenders are categorised, as follows:

Category 1 – Registered sexual offender

Category 2 – Murderer or an offender who has been convicted of an offence under Schedule 15 of the Criminal Justice Act and:

– who has been sentenced to 12 months or more in custody; or

– who has been sentenced to 12 months or more in custody and is transferred to hospital under s.47/s.49 of the Mental Health Act 1983 ('MHA 1983'); or

– who is detained in hospital under s.37 of the MHA 1983 with or without a restriction order under s.41 of that Act.

Category 3 – Other dangerous offender: a person who has been cautioned for or convicted of an offence which indicates that he or she is capable of causing serious harm and which requires multi-agency management...[29]

MAPPA: SHARING INFORMATION

Under a duty to cooperate, agencies 'may' include the exchange of information. Guidance states that the responsible authorities and the 'duty to cooperate' agencies therefore have a statutory power to share information, under s.325 of the Act.

However, in the case of agencies not covered by s.325, the guidance notes that information could still be shared but on a different legal basis, effectively a common law power to do so, within limits:

Information-sharing between the MAPPA agencies and these third parties does not benefit from section 325(4) of the CJA 2003. In general, non-statutory bodies are able to share information provided this does not breach

---

26   Ministry of Justice. *MAPPA guidance 2012, version 4*. London: MoJ, 2012, para 7.1.

27   Criminal Justice Act 2003, ss.325–327.

28   Criminal Justice Act 2003, s.325(6). See: Ministry of Justice. *MAPPA guidance 2012, version 4*. London: MoJ, 2012, para 3.5.

29   Quoted from: Ministry of Justice. *MAPPA guidance 2012, version 4*. London: MoJ, 2012, para 6.1.

the law. They are bound by the common law duty of confidence. The key principle of the duty of confidence is that information provided should not be used or disclosed further in an identifiable form, except as originally understood by the provider, or with his or her subsequent permission. However, case law has established a defence to breach of confidence where an individual breaches the confidence in the public interest. The prevention, detection, investigation and punishment of serious crime and the prevention of abuse or serious harm will usually be sufficiently strong public interests to override the duty.[30]

The guidance states that any information sharing, in the context of MAPPA, must comply with the eight data protection principles in the Data Protection Act 1998. For example, information must be accurate and up to date; it must be stored securely; and it must not be retained any longer than necessary.

In addition, in relation to article 8 of the European Convention on Human Rights, the sharing must be necessary – 'in the interests of national security, public safety or the economic well-being of the country, for the prevention of disorder or crime, for the protection of health or morals, or for the protection of the rights and freedoms of others'.[31]

The guidance is clear that the sharing of information by MAPPA agencies is necessary under article 8 because it aims at preventing disorder or crime or administering justice: 'Provided the information shared is only used for MAPPA purposes the necessity test will be met, as information-sharing by way of MAPPA is not an excessive or unreasonable way of assessing and managing these risks.'[32]

Even then, the information sharing must be proportionate under both the Data Protection Act 1998 and the European Convention:

> For MAPPA agencies, this essentially means ensuring that information about the data subject is relevant to assessing and managing risk and that no more information is shared than is needed to manage that risk. For example, if what is actually needed is the names and addresses of individuals, sharing their race and religion as well would be likely to be disproportionate.[33]

In short, therefore, this means that information should not be shared casually, even in the context of MAPPA.

DISCLOSURE OF INFORMATION BY MAPPA AGENCIES TO THIRD PARTIES

Having discussed information sharing generally between MAPPA agencies, the guidance goes on to consider more specifically what it calls disclosure of information by a MAPPA agency to a third party, not part of MAPPA:

---

30   Ministry of Justice. *MAPPA guidance 2012, version 4*. London: MoJ, 2012, para 9.7.
31   Ministry of Justice. *MAPPA guidance 2012, version 4*. London: MoJ, 2012, para 9.7.
32   Ministry of Justice. *MAPPA guidance 2012, version 4*. London: MoJ, 2012, para 9.10.
33   Ministry of Justice. *MAPPA guidance 2012, version 4*. London: MoJ, 2012, para 9.13.

For the purposes of the Guidance, *information-sharing* is the sharing of information between all the agencies involved in MAPPA. *Disclosure*, on the other hand, is the sharing of specific information about a MAPPA offender with a third party (not involved in MAPPA) for the purpose of protecting the public. The third party could be a member of the public such as a victim, an employer, a person forming a relationship with an offender, or a person acting in a professional capacity but not party to the MAPP arrangements.[34]

It gives examples of when such disclosure might be needed:

- When there is evidence that grooming may be taking place, for example through leisure clubs, churches, employment.

- If there is a condition in a Sexual Offences Prevention Order/licence excluding offenders from a specific location or having contact with named persons.

- Where others may be at risk, for example in supportive accommodation. This may include other service users, but usually it will be staff and managers who are told for placement purposes and for greater vigilance to be exercised.

- Where there is a need to protect past or potential victims, in particular where offenders strike up new relationships with partners who have children or grandchildren. In some cases, this may include friends or neighbours who have children.

- Where the public may be at risk through the offender's employment, training or education.

- In schools and colleges if grooming needs to prevented. In the case of young offenders, limited and controlled disclosure may be made to school or college staff.

- Where a person may be in a position to actively assist in the risk management of an offender by being briefed about risk factors and scenarios.[35]

The guidance then notes that relevant law includes the common law power for the police to share information for policing purposes (for the prevention and detection of crime), Data Protection Act 1998, Human Rights Act 1998, Children Acts 1989 and 2004, Criminal Justice and Immigration Act 2008.

It goes on to note the importance of proportionality and the preferability of the offender knowing that disclosure is taking place. It also summarises the Child Sex

---

34   Ministry of Justice. *MAPPA guidance 2012, version 4*. London: MoJ, 2012, para 10.2.
35   Quoted from: Ministry of Justice. *MAPPA guidance 2012, version 4*. London: MoJ, 2012, para 10.5.

Offender Disclosure Scheme (members of the public registering a child protection interest in relation to a particular individual).

The following case, heard under previous legislation before registered housing providers were formally under the umbrella of MAPPA, would nowadays be the equivalent of a responsible authority sharing with a non-MAPPA agency – that is, what the guidance calls a third party disclosure case. The court made clear that information should be disclosed only after careful thought.

Starting point for sharing of information, and weighing up competing considerations. A 64-year-old man who had killed his wife was now being released, unconditionally, on licence. A report about his release concluded that the risk of reoffending was unlikely, although it might increase were he to engage in a personal relationship. He was going to live in sheltered accommodation. The probation service disclosed information about the man to the manager of the housing.

The court held that, as a matter of decision-making process, the disclosure was unlawful. This was because the probation service had approached the matter on the presumption that information would be disclosed. Rather, it should have begun with a presumption of non-disclosure and then used the risk assessment to displace that presumption. It should also have explicitly balanced the risk to other people of non-disclosure, with harm to the man flowing from disclosure.[36]

REQUESTS FROM THIRD PARTIES FOR MINUTES OF MAPPA MEETINGS

The guidance also deals with the question of requests for minutes of MAPPA meetings. It points out that requests might come from a variety of sources, including offenders, third parties and other organisations (such as the courts or the Crown Prosecution Service).

The guidance notes that such requests need to be considered in the light of the Human Rights Act 1998, the Data Protection Act 1998 (e.g. if the offender has made a subject access request) or the Freedom of Information Act 2000 (information requested about other people). The guidance notes that under the 2000 Act, a number of rules could apply that would make the requested information – the minutes – exempt from disclosure; in summary:

- information supplied by, or relating to, bodies dealing with security matters (section 23)

- national security (section 24)

- investigations and proceedings by public authorities (section 30)

- law enforcement (section 31)

- health and safety (section 38)

---

36   *R(A) v National Probation Service* [2003] EWHC 2910 (Admin).

- personal information (section 40)

- information provided in confidence (section 41).[37]

CRIME AND DISORDER ACT 1998, SECTION 115: POWER TO SHARE INFORMATION

Separately, there is a power under s.115 of the Crime and Disorder Act for any person to pass information to specified bodies, including the police, probation service, local authorities and NHS bodies. The reverse power, for authorities to give information to any person, is not included.

CRIME AND DISORDER STRATEGIES

Under the Crime and Disorder Act 1998, 'responsible authorities' have certain obligations. They are the local authority, police, NHS primary care trust, fire and rescue authority, probation service. They operate as community safety partnerships. These authorities must formulate and implement a strategy for the reduction of crime and disorder and for combating the misuse of drugs, alcohol and other substances in the area. In addition, each authority must have due regard to the effect of the exercise of its functions on – and to the need to prevent – these matters.[38]

CORONERS

The rules governing the role of the coroner are contained in the Coroners Act 1988, although this will be replaced by the Coroners Act 2009 (not yet in force).

Deaths in general must be reported to the local Registrar of deaths. Normally, a medical doctor provides the cause of death on a signed medical certificate, on receipt of which the death can be registered by the Registrar.

Deaths that are sudden, unexpected, violent or have occurred when a person has been in lawful custody are reported to the coroner. If, after a post-mortem, the coroner believes that the death was violent, unnatural or sudden (with causes unknown) or if the person died in prison or other particular place (e.g. police custody), then an inquest must be held.[39]

An inquest is held with or without a jury in open court. It hears evidence from witnesses but is not a trial. The purpose is to establish how a person died. Inquest verdicts include natural causes, accident or misadventure. These indicate that nothing untoward caused the death. These are in contrast to death through unlawful killing (including murder or manslaughter), self-neglect or neglect.

Neglect has been defined by the courts in this context as 'a gross failure to provide adequate sustenance, medical attention or shelter for a person in a position of dependency, whether by reason of a physical or mental condition'.[40]

---

37   Ministry of Justice. *MAPPA guidance 2012, version 4*. London: MoJ, 2012, para 13.39.
38   Crime and Disorder Act 1998, ss.5–7, 17.
39   Coroners Act 1988, s.8.
40   *R v North Humberside Coroner, ex p Jamieson* [1995] QB 1.

And coroners do have seriously to consider whether their legal functions are triggered. For example, the following case involved the deaths of residents at a care home in Birmingham in connection with allegations about antipsychotic drugs, inadequate antibiotic treatment for pneumonia and the restrictive effect of bucket chairs. The court found the coroner's decision not to hold an inquest to be unlawful.

Deaths in care home and holding of inquest. Expert evidence suggested that the death of a care home resident in 2002 had been caused or contributed to by excessive doses of an antipsychotic drug, coupled with the restrictive effect of a bucket chair and a possible failure to give adequate antibiotic treatment for pneumonia. The bucket chair was a low-slung seat from which elderly, and maybe restless, residents would have difficulty getting up unless assisted.

This gave reasonable cause to suspect that the death was unnatural under s.8 of the Coroners Act 1988. However, the coroner failed to hold an inquest; a successful judicial review case was brought challenging this decision. The death had taken place in the Maypole Nursing Home in Birmingham, operated by two general practitioners. Most of the residents were funded by social services and the NHS. A number of residents had died. The National Care Standards Commission had taken steps to close the home compulsorily, although the owner closed it voluntarily. The strategic health authority also investigated and disciplinary action was taken by the General Medical Council against the two general practitioners, who were suspended.[41]

CORONERS: SHEDDING LIGHT ON NEGLECT AND DEATHS OF VULNERABLE ADULTS

The findings of coroners continue to throw a window open on to the widespread neglect in care homes and hospitals. Sometimes, such findings may prompt police involvement and prosecution.

Prison sentence for wilful neglect, following coroner involvement. In one case, it was following the involvement of a coroner that a care home owner was charged and sent to prison for six months for wilful neglect. The resident concerned had died of septicaemia and pneumonia, having been found previously by his family in soiled clothing, sweating and unconscious, and having been dehydrated and lost two stone (12.7 kg) in weight in the period prior to his death.[42]

In another case, a 93-year-old man died, malnourished with multiple pressure sores on arms, back, hips, buttocks, groin, legs and feet and stuck in the foetal position, unable to uncurl. A 54-year-old woman had been living with him and had told police that she loved him and looked after him. The coroner found that the man's death had occurred 'aggravated by neglect' and that he would be writing to a number of agencies.[43]

It was a coroner in 2006 who threw light on standards of care at Tameside Hospital, when investigating the deaths of several patients,[44] and similarly at the

41   *Bicknell v HM Coroner for Birmingham/Solihull* [2007] EWHC 2547 (Admin).

42   Narain, J. 'Care home boss jailed after wilful neglect killed Alzheimer's patient.' *Daily Mail,* 21 May 2008.

43   'Inquest results in neglect verdict.' *Westmoreland Gazette,* 21 December 2001.

44   Fielding, F. (Professor Dame). *Independent review of older people's care at Tameside General Hospital.* Manchester: NHS North West, 2007, p.2.

Queen's Hospital, Romford, in relation to the suffering, neglect and death from pressure sores of an 89-year-old war veteran.[45]

And, in 2012, a coroner stated that she found:

> very alarming that such a vulnerable person who relied on professionals for her care and support was presented to hospital in the way she was. The vulnerable in our society must be properly cared for on all levels and their dignity protected. I think that Mrs Darby was not afforded the care and dignity she deserved on this occasion.

This was something of an understatement: the 94-year-old woman concerned had been admitted to hospital, five weeks after going into a care home in reasonable health. On admission to hospital, she had a chest infection, pneumonia, pressure sores, septicaemia and ear and urinary infections. She died about two weeks later.[46]

PRODUCTION OF FORMAL REPORTS BY CORONERS REQUIRING RESPONSES FROM OTHER AGENCIES

Rule 43 of the Coroners Rules 1984 was amended in 2008. It provides for the production of formal reports by coroners, sending them to relevant agencies and requiring a response.

Under this rule, coroners have a wider remit to make reports to prevent future deaths (and not necessarily the same type of death). The recipient of a coroner's report must send the coroner a written response. Coroners must provide the Lord Chancellor and other specified people with a copy of the report and the response, and can also provide copies to other interested persons. The Lord Chancellor may publish the report and response, or a summary of them, and also send copies to any other people or organisations with an interest.[47]

For example, in Southwark, the chief executive of the local authority was called on to respond to the concerns of the coroner following the death of an elderly woman.

Death of 88-year-old woman: report to social services requiring a response.
An 88-year-old woman lived alone following the death of her husband. She was not always compliant with her medication and was most reluctant to accept medical care. Neighbours had offered to help and became concerned when they had not seen her for some time.

The police and ambulance service were called on 21 July. They did not find her in need of medical attention; she seemed clean and well cared for, as did the property. Her blood sugar levels were low but were restored with sugared drinks and glucose. She was judged mentally competent to look after herself and the property. On 23 July, the ambulance service faxed the details through to social services.

---

45 Schlesinger, F. 'Coroner's fury as great-grandfather, 86, dies after being dumped on A&E trolley for 19 hours TWICE.' *Daily Mail*, 22 May 2009.

46 '"She looked like a concentration camp victim": Coroner slams care home after emaciated pensioner was admitted to hospital weighing five-and-a-half stone.' *Daily Mail*, 26 April 2012.

47 Ministry of Justice. *Guidance for coroners on changes to Rule 43: Coroner reports to prevent future deaths.* London: MoJ, 2008.

The referral was taken by a non-qualified, temporary member of staff and passed to the duty manager, who considered it non-urgent. That same day, a neighbour rang social services with her concerns. She rang twice more, the third call being four days later, on 28 July. A social worker visit was then scheduled for five days later on 4 August. By 30 July, however, the woman had been found dead.

The inquest recorded an open verdict, but the coroner sent a report under Rule 43 to the chief executive of the council. The coroner drew attention to the need for further training on eligibility criteria, better communication about how decisions were reached, better investigation where information is lacking, clear investigation and responses to external concerns, clearer distinction between social work and medical responses.[48]

In 2012, a six-monthly summary of Rule 43 reports showed that, of 233 reports issued under Rule 43, 88 – that is, 38 per cent – related to hospitals.[49]

48   Gardiner, D. *Assessment into the circumstances surrounding the death of Mrs E Lambert.* Report prepared on behalf of Southwark Council, 2009.

49   Ministry of Justice. *Summary of Reports and Responses under Rule 43 of the Coroners Rules: seventh report for period October 2011–March 2012.* London: MoJ, 2012, p.3.

Criminal justice support for vulnerable victims and witnesses

Key points
Special measures under the Youth Justice and Criminal Evidence Act
    Intermediaries
Achieving best evidence guidance
Admissibility of, and competence to give, evidence
    Competence to understand and answer questions
    Giving sworn or unsworn evidence

KEY POINTS

A number of 'special measures' are contained in the Youth Justice and Criminal Evidence Act 1999 to assist vulnerable and intimidated witnesses give their 'best' evidence in court.

In addition, the government has published guidance called *Achieving best evidence in criminal proceedings*. It is not legally binding, but a judge could raise a query as to why it has not been followed.

Within the 1999 Act, vulnerable witnesses are defined as witnesses whose quality of evidence the court considers will be diminished because they, in summary:

- have a mental disorder as defined in the Mental Health Act 1983, or

- are significantly impaired in relation to intelligence and social functioning – that is, witnesses with learning disabilities – or

- are physically disabled witnesses.[1]

A second category of witnesses are those who are intimidated. They are defined in s.17 of the 1999 Act as people suffering from fear or distress in relation to testifying in the case. Complainants in sexual offence cases automatically fall into this category, unless they wish to opt out.

SPECIAL MEASURES UNDER THE YOUTH JUSTICE AND CRIMINAL EVIDENCE ACT

Vulnerable and intimidated witnesses are eligible for special measures under the Youth Justice and Criminal Evidence Act 1999. These measures are, in summary:

---

1   Youth Justice and Criminal Evidence Act 1999, s.16.

- screens in the court room shielding the witness from the defendant (s.23)

- giving evidence via live video link from outside the court room (s.24)

- evidence given in private (clearing the public gallery in sexual offence cases and those involving intimidation) (s.25)

- removal of wigs and gowns (s.26)

- video recorded evidence in chief (s.27)

- video recorded cross-examination or re-examination (s.28, not yet in force)

- examination of a witness through an intermediary (s.29)

- aids to communication (s.30).

For instance, in the following case, evidence was given by live video link by two elderly women.

Giving live link evidence. In a theft case, two elderly women gave evidence from their living room, by means of a mobile video conferencing kit. They were giving evidence against a carer who had stolen money from them in their own homes. The carer was convicted and sentenced to prison for 18 months.[2]

In another case, evidence was given by video link, one of the victims blinking her eyes to answer questions.

Evidence given by severely disabled women to convict a care home worker of sexual assaults against them. A care home worker was jailed for 12 years after committing sexual assaults against four severely disabled women. Three had cerebral palsy and the fourth had brain injuries. One of the victims gave evidence by live video link, blinking her eyes in order to answer questions put to her. Another had, in a videotaped police interview, moved a pointer on a computer screen via the joystick on her wheelchair. A third could not communicate at all, and the fourth victim could no longer communicate by the time of the trial. Further evidence was provided by video link from Japan, by a former volunteer at the home, who had observed sexual touching of one of the victims by the man.[3]

INTERMEDIARIES

An intermediary communicates questions to the witness and answers from the witness, and explains these so that the witness or person putting the question can understand them. An intermediary might come, for example, from the speech and language therapy or social work professions and assist the witness to understand questions put to them and to be understood.[4]

Decisions on applications for special measures are for the court to determine after taking into account the views of the witness.[5] The appointment of an

---

2   *R v Atkins* [2004]. Reported in: Humberside Crown Prosecution Services. *Humberside Annual Report 2003–04*, 2004, p.5.

3   de Bruxelles, S. 'Evidence by blinking helps convict James Watts of sexual assaults.' *The Times*, 6 November 2009.

4   Ministry of Justice. *Achieving best evidence in criminal proceedings: guidance on interviewing victims and witnesses, and guidance on using special measures.* London: MoJ, 2011, para 2.117.

5   Youth Justice and Criminal Evidence Act 1999, s.16.

intermediary is discretionary, and the fact that an intermediary would improve the trial process does not necessarily mean that one must be appointed. It is a question of what the judge feels the need to do in order to achieve fairness.[6]

ACHIEVING BEST EVIDENCE GUIDANCE

Guidance outlines the stages through which a witness will pass. It covers identification and definition of vulnerable witnesses, competence, compellability, oath taking and how witnesses can be assisted. In summary:

(a) **planning and conducting interviews with vulnerable adult witnesses** (including support, interpreters, intermediaries, therapeutic help)

(b) **planning and conducting interviews with intimidated, reluctant and hostile witnesses**

(c) **witness support and preparation** (including supporters such as Victim Support volunteers, Witness Service volunteers, Witness Care officers, independent sexual violence advisers, independent domestic violence advisers, intermediaries, domestic violence officers, early special measures meeting, pre-trial therapy, risk assessment (e.g. in domestic violence) for managing a witness's safety during the pre-trial period)

(d) **witnesses in court** (explanation of special measures including role of intermediary to communicate questions and answers to and from the witness).[7]

Further specific guidance is available on therapy for vulnerable witnesses[8] and on working with intimidated witnesses.[9]

The guidance notes the importance of therapy for the welfare of the victim but also of taking precautions so that it does not contaminate the evidence to be given by the vulnerable witness. The guidance does state that, ultimately, if there is a tension, priority should be given to the best interests of the witness.[10]

This cautionary reminder is because witness training for criminal trials is prohibited. Nevertheless, this is not the same as pre-trial familiarisation arrangements, which do not include discussion about proposed or intended evidence and which are acceptable.[11]

In one case, concerning the prosecution of an NHS nurse for attempted murder, witness training was given to other staff, but the judge concluded that it did not

---

6   *R v Cox* [2012] EWCA Crim 549.

7   Ministry of Justice. *Achieving best evidence in criminal proceedings: guidance on interviewing victims and witnesses, and guidance on using special measures.* London: MoJ, 2011.

8   Home Office, Crown Prosecution Service, Department of Health. *Provision of therapy for vulnerable adults or intimidated witnesses prior to a criminal trial: practice guidance.* London: HO, CPS, DH, 2002.

9   Office for Criminal Justice Reform. *Working with intimidated witnesses: a manual for police and practitioners responsible for identifying and supporting intimidated witnesses.* London: Criminal Justice System, 2006.

10   Home Office, Crown Prosecution Service, Department of Health. *Provision of therapy for vulnerable adults or intimidated witnesses prior to a criminal trial: practice guidance.* London: HO, CP, DH, 2002, para 2.117.

11   *R v Momodu* [2005] EWCA Crim 177.

give the prosecution an unfair advantage. It had been an attempt to familiarise the witnesses with the giving of evidence coherently rather than to orchestrate the evidence.[12]

ADMISSIBILITY OF, AND COMPETENCE TO GIVE, EVIDENCE

The aim of government policy is to assist vulnerable and intimidated witnesses to give their best evidence with the assistance of the special measures and support before, during and after the trial. Thus, witnesses whose evidence might have been dismissed or simply not heard in the past might now have a better chance of access to justice. Basically, so that people get treated fairly.

However, even so, various rules apply as to admissibility of, and competence to give, evidence.

COMPETENCE TO UNDERSTAND AND ANSWER QUESTIONS

Under s.53 of the Youth Justice and Criminal Evidence Act 1999, the general rule is that all people, whatever their age, are competent to act as witnesses in criminal proceedings unless they cannot understand questions asked of them in court or cannot answer them in a way that can be understood (with, if necessary, the assistance of special measures).[13]

So, in the following case, the court held that the video evidence of an older woman with Alzheimer's disease should be admitted in spite of doubts about reliability.

Admissibility of video evidence of elderly woman in rape trial. The defendant was accused of attempting to rape and of indecently assaulting an 81-year-old woman who had long-standing delusional problems associated with early Alzheimer's disease. He attempted to have video testimony given by the woman excluded from the trial – partly on the grounds that the woman lacked competence to give evidence under s.53 of the 1999 Act.

The Court of Appeal upheld the judge's decision to admit the video. Considering the video, the judge had applied the test of whether the woman had 'been able to understand the questions being put to her' and whether she was 'giving answers which could be understood'. The court stated that it agreed with the judge's view on this. But, further, she 'prima facie has a right to have her complaint placed before a jury and a right to have a jury assess whether they are sure that the complaint is established and the putting of the video before the jury is the only way in which that right can be upheld'. The defence would then be able to bring medical evidence and argue as to the reliability of the video at the time it was made.[14]

In a further case, the court emphasised at the outset the presumption that everybody is competent to give evidence.

Giving of evidence by an 81-year-old person with Alzheimer's disease. The victim, an 81-year-old woman suffering from Alzheimer's disease, was spotted one morning

---

12   *R v Salisbury* [2004] Crown Court, Chester, 18 June 2004.
13   Youth Justice and Criminal Evidence Act 1999, s.53.
14   *R v D* [2002] EWCA Crim 990.

in someone's front garden, behaving strangely. The police were called. She made various rude comments suggestive of a sexual incident having taken place. She ultimately gave a video interview. At the time of the interview, and after it, she would not have been capable of giving evidence in court.

In respect of s.53 of the Act and her competence, the judge had taken the approach that she did not understand all the questions and not all her answers were understandable. But she understood, and was understood in part, sufficiently for a jury to evaluate her evidence. The Court of Appeal approved this approach, and the defendant's (a minicab driver) conviction for rape was upheld.[15]

GIVING SWORN OR UNSWORN EVIDENCE

Section 55 of the Youth Justice and Criminal Evidence Act 1999 sets out how courts are to decide whether a witness should swear an oath (or affirm) before giving evidence.

An adult can give sworn evidence if he or she has a sufficient appreciation of the solemnity of the occasion and of the particular responsibility to tell the truth that is involved in taking an oath. This is presumed if he or she is able to give intelligible testimony; intelligible testimony means that the witness can understand questions and give comprehensible answers.

If the witness cannot give intelligible testimony according to these rules, then, under s.56 of the Act, unsworn evidence can still be given as long as the witness is still competent (under s.53).

The question of the giving, and admissibility, of evidence by people with some form of mental impairment or disorder has been considered by the courts on a number of occasions. In summary, some of these cases have involved, in particular:

(a) **Video-recorded evidence:** s.27 of the Youth Justice and Criminal Evidence Act 1999. This allows for video-recorded evidence in chief in respect of vulnerable or intimidated witnesses. But any such recording does not have to be admitted by the court in certain circumstances – for example, if it is not in the interests of justice or the witness would not be available for cross-examination.

(b) **Presumption of competence to give evidence:** s.53 of the Youth Justice and Criminal Evidence Act 1999, discussed above.

(c) **Fairness of admitting evidence:** s.78 of the Police and Criminal Evidence Act 1984. This is about whether in all the circumstances, including how the evidence was obtained, it would be unfair to admit the evidence.

(d) **Hearsay evidence:** s.114 of the Criminal Justice Act 2003. This concerns admissibility of hearsay evidence, including whether it is in the interests of justice.

---

15   *R v Ali Sed* [2004] EWCA Crim 1294.

(e) **Admissibility of evidence not made orally in the proceedings:** s.116 of the Criminal Justice Act 2003. This concerns admissibility of evidence not made in oral evidence in the proceedings if certain conditions are satisfied, including that the person is unfit to be a witness because of his or her bodily or mental condition.

In the following case, the court disentangled a number of potentially complex issues surrounding these legal provisions. Having done so, it then questioned whether the case should have been brought to court at all, given the learning disabilities of both the alleged victim and alleged perpetrator.

Two children with severe learning disabilities: alleged indecent assault by one on the other. The accused and the alleged victim were both 13 years old at the time of the alleged offence. Both were pupils at the same special school, and both had severe learning disabilities. The boy was accused of having indecently touched the girl.

Initial interviews and evidence. Shortly after the initial complaint, the girl was interviewed on police camera. She gave an intelligible account. The boy was then interviewed under caution, with a solicitor and appropriate adult present. He appeared to admit he had touched the girl indecently.

Girl unable to remember events by the time of trial. By the time of the trial, the girl could not remember anything and could rely only on what she had said on the video-recorded original interview.

Boy unable to give meaningful evidence: s.53 of 1999 Act. The boy had subsequently been examined by a consultant clinical psychologist, who concluded that the boy was severely disabled, such that he was in the bottom 0.1 per cent of the population according to the Wechsler test. He could not remember why he was being brought to court. He was highly suggestible; a variation in voice intonation of the same question would elicit directly contradictory answers. The psychologist believed that the boy could give no meaningful evidence, either as a witness in court or at the time of the original interview. The case reached the High Court, where a number of points were clarified.

Competence to give evidence under s.53 of 1999 Act: to be considered both at interview and throughout trial. Under the Youth Justice and Criminal Evidence Act, the test of competence contained in s.53 should be addressed both when consideration is given as to whether to admit a video-recorded interview and also throughout the trial.

Admitting or excluding video interview under s.27 of 1999 Act. If it appeared that the witness was not competent at the time of the video interview, it would be a reason for declining to make a special measures direction under s.27 of the Act, and thus declining to admit the video interview.

However, in this case, the question about the girl's competence had arisen only at the time of the trial. If it was clear that the witness was not competent immediately before the trial, then the video interview would normally not be admitted because the witness would not be available for cross-examination. However, if the competence issue only arises after the video interview has been admitted, then it is open to the court to place little or no weight on it, precisely because it cannot be tested in cross-examination.[16]

---

16   *Director of Public Prosecutions v R* [2007] EWHC 1842 (Admin).

In another unusual case, preceding the Youth Justice and Criminal Evidence Act 1999, it was one of the defendants who wanted the video evidence, given by a severely disabled man, admitted, whilst her co-defendant sought its exclusion.

Admissibility of transcript made by social worker. An elderly man, living with his disabled son, had shown kindness to a female heroin addict. She went round to his flat with an acquaintance; they stole money, a television set and video recorder. The elderly man was punched and kicked such that he died 16 days later. The woman was convicted of robbery and manslaughter. However, she denied this, arguing that she had not inflicted any injuries, that there had been no agreement about using violence and that she had acted under duress from her companion.

Her version of events was supported by the elderly man's son (since deceased), whose interview had been videotaped. The son had been severely disabled, though with unimpaired mental faculties. He suffered from cerebral palsy, epilepsy, Parkinson's disease, severe speech difficulties and was confined to a wheelchair. He had acute difficulties in making himself understood, quite apart from a reluctance to speak to strangers.

Only the social worker could understand what he was saying in what had been supposed to be a police interview; in fact, the man did not answer the police officers, so the social worker asked all the questions. The social worker then made a transcript record of what the man had been trying to say. The court concluded that the video and transcript could be admitted; the question would then be to decide at trial how much weight to place on them.[17]

---

17   *R v Duffy* [1998] 3 WLR 1060 (Court of Appeal).

Criminal justice assistance for vulnerable suspects

Key points
Appropriate adult for vulnerable suspects or perpetrators
    Summary of Code C provisions for vulnerable suspects
    Examples of appropriate adult legal cases
    Not following appropriate adult rules will not necessarily
        undermine conviction
    Speech and communication difficulties
Provision of special measures in court for a vulnerable suspect
    Live link for suspects
    Intermediaries for suspects
Prosecution of mentally disordered offenders
    Fitness to plead and sentencing

KEY POINTS

The provisions outlined in the previous chapter are about assisting vulnerable witnesses to give evidence. However, the question of assistance for suspects who are vulnerable also regularly arises. The legal provisions are different. A few key points are as follows.

First is the Police and Criminal Evidence Act 1984, and in particular the statutory code of practice made under it, 'Code C'. This covers the provision of an 'appropriate adult' for vulnerable suspects being interviewed by the police. These rules are an important safeguard to ensure that a person's mental vulnerability does not lead to an erosion of their rights as a suspect and to unsafe conclusions being drawn at such interviews.

Second is the question of 'special measures' being made available for a vulnerable suspect, as opposed to a vulnerable witness. For example, fairness may require that an intermediary be appointed, so that the accused can follow proceedings, understand questions and have his or her answers communicated.

Third, mentally disordered offenders are sometimes 'diverted' away from the criminal justice system; for instance, Mental Health Act provisions may be used instead.

Fourth, sentencing by the courts will sometimes take account of the vulnerability of the perpetrator.

APPROPRIATE ADULT FOR VULNERABLE SUSPECTS OR PERPETRATORS

Vulnerable adults are sometimes suspects, rightfully or wrongfully accused. Separate, therefore, from the provisions described above for vulnerable or intimidated witnesses are rules for vulnerable suspects.

The Police and Criminal Evidence Act 1984 states that juries must be warned about the reliability of a confession made by a person with a learning disability ('mentally handicapped').[1]

The real detail is within 'Code of Practice C', made under the Police and Criminal Evidence Act 1984.[2] The code must be had regard to; whilst it is not legislation, it is 'statutory' and any departure from it would require strong justification in court. The details for mentally disordered or mentally vulnerable adults are summarised in Annex E of the code.

The code makes a general opening statement about the need to avoid discrimination against the groups of people now protected under the Equality Act 2010:

> The powers and procedures in this Code must be used fairly, responsibly, with respect for the people to whom they apply and without unlawful discrimination. The Equality Act 2010 makes it unlawful for police officers to discriminate against, harass or victimise any person on the grounds of the 'protected characteristics' of age, disability, gender reassignment, race, religion or belief, sex and sexual orientation, marriage and civil partnership, pregnancy and maternity when using their powers. When police forces are carrying out their functions, they also have a duty to have regard to the need to eliminate unlawful discrimination, harassment and victimisation and to take steps to foster good relations.[3]

It goes on to state about mental disorder:

> If an officer has any suspicion, or is told in good faith, that a person of any age may be mentally disordered or otherwise mentally vulnerable, in the absence of clear evidence to dispel that suspicion, the person shall be treated as such for the purposes of this Code.[4]

The code deals with the identification, treatment and interviewing of a mentally disordered or mentally vulnerable adult and the provision of an appropriate adult.

An appropriate adult is (a) a relative, guardian or somebody else responsible for their care or custody, (b) someone experienced in dealing with mentally disordered

1   Police and Criminal Evidence Act 1984, s.77.

2   *Police and Criminal Evidence Act 1984. Code C: code of practice for the detention, treatment and questioning of persons by police officers.* London: TSO, 2012.

3   *Code C revised: code of practice for the detention, treatment and questioning of persons by police officers.* London: TSO, 2012, para 1.0.

4   *Code C revised: code of practice for the detention, treatment and questioning of persons police officers.* London: TSO, 2012, para 1.4.

or mentally vulnerable people, (c) some other responsible adult over 18 who is not a police officer or employed by the police.[5]

SUMMARY OF CODE C PROVISIONS FOR VULNERABLE SUSPECTS

The provisions, in Code C, relating to mentally disordered and mentally vulnerable people, include, in summary:

(a) **Informing the appropriate adult:** If the custody officer authorises the detention of a person who is mentally vulnerable or appears to be suffering from a mental disorder, the custody officer must, as soon as practicable, inform the appropriate adult of the grounds for detention and the person's whereabouts, and ask the adult to come to the police station to see the person.

(b) **Legal advice requested:** If the appropriate adult, having been informed of the right to legal advice, considers legal advice should be taken, the provisions of *section 6* apply as if the mentally disordered or otherwise mentally vulnerable person had requested access to legal advice.

(c) **Clinical attention:** The custody officer must make sure a person receives appropriate clinical attention as soon as reasonably practicable if the person appears to be suffering from a mental disorder, or, in urgent cases, immediately call the nearest appropriate health care professional or an ambulance. It is not intended that these provisions delay the transfer of a detainee to a place of safety under the Mental Health Act 1983, section 136, if that is applicable. If an assessment under that Act is to take place at a police station, the custody officer must consider whether an appropriate health care professional should be called to conduct an initial clinical check on the detainee.

(d) **Assessment as soon as possible:** It is imperative a mentally disordered or otherwise mentally vulnerable person detained under the Mental Health Act 1983, section 136, be assessed as soon as possible. A police station should only be used as a place of safety as a last resort, but if that assessment is to take place at the police station, an approved social worker and registered medical practitioner shall be called to the station as soon as possible to carry it out. Once the detainee has been assessed and suitable arrangements have been made for his or her treatment or care, he or she can no longer be detained under section 136. A detainee should be immediately discharged from detention if a registered medical practitioner, having examined him or her, concludes he or she is not mentally disordered within the meaning of the Act.

(e) **Caution in presence of appropriate adult:** If a mentally disordered or otherwise mentally vulnerable person is cautioned in the absence of the

---

5   *Code C revised: code of practice for the detention, treatment and questioning of persons by police officers.* London: TSO, 2012, para 1.7.

appropriate adult, the caution must be repeated in the appropriate adult's presence.

(f) **Interview and signing of statements without appropriate adult not to be undertaken, other than in certain circumstances:** A mentally disordered or otherwise mentally vulnerable person must not be interviewed or asked to provide or sign a written statement in the absence of the appropriate adult unless the provisions of paragraphs 11.1 or 11.18 to 11.20 apply (relating to interference with evidence, physical harm, loss or damage of property).

(g) **Role of appropriate adult, not simply an observer:** If the appropriate adult is present at an interview, he or she shall be informed that he or she is not expected to act simply as an observer and the purposes of his or her presence are to:

 (i) advise the interviewee

 (ii) observe whether or not the interview is being conducted properly and fairly

 (iii) facilitate communication with the interviewee.

(h) **Review of detention:** If the detention of a mentally disordered or otherwise mentally vulnerable person is reviewed by a review officer or a superintendent, the appropriate adult must, if available at the time, be given an opportunity to make representations to the officer about the need for continuing detention.

(i) **Charging with an offence, presence of appropriate adult:** If the custody officer charges a mentally disordered or otherwise mentally vulnerable person with an offence or takes such other action as is appropriate when there is sufficient evidence for a prosecution, this must be carried out in the presence of the appropriate adult if he or she is at the police station. A copy of the written notice embodying any charge must also be given to the appropriate adult. See paragraphs 16.1 to 16.4A.

(j) **Intimate searches:** An intimate or strip search of a mentally disordered or otherwise mentally vulnerable person may take place only in the presence of the appropriate adult of the same sex, unless the detainee specifically requests the presence of a particular adult of the opposite sex. A strip search may take place in the absence of an appropriate adult only in cases of urgency when there is a risk of serious harm to the detainee or others.

(k) **Restraint:** Particular care must be taken when deciding whether to use any form of approved restraints on a mentally disordered or otherwise mentally vulnerable person in a locked cell.[6]

---

6   *Code C revised: code of practice for the detention, treatment and questioning of persons by police officers.* London: TSO, 2012, annex E.

EXAMPLES OF APPROPRIATE ADULT LEGAL CASES

If a police officer has any suspicion, or is told in good faith, that a person of any age may be mentally disordered or otherwise mentally vulnerable, or mentally incapable of understanding the significance of questions or his or her replies, that person must be treated as mentally disordered or otherwise mentally vulnerable. In the following case, however, there were no such suspicions.

Appropriate adult justifiably not perceived to be required: confession of murder by man of limited intelligence. An elderly man was strangled at home. A 23-year-old man of limited intelligence and abnormally suggestible was arrested. He denied the allegation that he was the murderer. He was then interviewed ten times over a period of six days. In the first nine interviews, there was no solicitor or independent person present. In the first six, he denied the murder; then admitted it in the next three. Only in the tenth was an appropriate adult, an independent social worker, present. The man appealed against his subsequent conviction. The appeal failed.

The medical evidence at the time did not suggest he had a learning disability. Furthermore, there was no evidence at the trial suggesting that the interviewing police officers knew or suspected or believed that the man might have had learning disabilities, thus requiring the presence of an independent person or appropriate adult at the interviews.[7]

In contrast, the following case involved a successful appeal against a conviction, based on a confession in the absence of an appropriate adult.

Confession by person with learning disabilities, without appropriate adult: successful appeal. The suspect had learning disabilities. He confessed to attempted murder and also, alternatively, to grievous bodily harm with intent. He had refused the presence of a solicitor. No independent adult was present. During 18 hours of interview, he had refused food, cried and been very emotional. The judge at the trial had found him not to be 'mentally handicapped'. He also failed to direct the jury under s.77 of the PACE 1984. This states that the jury must be warned about the special need for caution in convicting a 'mentally handicapped' person who has confessed without an independent person present.

The appeal succeeded. The judge should have given such a direction; the judge had also been wrong to suggest the absence of an appropriate adult was of little importance.[8]

Similarly, in another case, a man appealed against his conviction for burglary.

Excluding evidence obtained unreliably without an appropriate adult. When arrested, the man had informed the arresting officer that he could not read or write. He was interviewed without a solicitor or appropriate adult present. Evidence suggested that his mental capacity was that of a nine- to ten-year-old child. The trial judge found that there had been a breach of the code, but ruled that he was sure beyond reasonable doubt that the admissions were reliable and admitted them in. On appeal, the court held the judge should have considered whether the confession has been obtained in a way so as to make it unreliable. The evidence should not have been admitted; there was no other evidence and the conviction was overturned.[9]

7   *R v Foster* [2003] EWCA Crim 178.
8   *R v Lamont* [1989] Crim LR 813.
9   *R v Kenny* [1994] Crim LR 284.

NOT FOLLOWING APPROPRIATE ADULT RULES WILL NOT NECESSARILY UNDERMINE CONVICTION

Not following the appropriate adult rules will not necessarily result in a conviction being overturned. For example, in a drink driving case, involving a man suffering from depression (i.e. a mental disorder under the Act), the conviction was held to be safe and stood, even though no appropriate adult had attended. This was because the breath test had been properly administered. The police had acted in good faith. The man appeared to, and did, understand what was going on. The appropriate adult would not have made any difference to the administration of the breath test.[10]

Similarly, in a drug trafficking case, a confession was made by a man who was of low intelligence and mentally vulnerable, without an appropriate adult being present. The confession stood; the correct approach identified by the Court of Appeal was to consider what had been lost as a result of the absence of an appropriate adult at the time of the confession.[11] This followed from an older case in which a man with schizophrenia had not been afforded an appropriate adult when interviewed. He had said he didn't want anyone. The Recorder allowed the interview evidence because the man had been in an apparently lucid state at the time of interview, which meant he hadn't needed an appropriate adult. The Court of Appeal overturned this decision, noting that the correct question to ask was not whether the man's condition meant an appropriate adult wasn't needed, but whether the admission of the evidence would have such an adverse effect upon fairness that it should be excluded.[12]

SPEECH AND COMMUNICATION DIFFICULTIES

If a person appears to be blind, seriously visually impaired, deaf, unable to read or speak, or has difficulty orally because of a speech impediment, he or she must be treated as such for the purposes of this code in the absence of clear evidence to the contrary.[13]

Although the code does refer to the assistance to be given to people who are blind, seriously visually impaired, deaf, unable to read or speak, or who have difficulty orally because of a speech impediment, the appropriate adult rules apply only to people with mental disorder or mental vulnerability. If a person appears to be deaf or there is doubt about his or her hearing or speaking ability, he or she must not be interviewed in the absence of an interpreter unless he or she agrees in writing to being interviewed without one. That is, unless this would result in interference with evidence, interference or harm to other people, serious loss or damage to property and so on.[14]

10   *Stanesby v Director of Public Prosecutions* [2012] EWHC 1320 (Admin).

11   *R v Gill* [2004] EWCA Crim 3245.

12   *R v Aspinall* [1999] 2 Cr. App. R. 115.

13   *Code C revised: code of practice for the detention, treatment and questioning of persons by police officers.* London: TSO, 2012, para 1.6.

14   *Code C revised: code of practice for the detention, treatment and questioning of persons by police officers.* London: TSO, 2012, paras 11.1, 13.5.

PROVISION OF SPECIAL MEASURES IN COURT FOR A VULNERABLE SUSPECT

Aside from the rules about an appropriate adult is the more general point about vulnerable suspects getting a fair hearing. The following court case shows the importance of a basic recognition of a person's ability to give evidence in the light of a disability.

Making allowances for a vulnerable witness who had suffered a stroke. A man was conducting his own defence in respect of an alleged offence of failing to comply with a statutory notice under the Housing Act 1985. He had suffered a stroke, which had caused brain damage and affected his ability to work, concentrate and remember things. He waited all day in court before the hearing was held. He said to the judge that he was therefore physically and mentally unable to conduct his case due to the medical problems arising from the stroke. The judge insisted on proceeding. The Court of Appeal held that the man had not been given a fair hearing; the consequences of stress and fatigue on a person who had suffered a stroke had not been taken into account. The case would have to be reheard.[15]

In a related vein, the conviction of a man with learning disabilities was quashed after it became clear that, at the time of the trial, he suffered from a verbal memory impairment which affected his ability to put forward a proper defence, to instruct his lawyer and to follow the evidence. However, for various reasons, his lawyer was not aware of the extent of his disability. There was a reasonable explanation for this unawareness and no blame to be attached to the man himself.[16]

The special measures available under the Youth Justice and Criminal Evidence Act 1999 are primarily for vulnerable witnesses, not vulnerable suspects.

LIVE LINK FOR SUSPECTS

The 1999 Act does allow the court to direct that evidence be given by the accused person through a live link if certain conditions are met. These are: first, that the person has a mental disorder (as defined in s.1 of the Mental Health Act 1983) or a significant impairment of intelligence and social function; second, that because of this the person is unable to participate effectively in giving oral evidence in court; third, a live link would enable more effective participation.[17]

INTERMEDIARIES FOR SUSPECTS

The 1999 Act does not yet provide for intermediaries for an accused person (as opposed to a witness).[18] However, the courts retain an inherent power to take steps to ensure that a person has a fair trial. So, in particular circumstances, an intermediary could be appointed for a suspect.[19]

---

15   *R v Isleworth Crown Court, ex p King* [2001] EWCA 22 (Admin).

16   *R v Silcock* [2007] EWCA Crim 2283.

17   Youth Justice and Criminal Evidence Act 1999, s.33A.

18   Section 33BA of the Act does allow for the court to appoint an intermediary for the accused, but this section is not yet in force.

19   *C v Sevenoaks Youth Court* [2009] EWHC 3088 (Admin).

Intermediary for suspect with low IQ finding questions difficult. When a man of low IQ was accused of rape, the Court of Appeal confirmed that the courts had an inherent power to allow the equivalent of an intermediary, to give assistance to the defendant to understand questions, to be a supporter and to be the equivalent of an interpreter.[20]

Intermediary for suspect with learning disabilities. At an appeal hearing, a man convicted of murdering a television presenter was assisted throughout the hearing by a clinical psychologist. Her role was to help him follow the progress of the case. He had learning disabilities. His intellectual functioning was in the borderline range and he suffered from epilepsy and had severe cognitive impairment.[21]

However, the courts have pointed out that it is a power, not a duty, and the fact that trial process would be improved by use of an intermediary does not necessarily mean that one must be appointed.[22]

PROSECUTION OF MENTALLY DISORDERED OFFENDERS

The Code for Crown Prosecutors states that a prosecution may be less likely if the defendant is elderly or is (or was at the time of the offence) suffering from significant mental or physical ill health, unless the offence is serious or there is a real possibility of repetition. A balance has to be struck between the desirability of diversion away from the criminal justice system and the need to safeguard the public.[23]

This balance will not necessarily result in diversion. For example, a woman with learning disabilities, who had subjected a vulnerable man to extensive abuse, was nevertheless sent to prison indefinitely, with a minimum term of five years. She was sentenced for assaults and sexual assaults. She had beaten and sexually humiliated him over a nine-month period. The man was forced to do household chores and punished if he did not do them properly. He was forced to engage in sex and was set on fire.[24]

In contrast, when a man with dementia murdered a fellow care home resident over an argument about a seat in the television room, it was judged not to be in the public interest to prosecute. He was instead sent to a secure mental health unit.[25]

FITNESS TO PLEAD AND SENTENCING

In the case of alleged perpetrators of a crime, a number of matters might have to be considered, including mental disorder or vulnerability at the time of interview. In summary:

---

20 *R v H* [2003] EWCA Crim 1208.

21 O'Neill, S. 'Gunshot particle that helped to convict Dando's murderer should be discounted.' *The Times*, 6 November 2007.

22 *R v Cox* [2012] EWCA Crim 549.

23 Crown Prosecution Service. *Code for Crown Prosecutors.* London: CPS, 2013, para 4.12.

24 'Amanda Ford, woman who violently abused, sexually humiliated vulnerable man, jailed indefinitely.' *Huffington Post*, 23 November 2012.

25 Bingham, J. 'Pensioner died after attack by convicted killer in care home, inquest hears.' *Daily Telegraph*, 24 March 2009.

- fitness to stand trial at the time of trial under the Criminal Procedure (Insanity) Act 1964

- the question of insanity at the time of the alleged offence on the basis of *M'Naghten's Case*[26]

- diminished responsibility at the time of the offence, s.2 of the Homicide Act 1957, or

- mental disorder at the time of conviction (and the making of a hospital order under the Mental Health Act 1983).

For example, sometimes people are remanded to hospital under s.35 or s.36 of the Mental Health Act 1983, for assessment or treatment, whilst awaiting trial.

Fitness to plead may sometimes be decided before trial or during the trial. If a judge decides during a trial that the person is unfit to plead, the jury still must decide whether the person committed the act or omission in issue. If so, the court must make a hospital order under s.37 of the Mental Health Act 1983 (with or without a restriction under s.41), a supervision order (involving a social worker or probation officer) or give an absolute discharge.[27]

DIMINISHED RESPONSIBILITY

The Homicide Act 1957, s.2, states that a person cannot be convicted of murder if the following applies, leading to a finding of diminished responsibility.

First, he or she had an abnormality of mind (whether arising from a condition of arrested or retarded development of mind or any inherent causes or induced by disease or injury).

Second, this substantially impaired his or her mental responsibility for his or her acts and omissions in doing or being a party to the killing. This rule was applied in the following case in which both victim and perpetrator were vulnerable adults.

Care home resident with mental disorder prosecuted for killing another resident. An 82-year-old woman had spent many years in secure hospitals and had also been convicted ten years earlier for assaulting an elderly woman with a chair. However, her medical records and criminal history had not been passed to the home. She now bludgeoned to death, with an ornamental iron, a fellow resident, aged 93. She was convicted of manslaughter (rather than murder) because of diminished responsibility.[28]

26   *M'Naghten's Case* [1843] 10 Cl and Fin 200.
27   Criminal Procedure (Insanity) Act 1964, ss.4, 4A, 5, 5A.
28   Norfolk, A. 'Care home killer, 82, was violent psychopath.' *The Times*, 10 June 2005.

Physical harm and abuse: criminal offences

Seniority of perpetrator

Informal nature of caring role

Prosecutions and convictions for wilful neglect and ill-treatment

Selection of cases brought under section 127 of the Mental Health Act 1983

Selection of cases brought under section 44 of the Mental Capacity Act 2005

Health and safety at work legislation

Health and Safety Executive and safeguarding adults

Reporting of Injuries, Diseases and Dangerous Occurrences
Regulations 1995

HSE and systemic lapses in health care

Offence of causing death of vulnerable adult

Offence: commission of the act or failure to protect the victim

Wide definition of member of the same household

Definition of vulnerable adult

Reason to suspect that victim is at risk required

Reasonable steps taken to protect the victim

Vulnerability of victim essential for prosecution and conviction

Domestic homicide reviews

Slavery and servitude: Coroners Act 2009

Travellers convicted under the Act for treatment of labourers

Endangering life by wilful negligence

KEY POINTS

Physical harm, by way of abuse or neglect, might constitute a criminal offence such as assault, battery, manslaughter or murder. A number of these offences are summarised below and illustrated with examples concerning vulnerable adults.

In addition is an offence of wilful neglect or ill-treatment which is contained in both the Mental Health Act 1983 and the Mental Capacity Act 2005. And, under the Domestic Violence, Crime and Victims Act 2004, there is an offence of causing the death of – or serious physical harm to – a vulnerable adult, either by causing this directly or failing to take reasonable steps to prevent it.

Health and safety at work legislation has, on occasion, been used to prosecute in the case of abuse, where management failings effectively allowed the abuse to go unchecked.

ASSAULT AND BATTERY

The word 'assault' is used commonly to refer to physical attacks.

However, technically, common assault occurs when a person intentionally or recklessly causes somebody else to apprehend or anticipate any immediate and unlawful violence or touching.[1]

Battery occurs when a person intentionally or recklessly applies unlawful force to somebody else – that is, intentional touching of another person without the

---

1   *R v Savage and Parmenter* [1991] AC 699 (House of Lords).

consent of that person and without lawful excuse. It need not necessarily be hostile, rude or aggressive.[2] So, if there has been a battery, the charge should be 'assault by beating'.[3]

These are (probably) still to be regarded as common law offences, although sentences are governed by s.39 of the Criminal Justice Act 1988, with a maximum six months' imprisonment. This should be contrasted, for example, with the maximum of five years' imprisonment for the offence of ill-treatment (of a mentally disordered or mentally incapacitated person: see below), which offence could comprise assault and battery.

Assault and battery might typically be charged for injuries such as grazes, scratches, abrasions, minor bruising, swellings, reddening of the skin, superficial cuts or a black eye.[4]

In the context of vulnerable adults, practices that may lead to prosecution and conviction for battery and assault include the following, ranging from shaving the word 'fool' into a person's hair to kicking a resident with dementia.

Daughter, a retired nurse, spitting at her mother. A former nurse was convicted of common assault on her 91-year-old mother after she was caught on a hidden camera, placed by her brother in their mother's kitchen. She ripped her mother's clothes and was spitting, screaming and elbowing. She was given a 12-month community sentence of 100 hours' unpaid work and ordered to attend five sessions on stress management. Her defence was that she had been ground down by stress and criticism, she was highly regarded in the community and the offence was out of character. A restraining order was imposed, prohibiting her visiting her mother without other family members present. The judge said: 'It is a very sad case and I think everybody can relate to it in some way.'[5]

Shaving the word 'fool' into the hair of a person with learning disabilities. A barber was convicted of assault on a person with learning disabilities after shaving the word 'fool' into the hair of a person with learning disabilities. Before staring work at the hair salon, he had been a support worker in a care home. He was sentenced to an 18-month community order and a three-month curfew. He had to pay £775 costs and £300 compensation to the victim.[6]

Bending thumbs back. When a care assistant bent back the thumbs of residents as part of the way she handled them, she was found guilty of six offences of assault.[7]

Stuffing deodorant into a person's mouth. A nurse at a care home was jailed for 15 months on various charges, including assault, for stuffing a deodorant can into the mouth of a 95-year-old man to stop him shouting.[8]

---

2   *Faulkner v Talbot* [1981] 3 All ER 468 (Court of Appeal).

3   *DPP v Little* [1992] 1 All ER 299.

4   Crown Prosecution Service. *Offences against the person, incorporating the charging standard: guidance*, undated. Accessed on 23 November 2012 at: www.cps.gov.uk/legal/p_to_r/public_order_offences.

5   Cooper, R. 'Son who feared his 91-year-old mother was being abused left shocked when hidden camera reveals his own SISTER spitting in her face.' *Daily Mail*, 6 July 2012.

6   'Barber who shaved word "fool" into hair of customer with learning difficulties is spared jail.' *Daily Mail*, 4 November 2011.

7   *Mwaura v Secretary of State for Health* [2006] 687 (PVA)/688 (PC) (Care Standards Tribunal hearing: conviction mentioned in report of hearing).

8   Davidson, C. 'Nurse jailed for abuse of care home patients.' *The Scotsman*, 18 May 2007.

Tirade of abuse and slapping. A nurse, acting as matron, screamed a tirade of abuse at a mental health patient in a nursing home before slapping her twice across the face. The assault was witnessed by an inspector from the local NHS primary care trust. The nurse was sent to prison for three months for common assault.[9]

Painful use of massage. The deputy manager of a care home was jailed for three months for assault because of the manual method of massage which she used to relieve constipation of a resident. She and other staff had all been on a training course which had taught that this method was 'outlawed'. The resident, with dementia, had struggled and was screaming in pain; when staff members had asked the deputy manager to call a doctor, she had refused, saying it would look bad for the home.[10]

Punching, slapping, mishandling residents. Two care workers were sentenced for assault on evidence that they had punched, slapped and mishandled residents, whom they had been described as treating like animals on a cattle farm. The home had previously been heavily criticised by the Commission for Social Care Inspection for employing staff who had not been properly checked.[11]

Throwing a cup of tea at a resident. A care worker at a care home in Portsmouth was sent to prison for assaulting residents. She had thrown a cup of tea at a woman in her eighties who wouldn't get up from her chair; she had claimed to be following the example of a more senior colleague who used casual violence to get the residents to comply with a strict routine.[12]

Penalty-kicking a resident with dementia. A psychiatric nurse was sentenced to four months in prison for kicking a 55-year-old woman with dementia. He kicked her as she lay on her back on the floor of her room in Grennell Lodge, Sutton, run by Care Unlimited. She developed a massive bruise, and the kick was described as having the force of a penalty kick. The nurse had worked at the care home for seven years, had an unblemished work record and had been in nursing for 40 years.[13]

There does, however, have to be evidence of intention or recklessness for the offence to be committed. Thus, when three carers were accused of assault by pouring talcum powder into the mouth of an 87-year-old care home resident, they were acquitted. Whilst the district judge noted that the care had been below standard, and two of the carers admitted using unnecessary force when washing and handling the woman, nonetheless he could not be sure beyond reasonable doubt of intention or recklessness.[14]

---

9   'Nurse who slapped patient is struck off.' *Bury Times*, 2 November 2006.

10   Gould, M. and Revill, J. 'Adult care ban on 700 staff.' *The Guardian*, 24 July 2005.

11   'Improved staff checks came too late to prevent abuse.' *Community Care*, 30 August 2007.

12   'Care homes.' *File on 4*, BBC Radio 4, 18 September 2007.

13   'Nurse jailed for assaulting patient at Sutton care home.' *Your Local Guardian*, 12 September 2011.

14   Dayani, A. 'Ban them for life.' *Birmingham Evening Mail*, 4 February 2004.

ASSAULT OCCASIONING BODILY HARM

Assault occasioning bodily harm, under s.47 of the Offences Against the Person Act 1861, carries a maximum of five years' imprisonment. This offence is distinguished from common assault by the degree of injury resulting.[15]

Common assault might typically concern grazes, scratches, abrasions, minor bruising, swellings, reddening of the skin, superficial cuts or a black eye, whereas actual bodily harm could include loss or breaking of a tooth or teeth, temporary loss of sensory functions including consciousness, extensive or multiple bruising, displaced or broken nose, minor fractures, minor but not superficial cuts, psychiatric injury beyond fear, distress or panic.

For example, a nurse was convicted of actual bodily harm when he stamped on the foot of a care home resident who suffered from dementia. The resident had knocked over some furniture.[16]

Equally, in the following case, the harm was psychological.

Bodily harm in form of psychiatric harm resulting from harassment. For some eight months, a man subjected a woman to silent phone calls, distributed offensive cards in the street, sent threatening notes, appeared at her place of work and her home, and took photographs of her and her family. Such psychiatric harm as she suffered (a severe depressive illness) was capable of being actual bodily harm under s.47 of the Act or grievous bodily harm under s.20.[17]

UNLAWFUL WOUNDING OR GRIEVOUS BODILY HARM

Unlawful wounding or infliction of grievous bodily harm comes under s.20 of the Offences Against the Person Act 1861, carrying a maximum of five years' imprisonment. Wounding would cover more serious cuts or lacerations.

Grievous bodily harm is serious bodily harm including, for example, injury resulting in permanent disability or permanent loss of sensory function, more than minor, permanent, visible disfigurement, broken bones, compound fractures, substantial loss of blood, injuries resulting in lengthy treatment or incapacity, psychiatric injury.

Section 18 of the Act contains a similar offence, but there must also be intent to cause wounding or grievous bodily harm.[18]

The severe injuries in the following case, involving vulnerable victims and serious violence, attracted a long prison sentence.

Targeting of elderly couple: grievous bodily harm. The offender had been smoking crack cocaine at a house near to where the victims, an elderly couple, lived. Later that night, he broke into their house to steal money. He attacked the man, hit him, jumped on him and

15   Crown Prosecution Service. *Offences against the person, incorporating the charging standard: guidance.* London: CPS, undated. Accessed on 23 November 2012 at: www.cps.gov.uk/legal/p_to_r/public_order_offences.

16   'Jailed nurse struck off after Stockton assault.' *Evening Gazette* (Middlesbrough), 18 January 2012.

17   *R v Ireland* [1998] AC 147.

18   Crown Prosecution Service. *Offences against the person, incorporating the charging standard.* London: CPS, undated. Accessed on 23 November 2012 at: www.cps.gov.uk/legal/p_to_r/public_order_offences.

used his keys as a knuckle duster. He pushed the husband down the stairs. He kicked and punched the wife. He stole £80. The victims were taken to hospital for multiple bruising and abrasions. The woman was placed in a care home where, several days later, she fell off a commode, hit her head and consequently died. The court wished to make clear that 'those who select elderly or otherwise vulnerable people as victims and then invade their homes in search of gain will receive very severe sentences indeed'. A sentence of 12 years was given.[19]

ADMINISTERING A POISON OR NOXIOUS THING

Under ss.23 and 24 of the Offences Against the Person Act 1861 it is an offence to administer unlawfully or maliciously any poison or other destructive or noxious thing. Either with the effect of endangering life or inflicting grievous bodily harm – or with the intention of injuring, aggrieving or annoying.

For example, a nursing home carer was convicted of administering a poison or noxious drug. She was sentenced to three years in prison. Over a six-month period, she had sedated six elderly care home residents suffering from dementia by means of a cocktail of drugs – anti-insomnia, anti-depressant and anti-psychotic pills. The patients would become drowsy, enabling her then to lie down and sleep whilst on duty. Other staff began to notice that these residents only become drowsy when she was on duty. The drugs, which had not been prescribed, were eventually detected in hair samples taken from the residents.[20]

FALSE IMPRISONMENT

False imprisonment is a common law offence involving the unlawful and intentional or reckless detention of a person.

False imprisonment and death in a shed of vulnerable adult at the hands of those who had befriended him. A vulnerable and epileptic man died after being kept in a shed for a period of four months by three people who had befriended him. He was found dead with extensive bruising and burn marks. The prosecution could not prove that death was not due to his epilepsy; the three defendants were jailed for some ten years each for assault, causing actual bodily harm and false imprisonment.[21] However, a subsequent coroner's hearing concluded that he had been unlawfully killed, almost certainly due to a loss of blood.[22]

The act of false imprisonment must be unlawful. So, for instance, when a man lacking capacity was taken to hospital in his best interests and kept there for care and treatment, the courts held that 'necessity' justified what would otherwise have been unlawful in terms of the civil tort of false imprisonment.[23] The European

19   *R v Marcus* [2003] EWCA Crim 2005.

20   Griffith J. 'Carer Mirela Aionoaei jailed for drugging dementia patients.' *Uxbridge Gazette*, 4 October 2012.

21   de Bruxelles, S. 'Three tortured shed captive until he died.' *The Times*, 10 July 2007.

22   'Shed captive was unlawfully killed.' *Metro Newspaper*, 28 February 2008.

23   *R v Bournewood Community and Mental Health NHS Trust, ex p L* [1998] 1 CCLR 390 (House of Lords).

Court of Human Rights subsequently held that this breached the man's human rights for want of safeguarding legal procedures.[24]

GROSS NEGLIGENCE MANSLAUGHTER

Manslaughter divides into involuntary and voluntary manslaughter. Both may arise in the context of vulnerable adults.

Involuntary manslaughter may be by unlawful act (see below) or through gross negligence or recklessness.

On the other hand, a charge of murder is reduced to voluntary manslaughter in three instances: diminished responsibility, provocation or acting in pursuance of a suicide pact.[25]

MANSLAUGHTER THROUGH GROSS NEGLIGENCE

Gross negligence resulting in a person's death constitutes the basis of a criminal charge of involuntary manslaughter.

For example, when two medical doctors failed to realise the gravity of a patient's condition (toxic shock syndrome), with the consequence that he failed to get the require treatment and died, they were convicted of manslaughter by reason of gross negligence.[26] Likewise, an anaesthetist was convicted in connection with the death of a patient.[27]

Gross negligence contrasts with ordinary negligence, which may precipitate a civil legal case but not a criminal one.

Death by drowning in a care home: no prosecution for manslaughter, ordinary negligence not enough. A man with profound mental and physical disabilities, who was resident in a local authority care home, died by drowning in five inches (12.7 cm) of water. The police and Health and Safety Executive both concluded that there was inadequate evidence to prosecute. The Director of Public Prosecutions (DPP) concluded the same.

In the case of one of the care staff, it never crossed her mind that the man might be unsafe in the bath during the four to five minutes that he was left alone, since he had always kept his head out of the water in the past.

From an organisational point of view, there was a care plan, but it did not deal with the matter of bathing. The DPP had concluded that a formal policy on leaving a severely disabled person was not required because it was common sense. Furthermore, some risks were managed, some training was provided and staff members were appropriately experienced. The DPP decided that it would be difficult to find a guilty 'directing mind' at organisational level and that there was an absence of conduct so 'bad' as to be described as gross negligence.

---

24   *HL v United Kingdom* [2004] 40 EHRR 761 (European Court of Human Rights).
25   Homicide Act 1957, ss.2–3.
26   *R v Misra* [2004] EWCA Crim 2375.
27   *R v Adomako* [1994] 3 All ER 79 (House of Lords).

The court held that even if there had been ordinary common law negligence, criminality or badness still had to be established for a manslaughter case. The presence or absence of subjective recklessness was a relevant issue and the DPP had applied the right legal test.[28]

However, though necessary for the criminal law, gross negligence is not a necessary ingredient to argue a human rights case under article 2 of the European Convention.

Suicide of mental health patient: gross negligence not required for human rights case. When a patient detained under the Mental Health Act committed suicide, it was argued that a failure to take reasonable steps to prevent the risk of suicide constituted a breach of article 2 of the European Convention (a civil, rather than a criminal, offence). The NHS trust argued that in order to contemplate a breach of article 2, gross negligence (which would be sufficient to sustain a manslaughter charge), rather than ordinary negligence (which underpins a civil case for damages), was required. The court held that it was not necessary to show gross negligence in order to argue a breach of article 2.[29]

In the following case, a care home nurse was convicted of manslaughter.

Death from compression of neck in a care home. An 86-year-old care home resident with Alzheimer's disease, weighing six stone (38 kg), died from having her neck compressed and two fractured vertebrae. She also had cuts and bruises on her face. A prosecution took place but in the end the nurse's plea of manslaughter was accepted, death occurring through grossly negligent 'manhandling', which she had tried to cover up. The nurse was 62 years old, a devout Christian and mother of five. She was sentenced to 12 months in prison, suspended, because of time already spent in custody and at a bail hostel.[30]

Of course, things may not be as they seem. A nursing home matron was accused of manslaughter of a resident by force-feeding him with rhubarb and custard so that he choked to death. She was also charged with assaulting other residents. She was acquitted of all charges; she had denied feeding the man on the day of death, and a pathologist said food could enter the airway after death. The jury was also told that staff had fabricated the allegations because the matron had strict standards.[31]

CORPORATE MANSLAUGHTER

In the case of gross negligence or recklessness in care (and other organisational) settings, there are two main possibilities. The first is for individual employees, frontline staff or managers to be prosecuted under the common law.

The second is for the organisation to be prosecuted under the Corporate Manslaughter and Corporate Homicide Act 2007.

In summary, the 2007 Act is as follows. An organisation commits the offence of corporate manslaughter where (a) it owes a duty of care, (b) it grossly breaches

28   *Rowley v Director of Public Prosecutions* [2003] EWHC 693 (Admin).
29   *Savage v South Essex Partnership NHS Foundation Trust* [2008] UKHL 74.
30   Stokes, P. 'Nurse admits manslaughter after Alzheimer's victim dies of broken neck.' *Daily Telegraph*, 26 February 2009.
31   'Matron not guilty of manslaughter.' *BBC News*, 9 March 2005. Accessed on 17 October 2008 at: http://news.bbc.co.uk/1/hi/wales/4333015.stm.

that duty because of how its activities are managed or organised, and (c) a person's death results.

The way an organisation's activities are managed or organised by its senior management must be a substantial element of the breach in the duty of care. Senior management means the people who play significant roles in (a) the making of decisions about how the whole or a substantial part of the organisation's activities are to be managed or organised, or (b) the actual managing or organising of the whole or a substantial part of those activities.

A breach of the duty of care is gross if it falls far below what can reasonably be expected of the organisation in the circumstances. However, the Act does not apply to a duty of care in relation to matters of public policy and, in particular, the allocation of public resources or the weighing of competing public interests. The Act also does not yet apply to patients detained under the Mental Health Act 1983.

If the alleged breach, leading to death, has followed from a failure to comply with health and safety at work legislation, the jury has to consider how serious that failure was and how much of a risk of death it posed. The jury may also (a) consider the extent to which, on the evidence, there were attitudes, policies, systems or accepted practices that were likely to have encouraged any such failure, and (b) have regard to any health and safety guidance that relates to the alleged breach.

Conviction can result in an unlimited fine being imposed on the organisation. The Act provides for remedial orders being made by the court, forcing the organisation to remedy the problems that led to the breach, and also for publicity orders forcing the organisation to publish details of the conviction. However, imprisonment is not an offence penalty; you can't send an organisation to prison.

CARE SETTINGS: PROSECUTION FOR MANSLAUGHTER IN CASES OF SYSTEMIC POOR CARE AND NEGLECT

It might be expected that when there has been individual professional neglect, frontline staff would be prosecuted individually under common law. But when systemic and blatant failings were to blame, then organisations would be prosecuted corporately.

This is not the case, however; by the middle of 2012, no corporate convictions under the Act have been recorded against health and social care providers.

In fact, at the time of writing, very few convictions under the Act have occurred at all, in any setting. And, even before the coming into force of the Act, no prosecutions under common law for corporate manslaughter took place in the field of health and social care. This is significant because there have been a number of cases reported of scores of avoidable deaths in hospitals, contributed to by reckless policies and systems of care.

There is another trend to note. Although there has been prosecution of individual clinicians working in hospitals, these have been few and unrelated to systemic problems and large-scale mortality. In fact, death from neglect in basic nursing care – for example, in relation to pressure sores – seems more likely to be prosecuted in the context of care homes than hospitals. For example:

Pressure sores and death, leading to conviction for manslaughter of a manager of a care home and her deputy. In July 1999, Mrs Marion Dennis died from grossly negligent care of her pressure sores in Ballastowell Gardens nursing home on the Isle of Man. The manager and deputy manager of the home were both convicted. Mrs Dennis's pressure sores were as large as fists and gave off an overpowering smell of rotting flesh. The two nurses blamed the system, a defence rejected by the jury.[32]

In another care home, two nurses were convicted of manslaughter for failing to give an epileptic resident her medication and then failing, during a period of two and a half hours, to call an ambulance during a fit.[33]

And perhaps more likely still in relation to informal carers (see below).

SYSTEMIC FAILINGS IN CARE: MANY DEATHS BUT NO PROSECUTION

In at least two particular cases in recent years involving systemic failings in NHS hospital care, consideration was given to prosecution: at Stoke Mandeville and then in Kent. In neither case did it take place.

The reasons given at the time for not taking forward a prosecution do not read convincingly.

MAIDSTONE AND TUNBRIDGE WELLS NHS TRUST: NO MANSLAUGHTER PROSECUTION

Consideration was reportedly given to prosecution at Maidstone and Tunbridge Wells NHS Trust, where up to 90 people died of *Clostridium difficile*, in association with shocking standards of care.[34]

The statement by Kent police did not refer – as might have been expected – to evidence being insufficient to prove that the poor standards of care were causative of any one individual patient death. (One reason why causation may represent a problem is that if there is a very ill patient, with other potential causes of death in waiting, it might be difficult to conclude whether the neglectful care killed them.)

But the police statement did not seek to shelter in this particular lee. Instead, it referred to the lack of any grossly negligent act: 'having reviewed the report and interviewed the author and the experts engaged by the Healthcare Commission, Kent Police has concluded that there is no information to indicate that any grossly negligent act has occurred.'[35]

This is more surprising. The care standards at Maidstone and Tunbridge Wells NHS Trust were reported by the Healthcare Commission as appalling. Those care

32   'Nurses guilty of death by neglect.' *BBC News*, 27 October 2003. Accessed on 19 January 2011 at: http://news. bbc.co.uk/1/hi/england/3218847.stm.
33   'Nurse guilty of gross negligence.' *BBC News*, 19 March 2008. Accessed on 5 August 2010 at: http://news.bbc. co.uk/1/hi/england/west_midlands/7305598.stm.
34   Rose, D. 'Hospital ordered to halt pay off to chief after superbug scandal.' *The Times*, 12 October 2007.
35   Hawkes, N. 'No-one to be prosecuted over 90 C-difficile deaths at Kent hospitals.' *The Times*, 30 July 2008.

standards were associated with infection, and the infection was associated with up to 90 deaths. The NHS Trust was putting targets and finance before patient safety. As a result, it had over-occupied hospitals and inadequate staffing. If the following, drawn from the Healthcare Commission's report, does not represent a grossly negligent system of care, it is hard to know what would.

Healthcare Commission report: suggestive of reckless or grossly negligent system of care. In response to the initial outbreak of infection, the local infection control team had wanted to isolate patients, but an isolation ward was not made available by the Trust for four months. During this time, patients were nursed on open wards, with the result that the infection spread. Part of the reason for this delay was the Trust's preoccupation with using beds and wards consistent with meeting government targets.

The outbreak and poor handling of the infection was associated with poor prescribing of antibiotics, inadequate monitoring of patients for *Clostridium difficile* and its associated complications (e.g. dehydration), shortage of nursing staff, extremely poor basic nursing care, serious failures in hygiene and cleaning practices, proximity of beds (some bed heads were no more than 12 inches [30 cm] apart) and over-occupancy of beds.

Failures in washing of hands, emptying of commodes, cleaning of beds, wearing of gloves. Nurses, other clinical staff, patients and families revealed that nurses were too rushed to wash their hands, to empty and clean commodes, to clean mattresses and equipment properly, and to wear aprons and gloves appropriately and consistently. The high bed occupancy meant that the bed changeover period – between occupation by one patient and occupation by another – was so short that thorough cleaning was compromised.

Lack of continuity of care. The pressure on beds meant also that ad hoc 'escalation' areas were opened up for patients with inadequate bathroom facilities, laundry and cleaning services. Furthermore, these areas tended to be staffed by agency workers, which adversely affected continuity of care. These factors increased the risk of transmission of infection.[36]

Broken, worn and condemned equipment. The hospital had a history of broken and worn equipment, furniture, fittings, dishwashers, showers, chair covers and curtains. The Commission found eight bedpan macerators to be dirty, rusty and leaking. Bedpan washers were not working, so bedpans that had been washed were still visibly contaminated with faeces. There were shortages of equipment such as commodes and of supplies including hand wipes, linen and bandages. Nearly half the Trust's commodes needed to be replaced; months later, the condemned commodes were still in use.

Inadequate cleaning arrangements. Cleaning arrangements were inadequate; at Maidstone Hospital, cleaning took place only between 7.30am and midday. Patients and relatives reported dirty floors, commodes and toilets, as well as buckets full of dirty water, blood stains on trolleys and the sides of beds, unemptied bins, and walking frames being shared between patients without being cleaned.

Ninety-eight per cent of commodes soiled. An audit of commodes found 98 per cent to be soiled; staff were using alcohol to clean them, even though alcohol is not effective against *Clostridium*. Utility and treatment rooms were being used to prepare hot drinks and food. Refrigerators for clinical items were used for food. Hygiene practices – such as handwashing – were not observed by staff and not enforced generally.[37]

---

36 Healthcare Commission. *Investigation into outbreaks of* Clostridium difficile *at Maidstone and Tunbridge Wells NHS Trust, October 2007.* London: HC, 2007, pp.4–6.

37 Healthcare Commission. *Investigation into outbreaks of* Clostridium difficile *at Maidstone and Tunbridge Wells NHS Trust, October 2007.* London: HC, 2007, pp.44–58.

STOKE MANDEVILLE HOSPITAL: NO MANSLAUGHTER PROSECUTION

Death from infection at Stoke Mandeville Hospital also gave rise to deliberation about manslaughter charges against the Trust Board. Amongst other things, the Trust had persistently ignored the advice of its own infection control team and refused to use side rooms to isolate infected patients. The reason for not doing so related to performance and financial targets, not clinical priorities and patient safety.

In this instance, the more obvious reason of causation was given as the reason not to prosecute because no link could be made between the actions of any individual and patient deaths.[38] This is more understandable, for the reasons already given. Even so, it begs questions.

Even before the Corporate Manslaughter and Corporate Homicide Act 2007, it was possible to contemplate prosecution of the organisation if a senior mind could be implicated in what had occurred. The crux of the Healthcare Commission's report into events at Stoke Mandeville is that it pointed to the Trust Board's deliberate disregarding of infection control (and associated basic care) in the pursuit of other, essentially political, priorities and targets. This decision, in turn, led to the continuation of a whole range of poor practices associated with between 30 and 40 deaths. This might, one would have thought, have gone some way to serving up more than one 'senior mind' on a plate, enabling the organisation to be prosecuted corporately.

Furthermore, the following factors, unearthed by the Healthcare Commission, would, on surely any reasonable view, have been grounds for attempting a prosecution.

Healthcare Commission findings: suggestive of reckless or grossly negligent system of care. The first outbreak of infection, between October 2003 and June 2004, was associated with 174 new cases of *Clostridium* and the death of 19 patients, 16 of whom had acquired the infection in hospital. The infection control team made various recommendations to control the outbreak, but senior management and the Trust Board disregarded the advice.

The second outbreak ran from October 2004 to June 2005. It was linked to 160 new cases and the deaths of a further 19 patients, 17 of whom had contracted the infection in hospital.

Refusal of Trust Board to isolate patients. Even after the second outbreak, senior managers and the Board still failed to follow the advice of the infection control team and isolate patients. It was only when matters were leaked to the Department of Health and to the national press that the Trust took the necessary containment measures.

Board too preoccupied with meeting government targets. The Commission concluded, overall, that the first outbreak followed from a poor environment for caring for patients, poor infection control, lack of isolation facilities and insufficient priority being given to the control of infection by senior managers. Some changes were made but none that risked compromising strategic objectives. When the second outbreak occurred, it was not controlled because the Trust was too focused on reconfiguration of services and meeting

---

38   Health and Safety Executive. *HSE investigation into outbreaks of* Clostridium difficile *at Stoke Mandeville Hospital, Buckinghamshire Hospitals NHS Trust.* London: HSE, 2006.

the government's targets. The system of clinical governance was dysfunctional, the Board was not put fully in the picture, and there were serious failings at the highest level. The Trust had taken the advice of neither its own infection control team nor the Health Protection Agency.[39]

Obsession with targets and concealing the outbreak of infection and death. Contributory factors included an obsession with targets, shortage of staff, rushed staff not following hygiene procedures, concealment of the outbreaks from the public and failure to listen to staff concerned about patient safety. In addition were a lack of handwashing facilities, antiquated bedpan washers and utility rooms (with washbasins) cluttered with uncollected linen and waste bags.[40]

Avoidable deaths. Professor Sir Ian Kennedy, then chair of the Healthcare Commission, averred, in the Foreword to the Commission's report, that the deaths were avoidable: 'patients died when their deaths could have been avoided'.[41]

Whether prosecution in these two cases did not take place for political or genuinely legal reasons, it suggests that hospitals are operating with virtual immunity from prosecution, no matter how many patients they mistreat and neglect. In fact, it seems that the more people suffer and die, the less likely is any action to be taken.

Even more astonishing in the above two instances – and Mid Staffordshire (see below) – is that the Health and Safety Executive (HSE) declined to take any action, either.

Inexplicable because, in order to prosecute under s.3 of the Health and Safety at Work Act 1974, the Executive does not need to show that harm or death has resulted. In other words, the legal causation issue falls away. All it needs to prove is that the hospital did not take all reasonably practicable efforts to ensure the health and safety of patients. (This is discussed later in this chapter.)

MID STAFFORDSHIRE NHS FOUNDATION TRUST: NO PROSECUTION TO DATE

Other possible manslaughter prosecutions in relation to the NHS continue to be reported but have so far not materialised. Inevitably, the events in Mid Staffordshire, revealed in March 2010 by the Healthcare Commission, brought calls for a manslaughter investigation in relation to the many hundreds of patients who died as a result of grossly negligent care.[42]

No manslaughter charges have been brought, nor has the Health and Safety Executive brought a major prosecution. It is impossible to understand why, and all those involved in safeguarding – health care staff, social workers, police, Crown Prosecution Service, Health and Safety Executive – should surely regard the lack of criminal sanctions as a serious failure, given the following.

39   Healthcare Commission. *Investigation into outbreaks of* Clostridium difficile *at Stoke Mandeville Hospital, Buckinghamshire Hospitals NHS Trust, July 2006.* London: HC, 2006, pp.4–5.

40   Healthcare Commission. *Investigation into outbreaks of* Clostridium difficile *at Stoke Mandeville Hospital, Buckinghamshire Hospitals NHS Trust, July 2006.* London: HC, 2006, pp.5–9.

41   Healthcare Commission. *Investigation into outbreaks of* Clostridium difficile *at Stoke Mandeville Hospital, Buckinghamshire Hospitals NHS Trust, July 2006.* London: HC, 2006, p.2.

42   Davani, A. 'Police asked to consider corporate manslaughter charges at Stafford Hospital.' *Birmingham Post,* 9 March 2010.

Mid Staffordshire NHS Foundation Trust: summary of various findings, suggestive of reckless or grossly negligent system of care. The high mortality rate at Stafford Hospital was associated with a range of deficiencies in care, not just a specific infection. Nonetheless, *Clostridium difficile* had surfaced there as well; it was judged by the independent inquiry to be a significant contributor to deaths at the hospital and to be associated with the appalling care provided.[43]

Filthy wards and equipment: excrement trodden into floor, left for days. The Healthcare Commission reported that one patient had a chair by her bedside for the five days of her stay; it was covered in dried blood that was not cleaned during the entire period. Excrement trodden into the floor would remain for several days. Curtains were hanging off their hooks; high surfaces, window bars and curtains were dusty. Floors were basically only wiped. Corners were missed.[44]

Filthy toilets, overflowing bins, incontinence pads could not be disposed of. Toilets were filthy and covered in blood and urine. Relatives would clean toilets before patients used them. Bins would be overflowing, so there was nowhere to put used incontinence pads. In the patient discharge unit, toilets and rooms were filthy. The accident and emergency (A&E) department had dried blood and rubbish on the floor. A ward had excrement splashed on the bedside, armchair and lockers; it was not cleaned up.[45]

Isolation unit precautions not followed. Doors to isolation units were commonly left open; medical and nursing staff might not wash their hands, use alcohol gel or wear gloves when handling patients. Dirty commodes and soiled bed sheets were reported.[46]

Cleaners using same cloth to wipe faeces off bed frame and then patient's table. Balls of dust occupied the corners of rooms, hallways and stairs. Blood was in the lifts and trails of it in the corridors. Rubbish would be stacked in the corridors, including both normal and surgical waste. A cleaner was observed with a pink cloth. She used it to wipe faeces off a bed frame. Using the same cloth, she then cleaned the table, the sink, the patient's drip stand and the cupboard next to the table. An audit of commodes found that 35 needed to be replaced and that up to 50 per cent, supposedly ready for use, were soiled with faeces.[47]

Meals served up with bowls of vomit and soiled pads. The independent inquiry, too, noted that the same cloth might be used to clean both toilets and surfaces on the ward, that hand gel containers were often empty and that rooms vacated by patients with *Clostridium difficile* were not cleaned before admission of the next patient. The evidence suggested that such failures were not isolated.[48] Bins of soiled pads would be left in patients' rooms, creating a terrible smell; bowls of vomit would be left on patients' tables, even during mealtimes. Relatives would take matters into their own hands to try to clean things up themselves.[49]

---

43   Francis, R. (Chair). *Independent inquiry into care provided by Mid Staffordshire NHS Foundation Trust January 2005–March 2009.* London: TSO, 2010, p.446.

44   Healthcare Commission. *Investigation into Mid Staffordshire NHS Foundation Trust, March 2009.* London: HC, 2009, p.36.

45   Healthcare Commission. *Investigation into Mid Staffordshire NHS Foundation Trust, March 2009.* London: HC, 2009, p.36.

46   Healthcare Commission. *Investigation into Mid Staffordshire NHS Foundation Trust, March 2009.* London: HC, 2009, p.56.

47   Healthcare Commission. *Investigation into Mid Staffordshire NHS Foundation Trust, March 2009.* London: HC, 2009, p.85.

48   Francis, R. (Chair). *Independent inquiry into care provided by Mid Staffordshire NHS Foundation Trust January 2005–March 2009.* London: TSO, 2010, p.13.

49   Francis, R. (Chair). *Independent inquiry into care provided by Mid Staffordshire NHS Foundation Trust January 2005–March 2009.* London: TSO, 2010, pp.104–105.

Specifically, when Mrs Gillian Astbury died in 2007 at Stafford Hospital after she had not been given her insulin, a police investigation was conducted into possible manslaughter charges against three nurses. In the event, in August 2010, the CPS decided there was insufficient evidence. Instead, two nurses were sacked and the third suspended.[50] A month after this decision, an inquest jury would find that Mrs Astbury's death was due to gross defects in care.[51]

CONSIDERATION OF MANSLAUGHTER CHARGES IN CASES OF INDIVIDUAL DEATH

Elsewhere, but in 2010 also, it was reported that consideration was being given to a corporate manslaughter charge in relation to a younger adult who had reportedly rung the police the day before because he could not get a drink in hospital, where he was being treated. The case had been referred to the police by Westminster Coroner's Court.[52] A coroner eventually returned a narrative verdict, stating that he had died of dehydration contributed to by neglect.[53] At the time of writing, no criminal prosecution is reported.

Corporate manslaughter charges were also contemplated in 2009 against the Sussex Partnership NHS Trust, following several suicides at a mental hospital, the Woodlands Unit in Hastings.[54]

DENIAL AND COVER-UP IN CASES OF SYSTEMIC NEGLECT AND MANY DEATHS?

Suspicion must linger that an unspoken and perverted public interest test is being applied.

Prosecution in the case of systemic neglect in the health service – resulting from lack of staff, lack of beds and obsession with priorities other than patient welfare, and all connected to government policy – would prise open a can of highly unwelcome political worms. It is arguable, in the author's view, that the distinct reluctance to pursue systemic problems and large numbers of deaths is part of an institutional denial and cover-up about the state of some of the care in our hospitals.

The apparent reluctance to try to prosecute corporately or otherwise in the context of the health service, even in the case of shocking standards of care and many deaths, does seem to contrast starkly with manslaughter prosecutions in other contexts.

For instance, in the following case, a shortcut was taken in relation to the maintenance of an air-conditioning system. This resulted in an outbreak of

---

50 Corser, J. 'Two Stafford Hospital nurses sacked over patient death.' *Express and Star*, 30 August 2010.

51 Grainger, L. '"Appalling" standards in care led to the death of Hednesford grandmother.' *Cannock Chase Post*, 16 September 2010.

52 Moore-Bridger, B. 'Hospital manslaughter inquiry after patient dies begging for water.' *Daily Mail*, 8 March 2010.

53 Davies, C. 'London hospital blamed for man's dehydration death.' *The Guardian*, 12 July 2012.

54 Walker, E. 'Hastings hospital at centre of police inquiry will reopen.' *The Argus*, 10 April 2010.

Legionnaire's disease which resulted in a number of deaths. Both the council and the individual architect involved were prosecuted for manslaughter.

Shortcuts on maintenance and inspection contract for air-conditioning system: prosecution. A council architect and Barrow Council were both prosecuted for manslaughter after a number of people died of Legionnaire's disease at a council arts centre. The architect had cancelled a maintenance and inspection contract for the air-conditioning system. Five people died and another 172 were infected. The manslaughter case failed; both the architect and the Council were subsequently convicted of health and safety at work offences and fined.[55]

In terms of shortcuts being taken with people's lives, those at Stoke and Mandeville and in Kent dwarf those taken in Barrow, yet prosecution was taken in the latter but not the former cases.

An even greater contrast is afforded by the apparent eagerness of the criminal justice system to prosecute a particular type of domestic manslaughter case, involving vulnerable or inadequate perpetrators, whilst it leaves well alone far more culpable individuals and organisations who play with patients' lives recklessly and disingenuously in our hospitals. A few examples of these domestic manslaughter cases are given immediately below.

GROSS NEGLIGENCE MANSLAUGHTER BY VULNERABLE OR INADEQUATE PERPETRATORS

The question of manslaughter prosecutions, from gross negligence or recklessness, arises in relation not just to service providers but to family members or friends. In some cases, the perpetrators are arguably vulnerable themselves.

The following case involved the lack of care provided for a person by a close relative, which resulted in the person's death in the relative's home – death from toxaemia, spreading because of infected pressure sores, immobilisation and lack of food.

Informal carers guilty of manslaughter through gross negligence: vulnerable adults both victim and perpetrators. A partially deaf and almost blind man of low intelligence lived with a woman described as his mistress and as ineffectual and inadequate, together with the man's mentally impaired son. The man's sister came to live in the house as a lodger, in one room without ventilation, toilet or washing facilities save for a polythene bucket.

Brother and partner do nothing for his helplessly infirm sister in upstairs room. The sister was morbidly anxious not to put on weight, denied herself proper meals and spent days at a time in the room. After three years, she had become helplessly infirm. The mistress, who took the sister food, tried to wash the sister with the help of a neighbour, who advised her to contact social services. Also, the licensee of a pub frequented by the mistress and the man advised her to get a doctor. The sister refused to give the name of her doctor whom the man and mistress had attempted to locate. The man tried, unsuccessfully, to get his own doctor to attend. Neither the man nor the mistress made any further efforts

---

55   Hogg, D. 'Architect fined over deadly outbreak of disease.' *Yorkshire Post*, 1 August 2006.

to obtain professional assistance, not even mentioning anything to the social worker who visited the son.

Sister died of toxaemia from infected pressure sores. Three weeks after the attempt to wash the sister, she died of toxaemia, spreading because of infected pressure sores, immobilisation and lack of food. Had she received medical attention during those three weeks, she would probably have survived.

Reckless disregard by brother and his partner. The Court of Appeal upheld the conviction (although reduced the sentence) and described gross negligence in the following way:

> The duty which a defendant has undertaken is a duty of caring for the health and welfare of the infirm person. What the prosecution have to prove is a breach of that duty in such circumstances that the jury feel convinced that the defendant's conduct can properly be described as reckless, that is to say a reckless disregard of danger to the health and welfare of the infirm person. Mere inadvertence is not enough. The defendant must be proved to have been indifferent to an obvious risk of injury to health, or actually to have foreseen the risk but to have determined nevertheless to run it.[56]

In the following case, a man had been convicted of the manslaughter of his mother. A further legal case followed as to whether – as a matter of public policy – he should be deprived of what he inherited from her, as a result of his wrongdoing. The court felt not, given his inadequacy to meet the challenges presented by his mother's condition, an inability to recognise that inadequacy and a hesitancy in turning to outside help.

Son convicted of manslaughter of his mother. A woman was described as stubborn, domineering, hugely independent – and as one who shunned any type of 'officialdom', including doctors and home helps. Her son, in his fifties, lived with her. He had limited education, had never had a girlfriend and had worked as a labourer from the age of 15. He rarely went out except to visit his father's grave; his only friend was his aunt. In January 2004, he called an ambulance. His mother was found suffering from severe pressure sores all over her body, with one sore penetrating to her sacrum, large enough to take two fists. She was suffering from breast cancer; her wounds were consistent with lying in urine and faeces for a period of time.

A few months earlier, she had suffered a fall. She had refused to go to hospital or have a doctor visit her. At her request, her son provided her with hot drinks, hot meals and whisky. By November, he was cleaning her pressure sores with antiseptic wipes and dressing them; he did not call the doctor. By December, his mother said it was too much for her to roll over, so he stopped attending to the wound in her back. When asked why he had acted as he did, he said he didn't really know. He accepted he should have called for help. He was prosecuted for manslaughter, pleaded guilty and was sentenced to four years in prison.[57]

In the following case, a man pleaded guilty to the manslaughter of his wife, by gross negligence, but the sentence was reduced to reflect a number of mitigating factors.

---

56   *R v Stone* [1977] 64 Cr App R 186.
57   *Land v Land* [2006] EWHC 2997 (Chancery).

Neglect of husband for nearly three weeks in not calling for ambulance. The appellant was convicted of manslaughter of his wife by gross negligence. He was the sole carer of his wife. She had lost a leg and had osteoporosis, which caused brittle bones liable to fracture. In March, she fell, suffering a number of broken bones. The husband did not call an ambulance for nearly three weeks. The wife then died in hospital a few weeks later from pneumonia. The husband was convicted and sentenced to four years in prison. He appealed.

The sentence was reduced to 30 months. His wife had not wanted to go to hospital. She could have called for assistance herself. Although the neglect lasted nearly three weeks, she did not die during that time; her death was not wholly through the husband's lack of care and gross neglect.[58]

Convictions and sentences continue in such cases. In the following case, the sentence of two years and eight months' imprisonment was upheld on appeal, against a brother who had stood back and let his sister die.

Sister, in care of brother, found dying in profound squalor. The appellant was the brother and carer of his 58-year-old sister who shared a house with him and who was the deceased in this case. She suffered from a mild learning disability and a low IQ. She was diabetic, grossly obese and suffered from panic attacks relating to travel, agoraphobia and inability to care for herself. She also suffered from hypertension and poor vision.

On the afternoon of 9 February 2010, the appellant called the emergency services. When they arrived at the house at about 4.45pm, they found the sister lying on the floor in an upstairs bedroom in a state of profound squalor. The appellant told the paramedics that she had been lying there for about two and a half weeks following a fall. During that period, the temperatures had been very cold and the house had limited heating facilities. There was no central heating and no water supply, and although there were two electrical heaters, only one was working and that was downstairs. The bedroom was cold and she was scantily clad in a nightgown, on wooden floorboards, covered in excrement and urine. She was barely conscious. Her toes and feet were gangrenous and there were pressure sores down her left side. On arrival at hospital, her core temperature was 27°C, which was ten degrees below normal. She suffered a number of cardiac arrests in hospital but died in the early hours of the following day, primarily from hypothermia.

The brother could have called for help but had not done so:

> The appellant was the only person who could have alerted the authorities to her condition and he had been grossly negligent in failing to provide for her basic needs of care, warmth and clothing and to summon assistance when her condition deteriorated. As the judge was to remark in his sentencing remarks, the appellant must have entered her room every day because he had provided food to her, but the only other care he had given her, until calling for the emergency services when it was too late, was to reposition her television set.

The sentence, while upheld, would have been longer but for the fact that the brother had grown up in a grossly abnormal family and simply didn't appreciate the abnormal living conditions in the house. This had impaired his ability to respond to his sister's needs.[59]

---

58   *R v Hood* [2003] EWCA Crim 2772.
59   *R v Barrass* [2011] EWCA Crim 2629.

In contrast, the next case was about whether a man's partner (a nurse) was potentially guilty of manslaughter for failing to call for medical attention for the man who had a gangrenous foot and was adamant in not wanting medical help. The coroner thought not and the court agreed.

Not calling for a doctor to help man with a gangrenous foot at home: no duty on his partner (a nurse) to call for help. A man died of gangrene resulting from diabetic neuropathy after an injury to his foot. The question was whether the coroner should have returned a finding of unlawful killing, on the basis of gross negligence manslaughter, instead of the 'narrative verdict' that he had in fact returned.

The man had very particular beliefs, which included the idea that physical ailments were symptomatic of emotional turmoil. As a result, he was opposed to traditional medical remedies. His GP had previously explained the dangers that could arise from broken skin and as a result of his diabetes. He became personally close to a registered nurse, who looked up to him as a spiritual teacher. He injured his foot when he stepped on an electric plug. The condition of the foot slowly deteriorated. As it got worse, he insisted that a doctor not be called; accordingly, the nurse did not call for one.

The coroner decided that, given the man's total opposition to medical help and his knowledge of the risks he was running, there was not a duty on the nurse, breach of which was gross and which in turn could be characterised as manslaughter.

One last question arose. Before he lapsed into unconsciousness for the last two hours of his life, he had not instructed the nurse not to call a doctor. So she was no longer bound by what he said when conscious. The coroner decided that, in any event, even if she had acted, it would have made no significant difference to his dying. The court therefore upheld the coroner's decision.[60]

MANSLAUGHTER BY UNLAWFUL ACT

Involuntary manslaughter by an unlawful act is a different type of manslaughter to manslaughter by gross negligence or recklessness.

The former must be an act, as opposed to an omission, which a reasonable person would realise would subject the victim to some risk of physical harm, albeit not serious harm, whether or not the perpetrator realised this.[61]

Physical abuse of man with learning disabilities by teenagers before death in river. A man with learning disabilities was subjected to a campaign of physical abuse in his home by a group of teenagers. Having previously shaved clumps of hair from his head, daubed make-up on his face, urinated in his drinks, smoked cannabis in his flat, scrawled graffiti on his walls and poured bleach on him, they then beat him and threw him into the River Mersey where he died. They were jailed for life for manslaughter. He had learning disabilities, was a heavy drinker and had the capacity to make his own decisions, but his vulnerability meant that he 'couldn't say no to the people who came to his door'.[62]

---

60 *R(Jenkins) v HM Coroner for Portsmouth and South East Hampshire* [2009] EWHC 3229 (Admin).

61 Crown Prosecution Service. *Homicide: murder, guidance.* London: CPS, undated.

62 Carter, H. 'He couldn't say "no".' *The Guardian (Society)*, 15 August 2007.

With the bullying or harassment of vulnerable adults in mind, the following conviction is notable because the actual act causing death was committed by the victim herself, but the perpetrators of the bullying were still convicted.

Bullying leading to manslaughter conviction. A 19-year-old woman and 15-year-old girl were found guilty of manslaughter, committed two years earlier, of a 19-year-old woman who had thrown herself out of a window. This had followed a number of incidents of escalating violence leading up to the day of the woman's death. On that day, the campaign of bullying had included punching, kicking, violent hair pulling, derogatory name calling, grabbing and ripping clothing. The woman had then thrown herself out of a window to escape threats, verbal abuse and physical assault.[63] One of the perpetrators was given a hospital order under ss.37 and 41 of the Mental Health Act 1983. The other was sentenced to eight years in prison.[64]

VOLUNTARY MANSLAUGHTER THROUGH DIMINISHED RESPONSIBILITY

The charge of murder may, in some circumstances, be reduced to voluntary manslaughter because of diminished responsibility. This is where the person was suffering from such abnormality of mind – whether arising from a condition of arrested or retarded development of mind or any inherent causes or induced by disease or injury – so as substantially to have impaired his or her mental responsibility for his or her acts or omissions in doing or being a party to the killing.[65]

One such case involved a 72-year-old man who started a relationship with a woman on a low-security, mixed-sex mental health ward in a care home. He had a history of assaults on women. He stabbed the woman to death after he had failed to receive a three-weekly injection of antipsychotic drugs. He was jailed for life.[66]

It was similarly manslaughter through diminished responsibility when an 82-year-old care home resident bludgeoned a fellow resident to death with an iron.

Care home killing: diminished responsibility through undetected psychopathic illness. An 82-year-old woman, charged with murder, was convicted of manslaughter on grounds of diminished responsibility. Using an ornamental iron, she had bludgeoned to death a 93-year-old fellow resident in a care home in Newcastle-upon-Tyne. She told police she had not hit the woman enough. She suffered from a psychopathic illness, having previously spent 14 years in secure hospitals and been convicted ten years earlier of grievous bodily harm for attacking a 72-year-old woman with a chair. Her medical records and criminal history had not been passed on to the care home.[67]

A very different type of case, though resulting in a similar verdict, also reached the courts, involving family carers who had reached breaking point through stress.

---

63   Siddique, H. 'Teenage bullies guilty of killing vicar's daughter who jumped from window.' *The Guardian*, 18 November 2009.

64   Siddique, H. 'Girl, 15, sentenced to eight years over bullying death of Rosimeiri Boxall.' *The Guardian*, 15 December 2009.

65   Homicide Act 1957, s.2.

66   Brody, S. 'Council seeks stronger safeguards after killing at Surrey home.' *Community Care*, 12–18 January 2006.

67   Norfolk, A. 'Care home killer, 82, was violent psychopath.' *The Times*, 10 June 2005.

They then killed in desperation and with diminished responsibility – as in the following case of a mother of a 36-year-old man with Down's syndrome.

Mother killing disabled son, unbearable pressure, diminished responsibility, role of social services. A mother killed her 36-year-old son who had Down's syndrome. She gave him 14 sleeping pills and suffocated him with a plastic bag. She then swallowed some pills herself and attempted to kill herself with a kitchen knife.

The judge acknowledged the exceptional nature of the case and the unbearable pressure she had been under for more than 30 years. She had pleaded for help from the local authority (social services) and from her GP. Her eldest son gave evidence that her devotion to her disabled son had been saintly. Her son had flourished in early life before developing autism in his twenties and harming himself; he blinded himself in one eye. He had been enrolled in a day centre but was excluded for disruptive behaviour. He did better when he was assisted by a social integration team, but this was disbanded for lack of funds.

Most recently, social services had not provided a care manager, although it acknowledged the urgency of her situation. Social services stated that it had offered services, but the mother had refused them. She was convicted of manslaughter on the grounds of diminished responsibility and given a suspended two-year prison term.[68]

Questions about social services involvement also arose in a case where a mother was convicted of manslaughter by reason of diminished responsibility after drugging and suffocating her two adult sons, both of whom had cerebral palsy. She was suffering from depression, as well as a degenerative neurological condition. The judge criticised social services and called on them to conduct an inquiry.[69]

The following case had each of these elements: an arguably vulnerable perpetrator, a vulnerable victim and no outside help, all leading to abnormal stress.

Brutal killing of woman with dementia by 'inadequate' man in situation of abnormal stress. A 20-year-old man pleaded guilty to manslaughter through diminished responsibility. He had killed a 91-year-old woman. She had been living at home with the man and his wife. This had been arranged by the woman's nephew. The wife was the niece of this nephew. The nephew basically said they could live there if they looked after his aunt. The woman had dementia. She needed assistance 24 hours a day. The couple expected they would have help, either arranged by the nephew or through the local authority. This didn't happen. One evening, after drinking eight bottles of beer, the man snapped. He went up to the woman's room and launched a sustained attack, leaving her with such severe injuries that she died a few days later in hospital.

The man had had a troubled upbringing involving beatings and emotional and sexual abuse. He suffered from long-standing emotional instability and, at the time of the offence, from severe clinical depression. The offence was out of character; there was no continuing risk to anybody else.

The sentencing had to weigh up a brutal killing against the man's youth, inadequacy mental impairment (mild) and the fact that the nephew had abdicated his responsibility,

---

68   Laville, S. 'Mother who killed son with Down's syndrome gets suspended sentence.' *The Guardian*, 3 November 2005.
69   Kelso, P. 'Woman who killed disabled sons is freed.' *The Guardian*, 24 June 2000.

leaving the couple to cope with a very sick and demanding woman, which led to abnormal stress. On appeal, the sentence was reduced from six to four and a half years.[70]

When a father suffocated his mentally ill daughter, he was convicted of manslaughter due to diminished responsibility and given a two-year suspended jail sentence. She had repeatedly tried to kill herself, suffered from severe personality disorder and deep depression, and was an alcoholic. She had been asked to leave a specialist NHS unit the day before. The daughter had leaned towards her father for him to cover her head with a plastic bag; when that failed, he suffocated her with a pillow.[71]

A similar verdict was reached in the case of a man who helped his wife kill herself; she was suffering from the degenerative effects of multiple sclerosis. She had previously attempted to kill herself on a number of occasions. He suffocated her after she had taken an overdose of pills.[72]

Further along the spectrum, such killings may amount to murder, rather than manslaughter through diminished responsibility. When a man killed his wife of 33 years (who suffered from an irritable bowel condition), after she had persuaded him to help her die, he was convicted of murder. He had bought her nearly 100 paracetamol tablets, roses and two farewell cards. He placed a plastic bag over her head and smothered her with a pillow.[73] Likewise:

Mother convicted of murder of her own son. A woman killed her son with an injection of heroin at the nursing home where he was resident. This was following a catastrophic accident when he fell out of an ambulance, could not move, could communicate only by squeezing his hands and had to be tube-fed. She claimed she did it out of love; she was sentenced to life imprisonment with a minimum period of nine years.[74]

MURDER

Murder consists of a person of sound mind unlawfully killing a human being with intent to kill or cause grievous bodily harm.[75]

The following examples make clear the relevance to vulnerable adults. For instance, in the following case, a vulnerable adult was murdered, despite a measure of social services involvement.

Man with learning disabilities befriended by gang and then murdered. A man with severe learning disabilities was befriended by a 'gang'. He thought they were his best friends. For a year, they exploited and cheated him, taking control of his money, his flat and his life, dragging him around his bedsit on a dog's lead. They then tortured him into confessing falsely that he was a paedophile, sentenced him to death, forced him to swallow 70 painkilling tablets, marched him to the top of a viaduct, forced him over and stamped on his hands as he hung on. He fell 30 metres and died. Three of the gang were convicted of

70   *R v Slater* [2005] EWCA Crim 898.
71   Smith, L. 'Father who suffocated sick daughter is freed.' *The Times*, 9 June 2001.
72   Fletcher, H. 'Husband is spared jail for suffocating sick wife who wanted to die.' *The Times*, 2 February 2008.
73   Batchelor, W. 'Man guilty of murdering wife in assisted euthanasia.' *The Independent*, 10 May 2007.
74   Bannerman, L. 'Jury heckled over murder verdict for mother who "acted out of love".' *The Times*, 21 January 2010.
75   Crown Prosecution Service. *Homicide, murder and manslaughter: guidance.* London: CPS, undated.

murder, another of manslaughter. During the period in question, social services had been visiting him but stopped before his death, apparently in response to his wishes.[76]

Two teenagers, both trained boxers, and an older man were involved in a bet made at a bus stop about whether they could knock out a man with learning disabilities. They repeatedly hit him and then chased him across two housing estates, continuing to attack him by punching, stamping, kicking and headbutting. After the murder, they posed for pictures. All three were convicted of murder.[77]

A vulnerable, timid adult was taken to a remote hillside where he was strangled, hit with a brick, kicked and stamped on, before being set on fire, by two cousins who wrongly believed he was a paedophile. They were given life sentences; the planning, mental and physical suffering of a vulnerable man and the attempt to conceal the body were aggravating features.[78]

A man with learning disabilities was humiliated, tortured and then thrown into a river to drown by four of his neighbours who suspected he was a paedophile.[79] Another man with learning disabilities, also wrongly believed by his killers to be a paedophile, was gagged, bound, tortured, stabbed and disembowelled. His two killers were, on appeal, sentenced to 28 years and 22 years in prison.[80]

In contrast, the murder charge may relate to a senior health care professional, such as a hospital matron, described as eccentric, bossy, popular and well respected. Charged with poisoning three patients, although suspected of having murdered many more, she committed suicide before trial.[81]

Another nurse drugged an 84-year-old care home resident, who suffered from senile dementia, by giving her an overdose of a sedative (heminevrin). The judge stated that she had committed murder largely because she didn't want the trouble of caring for the woman, who needed up to half an hour's care and attention from staff every two hours.[82]

In March 2008, a staff nurse was convicted of murdering four elderly patients and attempting to murder a fifth by means of administering insulin to induce hypoglycaemic coma and death. The judge stated that he was an essentially lazy man who believed that the elderly required too much care. All the victims were frail elderly women admitted to the orthopaedic ward following hip fractures.[83]

76   Morris, S. 'Tortured, drugged and killed a month after the care visits were stopped.' *The Guardian*, 4 August 2007.

77   'Boy convicted of "£5 bet" murder.' *BBC News*, 22 January 2008. Accessed on 17 October 2008 at: http://news. bbc.co.uk/1/hi/england/wear/7202351.stm.

78   'Hillside murderers get life terms.' *BBC News*, 4 May 2007. Accessed on 17 October 2008 at: http://news.bbc. co.uk/1/hi/wales/south_east/6624515.stm.

79   Payne, S. 'Four "drowned man they thought was pederast".' *Daily Telegraph*, 22 March 2007.

80   'Murder terms increased by judges.' *BBC News*, 16 February 2006. Accessed on 17 October 2008 at: http://news. bbc.co.uk/1/hi/england/tees/4720642.stm. Also: Vinter, P. 'Killer preyed on "kind Sean".' *Oxford Mail*, 20 April 2007.

81   Jenkins, R. 'Nurse found dead may have killed 23 patients.' *The Times*, 31 August 2005.

82   'Nurse convicted of murder.' *BBC News*, 19 June 2001. Accessed on 17 October 2008 at: http://news.bbc. co.uk/1/hi/health/1396950.stm.

83   Jenkins, R. 'Killer nurse must serve at least 30 years.' *The Times*, 5 March 2008.

VOLUNTARY EUTHANASIA

Currently, a person, medical doctor or otherwise, who actively brought about a person's death would be open to the charge of murder.

This situation was challenged in 2012 by a man who had survived a stroke and led what he considered to be a miserable existence. He could communicate via his eyes only. He wanted, at a time of his choosing, for a doctor to end his life without facing prosecution for murder. His legal challenge gave rise to the following key questions about murder. Was voluntary euthanasia a possible defence to murder? And was the mandatory life sentence for murder incompatible with the European Convention on Human Rights in a case of genuine voluntary euthanasia? The answer to all three questions was in the negative.[84]

ATTEMPTED MURDER

Under s.1 of the Criminal Attempts Act 1981, attempted murder is when a person does an act that is more than merely preparatory to murder, with an intention to kill.

For instance, a few days after her father had been diagnosed with inoperable stomach cancer, a woman simply decided, unbidden, to kill him by trying to smother him with a pillow. He tried to push her away and called for help, and her daughter rushed into the room and managed to pull her mother away. She was charged with attempted murder, given a suspended prison sentence and sentenced to 150 hours' community work.[85]

In a very different type of case, an 84-year-old man was convicted of attempted murder of his wife following threatened withdrawal of care by social services.

Manual handling dispute about care of woman with Alzheimer's disease leads to attempted murder by husband. An elderly couple were due to celebrate their diamond wedding anniversary in two weeks' time. The wife had Alzheimer's disease; she was doubly incontinent and immobile, receiving visits from two carers three times a day, seven days a week. The council then allegedly told the husband that unless they accepted a hoist, the carers would be withdrawn. On one particular day, the carers refused to lift the wife manually, leaving him unable to feed or clean her. The husband became distraught and anxious and tried to kill both himself and his wife by attaching a hose to the exhaust of his car and leading it into the couple's bedroom. A neighbour saved them. He had left a typed note, referring to the social worker and owner of the private care company as two of the most 'evil people' he had encountered in recent years. His wife was placed in a care home where she died a month later from an unrelated infection.

The husband confessed to attempted murder and was put on a year's probation by the judge. The latter condemned the decision of the Crown Prosecution Service to bring the case at all.[86]

---

84   R(Nicklinson) and R(AM) v Director of Public Prosecutions and Ministry of Justice [2012] EWHC 2381 (Admin).

85   Wood, A. 'Daughter spared jail over attempted "mercy killing".' Yorkshire Post, 21 December 2008.

86   R v Bouldstridge [2000] unreported (but see: Kelso, P. 'He only wanted to end his wife's pain. He ended up in court, at 84.' The Guardian, 7 June 2000, p.1).

ASSISTED SUICIDE

Under the Suicide Act 1961, it is an offence to do something that is capable of encouraging or assisting the suicide or attempted suicide of another person or was intended to encourage or assist suicide or an attempt at suicide. The offence can be committed even if the act does not result in suicide or attempted suicide.

In addition, if a person arranges for a second person to commit such an act, then the first person as well as the second will be liable.

Legally, there is encouragement or assistance even when the act could in reality never have constituted *effective* encouragement or assistance. An illustration would be giving a person a supposedly lethal drug that was in fact a vitamin pill.

The offence itself was initially considered to be consistent with human rights. This was established in a case involving a woman with motor neurone disease who wanted an assurance that her husband would not be prosecuted if he assisted her to commit suicide. It was held that the offence did not contravene article 2 (right to life), article 3 (inhuman or degrading treatment) or article 8 (right to respect for private life).[87]

In 2009, however, a further case was brought, which established that, under human rights law, a reasonable amount of guidance was required to make clear when it was likely that a prosecution would take place.

Question of prosecution for assisting a person to travel to a clinic abroad for assisted suicide. The question was whether a woman's husband would be prosecuted for helping his wife (who had multiple sclerosis) travel to a country (Switzerland) where assisted suicide was legal. The destination would be a clinic that assists people to commit suicide. It was argued that the *Code for Crown Prosecutors* used by the Crown Prosecution Service was inadequate to deal with such cases and that article 8 of the European Convention demanded accessibility and foreseeability in relation to how decisions to prosecute would be taken.

The House of Lords agreed with this argument and found a breach of article 8 of the Convention.[88]

Following this case and a great deal of publicity, the Director of Public Prosecutions produced guidelines, in order to make clearer the effect of the law. These guidelines set out two lists of factors, one which would tend to result in prosecution and the other which would tend not to. Factors that would make prosecution more likely are as follows, in summary:

(a) **Age:** The victim was under 18 years of age.

(b) **Mental capacity:** The victim lacked mental capacity.

(c) **No clear decision:** The victim had not reached a voluntary, clear, settled and informed decision to commit suicide.

---

87   *Pretty v United Kingdom* [2002] 2 FCR 97 (European Court of Human Rights).

88   *R(Purdy) v Director of Public Prosecutions* [2009] UKHL 45.

(d) **No clear communication:** The victim had not clearly communicated the decision to commit suicide.

(e) **Victim did not ask for help:** The victim did not seek the encouragement or assistance of the suspect personally or on his or her own initiative.

(f) **Motives other than compassion:** The suspect was not wholly motivated by compassion – for example, he or she was motivated by the prospect of gain from the persons' death.

(g) **Pressure:** The suspect pressured the victim to commit suicide.

(h) **No reasonable steps by suspect:** The suspect did not take reasonable steps to ensure that any other person had not pressured the victim to commit suicide.

(i) **Suspect's history:** The suspect had a history of violence or abuse against the victim.

(j) **Victim's capability:** the victim was physically able to undertake the act that constituted the assistance him- or herself.

(k) **Suspect unknown to victim:** The suspect was unknown to the victim and encouraged or assisted the victim to commit or attempt to commit suicide by providing specific information via, for example, a website or publication.

(l) **Activities of suspect:** The suspect gave encouragement or assistance to more than one victim who were not known to each other.

(m) **Payment:** The suspect was paid by the victim or those close to the victim for his or her encouragement or assistance.

(n) **Professional involvement:** The suspect was acting in his or her capacity as a medical doctor, nurse, other health care professional, a professional carer (whether for payment or not) or as a person in authority, such as a prison officer, and the victim was in his or her care.

(o) **Public place:** The suspect was aware that the victim intended to commit suicide in a public place where it was reasonable to think that members of the public may be present.

(p) **Organisation or group involvement:** The suspect was involved in an organisation or group, a purpose of which is to provide a physical environment (whether for payment or not) in which to allow another to commit suicide.[89]

Conversely, a prosecution would be less likely in the following circumstances, in summary:

---

89   Director of Public Prosecutions. *Policy for prosecutors in respect of cases of encouraging or assisting suicide.* London: DPP, 2010. Accessed on 23 November 2012 at: www.cps.gov.uk/publications/prosecution/assisted_suicide_policy. html.

(a) **Clear decision:** The victim had reached a voluntary, clear, settled and informed decision to commit suicide.

(b) **Compassion:** The suspect was wholly motivated by compassion.

(c) **Minor assistance:** The actions of the suspect, although sufficient to come within the definition of the offence, were of only minor encouragement or assistance.

(d) **Dissuasion:** The suspect had sought to dissuade the victim from taking the course of action that resulted in his or her suicide.

(e) **Reluctance:** The actions of the suspect may be characterised as reluctant encouragement or assistance in the face of a determined wish on the part of the victim to commit suicide.

(f) **Reporting to police:** The suspect reported the victim's suicide to the police and fully assisted them in their enquiries into the circumstances of the suicide or the attempt and his or her part in providing encouragement or assistance.[90]

The Director of Public Prosecutions warned that practitioners such as social workers run the risk of being prosecuted if they discuss assisted suicide with service users and that they should seek legal advice before doing so.[91]

Even a successful prosecution may not result in a heavy sentence, depending on the case.

Helping wife with multiple sclerosis to commit suicide. A man helped his wife to commit suicide. She had already tried to commit suicide twice before. One day, he came home from work. She had left a note saying she had taken 175 valium tablets. She was still alive but had a plastic bag over her face. He tightened the bag, rather than see another failed suicide attempt – she had blamed him for the previous failures. He was sentenced to nine months in prison, suspended for a year, and had to do 50 hours of unpaid work. He was otherwise entirely of good character and no risk to the community.[92]

ILL-TREATMENT OR WILFUL NEGLECT

Criminal offences of ill-treatment or wilful neglect apply against people who lack mental capacity or have a mental disorder. These offences apply in any setting, in hospital or otherwise. They come under both the Mental Capacity Act 2005 and Mental Health Act 1983. The maximum sentence is five years in prison.

The offences have been prosecuted on a significant number of occasions, particularly in relation to people in care homes; none seem to have been reported in connection with failure to provide basic hospital care, certainly not in the context

---

90   Director of Public Prosecutions. *Policy for prosecutors in respect of cases of encouraging or assisting suicide.* London: DPP, 2010. Accessed on 23 November 2012 at: www.cps.gov.uk/publications/prosecution/assisted_suicide_policy.html.

91   Pitt, V. 'Social care workers warned about discussing suicide with client.' *Community Care,* 25 February 2010.

92   Cumming, J. 'Man aided his ailing wife's suicide.' *The Scotsman,* 15 September 2006.

of systemic neglect of vulnerable patients. It does not follow that this is because care in the health service has not sometimes sunk sufficiently low.

ILL-TREATMENT OR WILFUL NEGLECT: MENTAL DISORDER (SECTION 127 MENTAL HEALTH ACT 1983)

Under s.127 of the Mental Health Act 1983, it is an offence for employees or managers of a hospital, independent hospital or care home to ill-treat or wilfully neglect a person receiving treatment for mental disorder as an inpatient in that hospital or home; likewise, ill-treatment or wilful neglect, on the premises of which the hospital or home forms a part, of a patient receiving such treatment as an outpatient.

It is also an offence for any individual to ill-treat or to wilfully neglect a mentally disordered patient who is subject to his or her guardianship under the 1983 Act or otherwise in his or her custody or care.

In sum, it seems that the offence can be committed by anybody caring for a person with a mental disorder.

ILL-TREATMENT OR NEGLECT: MENTAL INCAPACITY (SECTION 44 MENTAL CAPACITY ACT 2005)

Section 44 of the Mental Capacity Act 2005 creates offences of ill-treatment or wilful neglect by any person who has the care of another person who lacks, or who the first person reasonably believes to lack, capacity, or by any deputy or person with lasting power of attorney under the 2005 Act, or any person with enduring power of attorney as created under previous legislation.

ILL-TREATMENT AND WILFUL NEGLECT MUST BE CHARGED SEPARATELY

The courts have held that ill-treatment and wilful neglect are not the same and need to be charged separately.

Ill-treatment must (a) be deliberate conduct which could be described as such, irrespective of whether it damages or threatens to damage the health of the victim, and (b) involve a guilty mind (*mens rea*) – namely, an appreciation by the perpetrator that he or she was inexcusably ill-treating a patient or was reckless as to whether he or she was acting in that way.[93]

Criticism was levelled previously at limits to the sentencing powers available under the 1983 Act (before they were increased) – a maximum of two years in prison (although subsequent legislative amendment increased this to five years from October 2007).

For example, the judge in the 'Longcare' case – a care home in Buckingham where adults with learning disabilities were systematically abused – did so. One manager, sentenced to 30 months in prison under s.127 of the 1983 Act, had

---

93   *R v Newington* [1990] 91 Cr App R 247.

ordered a woman to eat meals outside as a punishment, pulled another down the stairs by her hair and deprived two other residents of toiletries in order to save money.[94]

MEANING OF ILL-TREATMENT AND WILFUL NEGLECT

The terms 'ill-treatment' or 'wilful neglect' are not defined in either the Mental Health Act 1983 or the Mental Capacity Act 2005.

The Mental Capacity Act 2005 code of practice notes that the offences are separate, that ill-treatment involves deliberation or recklessness and that wilful neglect usually means deliberate failure to do something that was a duty.[95]

In fact, as the Court of Appeal has stated, recklessness will suffice in relation to wilful neglect as well.[96]

ILL-TREATMENT (COURSE OF ACTION), WILFUL NEGLECT (OMISSION)

In addition, the courts have also contrasted the two offences, the one more about omission, the other more about a deliberate course of action.

Distinction between omissions and courses of action. Wilful neglect is a failure to act – typically an omission – when a moral duty demands it, whereas ill-treatment is a deliberate course of action.

This was considered in a case involving the owner of a residential home and allegations of assault and ill-treatment. The wider backdrop to the charges was described at trial by former members of staff. The owner referred to the older residents as 'babies', the home smelt of urine, there were insufficient staff, the food was inadequate, wet mattresses were never dried out, there were insufficient linen and blankets, residents' clothing was regarded as communal, residents were washed with a common flannel and soap.[97]

ILL-TREATMENT (DELIBERATE COURSE OF ACTION, APPRECIATING, OR RECKLESS ABOUT, THE OUTCOME)

The courts have considered further the meaning of ill-treatment. They have stated that it involves:

- deliberate conduct which could be described as such, irrespective of whether it damages or threatens to damage the health of the victim, and

- involves a guilty mind (*mens rea*), namely an appreciation by the perpetrator that he or she was inexcusably ill-treating a patient or was reckless as to whether he or she was acting in that way.[98]

---

94   'A punishment to fit the crime.' *Disability Now*, December 2003.
95   Lord Chancellor. *Mental Capacity Act 2005: code of practice*. London: TSO, 2007, p.252.
96   *R v Salisu* [2009] EWCA Crim 2702.
97   *R v Newington* [1990] 91 Cr App R 247.
98   *R v Newington* [1990] 91 Cr App R 247.

On this definition of ill-treatment, deliberate conduct is required, but not necessarily an explicit intention to ill-treat; recklessness as to whether the conduct was ill-treatment could be enough.

Furthermore, a notable feature, perhaps overlooked in practice, is that harm is not required.

The courts have also commented on the issue of violence and ill-treatment:

> Violence would not amount to ill-treatment if it was, for example, necessarily used for the reasonable control of a patient. We consider that the judge did not sufficiently deal with the appellant's explanation for some of the conduct, other than violence, alleged by the Crown as ill-treatment which could be said to be conduct necessary for the treatment, rehabilitation or otherwise perpetrated in the best interests of the patient. If, let it be supposed, the appellant genuinely believed that in using such conduct she was acting in the best interests of a patient and the jury accepted that, she would not be guilty of the offence alleged.[99]

WILFUL NEGLECT: OMISSIONS (RECKLESSNESS OR 'COULDN'T CARE LESS')

The courts have held also that recklessness – in the form of a 'couldn't care less attitude' – could constitute an ingredient of wilful neglect.[100]

This was against the background of previous consideration of the offence of wilful neglect of a child under the Children and Young Persons Act 1933 and the necessity of showing both objective and subjective elements to the offence. First, the child must have objectively been in need of help. Second, the parents must subjectively have been aware of this or simply not have cared whether their child was at risk.[101]

So, in the following Court of Appeal case under s.127 of the Mental Health Act 1983, involving a man's death in a care home, the courts stated that there needed to be both an objective breach of a duty of care and an element of subjective (i.e. in the mind of the perpetrator) intention or recklessness.

Leaving highly dependent man to die unattended, wilful neglect. Two of a number of people convicted of wilful neglect appealed against conviction. The first was a qualified staff nurse who was in charge of night duty. The second was the overall care manager responsible for staff rotas.

Man with dementia left to die alone during the night. The circumstances were that a 53-year-old man with frontal lobe dementia died during the night in question. For ten days before his death, he had required one-to-one attention, 24 hours a day. He had also lost the power of speech. The crux of the prosecution (originally brought against seven other people) was that the one-to-one system of attendance had broken down and that the patient had died unattended.

---

99   *R v Newington* [1990] 91 Cr App R 247.
100   *R v Salisu* [2009] EWCA Crim 2702.
101   *R v Sheppard* [1981] AC 394.

The court started from the premiss that, for neglect to be proven, there needed to be not just an objective breach of a duty of care but also the element of subjective intention or recklessness.

Care manager on holiday: no evidence that she couldn't care less. The overall care manager was on holiday at the time but responsible for instituting the one-to-one attention, for which the care home had receive additional funding. The court stated that to show that the system of care drawn up was less than perfect was not enough. For the conviction to stand, evidence would be required that the manager had either intentionally fallen below a reasonable standard or simply could not have 'cared less' about what happened. There was no evidence of this.

Staff nurse: reckless disregard for attention required by man. It was different in the case of the staff nurse. In the court's view, there was not just an objective failure to meet standards but subjective recklessness on his part. First, he had not given any instruction or briefing at the outset of the session to ensure one-to-one attendance was maintained. Second, no one had been with the man when he died. Third, he maintained that he had carried out hourly checks, but the evidence (including that relating to rigor mortis) suggested he was covering up his own failures or those of other staff. All this was capable of showing reckless disregard for the one-to-one attendance required. There were no grounds for overturning the jury's decision about his guilt.[102]

STRENGTHS AND WEAKNESSES OF THE OFFENCES OF ILL-TREATMENT AND WILFUL NEGLECT

The potential application of the offences is clearly limited but, at the same time, also wider than might be supposed.

LIMITATION: MENTAL DISORDER OR MENTAL CAPACITY REQUIRED

A limitation is obviously that there must be a lack of mental capacity or a mental disorder.

Indeed, there is no equivalent offence in criminal law for people who do not lack capacity or who do not have a mental disorder, no matter how ill, vulnerable or helpless those people may be. This makes no sense and is a serious loophole in the law. The Law Commission has drawn attention to the issue, but at the time of writing there is no sign that government is intending to do anything about it.

Another limitation is therefore that, in addition to proving the circumstances of the neglect, lack of capacity or mental disorder at the relevant time also has to be proved. This might be problematic if a formal diagnosis or judgement about this was not made and recorded at the relevant time.

An obvious difficulty is that the patient might now be dead. For instance, at the Briars residential home in Southampton, the police investigation into the terrible conditions and the pressure sores of residents was made more difficult by the fact that many of the victims, nine in number, had died. Convictions for wilful

---

102 *R v Salisu* [2009] EWCA Crim 2702.

neglect (subsequently overturned) did eventually follow in 2010 but only after an 18-month investigation.[103]

The courts have also expressed the view that respect for a person's autonomy, even if it resulted in neglect, will not be wilful neglect:

> Therefore, actions or omissions, or a combination of both, which reflect or are believed to reflect the protected autonomy of the individual needing care do not constitute wilful neglect. Within these clear principles, the issue in an individual prosecution is fact specific.[104]

Always assuming a lack of capacity. A person might lack capacity to make financial decisions but their carer reasonably might believe that the person had capacity to refuse help with personal hygiene, toenail cutting and cleaning in her room.[105]

LIMITATION: NO OFFENCE OF CORPORATE NEGLECT

Just as there exists an offence of corporate manslaughter, so too is there a crying need for an offence of corporate wilful neglect. This would precisely be so that organisations could be prosecuted for systemic failings that lead to neglect not just of one person but of many people.

The offences as they currently stand mean that, for the most part, it is frontline, hands-on carers who are in the sights of the police and Crown Prosecution Service. Whereas a corporate offence would enable the behaviour and decisions of reckless chief executives and senior managers, who cut staff and basic care to the bone without a thought, to be brought into the reckoning.

Prison would not be a penalty; you cannot send organisations to prison. But large fines and the ruin of reputation would be a great disincentive to recklessness with people's welfare, particularly in a health and social care world of competition, free markets, commercialisation, spin and reputation.

RESTRICTION ON PROCEEDINGS UNDER 1983 ACT

Under the Mental Health Act 1983, local authorities, as well as the Director of Public Prosecutions (DPP), can prosecute this offence, although only with consent of the DPP.

Under the 1983 Act, no proceedings can be brought under s.127 unless the Director of Public Prosecution brings, or at least gives consent to, such proceedings. It has been pointed out that proceedings for most offences under the Mental Health Act 1983 can only be brought in respect of an act committed in bad faith or without reasonable care. However, this rule does not apply to s.127.[106]

---

103 Bennett, R. 'Women convicted of wilful neglect at filthy care home for elderly.' *The Times*, 7 August 2010.

104 *R v Nursing* [2012] EWCA Crim 2521.

105 *R v Nursing* [2012] EWCA Crim 2521.

106 This is because of s.139 of the MHA 1983, as pointed out by: Jones, R. *Mental Health Act manual* (14th edition). London: Sweet and Maxwell, 2011, para 1–1117.

STRENGTH: APPLICATION OF OFFENCES TO WIDE VARIETY OF SETTINGS AND CARE

Notwithstanding these caveats and limitations, the existing offences are, in some respects, of wider import than is sometimes appreciated. Under s.127 of the Mental Health Act 1983, it is enough that a person has a mental disorder and is in the care of somebody else – including in a hospital. Under s.44 of the Mental Capacity Act 2005, it is likewise sufficient that the person lacks capacity and is in somebody else's care, including – but not necessarily – in a hospital. These offences could be committed in a domestic setting.[107]

STRENGTH: POTENTIALLY WIDE APPLICATION OF MENTAL DISORDER OR LACK OF MENTAL CAPACITY

Furthermore, for example, an elderly person in hospital may develop depression (even as a result of poor care), in which case he or she will have a mental disorder, now defined broadly in s.1 of the amended Mental Health Act 1983.

Equally, a person may go into hospital with full mental capacity but – owing to infection, dehydration, malnourishment or serious constipation – become sufficiently confused as to lack capacity at the time of the neglect or ill-treatment.

STRENGTH: ENOUGH THAT PERPETRATOR BELIEVED PERSON LACKED CAPACITY

If, under s.44 of the Mental Capacity Act 2005, a person did not in fact lack capacity, but the perpetrator reasonably believed that he or she did lack capacity, then a prosecution can still take place.[108]

STRENGTH: HARM DOES NOT HAVE TO BE PROVED

For the offences of wilful neglect and ill-treatment, the Court of Appeal has confirmed that harm does not have to be proved: 'We note that Section 44 does not require proof of any particular harm or proof of the risk of any particular harm.'[109]

STRENGTH: OFFENCES CAN BE COMMITTED BY SENIOR STAFF OR MANAGERS, EVEN IN HANDS-OFF ROLE

Another point that might not always be appreciated is that the offences, particularly perhaps wilful neglect, need not lie only against staff providing the hands-on care. It is possible to bring in managers with a hands-off role – and even, in one case, a manager who was away on holiday at the relevant time. This is discussed below.

NATURE OF LACK OF MENTAL CAPACITY FOR PURPOSE OF WILFUL NEGLECT OR ILL-TREATMENT

A consideration specific to the offences under the Mental Capacity Act, rather than the Mental Health Act, is the nature of the incapacity of the person.

---

107 *R v Nursing* [2012] EWCA Crim 2521.
108 Crown Prosecution Service. *Guidance on prosecuting crimes against older people.* London: CPS, 2008, p.31.
109 *R v Hopkins, R v Priest* [2011] EWCA Crim 1513.

Under sections 3 and 4 of the Mental Capacity Act, lack of capacity is issue-specific. The Court of Appeal has stated that this creates some difficulty because s.44 is not drafted in such a way as to make clear the nature of the lack of capacity required for the offence to be made out. In one case, the court pointed out that, in relation to s.44, there might be various possibilities:

> This court could make suggestions as to what Parliament had in mind, for example, capacity to make a decision as to (1) residence, (2) personal hygiene and care, (3) personal finances, and (4) the identity of personal carers. We can think of more examples. The question for this court is whether any of them necessarily must be implied or is capable and should be implied into the wording of Section 44 (1)(a).[110]

The Court of Appeal pointed towards the relevant mental capacity being about the care involved in the case and which amounted to wilful neglect:

> Although…there is something of a disconnection between the simple criminal offence created by section 44 of the Act and the elaborate definition sections which are directed to the more general questions of mental capacity in the wide context of the legislation as a whole, nevertheless the stark reality is that it was open to the jury to conclude that the decisions about the care of each of these residents at the time when they were subjected to ill-treatment were being made for them by others, including the appellant, just because they lacked the capacity to make these decisions for themselves. For the purposes of section 2, this was 'the matter' envisaged in the legislation.[111]

The overall offence has to be proved to the criminal standard, but the standard for proving lack of capacity for the issue in question is the civil standard:

> The effect of this construction is not to change the criminal standard of proof of the offence but only of the state of affairs in which the offence was committed. In other words, the prosecution must prove (1) to the criminal standard that the defendant ill-treated or wilfully neglected a person in his care, and (2) that on a balance of probability that person was a person who at the material time lacked capacity.[112]

A comparable issue does not arise under the Mental Health Act; for the purpose of the offences, the specific type of mental disorder, and whether it in some way relates to the neglect or ill-treatment, is immaterial.

SENIORITY OF PERPETRATOR

Notable in the *Salisu* case (see below) is that the court was prepared to consider whether an absent manager might be guilty of wilful neglect – and not just the

---

110   *R v Hopkins, R v Priest* [2011] EWCA Crim 1513.
111   *R v Dunn* [2010] EWCA Crim 2935.
112   *R v Hopkins, R v Priest* [2011] EWCA Crim 1513.

staff on actual duty. It is true that the manager (who was on holiday) eventually had her initial Crown Court conviction overturned. Crucially, nevertheless, the court suggested that the conviction would have stood, had it been proved that she set up an inadequate system of care either intentionally or on the basis that she couldn't have 'cared less' what happened.

The implications of this would seem to be that when institutional neglect takes place – owing not to individual frontline staff but to a grossly flawed care system – more senior managers might be at risk of being held liable.

CONSIDERATION OF NEGLECT IN CASE OF HANDS-OFF MANAGERS

In a wilful neglect case involving deaths of residents from pressure sores in a care home, the court noted that the manager and owner of the home, who were prosecuted, both had a hands-off role. The court clearly accepted that they could be prosecuted but that proper consideration had to be given to *whether they had fallen short in respect of that specific hands-off role.*

> The jury needed to ask in respect of each one (1) are we sure lack of care is proved?; (2) if so, are we sure that it amounted to neglect?; (3) if so, are we sure either (i) that the defendant knew of the lack of care and deliberately or recklessly neglected to act, or (ii) that the defendant was unaware of the lack of care and deliberately or recklessly closed her mind to the obvious?
>
> We do not suggest that this is the form of question required in every case. But in this case the appellants were persons whose primary responsibility was supervision and management rather than hands-on care. The issue whether or not either or both of them was aware of the failing was a principal fact about which the jury required direction or, in the alternative, if unaware of that failing, whether the jury were sure that it was the consequence of a deliberate or reckless closing of the eyes to the obvious.[113]

The court went on to draw attention to the crucial distinction between wilful neglect and the honest, but overworked, efforts of a manager:

> The jury needed careful directions on the issue of delegation of tasks and upon the difference between wilful neglect of the welfare of residents on the one hand, and failure of honest efforts of an overworked but caring manager on the other.[114]

These points are important; the failure of the judge to direct properly the jury on such matters meant that the convictions of both the care home owner and the care home manager were overturned on appeal.[115]

---

113 *R v Hopkins, R v Priest* [2011] EWCA Crim 1513.
114 *R v Hopkins, R v Priest* [2011] EWCA Crim 1513.
115 *R v Hopkins, R v Priest* [2011] EWCA Crim 1513.

Quite how far up the chain a prosecution could go is an interesting point. In the following case, it was the care home manager who was convicted of wilful neglect and given an eight-month prison sentence, suspended for two years. Not the company, but the judge had strong words for it.

Suffering of 90-year-old woman with dementia. A 90-year-old woman was left unsupervised. She would tumble out of bed and crawl naked along the floors of the Dalton unit of Stonedale Lodge, Croxteth, Liverpool. She was not kept clean by staff. She was often hungry and thirsty. She suffered for two months before being admitted to hospital where she died.[116]

The prosecution lay against the manager. The resident had been largely funded by Liverpool City Council. The manager was given an eight-month prison sentence, suspended for two years, as well as 120 hours' unpaid work. She also had to pay £5000 costs. However, the judge criticised the company that ran the home, BUPA:

> BUPA hold themselves out as being the leading UK providers of dementia care, and as the home manager you were responsible for the care and well being of residents. It is clear from the evidence presented during the trial that the nursing home was run very badly and that there was a great deal of under-funding and cost cutting…
>
> This impacted significantly on the resources that were available, which meant there were often inadequate staffing levels and the unit itself was filthy and the premises were in a tired and dilapidated state…
>
> There was a financial interest to fill beds yet keep costs down. While I accept care of dementia sufferers is likely to be challenging there can be no excuses for no proper care and not giving value for money…
>
> A society has to be judged by the way it treats the elderly and vulnerable. Mrs Farrow fell into both categories. I am sure the public will be appalled to hear the way she was looked after at this home.

It transpired that unit managers had regularly told the manager of their concerns about staffing levels, but she did nothing about them; two managers had resigned over the issue. The judge put down the manager's inaction to her desire to please higher management:

> It seems to me you had little sympathy for the staff, some of whom were doing their best in difficult circumstances, as your priority was not the welfare of the residents but that BUPA higher management were satisfied with your performance…
>
> You did what they wanted without any real complaint and in that sense I am satisfied you were putting yourself ahead of the residents and the staff you should have been standing up for.[117]

---

116 Bunyan, N. 'Bupa put profit first at filthy and understaffed care home, says judge.' *Daily Telegraph*, 17 March 2012.
117 Bunyan, N. 'Bupa put profit first at filthy and understaffed care home, says judge.' *Daily Telegraph*, 17 March 2012.

The judge's comments bring to mind two issues. First, how far up the management ladder could the offences of wilful neglect and ill-treatment climb. Second, if care home managers are being prosecuted for wilful neglect, why not senior staff and managers in the NHS for the grossly defective systems of care that some of them have been operating, reckless as to patient welfare (see Chapter 7).

Similarly, in a case involving the now defunct care home company Southern Cross, the judge referred to the wider issue of shortcuts in care being taken because of the imperative for the company of making a profit.

Female resident left to die: endemic culture of neglect management failings. A female resident with dementia, in a Southern Cross care home, was in need of medical attention but was instead left to die. There was only one nurse looking after 29 residents on the night shift at the establishment in South Shields. The nurse pleaded guilty to wilful neglect, but, in imposing a community sentence, the judge was in no doubt that there were wider issues.

Endemic culture of neglect. 'Your neglect was part of an endemic culture of neglect. You had not been trained properly and that failure, which was not your responsibility, was directly relevant to the tragedy that happened.' The judge said the failings included management and leadership problems, not adhering to policies, a lack of training and care plans not followed. Justice Coulson said:

> Urgent medical attention was required, which did not happen. The evidence is [the resident] would not have died if you had summoned medical intervention earlier, which you now accept you should have done. On the other hand you cared for her and certainly did not want her to die. You failed that night mainly because you were not properly trained or managed. You were operating in a regime which was unfit for purpose.

Home run for profit and shortcuts taken by company. The judge went on to note that the care home was run for profit and suggested that this accounted for the shortcuts that had been taken:

> The bottom line is this [is] a care home run for profit, it is an example of privatisation of the health service, where elderly people who have funded the State for many years find themselves in nursing homes run for profit. These things are all very well but there can be no substitute for properly trained staff.

The sentence was nine months in prison, suspended for 12 months, with supervision and 60 hours' unpaid work.[118]

SALISU CASE: PROSECUTION OF SENIOR FIGURES INCLUDING GENERAL MANAGER AND CARE MANAGER (ON HOLIDAY AT THE RELEVANT TIME)

A resident died alone during the night, untended. A number of prosecutions followed, including a general manager, a senior nurse and an absent manager. The latter two were, at first instance, convicted. The case underlines the notion of a 'couldn't care less attitude', constituting recklessness and therefore the criminal element of the offence.

---

118 Kennedy, R. 'Nurse at Southern Cross home did not call doctor and Joyce Wordingham died, court hears.' *Evening Chronicle*, 3 March 2012.

Letting a highly needy and vulnerable patient die alone during night; wilful neglect: prosecution of staff, senior nurse and absent manager. An unnamed man died from natural causes in a nursing home on the night of 26 September 2004. The charge of wilful neglect, laid against a number of health care staff, was that he had died completely unattended, contrary to his care plan. He was 53 years old at the time and suffered from severe frontal lobe dementia, sufficient to warrant detention under the Mental Health Act 1983. Having remained in a hospital bed for a year, he was then moved to a care home in which he lived for two years prior to his death.

Professional observers were unanimous that he had received a good standard of care over that period, and his family had wished for him to stay there. By the time of his death, he had lost the power of speech. He was not aggressive but lacked spatial awareness, bumped into things and people, and might manhandle the latter out of the way. He was therefore a risk both to himself and to others. About ten days before his death, his care plan had been amended to state that he required attention 24 hours a day; without this, the risks would have become intolerable. Following his death, eight defendants were prosecuted, the essence of the case being that the one-to-one system of attendance had broken down and that the patient had died unattended.

The case involved prosecution of seven defendants working in the care home; a general practitioner was also prosecuted.

Care assistants, staff nurse, general manager, care manager all prosecuted. The identity of the first seven defendants repays analysis. They comprised four care assistants on duty that night, the staff nurse on duty that night, the general manager of the home and the care manager of the home. Convictions in the Crown Court were obtained against one of the care assistants, the staff nurse and the care manager (who had overall responsibility for the management of care and the one-to-one attendance of the deceased). The assistant did not appeal against conviction; the other two did. The Court of Appeal upheld the staff nurse's conviction, but the overall care manager's conviction was overturned.[119]

The Court of Appeal referred to the need to make out both objective and subjective elements of the offence.

Staff nurse's conviction upheld on appeal: objective and subjective elements of the offence made out. The essential elements that led to his conviction were that the court found that there was both an 'objective' failure to meet standards and also 'subjective' recklessness on his part.

This subjective failure included the fact that he had not given any instruction or briefing at the outset of the shift to ensure one-to-one attendance was maintained; he had simply left it all up to the carers. No one had been with the man when he died. And the staff nurse maintained that he had carried out hourly checks, but the evidence (including that relating to rigor mortis) suggested he was covering up his own failures or those of other staff.[120]

The court was clear that, had there been sufficient evidence to show that the care manager, away on holiday, had set up a care system betraying a 'couldn't care less attitude', then her conviction would have stood.

---

119 *R v Salisu* [2009] EWCA Crim 2702.
120 *R v Salisu* [2009] EWCA Crim 2702.

Overall manager on holiday: possible conviction for wilful neglect. The overall manager had been on holiday. The court was prepared, in principle, to consider whether absent managers – on holiday or indeed anywhere else – can be guilty of wilful neglect, not just the hands-on nurse in charge. True, the manager's conviction was overturned but not on the grounds that she was *in absentia*. Rather, the evidence did not support the contention that she had either deliberately or recklessly set up a care regime, and in particular a rota system, that was simply not good enough. In other words, had there been such evidence, not necessarily of intentionality but of a 'could not care less' attitude (as the court put it), then her conviction might have stood.[121]

INFORMAL NATURE OF CARING ROLE

It has already been pointed out that anybody caring, in any setting, for a person with a mental disorder or lacking capacity could commit the offences of wilful neglect or ill-treatment. In other words, a formal care setting is not a prerequisite.

For example, in 2012, a mother was convicted of neglect of her 18-year-old daughter. Despite her age, she looked about ten years old, because of the growth disorder Russell Silver syndrome; she also had epilepsy, encephalitis and learning difficulties. She needed care and attention all the time, but her mother had gone to a public house and got drunk, leaving her daughter alone. The police attended. The mother was prosecuted and convicted of neglect. The report of the case does not mention the legislation under which she was convicted, but, given the daughter's age, it was presumably s.44 of the Mental Capacity Act.[122]

Another wilful neglect case involved the perpetrator who was looking after a 79-year-old woman, apparently informally. There was serious neglect of the woman's hygiene and also too much intermingling of the 79-year-old's pension and the perpetrator's own money; the latter was appointee for the former (handling her state benefits). Originally, the perpetrator had run a care home in which the woman had lived. The home shut many years before, but the woman went on living there. She was given a community sentence of 100 hours' unpaid work and ordered to pay £3000 costs and £1500 compensation.[123]

PROSECUTIONS AND CONVICTIONS FOR WILFUL NEGLECT AND ILL-TREATMENT

Since the implementation of the Mental Capacity Act 2005 in April 2007, it has been reported that the police and social services have, in some areas, expressed uncertainty as to what sort of incidents could give rise to prosecutions for wilful neglect or ill-treatment or both. Often cited has been the lack of previous cases.

---

121 *R v Salisu* [2009] EWCA Crim 2702.
122 Allen, E. 'Mother, 40, left her disabled daughter home alone while she went to the pub and got so drunk she ended up at hospital.' *Daily Mail*, 6 July 2012.
123 'Carer fined £10,000 after OAP lived in squalor.' *Daily Echo*, 19 June 2012.

However, over the years there have been a number of convictions under s.127 of the Mental Health Act 1983. In addition, there are now, in any case, growing numbers of cases under s.44 of the Mental Capacity Act 2005.

The examples of cases below, under both Acts, are designed to illustrate, at a glance, the sort of circumstances that have underpinned a prosecution and conviction. It should be noted that they are mere examples and many other situations, not mentioned, could no doubt give rise to the offences.

SELECTION OF CASES BROUGHT UNDER SECTION 127 OF THE MENTAL HEALTH ACT 1983

The following is a sample of cases brought under the Mental Health Act 1983.

Hacking at the rotting flesh of pressure sores in filthy conditions (ill-treatment and wilful neglect). In a residential home near Oxford, relatives were encouraged to ring ahead of visiting, so that care workers could hide the stench of urine with air freshener and scrape faeces off the curtains. Upstairs, an 89-year-old man was lying with suppurating pressure sores that had rotted his flesh down to the bones. He was in too much pain to move and too much confusion to cry out. The owner attempted to clean the wounds by hacking at the skin around the sores with office scissors and ripping out pieces of rotting flesh – wearing gloves with which moments before he had scooped faeces from the sheets. The man was referred to by staff as the 'body in the attic'. The owner was charged with ill-treatment and wilful neglect under the 1983 Act and convicted; he served 12 weeks of a nine-month prison sentence.[124]

Kept in squalor (wilful neglect). When three mentally ill people were found living in squalor, a former mental health nurse and his wife admitted three counts of wilful neglect under the Mental Health Act 1983 and were sentenced to 200 hours' community service.[125]

Septicaemia, pneumonia, dehydration, death of resident (wilful neglect). Another care home owner, originally charged with manslaughter, was convicted instead of wilful neglect. The resident concerned had mental health problems, as well as Alzheimer's disease and Parkinson's disease. He had been awarded the Sword of Honour during his career in the armed forces. He died from septicaemia and pneumonia, and had been found previously by his family lying in soiled clothing, sweating and unconscious. He was severely dehydrated at times and during a period of ten days he lost two stone (12.7 kg). The home was also in breach of many of the regulations applying to care homes. The judge stated that 'those who wilfully neglect, with serious consequences, should expect to go to prison. This is the message that should go out.' The care home owner was sentenced to six months' imprisonment under s.127 of the 1983 Act. She had been arrested after the coroner had informed the police, so concerned was he about the man's appearance.[126]

Not administering medication to resident (wilful neglect). An 84-year-old woman died within five weeks of entering a nursing home. A nurse working there pleaded guilty to wilful neglect under the 1983 Act for not administering the correct medication.[127]

---

124 Hill, A. 'Tide of cruelty sweeps through our care homes.' *The Observer*, 18 February 2001.

125 'News.' *Community Care*, 25 June–1 July 1998.

126 Narain, J. 'Care home boss jailed after wilful neglect killed Alzheimer's patient.' *Daily Mail*, 21 May 2008.

127 'Neglect case "tragic" for nurse.' *BBC News*, 22 May 2008. Accessed on 17 October 2008 at: http://news.bbc. co.uk/1/hi/wales/south_east/7414850.stm.

Inciting residents racially to abuse and kick each other (wilful neglect and ill-treatment). When residents of a care home were incited racially to abuse each other and also to kick each other, the convictions of three carers and the manager of the care home followed for wilful neglect and ill-treatment under the 1983 Act.[128]

Sedatives, rough handling, verbal abuse, bullying, slapping (ill-treatment); not taking person to hospital (wilful neglect): prosecution of two managers and a nurse. Two managers of a South Wales nursing home and another nurse were convicted under s.127, one for wilful neglect, the other two for ill-treatment. The ill-treatment included the administering of sedatives to keep patients quiet, rough handling, neglecting requests to be taken to the toilet, verbal abuse and bullying. The ill-treatment perpetrated by the nurse, not just at this nursing home but another – for which he had already been sentenced to 12 months in prison – included kicking footballs at residents, giving heavy doses of medication to residents so he could sleep undisturbed on his shift, throwing a 75-year-old man across a room and leaving an elderly woman naked and exposed to the elements near open windows and doors. The wilful neglect included not taking a resident who had suffered two broken ribs to hospital for two days.[129]

Appeal by the nurse against conviction. The nurse who had been sentenced to 12 months' imprisonment for ill-treatment, referred to in the case immediately above, appealed on the basis that the judge had gone wrong procedurally on one group of the allegations. The allegations concerned a resident with Alzheimer's disease and dementia. These were (a) forcible administration of medication (so that the resident had to take the medication in order to breathe), (b) forcible administration of sedatives, (c) manhandling and ejecting a resident from the staff room, (d) flicking the resident's nose causing red marks, (e) throwing the resident across the lounge (causing him to fall into a footstool and then holding him down by the throat, causing him to choke and his face to go purple), and (f) regularly abusing the resident verbally. The Court of Appeal did reduce the sentence to nine months on the basis of procedural error, but the carer would still have to serve 12. This was because he had been anyway sentenced to 12 months on another count – namely, meeting the resident in the hallway, putting him in a double arm lock and pulling him to the floor.[130]

Care worker convicted. Another care worker at the same home admitted ill-treatment and was sentenced to 150 hours' community service for slapping a resident.[131]

Pulling hair (ill-treatment) and excessive isolation (wilful neglect). The carer was convicted of ill-treatment, under the 1983 Act, for pulling the hair and nipping the nose of a resident aged 37 with a developmental age of two years, suffering from epilepsy and severe learning disabilities. In addition, she was convicted of wilful neglect for leaving another male resident in a sensory room by himself for too long; he was 54 years old but with a developmental age of 12 months. He was severely physically and mentally disabled, suffered from meningitis, was epileptic, communicated by grunting only and was paralysed to some extent in all four limbs. The carer was sentenced to three months' imprisonment.[132]

128 Gadelrab, R. 'Patients abused at care home.' *Islington Tribune*, 22 December 2006.
129 'Care home bosses guilty of abuse.' *BBC News*, 28 June 2001. Accessed on 17 October 2008 at: http://news.bbc.co.uk/1/hi/wales/1412595.stm. And: 'Patient abuse – nurse struck off.' *BBC News*, 30 April 2003. Accessed on 17 October 2008 at: http://news.bbc.co.uk/1/hi/wales/2989241.stm.
130 *R v Spedding* [2001] EWCA Crim 2190.
131 'Care worker slapped patient.' *The Independent*, 3 January 2002.
132 *R v Lennon* [2005] EWCA Crim 3530.

Kicking, slapping, dragging hospital patients (ill-treatment). A four-month suspended sentence for ill-treatment, under the 1983 Act, was given to a hospital nurse who had kicked one patient, slapped another and dragged a third by his neck. She was subsequently struck off the nursing register.[133]

Placing a bag over the head of a resident (ill-treatment). A carer in a nursing home was convicted under s.127 of the 1983 Act for placing a bag over the head of an 88-year-old resident as he struggled to breathe. He told his horrified colleague not to worry, saying 'no bruise, no proof'. The convicted carer had almost completed his studies to become a doctor in his native Lithuania. He would be sentenced after an application for his deportation.[134]

Three-year regime of bullying, kicking, slapping, nipping, hair-tugging of residents (ill-treatment). In a Yorkshire care home, a regime of physical abuse had persisted for some three years. The eight victims with physical and learning disabilities had mental ages of less than two years old and could not speak for themselves. They suffered bullying, kicking, slapping, nipping, hair-tugging and other assaults. One resident was kicked five times in the groin by a female carer wearing high-heeled shoes; another had his face rubbed in urine as though he were a puppy; another resident was force-fed; another had incontinence pads changed roughly. One prevalent view was that these residents with learning disabilities did not feel pain in the normal way.

Of 33 charges, 23 were proven. Seven carers were sentenced to a total of 66 months in prison, mainly on grounds of ill-treatment and wilful neglect, under s.127 of the 1983 Act, variously; one (who had shown genuine remorse and shame) to ten months, another (a mother of three children and five months pregnant) to 12 months, a third to 12 months, his sister (who was pregnant) to 12 months, a fifth (a supermarket worker with a previous conviction for wilful neglect of a child but who had accepted her misbehaviour) to eight months, a sixth to nine months and a seventh to three months. Of the seven, six were women.[135]

Taking blood with a needle roughly and inappropriately (ill-treatment). Cleared of 15 charges of ill-treatment, a care home manager was convicted on the last charge under s.127 of the Mental Health Act 1983, concerning the taking of blood from the arm of a resident in her late eighties. He took the blood in a rough and inappropriate manner, such that the needle went right through the patient's arm, leaving her with bruises.[136]

Winterbourne View: range of abuse (ill-treatment). A BBC Panorama programme revealed extensive abuse of people with learning disabilities at a private hospital called Winterbourne View, run by Castlebeck Ltd. The abuse included, for example, staff poking residents' eyes, wrestling residents to the ground, slapping legs, bouncing on residents' laps, threatening to put residents' heads down the toilet, harsh hand-slapping, kicking, pinning people under chairs, threats with a cheese grater, the same resident being assaulted five times in one day, giving people showers fully clothed, tipping water from a flower vase over a resident's face.

---

133 'Nurse struck off.' *The Times*, 9 January 2002.

134 *R v Poderis* [2007] Chester Crown Court, 2007. See: McKeever, K. 'Cruel carer is guilty in landmark court case.' *Wilmslow Express*, 15 August 2007. Accessed on 23 October 2008 at: www.wilmslowexpress.co.uk/news/s/531/531529_cruel_carer_is_guilty_in_landmark_court_case.html.

135 Wood, A. 'Cruel care home abusers are jailed.' *Yorkshire Post*, 22 March 2005.

136 'Ex-care home boss cleared of 15 abuse charges.' *Cheshire Guardian*, 20 May 2004.

By August 2012, 11 members of staff had been convicted of ill-treatment. The prosecution argued that the ill-treatment amounted to disability hate crime.[137] In November of that year six members of staff were given prison sentences, the longest being two years. The other five staff received suspended prison sentences.[138]

SELECTION OF CASES BROUGHT UNDER SECTION 44 OF THE MENTAL CAPACITY ACT 2005

The second batch of cases is a selection of convictions under the 2005 Act.

Care home owner convicted: pressure sores (wilful neglect). A care home owner was convicted of wilful neglect for allowing horrendous pressure sores to develop and then doing nothing about them. The resident was 97 years old, immobile and unable to communicate. A pressure sore developed and the perpetrator told a carer to apply cream but no dressing. The sore got worse. Staff raised the issue but the care home owner did nothing and removed notes made by the staff about the sores. One of the sores was large enough to put a tennis ball in. After the resident was admitted to hospital following a fall, the sores were dressed. The care home owner took the resident home three hours later. A week later, the dressings had not been changed. Finally, social services sent a doctor to the care home and the woman was admitted to hospital. However, she picked up an infection and died there. The care home owner was sentenced to six months in prison, suspended for two years.[139]

Not attending to a nose bleed (wilful neglect). A care worker at a care home was convicted of wilful neglect. An elderly resident was found covered in dried blood in her room following a nose bleed. She had done her best to clean herself up, but there was blood in her room and in the bathroom. She was found in a distressed and confused state. The care worker admitted that he knew about the nose bleed but had been too busy to attend to the woman.

The carer was also convicted of ill-treatment, having pushed an elderly man, who had suffered a stroke and had dementia. He had been agitated. The carer said to him 'What the fucking hell do you want now?' He then pushed him over. Falling on his back, he lay motionless for five minutes before being helped by another member of staff. It was Christmas Day.[140]

Not attending to resident with dementia during the night (wilful neglect). Three care workers were convicted of wilful neglect, during the night, of an 85-year-old resident with dementia at a care home in Bromsgrove. He should, according to the care plan, have been checked every two hours. He was found in the morning wearing a pyjama jacket, daytime trousers, with one shoe and both socks on. He was very cold. The radiator was off.

The judge had directed the jury that they had to decide whether it was deliberate or reckless lack of care, or whether busy staff, with much to do, had forgotten the resident. It appeared that staff filled in the care plan book without having seen the resident. For instance, one of the carers had stated that the man had slept well. Yet it appeared he had

137 Ramesh, R. 'Winterbourne View abuse: last staff member pleads guilty.' *The Guardian*, 7 August 2012.
138 Brown, L. and Brooke, C. '"Culture of cruelty": 11 care home workers sentenced for shocking abuse of vulnerable residents exposed by Panorama probe.' *Daily Mail*, 26 October 2012.
139 Adwent, C. 'Care home owner spared jail.' *East Anglian Daily Times*, 5 July 2012.
140 Hickey, A. 'Flintshire carer abused and neglected elderly at Prestatyn nursing home.' *Daily Post*, 10 July 2012.

not been put to bed the previous evening and there were no impressions or creases on the bed.[141] They were given suspended jail sentences.[142]

Care home manager: unkempt residents, run-down environment (wilful neglect). A care home manager was convicted, under s.44 of the Mental Capacity Act, of wilful neglect of a number of mentally ill residents in her care in Colchester. She was given a suspended prison sentence. There was no heating, some patients were overdressed while others were not dressed properly, their bedding was damp and there was little food in the house. Some had what appeared to be long-standing scalp and foot infections.[143]

Not resuscitating a patient (wilful neglect). A nurse working at a care home was given a community sentence of 100 hours for failing to perform cardio-pulmonary resuscitation on a 90-year-old resident. The man would have died in any case, but the nurse did not know this at the time. The nurse failed to act, even though she was fully trained in the procedure and the home had a policy of giving resuscitation unless the resident was subject to a 'do not resuscitate' instruction.[144]

Care home manager locking people with learning disabilities in car on hot day (wilful neglect). A care home manager and an employee went to a betting shop and amusement arcade. For three hours during the visit, they locked three vulnerable people in a car on a hot and muggy day. The three had severe learning disabilities, autism and epilepsy. They were rescued when passers-by spotted them in distress and trying to get out. The police freed them and found them dehydrated and very hot.

The judge in the Crown Court sentenced the manager and employee to 300 hours and 250 hours of community service respectively for wilful neglect under s.44 of the Mental Capacity Act. They were in serious breach of their responsibilities, and the three men must have suffered very considerable stress and discomfort in the unventilated vehicle. They had been on the 'cusp' of going to prison but were previously model citizens. Both were sacked by their employer.[145]

Leaving service user in minibus (wilful neglect). On the day in question, a care assistant and another worker had taken two service users out in a minibus. They, and one service user, went for a coffee somewhere, leaving the other service user in the minibus for about an hour. He was 42 years old, could become very agitated and anxious in vehicles, had to be put in a harness in vehicles, could not articulate for himself and could not attend to his own personal care.

He could not see the others having coffee, and they could not see him. He became very distressed. The police were called. They arrested the care assistant and other worker. They were both convicted under s.44 of the 2005 Act and given a one-year community order and eight hours of unpaid work.[146]

Degrading photograph of 92-year-old semi-naked resident (wilful neglect). A nurse working in a care home made a photograph of a 92-year-old semi-naked resident and

141 'Trio convicted of neglect of 85-year-old at Bromsgrove care home.' *Bromsgrove Advertiser*, 19 July 2012.
142 'Bromsgrove care workers sentenced for neglect.' *Bromsgrove Advertiser*, 28 August 2012.
143 'Care home boss banned for neglect of mentally ill.' *Daily Gazette*, 9 July 2011.
144 Hunt, K. '"Negligent" nurse Parulben Patel spared jail after leaving man to die.' *KentOnline*, 18 April 2012. Accessed on 28 August 2012 at: www.kentonline.co.uk/kentonline/news/2012/april/19/nurse_spared_jail. aspx.
145 'Vulnerable patients locked in car for three hours while carers went to the bookies.' *Daily Mail*, 21 January 2008.
146 *Newton v Secretary of State for Health* [2009] UKFTT 19 (HESC). (Details of conviction recounted in this Care Standards Tribunal case.)

then circulated it. The woman was sentenced, for wilful neglect under s.44, to nine months' imprisonment, suspended for a year, together with 200 hours of community service.[147]

Filming a semi-naked resident having an incontinence pad changed, and encouraging a resident to swear: prison sentence (ill-treatment). A carer filmed a semi-naked elderly man having his incontinence pad changed. She encouraged another to swear. She was sent to prison for a year for ill-treatment under s.44 of the 2005 Act.

She was arrested after leaving her iPhone on a train. A member of the public handed it to police. There were three film clips of residents, at a Bupa-run care home, Elstree Court Nursing Home. The clips showed her asking a resident to open their eyes, clap their hands and give her a smile. In return for one of the requests, she was heard saying she would give their glasses back to them. The second showed a semi-naked man having an incontinence pad changed, with more staff in the room than necessary. The last clip showed her encouraging a woman to swear.[148]

Psychological and physical torment: throwing resident across the room, headlock, flicking orange juice, flicking ears, lying about a parcel the resident was expecting (ill-treatment). A care assistant working at a private hospital in Hexham, run by Castlebeck, was convicted of repeated ill-treatment of a 36-year-old man with learning difficulties, bipolar disorder and hyperactivity disorder. On one occasion, he was excitedly awaiting visitors and wouldn't move away from the door. The care assistant threw him across the room. On another occasion, after the resident had pressed his call bell, the care assistant put him in a headlock. Other instances included flicking orange juice into his hair, taunting him, flicking his ears and pretending that a parcel, with a model kit in it, had been sent back because of his bad behaviour. The judge referred not just to the physical assaults but to the psychological torment that had been inflicted. The carer was sentenced to 16 months in prison.[149]

Hitting people with learning disabilities on day trip (ill-treatment). A 21-year-old carer was convicted of ill-treatment of adults with learning disabilities on a day trip in Norfolk. One of the incidents involved her hitting one of the adults on the arm and laughing. She was sentenced to four months' imprisonment under s.44, suspended for 24 months, and to 200 hours of unpaid work.[150]

Hitting a vulnerable resident's head (ill-treatment). A care worker at a care home run by Calderstones Partnership NHS Foundation Trust was seen hitting a vulnerable resident round the head, such as to cause his head to hit the wall three feet (90 cm) away. The care worker was convicted of ill-treatment and given a community sentence, since it was a single incident and many letters of support from colleagues had been received.[151]

Humiliating resident by dressing him up in a bra and speaking in a derogatory way (ill-treatment). A support worker at the Southview Independent Hospital was convicted of ill-treatment under s.44. She had humiliated a man who had suffered a stroke by putting a bra on him. She had also referred to a 'fucking tsunami' when an incontinent woman had wet herself. In addition, she had assaulted another woman, after the latter had

147 Cambridgeshire County Council. 'UK nurse conviction makes legal history.' *News*, 24 August 2009.
148 'Eastbourne woman jailed after filming care home residents.' *Eastbourne Herald*, 22 July 2011.
149 Butcher, J. 'Hexham care assistant Michael Payne jailed for 16 months.' *The Journal*, 17 April 2012.
150 'Woman, 21, convicted of ill treatment.' *City Local*, 24 February 2012. Accessed on 13 August 2012 at: www.citylocal.co.uk/Thetford/news-in-Thetford/woman-21-convicted-of-ill-treatment-53292.
151 'Carer loses his job after passer-by sees him hit patient.' *Manchester Evening News*, 4 July 2012.

tried to strangle the support worker's dog during a therapy visit. The worker was sentenced to a 12-month community order and 120 hours of unpaid work.[152]

Hitting residents with dementia and flicking food at them (ill-treatment). A nursing home care worker worked on an 'intensive' ward at a nursing home, with responsibility for extremely vulnerable people who suffered from dementia. She banged the back of a 79-year-old man's head and ran away from him, pushed an 85-year-old woman and hit an 84-year-old man's head as though she were knocking on a door. She flicked food at an 89-year-old woman's face, hit her in the face with a metal bib, thought it was funny and stood there laughing. She was given six months in prison, suspended for two years, under s.44 of the 2005 Act.[153]

Using the arms of one resident to hit another resident in a care home (ill-treatment). An NHS care home manager used the arms of other residents as 'weapons' to hit a woman in a home for people with severe learning disabilities. This was in retaliation for having her hair pulled. Under s.44, she was given a six-month prison sentence, suspended for 18 months.[154]

Repeated assault of woman with dementia, in her bed at a care home (ill-treatment). A nurse, concerned about the treatment of her 80-year-old mother in a care home, installed a secret camera in her room. A care worker was then caught on film when suddenly striking the resident, repeatedly slapping her arms and then hitting her in the abdomen four times. He was convicted of both assault and ill-treatment, under s.44 of the Mental Capacity Act, and given an 18-month prison sentence.

The woman's daughter pointed out that there were wider issues within the care home and that rules were regularly breached – for example, two care workers should have been present when a resident was put to bed, and bathing and cleaning should have been carried out by a female care worker. Yet, in 2009, the care home had been judged excellent by the regulator.[155]

Smothering care home residents with fleece and pillow (ill-treatment). A care home worker was helping a resident into bed. The resident cried out in pain because of an injured hip. The care worker picked up a fleece and pulled it tightly over the old lady's face, telling her to 'shut up'. A second resident also cried out in pain when being moved because of a dislocated shoulder. The care worker grabbed a pillow and held it with both hands over the resident's face. Both residents were elderly and had dementia. The care worker was sentenced for ill-treatment, under s.44 of the Mental Capacity Act, to 12 months in prison.[156]

Carer: rough handling, dragging residents, sitting on resident, screaming at residents, prising open their mouths (ill-treatment). A senior carer at a care home in Widnes was convicted, under s.44 of the 2005 Act, on a number of counts of ill-treatment of female residents with dementia. She dragged two elderly women along a

152 'Court orders Billingham carer to work in community.' *Northern Echo*, 26 May 2012.

153 'Carer who abused elderly suffering with Alzheimer's and dementia avoids jail at Liverpool court.' *Liverpool News*, 13 February 2010. Also: 'Tammy Knox trial: care worker tells Liverpool crown court how he learned of patient abuse.' *Liverpool Echo*, 15 January 2010.

154 Dudgeon, O. 'Care home boss spared prison in abuse case.' *Yorkshire Post*, 17 November 2009.

155 'Nurse filmed assaulting dementia patient, 80, on daughter's secret camera.' *Daily Mail*, 13 April 2012.

156 'Jail warning for Cumbrian woman who ill-treated elderly women in care home.' *News & Star*, 12 November 2011. And: 'Care worker Kimberley Walker jailed for abusing women.' *BBC News*, 12 November 2011. Accessed on 13 August 2012 at: www.bbc.co.uk/news/uk-england-cumbria-16137039.

corridor, kicking their heels from behind, to make them walk 'like a rag doll'. She grabbed another resident so roughly that she banged her head on a bedstead. She sat on another woman to get her to take eye drops. She screamed at residents, forcing them to take their medication by prising open their mouths.[157]

Two carers: assault and verbal abuse of care home residents (ill-treatment). Two carers were convicted of ill-treatment at a care home in Farnworth, under s.44 of the Act. They were given prison sentences of 21 and 15 months respectively. The ill-treatment included assault and verbal abuse over a two-year period. The residents concerned had suffered several attacks, including being sprayed in the face with an air freshener and blocking bedroom doors with towels. On one occasions, a resident had been restrained with a towel across his face. Another patient was dragged to her room and locked inside.[158]

Carer punching and slapping a resident with dementia (ill-treatment). A carer was convicted of ill-treatment, under s.44 of the 2005 Act. She was given a suspended prison sentence of six months and ordered to do 140 hours' unpaid work.

The resident, of the Chestnuts care home in Grimsby, suffered from vascular dementia and could become agitated and aggressive. At 2.30 in the morning, the carer had entered his room and punched and slapped him repeatedly around the head, as well as swearing at him. He suffered several bruises to his forearms where he had put them over his face while trying to protect himself. The carer was witnessed as being in a red-faced rage.

The judge noted that she had showed no compassion towards the resident and that, by fighting a trial, she had shown no remorse.[159]

Nurse wrestling with and force-feeding patient (ill-treatment). A nurse working at Whitchurch Hospital, Cardiff, was convicted of ill-treatment of patients with dementia, under s.44 of the Mental Capacity Act. She was seen kneeling on top of one elderly man, force-feeding him medicine when he refused it. Another patient she was in charge of was spotted with a cut lip and skin tears on one arm after she had been at his bedside during an overnight shift. The nurse was given a six-month prison sentence, suspended for two years.[160]

Carer hitting resident of care home (ill-treatment). A carer was convicted of ill-treating, under s.44 of the 2005 Act, a resident at Huntleigh Lodge care home, Cleethorpes. She was given a suspended prison sentence of six months and also 60 hours' unpaid work. The resident had severe dementia, was hard of hearing, had cataracts, was frail, had poor mobility and could not look after himself. Without warning, the carer had swung his legs towards her as he lay on his bed. His body became twisted. He kicked out into her stomach. She picked up a towel, twisted it and used it to hit him in the stomach. She also punched him on the shoulder and slapped him with force on the shoulder. The injuries were minor, but the judge considered the matter serious.[161]

157 'Widnes mum Jeanette Judge found guilty on six charges of cruelty.' *Runcorn and Widnes World,* 1 February 2012. And: Jordan, B. '"Sentence is a damned insult", say families of abused victims.' *Runcorn and Widnes World,* 14 March 2012.

158 'Bolton women guilty of abusing care home patients.' *Manchesterwired,* 6 July 2012. Accessed on 13 August 2012 at: www.manchesterwired.co.uk/news.php/1439142-Bolton-women-guilty-of-abusing-care-home-patients.

159 'Is this justice for the elderly? Care worker who punched and slapped 87-year-old dementia sufferer walks free from court.' *Daily Mail,* 11 July 2011.

160 'Nurse sentenced for patient abuse.' *BBC News,* 23 November 2009. Accessed on 13 August 2012 at: http://news.bbc.co.uk/1/hi/wales/8375233.stm.

161 'Carer spared prison after hitting pensioner.' *Grimsby Telegraph,* 3 December 2011.

Care home worker slapping resident, putting vinegar and excess sugar in tea (ill-treatment). A care home worker was convicted and sentenced to six months in prison, under s.44 of the Mental Capacity Act, for ill-treating two elderly residents who suffered from Alzheimer's disease. She had slapped a wheelchair-bound resident on the back of the head. She had also put vinegar and excess sugar in the tea of another resident.

The court weighed up the effect on elderly residents of such treatment against the implications of conviction and prison for a carer of previous good character:

> Elderly people have a right to be treated with respect by everyone in the community. When they are ill and living in residential homes, they are entitled to expect, and we must demand, that they are properly cared for. What this appellant did was the opposite of that.

But the victims did not sustain distress or injury, the perpetrator was of good character and had two young daughters:

> However, we acknowledge that neither of the victims in fact sustained any distress or injury and they were very short incidents. The consequences for the appellant have been grave: she has lost her livelihood and has no realistic prospect of being able to work in her chosen field again and, if we may say so, rightly so. She has two young daughters at home. She is a woman in early middle age. The effect of a prison sentence upon someone like her, who was until now of previous good character, should not be underestimated.[162]

Manager of care home: incorrect hoisting, exposing a person, manhandling people by their clothing, abusive language, throwing walking aids (ill-treatment). The perpetrator was the manager of a care home in East London, whose residents were largely elderly people with dementia. She had provided good references, but a police investigation began when 14 members of the care home wrote a whistleblowing letter to the owner of the home. One resident in his eighties, utterly disoriented, was put in an incorrect position in a hoist and transported from the lounge into the conservatory with his genitals exposed. He was distressed by this and was incontinent of urine during the process. Afterwards, he was taken to hospital by ambulance.

A second resident, in her nineties, was described as a pleasant lady with no behavioural problems. She was ill-treated when the perpetrator held her by her clothing so as to cause discomfort and pain. Her trousers were pulled up very high, in a degrading way. She was thus held and then allowed to slump to the floor. She also suffered osteoarthritis of the spine, which meant that once she was on the floor she could not get up by herself.

A third resident, in his eighties, did have behavioural problems, including the molesting of female residents. The manager subjected him to abusive and offensive language and twice threw a walking frame at him.[163] Under s.44 of the 2005 Act, the manager was given a community sentence, consisting of 180 hours of unpaid work.[164]

Care worker: lifting resident and causing pain (ill-treatment). A care worker at a nursing home in Cannock was given a prison sentence of nine months under s.44. He had taken a shortcut when changing the man, by lifting him and causing pain, instead of turning

---

162 *R v Heaney* [2011] EWCA Crim 2682.
163 *R v Dunn* [2010] EWCA Crim 2935.
164 'Appeal dismissed for care home manageress who neglected Romford dementia patients.' *Romford Recorder*, 26 November 2010.

him. The resident's protests went unheeded. He then lashed out at the carer, who grabbed him by the wrists, leaving red marks.[165]

Care worker convicted of manhandling and swearing at a resident (ill-treatment). A care worker was convicted of ill-treatment, under s.44 of the 2005 Act, for pushing, manhandling and swearing at a mental health patient. She was witnessed grabbing a patient with early-onset dementia and schizophrenia by the shoulder, shouting and swearing at her, pushing her and causing her to fall on to a mattress. The patient was screaming, although there were no physical or mental injuries caused. The care worker was sentenced to four months in prison, suspended for two years, and ordered to pay £1000 costs.[166]

Tucking resident in so tightly she was trapped under the covers and leaving her in the dark (ill-treatment). A carer was convicted of ill-treatment for tucking a blanket so tightly around a 95-year-old resident with dementia that she was trapped under the covers. He then left her, switching off the light and leaving her in the dark, which she was afraid of, screaming in distress. On a separate occasion, he had tied her to a chair using a blanket. The care home, run by Prime Life, had already been rated 'poor' by the Care Quality Commission. The carer had also mistreated other residents.[167]

Verbal abuse, dragging across bedroom floor and failing to give medicine in care home (ill-treatment and wilful neglect). Two staff at a care home in Pontefract were found guilty of ill-treatment, one being given a prison sentence of four months, the other a community sentence. The family of one resident had left a camera in an alarm clock because of their fears about what was happening. The camera recorded five days of abuse including the resident being threatened with violence, dragged across the floor and not receiving her medicine. She was struck, and called a 'nasty old cow' and a 'horrible old lady'. The judge called the offences 'unforgivable and unacceptable'.[168]

Falsification of records, resident left during night, on floor, hypothermia, in faeces and urine (wilful neglect). Three care workers at a care home in Bromsgrove were convicted of wilful neglect of a resident during the night. In the documentation, the morning after, it was recorded that the resident had slept well. In fact, nobody had attended to him, and he had been found lying in the corner of his room, barely conscious, suffering from hypothermia. His clothes were soiled with urine and faeces. All three carers involved received suspended prison sentences and two were ordered to do community service.[169]

Frightening care home residents with a glove puppet (ill-treatment). Two care home workers were convicted of ill-treatment and given suspended prison sentences and community service. They had frightened a resident suffering from dementia by means of a sinister-looking, green glove puppet. One had brought out the puppet from behind her back, thrust it toward one of the residents and made a growling sound. The other carer had

---

165 'Prison term handed to care worker at Cannock nursing home.' *Express and Star*, 7 January 2012.
166 'Care home worker pushed patient.' *Evening Gazette*, 26 January 2010. And: 'Ex-care worker spared jail over treatment of vulnerable woman.' *Gazettelive*, 27 March 2010. Accessed on 13 August 2012 at: www.gazettelive.co.uk/news/teesside-news/2010/03/27/ex-care-worker-spared-jail-over-treatment-of-vulnerable-woman-84229-26118005.
167 Dolan, A. 'The cruelty of a "carer": judge jails worker who imprisoned Alzheimer's sufferers in bedrooms.' *Daily Mail*, 14 February 2012.
168 Peachey, P. 'Carer jailed after being caught on camera hitting and abusing a vulnerable 89-year-old woman.' *The Independent*, 29 August 2012.
169 Jackson, C. '"Neglectful" Bromsgrove care workers spared jail.' *Bromsgrove Standard*, 28 August 2012.

held the resident's hands in her lap so she couldn't fight back. The woman was so scared she slid down in her chair to try and get away. The carers laughed.[170]

HEALTH AND SAFETY AT WORK LEGISLATION

In some circumstances, health and safety at work legislation may be employed to prosecute in the context of adult protection.

The Health and Safety Executive (HSE) prosecutes offences committed under the Health and Safety at Work Act 1974. It normally prosecutes organisations but is able to, and sometimes does, prosecute individuals.

There are various duties contained within the 1974 Act. Under s.3, there is a duty on the employer to conduct its undertaking in such a way as to ensure, so far as is reasonably practicable, that non-employees who may be affected are not exposed to risks to their health and safety. In addition, under r.3 of the Management of Health and Safety at Work Regulations 1999, there is a duty to carry out a suitable and sufficient assessment of the risks to the health and safety of non-employees arising from, or connected with, the employer's undertaking.

Under s.7 of the 1974 Act, individual employees have a duty to take reasonable care of their own health and safety and also that of other people who may be affected by the employee's acts or failure to act.

And under s.37 of the 1974 Act, if an offence – such as under s.3 – is committed by the organisation, a director or manager will also be guilty individually if it is proved that the offence was committed with their consent, connivance or neglect.

HEALTH AND SAFETY EXECUTIVE AND SAFEGUARDING ADULTS

Adult protection has now and again come on to the HSE's radar.

For instance, in the following case, s.3 of the Health and Safety at Work Act 1974 (duty of employer towards non-employees) was used to prosecute both the company and individual managers of a care home for failing to investigate and prevent a sustained regime of physical abuse.

Health and safety obligations in relation to abuse at care home. People with physical and learning disabilities living in a care home in Hull had been subject to a regime of sustained abuse for three years. This included humiliation, rough behaviour, force-feeding, shouting, slapping, hair pulling, swearing and dragging residents across the floor. Most of the residents had a mental age of less than two years. Seven carers were sent to prison, under s.127 of the Mental Health Act 1983, for ill-treatment and neglect.

In addition, however, under the Health and Safety at Work Act 1974, the company was prosecuted and fined £100,000, together with £25,000 costs. It pleaded guilty to failing to take appropriate action to investigate and prevent the ill-treatment of vulnerable adults. Five senior managers were prosecuted as well for failing to protect residents from this

---

170 'Care workers use glove puppet to bully elderly women.' *BBC News*, 6 January 2011. Accessed on 20 January 2013 at: www.bbc.co.uk/news/uk-wales-south-east-wales-12125575.

ill-treatment; they had failed to act on reports of abuse. They were fined sums ranging from £4000 down to £360.[171]

Neglect or omission, more generally, may provoke a prosecution under s.3 of the 1974 Act. For instance, a local authority pleaded guilty in relation to the death in a care home of a 23-year-old man, who was quadriplegic and suffered from cerebral palsy. He was asphyxiated as a result of the failure to make sure the bed rails were maintained in effective working order and good repair and to ensure staff were properly trained in fitting, maintaining and using the bed rails.[172]

Likewise, another council was prosecuted under s.3 and fined £115,000 following the death of a severely disabled man in a bubble bath in a care home.[173] This followed the failure of the family, in a judicial review case, to challenge the Crown Prosecution Service's failure to bring a gross negligence manslaughter case.[174]

A couple who ran a private residential home were not only convicted of ill-treatment and wilful neglect (under s.127 of the Mental Health Act 1983) but also of breach of the Health and Safety Work Act 1974.[175] The judge found they had abused their position of trust and created a regime that centred on oppressive conduct and oppressive punishment; residents were repeatedly bullied, underfed (one man lost four stone [25.4 kg]) and given inappropriate medicines.[176]

REPORTING OF INJURIES, DISEASES AND DANGEROUS OCCURRENCES REGULATIONS 1995

Although harm is not a prerequisite for HSE intervention, prosecution and intervention, the HSE should not be turning a blind eye when harm – or even just a dangerous occurrence – happens.

This is because employers have an obligation to report to the Health and Safety Executive under the Reporting of Injuries, Diseases and Dangerous Occurrences Regulations 1995. In relation to non-employees – that is, members of the public (including therefore vulnerable adults) – these regulations include the duty to report on (in summary):

- the death of a person from an accident arising out of or in connection with work

171   Mark, D. 'Care home firm which failed to act on abuse claims is fined £100,000.' *Yorkshire Post*, 28 October 2005.

172   'Council admits safety breaches over man's care home death.' *24dash.com*, 22 November 2007. Accessed on 17 October 2008 at: www.24dash.com/news/health/2007-11-22-Council-admits-safety-breaches-over-mans-care-home-death.

173   'Care home death is reopened.' *Bolton Evening News*, 12 April 2004.

174   *Rowley v Director of Public Prosecutions* [2003] EWHC 693 (Admin).

175   'Care home pair guilty of neglect.' *BBC News*, 26 April 2004. Accessed on 17 October 2008 at: http://news.bbc.co.uk/1/hi/england/norfolk/3660605.stm.

176   'We just want to clear our names.' *Norwich Evening News*, 26 May 2006.

- injury of any person not at work as a result of an accident arising out of or in connection with work – and that person is taken from the site of the accident to a hospital for treatment in respect of that injury

- major injury of any person not at work as a result of an accident arising out of or in connection with work at a hospital, or

- a dangerous occurrence.

This reporting duty does not apply, however, if the death or injury has followed from medical examination, operation or treatment carried out, or supervised by, a medical doctor or dentist.[177]

HSE AND SYSTEMIC LAPSES IN HEALTH CARE

The Health and Safety Executive could, in principle, have a significant role to play in situations of systemic neglect or abuse in health or social care – that is, when the problem is a system of work rather than individual decision making. Major system lapses cause far more harm than isolated incidents. Yet the HSE has been shying away.

The following is a summary of what the HSE could, and arguably should, be doing under the relevant legislation.

SYSTEMS OF WORK RESULTING IN SYSTEMIC NEGLECT ARE WITHIN HSE'S REMIT

On the face of it, the HSE duties under the Health and Safety at Work Act 1974 are easily capable of covering systems of work in hospitals that directly lead to neglect – for example, grossly inadequate staffing levels, lack of hygiene, not helping people eat and drink, not taking people to the toilet, not managing pressure sores and not keeping equipment and the environment clean, hygienic and in working order.

ACTUAL HARM NOT REQUIRED FOR THE OFFENCES TO BE PROSECUTED

Furthermore, and most importantly, actual harm does not have to be demonstrated under the legislation; merely that reasonably practicable efforts have not been made to protect the health and safety of patients.

This contrasts, for example, with a prosecution for manslaughter which needs to show not just grossly negligent care but also that this directly caused the death of one or more patients. This absence, of the requirement of causation of harm, would suggest that frequent prosecutions would have taken place in relation to systems of neglectful care reported in the health service over the last decade and more. But it has not happened.

This takes a bit of disentangling.

---

177 SI 1995/3163. Reporting of Injuries, Diseases and Dangerous Occurrences Regulations 1995.

HSE NOT CONCERNED WITH CLINICAL STANDARDS AND JUDGEMENTS

Understandably, the HSE works to a self-imposed restriction of excluding clinical matters. This is on the basis that standards of clinical judgement and quality of care are the responsibility of the Department of Health and the Care Quality Commission (CQC). Whereas, the HSE claims, for its own, 'non-clinical' risks to patients including manual handling, trips, falls, scalding and some issues concerning health care-related infection.[178]

STOKE MANDEVILLE HOSPITAL: DECISION NOT TO PROSECUTE

For example, the HSE did consider whether a prosecution might be warranted when nearly 40 people died of *Clostridium difficile* at Stoke Mandeville hospital.[179]

The reason for not proceeding was thoroughly unconvincing, given the damning detail of the Healthcare Commission's report. This has already been set out above in this chapter. The HSE referred to an unrealistic prospect of securing a conviction. The HSE did at least concede that an outbreak of infection arising not from individual clinical judgement but instead from an NHS trust's system for managing infection was, in principle, within its purview.[180]

This concession is significant because the scandals affecting the NHS – including those at Stoke Mandeville, Maidstone and Tunbridge Wells NHS Trust and Mid Staffordshire NHS Foundation Trust – had their roots in grossly defective systems of work rather than individual clinical error or misjudgement. The logic of the concession made in this instance is that the HSE would and should look hard at systemic neglect. But it is not, in practice, doing so, even when the facts are staring it in the face.

At Stoke Mandeville, therefore, there was an NHS Trust that the Healthcare Commission had exposed as ignoring the advice of its own infection control team and failing to put in place basic precautionary measures. This was at least partly because to have done so would have jeopardised the hitting of finance and performance targets. As to whether such measures would have been reasonably practicable, the Trust changed its approach as soon as details of the infection and deaths were leaked to the national press. Plainly, if such measures were reasonably practicable following the leak, they were so before. Why, then, was a prosecution not attempted?

Stoke Mandeville: factors in favour of prosecution. The HSE did go into further detail; it listed the factors in favour of prosecution. These included the failure in clinical governance to ensure there were adequate criteria for declaring an outbreak of infection, absence of systems and procedures, failure to take sufficient steps to isolate patients and

178 Health and Safety Executive. *Priorities for enforcement of Section 3 of the HSWA 1974–July 2003 (rev. June 2011).* Accessed on 19 January 2012 at: www.hse.gov.uk/enforce/hswact/priorities.htm.

179 Health and Safety Executive. *HSE investigation into outbreaks of* Clostridium difficile *at Stoke Mandeville Hospital, Buckinghamshire Hospitals NHS Trust.* London: HSE, 2006.

180 Health and Safety Executive. *HSE investigation into outbreaks of* Clostridium difficile *at Stoke Mandeville Hospital, Buckinghamshire Hospitals NHS Trust.* London: HSE, 2006, p.1.

the paucity of recorded action and discussion which suggested that senior management did not appreciate how urgent the situation was.

Despite all this, the countervailing factors were deemed greater.

Stoke Mandeville: factors against prosecution. The HSE pointed out that the *Clostridium* strain was particularly virulent and there was limited information about it, that other NHS trusts were having the same problem with *Clostridium* infection rates, that the buildings were not ideal for isolating patients, that there had been discussion at Trust Board level (albeit not recorded) and that the Trust had reasonably not decided to spend more money on isolation facilities after the first outbreak because it believed that the infection was under control.[181]

This reasoning is far from persuasive. It omits the overwhelming evidence that reasonably practicable isolation measures could have been taken, that the infection control team had explicitly and urgently advised these and that the Board had equally explicitly rejected the advice, with wider performance and finance targets in mind.

It is not an exaggeration to suggest that the HSE effectively endorsed the priority given by this Trust – and, in effect, other trusts – to resources and targets over safety.

Just as concerning was the reasoning that, because other NHS trusts were also doing badly, this was not cause to single out Stoke Mandeville. Taken to its logical conclusion, such reasoning would mean that the worse a problem is within the health service, and the more widespread the breaches of safe systems of patient care, so the less likely it is that the HSE will do anything about it. And systemic problems with infection control in the health service had already, in 2004, been reported on by the National Audit Office.[182]

One can only speculate that the HSE may have had in mind a daunting vista of widespread prosecutions – for which it had neither the appetite nor the resources – or that it was simply warned off for political reasons.

MAIDSTONE AND TUNBRIDGE WELLS NHS TRUST: DECISION NOT TO PROSECUTE

If the HSE's explanation for not prosecuting at Stoke Mandeville is unconvincing, the statement it made in respect of Maidstone and Tunbridge Wells NHS Trust is more so.

It referred to lack of a causal link between management failings and the infection and deaths that were rampant within the hospital.[183] Yet some of the detail unearthed by the Healthcare Commission has been set out above in this chapter: the standards of care and system of work portrayed, including hygiene, were abysmal.

---

181 Health and Safety Executive. *HSE investigation into outbreaks of* Clostridium difficile *at Stoke Mandeville Hospital, Buckinghamshire Hospitals NHS Trust.* London: HSE, 2006, pp.14–15.

182 National Audit Office. *Improving patient care by reducing the risk of hospital acquired infection: a progress report.* London: NAO, 2004.

183 Health and Safety Executive. 'HSE and Kent Police decide not to investigate Maidstone and Tunbridge Wells NHS Trust.' *News*, 30 July 2010. Accessed on 5 August 2010 at: www.hse.gov.uk/press/2008/e08038.htm.

Taken at face value, the statement by the HSE betrays a misunderstanding of s.3 of the Health and Safety at Work Act 1974. This states that an employer must take reasonably practicable steps to ensure the health and safety of non-employees, amongst whom patients are numbered. *There is no requirement that harm be caused.*

Arguably, therefore, the HSE's statement about lack of a causal link between the failings and death of an individual patient is misconceived. The final sentence effectively dismisses the Healthcare Commission's report and findings because the Commission had explicitly found a veritable host of practices exacerbating the spread of infection.

It had identified a series of inadequacies in basic care given, or not given, to patients by nurses. Even if one concedes, according to the HSE's self-imposed policy of ignoring clinical issues, that eating and drinking and going to the toilet are 'clinical' (they are surely not), the HSE's approach does not add up. This is because, in addition, a shambolic system of work was glaringly exposed by the Commission, affecting the fabric of the environment, hospital equipment and patient safety.

The evidence for this conclusion included broken and worn equipment, furniture, fittings, dishwashers, showers, chair covers and curtains; dirty, rusty and leaking bedpan macerators; faulty bedpan washers leaving bedpans contaminated with faeces; shortages of commodes; over half of the commodes needing to be replaced; and overflowing sharps bins on the floors.[184] And these are but a few examples.

HSE PREPARED TO PROSECUTE IN INDIVIDUAL CASES, BUT NOT MULTIPLE CASES OF SYSTEMIC FAILINGS

What makes the absence of prosecution, in the above instances, even more notable is that the HSE is used to prosecuting for failures associated with equipment such as hoists and bed rails, *when individual patients meet with accidents.* It is therefore inexplicable that it should not have considered prosecuting for widespread failures in Kent – including those relating to equipment mentioned immediately above – which were clearly associated with infection that caused many deaths.

An example of this inconsistency came in June 2010. Basildon University Hospital Trust was convicted and fined for the death of a man with learning disabilities who had died with his head caught in bed rails. Essentially, this was because of a lack of systems to assess risk to particular patients on each ward.[185]

Similarly, when a care home resident fell from a worn and damaged sling being used on a hoist, the balancing mechanism of which was damaged. The HSE prosecuted on the basis of systemic failure covering equipment maintenance,

184 Healthcare Commission. *Investigation into outbreaks of* Clostridium difficile *at Maidstone and Tunbridge Wells NHS Trust, October 2007.* London: HC, 2007, pp.44–58.

185 Farmer, B. 'Basildon University Hospital trust fined £50,000 over patient's death.' *The Independent,* 8 June 2010.

training and supervision. Each of the two care home owners, prosecuted as an individual, was fined £50,000.[186]

The HSE also prosecuted a local council for not maintaining properly an air-conditioning system that led to deaths from infection at a leisure centre;[187] why, then, would it not prosecute for failure to maintain commodes and other equipment essential to hygiene and infection control in a hospital?

Similarly, University College London Hospitals NHS Trust was prosecuted successfully in 2002 after it failed to control the risk of injury or infection. It had left a sharps bin in a place accessible to the public, including a 21-month-old child.[188] If it will prosecute for one sharps bin, why not for a hospital in which over 50 per cent of commodes needed replacing, as was the case at Maidstone and Tunbridge Wells NHS Trust?

UNCONVINCING LINE BETWEEN CLINICAL AND NON-CLINICAL MATTERS

One further example anyway casts doubt on the claim that clinical matters are beyond the HSE's remit.

When two doctors were convicted of manslaughter for failing to diagnose and treat a fatal bacterial infection in a patient, Southampton University Hospitals NHS Trust pleaded guilty to inadequate management and supervision of the two doctors.[189] In other words, it was a defective system of clinical care. If the HSE could prosecute in this case, there is no reason it should not do so in numerous others described in this book.

Similarly, the Hertfordshire Partnership NHS Trust was fined nearly half a million pounds, after being convicted of breaching health and safety at work legislation, including s.3 of the Health and Safety at Work Act (duty to non-employees – i.e. the care workers in the care home). This followed the stabbing of a care worker at the residential home to which a mental health patient had been sent by the Trust. The breach in health and safety at work legislation was the failure to conduct a risk assessment – arguably, a clinical matter. The owner of the care home was also convicted for failing to ensure the safety of staff (s.2 of the Act) and fined £75,000 and told to pay costs of £388,000.[190]

In sum, one concludes that the HSE's hands-off approach to severe lapses of safety in the health service appears defensible in neither principle nor practice. Its self-imposed no-go areas might be justifiable if successful prosecutions were taking place at the hands of other enforcement bodies, such as the CQC or the Crown Prosecution Service. But they are not. In effect, then, it seems that the HSE has seen

---

186 'Pensioner suffered fatal fall from sling at nursing home.' *Safety and Health Practitioner*, 31 August 2012.

187 Hogg, D. 'Architect fined over deadly outbreak of disease.' *Yorkshire Post*, 1 August 2006.

188 Health and Safety Executive. *HSE successfully prosecutes University College London NHS Hospitals Trust.* Press release, 12 June 2002. London: HSE.

189 'Trust guilty over death doctors.' *BBC News*, 11 January 2006. Accessed on 7 September 2010 at: http://news.bbc.co.uk/1/hi/england/hampshire/4602228.stm.

190 Milligan, P. 'NHS trust fined £500,000 after female care worker was stabbed to death by dangerous bipolar patient "who never should have been sent to care home".' *Daily Mail*, 19 July 2012.

what is going on in the health service, doesn't like the look of the scale and political complexity of it all, and is now looking the other way.

It is perhaps time that all those involved in the safeguarding of vulnerable adults put some pressure on the HSE to act to protect vulnerable users of health and care services from systemic, institutional neglect.

OFFENCE OF CAUSING DEATH OF VULNERABLE ADULT

The Domestic Violence, Crime and Victims Act 2004 contains offences of causing or allowing the death of, or significant harm to, a vulnerable adult. In outline, it applies when, in summary:

- a vulnerable adult dies, or suffers significant harm, as a result of an unlawful act
- the person who committed the act was a member of the same household and had frequent contact with the victim
- the victim was at significant risk of serious physical harm by an unlawful act by such a member of the household
- the person either directly caused the victim's death or was or ought to have been aware of the risk, failed to take reasonable steps to protect the victim, and the act occurred in circumstances that the person foresaw or should have foreseen.

OFFENCE: COMMISSION OF THE ACT OR FAILURE TO PROTECT THE VICTIM

For the offence to be made out, the prosecution does not have to prove whether the person actually did the act or instead failed to protect the victim. The maximum sentence is 14 years' imprisonment in relation to death and 10 years' in relation to harm. The purpose of the offence is to overcome the problem of showing which of two perpetrators committed the act when, for example, each is blaming the other and the evidence is otherwise inconclusive.

WIDE DEFINITION OF MEMBER OF THE SAME HOUSEHOLD

A person could be classed as a member of the same household even if he or she does not live there but visits so often and for such periods of time that it would be reasonable to regard him or her as such a member.

DEFINITION OF VULNERABLE ADULT

A vulnerable adult means a person aged 16 or over whose ability to protect himself or herself from violence, abuse or neglect is significantly impaired through physical or mental disability or illness, through old age or otherwise.

REASON TO SUSPECT THAT VICTIM IS AT RISK REQUIRED

Guidance emphasises that no offence is committed under this Act if the harm or death is the result of an accident or natural causes.

It also points out that the existence of risk:

> is likely to be demonstrated by a history of violence towards the vulnerable person, or towards others in the household. The extended offence will not apply if there was no previous history of abuse, nor any reason to suspect a risk. Where there is no reason to suspect the victim is at risk, other members of the household cannot reasonably be expected to have taken steps to prevent the abuse.[191]

REASONABLE STEPS TAKEN TO PROTECT THE VICTIM

The Act states that it is a question of whether the relevant member of the household took reasonable steps to protect the victim. Guidance deals with the question of what those steps might be, particularly in relation to perpetrators who are themselves vulnerable:

> The definition of 'vulnerable adult' in section 5(6) of the 2004 Act applies to the *victim* of an offence but it is possible that *defendants* may be vulnerable for similar reasons. The 2005 circular specifically addresses the situation where defendants charged with the causing or allowing death offence are themselves victims of domestic violence and the issues relevant to the investigation of offences in such cases and these still apply.
>
> The same principles apply equally to the causing or allowing serious physical harm offence and to defendants who are vulnerable for other reasons. So, for example, the steps that someone with a learning disability could reasonably have been expected to take to protect a child or vulnerable adult from a foreseeable risk of serious physical harm may be more limited than the steps that someone without a learning disability could reasonably have been expected to take.
>
> For the avoidance of doubt, there is no question of defendants being deemed to have 'allowed' a child or vulnerable adult to die or suffer serious physical harm simply by living in the same household. As indicated in paragraph 10, the 'allowing' part of the offence has a high threshold.[192]

VULNERABILITY OF VICTIM ESSENTIAL FOR PROSECUTION AND CONVICTION

In 2008, the first reported conviction under the Act was as follows.

---

191 Ministry of Justice. *Domestic Violence, Crime and Victims (Amendment) Act 2012.* Circular 2012/03. London: MoJ, 2012, para 27.

192 Ministry of Justice. *Domestic Violence, Crime and Victims (Amendment) Act 2012.* Circular 2012/03. London: MoJ, 2012, paras 13–14.

Wife systematically beaten and abused by husband for months: four family members also convicted for doing nothing. A 19-year-old woman was systematically beaten and abused by her husband for three months. When she died, she had 15 broken ribs and bruising over 85 per cent of her body. Her husband was convicted of murder; however, his mother, two sisters and brother-in-law were all found guilty of allowing the death of a vulnerable adult. The Crown Prosecution Service commented that the family had chosen to do nothing and that if 'families or other people with a duty to look after those who need protection deliberately choose not to do so, their neglect will not be ignored by the law enforcement agencies, and prosecution will follow'.[193]

In this last case, those family members convicted under the Act appealed, arguing that the dead woman was not vulnerable within the meaning of the Act. The Court of Appeal dismissed this argument, pointing out that even a person who is physically young and fit can be vulnerable under the Act.

Vulnerability for the purposes of the Act. An 'adult who is utterly dependent on others, even if physically young and apparently fit, may fall within the protective ambit of the Act'. Thus, a major attack on the woman had occurred three weeks earlier; from that point on, she was vulnerable within the meaning of the legislation. The court noted that, in some circumstances, such a person might come within the Act even before the infliction of violent injuries if she or he was exposed to a serious risk of physical harm prior to such an attack.[194]

VULNERABLE ADULT UNDER THE 2004 ACT, BUT NOT UNDER SOCIAL SERVICES LEGISLATION

In 2010, three members of a family, with whom the victim had lived for many years, were convicted of the murder of Michael Gilbert. Four other members of the family were sentenced for 'familial homicide', referring to the offence of causing or allowing the death of a vulnerable adult under the 2004 Act.[195]

Details recounted by the court of what had occurred before his death and the finding of his headless body in a lake included the following.

Background to offences. The victim met one of the family at a children's home when they were in care and were about 15 years old. He was introduced to the rest of the family and began to live with them. He was a vulnerable adult who had been homeless for part of his life and was estranged from his own family.

Ingredients of offences. He was kept effectively as a slave. He was seriously assaulted and abused for entertainment on a fairly regular basis over a ten-year period. This included being beaten with fists and with weapons, including a baseball bat. He was pulled around by mole grips attached to his testicles. He would be made to stand in water hot enough to blister his feet for weeks. Snooker balls would be dropped on his genitals from a height. His benefit money would be confiscated.

If he managed to get away from the home, he was forcibly brought back. Some of the beatings were recorded on mobile telephones. All members of the household knew of the situation. Most took part in the abuse. None took any action to prevent the escalating

---

193 Jenkins, R. 'Women face prison for ignoring a murder under their own roof.' *The Times*, 6 February 2008.

194 *R v Khan* [2009] EWCA Crim 2.

195 '"Depraved" family sentenced for killing of man kept as a slave.' *Daily Telegraph*, 26 April 2010.

abuse. On occasions, the victim was handcuffed to a bed wearing only nightclothes in order to ensure that he did not escape.

After October 2008, the abuse got worse. It included actions such as doing press-ups on a piece of wood placed in his mouth and jumping on his stomach. In January, the victim had become doubly incontinent and his stomach was very badly swollen. He was complaining of stomach pains and asking for medicine. He could hardly walk.

As the month progressed, he was still alive but had suffered beating upon beating and was gravely ill. He was lying on a deflated blow-up bed. He had defecated and urinated where he lay. His stomach looked more swollen than before. He requested and was given medication. He could just about speak. They left him where he lay. He died that evening.[196]

The court was in no doubt that he was a vulnerable adult for the purposes of conviction under the Act; however, the local authority concerned had concluded previously that he was not a vulnerable adult under the community care legislation and therefore was not eligible for assistance from social services.

This was despite the fact that, as a child, he had been in the care of the local authority in a children's home. And that to professionals he was known at various times as:

> an alleged child sex offender, a care-leaver, homeless, a glue sniffer, a user of cannabis, an associate of criminals and responsible himself for crimes against the person, against property and crimes of theft, long term unemployed and latterly, as experiencing auditory hallucinations.[197]

DOMESTIC HOMICIDE REVIEWS

Under s.9 of the Act, there is a duty to carry out domestic homicide reviews.

The duty is triggered on the death of a person aged 16 or over which has, or appears to have, resulted from violence, abuse or neglect by (a) a person to whom he or she was related or with whom he or she was or had been in an intimate personal relationship, or (b) a member of the same household as him- or herself.

The review is held with a view to learning lessons. Relevant agencies for such reviews are the police, local authority, strategic health authorities (in future the NHS Commissioning Board), primary care trusts (in future Commissioning Consortia Groups) and the probation service.

Statutory guidance states that the ultimate responsibility for convening a review rests with the local community safety partnership and also sets out in detail how such reviews should proceed, disclosure issues and parallel criminal proceedings.[198]

SLAVERY AND SERVITUDE: CORONERS ACT 2009

The Coroners Act 2009, section 71, contains offences concerning slavery or servitude and also of forced compulsory labour.

---

196 *R v Watt* [2011] EWCA Crim 1325.

197 Flynn, M. *The murder of Adult A (Michael Gilbert): a serious case review.* Luton: Luton Safeguarding Adults Board, 2011, pp.3, 13.

198 Home Office. *Multi-agency statutory guidance for the conduct of domestic homicide reviews.* London: HO, 2011.

The first offence consists of the perpetrator holding a person in slavery or servitude. The second is that the perpetrator requires a person to perform forced or compulsory labour.

For both offences to be made out, the perpetrator must either have known, or ought to have known, what was going on.

The references to slavery, servitude, forced or compulsory labour must be interpreted in accordance with article 4 of the European Convention on Human Rights, which prohibits these things. There is a maximum sentence of 14 years in prison.

TRAVELLERS CONVICTED UNDER THE ACT FOR TREATMENT OF LABOURERS

In 2012, four members of a group of travellers were found guilty under this Act for how they treated labourers. Of the 23 men found at the site, 13 cooperated with police in a vast investigation that was seen as a test case in the use of this new anti-slavery legislation.

Labourers kept on travellers' sites. The labourers lived at the travellers' sites and were paid little or nothing, working six days a week and doing door-to-door selling on Sundays. They might get one meal a day. One of the labourers lived, dirty and frightened, in a shed, with barely enough room to walk. There was no lavatory on one site, and he had to shower at a local leisure centre. The intervals between showers sometimes stretched to months rather than days. Sometimes, he did not get even one meal a day. He could not visit local shops without permission. Over 15 years, he had been paid £80. He was sometimes punched, was attacked with a broom handle and scratched.

During a 13-week trial, the court heard that vulnerable men – many of them homeless, addicted to alcohol or drugs – were recruited in soup kitchens and outside dole offices and promised cash payments for manual labour. Once in the family's grip, however, they were forced to work up to 19 hours a day for no pay while being routinely abused, underfed and housed in filthy sheds and horseboxes.

A pre-dawn raid in September released 23 men from a caravan site, in a significant operation involving armed police, sniffer dogs and helicopter support, when a worker contacted officers after fleeing the site.

State of site and living quarters. The site, a mixture of pristine chalets and smaller caravans sitting on well-kept paved yards, was the scene of abuse and exploitation, according to police. Destitute men were picked up and made to perform manual labour such as tarmacking and laying paving stones, and menial tasks such as cleaning their bosses' homes.

When police found them, they were living in sheds that were 'unfit for human habitation' with no heating. One picture of the sheds in which the men lived showed a sheet covered in human excrement, with discarded budget food wrappers littering the floor.

The prosecution argued that:

> They were controlled in such a way that in many cases they could not see it. They became conditioned to do what the defendants wanted. The reason for their

exploitation was money. They may not in the strict sense have been slaves, members of the jury, but the prosecution say this: they were not free men.[199]

ENDANGERING LIFE BY WILFUL NEGLIGENCE

When elderly residents in a care home in Clacton were forced to drink vast amounts of liquids by the owner, who was obsessed with avoiding dehydration in residents, two of them died. It was reported that the owner was given a suspended 15-month prison sentence under a common law offence not used for 200 years: endangering human life or health by wilful negligence.[200]

---

199 Ward, V. 'Travellers recruited slaves for "concentration camp".' *Daily Telegraph*, 19 April 2012. And: Topping, A. 'Four found guilty of forcing vulnerable men into servitude.' *The Guardian*, 12 July 2012.
200 Horsnell, M. 'Fluids force fed to elderly in care.' *The Times*, 20 October 2001.

22

Sexual offences

KEY POINTS

The Sexual Offences Act 2003 reformed the law on sexual offences.

In relation to adult protection, there are, in addition to the basic offences (rape, sexual assault, etc.), a number of offences specifically related to victims with a mental disorder, with special rules attached. Of particular note is that, of three sets of offences concerning victims with a mental disorder, two do not require that the victim lacked capacity to consent to the sexual activity.

OVERVIEW OF OFFENCES

The general offences are, of course, relevant to vulnerable adults.

RAPE

These general offences include rape which consists of (a) intentional penetration of vagina, anus or mouth of the victim with the penis, (b) lack of consent, and (c) the perpetrator does not reasonably believe that the victim consents.[1]

The question of whether the perpetrator reasonably knows whether the victim is consenting – in the case of alleged rape, for example – may, however, not be straightforward in the case of a vulnerable adult who is the perpetrator.

---

1   Sexual Offences Act 2003, s.1.

For instance, when a man was convicted of rape and indecent assault on his estranged wife, a successful appeal was made. This was on the basis that the evidence of a consultant forensic psychiatrist showed that he suffered from Asperger's syndrome which would affect his ability adequately to determine somebody else's intentions and desires or to understand their wishes. This was relevant to the question of *mens rea* (the guilty mind), to the jury's view of the honesty of his evidence about what he believed to have been the situation and to why he had behaved so oddly during the trial. A retrial was ordered.[2]

ASSAULT OR CAUSING SEXUAL ACTIVITY WITHOUT CONSENT

Assault by penetration consists of (a) intentional penetration of the vagina or anus with a part of the perpetrator's body or with anything else, (b) the penetration being sexual, (c) lack of consent, and (d) the perpetrator does not reasonably believe that the victim consents.[3]

Sexual assault consists of (a) intentional touching of another person, (b) the touching being sexual, (c) lack of consent, and (d) the perpetrator does not reasonably believe that the victim consents (s.3).[4]

Causing sexual activity without consent consists of (a) intentional causing of another person to engage in an activity, (b) the activity being sexual, (c) lack of consent, and (d) the perpetrator does not reasonably believe that the victim consents (s.4).[5]

SEXUAL OFFENCES, MENTAL DISORDER AND INABILITY TO REFUSE

In addition are a number of offences specifically related to the situation where the victim suffers from mental disorder. Mental disorder bears the same meaning as in s.1 of the Mental Health Act 1983.

Sections 30–33 of the 2003 Act contain certain offences that rely on the victim being unable, because of his or her mental disorder or for a reason related to it, to refuse the sexual activity.

The offences are (a) sexual activity with a mentally disordered person, (b) causing or inciting a person with a mental disorder to engage in sexual activity, (c) engaging in sexual activity in the presence of a person with a mental disorder for the purpose of sexual gratification of the perpetrator, and (d) causing a person with a mental disorder to watch a sexual act for the purpose of sexual gratification of the perpetrator.

For the purposes of ss.30 and 31, the sexual activity constituting an offence is defined as touching involving (a) penetration of the victim's anus or vagina with a

---

2   *R v TS* [2008] EWCA Crim 6.
3   Sexual Offences Act 2003, s.2.
4   Sexual Offences Act 2003, s.3.
5   Sexual Offences Act 2003, s.4.

part of the perpetrator's body or anything else, (b) penetration of the victim's mouth with the perpetrator's penis, (c) penetration of the perpetrator's anus or vagina with a part of the victim's body, or (d) penetration of the perpetrator's mouth with the victim's penis.

INABILITY TO REFUSE (i.e. LACK OF MENTAL CAPACITY) OR TO COMMUNICATE CHOICE

The inability to refuse must be because either (a) the victim 'lacks the capacity to choose whether to agree to the touching (whether because he lacks sufficient understanding of the nature or reasonably foreseeable consequences of what is being done, or for any other reason), or (b) is unable to communicate such a choice'.[6]

In the following case, the victim probably understood about sex and had the capacity to refuse, but was unable to communicate her choice.

Inability to communicate choice. The victim lived in a public house with her parents. She was 27 years old (but had a much lower developmental age) and had cerebral palsy. A 73-year-old man, of previous good character, allegedly touched her over her clothing in the area of her vagina, whilst exposing himself and placing her hand on his soft penis. The defence accepted that the woman suffered from a mental disorder but argued that she did not lack the capacity to agree to the touching.

The magistrates' court had accepted that she understood the nature of sexual relations but did not have the capacity to understand that she could refuse. The High Court took this reasoning to mean that, whilst she might have understood about sexual activity, she was unable to communicate her choice.[7]

In a more recent case, the 25-year-old victim was literally unable to refuse because a feature of her extreme autism was that she did whatever she was asked. She had the communication skills of a three-year-old. A 77-year-old retired bus driver saw her at a bus stop and went round to her home for sex. She was so distressed at what had happened that she gave up living independently. He was sentenced to nine and a half years in prison. He claimed that he could not reasonably have known about her mental disorder; this claim was rejected.[8]

PERPETRATOR KNOWING, OR REASONABLY EXPECTED TO KNOW, OF MENTAL DISORDER

The offences under sections 30–33 of the Act also rely on the perpetrator knowing, or reasonably being expected to know, of the mental disorder, and that because of it, or a reason related to it, the person was likely to have been unable to refuse. For example:

Sexual activity involving a mentally disordered woman. A neighbour took advantage, on a number of occasions, of a 20-year-old woman with severe learning disabilities who lived with her parents. This took place first at the neighbour's house, to

---

6   Sexual Offences Act 2003, ss.31–33.
7   *Hulme v Director of Public Prosecutions* [2006] EWHC 1347 (Admin).
8   'Sex offender jailed for nine years.' *North Devon Journal*, 10 May 2012.

which the woman had gone invited, and then elsewhere (social club and a lay-by). He was convicted under s.30 of the Sexual Offences Act 2003 and sentenced to four years in prison, increased to five and a half years.[9]

Likewise, in the following case, the perpetrator should reasonably have known that the victim was unlikely to have been able to refuse.

Sentence for touching partner's granddaughter. The 74-year-old defendant lived with the victim's grandmother. The victim was in her twenties, but with a mental age of between four and eight years old. The defendant's partner found him with his hand down the front of the victim's trousers. No digital penetration took place. He ultimately pleaded guilty and accepted that he had closed his mind to the reasonable expectation that, by reason of her mental disorder, the victim was likely to be unable to refuse the sexual touching.

He had been cautioned four years before for sexual touching of the same victim. He was now sentenced, under s.30 of the Sexual Offences Act, to three years and nine months in prison (12 months custodial, the rest an extended sentence). On appeal, taking account of his age, medical condition and all the circumstances of the offence, the court reduced the custodial element from 12 to six months.[10]

(Under s.227 of the Criminal Justice Act 2003, an extended sentence consists of a custodial element and a period for which the offender is subject to a licence.)

TEST FOR CAPACITY – AND PUBLIC INTEREST AS TO WHETHER TO PROSECUTE

It has been pointed out above in Chapter 13 that, under the Mental Capacity Act, the courts have run into difficulties in identifying the right test of capacity for sexual activity, and also the management of problems resulting from such difficulties.[11]

It has been suggested that the following case, albeit in the criminal sphere, touches on such matters, not least because of the lower sentence given for what was, on its face, a serious offence under s.30 of the Sexual Offences Act. Questions of capacity and degree of criminal responsibility arise.

It is also a notable case because, under the Mental Capacity Act, the courts have been confined largely to considering sexual activity involving younger adults with learning disabilities. Whereas the following case revolved around a care home for older people. For that reason, it is worth setting out the facts in a little detail.

Perpetrator, the 'chocolate man', regular visitor to care home to visit wife. The appellant's wife suffered from Huntington's disease and was a long-time resident at a care home where he visited her on virtually a daily basis. As she could not communicate with him, he frequently visited other residents at the home and gained a reputation as the 'chocolate man' because he often gave residents chocolate mints.

Victim: pattern of sexual behaviour and other disinhibited behaviour. The 57-year-old victim, BG, had been a resident at the home since 2000. She had suffered a severe stroke in 1999 which had left her with significant cognitive difficulties and unable to care for herself. She had been left with poor vision, little capacity for short-term memory

---

9   *R v Charles* [2007] EWCA Crim 2266.
10   *R v D* [2005] EWCA Crim 1459.
11   *D Borough Council v AB* [2011] EWHC 101 (COP).

and only patchy long-term memory. She was unable to care for her basic needs without prompting and was generally apathetic, lacking in initiative and incapable of even asking for a glass of water.

If she was left alone, she would drift off to sleep and she could not hold full conversations with people but restricted her answers to 'yes' and 'no'. Over her years at the home, BG had displayed both sexual and non-sexual disinhibited behaviour, although there was no evidence that the appellant knew of this. Her behaviour had been managed through a behavioural management programme, but she was not someone who was able to decide whether or not to take part in a physical relationship with someone.

On 18 August 2008, the appellant visited his wife at the home. He was seen by two care assistants sitting with BG in the residents' lounge. It was noticed that her dress was up over her knees and he was rubbing her vagina through her underwear. A few minutes later, he was seen to be holding her hand and rubbing her right breast. The two care assistants noted that both the appellant and BG appeared to be smiling. They reported the matter to the manager who informed the police, and on 20 August 2008 the appellant was arrested.

Perpetrator claims victim was consenting. When he was interviewed under caution, he confirmed the observations of the care assistant. He added that such activity with BG had first occurred a few weeks earlier, that he had rubbed her breasts on three or four occasions and had inserted his finger into her vagina twice. On each occasion, he stated that he held his hand and put it against her breast or vagina, thus initiating the activity. He insisted that she had her own mind and was capable of refusing anything if she wanted to.[12]

The judge found plentiful evidence that the woman lacked capacity to consent and that the perpetrator should reasonably have known this, and not only found him guilty but also concluded that he posed a high risk to vulnerable females.

Section 30(1) of the Act provided for a sentencing range of between eight and 13 years. Yet the judge departed from this range, arriving at a sentence of four years. The Court of Appeal subsequently reduced this still further to three years. It noted the grey area surrounding the line of criminality which the man had crossed:

We return to the basis of plea because the sentence had to reflect it. On that basis of plea there is force in the submission…that this was a case of ostensible consent, where the defendant's criminality arose out of his lack of judgment in acquiescing to the victim's request. He submitted there was no evidence that the defendant had planned the activity, nor that the victim had suffered mentally or physically as a result of that activity. The care home had in earlier years allowed the victim to behave in this way with others, and the records made it plain that she made sexual demands from time to time of those around her.

The appellant was 62 years old at the time of the offences. He was a man of previous good character. There were many witnesses (18 in all) who wrote of his devotion to his wife and to his two daughters, whose childhood was blighted by their mother's condition, of his exemplary employment record and of his standing in the community.[13]

12   Bartlett, P. 'Sex, dementia, capacity and care homes.' *Liverpool Law Review 31*, 2010, 137–154.
13   *R v Adcock* [2010] EWCA Crim 700.

Guidance published by the Crown Prosecution Service states of offences under the Sexual Offences Act 2003:

> A prosecution will usually take place unless there are public interest factors tending against prosecution which outweigh those tending in favour. Rape is so serious that a prosecution is almost certainly required in the public interest.[14]

Given the ambiguities and complications around sex and capacity, it has been suggested that the CPS should produce further guidance, indicating factors that would tend to lead to prosecution and factors that, in the public interest, would not. Such guidance would be similar to that produced for assisted suicide prosecutions.[15]

For example, it has been asked whether it is in the public interest to prosecute if a man visits his wife in a care home, they have had a long and happy marriage, his wife enjoys sexual activity that now takes place – but she now lacks capacity. Should the husband be treated as a criminal and sent to prison?[16]

CAPACITY, IRRATIONAL FEARS AND INABILITY TO COMMUNICATE

The House of Lords (now the Supreme Court) considered the following questions about an offence under s.30, in these circumstances.

Inability to communicate because of fear. A woman with serious mental health problems was effectively picked up on the streets and taken advantage of. The defendant took her to a friend's house, sold her mobile phone and bicycle, gave her crack cocaine and then asked her to give him a 'blow job'. She gave evidence that she was in a panic and afraid of what else they might do to her; so she stayed and just went along with it.[17]

The first question was whether a lack of capacity to choose was person- and situation-specific. The answer was yes:

> Once it is accepted that choice is an exercise of free will, and that mental disorder may rob a person of free will in a number of different ways and in a number of different situations, then a mentally disordered person may be quite capable of exercising choice in one situation but not in another.[18]

The second was whether an irrational fear, preventing the exercise of choice, equated to lack of capacity to choose; the answer to this was also yes. The question was whether it did so in the particular situation. The jury had been entitled to decide that it did.[19]

Third was whether the inability to communicate a choice could stem only from a person's *physical* inability related to the mental disorder (and not, for example,

---

14   Crown Prosecution Service. *Sexual Offences Act 2003: legal guidance.* London: CPS, 2010.
15   Bartlett, P. 'Sex, dementia, capacity and care homes.' *Liverpool Law Review 31*, 2010, 137–154.
16   Bartlett, P. 'Sex, dementia, capacity and care homes.' *Liverpool Law Review 31*, 2010, 137–154.
17   *R v C* [2009] UKHL 42.
18   *R v C* [2009] UKHL 42.
19   *R v C* [2009] UKHL 42.

from an irrational fear). The answer was no: an irrational fear could rob a person of the ability to choose or to communicate that choice.[20]

CHARGE OF RAPE OR OF SPECIAL OFFENCE AGAINST VICTIM WITH MENTAL DISORDER

The courts have considered when an offence should be prosecuted as rape rather than as an offence against a victim with mental disorder. In the House of Lords case *R v C* (summarised above), the court decided as follows.

In short, one judge stated that it should be rape if (a) a victim has capacity to choose whether to agree to the sexual activity, (b) she chooses not to consent, (c) she is unable to communicate this because of a physical disability, and (d) the perpetrator does not reasonably believe that she consents.

On the other hand, if, in such circumstances, the inability to communicate is related to the mental disorder, then the special offences relating to a victim with a mental disorder apply.

Another judge in the same case provided a more detailed response and felt that, in the circumstances, three different charges would have been possible. The first was rape which would have required the perpetrator not reasonably believing that the woman was consenting.

The second was a charge under s.30 (the actual charge) which required that the perpetrator knew, or could reasonably have been expected to know, that the person had a mental disorder and would be unlikely to be able to refuse. This puts a greater burden of restraint on the perpetrator because the rape test is about the actual consent of the other person, whereas the s.30 offence is about whether there was an inability to refuse.[21]

The third would have been an offence of inducement or threat (see below) which would not have had to rely at all on matters of consent or ability to choose.

It is worth quoting the relevant passage.

Appropriate criminal charge: rape, sexual activity without consent of person with mental disorder, or sexual activity through inducement or threat to person with mental disorder. The judge dealt with each question in turn.

Mental disorder offence easier to prove than rape. She stated first that:

> We are told that the defendants were originally charged with rape, but that charges under section 30 were substituted at a late stage. The view may have been taken that the offence under section 30 is somewhat easier to prove. The prosecution has only to prove the inability to refuse rather than that the complainant actually did not consent.
>
> This may not make much difference (although the Law Commission apparently thought that it did), given that both offences relate to a specific sexual act, and the Act provides that 'a person consents if he agrees by choice, and has the freedom and capacity to make that choice'...

---

20   *R v C* [2009] UKHL 42.
21   *R v C* [2009] UKHL 42.

But the *mens rea* under section 30 is that the defendant knows or could reasonably be expected to know that the complainant has a mental disorder and that because of it or for a reason related to it she is likely to be unable to refuse…

Greater burden on accused by charging mental disorder offence. She pointed out the different burden on the accused:

The *mens rea* for rape is that the defendant does not reasonably believe that the complainant consents… This puts a greater burden of restraint upon people who know or ought to know that a person's mental disorder is likely to affect her ability to choose. This may explain why the decision was made to charge the section 30 offence in this case.

Inducement, threat or deception. She was uncertain why the charge of inducement or threat was not used:

Less easy to understand is why the offence under section 34 was not charged in the alternative. This involves the same range of sexual acts as does the offence under section 30 and attracts the same levels of punishment. It covers intentional sexual touching with the agreement of the person touched…where the defendant has obtained that agreement by means of an inducement offered or given, a threat made or a deception practised for that purpose…and the defendant knows or could reasonably be expected to know that the complainant has a mental disorder…

Perhaps the view was taken that the evidence of lack of capacity was more robust than the evidence of any inducement, threat or deception. This is pure speculation. But the alternative charges would have enabled the judge to explain the various concepts by distinguishing them from one another and relating them to the evidence: a lack of consent arising from the lack of either the freedom or the capacity to make that choice; a lack of capacity to make that choice arising from or related to a mental disorder; and a choice procured by threats, inducement or deception of a person with a mental disorder.[22]

SEXUAL OFFENCES: INDUCEMENT, THREAT OR DECEPTION

A further number of offences, under sections 34–37 of the Act, do not require an inability to refuse on the part of the mentally disordered victim. In other words, these offences don't demand that the victim lack capacity to decide. However, they do still require the perpetrator to know, or reasonably be expected to know, that the victim has a mental disorder.

These offences concern inducement, threat or deception to (a) procure sexual activity with a person with a mental disorder; (b) cause a person with a mental disorder to engage in sexual activity by inducement, threat or deception; (c) engage in sexual activity in the presence, procured by inducement, threat or deception, of a person with a mental disorder; or (d) cause a person with a mental disorder to watch a sexual act by inducement, threat or deception.[23]

Explanatory notes accompanying the Act state that the purpose of these offences is to criminalise the exploitation of a person with a mental disorder who may have

22   *R v C* [2009] UKHL 42.
23   Sexual Offences Act 2003, ss.34–37.

capacity but who is vulnerable to exploitation. For instance, such a person may engage in sexual activity in return for a packet of sweets.[24]

SEXUAL OFFENCES, MENTAL DISORDER AND CARE WORKERS

A third set of offences, under ss.38–41 of the Act, applies in the context of care workers and mentally disordered people.

The offences also do not rely on lack of capacity of the victim to decide. In effect, consent or the absence of it is immaterial. The perpetrator must have known or reasonably be expected to have known that the victim had a mental disorder. However, if it is proved that the victim has a mental disorder, then it is assumed that the care worker knew or should reasonably have known this, unless sufficient evidence is led to question such an assumption.

The offences apply to a care worker, in summary:

- engaging in sexual activity with a person with a mental disorder

- causing or inciting sexual activity

- engaging in sexual activity in the presence of a person with a mental disorder

- causing a person with a mental disorder to watch a sexual act.

A care worker is defined as somebody having functions in the course of his or her employment that brings, or is likely to bring, him or her into regular face-to-face contact with the mentally disordered person.

These include (a) in a care home or (b) in the context of the provision of services by the NHS or an independent medical agency or in an independent hospital or clinic. Alternatively, whether or not employed to do so, the perpetrator provides care, assistance or services to the victim in connection with the victim's mental disorder and so has, or is likely to have, regular face-to-face contact with the victim.[25]

EXCEPTIONS TO CARE WORKER RULE: MARRIAGE OR PRIOR RELATIONSHIP

The care worker offences do not apply where (a) the mentally disordered person is 16 years old or more and is lawfully married to the care worker, or (b) a sexual relationship existed between the mentally disordered person and the other person, immediately before the latter became involved in the care of the mentally disordered person.[26] These exceptions would cover, for instance, one partner or spouse now providing care at home for the other who has become mentally disordered during the relationship.

EXAMPLES OF CARE WORKER CONVICTIONS

An example of a conviction of a social worker under these provisions was as follows.

---

24 Sexual Offences Act 2003, explanatory notes, para 67.

25 Sexual Offences Act 2003, s.42.

26 Sexual Offences Act 2003, ss.43–44.

Conviction for sexual activity with mentally disordered service user. A senior social worker (approved under the Mental Health Act) was helping a service user suffering from a mental disorder, depression. Her depression was rooted in postnatal depression. She suffered from low self-esteem. A more intimate relationship developed; she felt sexually attracted to him but could not believe he would be interested in her. They started to touch. She became more and more dependent on him, to the point of obsession. She was still vulnerable, suffering panic attacks and inflicting a degree of self-harm if he did not ring her. He suggested she have a break in a residential home; he visited her there and sexual intercourse took place. She subsequently told the pastoral director at the home. When accused, the social worker denied it, even when forensic examination of a towel showed semen stains.

In passing sentence, the judge characterised the offence as extremely serious. He said that it had devastated the victim, an extremely vulnerable woman who had been in the social worker's care. The fact that she was willing was irrelevant to the sentence. Supporting statements in mitigation showed the social worker was a good husband and father, and a good professional. There was a moving letter from his wife (although, by the time of the appeal, she had withdrawn this support and left the marital home with the children). The judge sentenced the social worker to 17 months in prison; this sentence was upheld on appeal.[27]

Similar was the conviction of a senior mental health worker for the Cornwall Partnership NHS Foundation Trust. He had fallen in love with a patient 20 years younger than him and had a sexual relationship with the woman, who had a borderline personality disorder and was mentally unstable. It was a consensual relationship. He was nonetheless convicted under s.38 of the Act, sentenced to prison for 16 months, received an indefinite sexual offences prevention and had to sign the sex offenders register for ten years.

The judge explained why the offence was serious.

Seriousness of abuse of professional position of trust: irrelevant whether love involved.

> You were her principal carer and for you to become involved was not only totally unprofessional but was an abuse of your professional position and the integrity of the mental health service provided in this county. You were a figure of authority and whether or not you loved her you took advantage of her to have a relationship and she has suffered the consequences. There is no alternative to immediate custody to show the public abhorrence of what you did and the grave breach of trust you committed.[28]

In the following case, a heavy sentence was imposed on a care worker, even though he had significant learning disabilities and was working on his own in a care home.

Care worker convicted for incident in care home. The victim was a 76-year-old woman with severe dementia, resident in a care home. One evening, contrary to policy and rules, a 22-year-old care worker, who had significant learning disabilities, was working on his own. He claimed that he had been left on his own and he took the woman to her bedroom

---

27   *R v Bradford* [2006] EWCA Crim 2629.
28   'Married carer "fell in love" with mentally ill woman.' *West Briton*, 5 April 2012.

to put her to bed. Shortly after, he activated the emergency alarm and the woman was taken to hospital for emergency surgery for tears to her perineum. There was grave risk of serious injury or even death. The evidence was that the injuries had been caused by a penis or penis-size object. He was convicted under s.38 of the Sexual Offences Act 2003 and, on appeal, sentenced to seven years' imprisonment.[29]

A nurse was convicted under the care worker sections of the Sexual Offences Act after having a sexual relationship with a 16-year-old boy at a secure mental health unit.[30]

Other examples of care workers convicted under the 2003 Act (the reports do not explicitly mention which section of the Act conviction was achieved under) include the following.

Sexual assault on care home resident. A sentence of eight years in prison was given to a care worker convicted of sexual assault on an 82-year-old care home resident with dementia, in whose room he was discovered partially clothed. The woman herself was unable, because of her dementia, to give any details of what had happened. The man was also put on the sex offenders register and made subject of a sexual offences prevention order, which barred him taking employment as a care worker. He was a man of hitherto good character, a family man and with a child on the way.[31]

Attempted rape of care home resident. A care home assistant was imprisoned for over five years after attempting to rape an 84-year-old care home resident. He was supposed to be checking on residents in the early hours of the morning. He climbed on top of her but was unaware that a 'wandering' alarm had recently been installed. He had been a school teacher in Poland, where his disabled wife and family still lived, before coming to work in England. He was ashamed and could not explain the offence, only that he missed his wife. He was placed on the sex offenders register for life.[32]

Assault on two women with learning disabilities. A man who sexually assaulted two women with learning disabilities, one on a park bench, one in a garden, had to sign the sex offenders register for five years, was given a three-year community order and ordered to attend a sex offenders treatment programme. But he was not sent to prison because the perpetrator himself had learning disabilities and mental health problems.[33]

Another case didn't involve a care worker but the 73-year-old caretaker of a care home. He was convicted of sexually abusing three elderly residents with dementia (probably under s.30 of the Sexual Offences Act) and sentenced to 12 years in prison.[34]

29 *R v Jones* [2009] EWCA Crim 237.
30 'Married nurse, 52, had sexual relationship with mentally-ill 16-year-old boy in secure unit.' *Daily Mail*, 11 July 2012.
31 'Disgraced Norwich care worker jailed for eight years.' *Eastern Daily Press*, 6 September 2011.
32 'Jail for rape of care home resident.' *Yorkshire Evening Post*, 18 October 2011.
33 'Sex attacker targeted women with learning difficulties.' *Hull Daily Mail*, 16 November 2011.
34 'Pensioner jailed for sexually abusing dementia sufferers.' *Dartford Messenger*, 29 February 2012.

SEX OFFENDERS REGISTER

Conviction for a sexual offence may lead to a person being placed on the sex offenders register under s.80 and schedule 3 of the Act. Such registration means that the offender becomes subject to notification requirements (a duty to register with the police) under the Act.

Notification periods vary depending on the offence and how it is dealt with by the courts. Indefinite notification, without the possibility of review, was held by the courts to be incompatible with human rights.[35]

Consequently, the Sexual Offences Act 2003 (Remedial) Order 2012 provides for offenders to seek a review after 15 years (or eight years in the case of juveniles). Application is first made to the police and then to a magistrate if the police refuse.

SEXUAL OFFENCES PREVENTION ORDER

A sexual offences prevention order can be made either at the time of conviction or, on application by the police, after conviction, if it is necessary to protect the public from serious sexual harm by the offender. The order can be wide-ranging in terms of prohibitions placed on the person. It must be for a minimum of five years.[36]

---

35   *R(F and Thompson) v Secretary of State for the Home Department* [2010] UKSC 17.
36   Sexual Offences Act 2003, ss.104–109.

Financial harm and abuse: criminal offences

KEY POINTS

Financial abuse of vulnerable adults is perceived to be a serious and widespread problem.

It might involve a range of individual people in positions of trust, including close family members, friends, neighbours, informal and paid carers, nurses, social services staff, solicitors and the clergy. Action on Elder Abuse believes that financial abuse in families is significant and that 'middle-aged sons and daughters are the people most likely to rob older people of their cash, valuables and even their homes'.[1]

In criminal law, financial abuse may be tantamount to various offences, including theft, burglary, robbery, fraud, false accounting and forgery. The number

---

1   Action on Elder Abuse. £Millions stolen, defrauded or conned from older people by their own sons and daughters each year. News release, 30 January 2007. London: Action on Elder Abuse.

of convictions involving financial abuse, both by carers and other professionals in positions of trust, might suggest that the problem is more than trivial. It is tempting to conclude from these cases that financial abuse on a smaller or larger scale is regarded by some as a perquisite of the job of caring for or handling the financial affairs of vulnerable older or disabled adults.

In addition, difficult to deal with, both legally and practically, is what has become known as 'cold calling', whereby vulnerable people are tricked or pressurised into parting with sometimes large sums of money in return for little or no work carried out by dishonest or simply bogus tradespersons.

Civil legal cases concerning property and money – involving, for example, negligence, contract law or undue influence – are about getting the property back. Criminal cases primarily are about guilt, conviction and sentencing. However, following conviction for a criminal offence, the court can, for example, make compensation orders under s.130 of the Powers of the Criminal Courts (Sentencing) Act 2000. Confiscation orders can also be made under the Proceeds of Crime Act 2002.

This chapter outlines some of the relevant law, illustrating it with various examples to bring home just how vulnerable some people are and how other people – in a position of trust to a greater or lesser extent – are only too ready to take advantage.

Note. Financial abuse by large organisations. Financial abuse can also involve both local authorities and NHS bodies who deliberately, or at least recklessly (with a 'couldn't care less' approach), ignore the law relating to charges and payment for care and end up taking sometimes significant sums of money, unlawfully, from vulnerable adults.

However, local authorities and NHS bodies consistently but unsurprisingly fail to recognise this as financial abuse. This has been discussed in Chapters 5 and 6. It is possible to challenge local authorities and the NHS on such matters, but not normally by way of the legal remedies outlined in this chapter. Rather, legally, by trying to bring a judicial review case and getting the courts to rule on the unlawfulness of the charge. Or, alternatively, complaining to the health service ombudsman or to the local government ombudsman.

In addition, other large organisations might blatantly exploit vulnerable adults on a large scale but not be prosecuted or labelled criminal.

For example, in late 2011, the Financial Services Authority announced that it had fined the bank HSBC over £10 million. HSBC had already agreed to pay back nearly £30 million in redress to elderly customers. The problem was the activity of NHFA, an HSBC subsidiary, which had sold, on a large scale, five-year investment bonds to fund long-term care for thousands of elderly people.

However, the mis-selling was blatant in 87 per cent of cases:

> The advice and sales were unsuitable because in a number of cases the individual's life expectancy was below the recommended five-year investment period. As a result customers with shorter life expectancies had to make withdrawals from these investments sooner than is recommended. The combination of withdrawals and product charges led to faster reduction of capital than should have been the case if customers had received

the right advice. A review by a third party of a sample of customer files found unsuitable sales had been made to 87% of customers involving these types of investments.[2]

The FSA issued a final notice under s.390 of the Financial Services and Markets Act 2000, imposing the fine. It could have required that restitution be made but HSBC had already started the redress process. The Act also confers powers on the FSA to prosecute.

FINANCIAL CRIME: OVERVIEW

A City of London Police document lists financial crime against vulnerable adults as including the following:

(i) People not receiving the benefits or allowances to which they are entitled.

(ii) An appointee, deputy or attorney…receives payment on behalf of the individual and does not:

   ○ pay money towards the cost of care for the adult

   ○ pass on money for food, clothes etc.

   ○ pass on the weekly personal allowance for people in residential care.

(iii) An individual befriending a vulnerable adult to gain access to their benefits. In one particular case, a perpetrator targeted six to seven people in one housing area.

(iv) People unable to get out of the house (due to, for example, frailty, disability, mental health problem) and depending on others to withdraw/collect money or essential items for them. Where others abuse this (taking out money or buying items for themselves), some victims may be unaware, while others may tolerate abuse because they have no one else on whom to depend.

(v) Withdrawals of cash and transfer of property, by those with registered and unregistered Power of Attorney. Reports indicate that some relatives and friends have presented 'fake Power of Attorney documents'.

(vi) People being persuaded to give away assets or gifts.

(vii) Thefts from care home residents and people in hospital by staff, including unauthorised use of payment cards, or taking items and replacing them with cheaper ones.

(viii) Care home manager gaining trust of residents and taking over their finances unlawfully.

---

2   Financial Services Authority. *FSA fines HSBC £10.5million for mis-selling products to elderly customers.* London: FSA, 2011. Accessed on 4 September 2012 at: www.fsa.gov.uk/library/communication/pr/2011/105.shtml.

(ix) Financial institutions or solicitors exploiting vulnerable adults. For example, corrupt bank insiders targeting vulnerable adults' funds, or a solicitor exploiting an adult's finances.

(x) Non-investment fraud – rogue traders providing goods or services that are unnecessary, of a poor standard, or at a higher cost than the market value.

(xi) Share purchase fraud – unsolicited callers putting pressure on or harassing a vulnerable person into investing in fraudulent shares.

(xii) Mass-marketing fraud – perpetrated, for example, through direct mail as lottery scams/advance fee fraud, encouraging people to send money.

(xiii) Identity theft – for example, stolen identity, or customer impersonation, to obtain bank accounts or mortgages. Stolen identity may be through a phishing scam, or grooming the person for information.[3]

THEFT

Under s.1 of the Theft Act 1968, a person is guilty of theft if he or she dishonestly appropriates property belonging to somebody else. This must be with the intention of permanently depriving the other person of it.

Such an appropriation is not dishonest if the person believes he or she had a right in law to deprive the other person of it. Alternatively, it is not dishonest if he or she believed that the other person would consent if the other person knew of the appropriation and the circumstances.

MENTAL CAPACITY, THEFT AND EXPLOITATION OF VULNERABLE ADULTS

One particular issue that has arisen is whether a prosecution and conviction may lie in the case of the victim who is judged to have mental capacity to have given away the property in question, or, at least, where there is a lack of evidence, on the balance of probability, to determine that they lack capacity.

There are many vulnerable adults, with mental capacity to handle the money or property in question, who are vulnerable precisely to exploitation, sometimes ruthless. Is such exploitation capable of constituting a criminal offence?

It can be in some circumstances. The significance therefore of the following legal case is that theft could be made out on the basis of the jury's overall view of whether there had been dishonesty, and that this would not necessarily depend on the man being shown to have lacked the requisite capacity to make a gift of the money involved.

Financial exploitation of and theft from a vulnerable person. A man of limited intelligence, 53 years old, was assisted and cared for by a 38-year-old woman on a private

---

3   Quoted from: City of London Police; National Fraud Intelligence Bureau. *Assessment: financial crime against vulnerable adults.* London: Social Care Institute for Excellence, 2011, p.10.

basis. Over a period from April to November, he made withdrawals almost every day up to the maximum £300 allowed from the building society, to the amount of £60,000 (his inheritance from his father).

Lack of decisive evidence that victim lacked mental capacity. The money ended up in the carer's bank account. The building society employees stated that the carer did most of the talking and would interrupt the man if he tried to talk. A consultant psychiatrist gave evidence that the man's IQ was between 70 to 80 (as opposed to the average of 90 to 110), that he could lead a normal if undemanding life (he had worked in a dairy as a packer for 30 years) and that he was naive and trusting and had no idea of the value of his assets or the ability to calculate their value. The consultant, however, accepted that he would be capable of making a gift and understood the concept of ownership and so would be able to divest himself of money but could probably not take the decision alone.

Jury entitled to find dishonesty, even if man had mental capacity to make a gift of the money. The carer was convicted of theft in the Crown Court; the case went on appeal to the House of Lords, which refused to interfere with the conviction. The court placed great weight on leaving the matter to the jury to decide about whether there had been dishonesty in all the circumstances. It was not crucial whether the man had the mental capacity to make a gift of the money. This was because the court was not prepared to read into s.1 of the Theft Act the words 'without the owner's consent'. In other words, consent was not necessarily fatal to the success of a charge of theft (it had been argued that, as a matter of law, it could not be theft if the man did have the capacity to make a gift, and that the Crown Court judge should have directed the jury to that effect).[4]

The *Hinks* case effectively overruled a slightly earlier Court of Appeal case, in which a maid, employed by an elderly woman aged 89 years, was prosecuted for allegedly cashing cheques to the value of £37,000 and stealing a brooch and crystal ornament. The appeal against conviction was allowed on the basis of the failure of the judge's directions to be clear about the relevance of mental capacity. This meant the jury had felt able to make a moral judgement about the maid, instead of deciding whether there was theft.[5]

Nevertheless, the *Hinks* case, which takes precedence because it was a House of Lords case, did not follow the *Mazo* approach. Instead, it took the approach followed by the Court of Appeal in another earlier case, which had held that mental capacity to transfer the property by way of a 'gift' was not decisive.

Theft of 99-year-old care home resident's assets: capacity and consent for gift not decisive. A 99-year-old woman lived in a care home. She was virtually blind. She went to live there in 1991; her daughter died in 1992 and at this point the two owners of the home took control of her affairs. A large number of cheques were drawn on her account; they argued that they were gifts. The owners obtained power of attorney and liquidated the woman's gifts and stocks; the proceeds were paid into a bank account held in their names and the woman's. Only one signature was required. A series of payments was subsequently made from that account for the benefit of the owners of the home. They were prosecuted for theft.

---

4   *R v Hinks* (2001) 2 AC 241 (House of Lords).
5   *R v Mazo* [1997] 2 Cr App R 518.

They appealed against their conviction on the grounds that the judge should have directed the jury that there could be no theft if the woman consented to the 'gifts' (and thus had the capacity to give that consent). Furthermore, the judge had failed to indicate the level of mental capacity required in order to make the acts of appropriation dishonest.

The appeal failed. The court held that the relevant term in s.1 of the Theft Act 1968 was 'dishonest appropriation'; this did not necessarily mean 'without the consent of the owner'.[6]

The significance of the *Hinks* case appears not always to be appreciated within the criminal justice system. Anecdotally, it seems that often the police and Crown Prosecution Service take the view that if a person has mental capacity to give something away and has done so, then they discount the possibility of prosecuting a theft case. In spite of the fact the *Hinks* case is clear authority for theft being made out, even if the person has the capacity to make a gift, if that gift was dishonestly obtained through, for example, coercion or undue influence.

GIFT MADE OF A PERSON'S FREE WILL?

In the *Jouman* case, the judge's direction to the jury, taken at face value, seems to omit the possibility that the 'gift' of thousands of pounds could nonetheless have been a theft. Yet the *Hinks* case involved a 'gift'. The judge said that either it was a gift, in which case the perpetrator was innocent, or it was not a gift, in which case it was theft. This is just about consistent with *Hinks* if one focuses on the phrase 'given of her own free will'. Because a gift given, but not through the untrammelled exercise of free will, could (according to *Hinks*) still be theft:

> But if, as the judge had directed them, they were sure it was or might have been a gift, the result must be an acquittal of the appellant. If they were sure it was not, there were on the evidence no circumstances in which the appellant could have believed that she was honestly entitled to have received it. She did not suggest that it was given for some other purpose, but that she honestly believed it to be a gift. It was either a gift 'given of her own free will' or it was not. That in a nutshell was the case that the judge left to the jury in a short but effective direction.[7]

The case had involved an 85-year-old woman who had known the perpetrator when the latter worked at the Post Office. The perpetrator no longer worked there but visited the woman weekly. She was given thousands of pounds by the victim who had suddenly cashed in tens of thousands of pounds of savings.[8]

Another slightly unusual case also involved gifts and a conviction for fraud (rather than theft) without there being a suggestion of lack of mental capacity on the part of the victim. Instead, the victim suffered from a psychiatric disorder involving compulsive or obsessive spending. The perpetrator had been the carer of

---

6   *R v Kendrick* [1997] 2 Cr App 524.

7   *R v Jouman* [2012] EWCA Crim 1850.

8   *R v Jouman* [2012] EWCA Crim 1850.

the victim's husband before becoming carer for the victim. One of the activities she helped with was the shopping. She benefited from 'spectacular generosity' on the part of the victim, who bought gifts worth £3000 for the carer over a period of six months. The carer was convicted of fraud and given a suspended prison sentence.[9]

DISHONESTY

The *Hinks* case, above, indicates the importance of the word 'dishonesty' in defining theft. In that case, involving a gift, the court left it up to the jury to decide whether, in all the circumstances, acceptance of the 'gift' constituted dishonesty.

The courts had previously given guidance about dishonesty, stating that, in order to establish guilt, there were two tests to apply – the objective and subjective. The objective test, to be applied first, was whether, according to the ordinary standards of reasonable and honest people, the defendant had acted dishonestly. If not, then that was the end of the matter. However, if, according to this objective standard, there was dishonesty, then the subjective test came into play. This was about whether the defendant would have realised that he or she was acting dishonestly by those standards.

In a much later case, the *Jouman* case (outlined immediately above), the court stated that the application of the second test did not follow automatically but only 'if the state of the evidence is such that the offender might have believed that what he or she is alleged to have done was in accordance with the ordinary person's idea of honesty'. However, in that case, there was no such evidence; the defendant's cognitive functioning was within the normal range. She displayed some features of autistic spectrum disorder, but these did not amount to a formal diagnosis to that effect. There was no suggestion she would not have understood dishonesty.[10]

TYPICAL EXAMPLES OF THEFT INVOLVING VULNERABLE ADULTS

The following headings and summaries of prosecutions and convictions for theft are intended to illustrate, for practitioners including social workers and criminal justice practitioners, different examples of theft (typically) perpetrated against vulnerable adults. Some of the headings and cases overlap. There are so many cases that the following are just a sample, in order to give a flavour.

Family members. A man was convicted of theft after stealing over £13,000 from his former partner and her mother who had dementia. He did this by using their bank cards and PINs, which he had stolen from the kitchen cupboard where they were kept. He also intercepted bank statements so that the theft would not come to light. Much of the money was spent on gambling machines in a betting shop.[11]

Friendly neighbours stealing large sums of money. When a social worker and police officer visited an elderly woman, they found her to be frail, dirty and unkempt, and the

---

9   'Carer admits fraud over £3k of gifts from client.' *The Star*, 1 April 2012.

10   *R v Jouman* [2012] EWCA Crim 1850.

11   'Gambler avoids jail term.' *Hartlepool Mail*, 31 March 2012.

house to be dirty and smelling of urine. She was apparently happy but mentally confused and forgot who her visitors were after five minutes. It became clear subsequently that two friendly neighbours (a married couple) had, over a period from 1995 to 2001, obtained sums of money from the woman amounting to £110,000. The couple unsuccessfully challenged the admissibility of evidence relating to the woman's dementia and mental capacity (some of the offences for which they were charged and convicted were also under the Forgery and Counterfeiting Act 1981).[12]

Woman stealing from a terminally ill neighbour. A 34-year-old woman stole more than £20,000 from a terminally ill neighbour, who was living in a nursing home. Having been trusted by her neighbour to withdraw small amounts of money with a bank card, she began by taking loans with the woman's knowledge. This then escalated to systematic theft, amounting to over £20,000. She was ordered to repay money to the bank within 28 days and given a suspended 12-month jail sentence.[13]

Neighbour stealing from man with senile dementia. A neighbour was convicted of conspiracy to steal. She (and her half-sister) had befriended an elderly man with some form of senile dementia or Parkinson's disease. She began to visit him frequently. Soon, his building society balance dropped dramatically and, over a period of three months, £5980 was withdrawn. The building society staff noticed that he always seemed to be accompanied when he came in to make the withdrawals. The money was given to the women and spent on drugs.[14]

Elderly couple stealing from woman who had suffered a stroke. A woman who had suffered a stroke hired a man to do the gardening. She came to trust him and his partner. He was 77 and his partner was 68 years old. They gained the woman's trust. They then withdrew £2000 from her bank after promising to take care of her bills, tried to change her will and had her £3000 car signed over to them. They were given ten-month jail sentences, suspended for a year. They had to repay the money, were placed under a curfew and fitted with electronic tracking devices.[15]

Neighbourhood Watch volunteer stealing life savings of 89-year-old woman. A Neighbourhood Watch volunteer stole the life savings – £60,000 – of an 89-year-old woman, whom he had befriended. He left her with £550. The money was used to pay for cocaine, a car and a computer. He had gained her trust because of his position in the Neighbourhood Watch scheme and also as head of a residents' group. He had initially run errands for her. She handed her bank cards to him. He also gained a lasting power of attorney which was registered. In addition, she amended her will, making him executor and sole beneficiary.

However, a social worker became concerned on discovering that he had the keys to the woman's flat and also use of her credit cards. He was convicted of both fraud and theft.

He had previously been well regarded locally and had helped the police tackle anti-social behaviour of drug addicts. He was sentenced to 28 months in prison.[16]

---

12   *R v Bowles (Lewis) and Bowles (Christine)* [2004] EWCA Crim 1608.
13   'Theft shame nurse struck off.' 5 August 2007. Accessed on 2 December 2012 at: www.walesonline.co.uk/news/wales-news/2007/08/05/theft-shame-nurse-struck-off-91466-19570303.
14   *R v Stockdale* [1994] 15 Cr App R (S) 48.
15   'UK's oldest tagged couple: pair with a combined age of 145 fleeced vulnerable pensioner who trusted them.' *Daily Mail*, 26 July 2012.
16   Smith, G. 'Neighbourhood Watch volunteer who helped jail drug gang stole £60,000 from pensioner to fund secret cocaine habit.' *Daily Mail*, 25 June 2012.

Head of residents' association stealing £750,000. Over £750,000 was stolen in a theft and conspiracy to steal case involving share certificates, by the head of a residents' association, a mortgage broker and an unqualified accountant. The victim was an elderly man, in poor health, living near the head of the residents' association. When going into a care home, he entrusted the keys to his home to the latter, who took (on the man's behalf and legitimately) some share certificates to a solicitor (who had power of attorney) for cashing in. However, following that, more shares were sold – without the man's knowledge or approval – via the mortgage broker and unqualified accountant. There were also other documents of authority discovered with the man's forged signature. The solicitor discovered the illegal sale of the shares and contacted the police.[17]

Social worker stealing from mental health patients. A social worker, in the grip of a loan shark, was convicted of theft, having stolen money from four mental health patients. She worked in a hospital, obtaining money from patients and pretending to buy things for them. She also stole money from the office lottery scheme. She was sentenced to ten months in prison, suspended for two years, and ordered to do 150 hours community service.[18]

Mental health team social worker taking money from patients. A social worker in a mental health team had duties that included looking after the finances of service users. She falsely claimed she bought items for a male patient with £680. She had taken the money on the pretext of buying carpets and a mobile phone for the person. She also took money from a female patient in hospital. The judge referred to her cynical abuse of trust. She would have been sent to prison except for her remorse and her young son.[19] The social worker was also removed from the General Social Care Council's register.[20]

District nurse stealing from cancer patient. A district nurse in Hereford was convicted of stealing £34,000 from a patient with cancer, whom she was caring for and had befriended. She was sentenced to three years in prison.

Evidence included images on a CCTV camera. This showed her paying money, which she had withdrawn from the victim's account, into her own bank account. She made 119 withdrawals, each consisting of the maximum £300 allowed, amounting to nearly £34,000. This was in addition to a £70,000 gift which the victim had made to her and which she had not declared. She was able to steal the money after obtaining from the victim the code to a safe in which the victim kept her bank card. Police were unable to trace the money; it had been apparently spent.[21]

Financial adviser stealing millions from vulnerable adults. A financial adviser was convicted of theft, false accounting and forgery. The total amount stolen was some £2 million. His victims included a man with severe learning disabilities, a chronically ill woman and even a member of his own family. He took money he had been given to invest on people's behalf and also borrowed a client's credit card, before failing to pay back the amount he had 'borrowed'.[22]

Solicitor overcharging amounting to theft. A solicitor (also a coroner) charged 250 per cent more than would have been reasonable from the estates of dead clients. He was

17 *R v Ryan* [2001] EWCA Crim 1956.
18 Hunt, K. 'Social worker faces judge after stealing from vulnerable patients.' *Medway Messenger*, 11 July 2008.
19 NHS South Coast Audit's Counter Fraud Investigation Team. *Newsletter*, June 2009.
20 *Buchanan v General Social Care Council*, Conduct Committee, July 2009.
21 Tanner, B. 'Nurse stole £34,000 from cancer patient.' *Worcester News*, 16 March 2012.
22 Jenkins, R. 'Financier stole from elderly clients.' *The Times*, 13 September 2006.

found guilty of six counts of theft, amounting to £155,000. Among beneficiaries that lost out were the Royal National Lifeboat Institute, the Salvation Army and a cottage hospital in Thirsk.[23]

Befriending people. A 41-year-old woman befriended an elderly woman and acted as private carer. She was charged with ten counts of theft. One charge concerned the taking of a frail 89-year-old woman to the bank and cashing a cheque; the others to withdrawing money from the woman's account using her cash card. The carer pleaded guilty to seven cash withdrawals and was sentenced to 12 months in prison.[24]

Befriending in care home. A woman befriended an elderly woman living in a care home. Twice she forged woman's signature in letters to the bank, obtaining a total of £11,000. She was sentenced to four months in prison.[25]

Systematic befriending and theft. The befriending and subsequent theft may be systematic, as in the following case involving a heroin addict, who also used her daughter. The judge referred to the perpetrator as an evil and calculating woman who was a danger to old and infirm people.

Pushing into house and offering sexual services.

Counts 1 and 2 concerned a dwelling burglary and sexual assault. A man aged 58 was at his home address on 20th July 2010 when the defendant rang the door bell. She pushed past him and entered his flat. Once in the living room the defendant offered the victim sexual services and sexually assaulted him. The defendant then picked up the victim's wallet and removed £80 before leaving.[26]

Picking up a vulnerable victim at the supermarket.

...count 3, which was theft. Another man, aged about 80, was walking to his local supermarket on 21st August 2010 when he was approached by the defendant and her daughter. They engaged him in conversation. They walked with him to the supermarket and said they would wait outside for him. The victim left by another exit and went home. Whilst in the communal passageway inside the block of flats where he resides, the two women came to the front door and were allowed entry by another resident. The defendant and her daughter then took him by the arms and walked him to his front door, which he opened. They all entered his flat. Whilst the defendant spoke to him in the living room, the daughter took £110 from his coat pocket in the hallway.[27]

Selling mobility scooter and keeping money.

...count 7, another offence of theft. A third man, aged 59, had been a friend of the defendant for over a year and had allowed her to stay at his home address from time to time. On one occasion in August 2010 the defendant suggested that she could sell a mobility scooter that the victim had inherited from his brother. The victim agreed as he needed the money, but the defendant then sold the scooter and, apart from £5, never gave him any of the proceeds.[28]

23   Norfolk, A. 'Coroner who stole £155,000 from the dead.' *The Times*, 8 February 2003.

24   *R v Singh* [2007]. Reported in *London Borough of Hounslow News*. 'Callous carer jailed for theft from 89-year-old woman.' 14 September 2007. Accessed on 23 October 2008 at: www.hounslow.gov.uk/news_mod_home/news_mod_year/news_mod_month/news_mod_show?year1=2007&month1=9&NewsID=30078.

25   *R v Clarke* [2003] EWCA Crim 1764.

26   *R v Law* [2012] EWCA Crim 40.

27   *R v Law* [2012] EWCA Crim 40.

28   *R v Law* [2012] EWCA Crim 40.

Collecting pension and using money of victim.

Count 9 was another theft offence. A fourth man, whose age is unknown but who was elderly and with mobility problems, was an acquaintance of the defendant. On 24th January of last year the defendant was at his home address with two other friends of his. It was discussed that one of the friends who usually collected his pension would be unable to do so the next day, and therefore on 25th January the defendant visited him and offered to go to the post office for him to collect his pension. He gave her his bank card and PIN number, and when she returned she told him that she had used the money to pay a debt she owed to a money lender and would pay it back to him the following Friday. No money was ever paid back. £117-odd was removed from his account.[29]

Controlling and directing an elderly confused man to withdraw money from the building society. An elderly confused man living alone in Birmingham had a number of building society accounts with significant balances. He came under the control or direction of the perpetrator, who would take him to the building society. Acting ostensibly on the man's behalf and pretending to be his grandson, the perpetrator would ask for a cheque to be made out to the man and specify the amount and the payee (always one of the perpetrator's associates – one of whom was ordered to pay £27,000 compensation to the victim). He was convicted of theft and sentenced to four years in prison.[30]

Bank worker stealing £2 million from vulnerable customers. A bank staff member stole more than £2 million from elderly and vulnerable bank customers, in order to fund his obsession with exotic birds, including gold macaws at £20,000 a pair and black cockatoos at £20,000 each. He admitted 24 counts of theft and asked for 203 similar offences to be taken into consideration.[31]

Bank manager committing theft. A Barclays Bank manager in Twickenham investigated a £20,000 theft from a customer aged 95, committed by a colleague at the bank. The manager then decided to steal a further £23,000 himself. The manager was convicted of fraud and given a prison sentence of two and a half years.[32]

Bank cashier stealing from 83-year-old customer. Another Barclays Bank employee, a cashier, stole £42,000 from an 83-year-old former teacher, now with health problems and confused, by simply transferring money out of his account into other accounts. The theft came to light when a solicitor took charge of the man's affairs as his mental condition worsened.[33]

Housekeeper stealing possessions. The perpetrator stole valuable heirlooms (silver and jewellery) and war memorabilia from elderly and vulnerable clients. She gave them to a dealer who in turn sold them to a pawnbroker. One victim was 86 years old and confined to a wheelchair; another had a degenerative brain condition. The perpetrator had concealed a previous conviction in order to secure a housekeeping role with a locum agency. The judge

29   *R v Law* [2012] EWCA Crim 40.
30   *R v Kelly* [1997], Court of Appeal, 14 November 1997.
31   Barkham, P. 'Fraudster that fluttered inside a suburban banker.' *The Times*, 3 September 2003. Also: 'Banker stole to buy parrots.' *BBC News*, 2 September 2003. Accessed on 17 October 2007 at: http://news.bbc.co.uk/1/hi/england/kent/3201135.stm.
32   'Bank manager investigating colleague's theft from customer aged 95 stole £23,000 himself.' *The Mirror*, 6 September 2011.
33   'Ruthless bank cashier stole thousands from Wood Green pensioner.' *Tottenham & Wood Green Journal*, 7 June 2012.

stated that the thefts were cynical, hard-hearted and cruel. She was jailed for 15 months for theft and the dealer for nine months (for handling stolen goods and perverting the course of justice).[34]

Care home worker using bank card of 92-year-old. A 21-year-old care home worker was jailed for eight months after stealing £6400 from the bank accounts of two care home residents, aged 92 years and 71 years. Her duties had included taking the residents out shopping; she had dishonestly used their bank cards to take money for herself.[35]

Nurse using bank cards of care home residents. A nurse was both struck off from the nursing register and sentenced to prison after she was found guilty of 55 counts of theft. Using the bank cards of a man and woman with learning disabilities, residents at care homes where she worked, she stole some £13,000 over a five-year period. She blamed the thefts on the financial pressures following the break-up of a relationship.[36]

Care home worker using Post Office card of 91-year-old. A care home worker stole a Post Office card from the room of a 91-year-old resident where he had found it together with the PIN. He admitted using the card fraudulently to take £100 from her account.[37]

Carer stealing from 76-year-old blind woman who treated her 'like a daughter'. A carer (a mother of two children) was treated like a daughter and with absolute trust by a 76-year-old blind woman, for whom she provided care twice a week. In order to obtain statements, she had been given the woman's savings account card and PIN, although she had never been asked to withdraw money. The woman regularly paid her late husband's mining pension into the account. In fact, over a 17-month period, about £200 at a time, the carer took over £5000. The thefts came to light when the woman realised she had only £190 left. The carer tried to stop the woman alerting the police. The carer was sentenced to one year's imprisonment.[38]

Ordering bank cards dishonestly. A carer working for a care agency in Winchester took advantage of a 90-year-old client after the latter had been admitted to hospital. She not only used the woman's bank cards but ordered further bank cards. She stole over £17,000 and was convicted of both theft and fraud and sent to prison, despite being pregnant.

The care company's logged records showed that the carer had been sorting out the woman's logs, something that was, of course, outside the remit of her responsibilities.

The bank paid back the missing money to the woman. The judge commented: 'cases like this are on the increase as the elderly are cared for more and the community must be protected from those like you who succumb to temptation.'[39]

Taping up letter boxes to intercept bank statements. A carer stole £46,000 from a bedridden elderly woman, leaving her only £255. Over a period of two years, she used her debit card to withdraw money from cash machines. She had also taped up the letter

34   Hills, S. 'Carer jailed for stealing £12,000 of valuable heirlooms and war memorabilia from elderly.' *Daily Mail*, 4 June 2012.

35·   'Care home worker jailed for theft.' *Craven Herald*, 20 December 2007.

36   'Theft shame nurse struck off.' *Icwales*, 5 August 2007. Accessed on 2 December 2012 at: www.walesonline.co.uk/ news/wales-news/2007/08/05/theft-shame-nurse-struck-off-91466-19570303.

37   'Carer sentenced for theft from 91-year-old woman.' *EDP 24*, 21 March 2008. Accessed on 17 January 2013 at: www.edp24.co.uk/news/carer_sentenced_for_theft_from_91_year_old_woman_1_1038650.

38   'Carer is jailed for theft of £5000.' *Northern Echo*, 6 November 2004.

39   Hendy, A. 'Jail for carer who stole £17k from pensioner.' *Daily Echo*, 8 April 2012.

box and put a new one on the outside of the door, so that she could intercept and destroy bank statements. She used the money on her wedding, expensive trips and concerts, and to set herself up as a hostess selling lingerie and sex aids. She was sentenced to prison for nine months.[40]

Nurse stealing cash card from dying war hero. A nurse (needing to pay her telephone bill) took an 83-year-old dying patient's cash card from a hospital locker. He had won the Croix de Guerre at the D-Day landings in the Second World War; the nurse was given a suspended three-month jail sentence.[41]

Opportunistic theft by nurse at clinic. A nurse working at a hospital in Leicester stole money from patients while they attended a breast-screening clinic, taking a total of £275 from the handbags of three of them. She was sentenced to 240 hours' community service and also struck off the nursing register.[42]

Care worker theft precipitates second stroke for care home resident. A 49-year-old care worker at a nursing home was sentenced to four months in prison after stealing more than £7000 from a 71-year-old resident – who, having suffered a paralysing stroke 30 years before, suffered another on learning of the theft. The carer had stolen the money after the resident had given her cash card and PIN, so the carer could do shopping for her.[43]

Carer stealing from bank account of care home resident. A care worker pleaded stress following the break-up of his marriage after he was convicted of 13 offences of stealing money from a resident with learning disabilities at a care home. The carer had been entrusted with managing the resident's financial affairs and had direct access to his bank account.[44]

Care home assistant taking money from wallets and purses. A nursing assistant at a care home was caught pilfering cash from residents after a suspicious manager installed a CCTV camera. He would take money from their wallets and purses. A marked note was placed in the wallet of one of the residents in order to entrap the perpetrator. The amounts taken were relatively small; the total was £120. He was given a suspended prison sentence.[45]

Cynical disregard for terminally ill residents: raiding of bank account by managing director of care home. A former matron, then the managing director of a care home, admitted 24 specimen counts of theft, false accounting and obtaining property by deception, involving a total of £5515. However, the total amount of money that might have had to be paid back was in excess of £100,000; a court order was already in place at the time of conviction freezing an estimated £138,000 of her assets. She had raided the bank accounts of terminally ill residents when she realised that accounting procedures were not as strict as they should have been. The judge referred to her 'cynical disregard' for the families who had relied on her to look after the physical and financial welfare of the residents. She was sentenced to 18 months in prison.[46]

40   'Carer steals bedridden gran's £46k life savings to start an Ann Summers business.' *Daily Mirror*, 1 September 2011.
41   'Nurse stole card from dying man.' *The Times*, 3 October 2007.
42   'Patient theft nurse is struck off.' *BBC News*, 17 December 2004. Accessed on 17 October 2008 at: http://news.bbc.co.uk/1/hi/england/leicestershire/4106257.stm.
43   'Law says "sorry" after theft leaves Mary £2000 in debt – and crook gets only 4 months.' *Liverpool Echo*, 18 February 2008.
44   'Carer convicted on theft charges.' *Swindon Advertiser*, 15 June 2001.
45   'Carer caught on CCTV stealing from residents.' *Bristol Evening Post*, 21 December 2011.
46   'Jail after theft spree revealed.' *Bromsgrove Advertiser*, 10 August 2006.

Care home manager stealing from people with learning disabilities. A care home manager stole over £14,000 from two residents with learning disabilities, at Priory Court care home in Lincolnshire, run by Southern Cross. Instead of using their benefits money to pay for care home fees, she bought goods for herself, including a fridge freezer, clothes, groceries and expensive chocolates.

She was caught out when a colleague checked a bank statement and realised that the listed transactions were nothing to do with the resident. She had also arranged for one resident's benefits to be paid into her account. That resident ended up £3000 in arrears with care home fees. She was convicted of theft and sentenced to one year's imprisonment. She was a trained nurse and previously of good character.[47]

Care home manager stealing from dying woman. A nursing home manager at Shandon House, Birkdale, stole £2300 from a dying woman, 85 years old with dementia, using the resident's bank card. She spent the money on lavish meals, cigarettes and clothes. She pleaded guilty on two counts of fraud and was sentenced to nine months in prison.[48]

Domiciliary carer stealing from wallet. A home carer was caught on closed-circuit television riffling through the wallet of her client, a man with multiple sclerosis whom a team of carers supported in his own home. Suspicions had arisen previously, and police had installed secret cameras. She was sentenced to four months' imprisonment, suspended for a year.[49]

Sacked carer returns to known clients to commit theft. Carers may use their acquaintance with clients to gain entry subsequently, not in their role as carer, in order to commit theft. For example, a carer had been sacked by a domiciliary care agency but visited clients nonetheless, pretending she was still working for the agency. She had stolen money from clients' wallets amounting to several hundred pounds.[50]

Former carer steals from three elderly women. The offences involved the theft of £20, £90 and £40 or thereabouts from elderly women in their own homes. The women concerned were aged 87, 69 and 85. Each had got to know the appellant when the latter had been engaged as a carer for them. She gained admission to their homes because she knew them in that capacity. In the course of the visits, she found opportunity to steal from them the sums mentioned. After the first offence, she had been arrested and given bail; she committed the other two offences while on bail for that first offence.

The carer appealed against a sentence of nine months' imprisonment, partly on the basis that they were only 'economic crimes' and involved small sums of money.

The Court of Appeal rejected the appeal, pointing out that it was a mistake to view them as such, since:

> Crimes such as these which target elderly and vulnerable victims in their home because they are precisely that, elderly and vulnerable, strike at such person's sense of security, increasing their vulnerability and rendering them more wary of others. They bear some of the characteristics of offences against the person.[51]

47   'Care home manager June Anne Walters jailed over "a monstrous breach of trust".' *Stamford Mercury*, 26 August 2011.

48   'Birkdale care home boss conned dying patient of savings to dine on steak and wine.' *Liverpool Daily Post*, 6 October 2011.

49   Alder, A. 'Suspended sentence for money-grabbing carer.' *Bedfordshire on Sunday*, 6 October 2007.

50   'Care worker jailed for theft.' *Dorset Echo*, 12 December 2001.

51   *R v Cutts* [2006] EWCA Crim 2208.

Carer stealing £135,000 from bed-bound woman, leaving her with £21.79. A bed-bound elderly woman inherited £180,000 from her husband. This was the cue for her carer to persuade the victim to trust her with her bank account details and bank cards. By writing out cheques and using the cards, she stole some £135,000 to pay for luxuries for her family. The victim was left with £21.79 in her bank accounts. Not all the inheritance was accounted for. When the police became involved, the carer sent highly threatening letters to the victim. A mother of four, she was sentenced to five years in prison for theft and fraud.[52]

Carers targeting and selling goods of elderly people. A carer targeted an elderly couple, stealing not only £7000 using a bank card (£300 a week withdrawn) but also paintings worth £3000 which she sold on eBay. She was sentenced to 18 months in prison. The husband died shortly after; he had trusted her completely, and the family believed the stress contributed to his death.[53]

Live-in carer abuses trust to arrange fake burglary in home of elderly couple. A live-in carer obtained a job to help a retired major-general and war veteran care for his wife. Within nine months, the carer had looked up the value of the antiques in the house and staged a fake burglary. Paintings, objets d'art, jewellery, furniture, silverware and many sentimental items were taken. The wife died two months later and the husband sold the house. The judge referred to the appalling breach of trust by the carer; she was convicted of conspiracy to steal and conspiracy to obtain property by deception.[54]

Loan of money turning into theft. A woman with multiple sclerosis employed a carer; there was genuine affection between the two women. However, first of all, the woman loaned £7500 to the carer; the carer then stole over £3000, which she was able to do because she had access to the woman's money (through credit cards) for doing the shopping. The carer was convicted of theft and sentenced to nine months' imprisonment.[55]

Stealing rings from fingers. A nursing home carer was convicted and imprisoned for stealing four rings from two bed-bound residents, aged 91 and 98, in the Coppice care home in Oldham. She sold them to obtain money to send back to her mother in the Philippines who had a kidney infection and also looked after the carer's daughter. Police recovered three of the four rings from pawnbrokers.

The judge noted:

> The effect of your crime is not just on the victims and fellow residents but also the public's confidence in the care system. The victims lost jewellery and you must have realised that those sort of items have sentimental value that goes way beyond the price in money. They are irreplaceable, not for their value, but for the memories that are attached to them when you reach such a ripe old age. Even when these rings have been returned, the victims are aware of what has happened to them, and those items' memories have now been hampered by what you did.[56]

52   Salkeld, L. 'Thieving carer took £135,000 from widow, 83, blew it on holidays and threatened to burn down her house.' *Daily Mail,* 1 March 2012.

53   Hemsley, A. 'Heartless care worker stole from elderly Winchelsea couple.' *Hastings and St Leonards Observer,* 22 August 2008.

54   'Carer stole antiques from war veteran.' *Daily Telegraph,* 28 November 2007.

55   'Carer jailed for nine months after stealing cash.' *Oxford Mail,* 14 January 2006.

56   'Jailed, carer who stole rings from women aged 91 and 98 from home in Oldham.' *Manchester Evening News,* 6 September 2011.

MOTIVES OF CARERS STEALING

In one sense, motive is irrelevant. Either the theft has been committed or it has not. In another, it may be relevant if it is argued in mitigation when sentencing takes place. We should also bear in mind that desperation and genuine hardship might tempt a carer, as pointed out in *Vanity Fair*:

> And who knows but Rebecca was right in her speculations – and that it was only a question of money and fortune which made the difference between her and an honest woman? If you take temptations into account, who is to say that he is better than his neighbour? A comfortable career of prosperity, if it does not make people honest, at least keeps them so. An alderman coming from a turtle feast will not step out of his carriage to steal a leg of mutton; but put him to starve, and see if he will not purloin a loaf.[57]

Yet this is not the whole story, because the pages of this part of this book are filled with cases of dishonesty perpetrated by the relatively well-off as well as the hard-up.

The motive might be greed and the wish to live in better style, in whatever form that may take. For example, in one case, a carer befriended a 78-year-old woman after working for her and stole nearly £4000 using the woman's debit card; most of the money went on slot machines. She was sentenced to one year in prison, suspended for 18 months, and ordered to repay some of the money. Her husband had left her and she had four children.[58]

It might be foreign holidays.

NHS care assistant caught by secret camera in teddy bear. A health care assistant attending a 75-year-old leukaemia sufferer stole in order to go on holiday to Las Vegas. After the family realised that money was going missing, they installed a small surveillance camera at the suggestion of the woman's granddaughter who was a forensic science graduate. It was placed in the eye of a pink teddy bear in the woman's room and it caught on film the care assistant stealing £60. She was convicted and sentenced to six months in prison. The judge referred to the seriousness of the offence, given the age and terminal illness of the victim. The carer worked for Liverpool NHS primary care trust.[59]

As has already been seen from some of the above examples, it might be pressing financial matters that are argued in mitigation, explanation or excuse – such as keeping up with mortgage payments and dealing with postnatal depression. So argued a pregnant carer convicted of theft for cashing cheques belonging to an 84-year-old woman for whom she cared and then keeping the money herself. She helped the woman with shopping and household chores. Her contract with the care company prohibited her from becoming involved with clients' finances.[60]

---

57   Thackeray, W.M. *Vanity Fair*. London: Thomas Nelson, undated, Chapter XLI, p.474 (originally published 1848).
58   'Dishonest carer told to pay up.' *Sunderland Echo*, 6 November 2007.
59   Hull, L. 'Camera hidden in a teddy bear catches carer stealing £100 from terminally ill pensioner.' *Daily Mail*, 18 August 2008.
60   Kelly, K. 'Pregnant carer jailed for theft from OAP.' *The Shields Gazette*, 9 May 2008.

It might be spending money on a two-year-old child.

Stealing money from 93-year-old woman by cashing cheques on the Market Hill. In Sudbury, Suffolk, an Age Concern carer paid – over a period of several weeks – nine visits to the bank on the Market Hill. She cashed cheques on behalf of the 93-year-old woman she provided care for, ostensibly for shopping, but in fact stealing £2575 for herself. The carer said the money was to spend on her two-year-old daughter. The judge referred to the 'particularly mean and wicked series of offences' in sentencing her to nine months in prison, suspended for 12 months, with 200 hours' community work and a repayment order starting with a lump sum of £500 and then £25 a fortnight.[61]

Similarly, a carer withdrew an 86-year-old woman's money for legitimate purposes, but then kept more than £1000. Her husband had lost his job, she had bills to pay and Christmas presents for the children to buy. She was sentenced to two months in prison.[62]

When the husband of a team leader in a residential home left her, she had mounting debts and eventually had to declare herself bankrupt and go to live with her parents. In order to try to stave this off, she used the cash cards and PINs of residents with Alzheimer's disease, stealing nearly £5000 before she admitted the offences to the police. She was sentenced to 12 months in prison, suspended for two years, with 100 hours' community service. Her family repaid the victims.[63]

Sometimes, the discovered theft seems less explicable, given the carer's background and other circumstances.

Inexplicable thefts by carer. A respected 57-year-old carer worked for the council; she had worked as a carer for 30 years. As her defence lawyer put it, there was no explanation since she had no debts and was not addicted to anything. She stole £50 from the victim, for whom she had been caring for six years. There were five separate incidents of theft until she was caught stealing on the camera the family had set up. She was sentenced to six months in prison, suspended for 18 months, with 200 hours' community service. The judge noted that these were serious breaches of trust, made all the more inexplicable because the carer looked after her own infirm mother.[64]

It might not only be money. One care home worker was convicted for stealing the pain relief tablets of a resident and substituting artificial sweeteners.[65]

Drug addiction might be the driver behind the theft.

Theft from man with learning disabilities driven by drug debts. A carer was entrusted with the money of a man with severe learning disabilities who lived in a sheltered housing complex. The carer had developed a cocaine habit and had to repay £11,000 to drug dealers. He made internet payments from the man's bank account and withdrew money from his account on shopping trips, stealing some £2000. He was sentenced to nine

---

61 'Carer who stole is spared prison.' *Sudbury Mercury*, 28 August 2008.

62 'Carer jailed over £1,150 theft.' *Lancashire Evening Telegraph*, 10 August 1999.

63 'Carer's theft from the sick.' *The Echo,* 6 January 2006.

64 Nowaczyk, W. 'Carer's reputation is ruined after theft.' *Walesonline*, 3 July 2008. Accessed on 23 October 2008 at: www.walesonline.co.uk/news/south-wales-news/pontypridd-llantrisant/2008/07/03/carer-s-reputation-is-ruined-after-theft-91466-21209746.

65 'Carer, 42, sentenced over theft.' *Shropshire Star*, 12 March 2008.

months in prison. The judge said that the carer presented 'the classic tale of an otherwise perfectly decent man' who became enmired in drug use and degradation which had led to his downfall.[66]

Or, perhaps, an addiction to shopping. An elderly woman in her eighties, with learning disabilities, was incapable of looking after her finances. A carer, employed by a care company, helped her do so by withdrawing up to £3650 on the woman's behalf from the latter's bank account. The carer claimed the woman went on extravagant shopping sprees; however, the woman's new carer noticed that the money withdrawn exceeded by far the total of receipts.[67]

A nurse, addicted to pethidine, was convicted on various charges, including theft, relating to controlled drugs. One count involved injecting an anodyne substance into the patient, who needed the painkiller on an orthopaedic hospital ward, and keeping the pethidine herself.[68]

BURGLARY

The offence of burglary comes under s.9 of the Theft Act 1968 and involves (a) a person entering a building as a trespasser with the intention of stealing or inflicting grievous bodily harm or doing unlawful damage; and (b) having entered a building, the person steals or attempts to steal something or inflicts or attempts to inflict grievous bodily harm.

Burglars sometimes specifically target vulnerable people.

Burgling the homes of elderly people, particularly the blind, deaf and partially sighted. One burglar raided 600 homes within 18 months and travelled hundreds of miles in order to steal £267,000 by deceiving vulnerable elderly people, some in their nineties. He posed as a policeman and targeted, in particular, blind, deaf and partially sighted people. Sometimes he would persuade people to give him their valuables to take to the police station for safe keeping; at other times he would simply rifle under beds for cash or other valuables. After being caught and admitting burglary by deception, he asked for 587 similar offences to be taken into account. He was jailed for seven years.[69]

Burglars offering to cut hedge. Two brothers called at the home of a 91-year-old man, offered to cut his hedge, entered the house, restrained the man, stole his wallet with money, cuttings of funerals (of his wife, older brother and stepson), documentation for his pacemaker and bank cards – 'exactly the sort of offence which is likely to cause extreme distress to an elderly man'. They were convicted of burglary and sentenced to seven and eight years in prison, given that they had been convicted previously for similar offences of targeting the elderly.[70]

Impersonation of police officer. A 22-year-old man impersonated a police officer and entered the home of a 93-year-old man, whom he proceeded to lock in the kitchen. He

66   Cox, C. 'Carer stole disabled man's cash for cocaine.' *Macclesfield Express*, 5 December 2007.
67   'Carer facing jail for theft from patient.' *Journal Live*, 16 November 2007. Accessed on 17 January 2013 at: www.questia.com/library/1G1-171430121/carer-facing-jail-for-theft-from-patient-mother-fleeced.
68   *R v Webster* [2007] EWCA Crim 619.
69   Bird, S. 'Conman jailed for 600 raids in just 18 months.' *The Times*, 8 February 2003.
70   *R v Cawley* [2007] EWCA Crim 2030.

then stole £140 in cash. The judge was in no doubt that he was targeting elderly people; when the perpetrator stated that he thought the victim was in his sixties rather than his nineties, the judge noted that he was not convinced 'had he shown you his birth certificate that you would have immediately backed away rather than thinking that you had a soft target in front of you'.

The perpetrator had a father involved in crime as a way of life, had been physically abused as a child, left home to live rough with travellers and had shown remorse. The judge had sentenced him to five years in prison; this was reduced to three and a half years on appeal.[71]

Burglar posing as police targeting elderly and vulnerable people. A man committed 38 burglaries within the space of a few months. He posed as a policeman. He visited houses, asking that people give him their cash and other valuables for safe keeping at the police station. He would even suggest that people speak on the phone to somebody pretending to be his superior. He targeted mainly elderly, or very elderly, people.

Aggravating features were professional planning, working as a group, targeting elderly and vulnerable people, inducing fear, the special trauma of posing as police and warning victims of the specific risk of burglary, planning entry into their homes when they were present and leaving them fearing that they might be attacked by criminals and – the last feature common to both appellants – the high value to the victims of the property stolen, either cash or jewellery. The two perpetrators (he had an accomplice) were sentenced to seven and 12 years in prison respectively.

Reference was made to s.143 of the Criminal Justice Act 2003 in relation to similar offences (before committing these burglaries, the man had just been released on licence, having been previously convicted for similar offences).[72]

Distraction burglary. A man claiming to be from the water board gained entry to a house where an elderly woman was living. Claiming to be checking the water, he went upstairs. He stole a watch from her bedroom, a mobile phone and £200 from her son's room. The offender had been sent to prison previously for the same type of offence. The court stated that burglary of this type 'casts a shadow on the lives of elderly people: they begin to dread the unexpected knock on the front door'. On appeal, he was sentenced to eight years in prison.[73]

Care agency carer committing burglary. A home help working for a care agency admitted four charges of burglary. For example, he went to the home of one 75-year-old woman to help her with the cleaning and took £75 from a fruit bowl. He was suspended and he resigned following this, but then returned to another client unofficially, again to help with cleaning, but took £120 from her purse; £400 savings in an envelope also went missing.[74]

Burglar masquerading as carer. A 77-year-old woman was watching television in her sheltered accommodation flat. The burglar entered her flat through the unlocked door. She said that the warden had let her in and that she was her care worker. The victim said her daughter was her care worker. The burglar took the victim's bag. The victim tried to take it back. She was struck on the back of the head with a kettle containing hot water. She

71   R v McInerney [2002] EWCA Crim 3003.
72   R v Casey [2007] EWCA Crim 2568.
73   R v O'Brien [2002] EWCA Crim 787.
74   Hudson, C. 'Carer stole from patients.' Macclesfield Express, 22 November 2006.

screamed for help. Her neighbours heard and the burglar was stopped outside by a group of people.

The perpetrator was sentenced to prison for some nine years. Her appeal failed. The effect on the victim was serious – not just physical hurt but fear, flashbacks, panic attacks. Previously, in 2004, for six almost identical burglaries of vulnerable people in their own homes, she was sentenced to 66 months' imprisonment. Straight away, whilst on licence, she did the same again – five more burglaries of vulnerable people in their own homes. She was sentenced to six years' imprisonment. She had been let out on four days of temporary release on licence when she committed the current offence, which, in contrast to the others, was accompanied by violence.[75]

ROBBERY

Under s.8 of the Theft Act 1968, a person is guilty of robbery if he or she steals and immediately before, or at the time of doing so and in order to do so, he or she uses force on any person or puts or seeks to put any person in fear of being subjected to force.

ROBBERS TARGETING KNOWN VULNERABLE ADULTS

In the following case, the three perpetrators went to the home of a victim whom they knew to be vulnerable.

Robbery at home of man known to be vulnerable and regularly pestered by children for money. Three men went to the home of the victim whom they knew to be vulnerable. He had learning disabilities and needed help in carrying out basic activities such as washing and shaving. He tended to be pestered by children for money. One of the children to whom he had given money was the stepson of one of the perpetrators. They pushed him into the hallway, demanded money and stole £100, the whole of his savings from benefits. He was punched in the face and suffered fractures to the cheek bone and eye socket. An initial sentence of three years for robbery was increased on appeal to five years, six months.[76]

An 84-year-old woman lived alone in a flat in Plymouth. The perpetrator's mother was her carer, and the perpetrator had previously been to her home to clean the windows. He visited her and stole her pension book and cash. He was arrested that evening, charged and released on bail. Four days later, he returned, grabbed her and dragged her into the bedroom, where she ended up on the floor. He stole her purse, pension book and £90 in cash. He gave himself up the following day. He was sentenced to six years in prison.[77]

In the following case, the three perpetrators, who were subsequently convicted, tricked their way into an elderly woman's home by pretending that urgent medical help was required.

---

75   *R v Collins* [2012] EWCA Crim 1161.
76   *R v Randall* [2005] 1 Cr App R (S) 60.
77   *R v Sowden* [2000] Criminal Law Reports 500, Court of Appeal.

Tricking their way into an elderly woman's home and threatening her with a meat cleaver. The perpetrator and her two co-accused went to the home of an 81-year-old woman. They rang the door bell. The victim got to her front door with the assistance of her Zimmer frame and when she opened the door she had taken the precaution of keeping it on the chain. However, one of the perpetrators presented a false story that her mother had collapsed and needed urgent medical help and, reluctantly, the victim opened her front door. The victim was particularly reluctant because she had had a previous unpleasant experience some three weeks before.

Once the chain was taken off the door, the three perpetrators forced their way inside. The victim resisted but was pushed back and ended up on the floor of her front room. They stepped over her and two of them, the females, searched the house while the male stood over the victim holding a meat cleaver, telling her not to move or she would be hit. During the course of the search of the premises, the intruders disabled more than one system by which the victim might have been able to summon help either during the offence or after it had taken place. Jewellery and a small amount of money were taken, together with two purses and other items. The taking of the jewellery included the pulling of a gold chain from the victim's neck in such a way as to break it.[78]

OBSERVING, THEN ROBBING VULNERABLE ADULTS

In one case, the perpetrator had been observed earlier that day paying attention to elderly pedestrians near sheltered accommodation. Eventually, he forced his way into the home of a 79-year-old frail man with severe arthritis, who had just returned from a shopping trip. The man was pushed to the floor and had money stolen before being punched in the face. The perpetrator was sentenced to four years in prison for robbery, a relatively lenient sentence.[79]

In another case:

Following vulnerable adult back to her home. A woman in her eighties had gone shopping on New Year's Day. She was vulnerable on account of her age. She lived in sheltered accommodation. The perpetrator, a drug addict, followed her back, knowing where she lived. As she took her keys out to open the door, he came up behind her, snatched at her purse and ran off with it. The robbery had a serious impact on her, making her fearful of going out. The perpetrator was convicted of robbery and sentenced to five years in prison.[80]

SYSTEMATIC GAINING OF PEOPLE'S TRUST, THEN ROBBING

The following case involved intensive targeting of a number of vulnerable people, all within the space of a month. In each instance, the woman involved first gained a degree of trust from the victims before robbing or stealing.

Intensive targeting of elderly people through gaining their trust: robbery and theft. The first offence of robbery concerned a couple living in a block of flats. The wife was bedridden and the husband suffered from Alzheimer's disease. The perpetrator, a 38-year-old woman, had befriended the husband and been invited into the flat. She told the

---

78   *R v Cleary* [2010] EWCA Crim 966.

79   *R v Johnson* [2001] 1 Cr App R (S) 123.

80   *R v Waters* [2008] EWCA Crim 1274.

wife that her husband owed £18 to the off-licence where the woman claimed she worked. She also offered to buy a new kettle because the existing one was leaking. She was given £40 by the wife (who had reached under her pillow for the money) and another £5 for food, and she borrowed the keys. She did not return (this was theft). However, ten days later, she returned, disguised, with an accomplice. The wife was pushed and hit, and her purse snatched. The perpetrator and her accomplice searched the room and left, stealing £300, papers and bank cards (this was robbery). Within a day, £1200 was withdrawn from the woman's bank account.

Befriending elderly lady before robbing her. Second, the same woman befriended an 80-year-old woman, for whom the perpetrator's son had apparently done some work. The perpetrator called at her home and, during a distraction, stole £400 from a wardrobe.

Befriending 90-year-old woman in pharmacy. Third, whilst at the chemist collecting her methadone prescription, she met a 90-year-old woman and assisted her out of the shop, during which time she stole her purse.

Befriending 88-year-old man in bank. Fourth, an 88-year-old man went to a bank to open an account, with £120 in his rear pocket. He was unsuccessful. The woman offered to help him open the account in another bank; she surreptitiously stole the £120.

Befriending 90-year-old man on street corner. Fifth, she struck up a conversation with a 90-year-old man on a street corner. Later that evening, he invited her in for a cup of tea; she stole £45 from a pair of trousers.

Befriending 79-year-old woman feeling unwell. Sixth, she approached a 79-year-old woman who was not feeling well and offered assistance. They had a cup of tea together. The woman put her handbag on the floor; her wallet, containing £70, was stolen.

Befriending 83-year-old man in Post Office. Lastly, an 83-year-old man went to the Post Office to collect his pension and had difficulty getting to his feet. The woman helped him to the bus stop, where she and her son helped him fasten his coat; on getting home, he discovered his pension book and £57 were missing.

She was convicted of robbery in relation to the first episode described above and of theft for the others. The offences involved targeting vulnerable people and gaining their trust with a display of false sympathy. She was sentenced to five years for the robbery, with three years for the thefts to run concurrently.[81]

FRAUD

The offence of fraud is contained in the Fraud Act 2006.

The three main offences are fraud by false representation, by failure to disclose information or by abuse of position.[82]

Previous offences under ss.15, 15A and 16 of the Theft Act 1968, of obtaining property, money transfer or pecuniary advantage by deception, were repealed by the Fraud Act and are, in substance, subsumed now within the 2006 Act. Some of the cases cited below refer to these previous offences.

Abuse of position is particularly relevant to safeguarding adults concerns. The ingredients are that a person (a) occupies a position in which he is expected to safeguard, or not to act against, the financial interests of another person, (b) dishonestly abuses that position, and (c) intends, by means of the abuse of that

---

81   *R v Moss* [2005] EWCA Crim 133.
82   Fraud Act 2006, ss.1–4.

position, to make a gain for himself or another – or to cause loss to another or to expose another to a risk of loss. Abuse can be made out even if the conduct consists of an omission rather than an act (s.4).[83]

EXAMPLES OF FRAUD PERPETRATED ON VULNERABLE ADULTS

The following are typical examples of fraud involving professionals, carers, neighbours, family members, rogue builders and so on.

Fraud perpetrated on former civil servant suffering from cancer. The court described this case as the 'worst crime of deception of the elderly ever to be before the courts in Scotland'. A builder was convicted of fraud and sentenced to ten years in prison. He had tricked a retired 77-year-old civil servant out if his life savings – almost £500,000 in cash – by pretending to lead a secret inquiry into police corruption, for which he required funds. The victim had been a former chief inspector of the pollution inspectorate. He had subsequently been forced to sell his home in order to pay for the care home in which he now lived, suffering from Alzheimer's disease and prostate cancer.[84]

Fiancée pretending to suffer from cancer. A woman, engaged to a lorry driver, pretended to be suffering from cancer and to be incurring high medical bills. She took £300,000 from him and spent it instead on a secret life of luxury with a lover. She was jailed for two years for fraud.[85]

Estate agents: taking money, fraudulently promising large investment returns. Two Hampstead estate agents carried out a sophisticated fraud on a rich, vulnerable and mentally ill (schizophrenia) middle-aged man. They were convicted of conspiracy to defraud, two counts of theft and one of obtaining money by deception. The fraud involved persuading the man to give them £200,000 for investment in property, on the promise of a £500 billion return. In addition, they duped him into giving them gold, jewellery (including his mother's ring) and share certificates worth £600,000. They were sentenced to five years in prison.[86]

Lawyer and parliamentary candidate overcharging two elderly sisters £50,000. A lawyer, who was also a Plaid Cymru parliamentary candidate and former head of administration for a county council, grossly abused the trust of two elderly sisters, obtaining some £50,000 from them by overcharging. For instance, he visited one of them in a nursing home, read poetry to her and then charged her hundreds of pounds for the privilege. He was sentenced to three years in prison for obtaining property by deception and theft and ordered to pay compensation.[87]

Solicitor stealing £3 million from estates of dead clients. A solicitor was sentenced to six years in prison for theft and obtaining property by deception. He had stolen money belonging to clients amounting to some £3 million, comprising sums from the estates of

83   Fraud Act 2006, s.4.
84   Harris, G. 'Builder cons man out of £450,000.' *The Times*, 2 March 2002. And: 'Conman jailed for 10 years.' BBC News, 22 March 2002. Accessed on 17 October 2008 at: http://news.bbc.co.uk/1/hi/scotland/1887420.stm.
85   'Conman jailed for 10 years.' *BBC News*, 22 March 2002. Accessed on 17 October 2008 at: http://news.bbc.co.uk/1/hi/scotland/1887420.stm.
86   Osley, R. 'Facing prison for £500,000 fraud.' *Camden New Journal*, 10 January 2008. And: Fletcher, H. 'Estate agents "swindled £m out of schizophrenic man".' *The Times*, 9 November 2007.
87   'Lawyer stole from elderly sisters.' *BBC News*, 3 October 2003. Accessed on 17 October 2008 at: http://news.bbc.co.uk/1/hi/wales/north_west/3159442.stm.

recently deceased clients – including £100,000 which was meant to provide income for the deceased client's son who had Down's syndrome.[88]

Directors of a will and probate service, fraud involving £5 million. In general, probate fraud is thought to be an increasing problem, with the Royal National Institute for the Blind estimating that it may amount to some £150 million a year, often involving solicitors or legal advisers.[89] Thus, in 2005, two directors of a wills and probate service were sentenced to three years, nine months (subsequently reduced by 13 months) and four years and six months in prison respectively for fraudulent trading under s.458 of the Companies Act 1985. The client account deficiency stood at nearly £5 million.[90]

Bank finance manager and financial adviser defrauding previous client. The victims were an 81-year-old man who had no close relatives and who lived alone, and an 84-year-old woman who also lived alone. Both had accounts at Lloyds TSB in Colchester. The perpetrator had been the financial manager there in 1997. In 1998, he was at Rothschilds and renewed contact with the two victims. Both were persuaded by him to invest money in Rothschilds. They subsequently paid over cheques in 1999 and 2000. He used the money for his own or his company's purposes, having pretended to the victims that he was going to invest the money on their behalf. In the first victim's case, this was £10,000; in the second case, £52,500.

There was complete recklessness with respect to the prospect of repayment of money obtained by persistently deceptive behaviour. The perpetrator undoubtedly selected his victims with care and subjected them to a cynical fraud.[91]

Investment adviser obtaining £360,000 from vulnerable people. A so-called investment adviser obtained £360,000 from vulnerable people (disabled, dying or bereaved), ostensibly to invest their money but in fact to put it into his own failing business. He was sentenced to four and a half years in prison for obtaining money by deception.[92]

Counter manager at bank taking £167,000 from elderly and sick people. A 59-year-old counter manager at Barclays Bank in the Rhondda Valley was a respected churchgoer and charity treasurer. She had been employed at the bank for 40 years. Yet she defrauded elderly and sick people of £167,000.

Many of the victims were friends or people she had known for years. They included a man with learning disabilities, retired people and recently widowed people. She also defrauded a hospital league of friends, for which she was treasurer. She massaged figures and transferred money in and out of accounts, making both withdrawals and credits to conceal what was going on. The bank reimbursed the victims in full. The perpetrator was described by many of her victims as apparently generous and thoughtful. She was sent to prison for two and a half years.[93]

Care home manager forging will and pretending to be daughter of resident. The manager of a care home forged the will of an 82-year-old resident, claiming to be his long-lost daughter, in order to inherit £300,000. She had tampered with her own medical records, inserting the resident's name as that of her father. She also stole tens of thousands

---

88   *R v Shaw* [1996] 2 Cr App R (S) 278.
89   'Fraud robs bereaved of £150 million.' *The Times,* 25 July 2004.
90   *R v Furr* [2007] EWCA Crim 191.
91   *R v Hooper* [2003] EWCA Crim 810.
92   Beattie, S. 'Conman jailed for £360,000 fraud.' *Teeside Evening Gazette,* 31 May 2008.
93   Stone, A. 'Bank clerk plundered pounds 167k from friends' accounts.' *Western Mail,* 25 February 2012.

of pounds from a 90-year-old resident. She was convicted on eight counts of fraud and two of theft, receiving a five-year prison sentence.[94]

Care home manger defrauding residents of £41,000. A care home manager defrauded two residents with dementia of over £41,000. This was by means of encouraging them to sign cheques or using their bank cards on 97 occasions. The fraud was detected by other staff who noticed problems with the accounts of the two residents, aged 82 and 93. She was of previously good character. She was sentenced to 30 months in prison. The victims would be compensated from her assets – £120 from a bank account and a television. The £40,000 was apparently missing.[95]

Care home manager stealing £330,000 from employer and residents. A care home finance manager, who called herself Lady Glanister, committed theft, false accounting and fraud. She was sentenced to 32 months in prison. She stole £330,000 from her employer, Oakfield Ltd, and from care home residents at two Northamptonshire care homes where she was responsible for the finances. She had become hooked on buying diamonds on a television channel, as well as going on cruises and buying champagne. She had been entrusted with debit cards, petty cash and residents' personal finances.

The woman had stolen from the company, using its accounts to cover her personal heating bills and petrol, and to inflate her salary and to pay her extra hours which she had not worked (but for which she forged spreadsheets). She also charged £17,000 of expenditure directly to the accounts of residents. In one case, when a resident needed a toothbrush, the perpetrator told the resident's mother that her daughter had no money to buy it.[96]

Sheltered housing manager using bank card of 78-year-old man. The manager of a sheltered housing complex was sent to prison after defrauding a 78-year-old widower of nearly £4000. She admitted six counts of abusing her position to commit fraud; this included using the resident's bank card on shopping sprees in Castleford. She was found not guilty on three other fraud charges, which related to him changing his will in her favour and fraudulently obtaining cash withdrawals of £10,000 and £2000 from his account.[97]

Fraud: making of elderly woman's will by impostor. A woman aged 87 had lived with her long-time male companion. Neither had ever married or had any children. He died at the age of 83 in January 1997 and the woman died on 12 March of that year. He had no surviving relatives, she only a cousin. Both had reciprocal wills with solicitors who had been appointed executors. She had very restricted mobility. The perpetrators, together with another female accomplice, arranged for the woman to make a new will. They arranged for her instructions to be transferred from her long-standing solicitors to a new firm with whom she had no previous dealings.

The new instructions were given and the will was executed. The accomplice posed as the woman, with the two perpetrators present when she signed the will. After the woman had died, they continued to represent that the new will was her true will. They were the main beneficiaries of the residue of the estate, which was valued in the region of £1.8 million,

---

94   "A despicable thief".' *Burton Mail*, 28 March 2012.

95   'Julie Close stole £41k from residents at Collins Green care home.' *Warrington Guardian*, 18 April 2012.

96   Dolan, A. '"Lady Glanister" stole £330,000 from the residents of her care homes to buy diamonds, cruises and champagne.' *Daily Mail*, 18 April 2012.

97   'Fraud carer jailed.' *Pontefract and Castleford Times*, 17 April 2008.

though there was a specific bequest of £10,000 in that will to the female accomplice (who, in fact, was the mother of one of the perpetrators).[98]

Senior local authority finance officer: taking £600,000 from vulnerable clients. A senior local authority finance officer, responsible for the finances of vulnerable adults who could not manage their own affairs, was convicted of fraud, having stolen some £600,000 from mentally ill and elderly service users.[99]

Carer impersonates dead client. The carer of a woman with multiple sclerosis fraudulently obtained a £5000 loan by pretending to be the dead woman. She was also convicted of dishonestly obtaining money from the dead woman's estate by pillaging her bank account after her death.[100]

Woman convicted for deceit and breach of trust against elderly people. A woman had obtained a job at a care home for vulnerable elderly people in January 2008 and had free access to the residents' rooms and personal effects. One of these residents, a 78-year-old woman, had a bank account and a cheque book which she kept in her handbag. The appellant stole that cheque book and wrote out a cheque to a loan company for £3100. However, she misspelt the name of the owner of the account and the cheque was dishonoured. The police were informed and she was arrested.

In a search of her home, another cheque from the same woman was discovered. That was made out to another company for £641.

As to other counts, another elderly lady of 88 lived over the road from the woman and regarded her as a friend. The woman had a bank card belonging to this lady. The woman would spend time with her, go shopping for her and give her general assistance. In fact, she had used the bank card to make a number of payments for herself.

The woman was convicted for deceit and breach of trust, in the words of the judge for 'sophisticated and sustained, serious, venal and stupid' crimes against elderly people'.[101]

Carer answering advertisements for carers in *The Lady* magazine. A carer was employed to look after a 90-year-old woman who had been discharged from hospital and required 24-hour care. The carer stole £3300 from a drawer, as well as blank cheques on which she forged the woman's signature (she was unsuccessful in drawing money on them). She left this employment without notice a day later. She then answered an advertisement in *The Lady* magazine and started work two months later, caring for an 88-year-old immobile woman. The carer was allowed to withdraw £250 cash per week, to cover her wages and housekeeping expenses. On six occasions, the carer exceeded this limit until a total of £3300 had been obtained. The carer pleaded guilty to theft, obtaining pecuniary advantage by deception and obtaining property by deception; she was sentenced to 30 months in prison, reduced on appeal to 18 months.[102]

Agency carer using signed, blank cheques. An agency carer cared for an 80-year-old housebound woman who was unable to walk. The carer collected her pension, did a bit of shopping, went to the launderette, cleaned the home and paid bills. At the carer's request, the woman would sign blank cheques, purportedly so the carer could then fill them in to

98   *R v Spillman* [2001] 1 Cr App R (S) 139.
99   Osley, R. 'Jail for £600k Town Hall fraud: "guilty, guilty" says trusted council finance man who bought home in Caribbean with elderly's cash.' *Camden New Journal*, 18 January 2007.
100 'Carer found guilty of fraud on dead woman's estate.' *Wirral Globe*, 1 April 1998.
101 *R v Lawson* [2010] EWCA Crim 193.
102 *R v Donaldson* [2001] EWCA Crim 2854.

pay the water and electricity bills. In fact, over a two-year period, she wrote out cheques to herself, amounting to £2875. She was convicted of obtaining a money transfer by deception and sentenced to 18 months in prison.[103]

Carer using cheques of 95-year-old woman. A carer was convicted of obtaining a money transfer by deception. She had been a carer working for a private care and support company for elderly and disabled people. She provided cover for the main carers of a 95-year-old woman. Her job was to prepare meals, do the cleaning and the shopping, to assist around the house and to help the elderly woman with getting up and going to bed. The woman's nephew had power of attorney over his aunt's affairs and was contacted by her bank in relation to a cheque for £4500, made payable to the carer's husband. The bank had stopped the cheque. Another cheque for £3000 had already been cashed. The body of the cheque was not in his aunt's writing; the signature appeared to be hers on one cheque but not on the other.[104]

Opportunistic obtaining and concealing pass book from social worker. A 65-year-old neighbour became friendly with an older woman. As the latter's mental health began to deteriorate, the neighbour began to act as her carer and discovered that she had substantial sums of money in various building society accounts. The neighbour arranged the transfer of one of the accounts into joint names. When she later handed over the woman's documents to a social worker, she retained the pass book, withdrew £44,000 and closed the account. She also obtained a watch, valued between £1200 and £1500, which the woman had left at a jeweller's. She was convicted of theft and obtaining money by deception.[105]

Woman defrauded by her son. A woman in her eighties was defrauded by her son, who managed to get her house transferred into his name in order to take out an £83,000 loan before falling behind on the payments. This resulted in bailiffs going to her home and her being at risk of losing her home. Her health deteriorated as she became more and more anxious and she died, aged 89 years. The judge stated that the son had asset-stripped his mother and had perpetrated a confidence trick of a particularly vile sort. He was sentenced to two and a half years in prison.[106]

Former RAF commander defrauding and ruining his two aunts. A former RAF flight commander defrauded three women, including two aunts, of over £300,000. He tricked them into investing their savings through him. He had simply used the money for himself, spending it on luxury items. He had obtained enduring power of attorney for one of his aunts who had dementia, whose money he then used for his own business. She was left £10,000 overdrawn, unable to pay care home fees and financially ruined.

Eventually, social services approached the Court of Protection, which removed him as attorney. He was sentenced to two years in prison.[107]

FALSE ACCOUNTING

Under s.17 of the Theft Act 1968, the offence of false accounting, in summary, requires dishonesty, with a view to gain or to cause loss to somebody else. It is about

---

103   *R v Roach* [2001] EWCA Crim 992.

104   *R v Seepersad* [2006] EWCA Crim 2998.

105   *R v Starsmeare* [2003] EWCA Crim 577.

106   'Liar son cons OAP mother.' *Eastwood and Kimberley Advertiser*, 19 March 2012.

107   Vinter, P. 'Ex-RAF flight commander who swindled his two aunties out of £312,000 is jailed for two years.' *Daily Mail*, 22 May 2012.

destruction, defacing, concealing or falsifying accounts, records or documents, or making use of these when the person knows they may be misleading, false or deceptive. The maximum penalty attached to this offence is imprisonment for seven years.

Care home owner stealing money from residents. When a care home owner was convicted of stealing money from residents with learning disabilities by withdrawing money from their bank accounts, she concealed the theft by false accounting.[108]

False accounting: care home manager taking over £100,000 from severely disabled residents. The manager of a nursing home had obtained well over £100,000 from sick and dying residents in order to fund an extravagant lifestyle, including six luxury holidays each year. She had access to residents' bank accounts – for example, as a signatory – as well as to residents' cash cards and PINs. She was eventually ordered to pay some £134,000 compensation. The manager appealed her conviction to the Court of Appeal and lost.

The false accounting had involved using the care home's cheque book to obtain items for herself, but falsely writing on the stub that the cheque had been paid to someone doing work for the home. The theft counts typically involved her withdrawing money from residents' accounts, amounts that bore no relationship to the actual expenditure of those residents. Obtaining property by deception involved, for example, using the care home's Barclaycard purportedly for items for the home or for residents but actually for herself.[109]

Supported living service: taking people to the bank. Mencap ran a supported living service for people with learning disabilities at a care home in Harborough. One of the staff took residents to the bank, where he withdrew sums for them and entered details in a log book. He falsified the entries, stole a total of £6720 and was convicted of false accounting and theft. He was sentenced to a 12-month community order and 120 hours of unpaid work.[110]

Social services manager: false accounting. When a social services manager took £4000 from elderly women in her care, she was convicted of forgery and of seven counts of false accounting.[111]

Solicitor: 50 offences of false accounting, £1 million stolen from paralysed man. A solicitor was convicted of more than 50 offences of false accounting, having stolen more than £1 million compensation money awarded to his client, who had been paralysed in a road accident. The solicitor was jailed for ten years.[112]

Solicitor abusing role of trustee and attorney. A solicitor was imprisoned for two years, having stolen money in his capacity as trustee of large sums of clients' money or of money belonging to the estates of dead clients and as holding power of attorney in relation

108 'Care home owner guilty of stealing from residents.' *Community Care*, 5 July 2007.

109 *R v Forbes* [2007] EWCA Crim 621. (See also: 'Nursing home matron jailed after stealing £100,000 from dying patients.' *Daily Mail*, 21 August 2006. Also: 'Matron ordered to pay compensation.' *Worcester News*, 11 May, 2007. Accessed on 3 December 2012 at: www.worcesternews.co.uk/archive/2007/05/11/Latest+%28eve_news_latest%29/1391124.Matron_ordered_to_pay_compensation.

110 'Carer abused trust by stealing from residents.' *Harborough Mail*, 1 September 2011.

111 'Social services manager stole from elderly.' *Isle of Thanet Gazette News*, 8 February 2002.

112 'Ten year jail sentence for solicitor who stole over £1m compensation from paralysed client.' *Solicitors' Journal*, 15 April 2008.

to clients' affairs. For example, he deprived a Weymouth-based charity, which operated an older persons' care home, of £168,000.[113]

Bank customer adviser transferring money from accounts of elderly and infirm people. A Barclays Bank customer adviser was sent to prison for 15 months after pleading guilty to 23 offences of false accounting over a period of three and a half years, involving £58,000. She had transferred money from customer accounts to her own, often via another account first. The four customers were elderly and infirm, including an elderly priest; none had noticed the missing money.[114]

FORGERY

Under section 1 of the Forgery and Counterfeiting Act 1981, a person is guilty of forgery if he or she makes a false document, intending that it be used to induce a second person to accept it as genuine and prejudicially to act (or not to act) in respect of that second person or somebody else.

A few examples are as follows.

Daughter-in-law forging cheques. When a Suffolk woman obtained more than £13,000 from her husband's vulnerable parents, she was jailed for six months for forgery. She had forged cheques and letters of authority to withdraw money from their bank account. She had started taking the money before her husband's father had died and had continued when the latter's wife had gone into a care home.[115]

Church minister forging powers of attorney and wills. A church minister befriended elderly parishioners before forging documents in order to inherit their property and possessions. He planned to wait until they were close to death before signing their properties over to himself. In one instance, he forged documents giving him power of attorney for a woman. When she moved into a nursing home, he gained control over her house. However, he was caught when one of the women involved made an unexpected recovery from a brain haemorrhage and stroke, after having received the last rites from the minister. She returned home from hospital to find that he had forged her will, which now left the house to him. He was sentenced to 240 hours' community service; one of his victims was appalled he had not been sent to prison.[116]

Social services manager. Under pressure from her drug-taking husband, who was physically and mentally abusing her, the manager forged the signature of an 84-year-old client in order to remove money from her savings account. She was convicted of forgery (and false accounting) but given a community sentence rather than prison because of her children.[117]

Carer of woman with multiple sclerosis forging a cheque for £8000. A care assistant employed by an agency was caring for a woman with multiple sclerosis who found it difficult to read. The carer would open and read her mail for her. The victim received a statement from her building society concerning an £8000 withdrawal. It transpired that the

113 Serious Fraud Office. *Former solicitor admits to plundering clients' accounts.* Press release, 6 June 2000. London: SFO.

114 'Mother stole £58,000 from bank to pay school fees.' *Bradford Telegraph and Argus,* 21 August 2008.

115 Hunt, J. 'Elderly couple victims of theft.' *East Anglian Daily Times,* 24 January 2006.

116 Britten, N. 'Trusted minister who fleeced his flock.' *Daily Telegraph,* 9 September 2006.

117 'Social services manager stole from elderly.' *Isle of Thanet Gazette News,* 8 February 2002.

carer had forged the victim's signature on a letter to the building society in order to pay a finance company for a car. The carer was convicted and sentenced to 15 months in prison.[118]

Nurse using pass book of 95-year-old woman. Another carer for a nursing agency acquired the National Savings pass book of a 95-year-old woman in her care. She forged the woman's signature twice, withdrawing a total of £5000. She was sentenced to 15 months in prison on appeal.[119]

Policeman stealing £280,000 from 89-year-old. A policeman gained the confidence of an 89-year-old woman and extracted some £280,000 from her over a period of three years. He was convicted of forgery and using a copy of a false instrument (this included selling her house).[120]

Financial adviser stealing tens of thousands of pounds from vulnerable adults. A financial adviser was convicted of forgery, false accounting, theft and money laundering. This included stealing £185,000 from an elderly woman, an £82,000 legacy bequeathed to a man with learning disabilities, and £31,000 from an 84-year-old man's estate (covered up by forged paperwork suggesting that the dead man had spent the money on foreign trips and double glazing).[121]

COLD CALLING, ROGUE TRADESMEN AND FRAUD

Door-to-door cold calling may result in abuse and may typically be aimed at older, vulnerable people. Clearly capable of constituting abuse and causing substantial harm, it may result in criminal offences being committed.

Relevant legislation includes the Pedlars Act 1871, Trade Descriptions Act 1968 and the Enterprise Act 2002. The Consumer Protection from Unfair Trading Regulations 2008 contain a number of offences relating, for instance, to misleading actions or omissions, aggressive practices and unfair practices.

The Cancellation of Contracts Made in Consumer's Home or Place of Work etc. Regulations 2008 provide for a seven-day cooling-off period. The regulations cover contracts made during both solicited and unsolicited visits for any value over £35. Cancellation must be clearly and prominently displayed in writing, whether or not there is a written contract.

It has been suggested that current legislation is inadequate to prevent the range of cold calling abuses, including:

- intimidation and persistence, false or no names and addresses being given

- token work being carried out so that the issue may be regarded as civil and contractual in nature, rather than criminal

- taking deposits and never returning

---

118 *R v Ross-Goulding* [1997] 2 Cr App R (S) 348.

119 *R v Mangham* [1998] 2 Cr App R (S) 344.

120 'Ex-PC conned victim out of home.' *BBC News*, 5 April 2006. Accessed on 17 October 2008 at: http://news.bbc.co.uk/1/hi/england/essex/4880720.stm.

121 Jenkins, R. 'Financier stole from elderly clients.' *The Times*, 13 September 2006.

- starting work immediately before people have had a chance to read the small print, driving people to the bank, there to pressure them into withdrawing large amounts of money etc.[122]

Legislation may be ineffective when traders' names and addresses are rarely known and large amounts of cash change hands on the spot. Fraud or deception might work, but the police may be reluctant to bring a case if at least some work has been carried out; they may characterise the issue as a civil, contractual matter rather than a criminal matter. It has been suggested by the Trading Standards Institute that cold calling for property services should be prohibited with a power of arrest attached.[123]

Apart from shortcomings in legislation, there is generally slow reporting of doorstep selling offences, a lack of resources to devote to prevention and detection, reluctance or inability of complainants to give evidence, poor evidence given and no agreed multi-agency approach. Alleged perpetrators may simply deny everything, and the police may then drop the criminal investigation and say instead that it is just a civil dispute.[124]

That said, convictions are sometimes secured. A number of convictions of rogue traders for fraud have already been highlighted above. The following are further examples.

Stairlift selling: theft and fraud. A man purporting to sell stairlifts was successfully prosecuted by Devon County Council (trading standards). He pleaded guilty to breach of the Theft Act 1968, Consumer Protection Act 1987 and Forgery and Counterfeiting Act 1981. He had posed as a stairlift repairer and installer, and targeted vulnerable elderly and disabled people. He would advise that a stairlift was irreparable, show customers advertisements from two well-known stairlift companies (he had no contract to supply their products or permission to use the trademarks), take their money, take away their existing stairlift and not deliver the new stairlift. He was an undischarged bankrupt and used a number of false names and addresses.[125]

Roofers sitting on roof drinking tea for a morning. In one case, two 'roofers' called, sat for most of a morning on the roof of the home of an 86-year-old woman with dementia, drinking tea, supplied less than £50 of labour and goods, and then charged her £600, escorting her to the bank to withdraw the money. In this case, the offenders were identified by CCTV at the bank and were convicted on the evidence (including that of a neighbour).[126]

Gross overcharging for roof work: fraud. A builder was sentenced to 100 hours' community service under s.2 of the Fraud Act 2006 (false representation of the price of work) after carrying out roofing work for an 81-year-old vulnerable woman. He had called

---

122 Quoted from: Trading Standards Institute. *Door to door cold calling of property repairs, maintenance and improvements: long overdue for statutory control.* Basildon: TSI, 2003, pp.6–13, 40.

123 Trading Standards Institute. *Door to door cold calling of property repairs, maintenance and improvements: long overdue for statutory control.* Basildon: TSI, 2003, pp.6–13, 40.

124 Office of Fair Trading. *Doorstep selling.* London: OFT, 2004, pp.93–94.

125 Devon County Council Trading Standards. *Devon Trading Standards successfully prosecutes stairlift fraudster.* Press release, 16 April 2007. Exeter: Devon County Council.

126 Trading Standards Institute. *Door to door cold calling of property repairs, maintenance and improvements: long overdue for statutory control.* Basildon: TSI, 2003.

uninvited. The work he had carried out was worth £562 plus VAT; he had, in fact, charged £4240.[127]

Building work, followed by bogus Customs and Excise officer: fraud of £120,000. In 2008, a builder was sentenced to seven and a half years in prison for fraud; a vulnerable 76-year-old man had been tricked into paying over £120,000 of his life savings. The builders had first approached him offering a free roof survey. They then carried out unnecessary and substandard building jobs for which they charged £66,000. The man then refused to pay for any more work, at which point a bogus Customs and Excise officer visited, claiming that the man had inadvertently become part of a VAT 'scam' and would have to make payments or go to prison. The man ended up paying a further £61,400.[128]

Builder gaining trust of vulnerable person first. A builder used his business to target elderly people by charging a modest price for an initial piece of work but then following up with subsequent works for which he charged excessive amounts. His customers were duped into parting with substantial sums of money. He was sentenced to five and a half years in prison for theft; a compensation order and a confiscation order were also made against him, each for £141,000. It was not quite a cold calling case; he distributed leaflets to obtain work.[129]

Rogue traders: fraudulent action after fraudulent action to clean out vulnerable elderly people of their assets. The victim was an elderly woman of 93. Some two years before the offence, she had been the victim of a fraud whereby work was carried out to her property over a period of 18 months at highly inflated prices. She paid more than £87,500. The matter was not reported to the police, and there is no evidence that this appellant was involved in that scheme.

On this occasion, the perpetrator went to her house, claiming he was a debt collector. He represented to her that he knew that she had been the subject of what he called a scam by others, who, he said, were now in prison. He said that he could get back £39,000 of what she had lost but that he needed to be paid what he called legal fees. She paid him over £1600. He then tried to persuade her to hand over £14,000 as what he called the debt collector's commission for recovering the debt. When she refused, he got a man he called Brian to speak to her over the telephone. He claimed to be the perpetrator's boss and persuaded her to hand over more money. She did so.

In total, she had handed over £4600 to the appellant over a period of five days. He then tried to get her to pay another £4000 in commission fees, and when she said that she did not have the money, he suggested that she borrow it. Fortunately, when she went to the building society to raise a loan, she was advised to contact the police. The perpetrator was arrested when he called at her home to collect more money.[130]

Works to drains: tens of thousands of pounds in fraud. The perpetrator and another man called on a house in Dulwich, where the 77-year-old victim lived. They told him that his drains had been investigated with a camera and needed repair. That was untrue. Over the coming weeks, they extracted money from him for the repairs they said were

127 Devon County Council Trading Standards. *Builder sentenced for defrauding elderly resident.* Press release, 16 July 2008. Exeter: Devon County Council.

128 Metropolitan Police Service. *Male imprisoned for seven and a half years for fraud.* July 2008. Accessed on 23 October 2008 at: http://cms.met.police.uk/met/boroughs/enfield/04how_are_we_doing/news/male_imprisoned_for_7_and_a_half_years_for_fraud.

129 *R v Williams* [2001] 1 Cr App R 23.

130 *R v Vinter* [2011] EWCA Crim 3327.

needed. He paid them £200 cash and then gave them a number of cheques. Two were cashed, totalling £10,000. That sum was immediately taken from the account into which it was paid. Cheques worth a further £19,000 were handed over, but fortunately the victim rang his insurers who investigated, and the confidence trick was discovered before that further amount was withdrawn from his account.[131]

Fraud causing victim to remortgage property. The fraud was committed whilst the perpetrator was on licence in respect of a six-year term of imprisonment. That had been imposed for a conspiracy to defraud. In that case, the appellant and others deliberately targeted a vulnerable individual, who was fraudulently advised that building works needed to be undertaken at his property. The cost of this unnecessary work was so high that the victim was persuaded to remortgage his property, to put money into an investment scheme (which, he was told, went bust) and then to sell his property to cover fictitious losses. As a result, that vulnerable victim lost all that he had – some £300,000.[132]

Fraud: roof tiles, driving victim to bank. The victim of the fraud was an 84-year-old woman who lived in a suburb of Birmingham. On 6 May 2011, the perpetrator and another man arrived at her home address. The other man had previously done some work at her house. They knocked on the front door. The other man spoke to her and said there were some loose tiles on her roof. He went up a ladder, came down and said they could repair the tiles but would need money up front.

They took her to a bank in the perpetrator's van. She went in and withdrew £2050 in cash which was the amount of the quotation she had been given for the work. When she got back to the van, there was a female in the front passenger seat. She handed the money to her. They returned to her street. They dropped her on the corner, saying they needed to go and buy the building equipment to make a quick start on the job. The victim went home but never saw the appellant or the other man or the woman again. A neighbour had been concerned about what he had seen at the house.[133]

Fraud: roofs and chimneys, 43 households defrauded, £800,000 obtained. The perpetrator was leader of a team of rogue builders who defrauded householders in the south-east of England by undertaking unnecessary repair works to houses, in particular roofs and chimneys, dishonestly charging for work that was not carried out and carrying out incompetent and substandard work.

Over a period from January 2003 until September 2007, about 43 householders were defrauded and about £800,000 was obtained. The perpetrator was involved throughout the conspiracy. The offences followed a very similar pattern. The victims were nearly all either elderly or otherwise vulnerable householders. They would be 'cold-called' and told that urgent work was required, usually to their roof or chimney. A price would be quoted for the work, but, as soon as the work commenced, further, more substantial, problems were 'found' which were said to require immediate attention. The work carried out would be cosmetic and unnecessary, and the amount charged for the work would be grossly excessive. Any work that was carried out would be to a very poor standard and frequently required rectification by competent contractors; other work was supposed to have been carried out but never was.[134]

---

131 *R v Cooper* [2012] EWCA Crim 162
132 *R v Cooper* [2012] EWCA Crim 162.
133 *R v Smith* [2012] EWCA Crim 1184.
134 *R v Baker* [2011] EWCA Crim 150.

Fraud: tarmac, initial quote followed by outrageous demand for money and intimidation of victim. The perpetrator and his associates would select a suitable victim. The victims, some ten of them in this case, varied in age from almost 60 to, in one case, 90. They would tell some story to the effect that they had been working in the area for this, that or the other organisation, and they had a quantity of material over, which they could use to tarmac the victims' drives.

Initial reasonable quote. When asked about the price, they would mention a figure of, say, £10. Since that seemed a good bargain, the victims would very often agree to have the work done. There would then be thrust in front of them a piece of paper, some form of contract – the material parts of which were concealed – and they would be invited to sign. They usually did so.

Presentation of enormous bill. In due course, that day or a day or two later, the perpetrator and his friends would come with chippings and tar. They would lay the chippings usually on a larger area than that contracted for and then present an enormous bill – £4000, £5000, £6000. When the customer demurred, as of course he or she always did, the contract would be produced and there it would appear that what the customer was said to have agreed to was not £10 for the whole job but £10 a square yard or a square foot or whatever. Hence, the appellant and his friends would seek to justify their exorbitant demand.

In the case of one woman, she was asked to offer a cup of tea to the workers when they came. Shortly afterwards, a lorry arrived and chippings were put on her driveway.

Intimidation of victim. At the end of the work, she was told that the cost was to be £4000. She was astounded. She said she could not and would not pay that ridiculous amount of money. Then there occurred the feature common to almost all of these cases, which is the particularly unpleasant aspect of this sort of fraud. The three men crowded around her. She became frightened. She pushed them away and returned to her house. But she was told that the money must be produced. It was the appellant who accompanied her to the building society, where she had some savings, who waited with her while she drew out the money and returned with her so that the money could be handed over. Which it was. She was defrauded of £4000.

It is worth pointing out that it is not even as though the work that was done came anywhere near in value to the sum charged. The view of the expert – as it happens her brother-in-law who worked in the trade – was that the labour was worth about £80, and subsequent enquiries revealed that the load of chippings had been bought for £31.

The perpetrator pleaded guilty and was sentenced to four years' imprisonment.[135]

Fraud: repairs, various techniques for extracting further sums of money, 29 vulnerable people defrauded, £140,000 stolen. The perpetrators were all members of the travelling community, largely based in Leicestershire. Between August 2007 and 24 July 2010, at least 29 vulnerable or elderly property owners or residents across the country paid a total of £140,528 in cash in consequence of the activities of the offenders and others.

Those sums frequently comprised the life savings of the victim and have not been recovered. In addition, a further £45,090 was sought from owners and occupiers, although not, in the result, obtained.

Property deliberately damaged. The victims were aged between 51 and 97 years. They would be approached at home, or even in the street near their home, and asked if they wanted work undertaken on their property, or they would be confronted with the

---

135 *R v Richards* [1989] 11 Cr App R (S) 286.

assertion that repairs were urgently required. Initial quotations were provided. It would then be alleged that further urgent work was required, when in fact it was not. On some occasions, the property was deliberately damaged by the offenders in order to demonstrate to the householder that further urgent work was required. Money would be taken from the victims for no work or for unnecessary work, or for shoddy, incomplete or inadequate work.

Different techniques to extract even more money after the initial fraud. Once the contact had been made, a recurring feature of this conspiracy was that different techniques were employed in order to extract further sums of cash, including the claim that additional work required special machinery or scaffolding, or that VAT or some other tax was due in respect of the payment. Some victims were promised repayment by way of a banker's draft or cheque. They would then be told that the banker's draft or cheque due to them had been completed for a sum greater than the repayment that the victim was due, and that the problem could only be solved and the money released if a further cash payment was made. When the cash was paid, the banker's draft or cheque would not be forthcoming.

Victims were frequently driven to the bank by the conspirators for the purpose that they be supervised while withdrawing the cash that had been demanded. On other occasions, they were followed into the bank. Some of the victims were subjected to threats or pressure, and it was clear that they complied with the demands made upon them by reason of fear or confusion. Casual theft took place from some of the victims' homes.[136]

Fraud: selling of useless alarm systems. The perpetrators set up Pentagon Security Systems, of which one perpetrator owned 75 per cent and the co-accused 25 per cent. From May 2007 to June 2008, the company operated a fraud which was directed mainly against elderly people by selling them virtually useless alarm systems for their homes. The alarms were faulty and regularly called the monitoring stations unnecessarily, which led to significant telephone bills of £400 to £500 per month.

Grossly inflated prices. A number of complainants had their phones cut off and struggled to pay the bills. The customers were led to believe that the alarm systems were tailor-made to their needs, but they were not. They were also led to believe that the system had National Security Inspection approval; that was not so. The prices charged were extortionate. In fact, the price fixed usually followed bargaining where grossly inflated prices were suggested and then reduced in order to make it appear as though the customers were receiving a good deal.

Fictitious maintenance, misleading information. The customers were charged for maintenance of the system, although there was none. The address given for the company did not exist. In some cases, perfectly good systems were replaced with the dud system. When customers contacted the company about the problems, their complaints received dismissive responses. Potential customers were either telephoned or had their doors knocked. They were given misleading information about the installation. On some occasions, they received leaflets about a home safety campaign. One of the perpetrators regularly said that he was calling about the home safety campaign. This was to encourage customers to take on the security system because it was said that it was necessary to keep them safe.

Large numbers of elderly people were deliberately targeted. Sometimes scare tactics were used, where customers were shown clippings from newspapers about attacks on the elderly.

---

136 *R v Newbury* [2011] EWCA Crim 2174.

The perpetrators' attitude towards the customers was dismissive. Paperwork later recovered revealed that they were described in disparaging and coarse terms.[137]

Serious consequences for victims: facing financial ruin. The judge observed that this was a gross and cynical deception, for the most part targeted at elderly and often vulnerable customers, the oldest of whom was 94. Not only had the perpetrator caused them anxiety, but in some cases the customers now refused to open the door and had lost their trust in people. In addition, some of the customers faced ruin because of the economic consequences. The inevitable inference was that the elderly had been deliberately targeted and they had been treated with disdain and contempt.[138]

SCAMS

The Office of Fair Trading notes that scams commonly include:

- **Letters predicting the future:** so-called psychics or clairvoyants promise to make predictions that will change the course of your life – but first you have to pay a fee.

- **Bogus foreign lotteries:** you are informed of a large lottery win – but you have to send off administration, tax and customs fees to claim your winnings. You get nothing.

- **Foreign money offers and advance-fee scams:** You are offered a huge sum of money in return for helping to get money out of a foreign country, or you are told you are the sole heir to an inheritance. You are asked for your bank details or told to send a fee. You will get nothing in return, and your bank account may be raided.

- **'Golden' investment opportunities:** you are offered the chance to invest money in things like shares, fine wine or gemstones. They are often over-priced, very high risk, and difficult to sell on.

- **'Miracle' health cures:** you are promised 'miracle cures' for ailments such as arthritis. The claims are often exaggerated to con you out of money.

- **Fake sweepstake and prize draw wins:** you are told you've won a large cash sum or another valuable prize. You are asked to send a processing fee, order goods from a catalogue or ring a premium-rate 090 number to claim your prize. You get a cheap prize or nothing at all in return.[139]

It offers suggestions as to what to do, such as encouraging the person to contact Consumer Direct, Citizens Advice Bureau, a social worker, trading standards officers or the police. Many scams will be potentially fraud.

---

137   *R v Kallian* [2012] EWCA Crim 652.
138   *R v Kallian* [2012] EWCA Crim 652.
139   Quoted from: Office of Fair Trading. *Can you stop the person you care for from being scammed? A guide for carers and care professionals.* London: OFT, 2008.

SUSPICIOUS ACTIVITY REPORTS

Under the Proceeds of Crime Act 2002, there are particular provisions relating to money laundering. Although these are mostly aimed at large-scale operations, including organised crime and terrorism, the provisions are drawn widely so as to be relevant to the financial safeguarding of vulnerable adults.

Sections 327 to 329 of the Act create a number of money laundering offences in relation to concealing, disguising, converting, transferring or removing from the jurisdiction criminal property; making arrangements for acquisition, retention, use or control of criminal property by or on behalf of somebody else; and acquiring, using, possessing criminal property. Criminal property is widely defined.

In addition, it is an offence for staff working for particular financial bodies such as banks and building societies to fail to report known or suspected money laundering. The grounds for reporting are that the person (a) knows or suspects or (b) has reasonable grounds for knowing or suspecting that another person is engaged in money laundering.

This means that if banks or building societies suspect criminal activity related to money laundering, including any such activity involving vulnerable adults, they must report it by means of a suspicious activity report (known as an SAR). The report goes to the Serious Organised Crime Agency (SOCA) who, in practice, might then feed the details back down to the local police force.

In terms of use of cashpoints by dishonest carers, for instance – a typical type of theft from vulnerable people – computerised systems can pick up unusual transaction patterns. However, if the theft has been regular over an extended period of time, this may not be identified. Alternatively, if, for example, people are coming to branches, staff might pick up suspicious activity.

The British Bankers' Association has published a good practice guide for bank staff. It includes two examples of suspicious activity.[140]

Case studies (British Bankers' Association). In the first case, there had been attempts to obtain several bankers drafts from an elderly customer, to the value of £31,000. The bank staff formed the view that the customer was being exploited by an individual pretending to be a relative. The suspicious activity report was passed on by the SOCA to the police, who were then able to protect the customer.

In a second case, an elderly person attended a building society branch with a carer and made several withdrawals up to a value of £2000. There were also cashpoint withdrawals, as much as £1500 in one week. The building society thought the cheque signatures might have been fraudulent; they blocked cashpoint withdrawals and cheques. A suspicious activity report was made. A trusted third party was appointed signatory. No action was ultimately taken against the carer, but the report had the effect of preventing further exploitation.[141]

---

140 British Bankers' Association. *Safeguarding vulnerable customers: banking best practice: advice for bank staff.* London: BBA, 2010.

141 British Bankers' Association. *Safeguarding vulnerable customers: banking best practice: advice for bank staff.* London: BBA, 2010.

The following are a few examples of legal cases involving banks and building societies.

Elderly man always accompanied to make withdrawals. A neighbour had befriended an elderly man with some form of senile dementia or Parkinson's disease. Her visits became frequent, and, over a period of three months, the man withdrew £5980 which he gave to the neighbour (and her sister-in-law). It was spent on drugs. Building society staff had noticed that he was accompanied whenever he came in to make a withdrawal. The neighour had persuaded him to make 37 withdrawals. She was sentenced for conspiracy to steal.[142]

Directing an elderly confused man to withdraw money from building society. An elderly confused man living alone came under the direction of somebody else who would regularly take him to the building society, pretending to be his grandson. The perpetrator would ask for a cheque to be made out, specifying not himself as a payee but one of several associates. He was convicted of theft and sentenced to four years in prison.[143]

Bank staff picking up on rogue traders extracting money. The victim was a 74-year-old woman who lived alone. The perpetrator called at her house and said to her: 'Do you remember me?' She did remember him; he had done some building work for her about seven years previously. He told her that her roof tiles needed some work done, which would cost £50. She agreed.

He returned with two accomplices. Roof tiles were removed and the complainant was then told that the job would cost more than £50 and that the loft needed insulating. They returned the next day. Some work was carried out on the loft, but the perpetrator told the complainant that the cost would now be £8900.

She went to her bank and attempted to withdraw the money. The bank was only able to hand over £2000. She took that and arranged to come back the next day for the rest. She gave the £2000 to the perpetrator and asked for a receipt and invoice. He said he would give those to her the following day. He did not. The next day, the victim returned to her bank to withdraw another £6900. The cashier at the bank was concerned about this second request to withdraw a large sum in cash and also by the fact that the victim had been driven there by one of the builders.

The police were called. They found a van with the perpetrators in it opposite the bank. They were arrested and convicted of fraud.[144]

Bank staff alert to person with learning disabilities being defrauded by rogue builders. One of victims was 46 years of age, a man with learning difficulties who lived with his elderly mother. He also owned the house next door. Some time before, he had won a large sum of money through a national savings scheme. In 2004, he was the victim of rogue builders, who charged him £12,500 for some work on a chimney. The perpetrator was not involved at that time.

Rogue builders come for second time. In 2006, builders again knocked at the victim's door. There were five in total, including the perpetrator and other rogue builders. They told the victim that he had some loose leading on his extension that ought to be seen to; otherwise, he would have water dripping on to his electrics. Over the next few weeks, they purported to carry out further work, which they persuaded the victim was needed. He was told that if the work was not done, he would be in a lot of trouble and his house might be

142 *R v Stockdale* [1994] 15 Cr App R (S) 48.
143 R v Kelly [1997] Court of Appeal, 14 November 1997.
144 *R v Frankham* [2010] EWCA Crim 1861.

condemned. He was told that the work would have to be done quickly. The prices charged for the work were extortionate. He was charged the inflated sum of £75,000.

Valueless work. A chartered surveyor later examined the properties and estimated that what work had been carried out was of no benefit or value.

Fraud upon fraud. On one occasion, two builders turned up asking for £9000, which the victim paid. Two days later, the other rogue builders said that they still had not received the £9000 and they persuaded the victim that the £9000 had been given to the wrong person. They asked for a further £2500 because they wished to hire a private detective to investigate the matter. The victim got the cash to pay the builders from the bank, and the builders drove him to the bank and parked a quarter of a mile away. They encouraged him to go to different branches of the bank so that the staff would not become suspicious.

Large withdrawal from bank. Matters came to a head on 20 March 2006 when the victim went to the bank at Margate and withdrew £10,000, which he gave to the builders. He returned to the same bank later that morning, saying he wished to withdraw a further £20,000. Staff were suspicious and took him into a private room to discover what had been going on; as a result, they phoned the police. Convictions for fraud followed.[145]

BANKS AND BUILDING SOCIETIES: CONFIDENTIALITY

A City of London Police document discusses the question of banks, building societies and customer confidentiality.

It notes that such confidentiality is governed generally by old case law which stated that disclosure could be made:

> (a) where disclosure is under compulsion by law; (b) where there is a duty to the public to disclose; (c) where the interests of the bank require disclosure; (d) where the disclosure is made by the express or implied consent of the customer.[146]

In addition, it points out that s.29 of the Data Protection Act 1998 allows disclosure for the prevention of detection and crime. And s.338 of the Proceeds of Crime Act 2002 states that the submission of a suspicious activity report, under the Act, does not breach any legal restrictions on disclosure that would otherwise apply.

Nevertheless, the document goes on to state that guidance for staff from the British Bankers' Association and the Building Society Association emphasises the importance of gaining customer consent – which is often not forthcoming. In which case, disclosure by the bank or building society would have to rest on the 1998 Act or 2002 Act.

Yet, the document observes, many reports made by staff purportedly under the 2002 Act might not, in fact, reflect the purpose of the Act, which is money laundering. In which case, it implies, the legal basis for such disclosure might be questionable:

> While some of these reports will demonstrate a suspicion of money laundering, many do not and they reflect a desire on the part of staff to

---

145 *R v Baker* [2011] EWCA Crim 150.
146 *Tournier v National Provincial and Union Bank of England* [1924] 1 KB 461.

act in the customer's best interests. However, the SARs regime is designed to provide financial institutions with an opportunity to comply with their statutory obligations around money laundering and is not intended to be used for the identification of vulnerable people. It is up to the receiving police service to determine how such reports are handled and, inevitably, most will place an emphasis specifically on the opportunity to restrain money held by criminals.[147]

---

147 City of London Police, National Fraud Intelligence Bureau. *Assessment: financial crime against vulnerable adults*. London: Social Care Institute for Excellence, 2011, p.23.

Undue influence: gifts, wills (law of equity)

Key points
    Express or presumed undue influence
    Undue influence and safeguarding
Undue influence: a social trend?
Express undue influence
Presumed undue influence
    Not necessary to show that anybody had done something wrong
    Relationships giving rise to trust and confidence
    Undue influence case succeeds where criminal case fails
Undue suspicion rather than undue influence
Safeguarding interventions and undue influence
Proprietary estoppel: relying on assurances or promises
Lack of capacity
    Wills: test of capacity
    Gifts: test of capacity
    Undue influence or lack of mental capacity?

KEY POINTS

In civil law, and apart from lack of capacity, there is sometimes an alternative ground on which a transaction may be set aside. This is on the basis of a legal, equitable concept known as undue influence. It can provide a legal remedy in relation to suspicious, improper transactions. Undue influence, in the law of equity, concerns lifetime gifts of property or money, or wills.

Generally speaking, undue influence can be summarised as follows. It is when a person has mental capacity to conduct the transaction – the will or the gift – but has had their will overborne not just by the influence but by the *undue influence* of somebody else.[1] This is in the sense that somebody is being unduly influenced precisely then to exercise their mental capacity to make a choice, albeit not a free and informed one.

EXPRESS OR PRESUMED UNDUE INFLUENCE

The undue influence can be either 'express' (in the case of gifts or wills) or 'presumed' (in the case of gifts only).

---

1   *Tchilingirian v Ouzounian* [2003] EWHC 1220 (Chancery).

If there is evidence of coercion or undue pressure, this is called 'express' undue influence. However, often there is no such evidence; instead, there might be presumed undue influence.

Undue presumed influence is particularly relevant to vulnerable adults.

First, it typically must involve a relationship of trust and confidence, which is unequal (e.g. because of one person's vulnerability).

Second, there needs to be a transaction which, if not suspicious, must at the very least call for an explanation.

Third, if the person who has benefited cannot give a plausible, innocent explanation, then the courts can set aside the transaction as invalid – even if there is no direct evidence that this person has done anything 'wrong'.

UNDUE INFLUENCE AND SAFEGUARDING

An obvious question is how knowledge of this legal rule will help practitioners involved in safeguarding. This is pertinent because many legal cases involving undue influence are brought after a person has died by relatives who want to retrieve inheritances. And a local authority, for example, would not normally be in the business of getting involved.

However, there are reasons for local authority involvement. These include (a) suggesting people seek professional advice if it seems they are subject to undue influence, (b) otherwise generally supporting them, (c) considering whether other law might be relevant, including criminal law or maybe the inherent jurisdiction of the High Court, (d) being aware that sometimes the financial issue might affect the local authority directly – for example, if the money changing hands represents future care home fees, in which case the authority might itself wish to take civil legal action.

UNDUE INFLUENCE: A SOCIAL TREND?

That undue influence is relevant to safeguarding adults would seem clear. In fact, the courts have observed the renewed interest in it, owing to the greater longevity of people now and their concomitant vulnerability to suggestion by family members.

The following case concerned a vulnerable 70-year-old man, described as physically and mentally disadvantaged all his life, who lost his house to the undue influence of his sister. The court set out at some length what it regarded as a social trend.

Lifetime gifts and transfers: importance of independent exercise of free will. With the increase in home ownership and the rising value of residential property, more people have more property to dispose of in their lifetime and on death, and more people expect to benefit substantially from inheritance.

People living longer, inheritors waiting longer. As people live longer, the inheritors have to wait longer. There is, however, the unwelcome prospect that the longer the wait, the greater the risk that even a modest estate will be seriously diminished by the high cost of care in the old age or infirmity of the home owner and by the impact of inheritance tax on death.

Elderly and infirm vulnerable to suggestions. The elderly and infirm in need of full-time residential care are vulnerable to suggestions that they should dispose of the home to which they are unlikely to return. In the author's view, these social trends are already leading to a renewed interest in the law governing the validity of lifetime dispositions of houses, both in and outside the family circle, by the elderly and the infirm. The transfer of a house is a substantial transaction. A house is the most valuable asset that most people own. If a transfer is made by one person on the dependent side of a relationship of trust and confidence to a person in whom trust has been placed, it must be shown by the trusted party that the disposition was made in the independent exercise of free will after full and informed consideration.

No need for reprehensible conduct for finding of undue influence. The court may grant relief to the transferor, even though the transfer was not made as the result of any specific reprehensible conduct on the part of the trusted transferee.[2]

EXPRESS UNDUE INFLUENCE

If undue influence is argued to be express, then evidence is required of how exactly the influence was exercised in terms of overt, improper pressure or coercion.[3]

For instance, a woman changed her will and left everything to her heavy-drinking son, with whom she lived and of whom she was afraid, whilst disinheriting her other son. The court found that the first son had exercised undue influence. It set aside the new will, finding sufficient evidence of express undue influence.

Mother frightened and unduly influenced by her son. The heavy drinking son (T) had every motive for persuading his mother to change the will. He was fearful for his own security in his mother's home and furious with the other brother and the latter's wife. He had already demonstrated vindictiveness towards them.

The judge concluded:

> There is also no doubt in my mind that T had the opportunity to use undue influence in persuading his mother to change her will. He had taken his mother back [to her own home from a nursing home] despite medical advice to the contrary; had deterred [his brother and wife] from visiting, even if there was no formal ban; and he had tried to push [his brother] out of the house on the day that the will was executed. She was frail and vulnerable and frightened of T. Did he take that opportunity? In my judgment he did.

There was no other reasonable explanation for the false allegations the mother made against the other son and for the reasons she gave for changing the will. She was 'simply doing as she was told'. Her discretion and judgement had been overborne. This was undue influence.[4]

In another case, the vulnerability of an 85-year-old woman and the forcefulness of her nephew meant that the latter had expressly unduly influenced her into resigning her position as trustee and landlord of a farm. This was after he had threatened

2   *Pesticcio v Huet* [2004] EWCA Civ 372.
3   *Royal Bank of Scotland v Etridge (no.2)* [2001] UKHL 44.
4   *Edwards v Edwards* [2007] EWHC 119 (Chancery).

court proceedings. Evidence was given that his aunt was distressed and upset, and frightened of both her nephew and court proceedings.[5]

An older case characterised express undue influence as having to involve 'some unfair and improper conduct, some coercion from outside, some over-reaching, some form of cheating and, generally though not always, some personal advantage obtained by a donee placed in some close and confidential relation to the donor'.[6]

Nonetheless, not all suspicious circumstances, even with evidence of pressure, will lead to a finding of express undue influence.

Changing of a will by person with early-onset Alzheimer's disease: persuasion and influence but not undue influence. An elderly woman suffering early-onset Alzheimer's disease was persuaded by her daughter to change her will largely in favour of the daughter. The daughter had written to her mother about how disappointed she had been over the previous will and how she had expected her mother would leave the estate to her only surviving child and not split it also with her grandchildren (children of the mother's deceased son).

The judge pointed out that not all influence is undue influence, not even necessarily strong persuasion or heavy family pressure. Furthermore, the judge found no evidence that the daughter had repeatedly pestered or badgered her mother.[7]

PRESUMED UNDUE INFLUENCE

Alternative to express undue influence is presumed undue influence. The latter relies on a relationship of trust and confidence and the relationship being abused, resulting in a disadvantageous transaction – or at least a transaction that 'calls for an explanation'.

Once these two elements are established, then the 'evidential burden' shifts to the other party to give an innocent explanation for the transaction. If this explanation is not forthcoming or convincing, undue influence will be made out. Importantly, it is not necessary to prove that the other party did anything 'wrong'. Relationships of trust and confidence are recognised by the law courts in well-known categories (such as doctor and patient) but also in other relationships (such as carer and cared-for person).

This second form of undue influence, presumed, can be relevant in the context of adult protection work and has been broken down in detail by the courts as involving the following, in summary:

(a) **Unfair advantage:** One person takes unfair advantage of another where – as a result of a relationship between them – the first person has gained influence or ascendancy over the second, without any overt acts of persuasion.

(b) **Trust and confidence assumed:** However, some relationships (e.g. parent and child, guardian and ward, trustee and beneficiary, solicitor and client,

---

5   *Daniel v Drew* [2005] EWCA Civ 507.

6   *Alcard v Skinner* [1887] 36 Ch D 145.

7   *Scammell v Scammell* [2008] EWHC 1100 (Chancery).

medical adviser and patient) will give rise to an irrebuttable presumption that a relationship of trust and confidence existed. The reposing of trust and confidence does not have to be proved.

(c) **Trust and confidence in other relationships:** However, such relationships are infinitely various; a key question is whether the one person has posed sufficient trust and confidence in the other.

(d) **Reliance, dependence, vulnerability:** It is not just a matter of trust and confidence; exploitation of a vulnerable person would be included, for example. Thus, trust and confidence, reliance, dependence, vulnerability, ascendancy, domination or control are all relevant terms.

(e) **Transaction calling for an explanation:** Undue influence must be proved by the person alleging it; however, a relationship of trust and confidence, coupled with a transaction that 'calls for an explanation', will normally be enough to discharge this burden of proof.

(f) **Shift of evidential burden; innocent explanation required:** The evidential burden then shifts to the other person to counter the inference of undue influence – that is, to rebut the presumption.

(g) **Degree of disadvantage:** Even within the special class of relationships (assuming trust and confidence), not every gift or transaction will be assumed to have been down to undue influence unless otherwise proved (otherwise, Christmas presents or the payment of reasonable professional fees would be caught); it should be only where the transaction calls for an explanation. The greater the disadvantage to the vulnerable person, the greater the explanation called for.

(h) **Independent advice:** The receipt of independent advice is a relevant consideration but will not necessarily show that a decision was free from undue influence.[8]

NOT NECESSARY TO SHOW THAT ANYBODY HAD DONE SOMETHING WRONG

In the context of safeguarding adults, when financial abuse takes place, the doctrine of undue influence may give interested parties (e.g. the exploited person or another member of the family) a civil remedy.

The courts have repeated that, for presumed undue influence, it is not necessary to show that anybody has done anything wrong.[9] Furthermore, even if the donor of a gift denies that he or she has been pressurised – for example, to transfer land

---

8   *Royal Bank of Scotland v Etridge (no.2)* [2001] UKHL 44.
9   *Pesticcio v Huet* [2004] EWCA Civ 372.

– presumed undue influence might still be made out since direct pressure for a particular gift is not necessarily required.[10]

In the case below, in which an elderly man was taken under the proverbial wing of a neighbour, the court emphasised the significance of the presumption of undue influence and of the carer having to provide an innocent explanation for what had occurred. In the absence of such an explanation, 'public policy' demanded a finding of undue influence, even in the absence of direct evidence of a wrongful act. The reference to the 'care authorities' and the 'care coordinator' might suggest (it is unclear) that the local social services authority was unwittingly involved in assisting the woman to exercise the undue influence.

Taken under the wing of a neighbour: £300,000 gift. A 72-year-old retired teacher and bachelor was living alone. He had become physically dependent on others because of limited mobility. His neighbour, whom he had met at a supermarket when he was holding on to railings and was in distress, 'took him under her wing'. Following a fall, hospital admission and then discharge, he became more dependent. She 'volunteered to the care authorities' to be responsible for giving him two meals a day. At the suggestion of the care coordinator, he then signed a third-party mandate, authorising her to draw on his current account. After further falls and hospital admission, he said he wanted to make a gift to her of certain investments; these amounted to nearly £300,000, nearly 91 per cent of his liquid assets.

No need for beneficiary to have done anything wrong or sinister. There was a relationship of trust and confidence; the gift was very large. These facts gave rise to a presumption of undue influence. It was for the woman to rebut this. Given that the man had received no advice, independent or otherwise, the presumption was not rebutted, and undue influence was made out. The court also made the point that this would be so even if the woman's conduct had been 'unimpeachable' and there had been nothing 'sinister' in it. This was because the court would interfere not on the grounds that any wrongful act had in fact been committed by the donee but on the grounds of public policy. Such public policy required that it be established affirmatively that the donor's trust and confidence had not been betrayed or abused.[11]

RELATIONSHIPS GIVING RISE TO TRUST AND CONFIDENCE

The relationships giving rise to a relationship of trust and confidence can be various, apart from those that automatically do so (see above). For instance, the relationship of aunt and nephew[12] or husband and wife[13] may do so. Similarly, presumed undue influence cases might involve carers.

The following court case illustrates how a live-in companion rapidly exercised such influence over the elderly man she was purporting to assist, to the point of having him 'at her mercy'. It also shows how supposedly independent advice might be suspect.

---

10   *Goodchild v Bradbury* [2006] EWCA Civ 1868.
11   *Hammond v Osborne* [2002] EWCA Civ 885.
12   *Randall v Randall* [2004] EWHC 2258 (Chancery).
13   *Royal Bank of Scotland v Etridge (no.2)* [2001] UKHL 44.

Depleting an elderly man's estate. An elderly man's wife died in 1958. Shortly after she died, he employed a woman as secretary-companion. In the last five years before he died in 1964, he made gifts to her of nearly £28,000; his estate had been reduced from £40,000 to £9500. His general practitioner's description of him was that he was elderly, weak, a little vacant, courteous, introspective, depressed at times; a gentle old man. His memory was not worse than that of many people of that age. He was not particularly fit and active; he was happy up to a point.

Solicitor involved subject to conflict of interest: no truly independent advice. The companion became increasingly entrusted with handling his financial and business affairs. He agreed to sell his house and to move to another house the companion had always wished to reside in. He made a gift of it to her; he was described on 'some government form' that had to be filled in as the 'lodger'. The judge concluded that at this point he was entirely at the mercy of the companion. The solicitor involved in the transaction was purportedly acting for both the man and the companion; he said nothing to the man about the desirability of independent advice. The man therefore did not receive the independent advice that could have supported the argument that he had exercised 'full, free and informed thought', which in turn could have removed the influence of the companion.

No direct evidence of pressure: but heavy onus on carer to rebut presumption of undue influence. The judge held that there was in fact a relationship of trust and confidence between the man and the companion and that there was a presumption of undue influence in the case of the gifts. It was for her to rebut this; she had failed to do this, even though there was no direct evidence of pressure being brought to bear by her. Furthermore, the onus on the carer was a heavy one because of the otherwise seemingly objectionable nature of her behaviour.[14]

Presumed undue influence might come in different guises, not necessarily in an obvious caring or family situation.

Undue influence from 'alternative' group. A woman in her sixties became involved with a group of people sharing an interest in art therapy, alternative medicine and spiritual writing. The group purchased a small estate, which they ran partly as a hotel and partly as a cultural centre; they formed a company. The woman first raised a mortgage on her house to loan £34,000 to the group; she subsequently sold her house and gave the proceeds of some £180,000 to the estate as a loan, repayable when the company/estate was dissolved or was sold.

Emotional reliance and dependence on group, influence going unchecked. The judge held that the second, larger loan had clearly been procured through undue influence. A relationship of trust and confidence existed; the woman had already allowed her house to be used by the defendants for two years before selling it; she was physically isolated at her house and emotionally reliant and dependent on the defendants. She also believed that one of the defendants had a gift of healing. It was a transaction that called for explanation, since by the sale she alienated her only remaining asset for the foreseeable future, if not forever. Furthermore, she did not receive proper, dispassionate advice from the defendants about the nature of the transaction, and her detachment from her past life and friends meant that the influence of the defendants went unchecked.[15]

---

14   *Re Craig* [1970] 2 All ER 390 (High Court).
15   *Nel v Kean* [2003] EWHC 190 (QB).

Obtaining of truly independent advice may indicate that presumed undue influence has not been exercised, but this is not decisive. For instance, it might have been inadequate advice.

Undue influence of sister exercised over 70-year-old disabled brother: and poor independent advice from solicitor. A 70-year-old man, physically and mentally disadvantaged for most of his life, lived at home with his widowed mother. She had made a gift of the house to him. Some 18 years later, he was admitted to hospital following a serious fall and discharged to a nursing home six months later. Shortly afterwards, having received some inadequate advice from his own solicitor concerning local authority rules about care home fees, he transferred the house to his sister who shortly afterwards sold it.

The court made a finding of undue influence. The sister had not obviously done anything wrong, but as a matter of public policy it could be set aside. The advice from his solicitor had been 'not such as a competent adviser would give' if acting solely in the interests of the man. (The solicitor had, in fact, been initially contacted by the sister.) It had not been so as to free him 'from the impairment of the influence on his free will and to give him the necessary independence of judgment and freedom to make choices'.[16]

UNDUE INFLUENCE CASE SUCCEEDS WHERE CRIMINAL CASE FAILS

The following case illustrates the importance of considering different legal avenues in safeguarding. A criminal prosecution was withdrawn, but a civil undue influence case succeeded against a nurse who had exploited a retired doctor.

Undue influence exercised by nurse over sick doctor. A nurse obtained £300,000 from the life savings of a doctor she was supposedly caring for, having been hired through a private care agency. He was suffering from a 'chronic brain wasting disease', was a bachelor and lived frugally. She had earned £36,000 a year as a live-in nurse. With the money, she booked an £8000 cruise, bought a house with a £100,000 loan from the doctor and persuaded him to change his will and sign over his £250,000 flat to her. A prosecution for theft was dropped, but an undue influence case was taken. She was ordered to repay the money, could not and was bankrupted. Two flats she owned were repossessed, and she faced being evicted from her £350,000 home.[17]

UNDUE SUSPICION RATHER THAN UNDUE INFLUENCE

Of course, not all transactions are suspicious. The doctrine is not about outlawing the making of gifts by elderly, or even dying, people.

Transfer of house to second wife by terminally ill man: no undue influence. A man transferred his house into the joint names of himself and his second wife as beneficial joint tenants. This followed the death of his first wife, although he had long since known his future second wife. Some months before the transfer, he had been diagnosed with terminal cancer. His children attempted to have the deed of gift set aside on grounds of undue influence. They failed.

---

16   *Pesticcio v Huet* [2004] EWCA Civ 372.
17   Scott, M. 'Nurse plunders £300k from dying patient.' *Sunday Mail*, 16 March 2008.

The court took account of various factors. He had been married to his second wife for 14 years, and the judge did not accept the children's view that she did not care for him properly when he was ill. He did not personally lose by the transaction (he continued to own half of, and to live in, the house), and the sons had previously upset the father in relation to family company payments. The judge also took the view that these facts 'did not speak for themselves' so as to raise the question of presumed undue influence. This meant that the burden did not fall on the second wife to explain the transaction; it remained with the children to try to show express undue influence. This could not be shown in this case.[18]

Likewise, generous gifts of provisions in wills might be innocent, as in the following case, and whether there had been express undue influence, even though the housekeeper had been present at two important meetings about the will.

Elderly woman's will in favour of housekeeper: no express undue influence. An elderly woman left her sizeable residuary estate to a live-in housekeeper and her husband. The woman's housekeeper had taken up her role in 1979; she and other members of her family lived in the woman's house until the latter's death in January 2000 at the age of 87. The woman was physically frail but had remained mentally alert. The will was dated May 1999. The woman's next of kin argued that either the woman had not known or approved of the contents of the will or that there had been undue influence.

The court noted that the housekeeper had been present at two important meetings concerning the will and that she had sometimes prompted the woman in respect of telephone calls about it. Furthermore, the woman was elderly and vulnerable, substantially dependent on the housekeeper; against this background, there could have been scope for the exercise of subtle undue influence.

Innocent explanation: genuine fondness for housekeeper. Nevertheless, the will was consistent with a 'perfectly innocent' explanation, which the judge preferred, when deciding the case in favour of the housekeeper. The woman had been highly intelligent, had possessed the mental capacity to make the will and had had the full extent of her estate explained to her only weeks before making it. Although elderly and vulnerable, she had remained intelligent, sensitive and independent-minded, capable of making her own decisions. She was genuinely fond of the housekeeper and her family.[19]

Sometimes, the suspicion of undue influence might arise not just in respect of friends or relatives but local authority staff. This occurred in the following case, but the local ombudsman declined to find maladministration, pointing out that genuine kindness could provide an explanation for the way in which the carer had behaved, resulting in the carer being a beneficiary in the will of a service user.

Making of will to benefit local authority care home assistant. A social services home care assistant was named as beneficiary in the will of a service user for whom she had provided care (£10,000 to her, £10,000 to each of his grandsons, the rest to his son). When he died, she expressed great surprise that she was a beneficiary. The son claimed that she had exercised undue influence and that the extra jobs she had done for him outside her duties (such as collecting a television and moving a bed downstairs for him) were evidence of her gaining that influence and playing on his father's gullibility.

---

18   *Glanville v Glanville* [2002] EWHC 1271 (Chancery).
19   *Re Ethel Mary Good* [2002] EWHC 640 (Chancery).

Carer unaware of provision in will. The council had a policy about refusing gifts or being named as beneficiary in a service user's will. However, the woman and her solicitor pointed out that this provision in the will was unsolicited and that she had been unaware of it, and that to terminate her employment would constitute unfair dismissal. The council's principal solicitor believed that she should not face disciplinary procedures if she kept the bequest. He thought it was common for conscientious workers to be remembered in wills; there was nothing wrong with this, and refusal to give up the bequest was not evidence of undue influence.

Acts of genuine kindness. The ombudsman stated that it was for the courts to decide about undue influence; it was his job to decide whether the care assistant's actions equated to maladministration. In his view, they did not; the evidence suggested neither coercion nor that she had known the contents of the will; and the television collection and bed moving appeared to be acts of genuine kindness.[20]

SAFEGUARDING INTERVENTIONS AND UNDUE INFLUENCE

Interventions by practitioners involved in safeguarding might not seem straightforward in relation to undue influence since many cases are brought by family members, often when the vulnerable person has died. However, there are various possibilities.

SEEKING OF INDEPENDENT ADVICE

First, in appropriate circumstances, if practitioners are sufficiently concerned about what they believe to be undue influence, it may be appropriate to suggest to the person that he or she seeks independent advice. For instance, it would be normal to seek advice from a professional such as a solicitor or accountant before entering a major financial transaction. This is bearing in mind that the courts regard the obtaining of genuinely independent advice as a safeguard against undue influence.

CRIMINAL OFFENCES

Second, it is possible, in some circumstances, that elements of undue influence could be associated with a criminal offence, in which case it might be a police matter. Although undue influence is a concept in civil, equitable law – not criminal law – nonetheless, it may, in substance, be relevant to a criminal conviction. This was explicitly mentioned in a major theft case, in which the courts confirmed that the making of a 'gift' by a person with capacity to make it could, in some circumstances, still amount to theft. This was on the basis of dishonesty, with reference to the fact that the notion of undue influence might be relevant to establishing that dishonesty.[21]

20   Local Government Ombudsman Investigation: *Bexley London Borough Council 1998* (97/A/2021). London: LGO, 1998.

21   *R v Hinks* [2001] 2 AC 241 (House of Lords).

NOT JUST THE DEAD BUT THE LIVING

Third, undue influence cases do not relate to dead people only. For instance, a living person can bring a case, arguing that he or she had been unduly influenced, but is no longer and now seeks redress.[22] In the following case, an elderly man had effectively lost his house because of the undue influence of his nephew.

Elderly man unduly influenced by his nephew. An elderly man's nephew persuaded him to sell his house and put the money (£43,000) towards a new house costing £83,000, which was in the nephew's name. This was on condition that the uncle could live there for the rest of his life. The nephew defaulted on the mortgage payments and the lender sought possession. The uncle argued that he had been unduly influenced and should be given his money back ahead of the lender. The Court of Appeal agreed, stating that he was entitled to money back, but only in proportion to the sale price (considerably less than the purchase price).[23]

In an unusual case, a deputy – the person's daughter – appointed by the Court of Protection went to court to try to regain money in the best interests of her father. The latter, when he still had capacity to manage his money, had, it was argued, been unduly influenced to give nearly £550,000 to a legal secretary employed by the man's own solicitors.

Deputy seeking to get back money given by her father under undue influence. A man, a retired lawyer in his seventies, became friendly with a legal secretary who worked for his solicitors. After suffering a stroke, she visited him regularly, becoming his carer. He cashed in his portfolio and ISAs, sold his Premium Bonds and paid her over £549,000. Meanwhile, he was 'living in squalor'. His estranged daughter found out what had happened. She was appointed deputy by the Court of Protection, but her father, having now lost capacity to manage his affairs, stated that he did not want a legal case to proceed and that the legal secretary should keep the money. However, the court ruled that it was in the father's best interests to proceed with the case and that there had been undue influence.[24]

INTEREST OF ORGANISATION IN THE MONEY OR PROPERTY

Fourth, undue influence cases might be brought by organisations, including those very organisations with a role in safeguarding adults at risk or children. This is when they have a particular interest in the money involved.

Hospital taking case against exploitative carers. A hospital went to court in a dispute over a woman's will. She had willed her farmhouse to the hospital; when she died (strangled by her own clothing on a stairlift), it transpired she had given it to two private carers. The hospital brought the case arguing alternatively lack of mental capacity to make the gift or undue influence.[25]

And a local authority brought an undue influence case against the son of a woman who had given her house to the son. This was, on the face of it, a safeguarding

---

22   *Royal Bank of Scotland v Etridge (no.2)* [2001] UKHL 44.

23   *Cheese v Thomas* [1994] 1 All ER 35 (Court of Appeal).

24   'Daughter of stroke victim who gave £500,000 to secretary in legal tussle.' *Daily Telegraph*, 12 October 2011.

25   *Special Trustees of Great Ormond Street Hospital v Rushin* [2001] WTLR 1137.

matter, but the local authority's motivation was not simply to restore the woman's property to her. She owed the local authority care home fees, which would be payable from the value of her house.[26]

PROPRIETARY ESTOPPEL: RELYING ON ASSURANCES OR PROMISES

As well as undue influence, other equitable principles surface in legal cases from time to time. One such is that of 'proprietary estoppel'.

The elements of this, roughly, have been that the person (e.g. a carer) making the claim has acted to their own detriment on the basis of assurances by the other person, by providing services to that other person. In the following case, the help given by a man to an elderly woman entitled him to some of her money, on the basis of promises made to him and all the help he had given her.

'This will all be yours one day.' A self-employed bricklayer had begun to provide gardening services to an elderly woman. As she became more incapacitated with arthritis and leg ulcers, he would do more and more for her, without payment. This included collecting prescriptions, helping her dress and go to the toilet, making sure she had food and drink, as well as helping in the garden. In the last few months of her life, he did even more. For the last ten years or so, she had stopped paying him. When he queried this, she had said not to worry, to the vague effect that 'this will all be yours one day'.

She died intestate, and the man challenged the extent of his entitlement. On the basis of proprietary estoppel, the court used its discretion – taking account of a number of factors – and held that his equitable interest amounted to £200,000 out of a house and furniture valued at some £435,000.[27]

In another case, a lodger had increasingly provided services and care to an elderly couple who had told him that, whatever happened, he would have a home for life. Instead, the house passed first to the man's wife and then, on her death, to her nieces. Far from him having exploited the couple in any way, the court held that he had an equitable interest amounting to £35,000 (out of a house valued at £160,000).[28]

LACK OF CAPACITY

Undue influence presupposes that the person who has been exploited had the mental capacity to make the gift or will, albeit subject to undue influence. However, alternatively, gifts or wills can be set aside by the courts if the person (the donor or testator) is shown to have lacked capacity at the time they were made.

WILLS: TEST OF CAPACITY

For wills, the common law test of capacity relates to an understanding of the nature of the act, the extent of the property, an appreciation of the claims of others, there

---

26   Woolcock, N. 'Widow, 91, sued over nursing home fees.' *Daily Telegraph*, 12 October 2002. See: *D v R* [2010] EWHC 2405 (COP); *Sharma v Hunters* [2011] EWHC 2546 (COP).

27   *Jennings v Rice* [2002] EWCA Civ 159.

28   *Campbell v Griffin* [2001] EWCA Civ 990.

being no disorder of mind poisoning the affections, and no 'insane delusions' influencing the disposal:

> It is essential…that a testator shall understand the nature of the act and its effects; shall understand the extent of the property of which he is disposing; shall be able to comprehend and appreciate the claims to which he ought to give effect; and, with a view to the latter object, that no disorder of mind shall poison his affections, pervert his sense of right, or prevent the exercise of his natural faculties – that no insane delusion shall influence his will in disposing of his property and bring about a disposal of it which, if the mind had been sound, would not have been made.[29]

However, when a highly educated pharmaceutical tycoon cut his son out of his will and instead left £10 million to the Conservative Party, the will was held to be invalid on grounds of lack of testamentary capacity. This was because his natural affection for his son had been poisoned or distorted by delusions about an international conspiracy of dark forces ranged against him, in which he believed his family members were implicated.[30]

GIFTS: TEST OF CAPACITY

In respect of gifts, the common law test of capacity demands that the degree of understanding required is relative to the transaction; a gift trivial in nature requires less understanding than, for example, at the other extreme, disposal of the person's only valuable asset. This latter would require as high a degree of understanding as required for a will:

> The degree or extent of understanding required in respect of any instrument is relative to the particular transaction which it is to effect… Thus, at one extreme, if the subject-matter and value of a gift are trivial in relation to the donor's other assets, a low degree of understanding will suffice. But, at the other, if its effect is to dispose of the donor's only asset of value and thus, for practical purposes, to pre-empt the devolution of his estate under the… will…then the degree of understanding required is as high as that required for a will, and the donor must understand the claims of all potential donees and the extent of the property to be disposed of.[31]

UNDUE INFLUENCE OR LACK OF MENTAL CAPACITY?

In some cases involving gifts, the court considers alternative arguments that the person either lacked capacity at the time – grounds for setting aside the gift – or, if

---

29   *Banks v Goodfellow* [1870] LR 5 QB 549.
30   *Kostic v Chaplin* [2007] EWHC 2298 (Chancery).
31   *Re Beaney (deceased)* [1978] 1 WLR 770.

capacity was lingering at the relevant time, had been unduly influenced. This then allows uncertainty to be overcome; one way or another, the gifts will not be valid.[32]

For example, the question of whether apparently rapacious carers could keep their ill-gotten gains from a vulnerable widow hinged in part on the latter's capacity at the particular time when she had made a gift of her farmhouse home. The court found, in the end, a lack of capacity to make the gift, but stated that if the woman had possessed the relevant capacity, it would have ruled that she had anyway been unduly influenced.

Death on stairlift preceded by gift of farmhouse and three cars to carers. An elderly couple live in a converted farmhouse just outside a village. The husband died and the woman received help and care on a private basis from two carers in the form of a mother and daughter from the local village.

In 1996, she was introduced by the mother to a solicitor who had been suspended by the Law Society. He prepared a statement which the woman signed, saying she wished to change solicitors. She never met the new solicitor, although she did meet the assistant solicitor twice. Otherwise, her 'instructions' were conveyed to the solicitor either by the suspended solicitor or by the mother.

Gift to carers. In February 1996, the woman met the assistant solicitor and agreed to transfer her home, a farmhouse worth nearly £300,000, for £50 and on terms that she would occupy it for the rest of her life and that the carers would provide care for her. She subsequently made a number of lifetime gifts to the mother-carer in order to enable the carer's family to buy three cars; in addition, regular withdrawals of £2000 to £3000 a month were made, with the mother-carer as co-signatory, for some months before the woman's death. The amounts were significantly larger than the woman had previously withdrawn.

Woman found dead. The woman was found dead, aged 77 years, in April 1997, with her clothing tangled in the stairlift. Great Ormond Street Hospital was one of the residuary beneficiaries of her will. The hospital subsequently brought a case to challenge the validity of the transactions that the woman had entered into, on grounds of her mental incapacity at the time to enter into them, of undue influence or of unconscionable bargain.

Transfer of property set aside: mental capacity or undue influence. The court decided that the transactions should be set aside since a wealth of evidence showed that she had been suffering from senile dementia at the time as a consequence of Alzheimer's disease. Had this lack of capacity not been proven, the court would in any case have made a finding of undue influence.[33]

---

32   For example: *Special Trustees of Great Ormond Street Hospital v Rushin* [2001] WTLR 1137. Or: *Burgess v Hawes* [2011] Central London County Court.

33   *Special Trustees of Great Ormond Street Hospital v Rushin* [1997] unreported (Chancery).

Harm and civil wrongs, including negligence

Key points
    Trespass to the person
    Negligence
    Negligence: sometimes about financial harm
    Public bodies: sometimes protected from liability in negligence
    Police protected by courts

KEY POINTS

Civil torts are legal 'wrongs' that give rise to civil actions for damages. Two such torts are trespass to the person and false imprisonment. Negligence is another.

They are relevant to safeguarding for a number of reasons. First, they require a lower standard of proof than is required in criminal proceedings. So a failed criminal prosecution does not necessarily preclude a civil action. Second, such cases may achieve significant and important financial compensation for the person who has suffered harm.

That said, there are circumstances in which the courts protect local authorities (and sometimes the NHS) from negligence cases if the alleged harm is associated with difficult statutory, policy or financial decisions made by the authority.

TRESPASS TO THE PERSON

Trespass to the person is the equivalent in civil law of assault and battery in criminal law.

In the following case, concerning an NHS trust's failure to withdraw a medical intervention on the request of the patient, the court concluded that the trust had acted unlawfully in terms of the tort of trespass to the person.

Unlawful failure to withdraw ventilator and trespass to the person. A former social worker suffered a haemorrhage in the spinal column of the neck. At the time, she executed a living will. This stated that if a time came when she could not give instructions but was suffering from a life-threatening condition, permanent mental impairment or permanent unconsciousness, then she wished for treatment to be withdrawn. She subsequently suffered another major bleed and became tetraplegic, following which she needed a ventilator in order to breathe. She asked for the ventilator to be switched off in March 2001. She could not do it herself. A year later, at the time of the court's judgment, it had still not been turned off.

Considering the evidence, the court started with the presumption of capacity; it considered that this had been displaced between April and August 2001. However, on the evidence, the court concluded that she had in fact had capacity from August 2001 onward. The court criticised the NHS trust's consistent failure for not attempting to resolve the dilemma urgently. The woman had been treated unlawfully by the trust (i.e. trespass to the person), for which a small award of damages should be made.

The court drew a distinction between the duties of the team of doctors and nurses and that of the trust as a whole; it was unfair that the burden of decision and responsibility had remained in the hands of the former when it was the trust's responsibility to act.[1]

Likewise, a caesarean section, carried out against a woman's will, constituted unlawful trespass to the person. It had been carried out in good faith, but was inconsistent with the law.

Unlawful caesarean section and trespass to the person. A woman in the late stages of pregnancy was suffering from pre-eclampsia; there was a risk to the lives of both herself and the unborn baby. She fully understood the potential risks and clearly rejected medical intervention; she wanted the baby to be born 'naturally'. After she had been detained in hospital unlawfully under the Mental Health Act 1983, the hospital then purported to act in her best interests from necessity – on the grounds that she lacked mental capacity – by performing a caesarean section. It did so, having obtained an emergency declaration from the High Court on the basis of inadequate and misleading information being given to the judge.

The woman subsequently brought a legal case against the approved social worker and the hospital. On the evidence, she had possessed capacity to decide about the operation, although she had ceased to offer resistance at the time, when told that the caesarean would go ahead anyway (following the court's emergency declaration). The court now pointed out that this had not been consent but submission; thus, the caesarean section, together with the associated medical procedures, constituted unlawful trespass to the person.[2]

In an ostensibly similar case, the outcome was different. A 40-week pregnant woman was refusing to have a caesarean section, required because the baby was in the breech position. The court held that to perform the operation would be in her best interests. This was because she was rendered temporarily incapable of making the decision by her all-pervasive fear of needles, which dominated everything and overrode the consent she had given in principle to the operation.[3]

NEGLIGENCE

Civil negligence cases can be brought for physical (and also sometimes psychological or financial) harm caused by carelessness. The standard components that have to be shown are the existence of a duty of care, breach of that duty, and causation in the sense that the breach caused the harm complained of.

---

1   *Re B (Adult: refusal of treatment)* [2002] EWHC 429.
2   *R v Collins, Pathfinder Mental Health Services NHS Trust and St George's Healthcare NHS Trust, ex p S* [1998] 1 CCLR 578 (Court of Appeal). And: *R v Collins, Pathfinder Mental Health Services NHS Trust and St George's Healthcare NHS Trust, ex p S (no.2)* [1998] 3 WLR 936 (Court of Appeal).
3   *Re MB (Adult: caesarian section)* [1997] 2 FCR 541.

For instance, negligence cases might be relevant in the context of adult protection, as in the following case involving neglect of an elderly man in hospital.

Dehydration and ill-nourishment in hospital causing death. Following the neglect and death of a man in hospital, a negligence case was settled out of court for some £15,000. A former metal worker, he had been admitted for a broken leg but within a few days became ill. He became dehydrated and ill-nourished, eventually dying of renal failure, septicaemia and a chest infection. Fluids and nutrition had not been administered and his poor state of health was only identified when he had been discharged to a rehabilitation unit. He was immediately readmitted to hospital intensive care but died.[4] Despite instructions from doctors to do so, staff had failed to provide a saline drip for 12 days. The hospital stated that it could have done things better but was under-funded.[5]

Another case involved an elderly man with senile dementia who went into a care home. Within two months, he was in a distressing state, heavily sedated, thin and bony, being shouted at to sit down and often sopping wet. He was admitted to hospital as an emergency, with a huge sore at the base of his spine which had rotted the skin to the bone. The family brought a negligence case against the care home and accepted an out-of-court settlement of £45,000.[6]

Cases involving pressure sores in hospitals are also regularly settled out of court. For instance:

Liability for pressure sore and death from septicaemia. In March 2010, the Belfast Health and Social Care Trust admitted liability and made a £40,000 out-of-court settlement in relation to the death of a woman in the care of the hospital. Her family had claimed she was not treated properly and died from septicaemia as a result. She was admitted to Royal Victoria Hospital with a suspected broken hip. For about two weeks, staff were undecided about whether it was broken; in the meantime, she was allowed to develop a pressure sore on her heel, which deteriorated until the whole heel turned black and gangrenous.[7]

When NHS trusts have taken shortcuts with infection control and people have suffered or died as a consequence, a negligence case might be possible. For instance, an actress and model was compensated with £5 million for negligence on the part of a hospital which led to her contracting the MRSA infection.[8]

Following the scandal at the Mid Staffordshire NHS Foundation Trust, where many hundreds of people died following poor care and neglect, the hospital settled claims worth over £1 million on the basis of human rights breaches and clinical negligence claims.[9]

4   'Settlement over pensioner's death.' *BBC News*, 3 March 2004. Accessed on 17 October 2008 at: http://news.bbc.co.uk/1/hi/england/west_midlands/3530283.stm.

5   Wright, O. and Carson, V. '86-year-old is killed by hospital's cruel neglect.' *The Times*, 8 August 2002.

6   *Pannone wins care home negligence settlement of £45,000.* Press release, 12 December 2006. Manchester: Pannone.

7   'Belfast Trust pays damages over pensioner's death.' *BBC News*, 1 March 2010. Accessed on 1 September 2010 at: http://news.bbc.co.uk/1/hi/northern_ireland/8544259.stm.

8   Sanderson, D. 'Leslie Ash gets £5m payout from hospital where she caught MRSA.' *The Times*, 17 January 2008.

9   Leigh Day & Co. 'Mid Staffs cases start to settle.' *News*, 2 March 2010. Accessed on 11 January 2012 at: www.leighday.co.uk/News/2010/March-2010/Mid-Staffs-cases-start-to-settle. See also: www.leighday.co.uk/News/2011/August-2011/17-more-Stafford-Hospital-families-receive-compens.

In sexual abuse cases involving children, the courts have held that it is possible to bring a civil case in tort against the employer of the abuser on the basis of vicarious liability of the employer for the acts of the employee.[10]

There is no reason why this principle might not apply in the context of adults. For instance, when three carers were acquitted of assault (feeding talcum power to an elderly woman), nonetheless two other courses of action followed. First, the local authority terminated its contract with the agency that employed the carers. Second, the woman then brought a civil case against the agency. It was settled out of court, the agency admitting negligence and agreeing to pay over £10,000 in compensation.[11]

NEGLIGENCE: SOMETIMES ABOUT FINANCIAL HARM

Negligence need not always be about physical harm; it can sometimes relate to psychological or financial harm.

In the following case, an elderly man in Eastbourne, with uncertain understanding and partial memory, had fallen into the hands of a confidence trickster who first cleared out his savings account and then put him up to raising a mortgage on his house, which money was then also taken. However, the court held a solicitor liable for loss of the mortgage money for blatant breach of his duty of care in facilitating the mortgage, even though the money had been appropriated by an unknown third party, for whom the solicitor was, of course, not responsible.

Confidence trick on elderly man facilitated by negligent solicitor. An elderly man had fallen into the hands of an unknown confidence trickster. The latter first of all took all the man's savings via his bank account. Then a mortgage application was drafted, which the man was persuaded to sign. The court found that if his solicitor had done his job, he would immediately have realised that the man did not want the mortgage, did not need it and could not afford it (inevitably, he defaulted on the first interest repayment, with the predictable outcome that the mortgage lenders sought repossession of the house). The solicitor would have realised that the mortgage application was to benefit somebody else. Nonetheless, the solicitor went ahead and arranged a £55,000 mortgage against the house worth £70,000.

Breach of duty by solicitor. The solicitor was held to have breached his duty of care by arranging the mortgage transaction. Had the solicitor exercised his duty of care, it would have been patently obvious that 'as soon as the money was advanced it would have been out the other door again'. The specific breach of duty here was the solicitor's failure to check (with the man) the mortgage proposal agreement, which the lenders had sent back by fax to the solicitor precisely in order that it should be checked. Had the solicitor done this, it would have become apparent that the man could not afford the mortgage. The lenders had been supplied with untrue information relating to affordability and the man's wish to purchase a second house; this would have come to light if the solicitor had taken care. The solicitor also owed a duty to the lender by ensuring that the man understood the obligation he was incurring and the resources he would need to repay the capital and interest.

---

10   *Lister v Hesley Hall* [2001] UKHL 22.

11   Dayani, A. 'Ban them for life.' *Birmingham Evening Mail*, 4 February 2004. And: Carvel, J. '£10,000 for widow, 89, "fed talcum powder" by carers.' *The Guardian (Society)*, 12 July 2006.

The judge described the facts of this case as quite exceptional and held that the solicitor was liable for the mortgage capital and interest repayments – even though it was the confidence trickster, an unknown third party, who had ultimately walked off with the money.[12]

PUBLIC BODIES: SOMETIMES PROTECTED FROM LIABILITY IN NEGLIGENCE

The courts sometimes protect local public bodies from certain types of negligence case by holding that the local authority or NHS body did not have a duty of care in the first place. This means that even if there is ostensible carelessness, it is irrelevant because there is effectively no duty to breach.

This approach may become evident when the alleged failure is closely connected with what the court perceives to be the public body's statutory duties, or where policy and resource issues are in play. For example, the issue has arisen as to whether it is fair, just or reasonable to impose a duty of care in child protection,[13] aftercare under s.117 of the Mental Health Act 1983[14] and protection of witnesses by the police.[15]

The courts have struggled to state exactly what the law is and to maintain a consistent line. All of which makes potentially significant the following case, involving a local authority's failure to safeguard and protect two highly vulnerable adults with learning disabilities from being tortured by a third party.

The local authority had argued that it simply owed no duty of care in negligence (whether or not it had acted carelessly) and that any challenge should be by way of judicial review (to review the lawfulness of its actions) rather than negligence (concerning the payment of damages). The judge's decision, in finding the local authority liable, might seem plausible but was in fact overturned by the Court of Appeal (see below).

Torture of couple with learning disabilities over a weekend; local authority failure to act: negligence? The two claimants, represented by the Official Solicitor, had learning disabilities. They lived together in a flat, together with the woman's two children, one of whom also had learning disabilities. The family was able to live as a unit in the community but functioned at a low level in some respects. It was vulnerable. Two parts of the local authority's social services department had been involved with the family before the relevant weekend.

Background to weekend.

For a period of time prior to the relevant weekend the claimants had been befriended and then taken advantage of by a number of youths. It is not known exactly when this began to happen, but the evidence suggests that it probably did so at or about the end of the summer of 2000. As time went by some of these youths would use

---

12 *Finsbury Park Mortgage Funding v Burrows and Pegram Heron* [2002], Brighton County Court, 22 February 2002 and 3 May 2002.

13 *X(Minors) v Bedfordshire County Council* [1995] 2 AC 633. Also: *Barrett v Enfield London Borough Council* [2001] 2 AC 550.

14 *Clunis v Camden and Islington Health Authority* [1998] 3 All ER 180 (Court of Appeal).

15 *Chief Constable of Hertfordshire v Van Colle; Smith v Chief Constable of Sussex* [2008] UKHL 50.

the claimants' flat as a place at which to live, take drugs, engage in sexual activity, leave stolen goods, and generally misbehave. X was assaulted quite seriously in a McDonald's restaurant on 11th October 2000 by one of the youths, who believed that X had 'grassed' on him in relation to some stolen goods found by the police at [the claimants' flat] on the previous day.[16]

The weekend.

During the relevant weekend the claimants were effectively imprisoned in their own home, and repeatedly assaulted and abused, often in the presence of the two children. Both claimants later made statements to the police, describing their ordeals. What follows is intended only as a brief summary. X said that at one stage the youths confined him and Y to their bedroom, and made them perform sexual acts. They threw many of X's and Y's possessions over the balcony. They forced pepper and fluid into X's eyes. They locked him in the bathroom for a time, in the dark. They made him drink urine, eat dog biscuits, dog faeces and the faeces of one of the youths, threatening him that he would be stabbed if he did not. They made him put a vibrator up his bottom, and then lick it. They sprayed kitchen cleaner in his mouth, face and hair. They slashed him repeatedly all over his body with a knife or knives. Y's statement was to similar effect, adding that she too was made to put the vibrator in her mouth. The children too were abused, assaulted and locked in their bedroom from time to time. Even the family dog was abused. It is unnecessary to go into further detail, or into the physical and psychological injuries suffered by the claimants as a result.[17]

Local authority's failure to act and duty of care. The judge considered in detail both the local authority's responses to the deteriorating situation leading up to the weekend and the relevant case law. He acknowledged the past reluctance of the courts to impose a duty of care where there has been a negligent failure in the exercise of a statutory function by a public body. Nonetheless, he concluded that, before the weekend in question, the council's emergency procedure for moving the couple from their flat should have been triggered. The fact that this did not occur resulted from a lack of cooperation and communication between the social services and housing departments, a failure to appreciate the gravity and urgency of the situation indicated by the evidence, and a failure to give the case the priority it warranted. In all the circumstances, it was fair, just and reasonable to impose a duty of care.[18]

The Court of Appeal stepped in, however, and overruled the High Court's decision. First, uncontroversially, it concluded there had, in any case, been no negligent actions on the part of the social worker involved. Second, more notably, the court held that, because the judgements made by the local authority staff were inextricably linked to its statutory duties under the Housing Act 1996, it would not be fair, just and reasonable to impose liability. This was so, even had there been negligent or careless actions by local authority officers.

The legal argument was that, under either housing legislation (s.188 of the Housing Act 1996) or social services legislation (s.21 of the National Assistance Act

---

16   *X & Y v Hounslow London Borough Council* [2008] EWHC 1168 (QB).
17   *X & Y v Hounslow London Borough Council* [2008] EWHC 1168 (QB).
18   *X & Y v Hounslow London Borough Council* [2008] EWHC 1168 (QB).

1948), the council should have moved the vulnerable couple before that weekend. And that, by failing to do so, the local authority was liable in the common law of negligence. The Court of Appeal confirmed that whilst a judicial review case (a different type of legal case not involving suing for money) might have been possible, no common law duty of care in negligence automatically attached to that legislation. In some limited circumstances, a separate duty of care might arise in negligence.[19]

So the case was argued in respect of both the social services and the housing duties of the local authority. Its outcome was in line with a number of decisions involving housing. For instance, the courts have in the past held that local authorities are not liable in the law of nuisance caused by one tenant to another.[20]

Likewise, they have held that a social landlord does not owe a duty of care under negligence law for failing to take steps against tenants indulging in anti-social behaviour. The case in question revolved around a tenant who, over a period of years, had been violent towards another tenant and the failure of the local authority to start eviction proceedings sooner and to inform the victim about a meeting it held with the perpetrator, threatening him with eviction. Following that meeting, the perpetrator killed the victim. The Supreme Court was clear that it would not be fair, just and reasonable to impose a duty of care on the local authority.[21]

POLICE PROTECTED BY COURTS

The protection might extend to the police. For instance, in the following case, it was clear that the man was not responsible for the offence of which he had originally been suspected, but information about the original suspicion was still supplied on a criminal record certificate. Again, in a pattern similar to the *Hounslow* case above, the High Court judge considered that the police might be liable, only to be overruled by the Court of Appeal.

Need to be reasonably careful about accuracy of information provided. In one case, a man was initially accused of indecent assault and attempted rape. The police later recorded that he was not responsible for the crime and closed the case. When the man was later applying for a teaching post, a criminal record certificate was required; it contained details of his arrest for the suspected offences. The man then spent nearly a year trying to persuade the police that this information should not have been included. A subsequent certificate provided omitted the information.

The man complained of psychiatric illness and financial loss and sued in negligence. The High Court refused to strike out the negligence action, meaning the case could at least go to trial. This was because, although the police owed no duty of care generally in the investigation or suppression of crime, they could sometimes still be liable on 'ordinary' principles of negligence. This could be particularly where they had 'assumed a responsibility' to act with reasonable care towards an individual. The putting together, on specific request,

---

19   *X & Y v Hounslow London Borough Council* [2009] EWCA Civ 286.

20   *Mowan v Wandsworth LBC* [2001] 33 HLR 56.

21   *Mitchell v Glasgow City Council* [2009] UKHL 11.

of information in relation to a criminal record certificate might constitute this assumption of responsibility.[22]

Even though the High Court recognised that police did not have a wide-ranging duty of care, it felt that in these particular circumstances they did.

The Court of Appeal thought otherwise and found in favour of police immunity, stating that a duty of care did not arise under the Police Act (even had the police behaved negligently). One of the reasons given for this decision was that any such duty of care could conflict with the duty to protect young people:

> Not only is there no proper basis for concluding that the chief officer is to be taken to have assumed responsibility to [the claimant] in the performance of a responsibility imposed by statute, but the structure and purpose of the statute strongly suggests that there should be no duty of care. If there were, there would be a plain conflict between the chief officer's putative duty to [the claimant] and the statutory purpose of protecting vulnerable young people.[23]

Notwithstanding this protection, it does not mean that the police might not in some circumstances be held liable – or simply decide to settle out of court, without admission of liability.

For instance, in the case of Fiona Pilkington, who killed herself and her disabled daughter after suffering years of anti-social behaviour, the police had failed to identify them as vulnerable, despite numerous referrals and complaints over a ten-year period. The Independent Police Complaints Commission made adverse findings in respect of the Leicestershire police. A legal action, brought by Fiona Pilkington's mother, was settled out of court by the police with no liability admitted.[24]

22   *Desmond v Chief Constable of Nottinghamshire Police* [2009] EWHC 2362 (QB).
23   *Desmond v Chief Constable of Nottinghamshire Police* [2011] EWCA Civ 3.
24   'Family of Fiona Pilkington settle claim against police.' *BBC News*, 9 March 2012. Accessed on 28 August 2012 at: www.bbc.co.uk/news/uk-england-leicestershire-17309285.

Restraint

KEY POINTS

The physical restraint of adults, as well as of children, remains a substantial issue. On the one hand, total prohibition on restraint might sometimes result in harm to both the service user and other people. Equally, improper restraint runs the risk of resulting in, for example, injury to the restrained or the restrainer, breach of human rights, the criminal offence of assault and battery, and the civil tort of trespass to the person.

This chapter refers to the rules under the Mental Capacity Act 2005, Department of Health guidance on restraint and to a number of key legal cases illustrating the sometimes fine line between acceptable and unacceptable practices.

DEPARTMENT OF HEALTH GUIDANCE

In response to such concerns, the Department of Health issued guidance in 2002 on physically restrictive interventions for people with learning disabilities or autism in health, education and social care settings.

In summary, the guidance emphasises that interventions are legally permissible in certain circumstances (e.g. self-harm or injury to others) and that any interventions should be the least restrictive necessary. They should be planned as far as possible, result from multi-disciplinary assessment and be part of a wider therapeutic strategy detailed in individual care plans. Prevention should be the primary aim, in order to avoid the use of restraint if possible. There should be clear organisational policies and adequate training.[1]

Following the scandal of abuse at Winterbourne View independent hospital in 2011, the Care Quality Commission undertook inspections in 2011 and 2012 at 150 locations of care for people with learning disabilities, including NHS providers, independent health care services and adult social care residential providers. A major concern was in relation to restraint, with 25 per cent of providers not complying in terms of recording, monitoring, reviewing and learning lessons from incidents of restraint.[2]

RULES ABOUT RESTRAINT UNDER THE MENTAL CAPACITY ACT

Section 6 of the Mental Capacity Act 2005 specifically deals with restraint in the case of people lacking the relevant capacity, permitting it but only where it is to prevent harm to the person and it is employed proportionately. The code of practice points out, more generally, that the common law also imposes a duty of care on health care and social care staff to take appropriate and necessary action to restrain or remove a person – with challenging behaviour or who is in the acute stages of illness – who may cause harm to themselves or other people.[3] The Mental Health Act 1983 code of practice also contains guidance on restraint.[4]

CARE STANDARDS REGULATIONS

Care standards regulations, governing the provision of care by registered providers of health and social care, state that:

> Where any form of control or restraint is used in the carrying on of the regulated activity, the registered person must have suitable arrangements in place to protect service users against the risk of such control or restraint being –
>
> (a) unlawful; or
>
> (b) otherwise excessive.[5]

COMMISSION FOR SOCIAL CARE INSPECTION REPORT ON RESTRAINT

In 2007, the Commission for Social Care Inspection published a report on the use of restraint in the care of older people. It found a range of examples of the use of restraint which it considered were unacceptable and arguably constituted a breach

1   Department of Health. *Guidance on physically restrictive interventions for people with learning disability and autistic spectrum disorder in health, education and social care settings.* London: DH, 2002.
2   Care Quality Commission. *Learning disability services inspection programme: national overview.* London: CQC, 2012, p.7.
3   Lord Chancellor. *Mental Capacity Act 2005: code of practice.* London: TSO, 2007, para 6.43.
4   Department of Health. *Code of practice: Mental Health Act 1983.* London: DH, paras 19.1–19.14.
5   SI 2010/781. The Health and Social Care Act 2008 (Regulated Activities) Regulations 2010, r.11(2).

of human rights. These included people fastened into wheelchairs or kept in chairs by means of trays, use of low chairs to stop people getting up, wrapping up people in bed to the point of immobility so they could not remove their incontinence pads, excessive use of bed rails, dragging a person by her hair and tying her to a chair, excessive drug-based sedation, not taking people to the toilet when they want to go, punishing people by leaving them sitting in soiled pads – and so on.

The Commission referred to restraint as including physical intervention, physical restraint, denial of practical or staff resources to manage daily living, environmental restraint, chemical restraint, electronic surveillance, medical restraint and forced care. It emphasised that restraint had to be justified in each case and might be if, in summary:

- consideration is given to the best interests of the individual and others
- there is a serious risk of harm to older people or others
- other methods to control the situation, such as de-escalation, have been tried and found to be unsuitable or have failed
- the least practicable amount of force is used for the shortest time
- it is used according to agreed guidelines, on the basis of a risk assessment and recorded decisions
- it is a last resort.[6]

SAFEGUARDS AND NARROW DIVIDING LINE BETWEEN ACCEPTABLE AND UNACCEPTABLE RESTRAINT

On any view, the effect of all these legal and guidance provisions is that safeguards are required. In the following case, the health service ombudsman found they were absent: policy, planning, training and an individual care plan were all lacking.

No policy or care plan for restraint. An elderly man in hospital had chronic obstructive airways disease, peripheral vascular disease, and had suffered a stroke that left him with right-sided weakness. Previously, whilst at home, he had displayed signs of irritability and frustration, and verbal and physical aggression towards his wife. He was admitted to hospital for respite care for social reasons, since he could not cope whilst his wife, his main carer, herself required hospital treatment. He became disturbed during the night after going to the day room to use his nebuliser. Nursing staff restrained him. When his daughter visited, she found that he had an injured arm, carpet burns on his face and a cut on his hand.

The health service ombudsman found that the NHS trust had no policy on control and restraint, and in that respect there was no particular plan for this particular patient. This latter failing was made worse by the fact that there had been a previous incident of restraint a few nights earlier involving the same patient. The ombudsman severely criticised the lack of planning and training that led a disabled, elderly man to be restrained in such a way.[7]

6   Commission for Social Care Inspection. *Rights, risk and restraints*. London: CSCI, 2007.
7   *Oldham NHS Trust 1999* (E.1780/97–98). Published in: Health Service Ombudsman. HC 497. *Investigations completed October 1998–March 1999*. London: TSO, 1999.

The dividing line between what constitutes reasonable and unreasonable restraint might be difficult to discern.

Use of armchair with fitted table at mealtimes: limited use acceptable. During the course of a defamation court case concerning an undercover BBC investigation of practices at a Scottish nursing home, it came to light that a Parker Knoll chair with fitted table was used to restrict the movements of one of the residents. However, the court found that it was acceptable that, for example, at mealtimes the chair should play a useful part in the care of a resident with dementia. Likewise, because of his disruptiveness and the risk to himself, he was not always in his room at night but installed in his chair in the nurses' sitting room. The judge rejected the allegation that he was in his chair most days for 24 hours.[8]

Conversely, the findings of the Commission for Health Improvement, that patients at an NHS mental health hospital had been tied to commodes while they had breakfast or generally for restraint, left no doubt that unacceptable physical restrictions had been employed. Such incidents had been part of a culture that allowed unprofessional, counter-therapeutic and degrading – even cruel – practices to take root.[9]

BED RAILS

There has long been concern about the use of bed rails both as unacceptable restraint and when a proper assessment has not been carried out and health and safety hazards are created. However, matters appear not so simple as to warrant a blanket ban, which could itself lead to injury in individual cases.

Judging the use of bed rails. A report from the National Patient Safety Agency report found that accidents might occur without them, that individual assessment was most important, and that patients with bed rails were mainly positive or neutral about their use, with some patients being reluctant to manage without them. It concluded that the evidence suggested neither that there should be blanket policies not to use them nor that they should be used routinely.[10]

Thus, the family of a woman who fell out of bed at a care home and had to go to hospital complained about the 'new rule' in the care home banning the use of bed rails. They believed this was the reason their 94-year-old relative had fallen out of bed. The care home stated it was following Health and Safety Executive (HSE) guidance and that the modern approach was not to use bed rails unless there was no alternative and the safety benefits outweighed the lack of freedom of movement. It also referred to the fear that use of bed rails could be an unlawful deprivation of liberty.[11]

8   *Baigent v BBC* [1999] unreported, Court of Session, Outer House (Scotland).
9   Commission for Health Improvement. *Investigation into the North Lakeland NHS Trust, November.* London: CHI, 2000, p.10.
10   National Patient Safety Agency. *Bedrails – reviewing the evidence: a systematic literature review.* London: NPSA, 2007.
11   Hills, S. 'Great-grandmother, 94, suffers horrific injuries after falling out of hospital bed because 'elf and safety rules ban side-bars.' *Daily Mail,* 12 April 2012.

This press report is illustrative of the confusion that can arise. Long-standing HSE guidance has rightly urged careful, cautious use of bed rails, as a last resort; it has not banned them. In fact, it states that 'although not suitable for everyone, they can be very effective when used with the right bed, in the right way, for the right person'.[12]

The newspaper report was in fact probably referring to a Care Quality Commission report in 2012 about deprivation of liberty which had mentioned bed rails.[13] An incautious and incorrect reading of this report might have led some care providers to become wary about using bed rails.

UNPLANNED RESTRAINT OF PATIENT, EMPLOYER'S RESPONSE AND DUTY TO STAFF

The difficulties of caring for people with significantly challenging behaviour – and of balancing duties to patients and to staff and of applying the law – surfaced in a Court of Appeal case in early 2012. It is worth examining in some detail.

It concerned the care of an 87-year-old patient with dementia in a hospital in Bury St Edmunds, Suffolk.

Aggressive behaviour during the day: approved hands-on restraint. On the night of 22 September 2008, the two appellants, together with two health care workers, were the only staff taking care of 17 patients. It was clear from the handover notes from the previous shift that particular difficulties had been experienced in relation to the handling of JE. He was 87 and suffered from dementia. On the day in question, he had been agitated, aggressive, hitting things, spitting, swearing, throwing drinks, kicking and punching, and generally requiring particularly close attention. It was noted that the safe handling technique used by the staff on the previous shift had caused skin tears on his arms to be opened. Medication had to be administered forcibly because he was refusing both food and medicine.[14]

Because of the spitting, he had also had a mask placed on him. The hands-on manual handling and the mask, of course, represented restraint, which had been applied during the day shift, but the NHS Trust was subsequently not concerned about this. It seemed to have represented approved practice. This lack of concern was despite the fact that an experienced staff nurse had put in writing that during the daytime the patient was being cared for in 'a less than best way', that he had required on occasions two-to-one observation for safety reasons and that, as a result, the other patients had only their basic needs attended to.[15]

Come the night-time, the two nurses and two health care workers tried something different. The same staff nurse who had expressed her concerns about the daytime care was passing and reported that she had observed the following.

12   Health and Safety Executive. *Safe use of bed rails*. Accessed on 4 September 2012 at: www.hse.gov.uk/healthservices/ bed-rails.htm.

13   Care Quality Commission. *The operation of the Deprivation of Liberty Safeguards in England, 2010/11*. London: CQC, 2012, p.18.

14   *Crawford v Suffolk Mental Health Partnership NHS Trust* [2012] EWCA Civ 138.

15   *Crawford v Suffolk Mental Health Partnership NHS Trust* [2012] EWCA Civ 138.

Chair tied to dining room table, patient trying to get out of chair. She noticed night staff in the dining room surrounding a chair in which JE was sitting. She said he was restless and trying to get out of the chair. She noticed that the chair was secured to a dining room table by a sheet or two and that there was another sheet across his stomach. She was shocked, although she did not say anything to the nurses at the time. This was on a Monday evening. She did not make any complaint about this until she next came on shift on Thursday, when she reported to the ward manager what she had witnessed.

The two nurses were suspended and a referral to the police made. A month later, the police stated they would take no action, and an investigation and disciplinary hearing were instigated. The nurses accepted that they had tied the chair legs to the table but denied that the sheet round the patient's chest was tying him to the chair; they maintained that they had draped it around him to try to indicate that it was bedtime. The allegations against the nurses were assault, negligence and professional misconduct. The hearing found against them, with the penalty being dismissal. They appealed to a panel. The panel also found against them.

Nurses accused of physical assault by panel. The letter rejecting the appeal stated that the act of restraining the patient had been against the Trust's policy and the Mental Health Act code of practice and constituted physical assault. It concluded that the actions of the nurses represented a complete breakdown of trust and confidence. The panel was also critical of the failure to seek further advice about how to restrain the patient and of the failure to make a report of the restraint.[16]

The nurses took their case to an employment tribunal which they won; the NHS Trust then appealed successfully to an employment appeal tribunal. The nurses then took their case to the Court of Appeal; they won.

The Court of Appeal identified two procedural errors made by the Trust. First, the investigation had made conclusions about the third sheet (around the patient's chest) and conducted its own 'experiment', but without giving the nurses an opportunity to demonstrate their version of how the sheet had been used. This was unfair. Second, the Trust had failed to obtain the original statement of concern made by the staff nurse and to make it available to the two nurses. This, too, was procedurally unfair.

The Court went on to consider in more detail the nature of the restraint and the context in which it had been employed. It rejected the idea that tying the patient to the table was an assault.

Inappropriate accusation of assault. It no doubt prevented the patient from leaving the chair. That was the purpose. Given that he was on a drip at the time, it was reasonable to want to keep him in the chair, even if the means used were inappropriate. To describe the action – of tying the chair to the table – was not just an inept description but also had pejorative overtones and would have affected how the matter was investigated. This resulted in misunderstanding and exaggeration, on the part of the Trust, of the alleged wrongdoing.[17]

---

16   *Crawford v Suffolk Mental Health Partnership NHS Trust* [2012] EWCA Civ 138.
17   *Crawford v Suffolk Mental Health Partnership NHS Trust* [2012] EWCA Civ 138.

The court observed that it was not reasonable to dismiss staff with 20 years' service for using restraint on the night shift that was no more detrimental to his dignity than the approved restraint used during the day.

Perverse to dismiss employees with 20 years' service for employing restraint at night, no more (or even less) drastic than the approved restraint used during the day.

> I do not think that it would have been open to a reasonable employer to dismiss members of staff with twenty years' service simply for adopting this method for securing JE in his chair. It seems perverse to suggest that this is any more detrimental to his dignity than physically restraining him in other ways; one might have thought it less so. Moreover, the evidence showed that during the previous shift JE had been pinned to the chair in virtually the same way, save that instead of achieving this mechanically by tying the chair to the table, it was done by two nurses holding it there. To treat the one as permissible and the other as justifying the dismissal of employees with twenty years' service, simply it seems because it is not an approach permitted by the procedures, is in my view clearly perverse.[18]

The Court of Appeal approved, however, the reduction of compensation payable because of the failure of the nurses to report the unusual method of restraint. It added a footnote about the referral to the police.

Inappropriateness of referral to the police. The court found it:

> little short of astonishing that it could ever have been thought appropriate to refer this matter to the police. In my view it almost defies belief that anyone who gave proper consideration to all the circumstances of this case could have thought that they were under any obligation to take that step.[19]

TYING UP A PATIENT: MISCONDUCT BUT NOT SUCH AS TO MEAN CARER SHOULD BE BARRED FROM WORKING

The above Court of Appeal case is not to be taken, however, as approving ad hoc restraint; it was chiefly about the reaction of the employer and about a balanced approach.

Likewise, in the following case, a care assistant restrained a resident for a period of time and then forgot about her. It was clearly misconduct, and the woman had been placed on the Protection of Vulnerable Adults (POVA) list, which meant she was barred from working with vulnerable adults. She appealed. The tribunal was in no doubt that what she did was misconduct. But the question was whether, in all the circumstances of the case, the care assistant was unsuitable to work with vulnerable adults. She won her appeal,

Tying a person to chair as a temporary measure. A care assistant was working the night shift in a care home for people with dementia. Early in the morning, she faced an emergency situation. She was cleaning one resident who had soiled herself. Another resident was in the room hindering her. In order to attend to the first, she tied the second

---

18   *Crawford v Suffolk Mental Health Partnership NHS Trust* [2012] EWCA Civ 138.
19   *Crawford v Suffolk Mental Health Partnership NHS Trust* [2012] EWCA Civ 138.

resident to a chair using a sweater or fleece. Owing to pressure of work and then the need to get off shift for her children, she forgot about the second resident. When she was found about half an hour later, the resident was not physically hurt or psychologically affected. The care home alerted the police. The care assistant was dismissed.

In coming to its conclusion, the tribunal had to consider the number of incidents, the gravity, time elapsed since the misconduct, timing and degree of recognition by the person of the misconduct, steps taken by the person to minimise repetition and extenuating circumstances.

Taking account of her having to work alone that morning, her remorse and her work record, the tribunal was not satisfied that she was unsuitable to work with vulnerable adults. She won her appeal.[20]

INAPPROPRIATE RESTRAINT

The fact that there are grey areas of how to respond to incidents of restraint does not mean that anything goes.

Thus, a nurse was struck off by the Nursing and Midwifery Council for a form of restraint that involved covering the head of a resident with dementia with a towel to stop her spitting. The woman was small and slight and probably terrified.[21] And, in a further case, involving the regular restraint and seclusion of a 16-year-old with severe learning disabilities in the 'blue room' at his school, the court stated that it would expect the Mental Health Act code of practice to be followed as best practice.[22]

And the Care Standards Tribunal upheld the placing on the POVA list (barring him from working with vulnerable adults and children) of a domiciliary care worker for people with learning disabilities. He had placed a resident at risk of harm by barring his bedroom door with a mop between 11pm and 7am the next morning. The tribunal discussed the harm, or risk of harm, resulting.

Barring of resident's door with broomstick during the night: distress. The perpetrator argued that it had not been established that the victim had suffered great distress and showed signs of emotional and physical response to the restriction. It was not, however, necessary for the tribunal to make such a finding. It had to decide whether the misconduct harmed or placed at risk of harm a child or a vulnerable adult. The tribunal accepted the evidence that the victim would have suffered physical and mental distress when he was confined to his bedroom, as he would have been unable to understand why he was not able to move about the property.

The tribunal found that the misconduct placed the victim at risk of harm. He was unable to communicate his immediate needs and, in a confused and distressed state, he was at a greater risk of self-harm. His care plan noted the risk of self-harm when he was in pain or distressed. The tribunal found he did suffer distress as a result of the misconduct. There

---

20   *MK v Secretary of State for Health* [2009] UKFTT 150 (HESC).

21   'Dementia care nurse struck off.' *NL Group*, 13 July 2012. Accessed 13 August 2012 at: www.nlgroup.co.uk/dementia-care-nurse-struck-off.

22   *C v A Local Authority* [2011] EWHC 1539 (Admin).

could have been very much more serious consequences if he had choked or injured himself as no one would have known about the event until the door was opened.[23]

Other instances of seemingly disproportionate, and perhaps avoidable, restraint of people with dementia are sometimes reported. In the following case, a coroner severely criticised the actions of the police.

Confused, terrified man with dementia handcuffed and strapped to stretcher.
A retired engineer with dementia was in a care home. His mental state was deteriorating and it had been decided that he should be sectioned under the Mental Health Act. A meeting was called with the daughter but was then brought forward 24 hours, meaning she could not attend. So, without family involvement, he was – in a terrified state – handcuffed and strapped to a stretcher.

The police claimed that it was to protect everybody, including the man himself. They later accepted it had been inappropriate. The man died soon after. Of the police intervention, the coroner stated: 'This is totally ridiculous, officer, it beggars belief. [He] was an elderly, frail and frightened man with little understanding of the world around him and what would happen to him.' The coroner stated that he would be writing to the police about their handling of mental health patients and the use of handcuffs.[24]

Some months earlier, it was reported how another man with dementia, who needed to be taken from his own home to hospital but was struggling, was subject to several taser rounds when six policemen attended. He was then manhandled to the floor and carried out of the house.[25]

WIDE LEGAL RAMIFICATIONS OF INAPPROPRIATE RESTRAINT

The potentially wide legal ramifications of restraint were illustrated in a case brought against the police. It concerned their actions when a 16-year-old young man with autism and epilepsy became fixated with the water at a public swimming pool. He was there with four other pupils from his school as part of a familiarisation process; it was not intended that any of them would swim on that day.

Young man with autism: restrained by five police officers, handcuffed, leg restraints, placed in caged area of police van. The young man wouldn't move away from the water's edge, despite the attempts of his carers to persuade him. The police were called, via telephone, by the manager of the swimming pool who gave a misleading picture of what was happening, claiming that he was becoming aggressive when, in fact, he was not. By the time the police arrived, the young man had been standing by the water for 30–40 minutes.

The police did not consult with the young man's carers but went to touch the man. He shortly jumped into shallow water. Lifeguards formed a barrier to stop him moving to the deep end; eventually, he was lifted out of the water, where five police officers applied restraint before applying two sets of handcuffs and leg restraints. He was then placed in the caged area of the police van. During all this, he had lost control of his bowels. He

23   *Johnson v Secretary of State for Health* [2009] 1637 PVA.
24   Narain, J. and Parveen, N. 'Did police have to handcuff dementia patient?' *Daily Mail*, 5 July 2012.
25   Brooke, C. 'Outrage as police repeatedly TASER terrified Alzheimer's sufferer in front of his wife because he didn't want to go into care – then tie him up in his living room.' *Daily Mail*, 10 May 2012.

was greatly upset. The police claimed they acted as they did because the carers were so ineffective; the carers believed the police had overreacted.[26]

The judge went on to find multiple breaches of the law by the police. First, there had been assault and battery when they touched and then restrained him without consent. Had they complied with ss.5 and 6 of the Mental Capacity Act 2005, there would have been no liability. Under these sections of the Act, however, they had neither taken reasonable steps to ascertain what the young man's best interests were in the circumstances nor responded proportionately to the risks.

Disproportionate actions of police. Nor were the actions of the police proportionate in the circumstances, given that, as an alternative to such restraint, ZH could have been permitted to leave the pool by himself from the shallow end or, when on the poolside, been immediately released for his carers to deal with.[27]

By the same token, the police were also liable for his false imprisonment, without justification under ss.5 and 6 of the Mental Capacity Act 2005.

By not considering alternative strategies to deal with the situation, the police had, in addition, failed to make reasonable adjustments as demanded by the Disability Discrimination Act 1995 and so were in breach of that Act, too.

On top of all this, there were three separate breaches of the Human Rights Act 1998. First, a breach of article 3 of the European Convention.

Inhuman or degrading treatment. The duration of the force and restraint, injury sustained, and age, health and vulnerability of the young man, meant that there was a breach of article 3. The minimum level of severity had been attained when the whole period of restraint was taken into account. It was not just the application of handcuffs and leg restraints which had to be considered but the whole time when restraint on the poolside and in the van occurred. There was no intended humiliation, but nevertheless it was inhuman or degrading treatment.[28]

Second, article 5 was breached because he was deprived of his liberty, even though the period of restraint was no more than about 40 minutes.

Deprivation of liberty, even though only 40 minutes in duration. Even though the purpose and intention of the police (including safety of the young man) was relevant to article 5, a deprivation of liberty had occurred. The actions of the police were in general well-intentioned, but they involved the application of forcible restraint for a significant period of time to an autistic epileptic young man when such restraint was, in the circumstances, hasty, ill-informed and damaging. The restraint was neither lawful nor justified.[29]

Article 8, too, was breached, because the interference with the young man's private life was not in accordance with the law, as article 8 demands, since the judge had already found other domestic law being breached.[30]

---

26   *ZH v Commissioner of Police for the Metropolis* [2012] EWHC 604 (Admin).
27   *ZH v Commissioner of Police for the Metropolis* [2012] EWHC 604 (Admin).
28   *ZH v Commissioner of Police for the Metropolis* [2012] EWHC 604 (Admin).
29   *ZH v Commissioner of Police for the Metropolis* [2012] EWHC 604 (Admin).
30   *ZH v Commissioner of Police for the Metropolis* [2012] EWHC 604 (Admin).

SECLUSION

Department of Health guidance on restraint states that if seclusion is required, other than in an emergency, for periods of more than a few minutes or more than once a week, then advice should be sought about statutory powers under the Mental Health Act 1983 or Children Act 1989.[31]

The Mental Health Act code of practice states that seclusion should be a last resort, for the shortest possible time, and should not be used as a punishment, as part of a treatment programme, because of shortage of staff or where there is a risk of self-harm. It also sets out procedures in terms of length of time, periodic checking and reviewing.[32]

Adherence to the code in respect of such procedures was the subject of consideration by the courts.

Seclusion and the Mental Health Act code of practice. The courts have held that the code should be followed unless there is good reason not to in the case of an individual patient or individual group of patients. However, it should not be departed from as a matter of policy. Otherwise, this could be in breach of article 8 of the European Convention on Human Rights, because the interference with the right to respect for privacy (including physical and psychological integrity) would then not be in accordance with the law. This would be, in turn, because such interference would not have the necessary degree of predictability and transparency required by article 8. The court also accepted that although seclusion did not necessarily breach article 3 of the Convention, nevertheless it would do so if it resulted in inhuman or degrading treatment. Giving weight and status to the code of practice was precisely the sort of step and safeguard required in order to avoid breach of human rights.[33]

---

31   Department of Health. *Guidance on physically restrictive interventions for people with learning disability and autistic spectrum disorder in health, education and social care settings.* London: DH, 2002.

32   Department of Health. *Code of practice: Mental Health Act 1983.* London: DH, paras 15.43–15.62.

33   *Munjaz v Mersey Care NHS Trust* [2003] EWCA Civ 1036.

Index

05107014